Short Stories for Students

National Advisory Board

Short Stories for Students

Presenting Analysis, Context, and Criticism on
Commonly Studied Short Stories

Volume 22

Ira Mark Milne, Project Editor

Foreword by Thomas E. Barden

THOMSON
★
GALE

Detroit • New York • San Francisco • San Diego • New Haven, Conn. • Waterville, Maine • London • Munich

Short Stories for Students, Volume 22

Project Editor
Ira Mark Milne

Editorial
Sara Constantakis, Anne Marie Hacht, Gillian Leonard

Rights Acquisition and Management
Emma Hull, Sue Rudolph, Andrew Specht

Manufacturing
Drew Kalasky

Image Research & Acquisition
Kelly A. Quin

Imaging and Multimedia
Lezlie Light, Dan Newell

Product Design
Pamela A. E. Galbreath

Vendor Administration
Civie Green

Product Manager
Meggin Condino

ISBN 0-7876-7030-8
ISSN 1092-7735

Printed in the United States of America
10 9 8 7 6 5 4 3 2 1

Table of Contents

Why Study Literature At All?

Short Stories for Students is designed to provide readers with information and discussion about a wide range of important contemporary and historical works of short fiction, and it does that job very well. However, I want to use this guest foreword to address a question that it does *not* take up. It is a fundamental question that is often ignored in high school and college English classes as well as research texts, and one that causes frustration among students at all levels, namely why study literature at all? Isn't it enough to read a story, enjoy it, and go about one's business? My answer (to be expected from a literary professional, I suppose) is no. It is not enough. It is a start; but it is not enough. Here's why.

First, literature is the only part of the educational curriculum that deals directly with the actual world of lived experience. The philosopher Edmund Husserl used the apt German term *die Lebenswelt*, "the living world," to denote this realm. All the other content areas of the modern American educational system avoid the subjective, present reality of everyday life. Science (both the natural and the social varieties) objectifies, the fine arts create and/or perform, history reconstructs. Only literary study persists in posing those questions we all asked before our schooling taught us to give up on them. Only literature gives credibility to personal perceptions, feelings, dreams, and the "stream of consciousness" that is our inner voice. Literature wonders about infinity, wonders why God permits evil, wonders what will happen to us after we die. Literature admits that we get our

hearts broken, that people sometimes cheat and get away with it, that the world is a strange and probably incomprehensible place. Literature, in other words, takes on all the big and small issues of what it means to be human. So my first answer is that of the humanist: we should read literature and study it and take it seriously because it enriches us as human beings. We develop our moral imagination, our capacity to sympathize with other people, and our ability to understand our existence through the experience of fiction.

My second answer is more practical. By studying literature we can learn how to explore and analyze texts. Fiction may be about *die Lebenswelt*, but it is a construct of words put together in a certain order by an artist using the medium of language. By examining and studying those constructions, we can learn about language as a medium. We can become more sophisticated about word associations and connotations, about the manipulation of symbols, and about style and atmosphere. We can grasp how ambiguous language is and how important context and texture is to meaning. In our first encounter with a work of literature, of course, we are not supposed to catch all of these things. We are spellbound, just as the writer wanted us to be. It is as serious students of the writer's art that we begin to see how the tricks are done.

Seeing the tricks, which is another way of saying "developing analytical and close reading skills," is important above and beyond its intrinsic literary educational value. These skills transfer to other fields and enhance critical thinking of any kind. Understanding how language is used to construct texts is powerful knowledge. It makes engineers better problem solvers, lawyers better advocates and courtroom practitioners, politicians better rhetoricians, marketing and advertising agents better sellers, and citizens more aware consumers as well as better participants in democracy. This last point is especially important, because rhetorical skill works both ways when we learn how language is manipulated in the making of texts the result is that we become less susceptible when language is used to manipulate us.

My third reason is related to the second. When we begin to see literature as created artifacts of language, we become more sensitive to good writing in general. We get a stronger sense of the importance of individual words, even the sounds of words and word combinations. We begin to understand Mark Twain's delicious proverb "The difference between the right word and the almost right word is the difference between lightning and a lightning bug." Getting beyond the "enjoyment only" stage of literature gets us closer to becoming makers of word art ourselves. I am not saying that studying fiction will turn every student into a Faulkner or a Shakespeare. But it will make us more adaptable and effective writers, even if our art form ends up being the office memo or the corporate annual report.

Studying short stories, then, can help students become better readers, better writers, and even better human beings. But I want to close with a warning. If your study and exploration of the craft, history, context, symbolism, or anything else about a story starts to rob it of the magic you felt when you first read it, it is time to stop. Take a break, study another subject, shoot some hoops, or go for a run. Love of reading is too important to be ruined by school. The early twentieth century writer Willa Cather, in her novel *My Antonia*, has her narrator Jack Burden tell a story that he and Antonia heard from two old Russian immigrants when they were teenagers. These immigrants, Pavel and Peter, told about an incident from their youth back in Russia that the narrator could recall in vivid detail thirty years later. It was a harrowing story of a wedding party starting home in sleds and being chased by starving wolves. Hundreds of wolves attacked the group's sleds one by one as they sped across the snow trying to reach their village. In a horrible revelation, the old Russians revealed that the groom eventually threw his own bride to the wolves to save himself. There was even a hint that one of the old immigrants might have been the groom mentioned in the story. Cather has her narrator conclude with his feelings about the story. "We did not tell Pavel's secret to anyone, but guarded it jealously as if the wolves of the Ukraine had gathered that night long ago, and the wedding party had been sacrificed, just to give us a painful and peculiar pleasure." That feeling, that painful and peculiar pleasure, is the most important thing about literature. Study and research should enhance that feeling and never be allowed to overwhelm it.

Thomas E. Barden
Professor of English and
Director of Graduate English Studies
The University of Toledo

Introduction

Purpose of the Book

The purpose of *Short Stories for Students* (*SSfS*) is to provide readers with a guide to understanding, enjoying, and studying short stories by giving them easy access to information about the work. Part of Gale's "For Students" Literature line, *SSfS* is specifically designed to meet the curricular needs of high school and undergraduate college students and their teachers, as well as the interests of general readers and researchers considering specific short fiction. While each volume contains entries on "classic" stories frequently studied in classrooms, there are also entries containing hard-to-find information on contemporary stories, including works by multicultural, international, and women writers.

The information covered in each entry includes an introduction to the story and the story's author; a plot summary, to help readers unravel and understand the events in the work; descriptions of important characters, including explanation of a given character's role in the narrative as well as discussion about that character's relationship to other characters in the story; analysis of important themes in the story; and an explanation of important literary techniques and movements as they are demonstrated in the work.

In addition to this material, which helps the readers analyze the story itself, students are also provided with important information on the literary and historical background informing each work. This includes a historical context essay, a box comparing the time or place the story was written to modern Western culture, a critical overview essay, and excerpts from critical essays on the story or author. A unique feature of *SSfS* is a specially commissioned critical essay on each story, targeted toward the student reader.

To further aid the student in studying and enjoying each story, information on media adaptations is provided (if available), as well as reading suggestions for works of fiction and nonfiction on similar themes and topics. Classroom aids include ideas for research papers and lists of critical sources that provide additional material on the work.

Selection Criteria

The titles for each volume of *SSfS* were selected by surveying numerous sources on teaching literature and analyzing course curricula for various school districts. Some of the sources surveyed include: literature anthologies, *Reading Lists for College-Bound Students: The Books Most Recommended by America's Top Colleges*; *Teaching the Short Story: A Guide to Using Stories from around the World*, by the National Council of Teachers of English (NCTE); and "A Study of High School Literature Anthologies," conducted by Arthur Applebee at the Center for the Learning and Teaching of Literature and sponsored by the National Endowment for the Arts and the Office of Educational Research and Improvement.

Input was also solicited from our advisory board, as well as educators from various areas. From these discussions, it was determined that each volume should have a mix of "classic" stories (those works commonly taught in literature classes) and contemporary stories for which information is often hard to find. Because of the interest in expanding the canon of literature, an emphasis was also placed on including works by international, multicultural, and women authors. Our advisory board members—educational professionals—helped pare down the list for each volume. Works not selected for the present volume were noted as possibilities for future volumes. As always, the editor welcomes suggestions for titles to be included in future volumes.

How Each Entry Is Organized

Each entry, or chapter, in *SSfS* focuses on one story. Each entry heading lists the title of the story, the author's name, and the date of the story's publication. The following elements are contained in each entry:

- **Introduction:** a brief overview of the story which provides information about its first appearance, its literary standing, any controversies surrounding the work, and major conflicts or themes within the work.

- **Author Biography:** this section includes basic facts about the author's life, and focuses on events and times in the author's life that may have inspired the story in question.

- **Plot Summary:** a description of the events in the story. Lengthy summaries are broken down with subheads.

- **Characters:** an alphabetical listing of the characters who appear in the story. Each character name is followed by a brief to an extensive description of the character's role in the story, as well as discussion of the character's actions, relationships, and possible motivation.

    Characters are listed alphabetically by last name. If a character is unnamed—for instance, the narrator in "The Eatonville Anthology"—the character is listed as "The Narrator" and alphabetized as "Narrator." If a character's first name is the only one given, the name will appear alphabetically by that name.

- **Themes:** a thorough overview of how the topics, themes, and issues are addressed within the story. Each theme discussed appears in a separate subhead, and is easily accessed through the boldface entries in the Subject/Theme Index.

- **Style:** this section addresses important style elements of the story, such as setting, point of view, and narration; important literary devices used, such as imagery, foreshadowing, symbolism; and, if applicable, genres to which the work might have belonged, such as Gothicism or Romanticism. Literary terms are explained within the entry, but can also be found in the Glossary.

- **Historical Context:** this section outlines the social, political, and cultural climate *in which the author lived and the work was created.* This section may include descriptions of related historical events, pertinent aspects of daily life in the culture, and the artistic and literary sensibilities of the time in which the work was written. If the story is historical in nature, information regarding the time in which the story is set is also included. Long sections are broken down with helpful subheads.

- **Critical Overview:** this section provides background on the critical reputation of the author and the story, including bannings or any other public controversies surrounding the work. For older works, this section may include a history of how the story was first received and how perceptions of it may have changed over the years; for more recent works, direct quotes from early reviews may also be included.

- **Criticism:** an essay commissioned by *SSfS* which specifically deals with the story and is written specifically for the student audience, as well as excerpts from previously published criticism on the work (if available).

- **Sources:** an alphabetical list of critical material used in compiling the entry, with bibliographical information.

- **Further Reading:** an alphabetical list of other critical sources which may prove useful for the student. Includes full bibliographical information and a brief annotation.

In addition, each entry contains the following highlighted sections, set apart from the main text as sidebars:

- **Media Adaptations:** if available, a list of film and television adaptations of the story, including source information. The list also includes stage adaptations, audio recordings, musical adaptations, etc.

- **Topics for Further Study:** a list of potential study questions or research topics dealing with the story. This section includes questions related to other disciplines the student may be studying, such as American history, world history, science, math, government, business, geography, economics, psychology, etc.

- **Compare and Contrast:** an "at-a-glance" comparison of the cultural and historical differences between the author's time and culture and late twentieth century or early twenty-first century Western culture. This box includes pertinent parallels between the major scientific, political, and cultural movements of the time or place the story was written, the time or place the story was set (if a historical work), and modern Western culture. Works written after 1990 may not have this box.

- **What Do I Read Next?:** a list of works that might complement the featured story or serve as a contrast to it. This includes works by the same author and others, works of fiction and nonfiction, and works from various genres, cultures, and eras.

Other Features

SSfS includes "Why Study Literature At All?," a foreword by Thomas E. Barden, Professor of English and Director of Graduate English Studies at the University of Toledo. This essay provides a number of very fundamental reasons for studying literature and, therefore, reasons why a book such as *SSfS*, designed to facilitate the study of litererture, is useful.

A Cumulative Author/Title Index lists the authors and titles covered in each volume of the *SSfS* series.

A Cumulative Nationality/Ethnicity Index breaks down the authors and titles covered in each volume of the *SSfS* series by nationality and ethnicity.

A Subject/Theme Index, specific to each volume, provides easy reference for users who may be studying a particular subject or theme rather than a single work. Significant subjects from events to broad themes are included, and the entries pointing to the specific theme discussions in each entry are indicated in **boldface**.

Each entry may include illustrations, including photo of the author, stills from film adaptations (if available), maps, and/or photos of key historical events.

Citing Short Stories for Students

When writing papers, students who quote directly from any volume of *SSfS* may use the following general forms to document their source. These examples are based on MLA style; teachers may request that students adhere to a different style, thus, the following examples may be adapted as needed.

When citing text from *SSfS* that is not attributed to a particular author (for example, the Themes, Style, Historical Context sections, etc.), the following format may be used:

"The Celebrated Jumping Frog of Calavaras County." *Short Stories for Students*. Ed. Kathleen Wilson. Vol. 1. Detroit: Gale, 1997. 19–20.

When quoting the specially commissioned essay from *SSfS* (usually the first essay under the Criticism subhead), the following format may be used:

Korb, Rena. Critical Essay on "Children of the Sea." *Short Stories for Students*. Ed. Kathleen Wilson. Vol. 1. Detroit: Gale, 1997. 39–42.

When quoting a journal or newspaper essay that is reprinted in a volume of *Short Stories for Students*, the following form may be used:

Schmidt, Paul. "The Deadpan on Simon Wheeler." *Southwest Review* Vol. XLI, No. 3 (Summer, 1956), 270–77; excerpted and reprinted in *Short Stories for Students*, Vol. 1, ed. Kathleen Wilson (Detroit: Gale, 1997), pp. 29–31.

When quoting material from a book that is reprinted in a volume of *SSfS,* the following form may be used:

Bell-Villada, Gene H. "The Master of Short Forms," in *García Márquez: The Man and His Work.* University of North Carolina Press, 1990, pp. 119–36; excerpted and reprinted in *Short Stories for Students*, Vol. 1, ed. Kathleen Wilson (Detroit: Gale, 1997), pp. 89–90.

We Welcome Your Suggestions

The editor of *Short Stories for Students* welcomes your comments and ideas. Readers who wish to suggest short stories to appear in future volumes, or who have other suggestions, are cordially invited to contact the editor. You may contact the editor via E-mail at: **ForStudentsEditors@thomson.com.** Or write to the editor at:

Editor, *Short Stories for Students*
Thomson Gale
27500 Drake Road
Farmington Hills, MI 48331-3535

Literary Chronology

1865: Rudyard Kipling (Joseph Rudyard Kipling) is born on December 30 in Bombay, India.

1894: Rudyard Kipling's "Mowgli's Brothers" is published.

1898: Stephen Vincent Benét is born on July 22 in Bethlehem, Pennsylvania.

1899: Elizabeth Bowen is born on June 7 in Dublin, Ireland.

1902: John Steinbeck is born on February 27 in Salinas, California.

1915: Saul Bellow is born on June 10 in Lachine, Quebec, Canada.

1928: Cynthia Ozick is born on April 17 in New York City.

1932: Stephen Vincent Benét's "An End to Dreams" is published.

1936: Lars Gustafsson is born on May 17 in Västerås, Sweden.

1936: Rudyard Kipling dies on January 18 of peritonitis caused by a hemorrhaging gastric ulcer.

1941: Simon J. Ortiz is born on May 27 and raised on the Acoma Pueblo, near Albuquerque, New Mexico.

1943: Stephen Vincent Benét dies of a heart attack on March 13 in New York City.

1945: Robert Olen Butler is born on January 20 in Granite City, Illinois.

1947: John Steinbeck's "The Pearl" is published.

1954: Louise Erdrich is born in Little Falls, Minnesota.

1955: Elizabeth Bowen's "A Day in the Dark" is published.

1964: Aleksandar Hemon is born in Yugoslavia in Sarajevo, the capitol of what is, in 2005, Bosnia-Herzegovina.

1965: Mary Yukari Waters is born in Kyoto, Japan.

1968: John Steinbeck dies on December 20 in New York City, and at his request his ashes are buried in the Garden of Memories Cemetery in Salinas, California.

1973: Elizabeth Bowen dies of lung cancer on February 22 at her home at Hythe, England.

1974: Simon J. Ortiz's "The End of Old Horse" is published.

1978: Saul Bellow's "A Silver Dish" is published.

1981: Lars Gustafsson's "Greatness Strikes Where It Pleases" is published.

1983: Cynthia Ozick's "Rosa" is published.

1986: Louise Erdrich's "Fleur" is published.

1996: Robert Olen Butler's "*Titanic* Survivors Found in Bermuda Triangle" is published.

1998: Aleksandar Hemon's "Islands" is published.

1999: Samrat Upadhyay's "The Good Shopkeeper" is published.

2001: Mary Yukari Waters's "Aftermath" is published.

2005: Saul Bellow dies on April 5 in Brookline, Massachusetts.

Acknowledgments

The editors wish to thank the copyright holders of the excerpted criticism included in this volume and the permissions managers of many book and magazine publishing companies for assisting us in securing reproduction rights. We are also grateful to the staffs of the Detroit Public Library, the Library of Congress, the University of Detroit Mercy Library, Wayne State University Purdy/Kresge Library Complex, and the University of Michigan Libraries for making their resources available to us. Following is a list of the copyright holders who have granted us permission to reproduce material in this volume of *Short Stories for Students (SSfS)*. Every effort has been made to trace copyright, but if omissions have been made, please let us know.

COPYRIGHTED MATERIALS IN *SSfS*, VOLUME 22, WERE REPRODUCED FROM THE FOLLOWING PERIODICALS:

America, May 17, 1997. Copyright © 1997. All rights reserved. Reproduced with permission of America Press, Inc., 106 West 56th Street, New York, NY 10019. For subscription information, visit www.americanmagazine.org.—*Booklist*, v. 95, August, 1999. Copyright © 1999 by the American Library Association. Reproduced by permission.—*Chicago Tribune*, September 4, 1988 for "Enthralling Tale: Louise Erdrich's World of Love and Survival," by Thomas M. Disch. Copyright © 1988 by Chicago Tribune Co. Reproduced by permission of the author.—*Children's Literature*, v. 20, 1992. Copyright © 1992 by Yale University Press. Reproduced by permission.—*Irish University Review*, v. 27, June, 1997. Copyright © 1997 Irish University Review. Reproduced by permission.—*Journal of the Short Story in English*, spring, 1987. Copyright © 1987 by Presses de l'Universitè d'Angers. Reproduced by permission.—*Kipling Journal*, v. 57, September, 1983 for "Mowgli's Jungle," by Roger Lancelyn Green. Reproduced by permission of the Literary Estate of Roger Lancelyn Green.—*Kirkus Reviews*, February 1, 2003. Copyright © 2003 by The Kirkus Service, Inc. All rights reserved. Reproduced by permission of the publisher, Kirkus Reviews and Kirkus Associates, L. P.—*Lancet*, v. 356, December 2, 2000. Copyright © by *Lancet*. Reprinted with permission from Elsevier.—*Library Journal*, v. 113, September 1, 1988; September 1, 1996; v. 125, July 1, 2000; v. 128, March 15, 2003. Copyright © 1988, 1996, 2000, 2003 by Reed Elsevier, USA. All reprinted by permission of the publisher.—*Modern Fiction Studies*, v. 43, 1997. Copyright © 1997 by Purdue Research Foundation, West Lafayette, IN 47907. All rights reserved. Reproduced by permission of The Johns Hopkins University.—*Nation*, v. 259, August, 1994. Copyright © 1994 by The Nation Magazine/The Nation Company, Inc. Reproduced by permission.—*New York Times Book Review*, June 8, 2003. Copyright © 2003 The New York Times Company. Reproduced by permission.—*Partisan Review*, summer, 1991 for "Text and Stories," by Rachel Hadas. Reproduced by permission of the author.—*Publishers Weekly*, v. 246, August

9, 1999; v. 247, May 15, 2000; v. 250, April 28, 2003. Copyright © 1999, 2000, 2003 by Reed Publishing USA. All reproduced from *Publishers Weekly*, published by the Bowker Magazine Group of Cahners Publishing Co., a division of Reed Publishing USA, by permission.—***South China Morning Post (Hong Kong)***, April 13, 2003. Copyright © 2003 South China Morning Post Ltd. Reproduced by permission.—***Studies in Short Fiction***, v. 21, fall, 1984; v. 27, summer, 1987; v. 33, fall, 1996. Copyright © 1984, 1987, 1996 by Studies in Short Fiction. All reproduced by permission.—***The Sunday Tribune***, April 27, 2003. Copyright © 2003 *The Sunday Tribune*. Reproduced by permission.—***Wall Street Journal***, September 29, 1989 for "Change of Pace for a Pair of Heavyweights," by Bruce Bawer. Copyright © 1989 by Dow Jones & Company, Inc. All rights reserved. Reproduced by permission of the publisher and author.—***World Literature Today***, v. 66, spring, 1992; v. 74, winter, 2000; v. 75, spring, 2001. Copyright © 1992, 2000, 2001 by *World Literature Today*. All reproduced by permission.

COPYRIGHTED MATERIALS IN *SSfS*, VOLUME 22, WERE REPRODUCED FROM THE FOLLOWING BOOKS:

Angley, Patricia. From "Fleur Pillager: Feminine, Mythic, and Natural Representations in Louise Erdrich's *Tracks*," in ***Constructions and Confrontations: Changing Representations of Women and Feminism, East and West***. Edited by Cristina Bacchilega and Cornelia N. Moore. University of Hawaii, 1996. Copyright © 1996 by College of Languages, Linguistics and Literature. All rights reserved. Reproduced by permission.—Baxter, Charles. From an Introduction in ***You've Got to Read This: Contemporary American Writers Introduce Stories That Held Them in Awe***. Edited by Ron Hansen and Jim Shepard. HarperCollins, 1994. Copyright © 1994 by Ron Hansen and Jim Shepherd. Reproduced by permission of the authors.—Dübois, Ia. From "Lars Gustafsson," in ***Dictionary of Literary Biography,*** Vol. 257, ***Twentieth-Century Swedish Writers After World War II***. Edited by Ann-Charlotte Gavel Adams. A Bruccoli Clark Layman Book, 2002. Reproduced by permission of Thomson Gale.—Gray, Donald. From "Rudyard Kipling," in ***Dictionary of Literary Biography,*** Vol. 156, ***British Short-Fiction Writers, 1880–1914: The Romantic Tradition***. Edited by William F. Naufftus. A Bruccoli Clark Layman Book, 1996. Reproduced by permission of Thomson Gale.—Hoilman, Dennis R. From "Simon J. Ortiz," in ***Dictionary of Literary Biography***, Vol. 256, ***Twentieth-Century American Western Writers, Third Series***. Edited by Richard H. Cracroft. A Bruccoli Clark Layman Book, 2002. Reproduced by permission of Thomson Gale.—Izzo, David Garrett. From "Stephen Vincent Benét," in ***Dictionary of Literary Biography***, Vol. 249, ***Twentieth-Century American Dramatists, Third Series***. Edited by Christopher Wheatley. A Bruccoli Clark Layman Book, 2001. Reproduced by permission of Thomson Gale.—Nordgren, Joe. From "Robert Olen Butler," in ***Dictionary of Literary Biography***, Vol. 173, ***American Novelists Since World War II, Fifth Series***. Edited by James R. Giles and Wanda H. Giles. A Bruccoli Clark Layman Book, 1996. Reproduced by permission of Thomson Gale.—Opdahl, Keith M. From "Saul Bellow," in ***Dictionary of Literary Biography***, Vol. 28, ***Twentieth-Century American-Jewish Fiction Writers***. Edited by Daniel Walden. A Bruccoli Clark Layman Book, 1984. Reproduced by permission of Thomson Gale.—Rosenberg, Ruth. From "Louise Erdrich," in ***Dictionary of Literary Biography***, Vol. 152, ***American Novelists Since World War II, Fourth Series***. Edited by James Giles and Wanda Giles. A Bruccoli Clark Layman Book, 1995. Reproduced by permission of Thomson Gale.—Smith, Laurel. From "Elizabeth Bowen," in ***Dictionary of Literary Biography***, Vol. 162, ***British Short-Fiction Writers, 1915–1945***. Edited by John H. Rogers. A Bruccoli Clark Layman Book, 1996. Reproduced by permission of Thomson Gale.—***The Times Literary Supplement***, January 25, 1936. Copyright © 1936 by The Times Supplements Limited. Reproduced from the Times Literary Supplement by permission.

Contributors

Bryan Aubrey: Aubrey holds a Ph.D. in English and has published many articles on contemporary literature. Entry on *Greatness Strikes Where It Pleases*. Original essays on *The Good Shopkeeper* and *Greatness Strikes Where It Pleases*.

Michael Becker: Becker has an M.M. in musicology from the University of Texas at Austin. As of 2005, he is completing his Ph.D. in musicology from the same school. Original essay on *"Titanic" Survivors Found in Bermuda Triangle*.

Laura Carter: Carter is a freelance writer. Original essay on *"Titanic" Survivors Found in Bermuda Triangle*.

Sheldon Goldfarb: Goldfarb has a Ph.D. in English and has published two books on the Victorian author William Makepeace Thackeray. Original essay on *An End to Dreams*.

Joyce Hart: Hart is the author of several books. Entry on *The Good Shopkeeper*. Original essay on *The Good Shopkeeper*.

Anna Maria Hong: Hong is a writer-in-residence at the Richard Hugo House in Seattle. Nominated for a 2004 Pushcart Prize, she has published poems in numerous journals and is the editor of the fiction and memoir anthology *Growing Up Asian American* published by William Morrow and Avon Books. Entry on *Aftermath*. Original essay on *Aftermath*.

David Kelly: Kelly is an instructor of literature and creative writing at College of Lake County and Oakton Community College in Des Plaines, Illinois. Entries on *The End of Old Horse*, *A Silver Dish*, and *"Titanic" Survivors Found in Bermuda Triangle*. Original essays on *The End of Old Horse*, *A Silver Dish*, and *"Titanic" Survivors Found in Bermuda Triangle*.

Anthony Martinelli: Martinelli is a Seattle-based freelance writer and editor. Entry on *Mowgli's Brothers*. Original essay on *Mowgli's Brothers*.

Wendy Perkins: Perkins is a professor of American and English literature and film. Entries on *A Day in the Dark*, *An End to Dreams*, and *The Pearl*. Original essays on *A Day in the Dark*, *An End to Dreams*, and *The Pearl*.

Laura Pryor: Pryor has a bachelor of arts degree from the University of Michigan and twenty years experience in professional and creative writing with special interest in fiction. Entry on *Rosa*. Original essay on *Rosa*.

Scott Trudell: Trudell is an independent scholar with a bachelor's degree in English literature. Entries on *Fleur* and *Islands*. Original essays on *Fleur* and *Islands*.

Bonnie Weinreich: Weinreich has a bachelor's degree in English and has worked as a staff reporter for a daily newspaper. Original essay on *The Good Shopkeeper*.

Aftermath

Mary Yukari Waters

2001

Mary Yukari Waters's "Aftermath" was first published in the journal *Manoa* in 2001 and is found in her first short story collection, *The Laws of Evening,* published by Scribner in 2003. The short story was also included in the anthology *The Best American Short Stories 2002.* As of 2005, *The Laws of Evening* remains Waters's only published book.

Like most of the stories in *The Laws of Evening*, "Aftermath" focuses on the life of an individual trying to cope with dramatic change in Japan after the end of World War II. The story's main character Makiko is a young Japanese widow, whose husband was killed while fighting American forces during the war. Following Japan's surrender to the Allied forces, Makiko struggles to raise their seven-year-old son Toshi in the years right after World War II, as the United States occupies Japan and subsidizes its recovery from the war. Makiko tries to instill traditional Japanese values and habits in Toshi, as he inevitably takes in the influences of American culture and Japan modernizes. Makiko also grapples with her memories of the pre-war period and how Japan then contrasts with the more complex and difficult world she lives in now. In addition to exploring the tension between tradition and change, the story focuses on themes of loss, memory, and grief and how individuals come to terms with those phenomena.

Author Biography

Mary Yukari Waters was born in 1965 in Kyoto, Japan. The daughter of a Japanese homemaker

and an Irish American physicist, Waters lived in Kyoto until the age of nine, when her family moved to a small logging town in Northern California, where she spent the rest of her childhood and adolescence. Although she lived in the United States after the age of nine, Waters frequently visited relatives in Japan after moving to California. After studying economics in college, Waters worked as a certified public accountant in Los Angeles for many years, before starting to write fiction at the age of 30.

In 2003, Waters published her first collection of short stories entitled *The Laws of Evening*, in which "Aftermath" appears. The short stories in *The Laws of Evening* focus on the lives of people living in Japan after World War II, and although the stories are not autobiographical, Waters has said that she drew on the experiences of her grandmother and other elderly people she knew while growing up to write about Japanese culture during the time in which the book is set.

Most of the short stories in *The Laws of Evening* were previously published in literary journals such as *Shenandoah*, *Triquarterly*, *The Missouri Review*, and *Zoetrope: All-Story*. "Aftermath" was first published in the journal *Manoa* and was also reprinted in the collection *The Best American Short Stories 2002*. Other short stories in Waters' collection have appeared in the anthologies *The O. Henry Prize Stories 2002*, *The Pushcart Book of Short Stories: The Best Short Stories from a Quarter-Century of the Pushcart Prize*, and *The Best American Short Stories 2003*.

Waters earned her master of fine arts degree in creative writing from the University of California at Irvine. She is the recipient of a 2002 National Endowment for the Arts literature grant and a 2004 Kiriyama Prize Notable Book Award.

Plot Summary

"Aftermath" begins with the protagonist Makiko watching her seven-year-old son Toshi playing dodge-ball in Imamiya Park. As she watches Toshi play the "new American" game, Makiko thinks about how fast Toshi is growing and worries about how quickly Japan is becoming Americanized in the years after Japan's defeat in World War II. She particularly worries about how Toshi is being influenced by this process of modernization, including eating American food at school, which is

provided by the American government that is now supporting Japan's recovery from the war.

As she continues to watch her son play, Makiko also recalls Toshi's toddler years, when her husband Yoshitsune was still alive. With sadness, she remembers a playful routine Toshi and Yoshitsune used to enact. As she reminisces, Makiko compares days gone by with her current life, which is marked by the presence of American Army jeeps and soldiers, who are occupying Japan. She thinks about how the day before, she had gotten angry with Toshi for accepting candy from an American soldier and how she'd struck the pieces of candy out of Toshi's hand, reminding him that American soldiers had killed his father. Feeling remorseful, Makiko comes to the park with caramels for Toshi in an effort to redirect his desire for sweets toward her. When Toshi is finally hit in the dodge-ball game, Makiko thinks about how easily the children switch sides in the game, without allegiance to a particular team.

The next section of the story begins with Makiko encouraging Toshi to remember his father in a nightly prayer ceremony. She lets Toshi light the incense before a family altar that displays photographs of Yoshitsune and other things that belonged to her husband such as letters and scented silk bags. Makiko rotates the items on the altar in an effort to engage her son's interest in memories of Yoshitsune. Although he enjoys lighting the matches, Toshi resists his mother's attempts to get him to think about his deceased father, and Makiko scolds him. Makiko thinks about how Toshi's only memory of his father is of being carried by him on one arm before a sunny window.

After quickly finishing the prayer ceremony, Toshi heads for the dinner table. Since her previous reprimand of him is so recent, Makiko resists scolding Toshi again and allows him to eat his dinner, which is meager. Like everybody else living in Japan during the postwar years, Makiko receives food rations that are given out by the government, since food supplies are scarce. At the end of dinner, Toshi asks Makiko a question about forgetting the past, and Makiko assures him that from now on, he'll remember everything.

In the next scene, Makiko wakes from a dream in which Yoshitsune is hitting her with a flyswatter. Disturbed by the dream, Makiko thinks about how since his death, she has recalled other small injustices from her life with Yoshitsune, and she wonders what to do with those memories. She struggles with the need to create a positive legacy of Yoshitsune for Toshi and her ambivalent feelings about the past.

Following the dream scene, Makiko and Toshi anticipate going to Tanabata Day, a traditional Japanese festival. Also called the "star festival," Tanabata takes place once a year on either the seventh of July or August and is celebrated throughout Japan with colorful activities. The festival honors the Chinese legend of two stars, Altair and Vega, which though usually separated by the Milky Way, are allowed to meet on the day of Tanabata. One custom is to write names on pieces of paper and hang the paper on bamboo trees in the hope of having wishes come true.

On the evening of the festival, Makiko's younger brother Noboru comes by to accompany Makiko and Toshi to the event. A student at the local university, Noboru teases Makiko about her place being too clean. As they walk to the festival, Makiko is struck by a mixture of nostalgic odors that come from a neighbor's open door, and as they walk, Noboru talks about how Japan needs to reinvent itself to keep pace with the modern world and free itself from the American occupation. Makiko warns Toshi to not run too far ahead. As Makiko comments that the changes are taking place too quickly, they pass Mr. Watanabe, an elderly neighbor watering his plants, who mistakes Noboru for Yoshitsune. Mr. Watanabe's mistake makes Makiko recall a pleasant memory of strolling with her husband on a summer evening. Makiko again tells Toshi to slow down and ruminates about her future.

Upon arriving at the festival, Makiko is disappointed to see how different the festival appears from those of her youth. Unlike the colorful festivals of her childhood, the current Tanabata festival sports tattered lanterns and makeshift canopies and grills for roasting corn. The surroundings make Makiko feel ashamed about Japan's defeat in the war. As Toshi tries to run off to meet a friend, Makiko grabs him. Noboru applauds the festival's efforts, as his date, a young female classmate from the university approaches them. Buying two small ears of corn with her ration stamps, Makiko finds herself crying as she eats the corn, which tastes exactly the way it did during previous festivals. After Toshi devours his corn, Makiko gives him the rest of hers, and Noboru teases Toshi for being a piglet. Noboru and his date discuss the legend of the stars honored by the Tanabata festival.

After the festival, Makiko stands on her veranda at home, fanning herself with a paper fan.

Media Adaptations

- An interview with Waters by Stewart Wachs in *Kyoto Journal*, Vol. 56, appears online at www.kyotojournal.org/kjselections/waters.html under the title "The Clarity of Double Vision: An Interview with Mary Yukari Waters."

- The University of California at Los Angeles Asia Institute online magazine *Asia Pacific Arts* features a textual and real video interview with Waters at www.asiaarts.ucla.edu/article.asp?parentid=12287 under the title "The Laws of Mary Yukari Waters."

While Toshi sleeps, she thinks about what a pleasant surprise the festival turned out to be. In spite of its shabbiness, Makiko enjoyed the event more and more as night descended and children lit sparklers over the water, and she attributes her enjoyment of the festivities to her memories of previous celebrations' charms. She hopes that Toshi will remember the festival fondly and recall other memories from his childhood as well.

Characters

A Girl

An unnamed girl is Noboru's date for the Tanabata Day festival. Like him, she is a university student who embraces the changes wrought by the modernization of Japan.

Makiko

The protagonist of the story, Makiko is a young Japanese widow living in Kyoto, Japan after World War II. She struggles to raise her son Toshi to abide by and respect traditional Japanese values, as Japan becomes more and more Americanized during the post-war period. Makiko is also determined to make Toshi remember his father Yoshitsune, who was killed while fighting American soldiers during the war. Throughout the story, Makiko comes to terms with her own pre-war memories and nostalgia for easier and less complicated times.

Noboru

Noboru is Makiko's younger brother and Toshi's uncle. An energetic second-year student at the local university, Noboru openly embraces the American-driven process of modernizing Japan. He argues with Makiko about this process, telling her that Japan needs to adapt to the modern world.

Toshi

Toshi is Makiko's seven-year-old son. He attends an elementary school subsidized by the American government. In spite of his mother's instructions and wishes, Toshi inevitably absorbs the process of Americanization, eating snacks that the American government and soldiers give him and playing dodge-ball with his classmates.

Mr. Watanabe

A minor character, Mr. Watanabe is an elderly neighbor of Makiko and Toshi, whom they encounter briefly on the way to the Tanabata Day festival.

Yoshitsune

Yoshitsune is Makiko's deceased husband, a Japanese soldier who was killed while fighting the Allied forces during World War II. Yoshitsune appears in the story only through Makiko's memories of him, which focus on their brief marriage and his relations with Toshi.

Themes

Memory

One of the major themes of the story is memory, particularly how memory influences the present and how individuals hold onto and let go of memories. The main character Makiko is preoccupied with retaining memories of the pre-war years, and she tries to recall specific events and feelings from the time her husband was alive. She also encourages Toshi to recall memories of his father, and she is disappointed by the fact that he only remembers one moment when his father was carrying him by a window. Makiko attempts to prod more memories of Yoshitsune out of Toshi by having him honor Yoshitsune's memory in a prayer ceremony each evening and by asking him questions

about his father. Makiko wants to instill positive images of Yoshitsune in Toshi's mind, and she tries to preserve "good" memories of the past, while leaving behind less pleasant ones.

For Makiko, memory is also tied to preserving a past that no longer exists, since Japan has changed so dramatically in the wake of World War II. In her eyes, the current situation compares unfavorably with her memories of pre-war Japan, in which traditions and cultural habits were strong. At the Tanabata festival, Makiko is at first distressed by the shabby appearance of the fair, since in her memory past festivals were so much more glorious. However, by the end of the festival, Makiko changes her mind, enjoying the new situation, and she believes that her pleasure derives from the fact that her old memories have given the present a kind of luster, even as those memories are dissolving. As she acknowledges the elusiveness of memory, Makiko wishes for Toshi to remember the evening and other pleasant memories from that time.

Postwar Society

The story takes place in Japan right after the end of World War II, at the end of which Japan surrendered to the Allied forces, led by the United States. Following its defeat, Japan was occupied by American troops, who were part of the process of rebuilding the nation. The presence of U.S. Army personnel creates tension in the story, as the locals are warned to "Keep your young women indoors," and Makiko observes the "American Army jeeps with beefy red arms dangling out the windows roar down Kagane Boulevard, the main thoroughfare just east of Toshi's school." She particularly resents how American soldiers give Toshi candy, when she can barely afford to feed him on the rations everybody is living on, and she scolds Toshi for accepting chocolates from an American soldier, telling Toshi that those men killed his father. She is likewise distressed by the fact that Toshi eats American food at school, as the school is being subsidized by the American government, and she fears that Toshi will become more and more Americanized, forgetting Japanese traditions. Throughout the story, the difficulty of life in postwar Japan is emphasized, as Waters highlights how scarce food is for Japanese civilians who live on meager rations and how their enemy had so quickly become their ally.

Loss

Related to the theme of memory, the theme of loss also informs the story, as Makiko grapples with several losses. Throughout the story, she grieves for

Topics For Further Study

- Consult and read magazines, newspapers, and other media sources to research theories of how memory works. Prepare and deliver a presentation on different theories of memory, using diagrams and pictures to aid your presentation.

- Imagine that it is 1947 and you are living in Japan, Italy, or Germany. Write a short journal entry that describes what your life is like on a typical day. Be creative, and try to use details that show what daily life is like. You may need to research what was going on in the country of your choice before you write.

- Research how Japan developed its modern industries during the late twentieth century. Pick one industry such as automobile manufacturing and write and then give a speech explaining how

that industry transformed the Japanese economy into the world power that it is in the early 2000s. Use supplementary photos, charts, or other information graphics, if possible.

- Find some poems by Japanese poets from the Edo Period such as Basho or Buson. Read their poems and create sketches based on the poems. Present your drawings to the class and read the poems aloud.

- Research festivals in Japan such as the Tanabata Day festival. Pick one festival and write a play that takes place during the festival. Include details such as time of year, the food eaten and activities engaged in by participants. Perform the play or do a staged reading, with different people reading different parts.

---

the loss of her husband, who was killed during the war. In addition, she mourns the loss of the world and culture she knew before the war. Makiko's obsessive efforts to preserve memories and traditional rituals such as the prayer ceremony are her attempts to overcome the sense of loss she feels in the face of enormous changes in her personal and social worlds. Unlike her brother Noboru who embraces the process of modernization as a way for Japan to get on its feet again, Makiko wants to hold onto her memories and the traditional ways, since they are what remains for her in the wake of loss.

Customs and Traditions

Several Japanese customs and traditions make an appearance in the story, including the Tanabata festival, the prayer ceremony, and the ball game Makiko tries to teach Toshi at the beginning of the story while chanting a traditional Japanese song. These customs and traditions serve to both illustrate Makiko's desire to preserve the past and to show how much things have changed in postwar Japan. The Tanabata festival points up how impoverished the town has become after the war, with faded lanterns trotted out and makeshift barrels used for the

festivities. However, the festival also highlights how old traditions and enjoyments persist even in the face of defeat and the process of Americanization.

Style

Setting

The short story takes place in Kyoto, Japan, shortly after the end of World War II. When the story opens, Toshi is playing dodge-ball in a city park called Imamiya, and other scenes in the story take place in Makiko and Toshi's home and on the grounds of the Tanabata Day festival in the city. Although Kyoto was spared bombings and severe damage during the war due to its historic value as a center for art, Kyoto was occupied like other Japanese cities by American troops after World War II, and the occupation informs the story's setting, creating an atmosphere of tension and forced intrusion.

Point of View and Conflict

The story is told from the third person point of view, emphasizing the protagonist Makiko's thoughts, feelings, and observations. The primary conflict in the story is internal, with Makiko struggling to come to terms with her own feelings of loss and nostalgia, as she tries to preserve what she has known in the face of inevitable change. At the end of the story, the conflict is resolved by Makiko's newly found pleasure in current activities that remind her of her pre-war life. Most of the story is propelled by Makiko's thoughts and feelings, as no highly dramatic events occur in the story.

Flashback

Several times in "Aftermath" Waters uses the device of flashback to present action that occurred before the beginning of the story. The first flashback occurs while Makiko watches Toshi playing dodge-ball: she recalls how Yoshitsune would affectionately tease Toshi by asking if he was a man, when Toshi was only a toddler. The second flashback occurs after Makiko dreams of Yoshitsune swatting her with a flyswatter, and she wakes to recall other unpleasant memories such as the time Yoshitsune grabbed and shook her in anger. Other smaller incidents from Makiko's past resurface throughout the story, as current events remind her of past ones. The flashbacks give the reader information about Makiko's life with Yoshitsune before the war and also reinforce the theme of memory and how memory both haunts and eludes individuals.

Motifs

Waters uses the motifs of light and water throughout the story. Sun and sunlight convey a sense of nostalgia, representing the golden light of the pre-war past. As Makiko tries to recall the time Yoshitsune held up Toshi on one arm by a sunny window, she conjures the picture of "How the afternoon sun would seep in through the nursery window, golden, almost amber, advancing with the slow, viscous quality of Tendai honey, overtaking sluggish dust motes and even sound." At the end of the story, Waters again invokes light as a positive force from the past, as Makiko attributes the Tanabata Day's success to previous celebrations that "emit[ted] a lingering phosphorescence through tonight's surface."

The motif of water, on the other hand, represents the movement of the present. From the beginning of the story, Waters likens Makiko's situation to being caught up in a wave, as Makiko "feels unmoored, buffeted among invisible forces that surge up all around her." The water motif occurs again later in the story, after Makiko wakes from the bad dream about Yoshitsune, and Waters has Makiko thinking, "Tonight she senses how far beneath the surface her own past has sunk, its outline distorted by deceptively clear waters." Here, the present is compared to a pool that appears calm but is not. The water motif reinforces the sense that the present is constantly in motion, since water is an element that moves and, unlike earth, is inherently unstable. As Makiko is the character who invokes water imagery repeatedly, the motif also points up how distressed Makiko feels in the midst of dramatic and constant change.

Historical Context

Although Waters published "Aftermath" in 2001, the work is set in Japan right after the end of World War II. On August 14, 1945, following several military defeats and the United States' dropping of an atomic bomb on the Japanese cities of Hiroshima and Nagasaki, Japan's emperor Hirohito surrendered unconditionally to the Allied powers, which included the United States, France, and Great Britain. Japan had been devastated during the war, with all its major cities except for Kyoto suffering from severe bombing damage. Following Japan's surrender, the Allied powers led by the United States occupied Japan from August 1945 through April 1952. General Douglas A. MacArthur was the first supreme commander of the occupation.

In 1947, a new Japanese constitution went into effect, with the emperor losing all political and military power and becoming instead a figurehead (a head of state without real power). The constitution forbade Japan from maintaining an army or leading another war. MacArthur and other American leaders instituted other rules during the occupation to break up strongholds of economic and religious power in Japanese society. American occupiers imposed a series of social reforms, including a reorganization of the educational system. In addition, the Allied forces censored Japanese media during the occupation, forbidding any anti-American statements and topics deemed controversial from being discussed.

During the occupation, Japanese industries and transportation networks that had been destroyed during the war had to be rebuilt. Food shortages and rationing programs continued for many years after the end of World War II. Although the occupation went relatively smoothly due to cooperation

Compare & Contrast

- **Postwar Japan:** The economy and infrastructure of the nation are in ruins. Whole cities have been destroyed and need to be rebuilt from the ground up. Civilians suffer from food shortages and rely on rationing to get food and other necessities.

  Today: Japan is the leading industrial state of East Asia and supports one of the most advanced economies in the world. Following its crushing defeat in World War II, Japan created the fastest growing economy in the postwar period from 1955 to 1990. A world power in the early 2000s, Japan is outproduced only by the United States.

- **Postwar Japan:** From 1945 to 1952, Japan is occupied by Allied forces led by the U.S. military.

  Today: Japan is an independent nation and world power known for its peacetime economic might.

- **Postwar Japan:** Individuals in Japanese cities and in the countryside experience the effects of modernization, as the American occupation continues and Japan develops the modern industries that will make it a world power.

  Today: With rapid industrialization, Japan has become a thoroughly modern culture. One of the most urbanized countries in the world, Japan supports numerous metropolises such as Tokyo, one of the largest cities in the world. City dwellers use modern conveniences such as commuter trains, cars, and appliances. However, along with embracing technological advances and other emblems of modern life, Japan maintains traditional customs and culture, with modern and traditional values existing side by side.

---

between Japanese and Allied forces, criticism of the American occupation increased as the situation continued. The occupation ended in 1952, after the signing of a peace treaty between Japan and the Allied forces in 1951.

Critical Overview

The Laws of Evening, the collection that includes "Aftermath" has received much acclaim from critics, who have noted the precision and elegance of Waters's stories. Many reviewers have praised Waters for creating stories that give a human face to the generation that lived in postwar Japan. As Edel Coffey noted in the preface to an interview with Waters in Ireland's *Sunday Tribune*, "Indeed the stories certainly surpass the usual images we are offered of Japanese culture and Yukari Waters manages to show the humanity behind the societal rules." Similarly, an anonymous reviewer writing

in *Publishers Weekly* lauded Waters's collection noting its sad but hopeful tone: "Wistful yet optimistic, these tales of inevitable cultural mutation, and of the unspoken fear and shame of an older generation wrenched from its prewar world, herald the arrival of a brave new voice that, like the characters herein, speaks with a serenity from a 'limbo for which there are no words.'"

While praising the collection overall, other reviewers such as Mary Park, who reviewed the book for the *New York Times*, have pointed out the lack of dramatic plots in the stories, stating that reading the collection requires a certain amount of patience. Some critics have offered a mixture of positive and negative criticism, as an anonymous reviewer in *Kirkus Reviews* did who noted that "Waters relies heavily on nostalgia and predictions of a future that has already come to pass, and clings to a habit of melodrama ('. . . skimming her consciousness like skipped pebbles over water'), but her stories are as finely wrought as miniature Japanese sculptures in balsa wood."

Army soldier pushing a Japanese youth on a swing in Sendai, Japan, 1951 AP/Wide World Photos

Criticism

Anna Maria Hong

Hong is a writer-in-residence at the Richard Hugo House in Seattle. Nominated for a 2004 Pushcart Prize, she has published poems in numerous journals and is the editor of the fiction and memoir anthology Growing Up Asian American *published by William Morrow and Avon Books. In the following essay, Hong discusses Waters's use of water and light motifs to reinforce the themes of memory and loss.*

Like many of the stories in Waters's acclaimed collection *The Laws of Evening*, "Aftermath" focuses on the life of an individual dealing with post–World War II conditions in Japan. The protagonist, Makiko, is a young widow whose husband has been killed while fighting the Allied forces during the war, and the plot is driven by Makiko's attempts to hold onto her pre-war past in the face of rapid modernization. Makiko is particularly concerned with preserving memories and traditional customs as a way to provide a legacy for her seven-year-old son Toshi, who seems to become more and more Americanized, as she raises him in the years

right after the war. Waters uses the motifs of light and water to convey Makiko's sense of distress over her situation and to elucidate the story's central theme of memory and how memory influences people coping with difficult pasts.

Throughout the story, much of the dramatic conflict centers around Makiko's attempts to preserve memories of Yoshitsune, her deceased husband, for herself and for Toshi. Makiko is disturbed by the fact that Toshi only recalls one memory of his father, and she encourages him to remember more by asking him questions and having him participate in a nightly prayer ceremony to honor the memory of his father. To keep Toshi engaged with the ritual, Makiko rotates the items associated with Yoshitsune, sometimes displaying letters or different photographs. However, although Toshi enjoys lighting the incense on the prayer altar, he hurries through the ceremony, so that he can eat his dinner sooner, much to Makiko's dismay. Obsessed with preserving the past, Makiko scolds Toshi for rushing, telling him that "A man who forgets his past . . . stays at the level of an animal" while she scoops rice into his bowl.

Through her portrayal of Makiko, Waters conveys that memory is a slippery and uncontrollable process. Although Makiko doggedly tries to preserve "good" memories of her pre-war life with Yoshitsune, dwelling on the times when her husband affectionately interacted with their son, she also attempts to banish less pleasant memories, but with little success. In one scene, Makiko wakes up from a dream in which Yoshitsune is hitting her with a flyswatter, and she then recalls other disagreeable memories such as the time during the early years of their marriage when Yoshitsune shook her in anger. This scene illustrates how all types of memories persist and influence Makiko's current post-war life, even as she attempts to control what kinds of memories get through. Waters emphasizes Makiko's distress, as she describes her at the end of this scene: "She has tried so hard to remain true to the past. But the weight of her need must have been too great: her need to be comforted, her need to provide a legacy for a small, fatherless boy. Tonight she senses how far beneath the surface her own past has sunk, its outline distorted by deceptively clear waters."

Here, as elsewhere in the story, Waters uses the motif of water to describe Makiko's present, likening Makiko's current life to a pool, which appears calm but is roiling with memories below the surface. The comparison of Makiko's life to a body of water occurs again when her younger brother Noboru teases her for being so zealously clean, invoking the expression, "Nothing grows in a sterile pond" and then jokingly extolling the virtues of dirt.

Earlier in the story, Waters compares Makiko's situation to being pushed around in a wave, as Makiko "feels unmoored, buffeted among invisible forces that surge up all around her." By associating water with Makiko's life in post-war Japan, Waters conveys the idea that the present is constantly shifting, as the element of water is—unlike wood or earth—always moving. In using this motif, Waters also points up Makiko's sense of fear regarding how quickly things are changing, as water is an inherently unstable element that threatens to obscure or wash away what is left of the past.

Makiko's relentless efforts to preserve memories and rituals such as the prayer ceremony can be seen as her attempts to hold onto something definite in the face of enormous personal and cultural changes. In addition to grieving her husband, Makiko also mourns the loss of an entire way of life, as she sees traditional Japanese customs and values disappear when Japan embraces the process of modernization during the American occupation. Waters contrasts Makiko's reactions to the situation with those of Noboru, who heartily welcomes industrialization as a way for Japan to recover, rebuild, and free itself from U.S. occupation. Makiko, by contrast, resists these changes, wishes that her son and her culture were not growing so rapidly. She longs for a time when her life and Japanese society as a whole were undisturbed by the trauma of war and by recovery from its aftermath.

Waters uses light to show how nostalgically Makiko sees the past, casting her memories of the pre-war years in a golden sunlight. Although she herself cannot recall Toshi's one memory of his father—a seemingly inconsequential moment when Yoshitsune carries him on one arm next to a sunny window—Makiko imagines, "How the afternoon sun would seep in through the nursery window, golden, almost amber, advancing with the slow, viscous quality of Tendai honey, overtaking sluggish dust motes and even sound." Sunlight also imbues the present with a kind of nostalgic quality. On the way to the Tanabata festival, Makiko notices the setting sun "casting a pink and orange glow on the charred wooden lattices where shadows reach" and Toshi's "long shadow sweeping the sunlit fence as sparrows flutter up from charred palings." In these descriptions, Waters conveys how Makiko's focus on the past affects her perceptions

> **In this description, moonlight leads her to consider memory as a transformative force that imbues the shabby, difficult present with a kind of beauty that Makiko finds consoling."**

of the present, giving even current events a sad, lovely, and fleeting feeling. In these ways, Waters uses sunlight to convey a sense of nostalgia and Makiko's particular longings for a less complicated earlier life.

At the end of the story, however, as night descends, and the softer glow of moonlight emerges, Waters alters the motif slightly. Following the Tanabata festival, Makiko stands alone on her veranda thinking about the night's festivities and feeling happy for the first time within the time frame of this story. After noticing the moon and how bright and strong it is "awash with light, pulsing with light," Makiko attributes her contentedness to the fact that, for her, it is the past and her memories of former festivals of her youth that have imparted a sense of joy to her recent experiences at the new Tanabata festival. She thinks: "Surely tonight's festival owed its luster to all that lay beneath, to all those other evenings of her past that emit a lingering phosphorescence through tonight's surface." In this description, moonlight leads her to consider memory as a transformative force that imbues the shabby, difficult present with a kind of beauty that Makiko finds consoling. In this final scene, memories of the past have become less haunting and more reassuring, as the protagonist finds a way to envision her future.

In the last few paragraphs of the story, Waters also mixes the motifs of water and light, with the reference to "tonight's surface" referring back to the pond motif that is used earlier in the work. In addition, Makiko acknowledges that her beloved memories are "dissolving in her consciousness" like liquid beads, reinforcing the idea that memory is uncontrollable in spite of her fervent efforts. And in the last paragraph, Waters employs the light

What Do I Read Next?

- Haruki Murakami's *The Wind-up Bird Chronicle: A Novel* (1998) traces the story of Toru Okada, an ordinary Japanese man who experiences a strange, unsettling journey when his cat and his wife disappear and he goes searching for them. Murakami is one of Japan's most highly regarded contemporary fiction writers, known for his imaginative stories.

- Cynthia Kadohata's novel *The Floating World* (1989) tells the story of a Japanese American family traveling around the United States during the 1950s in search of work and a home. Narrated by the twelve-year-old Olivia, the novel depicts family dynamics against a backdrop of the "floating world" of menial jobs and shifting locales that the family inhabits.

- In *Underground: The Tokyo Gas Attack and the Japanese Psyche* (2001), Japanese novelist Haruki Murakami gives a riveting non-fiction account of the tragic events that took place in Tokyo on March 20, 1995, when followers of the religious cult Aum Shinrikyo unleashed deadly sarin gas into the Tokyo subway system, killing and injuring many commuters.

- Mary Yamamoto's *Grassroots Pacifism in Postwar Japan: The Rebirth of a Nation* (2004) discusses the peace movement led by Japanese workers and housewives during the years after World War II.

- Ronald Takaki's *Strangers from a Different Shore: A History of Asian Americans* (1989) provides a comprehensive history of the contributions and struggles of different Asian Pacific Islander American groups, including Japanese Americans in the United States from the early 1800s through the twentieth century.

---

motif once again, as she describes Makiko hoping that Toshi will recall their life when he is older: "Perhaps Toshi will remember this night. Perhaps it will rise up again, once he is grown, via some smell, some glint of light, bringing indefinable texture and emotion to a future summer evening." By drawing on both of the major motifs of the story in these concluding descriptions of Makiko's shifting perceptions, Waters conveys how the character has experienced a moment of happiness and a reprieve from grieving, as she is able to feel how the light of the past informs her uncertain present and will continue to glimmer into the future.

Source: Anna Maria Hong, Critical Essay on "Aftermath," in *Short Stories for Students*, Thomson Gale, 2006.

Mary Yukari Waters and David Wilson

In the following interview-review, Waters discusses her accounting background and how a combination of guilt, anxiety, and persistence contribute to her success as a writer.

If you want to be a writer, consider becoming an accountant. Number-crunching worked for Mary Yukari Waters, the award-winning author of *The Laws Of Evening: Tales From The Twilight Of A Civilisation* (Scribner $130).

The 37-year-old Japanese-American, who was employed by several Los Angeles accounting firms between 1990 and 2000, explains why: "Because you deal with numbers and things all day so when you start writing at home you really are much fresher. Your brain starts dealing with words and images and it's easier, I think, than if you were doing, say, copy-editing all day—that would be terribly draining."

Waters would write at night which was also helpful. It taught her not to be "finicky and diva-ish".

She can work almost anywhere. "Some people claim that they can only write in the morning and only write between eight and 10 and I think that's great. But if you don't have that luxury, then you learn to make do pretty fast."

A fast talker, Waters quivers with energy that may stem from her quotidian workout routine and diet incorporating nine servings of fruit or vegetables a day. She looks good, too. It's her height, her porcelain skin and those cheekbones "packed high like an Eskimo's", to quote from "Egg-Face," a *Laws Of Evening* story about a girl who, despite this feature, has reached the age of 30 and never been on a date.

"Egg-Face" is, in sharp contrast with Waters' persona, full of melancholy. So, too, is "Aftermath," which explores life after the bombing of Hiroshima leaves a widow with little solace except the memory of her dead husband. Likewise, in "Rationing," a son struggles to tell his dying father, a member of the generation that rebuilt Japan from the ashes, how much he admires him. In "Circling The Hondo," an old woman who is winding down her life recognises "the sorrow of things passing" in the smile of a water Buddha statue.

Sure, other stories such as "Mirror Studies," a meditation on monkeys, are quirky. Likewise, "The Way Love Works," a look at family bonding, exudes affection and humour.

Even so, sadness prevails. "That's what people always say! You know, I am very surprised."

She gradually acclimatises to the idea, slowly saying, "I guess it's sort of like seeing your face on a videotape or something. It's like, Oh!" But she adds that ultimately the book does not leave readers depressed. She thinks it uplifts them: "It's not nihilistic. That's just not me."

Her own resilience sometimes flounders, however. Indeed, some days, she feels "completely out of control" and then resorts to reading "chick lit" (trashy women's literature). In an aside, she goes further, saying "life sucks". But then, as if she had just uttered a heresy, she takes it back, adding that you "kind of just muscle your way through".

She has certainly done that. Her stories have appeared in three major anthologies: *The Best American Short Stories 2002* (Houghton Mifflin), *The O. Henry Prize Stories 2002* (Anchor) and *Pushcart Book Of Short Stories: The Best Stories From A Quarter-Century Of The Pushcart Prize* (WW Norton). Waters, who lives in Los Angeles, also won a 2002 NEA Creative Writing Fellowship award of US$ 20,000 (HK$ 156,000).

Her explanation of how she contrives to be so successful is more sophisticated and complex. She compares the business of being a writer to being on a diet: "There's a sense of guilt that you're always with. I always get this sense of guilt when I'm not writing because I'm taking time off—any time I'm shopping at the grocery store or just hanging out, I feel guilty. When the guilt gets too much, you just have to carve it out," she says, miming the action by digging the thumb and finger of one hand into the palm of the other.

In addition to guilt, her University of California Master's degree in creative writing has played a part in her success. "Impelling" is the word she uses to describe its effect. The course, which she completed in 2000, gave her time and it was "just nice to be in an environment where you could just focus on one thing instead of being split and saying, Okay, part of my mind is here and part of my mind is there."

When facing writer's block, she keeps at it because she never knows when inspiration will strike. She does, however, become frustrated and find herself wishing she had just spent the last four or so barren hours doing something else such as shopping.

She says that it would be nice if the process of writing "was highly . . ."—she leans on the word with all of her poised energy—"efficient". But she is not there yet.

Indeed, it takes her so long to complete a story that if she takes what she earns for it and divide it by the time expended . . . she pauses, and says: "I don't want to even do the math. It would be so appalling."

Another source of anxiety is determining whether a story is completed. All she knows is that when the reader finishes, he or she should think, "Wow!" And that feeling should linger. She can never tell whether a story of hers has turned out well. "It's scary. We were talking last night—I was having dinner with some people and they were saying how comics have it easy because people either applaud or heckle them."

The Laws Of Evening should win Waters applause. One of her heroes, that king of understatement Raymond Carver, might have been proud of the collection. It contains scarcely a duff sentence and is studded with some breathtaking cameos, as when in "Mirror Studies" a character named Dr Ogawa reminds the protagonist of alpha male apes he has studied: "Not in any aggressive sense, but rather in the quiet force of his linear focus, that unrelenting, almost brute push of each thought to the very end."

All the stories are set in her native Japan. Raised in Kyoto, she was nine when her American

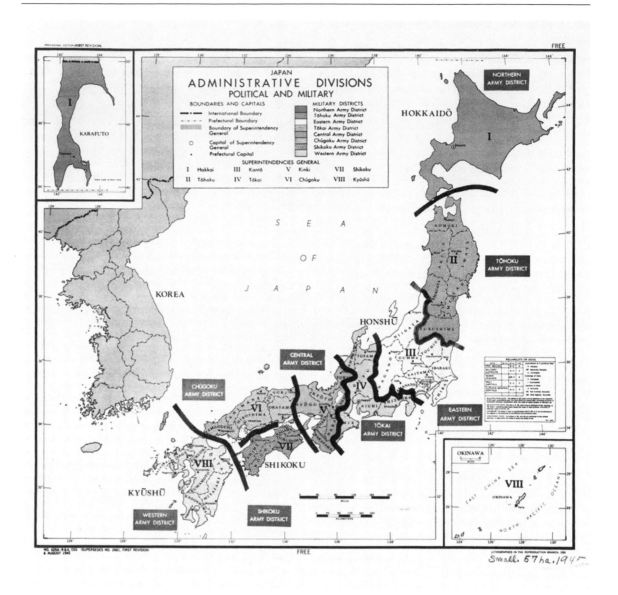

Map showing the administrative divisions of Japan following its surrender to the Allied Occupation forces in World War II   Reproduced by permission of Thomson Gale

computer scientist father and Japanese mother took her to the US for "no particular reason, I suppose they just felt like a change".

She found she missed the gentleness with which the Japanese interact. Life, nevertheless, ran fairly smoothly until her father's death in 1995. It sparked what she calls "a quarter-life crisis" and led her to quit accountancy and begin writing full-time. *The Laws Of Evening* is the result.

Next, she plans a novel, if she can manage it. "I hear that some people are much better at short stories than they are at novels, and vice versa. And of course there are some people that do both well, and I am hoping to God that I am one of those."

The novel's plot has yet to come into focus. She nonetheless appreciates the form's comparatively leisurely pace and the opportunity to lace her writing with more layers, details and "flavouring".

Or rather, as she then puts it bluntly, she likes the way the author can "just sort of put things in there—just for the hell of it".

Writing books apparently beats balancing them any day.

Source: Mary Yukari Waters and David Wilson, "Sum of Her Success," in *South China Morning Post* (Hong Kong), April 13, 2003, p. 5.

Mary Yukari Waters and Edel Coffey

In the following interview-essay, Waters describes her experience with Japanese culture and how it informs the stories in The Laws of Evening.

Having worked as a certified public accountant for 10 years, Mary Yukari Waters came to writing a little later in life. "I did corporate taxes for almost 10 years and pretty much knew from the first year that I had chosen the wrong profession." It wasn't until her father died, when she was 30, however, that she started to think about what she really wanted to do. "My father died and that was a turning point where I started thinking I should spend more time doing what I really love instead of spending time doing what I have to do." So she took a course in creative writing and the result was her collection of short stories. *The Laws of Evening.*

The stories evoke the melancholic beauty of post-war Japan and go beyond the mere facts and into the everyday lives of those affected. Yukari Waters has the advantage of having a deep understanding of both American and Japanese culture. "I've been living in America ever since I was 11 and that's my home but I was born in Japan and went to school there. I think in many ways—although America is my home now—because my childhood experiences all took place in Japan with my Japanese family, in some deep, weird way it feels more like home."

While the stories are not autobiographical they are taken indirectly from her childhood memories, from half-remembered snippets of overheard conversations or local gossip. "I think it's less a concrete history of Japan, maybe a history of the way it feels. That's what I was going for and hopefully some of the sensibilities might make perfect sense to an English-speaking person, to not see it as strange and foreign and inexplicable but something that does make sense if it's presented the right way." Indeed the stories certainly surpass the usual images we are offered of Japanese culture and Yukari Waters manages to show the humanity behind the societal rules. "Japanese culture is seen as inscrutable. I know when you see Japanese people on the street they have a very cold, impenetrable front but once you get past that barrier and go into

their homes you'll find that they're still gossipy and bitchy and funny in a way that isn't obvious to any foreigner." While the stories are bitchy and funny, they all have a thread of melancholy running through them, which, through Yukari Waters's elegant writing, manages to be more beautiful than depressing. "I think a lot of the feelings were driven by the fact that my father died and when you write in the presence of an absence sometimes that happens. I lost my mother when I was 20 and she was 45 and my grandmother's family lost people in the war, so as an adult having lost both my parents there were already huge kinds of losses or gaps. I think that even when I write about the war or Japan after the war—I've only realised this after the book—I've never been that interested in the actual war and the bombing, so that's rather curiously absent in the book. For me what was interesting was how life goes on after a calamity and I've noticed there is a similarity between the actual war in Japan, which is what is superficially in the stories, and with my experience. You lose people that are important and then what happens? How do people come to terms with that? I think that's been the important theme that has come out of it because the characters all find a way to transcend it and move it to the next level. There's so many ways you can deal with loss and things that have happened in your life and through that there's a beauty, a sad but wonderful beauty, and for me that's a force that overlies the book."

Source: Mary Yukari Waters and Edel Coffey, "Living Life after Loss," in *Sunday Tribune* (Ireland), April 27, 2003, p. 8.

Mary Park

In the following review, Park comments on the patience needed to understand Waters' stories in The Laws of Evening, *describing the collection as having a "deceptively smooth and elegant surface."*

Like the spare and prescribed movements of a Japanese tea ceremony, the stories in *The Laws of Evening*, Mary Yukari Waters' first collection, present a deceptively smooth and elegant surface. Underneath this unruffled exterior, however, the smallest nuances convey real depth of feeling. *The Laws of Evening* moves in a cohesive arc from "Seed," in which the drumming made by a procession of Chinese prisoners announces the end of a housewife's cloistered prewar life, to "Mirror Studies," which observes the popularity of nostalgic "wartime" cuisine among jaded city dwellers. In between, a series of Japanese men and women grow old in the wake of their generation's great calamity. Alone late in life, the narrator of the title story spends evenings wandering the grounds of a temple, her mind floating through a world gone pleasantly abstract: "Having little left to lose, little left to desire, had lifted her onto a halcyon mountaintop from which she saw all the sufferings of mankind blending beautifully, like tiny trees, into the landscape below." In "Aftermath," a war widow struggles to salvage her memories in a country that seems bent on forgetting as quickly as possible, while "Rationing" explores the demands strong emotions place on a father and son unaccustomed to such exercise: "It reminded him of track days: anguish escalating unbearably in oxygen-deprived lungs, the blind rush down the homestretch on legs that were too slow." Measured, deliberate and often nearly plotless, these stories require a certain patience, and the delicacy of their construction is not always apparent until the second reading.

But such effort is amply repaid. You come away from this collection wondering, like the scientists in "Mirror Studies," "Isn't life a resilient force ... turning the worst of its disasters into something like this?"

Source: Mary Park, "Lacquer on Everything," in *New York Times Book Review*, June 8, 2003, p. 24.

VNU US Literary Group

In the following review, the reviewer asserts that Waters "relies heavily on nostalgia" and "clings to a habit of melodrama," but concludes that her stories are "finely wrought."

Eleven debut stories about Japanese life circa WWII from Japanese-American Waters. How Japan came to reimagine itself is almost the exclusive theme here. In "Since My House Burned Down," a woman born in the year of the snake is told by her mother that "Snake people lie close to the ground. They feel the earth's forces right up against their stomachs." But after the war years burn down the house of Japan, she reconsiders: "My whole life has been a process of losing security. Or identity. Perhaps they are the same thing. I may not be a true snake." In "Seed," a young Japanese woman lives with her family in an occupied China—a chance to compare cultures and topography: "The immensity of this land. . . . Ancient land, stretching out to desert beneath the blank blue sky of late summer." Dr. Kenji Endo moves to a rural town in Japan to study aggressive primates ("Mirror Studies"), but how will the monkeys here, among the most violent in the world, react to mirrors and endo's arrhythmia? Mysteriously is "The Way Love Works,"

the story of a girl visiting her native Japan with her mother—who will soon die, of course, of heart failure. Best American 2002 selection "Aftermath" finds a woman struggling in a postwar Japan controlled by Americans: What will she do when her son develops an unavoidable affinity for the culture that killed the boy's father? Waters relies heavily on nostalgia and predictions of a future that has already come to pass, and clings to a habit of melodrama (". . . skimming her consciousness like skipped pebbles over water"), but her stories are as finely wrought as miniature Japanese sculptures in balsa wood. Sure to be devoured by fans of Amy Tan and Susan Power.

Source: VNU US Literary Group, Review of *The Laws of Evening*, in *Kirkus Reviews*, February 1, 2003, p. 1.

Bowker Magazine Group

In the following review, the reviewer calls Waters' stories "wistful yet optimistic" and praises her "brave new voice."

The tension between tradition and the "white noise" of Western culture and technology in post-WWII Japan is captured with great poise and delicacy in this debut collection of 11 stories by Japanese-American Waters. As evidence of this clash of cultures, a television rests beside the widow Hanae's family altar in "Kami"; meanwhile, it is only the music of the traditional koto that is in sync with her biological clock (unlike "that tiresome Beethoven, who gives her a headache"). In many of the stories, women contemplate the untimely deaths of their husbands, brothers and fathers, and grow anxious as their children learn who Magellan was, how to use silverware and how to stomach alien foods. Makiko watches her son, Toshi, play dodgeball in "Aftermath," distressed by his willingness to "[heave] the ball at his former teammates without the slightest trace of allegiance," just as she is horrified by her nation's reverence for the American soldiers who killed her husband. "Shibusa" features a mother who cannot bear to meet the eyes of an old friend, whose startled look reminds her of her five-year-old's death in a bombing raid on her neighborhood. Several characters who escape death in combat fall victim to cancer or, in one case, food poisoning, which kills a set of identical twins and convinces their mother that imported bacteria is to blame for the tragedy in the title story. Wistful yet optimistic, these tales of inevitable cultural mutation, and of the unspoken fear and shame of an older generation wrenched from its prewar world, herald the arrival of a brave new voice that, like the characters herein, speaks with serenity from a "limbo for which there are no words."

Forecast: Until recently, the aftereffects of war on the losing countries in World War II have been little discussed. WG. Sebald's recent, nonfiction work, *On the Natural History of Destruction*, provoked a surge of interest in Germany's fate; Waters' collection may spark similar interest in postwar Japan.

Source: Bowker Magazine Group, Review of *The Laws of Evening*, in *Publishers Weekly*, Vol. 250, No. 17, April 28, 2003, p. 46.

Cheryl L. Conway

In the following review, Conway praises Waters' "lyrical descriptions" that help the reader gain "insight into Japanese culture and philosophy."

In her first short story collection, Waters (winner of O. Henry and Pushcart awards) explores the themes of loss, memory, grief, and cultural change in Japan during and after World War II. These compelling stories describe the daily lives of Japanese women and men who have coped with the effects of the war on their lives. Some stories, like those narrated by Japanese widows whose children died because of the poor living conditions, reveal the enlightenment and redemption one can experience over time. Others concentrate on the effect of cultural change. A young widow, who watches her son adapt to Western ways and forget his father, learns to accept these changes for her son's sake. But a young woman in another story lives with her parents and cannot adjust to modern Japan. Through Waters's lyrical descriptions of nature and Buddhist shrines, the reader gains insight into Japanese culture and philosophy. Recommended for public and academic libraries, especially those with strong short story or multicultural collections.

Source: Cheryl L. Conway, Review of *The Laws of Evening*, in *Library Journal*, Vol. 128, No. 5, March 15, 2003, p. 119.

Sources

Park, Mary, "Lacquer on Everything," in *New York Times*, June 8, 2003, sec. 7, col. 2, p. 24.

Review of *The Laws of Evening*, in *Kirkus Reviews*, February 1, 2003.

Review of *The Laws of Evening*, in *Publishers Weekly*, Vol. 250, April 28, 2003, p. 46.

Wachs, Stewart, "The Clarity of Double Vision: An Interview with Mary Yukari Waters," in *Kyoto Journal*, Vol. 56 (See also www.kyotojournal.org/kjselections/waters.html).

Waters, Mary Yukari, "Aftermath," in *The Laws of Evening*, Scribner, 2003, pp. 39–54.

Waters, Mary Yukari, and Edel Coffey, "Living Life after Loss," in *Sunday Tribune* (Ireland), April 27, 2003, p. 8.

Wilson, David, "Sum of Her Success," in *South China Morning Post* (Hong Kong), April 13, 2003, p. 5.

Further Reading

Henshall, Kenneth G., *A History of Japan: From Stone Age to Superpower*, Palgrave Macmillan, 2001.
    Henshall, a New Zealander professor of Japanese Studies, provides a sweeping and lively account of the history of Japan, focusing on both political and cultural history.

Ikeno, Osamu, and Roger Daniels, eds., *The Japanese Mind: Understanding Contemporary Culture*, Tuttle Publishing, 2002.
    The editors, a Japanese and a British professor living in Japan, provide a guide to some aspects of contemporary Japanese culture, including rituals, myths, and ideas about social organization.

Sugimoto, Etsu I., *A Daughter of the Samurai: How a Daughter of Feudal Japan, Living Hundreds of Years in One Generation, Became a Modern American*, Doran, 1933.
    Sugimoto's autobiography tells the true story of her upbringing in traditional Japan and transition to life in the twentieth century in Japan and the United States. The book provides personal insight into Japanese culture as it switches from traditional to twentieth-century norms.

Takaki, Ronald, *A Different Mirror: A History of Multicultural America*, Back Bay Books, 1994.
    Takaki, a Japanese American historian, traces the economic and political history of several groups in the United States, including African Americans, Japanese Americans, Chinese Americans, Mexican Americans, Irish Americans, and Jewish Americans. Takaki focuses on how racism has shaped the experiences of each group.

Varley, H. Paul, *Japanese Culture*, 4th ed., University of Hawai'i Press, 2000.
    Since 1975, this book has been praised as an introductory text on Japanese history and culture.

A Day in the Dark

Elizabeth Bowen

1955

"A Day in the Dark" was first published in the journal *Botteghe Oscure* in 1955 and later in a collection of Elizabeth Bowen's short stories in 1965. Bowen gave the title of the collection the same name as the story, which she placed at the very end as an important closing statement to the work. "A Day in the Dark," considered a "timeless gem" by many readers including F. L. H. Jr. in his review of the collection, focuses on one afternoon in the life of a fifteen-year-old girl in a small town on the west coast of Ireland. What she learns that day forever changes her perspective on the relationships between men and women.

Barbie sets out to ask Miss Banderry, a descendent of one of the town's wealthiest families, a favor for her uncle, for whom she feels an innocent but powerful love. During her conversation with Miss Banderry, however, Barbie learns of the darker side of human passions, which fills her with a sense of dread. By the end of the story, she recognizes that she cannot retreat into the safety of her childhood beliefs after being indoctrinated into the complexities of the adult world.

Author Biography

Elizabeth Bowen was an only child, born in Dublin, Ireland, on June 7, 1899 to Henry Cole Bowen and Florence Colley Brown. Her father worked in the law and this kept the family between their two homes in Ireland, one in Dublin and another in Bowen's Court, her family house in County Cork. Bowen had a happy childhood until 1905, when her father had a nervous breakdown. Due to her father's long convalescence for the next several years, a family physician recommended that Elizabeth and her mother go stay with various aunts in England. Bowen's father recovered from his breakdown when Elizabeth was 12. However, her happiness at the family being reunited was short-lived since her mother died of cancer the following year. Her sense of displacement and loss of innocence as a result of her parent's death became major themes in her work.

After her mother's death, Bowen was sent to Downe House, a boarding school in Kent, England, where she stayed for the next three years. She wrote a great deal of short stories at Downe House, and decided this was what she was meant to do. Bowen was able to get started with her career as a writer partly due to Rose Macaulay, a friend who attended Downe House and who introduced her to influential editors and publishers.

Encounters, her first volume of short stories, was published in 1923. The same year, Bowen married assistant secretary for education in Northampton, Alan Charles Cameron. Bowen was soon immersed in the intellectual atmosphere of Oxford, due to her husband's promotion to secretary of education for that city.

Over the next several decades, Bowen's literary output was prolific. She published several novels, including *The Hotel* (1927), *The Last September* (1929), *Friends and Relations* (1931), and *To the North* (1932). Her literary reputation was firmly established with the publication of *The House in Paris* in 1935, *The Death of the Heart* in 1938 and *The Heat of the Day* in 1948. She also published collections of short fiction, including *The Demon Lover and Other Stories* (1945), and *A Day in the Dark and Other Stories* (1965).

In 1935, Bowen moved with her husband to Regent's Park in London, where she wrote essays for several journals, including the *Tatler*, the *New York Times Magazine*, *Harpers*, and the *Saturday Review of Literature*. During this time, she was also the associate editor of *London Magazine*. Bowen incorporated the subject of World War II in much of her writing. She was an Air Raid Precautions warden during the war, and she and Cameron often suffered through bombing raids in Regent's Park, which gave her firsthand exposure to the war. Bowen continued to write after the war. Her most well-received work was *Eva Trout, or Changing*

Elizabeth Bowen   The Library of Congress

Scenes, which earned her the James Tait Black Memorial Prize in 1970. On February 22, 1973, Elizabeth Bowen died of lung cancer at her home at Hythe, England.

Plot Summary

"A Day in the Dark" is set in Moher, a town on the west coast of Ireland. The story is narrated by Barbie, who looks back on herself as a fifteen year-old-girl and begins this story with a description of a row of houses under the bridge and the center of her town—its intermingling of houses with a "faded air of importance" and a main street that "prospers." She then turns to a history of Miss Banderry, one of the last of a once prominent family. Miss Banderry, who now owns some property and a profitable farm nearby, had insisted on getting half of the profits of the family mills, which eventually drove her "hopeless" brother to suicide. The narrator's uncle has had "dealings" with Miss Banderry and the two have fallen "into talk," especially about magazine and journal articles that she gave him to read.

One afternoon, the narrator pays Miss Banderry a visit to return a magazine and to ask if her uncle can borrow a farming tool from her. She has thought to bring some roses for her, which she pretends are from her uncle. At the door, she meets Mrs. Banderry's widowed niece, Nan, who informs Barbie that her aunt is resting and instructs her to wait. As Barbie passes the time, she notes the interior of the house, "peopled" with portraits of generations of Banderrys. She also examines her "thin" reflection in a mirror, with "no sign yet of a figure."

When Mrs. Banderry finally arrives, she appears disappointed that Barbie's uncle has not come himself. She begins bantering with Barbie, insisting to the girl, "I hear wonders of you," which Barbie recognizes is a lie. Mrs. Banderry pretends that she believes that Barbie's uncle has sent the flowers and thanks for the magazine he had borrowed. When she notices the marks on the magazine, she tries to embarrass Barbie by suggesting that her uncle reads during meals, obviously ignoring his niece. Yet, she immediately counters the stinging comment with "Oh, I'm sure you're a great companion for him."

Barbie imagines that Mrs. Banderry can read her thoughts and emotions, fearing that the woman will discover her love for her uncle. Her thoughts about him have been innocent: "There was not a danger till she spoke."

When Mrs. Banderry tries to conclude the visit, Barbie admits that her uncle wants to again borrow a farming tool. This point upsets the woman who calls him a "brute" and insists, "Time after time, it's the same story." When she declares that she does not like to lend out machinery, Barbie responds haughtily that she will relay the message to her uncle. At this, Mrs. Banderry reconsiders and says that she will think about it and teases that she might agree and she might not. She then returns her attention to Barbie. After a close examination of the girl, she concludes that her uncle should not "hide behind" her skirts, suggesting that he should have come himself. Barbie insists that her uncle is too busy to come that day.

Barbie's memory of the conversation stops after Mrs. Banderry compares Barbie's uncle to her dead brother. The narrator shifts to the present when she is older and more informed; she refuses to fill in any details about the woman that she later gained, insisting that she describe only what she experienced that day from her fifteen-year-old and innocent perspective. She understands that the woman felt an ambivalent "amorous hostility" toward her uncle but questions its cause. Barbie insists that she and her uncle felt no guilt about their relationship that summer, that they "did each other no harm." They "played house together on the margin of a passion which was impossible."

Barbie returns to her memories of that afternoon, relating that she left Mrs. Banderry's home with a little "ceremony," accepting a "thimble glass" of raspberry cordial. As she leaves, Nan asks her "conspiratorially" if she is going to meet her uncle. Barbie admits that she does not know he is in town and that she has planned to take the bus home. After practically shoving her out of the door, Nan watches Barbie as she walks away from the house.

As Barbie walks into town, she sees her uncle's car parked near the hotel. She searches for the bus that will grant her "independence" but discovers it has already departed. Her visit with Mrs. Banderry seems to have changed her attitude toward her uncle, of whom she thinks, she "did not want to be bothered." She feels people watching her from the shops as she walks toward the hotel. As she watches her uncle standing on the porch, she determines that "he was not a lord, only a landowner." He appears to have not been waiting for her. When the two meet at his car he asks how her meeting has gone, whether "the old terror" has eaten her. He is relieved that Miss Banderry has not sent him another magazine. The story ends as he touches Barbie's elbow, reminding her to get in the car.

Characters

Miss Banderry

Given the status her family once held in the town of Moher, Miss Banderry is most likely Anglo-Irish, a group in Ireland that made up the governing class. Her family was in the milling business and owned a profitable farm nearby. After her brother lost control of the family mills, she gained ownership of all the homes in the terrace, some property in another part of town, as well as a profitable farm. Although she is probably one of the wealthiest inhabitants of Moher, her house has a "faded air of importance." Presumably, she has lost the power her family once had when Barbie describes the oil portraits that hang from the walls of her home, depicting the "vanished Banderrys."

Her controlling, selfish nature becomes evident in her treatment of her "hopeless" brother, who sold the family business. After she demanded her share of the profits, he was unable to meet his debts and hanged himself. Later in the story, she callously compares him to Barbie's uncle, insisting that the two were quite "busy" men, ignoring the fact that she drove her brother to suicide.

Aware of her advancing years, she tries desperately to convince others that she is still desirable, as when she greets Barbie with a "racy, indulgent smile, to counteract the impression she knew she gave." She continues to insinuate that she and Barbie's uncle have an intimate relationship by insisting when she sees his thumbprints on her magazine, "I'd know *those* anywhere!" Later, she suggests, with distinctly sexual undertones as she "rub[s] her palms on her thighs," that Barbie's uncle often asks her for favors, referring to him as "my lord" and insisting that he must come to her himself.

She also cruelly taunts Barbie, whom she realizes is in love with her uncle. At times she plays along with the game as Barbie pretends to offer her tokens of her uncle's affection. Just as quickly, though, she tries to undermine Barbie and her uncle's relationship by insinuating that Barbie is too young and inexperienced to maintain his attention.

Barbie

Fifteen-year-old Barbie has an innocent view of love before she goes to visit Miss Banderry. When she meets her, she is "unread," her "susceptibilities were virgin." She admits that she is in love with her uncle, and so will do what she can to "stand between him and trouble." Whenever Miss Banderry tries to attack his character, she defends him, even if it means she must lie to her. Barbie describes her feelings for her uncle as a slow process of transition, like beech trees turning from pink to purple. She is the one who sits in his chair and watches "the lassitude of his hand hanging caressing a dog's ear."

Miss Banderry's insinuations about her own relationship with the uncle as well as Barbie's, however, soon fill Barbie with dread and make her reevaluate her views on male/female interaction. Miss Banderry makes her feel defensive about her relationship with her uncle, so much so that she twice swears that she felt no guilt about their feelings for each other. Later, though she admits that they "played house together on the margin of a passion which was impossible" and that "convention was [their] safeguard," suggesting a certain danger.

She continues to feel a sense of danger and dread when she leaves Miss Banderry's, feelings that are reinforced by the appearance of her uncle at the hotel. Barbie longs to return to the innocence she felt before that afternoon but recognizes that she cannot get "out of reach" of the risks of sexuality. When her uncle touches her elbow as she gets into the car, she crosses over into the darker world of experience.

Nan

The widowed Nan is Miss Banderry's niece, who greets Barbie at the door of her aunt's house and shows her out at the end of the visit. She reinforces the dark, cynical view of sexuality that her aunt relates to Barbie. Nan, "ready to be handsome, wore a cheated ravenous look." While Nan waits for her inheritance from her aunt, the older woman has reduced her into servitude. Nan scoffs at the "overblown" roses that Barbie brings and doubts that they came from her uncle.

Apparently Nan makes it her business to know everyone else's. She tells Barbie that her uncle is at the hotel, thinking that he is waiting to drive home his niece, glancing "conspiratorially" at the girl. Nan claims that Barbie is "mad" for not wanting to ride home with her uncle.

Uncle

Most of the information readers gain about Barbie's uncle comes from her discussions with Nan and Miss Banderry. He does not actually appear until the end of the story. He obviously relies on Barbie, as she appears used to standing "between him and trouble." The "winning, versatile and when necessary inventive talker" appears to be a charmer, who likes having relationships with women but hates "to tax his brain."

Barbie had felt comfortable in her relationship with him until her visit with Miss Banderry. She recognizes that he was fond of her companionship. After Miss Banderry's cynical insinuations about her uncle, Barbie feels a sense of danger about her relationship with him that she had not previously felt. This danger is reinforced when she meets him after her afternoon with Miss Banderry. Her uncle has been at the hotel, and Nan suggests "conspiratorially" that he may have been waiting there for Barbie. His surprise when he sees her, however, indicates that he was at the hotel for another reason, perhaps a secret assignation since he never explains to Barbie what he is doing there. He appears almost sinister at the end of the story as he touches her elbow as she gets in the car.

Themes

Innocence and Experience

In "Day in the Dark," Bowen presents a version of the conflict between innocence and experience. The innocents in the story are not necessarily pure, and the experienced become sinister. Barbie arrives

Topics for Further Study

- Read over the passages in which Barbie describes the landscape of Moher. Write a poem or a short sketch describing a scene in nature and your own or a character's emotional response to it.

- Read Bowen's "The Demon Lover" and compare its themes to those of "A Day in the Dark."

- Bowen lived in a "big house" much like the one occupied by Miss Banderry. Investigate the history of the region of Moher to get a sense of the changes that occurred that would have affected Miss Banderry. How do you think a woman like her would have lived before her family lost the milling business? How do you think this loss affected her? Use details from the story to back up your views.

- Bowen had a difficult childhood as she continually moved from house to house and she eventually lost both her mother and father. Read biographical materials on her to determine whether you see any autobiographical details in the story. Do you think she would identify more with Barbie or with Miss Banderry?

---

at Miss Banderry's with an innocent heart, firmly believing that her love for her uncle is above reproach. But during her conversation with Miss Banderry, she begins to view her uncle and his relationship with her as well as others as potentially "dangerous."

Miss Banderry is a "formidable reader" of human nature. She immediately understands that Barbie's uncle has sent his niece to gain a favor from her and that Barbie has played a part in this deceptive game. Barbie willingly agrees to deceive Miss Banderry with her offering of roses because she is trying to protect her uncle, with whom she has fallen in love.

After listening to Miss Banderry's insinuations about the nature of Barbie's relationship with her uncle, Barbie becomes defensive, asserting to herself that she has no reason to feel guilty about it. Part of the narrative suggests that there has been no physical contact between Barbie and her uncle, but Barbie admits that the two of them "played house together on the margin of a passion which was impossible.

Miss Banderry introduces Barbie into the adult world of sexuality with her intimations concerning her own relationship with Barbie's uncle. Miss Banderry is also guilty of deceit as Barbie catches her "dealing the lie to me like a card" when she accepts the roses and reports that she has heard good things about Barbie. Miss Banderry, Barbie claims, "took a long voluptuous sniff at [the roses], as though deceiving herself as to their origin— showing me she knew how to play the game." The game becomes more sinister as Miss Banderry talks about Barbie's uncle, calling him both a "brute" and "my lord," and complaining about "what blows in off his dirty land." Ironically, while she is trying to assert her influence over Barbie's uncle, Miss Banderry is warning the girl about the dangers women face in their relationships with men.

Barbie feels a sense of betrayal after she leaves Miss Banderry's and sees her uncle at the hotel, which appears to confirm Miss Banderry's dark vision of him. Barbie has sacrificed her innocence in the process as she "sacrificed a hair ribbon to tie the roses." She sees her uncle as "all carriage and colouring" when he is "finished with the hotel." By the end of the story, she has discovered that "he was not a lord, only a landowner."

Guilt

Barbie swears twice that she feels no guilt about her relationship with her uncle. Yet she admits feeling that people are spying on her, which seems to contradict her assertion. Before she arrives at Miss Banderry's house, she imagines that the vines on the terrace "leaned on the balustrade spying down upon [her], or so [she] thought." This initial sense of guilt may be a result of her involvement in her uncle's deceitful game with Miss Banderry.

After her visit with Miss Banderry, however, Barbie's guilt emerges from a darker source: her reexamination of her relationship with her uncle. She feels Nan watching her walk down the street to the hotel where her uncle is. As she walks, she insists, "people started to come to the shop doors in order to look at me in amazement. They knew who I was and where he was. . . . They speculated." As she looks for the bus to take her home, she feels that the people watching her are wondering, "what should *I* be wanting to catch the bus for?" Barbie longs to escape to the innocence of her past but she recognizes that the bus that would have taken her there is now "out of reach," and so she allows her uncle to help her into his car.

Style

Point of View

In his review of *A Day in the Dark*, Edwin Morgan writes, "in this rich selection of her short stories the communication is often an ambiguity or a mystery which the imagination of the reader must try to unravel or complete." One way Bowen accomplishes this is by relating the plot through the narrator's limited point of view. Barbie tells the story as an adult but refuses to add any details that she did not observe or conclusions she did not make during that afternoon. At one point, she claims that memory has failed her and that she has lost half of her conversation with Miss Banderry. This truncated version forces readers to think about omitted parts of the experience and ambiguous parts of the story, like Barbie's sense of danger and dread. Yet this narrative technique provides a truer portrait of Barbie's experience, that of a young girl confronted with disturbing realities and trying to make sense of them.

Setting

Bowen's vivid descriptions of the setting provides meaning that deepens readers' understanding of the story. In his review of her collection of short stories, F. L. H. quotes Bowen as writing (in the Preface to her collection of short stories): "On the whole, places more often than faces have sparked off stories. To be honest, the scenes have been before me before the characters." She spends a good deal of time in "A Day in the Dark" setting the scene in which Barbie learns about the complex adult world she is to enter.

In the beginning of the story, Bowen juxtaposes images of life, transition, and decay, suggesting the movement from innocence to experience, which becomes the story's main theme. The opening image is one of transition, of one coming over the bridge and seeing the "faded air of importance" that characterizes the terrace, where, appropriately, Miss Banderry lives, and nearby the ruined castle. Barbie is literally the one in transition, as she walks from the prosperous town square to Miss Banderry's faded house, where she is to lose her innocent vision of the relationships between men and women.

Also, the castle juxtaposed with the row houses under the bridge suggest the transition in generations of Miss Banderry's Anglo-Irish ancestors, who were themselves land lords (literally lords over the land worked by poor Irish laborers) and later became merely owners of the land.

Bowen also makes good use of interior details in Miss Banderry's house, decorated with pictures of ancestors and a stopped clock. In the parlor where Barbie waits, she has the chance to inspect herself in the mirror at the beginning of an afternoon in which she is forced to reexamine her relationship with her uncle. Nan notes that the roses Barbie brings are "overblown" and did not "travel well" as they drop petals on the doorstep. Miss Banderry, of course, recognizes the lie when she grabs them "thorns and all" and begins the malicious game she plays with Barbie. The roses are an apt symbol of Barbie's situation. Traditionally roses are given as a token of affection, and they can be used to suggest sexuality. But these are past their prime and thorny. By dropping their petals, they suggest the loss of Barbie's sexual innocence; their thorns suggest the thorny lie she is obliged to act out. Barbie's innocent vision of love, like the petal-dropping roses, dies as Miss Banderry introduces Barbie into the adult realities of relationships. The knowledge Barbie gains is later symbolized by "the copper beeches" that surround the house she and her uncle live in that summer "turning from pink to purple," colors that suggest a transformation from bright innocent affection to dark physical passion.

At the end of the story, Bowen uses setting details to further illuminate Barbie's transition. She becomes as powerless as the paper boat the river carries away, "traveling at uncertain speed on the current, list[ing] as it vanished under the bridge." She does not have "the heart to wonder how the boat would fare." But readers may well wonder how Barbie will fare. When she sees her uncle at the hotel, her impulse is to escape. Here the bus becomes the symbol of her freedom from this adult world. She longs to take the bus back to "scenes of safety . . . and solitude." But the innocence of that world is past; a means of escape is "out of reach."

Historical Context

The Decline of the Big Houses

After civil war broke out in Ireland in 1921, ancestral homes known as Big Houses went into decline. They were owned by the Anglo-Irish, British

Compare
&
Contrast

- **1950s:** Girls who engage in sexual activities continue to be sent to convents in Ireland to remove them from such opportunities and to teach them a sense of morality.

  Today: Reflecting the relaxed sexual mores of the twenty-first century, sexual acts involving young adults can be viewed on cable television as well as on the Internet.

- **1950s:** Ireland is plagued by high unemployment figures. This situation makes it even more difficult for women to find work. Women in the cities tend to stay home, but in rural areas, women often work farms alongside men. Both young men and women emigrate to other countries, including England and the United States, in search of better employment opportunities.

  Today: Many young Irish stay in Ireland, which in the early 2000s experiences strong economic growth, especially in the cities where employment opportunities are expanding.

- **1950s:** On both sides of the Atlantic, women feel a growing sense of dissatisfaction about the unequal treatment they receive in the home, the workplace, and in other institutions.

  Today: Women have made major gains in their fight for equality. Discrimination against women is against the law in Ireland, in Britain, and in the United States.

Protestants who made up the occupation governing class in Ireland and who had taken the land away from the Irish Catholics. During the war, many of these homes, like Bowen's Court, Elizabeth Bowen's family estate, were either taken over by soldiers or destroyed by anti-British mobs who regarded them as symbols of social and economic oppression.

Richard Tillinghast, in his article on Bowen, writes that she "was born into a Protestant ascendancy that rose to power and distinction in the eighteenth century and went into decline by the late nineteenth." Tillinghast reveals the influence this movement had on her when he concludes, "The alienation of the Anglo-Irish landowner, set above and isolated from the 'native' population, is a vantage point to which Bowen refers often when writing of Ireland."

In 1903 the Wyndham Act was passed in Ireland, which helped displaced Catholics buy back their lands from the Anglo-Irish. By the second decade of the twentieth century, landlords who had sold off their farms were left with not much more than their big houses. The wealth they had accumulated from the sale of their lands left them with little to occupy their time in a place where they felt a growing sense of isolation.

Girls and Sexuality in Ireland

A celebrated 2003 film *The Magdalene Sisters* depicts the harrowing consequences for Irish girls who experimented with sex during the first half of the twentieth century. Girls who became pregnant or engaged in sexual activities were often handed over to the Catholic Church by their families. Some of them ended up in convents that turned them literally into slaves, working in laundries or other money-making operations. The film paints a bleak picture of convent life, in which it claims the girls were brutalized.

Sexuality in the 1950s

Traditional attitudes about sex began to change during this era. Still heavily influenced by the church, the Irish tried to encourage the young to refrain from sexual experimentation. But new attitudes in America began to filter into the Irish culture. Alfred Kinsey's reports on the sexual behavior of men and women (1948, 1953) helped bring discussions of this subject out in the open in the United States and overseas. Although many Irish clung to oppressive Catholic ideas about sexuality, they could not suppress questions that began to be raised about what constituted normal or abnormal sexual behavior.

Cliff Moher along the Irish coastline Photograph by Daniel L. Gore. © Daniel L. Gore. Reproduced by permission

Movie stars such as Marilyn Monroe and Brigitte Bardot, who openly flaunted their sexuality, intrigued the public on both sides of the Atlantic and magazines like *Playboy*, begun in 1953, gained a wide audience. In the 1960s relaxed moral standards resulted in an age of sexual freedom in Europe and the United States. Yet, most Irish in the 1950s retained conservative attitudes toward sexuality: they did not openly discuss sexual behavior, and promiscuity, especially for women, was not tolerated.

Critical Overview

"A Day in the Dark" was first published in the journal *Botteghe Oscure* in 1955. It appeared in *Mademoiselle* magazine in 1957 and then became the title story in Bowen's 1965 collection of short stories. In a review of that collection, F. L. H. Jr. praises Bowen's detailed descriptions of setting, concluding that "Miss Bowen carries over a novelistic technique to her short stories." Many other scholars have applauded Bowen's attention to detail in these stories, including Edwin Morgan who writes in his review of *A Day in the Dark* that in

this "rich selection of her short stories," "Miss Bowen shows again and again her skill in evoking atmosphere, weather, gardens, houses, brooding human feelings." He also finds a strong connection between place and the "convincing psychological realism" of her stories. Echoing this conclusion, Laurel Smith, in her article on Bowen in the *Dictionary of Literary Biography* determines that "Bowen unobtrusively steers readers through the geography of motives and interactions on which human identity and human character depend."

Turning to "A Day in the Dark," F. L. H. Jr. insists that the story is "a timeless gem about a girl's recognition of the complexities of love." In her article on the story, Lis Christensen claims that it "has been hailed as a Bowen classic." She echoes the positive reviews of the collection when she notes "the dominant role played by rooms and houses and landscapes" in the story. She also praises the story's narrative voice, commenting that "The handling of the narrator provides a degree of ambivalence and complexity . . . that places it among the most sophisticated of Elizabeth Bowen's writings." F. L. H. Jr. illustrates the appeal of this collection and specifically of "A Day in the Dark" with the conclusion that "It's great to be a reader in the same world in which Elizabeth Bowen writes."

Criticism

Wendy Perkins

Perkins is a professor of American and English literature and film. In this essay, Perkins examines the theme of innocence and experience in the story.

Laurel Smith, in her article in the *Dictionary of Literary Biography*, notes that the central concerns in Bowen's short stories are "the complex truths of human relationships." In one of her most poignant stories, "A Day in the Dark," Bowen explores the complex truths in the relationships a fifteen year-old Irish girl has with her uncle and a woman in her town. Barbie's interactions with these two influential figures in her young life cause her to discover the darker nature of sexuality and so to be initiated into the realities of the adult world.

Angus Wilson, in his introduction to *The Collected Stories of Elizabeth Bowen*, concludes that Bowen's best stories focus on the "never changing conflict of youth's hopeful imagination and the regretful doubts of the ageing." In "A Day in the Dark," Bowen alters this conflict a bit to one between "hopeful imagination" and a cynical vision of the adult world. Barbie's and Miss Banderry's conflicting visions center on the issue of sexuality. On the afternoon of her visit Barbie admits that she is in love with her uncle, exclaiming, "with him I felt the tender bond of sex." Since she had not known him when she was a child, she came upon his "manhood" without warning. She had not felt any danger in their relationship, "growing into love . . . like the grass growing into hay on his uncut lawns." Not at least until she visits Miss Banderry that day.

Barbie makes the trip for her uncle, who needs to return a magazine and borrow a farming implement. She insists that he has evaded meetings with Miss Banderry because although "a winning, versatile and when necessary inventive talker, fundamentally [he] hated to tax his brain," and Miss Banderry liked to discuss reading material that she often sent him. Barbie is hopeful that she can successfully perform the favor for her uncle and so brings roses as a gift.

She approaches the house with some trepidation, the cause of which is not immediately apparent. Perhaps it is due to her knowledge of Miss Banderry's hounding of her brother to the point of suicide or perhaps it is due to her understanding that her uncle has a certain relationship with the older woman. Bowen's subtle and indirect narrative style often forces the reader to follow barely detectable suggestions of plot line and character development. Soon after Barbie arrives, however, she confronts the complex realities of adult relationships, which will fill her with a sense of "dread."

Looking back from adulthood, Barbie admits that when she went to Miss Banderry's, she was "unread, [her] susceptibilities were virgin." Her innocence is immediately challenged by Nan, Miss Banderry's dependent niece, who "bets" that the "overblown" roses have not come from Barbie's uncle. The widowed Nan is a "regretful, doubting" older woman like the ones to whom Wilson refers. "[R]eady to be handsome," Nan "wore a cheated ravenous look" as she waits for her inheritance, since she has no other opportunities.

Nan's response exposes Barbie to the complex games that men and women often play, prompting her to acknowledge that her uncle "*had* never thought of the roses. He had commissioned me to be gallant for him any way I chose." He had insisted, "She'll be mad. . . . Better say it was you." Her love for him, however, remains unshaken for she "sacrifices a hair ribbon to tie the roses" because "it rejoices [her] to stand between him and trouble." She again expresses her love when she wonders, "how dared [Nan] speak of my uncle with her bad breath?"

Miss Banderry will soon challenge that innocent love with her subtle treacheries and manipulations. Bowen refuses to make the relationship between Barbie's uncle and Miss Banderry clear since she relates it through the eyes of an inexperienced fifteen-year-old, but the older woman implies that at least from her point of view, there is a sexual tension between the two. She views the young girl as a threat to her relationship with the uncle as she indoctrinates Barbie into the darker side of human desires.

Before the two meet, Barbie observes the portraits of the "vanishing Banderrys" and the stopped clock, which suggest Miss Banderry's faded youth. Yet when Barbie becomes self-conscious under their gaze and so inspects herself in the mirror, she sees, "A tall girl in a sketchy cotton dress. Arms thin, no sign yet of a figure," not yet a woman. When Miss Banderry arrives, she continues the inspection, exclaiming "so he sent *you*, did he?" and sits down "the better to look at" her. Aware of her aged "angry" appearance, Miss Banderry, pastes a "racy, indulgent smile" on her face and begins her banter with Barbie concerning their relationship with Barbie's uncle. Miss Banderry's obvious regrets over her lost youth prompt her attacks on the girl, whom she recognizes as a challenge to the uncle's attentions.

Miss Banderry begins "the game" by pretending to believe that the roses come from Barbie's uncle. She suggests her intimacy with him when she spies his thumbprints on the returned magazine and exclaims, "I'd know *those* anywhere!" and later, when she admits, "he's a handsome fellow." She does her best to make Barbie feel uncomfortable and to undermine the girl's vision of her own relationship with her uncle. Noting that the thumbprints must have been made while he was dining, Miss Banderry insists to Barbie, "it's a poor compliment to you" for him to read at the table.

Her remarks sting Barbie, who is not much of a match for the older woman. She feels as if Miss Banderry can see into her heart and recognize that she is in love with him. Until this point, her love for her uncle has been innocent but Miss Banderry's challenging banter with her, with its obvious sexual undertones, has sounded a note of "danger." Here Barbie glimpses for a moment the implications for her future as she faces the adult world of competition and deceit.

Miss Banderry implies that Barbie's uncle has asked many things of her when she cuts off Barbie's request "My uncle wants" with "What this time?" She tries to suggest the man's dependence on her when she exclaims, "Looking to me to keep him out of jail?" After calling him "a brute," however, she backs down and instructs Barbie, "tell my lord . . . I'll think it over." She insists that if he wants an answer "let him come himself" and accuses him of hiding behind Barbie's "skirts." Barbie tries to defend him but knows that some of what the woman has said about her uncle's behavior is true.

Mrs. Banderry's comparison of her brother to Barbie's uncle fills the girl with "dread," an emotion she feels even as an adult whenever she sees the woman's house. Barbie recognizes that Miss Banderry's "amorous hostility" to her uncle "unsheathed itself when she likened him to the brother she drove to death." This knowledge apparently affects Barbie so greatly that her memory of the meeting breaks off at this point; she notes, "The other half is missing."

The meeting forces her to reexamine her own relationship with her uncle, yet she appears still to deny certain realities. She insists twice that she felt dread during her meeting with Miss Banderry, "not guilt." Twice also she "swears" that she and her uncle "did each other no harm." What she cannot

> " Soon after Barbie arrives, however, she confronts the complex realities of adult relationships, which will fill her with a sense of 'dread.'"

admit is that her encounter with Miss Banderry, arranged by her uncle, did damage her, as does her meeting with him at the end of the afternoon. She acknowledges that she and her uncle had "played house together on the margin of a passion which was impossible" but because of that passion, he had thrown her into the adult world of experience, which she realizes can be dangerous. Nan reads this on Barbie's face when she exclaims to the departing girl, "Anybody would think you'd had bad news!"

When Barbie leaves Miss Banderry's, she is surprised to see her uncle's car outside of the hotel since she told him that she would take the bus home. Her uncle's presence at the hotel suggests an alternate, secretive motive that he never explains. She recognizes that he did not go there to meet her. By the end of this afternoon, Barbie's world has become irreparably altered. The streets are now "filmed by imponderable white dust" that seems to her "the pallor of suspense." The bus that should have been there, granting her "independence" from her uncle and his adult world, has gone, denying her an exit to "the scenes of safety," and "hope of solitude." Her past, innocent relationship with him is now "out of reach," and so she determines that he is no longer her "lord." The end of the story signals Barbie's entrance into this adult territory as she gets in her uncle's car, prompted by his touch on her elbow.

Bowen ends the story on an ambivalent inconclusive note. Readers do not know what happens to Barbie and her relationship with her uncle. Bowen does show us, however, in her finely crafted narrative that she has left her hopeful innocence behind after her "day in the dark" adult world of experience.

Source: Wendy Perkins, Critical Essay on "A Day in the Dark," in *Short Stories for Students*, Thomson Gale, 2006.

What Do I Read Next?

- *Death in Venice* (1913), by Thomas Mann, is a tragic tale of an acclaimed author's obsession for a young boy and an exploration of the nature of beauty.

- *The Awakening* (1899), by Kate Chopin, is a novel of a young woman who struggles to find self-knowledge and inevitably suffers the consequences of trying to establish herself as an independent spirit.

- *Lolita* (1955), by Vladimir Nabokov, focuses on the relationship between a young girl and an older man.

- "The Demon Lover," one of Bowen's most popular stories, focuses on a woman whose lover is killed in the war.

Lis Christensen

In the following essay, Christensen examines Bowen's handling of the I-narrator and other ambiguities in "A Day in the Dark."

I-narrators are so rare in Elizabeth Bowen's fiction that interest naturally attaches to "A Day in the Dark", a first-person story that has been hailed as a Bowen classic. It first appeared in *Botteghe Oscure* in 1955, and ten years later it became the title story of the last collection of her stories to be published in her lifetime. From the point of view of technique, most of the few other I-narratives in Elizabeth Bowen's *Collected Stories* read like experiments in how to convey necessary information to the reader in a plausible manner; this goes for stories like "Love" (1939) and "The Cheery Soul" (1942), whose puzzling circumstances are finally explained to the wondering narrator by one of the characters, in set speeches, as it were. There is no such air of technical experimentation about "A Day in the Dark", which obviates any problems of information by making the narrator the heroine of her own story, and by choosing as narrator a woman with an almost self-advertising literary flair, for

whom it is quite in character to give a vivid rendering of a past experience. It is in many ways a recognisable Bowen story, both in its initiation theme—the sensitive adolescent thrown headlong into the power-games of the adults—and in its elements, from details like the propitiatory offering of flowers chosen by the heroine (roses, of course) to the dominant role played by rooms and houses and landscapes. The handling of the narrator provides a degree of ambivalence and complexity, however, that places it among the most sophisticated of Elizabeth Bowen's writings.

It will come as no surprise to Bowen devotees that there is more to the text than meets the eye, and for the uninitiated reader there are many pointers. The title itself, playing on the many overtones of the word "dark" as well as on the expression "to be in the dark", gives some forewarning of the ambiguities to come. The name chosen for the town on which the plot is centred, Moher, recalls a well-known landmark on the west coast of Ireland, the Cliffs of Moher: several miles of high cliffs falling sheer into the Atlantic—a spot readily associated with *danger* and *fall,* as befits a story concerned, at least on one level, with the loss of innocence. For readers with some knowledge of the Irish language, the name has the additional point the *mothar* (/mohar/) in Irish means a thicket, jungle; it is also used of a ruined *rath* or fort—as Moher in the story has its ruined castle. There are, moreover, early, scarcely veiled hints of wider perspectives in woods that "go back deeply", a "backdrop of Irish-blue mountains", and "elusive lights" in the valley beyond Moher. Reading between the lines in search of such perspectives, and focusing on what the narrator inadvertently reveals in the way she tells her tale, it becomes not so much a story of darkness as of light, luminously dwelling on an idyllic interlude of love-companionship between a charming, lonely man and a young girl on the threshold of sexual awakening. The first-person mould into which the story is cast leaves the author free to explore both the conscious and subconscious levels of her narrator's mind without forfeiting any of her habitual allusiveness, and to employ structural and stylistic features as part of that exploration. At the same time, the text is so overwritten as to approach metafiction, with a built-in distancing effect that appears partly in the guise of a take-off on the too professional text-book story; and the many echoes of Elizabeth Bowen's earlier writings suggest—again, unsurprisingly to her established audience—that it is she herself who is the object of her mockery.

"A Day in the Dark" is ostensibly the story of a young girl's terrifying encounter with the darkness of self-serving adult cynicism, told by herself many years later. Venturing into the neighbouring town on behalf of her farmer uncle to return a magazine and ask for the loan of a farm implement, the fifteen-year-old Barbie is met with snide suggestions about the nature of her relationship with her uncle, with whom she is spending the summer. Miss Banderry, the object of her visit, is an unprepossessing, unscrupulous woman who has hounded her own brother to death and now harasses Barbie's uncle, whom she pointedly refers to as "my lord", in a you-do-this-for-me-and-I'll-do-that-for-you game with unmistakable sexual undertones. On this occasion it is the young girl who has to bear the brunt of her hectoring manner, and she emerges from the ordeal with a lifelong feeling of "dread" (her own word). The story is divided into three sections, sharply marked off by linear spacing. The first section takes us through part of the visit and is abruptly broken off when Miss Banderry compares Barbie's uncle to her dead brother. The second contains the adult narrator's reflections. The third takes up the plotline with Barbie leaving Miss Banderry's house to find her bus, and meeting instead her uncle outside the hotel in the square.

The story shares certain features with other first-person narratives. One is that the sympathy of the reader tends to fall quite naturally on the side of the narrator-heroine; this is emphatically the case here, since Miss Banderry is clearly cast as the villain of the piece, the wolf in "Little Red Riding Hood." Her narrow, claustrophobic parlour is veritably "dark", crowded with mahogany furniture, curtained with heavy lace, looking on to a sunless dead-end road. Stagnation is the key-note. The only things reminiscent of life are the pictures on the wall, but they are all portraits of dead ancestors, and even the clock has stopped. The July afternoon, too, is "dead still", and the monotonous sound of the weir under the parapet of the terrace echoes the monotony of the houses. A liberating sense of movement is provided by the river running through the thriving little town of Moher, chiming in with the humming flour-mills and cheerful hotel, and the cars swishing by on the bridge. The reader is immediately drawn into the story by exclamations and direct address, and is moreover given a distinct identity as someone passing, or likely to pass, through Moher. This is signalled in the very first words of the story: "Coming into Moher over the bridge, you may see a terrace of houses by the river." The text goes on to describe the houses in the terrace, referring again twice to the

> "...Elizabeth Bowen created a narrator embodying many of the faults of the professional writer who knows all the tricks of the trade, yet succumbs repeatedly to the overriding sin of overemphasis."

brief imaginary visit of the reader. The contrast between stagnation and movement is thus established, even hammered home, already on the first page, with the readers on their travels firmly placed on the side of movement, against the Miss Banderrys of this world; and having enlisted us at an early stage as accomplices against Miss Banderry, the narrator can more easily presume on our sympathy with her teenage infatuation.

Again in common with other first-person narratives, the protagonist of "A Day in the Dark" is careful to establish her own credibility, insisting on the fact that she only sets down what she can actually remember. She makes a point of not filling in her here-and-now portrait of Miss Banderry, for instance, and draws attention to places where her memory has failed her; she has, so to speak, made it her business to be frank, and this is a part of that frankness. Frank, too, is the way she exhibits, even flaunts her schoolgirl infatuation with her uncle, orchestrating it with suggestively lush natural scenery: "With him I felt the tender bond of sex. Seven, eight weeks with him under his roof, among the copper beeches from spring to summer turning from pink to purple, and I was in love with him." The frankness is somewhat belied, however, by ambiguity as to what actually took place—notably where the narrator, commenting on a catty remark of Miss Banderry's, says: "It was as though she saw me casting myself down by my uncle's chair when he'd left the room, or watching the lassitude of his hand hanging caressing a dog's ear." Whether she in fact did one or the other is perhaps not so important as the impression we get that she is so lost in recollection—or fantasy—that she does not give a thought to making herself intelligible. The confessional tone is never far absent, however, and the narrator is clearly one of those ladies who protest too much: "It could be said, my gathering of foreboding had to do with my relationship with him—yet in that, there was no guilt anywhere, I could swear! I swear we did each other no harm." The appeal to the reader that ends this paragraph similarly defeats its own purpose: "All thought well of his hospitality to me. Convention was our safeguard: could one have stronger?"

Much of this might arguably have been conveyed by a third-person narrator with Barbie as reflector. But there is a very real advantage in the choice of the first person in the use of style and structure to reflect the subconscious of the narrator-heroine, as in the rhetorical question just quoted, and in the way past events and adolescent emotions are filtered through an adult mind inevitably open to the suspicion of repression. The depth of the narrator-heroine's feeling for her uncle appears nowhere more clearly than at the very end of the story when, after a graphic vignette of him standing in the porch of the hotel, she lets fall the words, "He was not a lord, only a landowner"—puzzlingly, and seemingly out of context, until we realise that it is Miss Banderry's references to her uncle as "my lord" all those years ago that are still uppermost in the narrator's mind when she is telling her story.

The story moves in its own rather cavalier fashion between different temporal planes and modes of narration. The initial paragraphs describing the setting are held in the present tense, with a future perspective in references to the reader-traveller and a potted history of Miss Banderry before the story proper begins with the words, "So much I knew when I rang her doorbell." Even then, there is room for a thumbnail sketch of the niece who opens the door to Barbie and a pre-past paragraph giving a revealing glimpse of her easy-going uncle, before she is shown into Miss Banderry's "narrow parlour." When the story finally gets under way in the narrative past, it is still anchored in the present; the past is referred to from a present standpoint as "that afternoon" or "that day", and there are repeated present-tense interruptions in the flow of the past narrative in the form of general and specific comment, even a sortie into pure metafiction: "I refuse to fill in her outline retrospectively: I show you only what I saw at the time." The narrative voice is almost insistently that of an adult recalling past events, interrupted only by snatches of direct speech—and even that may be accompanied by

narratorial comment: "'He told me to tell you, he enjoyed it.' (I saw my uncle dallying, stuffing himself with buttered toast.) 'With his best thanks.'"

It becomes increasingly clear, as the story progresses, that the narrator's mind is not really on the sleazy shadow cast by Miss Banderry on her relationship with her uncle, but rather on that relationship itself. Her subject is, in her own words, "Not what she [Miss Banderry] was, but *what she did to me*" [my italics]. Yet what Miss Banderry actually *did* is never explained in so many words; it is never made clear what exactly the narrator dreaded—whether it was a vague fear that Miss Banderry might harm her uncle, as she had caused her own brother's death; or that her insinuations were true, and the uncle-niece relationship might turn out to be not all that innocent; or, again, that it might lose its innocence. Perhaps this is what actually happens as soon as Barbie is made aware of the construction others may put on it; perhaps that is what is suggested by the use of words like "danger" ("There was not a danger till she spoke") and "foreboding" ("It could be said, my gathering of foreboding had to do with my relation with him"). Following this line of thought, we may pick up the word "suspense" towards the end of the story, taking it to mean that Barbie is on tenterhooks about meeting her uncle again in the light of what Miss Banderry has indirectly revealed: "That day the approach to Moher, even the crimson valerian on the stone walls, was filmed by imponderable white dust as though flourbags had been shaken. To me, this was the pallor of suspense." This would be quite in line with her longing to be alone, as in a prelapsarian state of innocence, in the peace and quiet of his house when he was not there. These are hints and guesses, however, in keeping with Elizabeth Bowen's customary narrative methods perhaps, but at variance with what we have been led to expect. Once the narrator has spelt out for us that it really is dread she is talking of—which she does quite literally: "When I speak of dread I mean dread, not guilt"—the word "dread" is not mentioned again. No analysis of the way Miss Banderry affected her is forthcoming, and the only direct information she offers as to any lasting effect of her visit is that she still "mislike[s] any terrace facing a river." The anticipation that has been encouraged in the reader is finally superseded by the interest surrounding the meeting between niece and uncle.

As the story gathers momentum, then, the emphasis veers away from Miss Banderry to the narrator's uncle. He is referred to throughout as "my uncle", with an appellative at once possessive and slightly distancing to the reader, who is not invited to share so much as his name (that he is feckless and devious and shirks responsibility we see for ourselves; the narrator withholds all comment, and perhaps all conscious knowledge, in this respect). The shift in emphasis accompanies the widely different presentation of the two contrasted adult characters, one commanding our attention at the beginning of the story, the other at the end. Miss Banderry is given an immense build-up: her name is introduced with awe, foregrounded in a simple sentence at the end of a paragraph: "You *could,* I can see, overlook my terrace of houses—because of the castle, indifference or haste. I only do not because I am looking out for them. For in No. 4 lives Miss Banderry." Then follows a brief review of her past history, and her handsome front door provides a concrete image of her substantial wealth. Her actual entrance is further delayed for several paragraphs, leaving time for a piece of stage business between the narrator and Miss Banderry's niece, and when she herself finally appears she is given a physical description such as we might expect when a new character enters a story: massive bust, choleric colouring, racy smile. The narrator seems to be following similar text-book guidelines (How To Introduce Your Characters) when she uses the gimmick of seeing herself in a mirror to describe her own appearance: "A tall girl in a sketchy cotton dress. Arms thin, no signs yet of a figure. Hair forward over the shoulders in two plaits, like, said my uncle, a Red Indian maiden's. Barbie was my name." She supplies her name almost as an afterthought, as though she knew it was something we should be told, a necessary piece of information that has to be fitted in somewhere. "Barbie" is never mentioned again and may seem superfluous; but it does serve to distance the narrator from her youthful persona, and to point up the fact that her hero is never given a name.

The uncle is introduced almost by the way. Indeed, he hardly gets a proper introduction at all, for he is first mentioned in the rundown of Miss Banderry's past merits, when the text assumes that we already know about him: "My uncle, whose land adjoined on hers, had dealings with her"; and mention of a blistered circle on *Blackwood's Magazine* "where my uncle must have stood down *his* glass" [my italics] suggests that the reader is well acquainted with the man's habits. Up to the very end of the story, this is how his picture is built up: the narrator concentrates on telling us something else, and the uncle is backgrounded—presupposing that we are in some degree familiar with him or at least

with his existence, and at the same time inducing us to take him as much for granted as his niece does. The glass I have just referred to comes in by the way when the narrator is telling of her errand to Miss Banderry. The uncle's farm, too, which is juxtaposed so markedly to Miss Banderry's terrace as a telling indication of his easygoing nature, is never made the focus of attention; that he has an overgrown garden appears à propos of picking roses for Miss Banderry, where familiarity is implied by the use of the definite article: "I would not do too badly with these, I'd thought, as I untangled them from *the* convolvulus in *the* flowerbed" [my italics]. His physical appearance is never described in so many words, moreover, and it is only through Miss Banderry's remarks that we learn that he is "a handsome fellow." It is not until the very last page that he appears "in the flesh", as Bowen might say, and by then he has fully won our sympathy, if only because of Miss Banderry's hostility to him. We see him before we hear him, nameless as ever and even thus in a class by himself, a princely figure framed in the porch of the hotel under the gold letters of its name (the lettering highlighted by being mentioned twice); "He tossed a cigarette away, put the hand in a pocket and stood there under the gold lettering." This is a well staged entrance if ever there was one, which the narrator nevertheless has thought well to point up by telling us a few paragraphs earlier that the square was "an all but empty theatre." And such is the aura surrounding the unnamed prince that one almost forgets how easily—charming as he is, gallant, lazy, fond of a glass and easygoing to a fault—he might, seen through other eyes than those of an adoring niece, have become yet another version of the cardboard cut-out that popularly does duty as the "typical Irishman."

In the final scene, the scene that stays in the reader's mind, the dread that the narrator initially seemed to have been leading up to has dissolved beneath the bantering tone of her uncle:

> We met at his car. He asked: 'How was she, the old terror?'
>
> 'I don't know.'
>
> 'She didn't eat you?'
>
> 'No,' I said, shaking my head.
>
> 'Or send me another magazine?'
>
> 'No. Not this time.'
>
> 'Thank God.'
>
> He opened the car door and touched my elbow, reminding me to get in.

This is an unusual note, surely, on which to end a story about dread. It is tempting to compare it with the very different ending of Joyce's "Araby", with which "A Day in the Dark" has a good deal in common: initiation theme, first-person narrator, opening description of a dead-end street, adolescent protagonist living with surrogate parent(s) and assuming the role of knight-defender of a less than perfect beloved. Joyce's story ends: "Gazing up into the darkness I saw myself as a creature driven and derided by vanity; and my eyes burned with anguish and anger."

The very last words in "A Day in the Dark" do nothing to resolve the story's ambivalence. The narrator ignores, or chooses to ignore, the intimacy of the uncle's final gesture, as she has a page earlier passed lightly over an earlier occasion when she and her uncle had "lingered, elbow to elbow" on the bridge—this in the same paragraph where she makes the Freudian slip of describing the battlements of the castle as being "kissed by the sky." She also seems blind to the suggestion that her uncle found her attractive, which appears when she quotes his rather novelettish comparison of her plaits to "a Red Indian maiden's." It is as though the narrator, while more than willing to reveal her own emotions, is at pains to avoid anything that might sully our impression of her hero. This leads her to assume a knowledge of his mind that is not quite in keeping with her necessarily restricted point of view: her own longing, she tells us, was not for an embrace, but for "him"; "as for him," she roundly goes on, "he was glad of companionship." Similarly, in the final scene she blandly asserts that he was not looking out for her with the same confidence that she tells us that he took her elbow to remind her—or rather, more ambivalently, "reminding" her—to get into the car. Whether she identifies so much with her uncle that she feels privy to his thoughts, or is playing down any suggestion of sexual attraction, her character has a psychological depth that is a major point of interest in the story.

It remains to consider the extraordinary degree of overemphasis by which the text constantly draws attention to itself as text. I have already pointed to early examples, such as the less than subtle contrast between stagnation and movement in the beginning of the story, and the introduction of Miss Banderry that reads suspiciously like a text-book example. The very creation of two so palpably contrasted characters as Miss Banderry and the narrator's uncle to represent darkness and light is in itself too neat to be overlooked, and their symmetrical

positions are further underlined by the opposition between their nieces and their relationship with them. Miss Banderry's treatment of her niece almost amounts to mental terror; poor Nan—even she has a name—has no more liberty than a slave, and her every movement is watched. "She was not in her aunt's confidence", the narrator tells us, thereby ensuring that we notice, by way of contrast, the perfect amity between herself and her uncle that appears in the brief snatches of dialogue between them. The dark/light symbolism is further pointed up by the difference between Miss Banderry's claustrophobic terrace and the uncle's farm, with butterflies flying in and out of the open windows.

There are many other kinds of overwriting, for "A Day in the Dark" is chock full of literary devices and clichés belonging to the stock-in-trade of the professional writer, and the narrator is apt to crowd on her effects. Even paragraphing and sentence-structure often have a distinct air of contrivance: Miss Banderry is first mentioned in a foregrounded sentence at the end of a paragraph, which I have quoted above, and when her door is opened, it is with the same end-of-paragraph foregrounding: "From the shabby other doors of the terrace, No. 4's stood out, handsomely though sombrely painted red. It opened." Even more melodramatically, change of time and mode is accompanied by spacing after Miss Banderry's last quoted words: "In my life I've known only one other man anything like so busy as your uncle. And shall I tell you who that was? My poor brother." The scene is cut off here by linear spacing, and when the text begins again it is with present-tense commentary.

Again, many images in the text are so obvious that they do not need drawing attention to, though this does not always prevent the narrator from being more than generous in her remarks. The dark terrace already referred to is a case in point: as if its claustrophobic description were not enough, we are told outright that years later it still "focuses dread." Similarly, Nan's frustrated life is clearly prefigured in the caged bird in the window, yet the two are neatly linked for us: "I think the bird above must have been hers"; and the moulting roses, which we might perhaps safely have been left to put our own interpretation on, occasion the niece's remark, "Overblown, aren't they!" plus the narrator's parenthetical comment, "I thought that applied to her". Moher's ruined castle is introduced prominently in the beginning of the story, singled out for our attention by rising "picturesquely", by being "likely to catch the tourist's eye"—and by being mentioned twice within three lines; towards the end of the story it reappears as "splendid battlements, kissed by the sun where they were broken." There are other glaring metaphors in the final scene: looking up the river Barbie sees a paper boat listing uncertainly into the current—the boat is seemingly unmotivated and invites the interpretation that the fragile young girl has now been caught up in the current of adult emotions. She recalls an earlier occasion when she and her uncle had seen a swan's nest—the nest is "now deserted", as, we supply, her innocence is now also lost. And the bus that might have carried her to "scenes of safety" has gone off, leaving only "a drip of grease on dust and a torn ticket" as a dismal image of the sordidness that she finds her romantic attachment reduced to in the eyes of the world.

As overwriting one might also include a tantalising literary allusion in the text, where Miss Banderry is knowingly discussed in terms of Irish and French literature: "She could be novelist's material, I daresay—indeed novels, particularly the French and Irish (for Ireland in some ways resembles France) are full of prototypes of her: oversized women insulated in little provincial towns." This must be enough to set anyone guessing what novels the narrator could possibly have in mind. An Irish reader might come up with one obvious example: Somerville and Ross's *The Real Charlotte* (1894), which is generally regarded as an Irish counterpart of Balzac's *La Cousine Bette* (1846). But how would the narrator expect a non-Irish (putative) audience to react? Were it not for the fact that the narrative voice is not that of the author, the slightly superior, self-promoting attitude might seem ill-judged; it fits in well enough, however, with the adult Barbie's less than discriminating use of structural and stylistic devices that I have been looking at.

For the purposes of "A Day in the Dark", then, Elizabeth Bowen created a narrator embodying many of the faults of the professional writer who knows all the tricks of the trade, yet succumbs repeatedly to the overriding sin of overemphasis. That she is also ridiculing her own foibles will not be lost on her established audience. The overemphasis itself would suggest that she was writing with her tongue in her cheek, for she was quick to find fault with any kind of overwriting, though much of her work in fact laid itself open to that accusation. The suspicion of self-parody in the present story is confirmed by the Irish setting and references to Irish literature, and the many echoes of her earlier writings. The reader-traveller addressed in the very first words of the story thus recalls countless other

travellers and journeys in her books (*The House in Paris* [1935], for instance), and scenes of departure from a favourite ending (cf. again *The House in Paris,* which ends with two of the characters waiting for a taxi). The protagonist in "A Day in the Dark" is one of countless Bowen children who are either orphaned or living apart from their parents, among them several nieces (Lois in *The Last September* [1929], for one), and dark, stuffy interiors with unimaginative or bigoted inhabitants are recurrent features. Many elements in fact turn out to be survivors from earlier contexts, for example, women examining their appearance in a mirror, couples leaning on a bridge, swans nesting; the sexuality in the touch of an elbow was there in her very first story, "Breakfast" (1923), and the pleasure of having an empty house to oneself in her second, "Daffodils" (1923). Tripartite structure recurs in both novels and short stories, while the present story's conceptual framework, demonstratively holding out prospects of self-analysis that are not fulfilled, exaggerates the famed Bowen allusiveness to the point of pastiche. Add to this the informal, even chatty style often adopted by Elizabeth Bowen and transferred to her narrator (including one or two familiar tricks of style, such as the coyly inventive adjective ending in -y: "the *wiry* hopping of a bird in a cage" [my italics], and the unusually placed adverb: "On the other side of the bridge *picturesquely* rises a ruined castle" [my italics]), and "A Day in the Dark" offers as neat a collection of Boweniana as one could wish for.

Given such a dominant element of parody and self-parody, it is all the more remarkable that the story conveys a very moving sense of two characters hovering "on the margin of a passion which was impossible." It is a fair question whether the overwriting I have been discussing has any hand in this. I think it has. The story gains in credibility, even poignancy, by drawing attention to the actual text, and the would-be romance lives its own life, as it were, quite independently of the obtrusive mechanics of the story-telling. It is precisely because the narrator is so heavy-handed, so obvious in her striving for effect and use of cliché, that we are disposed to take her artless backgrounding at face value. Because she is so often less that subtle, we do not suspect her of being designing.

On this showing, the title itself may be read as smoke-screening on the part of the author. Certainly light counts for as much as dark in this story, and the "elusive lights" that are juxtaposed at the beginning to the "chalk drawing" appearance of the little town are an apt metaphor for the subtler emotional currents underlying the sharply etched surface of the text.

Source: Lis Christensen, "A Reading of Elizabeth Bowen's 'A Day in the Dark,'" in *Irish University Review*, Vol. 27, No. 2, 1997, pp. 299–309.

Laurel Smith

In the following essay, Smith discusses Bowen's writing career.

Though not a literary giant of the stature of James Joyce or Virginia Woolf, Elizabeth Bowen is an important twentieth-century literary figure whose fiction has been well received. In presenting the complex truths of human relationships that are her central concerns, that fiction typically attends carefully to realistic details of both character and place. Indeed, in her best stories as well as in her novels Bowen unobtrusively steers readers through the geography of motives and interactions on which human identity and human character depend.

Elizabeth Bowen was born 7 June 1899 in Dublin, but her family home was Bowen's Court, near Kildorrey, County Cork, Ireland. Since the eighteenth century this ancestral home, built by the third Henry Bowen, had been the place that Elizabeth Bowen claimed had "made all the succeeding Bowens." The family can be traced to Welsh, not English, forebears, but critics and biographers have considered her heritage, as did Bowen herself, "classic Anglo-Irish." This heritage was inherently paradoxical: having both Dublin and rural residences, the family lived in a country house yet was separated from the indigenous people by politics and religion. Such families were steadfastly connected to Ireland yet also steeped in the narrower cultural traditions of their particular families. Their lives, according to Bowen, were "singular, independent and secretive." The psychological closeness that pervades the best of Bowen's fiction recalls the condition of Anglo-Irish society during her childhood.

Elizabeth was the only child of Henry Cole Bowen and Florence Colley Brown, whom Victoria Glendinning calls two "vague and dreamy people," and thus Bowen added the independence of being an only child to that of living an isolated country life. As a small child Bowen divided her residency between 15 Herbert Place, Dublin, and Bowen's Court. This pattern altered in 1905 when Henry Bowen became more and more withdrawn, eventually suffering a nervous breakdown. His wife was not prepared to deal with this change by herself, so

she and Elizabeth began living near cousins in southern England. Glendinning reports that Elizabeth saw these years as a time of "not noticing" harsh problems. She began to insulate herself from stress by paying close attention to place and to her childhood world; she found great solace in imagination. She also developed the stammer that persisted through her adulthood. Biographer Glendinning notes that a rich friend of Bowen once arranged for her stammer to be treated by an Austrian psychiatrist, who "laid bare before her his own personal anguishes, both private and professional." Elizabeth was "fascinated" by his disclosure but revealed nothing about herself—and consequently retained her stammer.

By the time Elizabeth was twelve Henry Bowen was recovering, preparing to reunite his family and resume his law practice. Unfortunately, Mrs. Bowen had been diagnosed with cancer and died when Elizabeth was thirteen, so from this time Elizabeth's upbringing was directed by her maternal aunts. They arranged for her to attend Downe House, a boarding school in Kent, from 1914 to 1917. The school, which Elizabeth enjoyed, had been Charles Darwin's residence; his study was the common room. When Elizabeth left the school to begin her adult life, her father had remarried and her main interests had shifted to England.

Even during her adolescence Elizabeth Bowen had thought that she would become an artist, and at age twenty she attended the London County Council School of Art for two terms in pursuit of this goal. She had also done much creative writing at Downe House, so she had been writing short stories even before she began art school. Writing was finally her dominant calling, but Bowen brought her awareness of visual arts into her vocation: she subsequently remarked years later that "often when I write I am trying to make words do the work of line and colour. I have the painter's sensitivity to light. Much (and perhaps the best) of my writing is verbal painting." Finding a first publisher took more than sensitivity and talent, however.

Bowen's first literary patron was Rose Macauley, who had been at Oxford with Downe House headmistress Olive Willis. By the early 1920s Macauley was an established critic and novelist who encouraged Bowen and introduced her to Naomi Royde-Smith, editor of the *Westminster Gazette*. Bowen's first published story appeared in this journal, and through Macauley and Royde-Smith, Bowen's circle of literary acquaintances expanded to include Edith Sitwell, Walter de la Mare, and Aldous Huxley. Although Bowen was not a member of the Bloomsbury group, she and Virginia Woolf did become friends. After her marriage Bowen was accepted into an Oxford intellectual circle that included David Cecil, Maurice Bowra, Cyril Connolly, Evelyn Waugh, Isaiah Berlin, Anthony Powell, and other major literary figures of the time.

In 1923 Bowen's first book, *Encounters: Stories*, was published by Sidgwick and Jackson. The value of a young person's perspective, one that Bowen would use repeatedly, can be seen in many of these stories. Adults become especially unsympathetic when they are self-indulgent, incapable of seeing with the cleaner, and sometimes more cruel, eyes of the young. An autobiographical story in this collection, "Coming Home," reflects some of the feelings and frustrations of the young Elizabeth, who had been sent away while her mother lay dying. In this story young Rosalind is disappointed to return from school and find her mother, "Darlingest," away. From disappointment Rosalind begins to feel worry and guilt that perhaps *she* is somehow responsible if something has happened to her mother. Once Darlingest safely returns, however, Rosalind sulks. When she later seeks forgiveness for her childish behavior, Rosalind must face the sad truth that Darlingest is more important to her than Rosalind is to her mother.

Her first book having been published, Elizabeth Bowen married Alan Charles Cameron in 1923. They had met in Oxford, where Elizabeth's cousin and lifelong friend Audrey Fiennes was living with her widowed mother. Cameron had attended Oxford, fought in World War I, and in the early part of their marriage seemed the dominant spouse. As Elizabeth was just launching her career, Alan did much to make her more sophisticated. Cameron began his own career as an Oxford schoolmaster, and his financial security as a civil servant in education eventually enabled Elizabeth to begin modernizing Bowen's Court when she inherited the ancestral home from her father in 1930.

During the first two years of their marriage, Elizabeth and Alan lived at Kingsthorpe, Northampton, where he was assistant secretary for education for Northamptonshire. There Bowen produced two more books, *Ann Lee's and Other Stories* (1926) and *The Hotel* (1927), the latter being her first novel. The title story of *Ann Lee's* had been first published in an abridged version by John Strachey in the *Spectator*. By this time Bowen had an agent, Curtis Brown. Her stories, however, were still largely rejected. In retrospect Bowen recognized that editors

> **The tight structure of the stories, comparable to that in the finely wrought stories of Henry James, allows Bowen to maintain control and to reveal, not state, those values and insights that present the truth of human feeling."**

may have thought she had incorporated too much experimental "atmosphere" and lost an earlier freshness. Many of these stories, she noted, represent "questions asked" and reflect a stylistic tension born of Bowen's looking back and transforming her own experience into fiction.

Alan Cameron became secretary of education for the city of Oxford in 1925, and there Elizabeth Bowen gained acceptance in a society that did not often accept outsiders. Part of her success can be attributed to the fact that she was a legitimate writer with work in print, but her strong personality and many qualities as both a hostess and a friend ensured her success. Cameron was the one socially outside these Oxford intelligentsia, but he did not begrudge his wife's success, as the two loved and depended on each other. Bowen may have been the famous wife, but she was always formally introduced as Mrs. Cameron at social events.

Following publication of her second novel, *The Last September* (1929), Bowen's other writing during her years at Oxford included two collections of short fiction, *Joining Charles and Other Stories* (1929) and *The Cat Jumps and Other Stories* (1934). By the time the second of these appeared, Bowen's audience was firmly established: the fifteen hundred first-edition copies sold out immediately. "The Cat Jumps" is an interesting story that presents Bowen's deft handling of the supernatural. "Her Table Spread," also included in the 1934 collection, features the "abnormal" Valeria Cuffe, a statuesque young heiress who is still "detained in childhood," sees herself as a princess, and wraps herself in fantasies about her possible princes. Unfortunately, her life on an isolated estate offers her few interests other than her search for the perfect suitor, a search that eventually sends her into the evening rain toward a navy destroyer anchored offshore. There is no landing party to join her for dinner, and Mr. Alban, the dinner guest who might have been a match, feels regret and dismay along with a stirring of passion for the girl in ruined red satin who comes home in the rain. The physical and emotional atmosphere of "Her Table Spread" is rich in its suggestion of social tension that is a psychological tension as well.

Another landscape that reflects emotional stress and the power of situation or place appears in "The Disinherited." Davina Archworth has brought her new friend, Marianne Harvey, to the shut-up home of Lord Thingummy for a gathering of an odd group of people without money or real profession or place. Oliver, the would-be lover of Davina, is "an enemy of society, having been led to expect what he did not get." Marianne has her married life with her husband, Matthew, but she too seems out of place in the company of these people, and even her husband senses something wrong when they are home together the next day. Prothero, the chauffeur of Davina's aunt, has literally gotten away with murder, but he too is disinherited, and he spends his nights writing to his murdered wife and burning the letters. The repercussions of failed expectations follow everyone in this Bowen tale.

Bowen had also published three more novels by 1935—*Friends and Relations* (1931), *To the North* (1932), and *The House in Paris* (1935)—and in that year Cameron and Bowen moved to 2 Clarence Terrace, Regent's Park, London, when he was appointed secretary to the Central Council of School Broadcasting at the BBC. This move, like the move to Oxford, enhanced Elizabeth's career. By this time she was writing reviews for the *Tatler* in addition to her regular writing of fiction, and in 1938 she published *The Death of the Heart*, a novel that many readers have considered her best and that continues to receive critical praise for its psychological realism and technical achievement.

Look at All Those Roses: Short Stories (1941), a collection of works written in the same period as *The Death of the Heart*, contains two important stories that focus on children. In "The Easter Egg Party" Eunice and Isabelle Evers are contented spinsters, "Amazons in homespuns" who wish to "restore childhood" to young Hermione. But Hermione already possesses a mixed identity of childishness and maturity, and the country idyll planned by the two middle-aged sisters becomes disturbing for all three. The Easter-egg party that delights the country children only alienates the unattractive Hermione, who demands to return to her own world, with all its scandal and lost innocence. This story voices Bowen's demand for honesty and her apprehensions about the self-delusive folly of seeking to protect others from corruption or somehow keep them innocent. Hermione shows the sisters the reality that Eden is not, in fact, made to order for anyone.

In "Tears, Idle Tears" seven-year-old Frederick Dickinson seems to have no reason to burst into tears and embarrass his elegant, widowed mother. Yet this behavior is not unusual for Frederick, as he and his mother walk in Regent's Park. His crying, another consequence of lost innocence, dates from his father's death when the boy was two years old. At that time his mother had saved all her sobs to pour onto his baby cot, where the boy had silently awakened without fully knowing the reason for her grief. Now touching her fox fur lightly and appearing as "a lovely mother to have," his mother seems more like an ornament than a person in Bowen's descriptions. Her perfect world is just as false as that of the sisters in "The Easter Egg Party." Meanwhile Frederick meets a girl in the park who is not appalled by him and who mentions another boy, George, who has the same senseless crying affliction. This disclosure represents hope of salvation, and when Frederick looks back on this day, he remembers "a sense of lonely shame being gone"—even as he completely forgets the story about George.

The title story from *Look at All Those Roses* also features a young character, Josephine, as well as Lou, a young woman whose love affair is faltering. Lou and Edward experience car trouble after a weekend away from London; when Edward seeks help, Lou is left in the home of Mrs. Mather and her daughter Josephine, who is confined to an invalid's carriage. The atmosphere is almost siren-like, as Lou lulls herself into thinking that Edward—like the runaway husband and father Mr. Mather—will not be coming back anymore. In fact, Lou begins to think that staying with the Mathers would be preferable: "No wonder I've been tired," she says, "only half getting what I don't really want. Now I want nothing." But Edward does return; Lou leaves, and the status of the affair remains vague. Both the reality and the humanity of the vagueness mark Bowen's art.

The complexity of a love affair and the ways in which others are touched by it are scrutinized in

"Summer Night." Robinson feels perfectly free to entertain Emma, a married woman, at his country house, but this freedom does not guarantee happiness or true love. The visit of Justin and his deaf sister Queenie before Emma arrives faintly suggests other possibilities: that Robinson might find greater satisfaction in traditionally courting Queenie, or that making a home for his absent sons might drive away boredom more effectively. And Emma's husband, the Major, does not deserve his wife's temporary desertion when he is left with Aunt Fran and the children. Only Queenie, in her world of silence and memory, seems truly satisfied. Even her brother Justin feels betrayed enough to write Robinson a wild letter before he goes to bed. In these stories Bowen does not dwell on madness or frantic eros: men and women are too easily bored, or simply restless, even in their passions.

World War II dominated much of Bowen's life in London and the writing she produced during this period. While Cameron joined the Home Guard, supervising the defense of the Broadcasting House during the raids, Bowen became an Air Raid Precautions warden. The war also became an important backdrop for her novel *The Heat of the Day* (1949) and for her short fiction written during the early 1940s and collected as *The Demon Lover, and Other Stories* (1945).

In his introduction to *The Collected Stories of Elizabeth Bowen* Angus Wilson notes that her stories may be some of the best records any future generation will have of London during the war and of the psychological violence and tenderness that the war evoked. Through the stories in *The Demon Lover, and Other Stories* readers may also gain an appreciation for Bowen's ghosts—spirits that are rarely malign but that seem to elucidate the "real" world. In "The Happy Autumn Fields" Mary prefers to dwell in a past peopled by ghosts inspired by letters that are more real than her own bombed house. London exists as its own moonlit ghost in "Mysterious Kor," a story that superbly displays Bowen's painting with words and also shows the threads of feeling that may become entangled in times of war. And the title story, "The Demon Lover," introduces the ghost or "demon" born of one woman's fickle nature.

There are other demons in the stories from this collection. In "Songs My Father Sang Me" a woman is haunted as much by her memory of the girl she had been with her father as by that of the long-absent father himself. In a conversation with her lover, the nameless woman recalls her mother's

aspiration for good appearances and "middle classdom" while her father remained a romantic who could not, and finally would not, be a traveling salesman. Her father's inability to finish any song he started was akin to his inability to get beyond his youth in World War I. These songs for another age, for love itself, are melodies in the end voiced by the daughter, herself thwarted in love. "The Inherited Clock" depicts another kind of haunting past when Clara inherits her rich Cousin Rosanna's clock. Clara and her fellow heir, her cousin Paul, have always known about Rosanna's will and their equal shares of her fortune. Neither Paul with his fickle nature nor Clara with her steadfast and hopeless love for a married man are likely to find that their inheritances improve their lives. Yet Paul is determined to have the skeleton clock, and Clara, though she loathes it, is unwilling to hand it over. Finally, when Paul recounts their stopping the clock as children, an incident that Rosanna had never discovered, other truths come to light. Rosanna's disdain, not affection, have directed this "gift" to Clara, and once that memory is recovered, Clara is changed. Thus truth, not love or money, is the real force that moves people.

Bowen's short fiction reiterates those themes found in her novels. Some critics find that the short story seems an even more appropriate form than the novel for Bowen's psychological portraits and powerful sense of the period. The tight structure of the stories, comparable to that in the finely wrought stories of Henry James, allows Bowen to maintain control and to reveal, not state, those values and insights that present the truth of human feeling. In "Ivy Gripped the Steps" the hero returns to an abandoned house he knew from childhood on the south coast of England, accessible now just after D day. The power of place holds him, because he is still crushed by the memory of himself as a boy, often a visitor here, in love with a beautiful older woman who saw him only as a charming diversion. The perception and the power of childhood, the intricacies of history and place, and the poignant forces of love are familiar Bowen themes that are masterfully handled in this single story.

After the war Bowen's novels, short stories, and essays continued to appear along with reflections on her childhood and other memoirs. Of particular importance is *The Heat of the Day*, generally considered to be Bowen's last major novel, which she intended to be a retrospective, blending public record with personal recollection. Although three more novels were to follow this—*A World of Love* (1955), *The Little Girls* (1964), and *Eva Trout; or,*

Changing Scenes (1968)—none of these demonstrates the mastery of Bowen's best fiction.

Bowen and Cameron had alternated between living in England and living at Bowen's Court throughout their marriage, but in 1952 the couple decided to live at Bowen's Court permanently. Unfortunately Cameron was seriously ill and died that same year. Following her husband's death Bowen remained at the family home until 1959, when she decided to sell Bowen's Court and return to England. Bowen, however much she was writing, remained an active traveler. From 1950 until her final illness she spent part of every year in the United States, where she visited campuses, lectured, and worked as a writer in residence. Glendinning states that the United States became as important to Bowen as Ireland, England, France, or Italy. When she returned from her travels, Bowen came home to Old Headington and later to Hythe in Kent, the place where her mother had died. Troubled by respiratory problems in the latter part of her life, she died of lung cancer on 22 February 1973 at Hythe.

Bowen was an energetic individual, a prolific writer, and a diligent woman of letters. A famous Bowen phrase from *The House in Paris* relates her philosophy of living: she feared having "a life to let." Bowen's lifestyle certainly precluded such an existence. During her career she had produced a new book almost every year, from fiction to history, autobiography, or criticism. She wrote essays and reviews for the *New Statesman and Nation*, the *Tatler*, the *Spectator*, the *Cornhill Magazine*, the *Saturday Review of Literature*, the *New Republic*, the *New York Times Magazine*, and *Harpers*. In the late 1950s she became associate editor of *London Magazine* after having been a contributor to this journal as well. But her life was not confined to writing and publishing. She entertained extensively in England and at Bowen's Court, and she moved beyond English and Irish literary circles to lecture in the United States, Canada, and Europe—and to be featured on radio and television.

As a strong woman who knew success in her lifetime and whose work has maintained a steady appreciation since her death, Bowen is a writer whose best short fiction, particularly that from the 1930s and 1940s, has confirmed critical regard for her as an important figure in English literature. Although the tight structure, the significant patterns, the impressionistic perception, and the psychological realism that may distinguish her writing have attracted the attention of some feminist scholars, Bowen was conscious of her literary success as something that she earned in an intellectual and literary milieu that was both male and female. Her themes are diverse and often uncomfortable, from incest and homosexuality to the absurdities of love and unpopular politics. Bowen appreciated independence on many levels, especially as an artist, but for her the heritage of that independence went beyond feminism.

Source: Laurel Smith, "Elizabeth Bowen," in *Dictionary of Literary Biography*, Vol. 162, *British Short-Fiction Writers, 1915–1945*, edited by John H. Rogers, Gale Research, 1996, pp. 49–56.

Mary Jarrett
In the following essay, Jarrett details Bowen's background in having an ambiguous identity and how that extends to the characters in her short stories.

Elizabeth Bowen felt early what she called the 'Anglo-Irish ambivalence to all things English, a blend of impatience and evasiveness, a reluctance to be pinned down to a relationship.' This, I would argue, richly affected her fiction.

Bowen may be compared with the Anglo-Indian Kipling, with his similar ambivalence to all things English. Each was early exposed to betrayal, alienation, and compromise, and each sought refuge through 'magical' fictions. Kipling, born in Bombay, was abandoned as a small child in England. The hell of bullying into which he was delivered laid, he says, 'the foundation of literary effort.' He played imaginary games in which he literally fenced himself off from the alien world in which he had been made a prisoner, making the later comment that 'The magic, you see, lies in the ring or fence that you take refuge in.' And it was in his House of Desolation that he learnt to read: 'on a day that I remember it came to me that "reading" was not "the Cat lay on the Mat," but a means to everything that would make me happy.'

Elizabeth Bowen suffered feelings of dislocation and betrayal as a child from the lies told to her about her father's mental breakdown and her mother's cancer, and Edwin J. Kenney has pointed out that she learnt to read, at the age of seven, precisely at the time 'when her family catastrophes began to enter her consciousness with her removal to England. As she said later, "All susceptibility belongs to the age of magic, the Eden where fact and fiction were the same; the imaginative writer was the imaginative child, who relied for life upon being lied to." So from this time on, she said, 'Nothing made full sense to me that was not in print.'

She instinctively connected being a grown-up with being a writer—that is, being in control of one's own fictions. For her, as for Kipling, fiction was a way of escape, a powerful magic, a means of a creating another, more tolerable, reality and identity.

Yet this identity could be a shifting one. Elizabeth Bowen, who was the first Bowen child to live and be educated in England since the family settled in Ireland in the seventeenth century, could never decide at school whether to present herself as Irish or as ultra-English, and this 'evasiveness' stayed with her all her life, this 'reluctance to be pinned down to a relationship' affected the way in which she presented her fictions. In all her best stories there is a refusal to pronounce on the validity of the worlds her characters create for themselves. Many of her characters share the fervent wish of Lydia in 'The Return': 'if she had only a few feet of silence of her own, to exclude the world from, to build up in something of herself.' But the nature of the silence, like the nature of the building up, in all her best stories is always left open to question. This is true too of Kipling: I would name in particular 'Mrs Bathurst' and 'The Wish House'. Kipling, however, draws attention to his ambivalence by the use of the frame of an outer narrator (in 'Mrs Bathurst' a double frame) in a way Elizabeth Bowen does not.

Nor do all Bowen's short stories have this richness of ambivalence. She wrote in 1959, of her art as a short story writer: 'More than half my life is under the steadying influence of the novel, with its calmer, stricter, more orthodox demands: into the novel goes such taste as I have for rational behaviour and social portraiture. The short story, as I see it to be, allows for what is crazy about humanity: obstinacies, inordinate heroisms, "immortal longings".' Some of this craziness and these immortal longings are made explicitly supernatural, for example in 'The Cheery Soul', 'The Demon Lover', 'Green Holly', and 'Hand in Glove'. That is to say, they are stories in which the surface of ordinary life cracks. This is to use Elizabeth Bowen's own image; in a broadcast discussion of 1948 she explained that she was fascinated with the surface of life not so much for its own sake, as for the dangerous sense it gives of being a thin crust above a bottomless abyss: 'the more the surface seems to heave or threaten to crack, the more its actual pattern fascinates me.' I would argue that in her finest stories the surface only seems to heave but never finally cracks.

One consistent cause of surface-heaving in Bowen is alienation, a loss of identity, like Mrs

> " One consistent cause of surface-heaving in Bowen is alienation, a loss of identity...."

Watson's in 'Attractive Modern Homes', who begins to doubt her own existence when she moves to a new housing estate, or that of the drifting Tibbie, 'The Girl with the Stoop', who 'had not learnt yet how to feel like a resident'. Bowen remarks of the Londoners in 'A Walk in the Woods' that 'Not to be sure where one is induces panic'. Yet in this same story the 'city woman' exclaims to the young lover she has brought to the woods, '"Before you came, I was walled in alive."' Imprisonment, the ultimate loss of control of one's environment, is another major preoccupation of the stories.

Imprisonment takes many forms. The prison can be one of vulgarity, an intolerable aesthetic assault, as it is for Mr Rossiter in 'Breakfast', trapped by the lodging-house's 'thick fumes of coffee and bacon, the doggy-smelling carpet, the tight, glazed noses of the family ready to split loudly from their skins'—an image in which even the family's noses become impatient prisoners. Cicely in 'The New House' make her escape into marriage, with the claim—which would be merely whimsical in another writer—that she was imprisoned in her life with her brother in the old house by the way the furniture was arranged. Oliver and Davina fail to escape into marriage, and their imprisonment is inaction: 'Their May had been blighted. Now, each immobile from poverty, each frozen into their settings like leaves in the dull ice of different puddles, they seldom met.'

Very often the imprisonment is the capture of one person by another. It can be deliberate, like the social capture of the young wife in 'Mrs Windermere': 'Firmly encircling Esmée's wrist with a thumb and forefinger she led her down Regent Street.' Or it can be involuntary, like the enslavement of the hapless Mr Richardson in 'Ann Lee's' by someone 'as indifferent as a magnet'. Ann Lee, the mysterious enslaver and hat-creator, incidentally appears to derive her power from the fact that she eludes identification: 'Letty Ames had said that she was practically a lady; a queer creature, Letty couldn't place her.'

For other characters, imprisonment can actually be the pressure of being a magnet, of feeling other people's needs. Clifford in 'A Love Story' feels that 'the nightmare of being wanted was beginning, in this room, to close in round him again.' In 'The Dancing-Mistress' Peelie the pianist, who wears a slave bangle on each arm, and Lulu, the male hotel secretary, are in thrall to their 'dancing mistress' Joyce James, whose name is perhaps an allusion to the 'paralysis' of James Joyces's *Dubliners,* since she is the prisoner of her own stupor of weariness. Bullying a clumsy pupil is all that affords her 'a little shudder of pleasure' and she is dismayed by Peelie's bright suggestion that the pupil might die, because 'She couldn't do without Margery Mannering: she wanted to kill her.' She wants, that is, the perpetual pleasure of hating and tormenting Margery. But, on another level, to kill Margery would mean that she need never do without her, for the Metropole ballroom in which Joyce and Peelie work is a vision of Hell. As Joyce says to her friend: "'Oh, Peelie, I'm *dead*!'", and when her would-be lover Lulu tries to hold Joyce's sleeping body in the taxi, Peelie implicitly warns him: "'You'll be as stiff as hell in a few minutes—I am, always.'" The story balances exactly between the real and the supernatural.

In many of the 'ghost' stories the ghost may be seen as the conscious or unconscious fiction of one of the characters. In 'Making Arrangements' a deserted husband is asked to send on all his wife's dresses, and his perception of her shallowness and her social dependence on him becomes his perception that 'From the hotel by the river the disembodied ghost of Margery was crying thinly to him for her body, her innumerable lovely bodies.' In 'The Shadowy Third' the second wife is haunted by the *idea* of the unloved first wife—although she does supply a technically correct explanation (murder) for the existence of a ghost by saying that she thinks "'that not to want a person must be a sort, a sort of murder.'"

Some ghosts are seen by the characters themselves as fictions. Thomas, a ghostlike figure himself who must never enter the world of the couple's children, visits Gerard and Janet. He is treated to a sickening, civilized display of luxurious acquisitions, but the fly in the ointment is Janet's acquisition of a ghost called Clara. It gradually becomes apparent that the ghost is the embodiment of Janet's own loneliness and unhappiness, so that Thomas feels how much less humiliating it would have been for Gerard for Janet to have taken a lover, and Gerard complains petulantly, "'She's seeing too much of this ghost.'"

In 'Dead Mabelle' the ghost is the dead film star whose films go on playing. Like Vickery in Kipling's 'Mrs Bathurst', Mabelle's fan William is drawn obsessively to her phantom image. The different worlds of reality comically collide when the distraught William returns home and jerks open a drawer for the pistol for a cinematic suicide, only to find a litter of odds and ends. Another collision of realities, or fictions, occurs in 'The Back Drawing-Room'. This story is relatively unusual for Elizabeth Bowen in having an outer framework of narrators. As one of the characters mutters disgustedly under her breath, "'Hell! . . . Bring in the Yule log, this is a Dickens Christmas. We're going to tell ghost stories.'" But the guileless little man who tells of his own supernatural experience in Ireland has no notion of the proper, literary way to tell a ghost story, despite hints about the House of Usher. He is actually presented as the prisoner of his ignorance as 'the others peered curiously, as though through bars, at the little man who sat perplexed and baffled, knowing nothing of atmosphere.' Mrs Henneker, the acknowledged arbiter of atmosphere, acts as a marvellous parody of Elizabeth Bowen herself as she urges the little man to recall correctly his entry into the phantom country house.

> 'You had a sense of immanence', said Mrs Henneker authoritatively. 'Something was overtaking you, challenging you, embracing yet repelling you. Something was coming up from the earth, down from the skies, in from the mountains, that was stranger than the gathered rain. Deep from out of the depths of those dark windows, something beckoned'.

This is a brisker, more peremptory version of the atmosphere Bowen herself establishes in 'Human Habitation', published in the same volume (*Ann Lee's,* 1926), in which two students on a walking tour blunder out of the rain into a heavily atmosphere-laden house. The pelting rain, and the physical exhaustion of the students, serve as the bridge into what one of them perceives as 'some dead and empty hulk of a world drawn up alongside, at times dangerously accessible to the unwary'. In his zombie-like state of weariness, he had already begun to doubt his own existence: 'He was, he decided, something somebody else had thought.'

Bowen uses a similar bridge in 'Look at All Those Roses', the story I would select as the best example of her delicate balancing of fictions against realities. Here the bridge is the 'endless drive' of Lou and Edward through the Suffolk countryside back to London. We are reminded that 'there is a point when an afternoon oppresses one with fatigue and a feeling of unreality. Relentless, pointless, unwinding summer country made nerves ache at the back of both of their eyes.' Beyond a certain point the route becomes pointless: unmappable. In any case it has always been a 'curious route', since Edward detests the main roads, and we are therefore prepared for the fact that when they break down 'Where they were seemed to be highly improbable'. They have already 'felt bound up in the tired impotence of a dream'. Lou and Edward may have driven over the borderline into another kind of reality—or they may not.

The title of the story becomes its first sentence.

'Look at All Those Roses'

Lou exclaimed at that glimpse of a house in a sheath of startling flowers.

The word 'sheath' has a sinister connotation. But the third sentence of the story runs, 'To reach the corner, it struck her, Edward accelerated, as though he were jealous of the rosy house—a house with gables, flat-fronted, whose dark windows stared with no expression through the flowers.' The curious syntax of 'To reach the corner, it struck her, Edward accelerated' emphasizes Lou's subjectivity. It is only her 'astounding fancy', later in the story, that the murdered father lies at the roses' roots.

The perhaps unsurprising lack of expression of the house's dark windows gains a resonance not only from Mrs Mather's greeting them with 'no expression at all,' but from Edward's and Lou's reaction when the car breaks down: 'He and she confronted each other with that completely dramatic lack of expression they kept for occasions when the car went wrong.' The car's breakdown itself is completely realistic and simultaneously a kind of magic spell: 'A ghastly knocking had started. It seemed to come from everywhere, and at the same time to be a special attack on them.' There is a 'magic' which is suggested by the curious isolation of the house and its dislocation: Edward speaks of the rest of the country looking like something lived in by '"poor whites'", although this is, on one level, Suffolk and not the American South. But Lou and Edward are themselves isolated and dislocated. Lou is perpetually anxious that Edward, who is not her husband, will escape her, whereas Edward feels that 'life without people was absolutely impossible'—by which he means life only with Lou. Lou is presented as rather less than a person: during the course of the story she is compared with a monkey, a cat, and a bird. When she says longingly of the 'rosy house', '"I wish we lived *there* . . . It really looked Like somewhere'", Edward replies tartly, '"It wouldn't if we did.'" Mrs Mather is also isolated, but it is a

powerful isolation, like Ann Lee's, and one disconcerting to Lou and Edward, who cannot make out whether she is a woman or a lady. She has no 'outside attachments—hopes, claims, curiosities, desires, little touches of greed—that put a label on one to help strangers.' By contrast, her crippled daughter Josephine has 'an unresigned, living face'. She asks Lou which are the parts of London with the most traffic, and her restlessness is expressed by her canary 'springing to and fro in its cage'. Josephine is described as 'burning', just as the rose garden has a 'silent, burning gaiety'.

Various interpretations of the 'rosy house' and its occupants are possible for the reader who is searching for a label. One is that Josephine's father had escaped after injuring her back. (This would have happened when Josephine was seven, the age at which Elizabeth Bowen left her father and felt abandoned by him.) As Lou, whose 'idea of love was adhesiveness', think bitterly: 'He had bolted off down that path, as Edward had just done.' Another is that he has been murdered by Mrs Mather, a view which obviously enjoys much local support. The murder weapon was possibly the lump of quartz, the 'bizarre object' which props open the front door, wielded by Mrs Mather's 'powerful-looking hands.' This leads to another interpretation, that the house and garden are in effect haunted, and that the murder is manifested by the over-profuse roses, 'over-charged with colour' and 'frighteningly bright'. When Lou sees the same roses that Josephine sees, 'she thought they looked like forced roses, magnetized into being. 'This would explain why the farm is '"unlucky'"', and why there is only one servant for the house, '"not very clear in her mind'." This in turn leads to another interpretation, that the 'rosy house' is a place of enchantment, which it is impossible to leave. Lou says jokingly to Josephine that she put the evil eye on the car, and when Lou refuses to eat tea, Josephine says, '"She thinks if she eats she may have to stay here for ever.'" (Eleanor in 'The Parrot' remembers Proserpine when she is offered figs by the Lennicotts.) The enchantment, however, may be either good or bad. Is Lou's 'ecstasy of indifference' to life, experienced as she lies beside Josephine's invalid carriage, an unaccustomed peep into the nature of things—one of her 'ideal moments'? Or is she succumbing to the lure of death, so that Edward rightly realizes that he had 'parked' her, like the car, in the wrong place? Lou realizes that she has always wanted 'to keep everything inside her own power', but to abandon this desire to control one's own fictions may be to abandon life.

The story is alive with ambiguities, like Josephine's "'We don't wonder where my father is.'" This reminds us of Edward's taunting Lou with "'You like to be sure where I am, don't you?'" Edward, who is a writer, comments on the episode, "'There's a story there'", which may reveal him either as a sensitive artist or a shallow journalist.

The title of the story is the first sentence, Lou's exclamation. It is also an exhortation to the reader to look at all those roses—and make what you can of them.

Source: Mary Jarrett, "Ambiguous Ghosts: The Short Stories of Elizabeth Bowen," in *Journal of the Short Story in English*, No. 8, Spring 1987, pp. 71–79.

Sources

Christensen, Lis, "A Reading of Elizabeth Bowen's 'A Day in the Dark,'" in *Irish University Review*, Vol. 27, No. 2, Autumn/Winter 1997, pp. 299–309.

H., F. L. Jr., Review of *A Day in the Dark*, in *Studies in Short Fiction*, Vol. 3, No. 2, Winter 1966, pp. 276–77.

Morgan, Edwin, "Shambling Man," in *New Statesman*, Vol. 70, August 6, 1965, p. 191.

Smith, Laurel, "Elizabeth Bowen," in *Dictionary of Literary Biography*, Vol. 162, *British Short-Fiction Writers, 1915–1945*, edited by John H. Rogers, Gale Research, 1996, pp. 49–56.

Tillinghast, Richard, "Elizabeth Bowen: The House, the Hotel, and the Child," in the *New Criterion*, Vol. 13, No. 4, December 1994, pp. 24–33.

Wilson, Angus, "Introduction," in *The Collected Stories of Elizabeth Bowen*, Knopf, 1981, pp. 7–11.

Further Reading

Chessman, Harriet, "Women and Language in the Fiction of Elizabeth Bowen," in *Twentieth Century Literature*, Vol. 29, Spring 1983, pp. 69–85.
    Chessman presents a feminist perspective of Bowen's work.

Dunleavy, Janet Egleson, "Mary Lavin, Elizabeth Bowen, and a New Generation: The Irish Short Story at Midcentury," in *The Irish Short Story: A Critical History*, edited by James Kilroy, Twayne, 1984, pp. 145–68.
    Dunleavy explores the Irish context of Bowen's work and compares it to that of other Irish writers.

Glendinning, Victoria, *Elizabeth Bowen*, Knopf, 1977.
    Glendinning's work is considered in the early 2000s to be the definitive biography of Bowen.

Sullivan, Walter, "A Sense of Place: Elizabeth Bowen and the Landscape of the Heart," in *Sewanee Review*, Vol. 84, Winter 1976, pp. 142–49.
    Sullivan explores the relationship between Bowen's technique and themes.

The End of Old Horse

Simon J. Ortiz

1974

"The End of Old Horse" is an excellent example of the understated, precise verbal control that Simon J. Ortiz wields in his fiction. Principally known as a poet, Ortiz has worked in all forms of literature since the 1960s. His stories tend to illuminate the subtle emotional forces at play in brief, supposedly inconsequential moments.

Ortiz was raised on the Acoma Pueblo in New Mexico, and most of his writing reflects this fact without dwelling on it. In "The End of Old Horse," two boys growing up on a reservation spend a quiet, eventless summer day trying to catch fish in a creek before their neighbor approaches to tell them that his dog strangled himself by straining too hard against the rope that tied him to a pole. The younger boy, Gilly, who has a supposedly grownup liking for obscenity, tries unsuccessfully to suppress his anger; the older boy, who is the story's narrator, nearly convinces himself that he does not care. Their actions are minimal, but with masterful control Ortiz conveys the suffering and confusion of children facing grief alone apparently for the first time.

"The End of Old Horse" was included in *The Man to Send Rain Clouds: Contemporary Stories by American Indians*, edited by Kenneth Rosen and published in 1974. It has also been included in Ortiz's short story collection *Men on the Moon*, published in 1999.

Author Biography

Simon J. Ortiz was born on May 27, 1941, and raised on the Acoma Pueblo, near Albuquerque,

Simon J. Ortiz   © Nancy Crampton. Reproduced by permission

New Mexico. His father was a stonemason and later a railroad worker, and his mother was a potter. As a child, he spoke the native Acoma language, Keresan. Early in his education, however, while attending a reservation school, he was forced to learn English, giving him a bicultural world-view that has characterized his writing.

In 1961 and 1962, Ortiz attended Fort Lewis College. He served in the army from 1962 through 1965, at the height of the Vietnam War. After his return, he attended the University of New Mexico, earning his bachelor of arts degree and then went on to earn a master's of fine arts from the International Writing Program at the University of Iowa. After graduating, he supported himself by working in public relations at Rough Rock Demonstration School in Arizona and as a newspaper editor at the National Indian Youth Council in Albuquerque. In 1974 and 1975 he was treated for alcoholism.

In 1969 Ortiz was awarded a National Endowment for the Arts Discovery Award, which gave him the motivation to keep writing. His first collection of poems, *Naked in the Wind*, was published in 1971. His first collection to be distributed by a major publisher was *Going for the Rain*, in 1976. Since that time, he has regularly published poetry, short fiction, and essays. His works have

consistently focused on his identity as an Acoma American, and he has served on numerous Native American committees, as well as the editorial staffs of Native American publications. He has won several awards, including being named a White House Salute to Poetry Honored Poet in 1981 and the Lila Wallace Reader's Digest Writer's Award. Since the mid-1970s, Ortiz has held a variety of teaching positions, starting at the Institute of American Arts in Santa Fe, New Mexico. As of 2005, he is a professor at the University of Toronto. His book *Out There Somewhere*, a collection of poetry, was published in 2002.

Plot Summary

"The End of Old Horse" begins with the narrator, an unnamed Native American boy, leaving home with his younger brother to go to the nearby creek to cool off on a hot summer day. They pass by Old Horse, a dog who is tied up with a rope, in front of the home of a neighbor, Tony. Old Horse jumps about wildly, chewing at his rope, trying to free himself. The boys tell Tony, who is fixing up an old horse stall so that he can park his truck in it, that the dog is overexcited, and Tony tells them to just ignore him. Gilly, the younger brother, curses about the dog, calling him stupid, awkwardly working the word "hell" into what he says.

The narrator muses about how boring life is. The only real excitement in the summer, he says, is when there are Grab Days during festivals for saints. Grab Days are a tradition of giving out candy and toys to children, similar to the practice of piñatas. It is here that he first points out the different perspectives of his mother and father: his father does not mind if the children hear graphic or explicit language, but his mother does.

At the creek, the boys chase trout into a trap that they made with some scrap tin. Gilly stops to wash some mud off of his jeans when Tony, the dog's owner, approaches, looking somber. Tony makes small talk about the cleaning that Gilly is doing before announcing that Old Horse, the dog who was straining against his leash, has strangled himself with the rope and is dead.

After a moment of silence, Gilly, trying to hold back his tears, eventually cries.

The narrator tells Tony that he should not have tied the dog up and is surprised that Tony's reaction is as emotional as it is: he reaches out and pushes the narrator, who falls into some bushes. But Tony immediately regrets having done this, and he reaches down and pulls the boy to his feet and brushes him off. He apologizes, tells the boys to go home, and then hops across the creek and walks off beside it.

On the way home, the boys glance mournfully over at the place where Old Horse had been tied up. Gilly curses, using a variety of words that he knows are offensive, and then cries openly. The narrator blames Tony for having tied the dog, when he could have let him roam freely or even asked the boys to take him to the creek with them. The narrator, angry and sad, tries to distract himself by asking Gilly to race him, but Gilly is not interested in running. The narrator swears at Gilly and takes off alone. He ends up running so hard that he makes himself sick and vomits on the side of the road. When Gilly catches up, the narrator apologizes for having sworn at him.

They arrive home after dark, and their mother is angry. She tells them to wash for supper. Their father seems to notice the mud on Gilly's jeans, but he does not point it out to their mother, instead changing the subject to an upcoming rabbit hunt.

When the subject of Tony comes up at the dinner table, the boys are silent. Gilly breaks the silence by saying that Tony choked the dog to death, immediately following his summary with the curse word "hellfire." Their mother warns him about using such language, but the narrator and the father do not react because they both understand the seriousness of the young boy's emotions and feel that swearing is his way of putting his mind to rest over this traumatic event.

Characters

The Father

The father is a quiet, practical man who works for the railroad. The fact that his sons look up to him is clear from the way that the narrator refers to funny stories his father sometimes told as an example of something interesting that would happen in his otherwise boring day.

At times, the father seems to be in collusion with his sons against the moral strictness of their mother. He tells stories that might be inappropriate for children, a point that his wife has to interrupt to remind him of. He notices the mud on Gilly's pants

Media Adaptations

- Ortiz discusses American Indian identity in literature with David Barsamian in an interview titled *Simon Ortiz*, available on audiocassette from Pacifica Radio Archives, 1986.

- Ortiz and five other writers from the American southwest are included on *Voices of the Southwest, 2003*, a six-disc recording of a conference that took place at University of New Mexico from June 9 to July 24, 2003. The recording is available from University of New Mexico Press.

- Ortiz's home page at www.uta.edu/english/tim/poetry/so/ortizmain.htm is rich with information about his life and his writings.

but does not point it out to their mother, in order to keep them from getting into trouble: what is more, he has covered for them before. At the end of the story, the narrator assumes that his father feels the same way that he does that the best way to cope with the day's traumatic event is by putting it aside and not talking about it ever again.

Gilly

Gilly is the narrator's younger brother. Early in the story, he displays his penchant for using foul language, frequently with no particular context: he likes to say crude words but does not seem to understand their meaning. When he hears Tony refer to Old Horse as a "dumb dog," he repeats the idea, calling him a "stupid dog" and then adds the word "hell." "He used to like cuss words when he was a kid," the narrator explains. In doing this, Gilly is copying the speech of Tony, who is a neighbor and distant relative.

After finding out that Old Horse is dead, Gilly tries to repress his sorrow and hold his tears in, crying only silently. After awhile, when the narrator is trying to get him to run, he sobs and hiccups openly, overwhelmed by grief.

By the time they are at the dinner table, Gilly is still upset, but not as upset as he had been earlier. Rather than spewing a list of obscenities, he just lets one, "hellfire," slip out while explaining the dog's death. Since he spends most of the story trying to wash mud off of his pants, it is clear that he knows his parents can be strict, and so it can be assumed that Gilly would not have uttered this one blasphemy if he could have held it in.

The Mother

The boys' mother represents logic over emotion. The narrator explains how, faced with a situation, she will try to explain it in a way that they will understand. In the story, she becomes angry with the boys, but her anger is never severe. When they come home late for dinner, she is described as being "more or less mad at us." Later, when Gilly uses "hellfire" at the dinner table, the extent of her anger is that she tells him to never do it again. She is not certain whether to respect his emotions, looking to her husband and other son for some sign of the right way to respond to what Gilly has done.

The Narrator

The story does not say how old the narrator is. He is a boy who is old enough to be cursing as a means of expression but too old to be fascinated with it, as his brother is. He has a philosophical bent, wondering, even before finding out about the death of Old Horse, about the nature of the world and in particular the fact that events happen that are out of human control. He thinks that the way to deal with important events is to not think about them, dismissing his mother's way of coping, which is to analyze and understand.

The news of Old Horse's death creates conflicting emotions in the narrator. He tries to remain dispassionate, but his emotions well up within him. He wants to run, and when his brother Gilly is not willing to let him channel his desire to run into a race he curses him and then runs as fast as he can anyway, to the point of exhaustion. Rather than accept the dog's death as a tragedy, he focuses on the ways his owner could have prevented it by letting Old Horse free from his rope. Though he did not offer to take the dog with them to the creek, he blames Tony for not asking him to take him.

In the end, the narrator copes with the sad news by adapting the indifference that he has seen in his father and in Tony, the "stoic Indian" stance that he has heard his father mock before.

Tony

Tony is related to the boys in the story in some undefined way: the story specifically does not say that they are unrelated, only that Tony "wasn't close family kinfolk." He is, however, familiar with the boys. Early in the story, when discussing Gilly's habit of swearing, the narrator points out that he did it in an attempt to copy Tony. Later, at the dinner table, their father asks what Tony has been doing lately, which indicates that the father knows Tony is an important part of their daily lives.

As a role model, Tony exudes a cool demeanor. When the boys tell him that his dog, tied to a clothesline pole, is acting crazy, he just laughs it off. His general calm is why his appearance by the creek where the boys are chasing fish is so frightening to the narrator, who is not used to seeing Tony behave seriously.

Tony seems to understand his responsibility as a role model. He loses his temper when the narrator blames him for Old Horse's death, shoving the boy into a bush, but he immediately reaches out to him and apologizes. The very fact that he sought the boys out after finding the dog dead suggests his need to talk to someone: when he finds that he cannot talk to them, that it just is not in his nature, he crosses over to the other side of the stream and walks away.

Themes

Language and Meaning

Ortiz uses language, and in particular obscene language, to represent the confused emotions that his characters are feeling. The narrator of this story shows his awareness of the special power of obscene language in the beginning of the story, when he notes that his younger brother Gilly liked to swear and that he did too, only not as much. At that point in the story, the use of obscenity just seems like a way for a younger boy to act older, like Gilly imitating Tony.

As the story progresses, though, it becomes clear that obscene language is not so much a posture, a way of acting cool, as it is an act of desperation, of venting emotions that one cannot show in any other way. When he first learns of Old Horse's death, Gilly does not swear, but instead becomes silent, in an attempt to stop all emotion: he does not let out a torrent of curse words until he passes Tony's house and is overcome with thoughts of the dog's death. His obscenities correspond with open sobbing. Later, when he uses the word "hellfire" at the supper table, it is clear that he does not

Topics For Further Study

- Research the newest technological restraining devices for dogs, and explain why they are safe.

- The narrator mentions gathering good presents at the tribe's "Grab Days" festivity. Research Grab Days and their significance to Indian culture.

- The obscenities that Gilly uses in this story are mild compared to things that are considered acceptable for television in the early 2000s. Do you think that his language is obscene if he

thinks it is? Explain what you think the rules should be for standards of obscenity.

- Tony performs the function of a big brother to the boys in this story. Look through other stories that you have read for similar big brother figures, and compare them to Ortiz's portrait of Tony.

- Ortiz is strongly associated with his Acoma heritage. Explore what religious significance the Pueblo Indians give to dogs and animals in general. Then decide what lasting effect the death of Old Horse may have on Gilly and his brother.

---

do it consciously but that it has slipped out of him in his sorrow while talking about what happened to Old Horse. The words that the boys use are powerful, but the story makes it clear that they use the power of these words, not as expressions of emotions, but as substitutes for them.

Stoicism

The central theme of stoicism is examined in this story when the narrator compares Tony, whose dog has just died, with a joke that his father often made about people being "blank as a stoic Indian." The characters here are in fact Indians, and they are struggling to remain stoic in the face of a terribly emotional experience.

The fact that Tony has to struggle to keep his stoic demeanor is obvious from the fact that he loses his composure temporarily and apologizes for it immediately. He is trying to be emotionless, but when the narrator angers him he responds angrily. He has every right to be angry, but anger is too emotional, and so he tries to bury his feelings, helping the boy to his feet almost the same moment that he reached out to shove him.

The narrator uses physical motion to put forth a stoic attitude. When he feels that he is about to cry, he runs instead, burying his feelings under the stress to his body. Just before he runs, he curses Tony and his brother Gilly: after he has run, those angry feelings are gone.

The end of the story shows how much stoicism is a preferred way of life for the grownups in general—the males, at least. When they hear Gilly curse out loud, the narrator and his father are not shocked, nor are they angry. They both recognize his cursing as being all that he can do, and they expect Gilly to quit grieving once he has gotten it out of his system. The story ends with the expectation that this emotional incident can now be forgotten: the narrator thinks that Gilly's use of a forbidden word will be "the end of everything that happened that day."

Gender Roles

In this story, the boys, their father, and Tony all share a similar outlook, trying to repress their emotions and forget about the problems that are upsetting them. The mother, on the other hand, is more inclined to examine problems, to encourage her sons to face up to what is upsetting them in order to understand it. These two different approaches to life might just reflect their different philosophies, but they come to indicate the parents' places in traditional gender roles. In this family, the mother is more upset than the father about appearance (she is the one they expect to raise a fuss about the dirt on Gilly's jeans, even though it is the father who notices it) and about obscenity. That she values such matters and the males do not divides the family along gender lines.

Poverty

The narrator of this story does not dwell upon the financial situation of the pueblo where he lives, but the story gives enough hints for discerning readers to understand it. For instance, when the boys first talk to Tony, he is working on an old horse stall, trying to nail it together so that it will cover his truck securely. He does not have a garage or the money to build a new structure or have one built but has to make do with fixing what is already old. Later, Gilly spends much time while they are at the creek trying to wash a smudge of mud off of his jeans. Insisting that they care for the condition of their clothes might reflect their parents' interest in having the boys look good in public, but since they are just going home at the end of the day, it is more likely that the parents are concerned that the clothes will not wear out from excessive washing and that he does not have many extra pairs of jeans to wear while these are being laundered. The boys' plan to catch trout in the creek and fatten them up indicates that they do not have much spending money and are conscious of finding the way to turn their playtime activity into cash.

Style

Conflict

One aspect that is particularly notable about "The End of Old Horse" is the story's lack of a general conflict. There are times when tension is raised, as when the narrator accuses Tony of being negligent and Tony shoves him or when Gilly curses at the family supper table and readers expect trouble to ensue. None of these problems develop into conflict, however: the story cannot be said to be "about" the conflict between Tony and the narrator or Gilly and his parents. Instead, Ortiz uses these tense moments to hold the reader's interest while pursuing a larger, less explicitly defined idea. The story is more about the characters' attitudes than it is about their interactions with each other: if one were intent on defining it in terms of conflict, it would be more accurate to say that it is about a series of internal conflicts.

Symbolism

Describing what the boys do at the creek, the narrator gives more attention to Gilly scrubbing his jeans than he does to their fishing project, which is supposedly their reason for being there. He mentions the mud on Gilly's jeans several times over

the course of three paragraphs then returns to the matter again when they arrive home. The mud is given almost as much focus as the obscene language that Gilly uses, and, in fact, can be seen as a symbol of Gilly's language: he fears his parents' reaction to seeing his Levis muddied just as much as he fears their reaction to hearing words like "hell." By focusing attention on the jeans and the fear of what the parents will think of them, Ortiz raises the expectation that the parents will be severe about language without having to call too much attention to what they will think of hearing Gilly say "hellfire": the story commands attention for its climactic moment without being too heavy handed about where it is going.

Narrator

The character in this story who draws the most attention is Gilly, the younger brother. Gilly is the one who is going through a phase of using colorful language. He is the one who has the greatest struggle with his emotions concerning Old Horse's death. And he is the one who is openly in trouble at the climactic moment at the supper table.

Still, it is the narrator who is the main character, as first person narrators of stories often are. Though readers know less about the narrator (for instance, his name), his complex emotions are important. While Gilly tries to be as dispassionate and stoic as his hero Tony is, he is unsuccessful and cries several times; the narrator, on the other hand, is much better at suppressing his sorrow. This is a story about a culture where people are expected to shrug off grief, the narrator is a much more sublime study of that state of mind than his younger brother is.

Historical Context

Ortiz was born and raised in the Acoma Pueblo in New Mexico, about 65 miles west of Albuquerque. For centuries, the Acoma Pueblo existed at the top of a mesa, 7000 feet above sea level, in what is now referred to as "Sky City." The Acoma people first came to the attention of Europeans in 1598, when the Spanish governor of New Mexico, Juan de Onate, sent troops to conquer the indigenous people of the area. Because of their location at the top of the mesa, the Acoma were able to hold off against the Spanish for a while, but a returning force the following year wiped out much of the population and burned many of the

Compare & Contrast

- **1970s:** The Indian unemployment rate is 10 times the national average, and 40 percent of the Native-American population live below the poverty line.

  Today: Half the total Native-American work-force remains unemployed, and nearly one-third live in poverty compared to 13 percent of the total U.S. population.

- **1970s:** Native-American life expectancy is just 44 years, a third less than that of the average American.

  Today: Life expectancy for Native Americans remains virtually unchanged.

- **1970s:** The American Indian Movement leads urban Indians, traditionalists, and young Indians along the "Trail of Broken Treaties" to Washington, D.C., seizes the offices of the Bureau of Indian Affairs in Washington, D.C., and occupies them for a week in order to dramatize Indian grievances.

  Today: Most Native Americans maintain an uneasy relationship with the BIA, which is responsible for managing Indian affairs, claiming that the BIA restricts their freedom and continues to demonstrate a paternalistic attitude towards Native Americans.

---

buildings. A truce with the Spanish was achieved in 1628, when the construction of the Catholic San Esteban del Rey mission was begun in Sky City. The church, a national landmark, remains to this day, making it the oldest Spanish mission in the United States.

As of 2005, only about fifty members of the Acoma tribe live at the ancestral location in Sky City, on top of the mesa. The rest live in the surrounding areas and only go to Sky City on holidays. The Acoma reservation consists of 378,114 acres around Sky City: the tribe owns most of that area, with 320 acres owned by individual tribal members.

Commerce has never been easy for the Acoma, since they are situated in the desert with just the barest hope of sustainable agriculture. Starting in the early 1900s, the chief commercial enterprise has been the tourist trade. For one thing, the reservation has the marvel of Sky City, which archeologists guess dates back to the middle of the eighth century. Early on, the tourist trade focused on the mission, with people of European descent ignoring the cultural significance of pueblo history. The city had no water or electricity and was difficult to reach until the 1950s or early 1960s, when a motion picture company making a John Wayne film restored

the road up the side of the mesa, making Sky City accessible to travelers.

Throughout the sixties, seventies, and eighties, interest in Native American culture grew, and the Acoma made use of the opportunity to make money while spreading awareness of their history. A tourism center was built at the base of the mesa, with water and electricity run in from the village of Acomita eleven miles away; this improvement gave the tribe the opportunity to control access to the ancient city via an old school bus that made the trip up and back throughout the day and offered visitors toilets and cold refreshments. This interest has put a premium on traditional Native American arts and crafts: the Acoma are especially known for their delicate clay pottery and beautiful weaving patterns, and the tourist trade provided a stream of interested buyers.

The citizens of the Acoma Pueblo are unique among the 29 pueblos that are scattered from Colorado to the Mexican border in that they have retained their own language. Many of the Acoma traditions and legends have remained intact, most likely because their isolation at the top of the mesa kept the Acoma from mixing with Spaniards and Americans for most of their history. Ortiz was raised in McCartys, the second largest city on the Acoma reservation after Acomita.

Old Horse was a dog that strangled himself on his own leash © Bettmann/Corbis

Critical Overview

Men on the Moon, that includes "The End of Old Horse," is Simon J. Ortiz's first collection of short stories: Ortiz has published children's literature, non-fiction, and memoirs, but he is best known as one of the preeminent voices in Native American poetry. When this book was published, Matt Pifer, reviewing the book in *World Literature Today*, observed that the stories in it "illustrate the sense Simon Ortiz has of the subtleties and power inherent in language, a sense he developed, in part, from the tradition of storytelling so deeply rooted in the culture of his Acoma people."

Ortiz's Acoma background is such an important part of his identity and the stories that he tells that few reviewers neglect to mention it. This is not to say that he has been pigeonholed by the reviewers: his heritage is a fact of Ortiz's life and has been a central frame of reference throughout his long publishing career. In an unsigned *Publishers Weekly* review of *Men on the Moon*, for instance, his background is acknowledged in the fact that the stories in the collection "demonstrate the diversity of Native experience in modern America." That review goes on to emphasize the fact that Ortiz is proud of his heritage and the fact that he is a gifted writer, as many reviewers of the book have done: "The language of these rich narratives reflect [sic] both Ortiz's poetic gift and his intimate knowledge of oral storytelling."

Criticism

David Kelly

Kelly is an instructor of literature and creative writing at College of Lake County and Oakton Community College in Des Plaines, Illinois. In this essay, Kelly looks at the story as a "coming of age" tale, questioning just who would be considered to have come of age.

Simon J. Ortiz's short story "The End of Old Horse" is clearly a coming of age story. It tells of two boys of indeterminate age who go fishing one hot, boring summer afternoon. They pass by the home of an older friend, Tony, and point out to him what he surely must already know: that his dog, Old Horse, is barking and straining at his rope. Later, Tony tells them that Old Horse has strangled himself, and the boys are filled with anger and sorrow. The younger brother uses the word "hellfire" at the dinner table, and his parents, who do not approve of such language, respect his sorrow and do not punish him. As with all coming of age stories, the focus here is on a young person having a realization that will change the way he looks at life.

The significance of the story's events, their unchangeable finality, is made clear in the story's two uses of the word "end." First of all, Ortiz uses it in the title, where it draws attention to itself by taking the place of the word "death." It would be more specific to say that Old Horse died: to say that he ended is not incorrect, but it is notably vague. Ortiz brings the word "end" back in the story's final line, when he writes that the boys' father decided "that what my little brother Gilly said was the end of everything that happened that day." This is a story about change, about a way of life that it is over for someone. Like any coming of age story, it represents the time when the old reality of childhood ends, and the reality of adulthood kicks in.

The question that arises, though, is just who is coming of age here. In many stories told in first-person point of view, the answer to this question is simple: traditionally, the story is about the narrator, who is the one most affected by the events. In "The End of Old Horse," though, there are plenty of reasons to see how the story works by understanding

> " Ortiz, a native of the Acoma Pueblo, whose people have been in 'the west' for nearly a thousand years, incorporates this Eurocentric literary tradition to imply that Tony, in his sorrow, is leaving his past behind."

characters other than the narrator as being recipients of the story's lessons.

Immediately upon reading it, one might assume that Ortiz means the story to focus on the younger brother, Gilly. Gilly is the one who is most clearly traumatized by the day's events. He cries twice, and at the story's climactic moment he clearly is unable to keep himself from using the kind of language at the dinner table that Ortiz has already shown to be forbidden in this household. The narrator, by contrast, acts as a silent observer: he has one emotional moment, when he wishes to drown his sorrow by running as fast as he can and he curses his little brother for refusing to run with him, but after exerting himself to the point of sickness he says that he "was okay" and he apologizes to Gilly.

If this really is a story about Gilly coming of age, it might not necessarily be about his realization of death. It might just fall into that subcategory of the coming-of-age story called the "fallen idol" story. From the third paragraph Ortiz makes it clear that Tony is a hero to Gilly; here, he likens the boy's use of obscenities to the way Tony uses them. When the boys arrive home, their father asks how Tony is, implying that he would naturally have expected them to have spent at least part of their time at his house.

Gilly's fascination with Tony might be exactly the innocence that he loses. As events transpire, the older boy focuses on ways in which Tony is responsible for the dog's death: he offends Tony by suggesting such, and later, when Gilly expresses his emotions with a string of random obscenities, the narrator focuses his own rage on Tony and the

What Do I Read Next?

- Ortiz's short story "To Change in a Good Way" is about a suburban Indian man coping with the death of his youngest brother. The story is included in *Growing Up Ethnic in America*, a collection of contemporary fiction, edited by Maria Mazziotti Gillan and Jennifer Gillan.

- Ortiz is just one of fourteen writers included in *Writing the Southwest* by David King Dunaway. The book profiles each writer with a brief biography, bibliography, interview, and sample works.

- Leslie Marmon Silko is a writer from the Laguna Pueblo, born and raised in Albuquerque, not far from Ortiz's home territory. Her collection *Storyteller* is considered groundbreaking for the way that its pieces weave poetry, fiction, and autobiography. Of the stories in the book, "Ceremony" is the one that has brought her the most widespread fame.

- *The Antelope Wife*, by Louise Erdich, has been commended for its sublime way of capturing the mood of contemporary Native Americans. Set in modern-day Minneapolis, the novel concerns two related Indian couples and their travails.

- *Speaking for the Generations: Native Writers on Writing*, edited by Ortiz, is an anthology containing essays from leading literary figures responding to the problem of living the dual life of being part of the Indian world as well as part of American culture. Included are essays by Roberta J. Hill, Gloria Bird, and Daniel David Moses.

- Navajo poet and short story writer Luci Tapahonso has written about modern Indian life with a sensibility that resembles Ortiz's. Readers can sample her works in her collection *Blue Horse Rush In: Poems and Stories* (1997), published by University of Arizona Press.

---

things that Tony could have done that would have kept Old Horse alive. In the end, Gilly's line, which is most noteworthy for its use of obscenity, is "Tony choked Old Horse to death, hellfire." If he believes this, after struggling with it over the course of the story, then he has lost faith in a person he looked up to, possibly the person he esteemed most. His understanding of the world is changed permanently.

It is also possible, though less likely, that it is Tony who is coming of age in this story. This would be unusual, because traditional coming of age stories occur when their subject is young and most impressionable: Tony is older than the brothers. Still, he is able to be affected by the event.

The story does not say how old Tony is. Obviously, he is old enough to own a truck, which he is in the process of building a shelter for, but there is no indication that he is building that shelter on his own land, and not on, say, his parents.' What is presented clearly enough is that the death of Old Horse is an event that affects Tony.

Tony struggles with his emotions after the death of his dog. When he first tells the boys about it, he is described as "stoic" and "blank." Ortiz refers to the cliché, "a stoic Indian," to show that this might be just the posture that Tony is trying to consciously adopt, a rôle that he is playing. When the narrator implies that Old Horse's death might be Tony's fault, his emotions flare, and he strikes out at the boy, though his rational mind regrets it and he immediately apologizes.

Reading this as a coming of age story makes apparent that Tony is awakening to adult responsibilities, realizing that his actions have consequences. The story starts with Tony ignoring his yelping dog, having tied Old Horse up with rope, unaware that an excited dog on a poorly designed restraint can die. It ends with Tony's remorse. Ortiz does not go into detail about the lasting effect on Tony, but readers are led to infer it. He jumps the creek, crossing to the other side of the water, a movement that many cultures use to symbolize someone leaving their past behind. In addition,

Tony is headed west: there is a tradition in white American literature of people abandoning the lives they knew and going westward, a tradition that dates back to the Europeans' arrival on the continent, when the west was considered unexplored, virgin territory (the most famous literary example of this is the way Mark Twain has Huckleberry Finn simply "light out" for the west at the end of his adventures). Ortiz, a native of the Acoma Pueblo, whose people have been in "the west" for nearly a thousand years, incorporates this Euro-centric literary tradition to imply that Tony, in his sorrow, is leaving his past behind.

Even though his reaction is the most understated of all those in the book, it could well be the narrator who is coming of age in "The End of Old Horse." As mentioned before, stories with a first-person narrator are often about that narrator. This narrator does not seem much changed by the events of the story but that may be the point: given these extreme circumstances (the sudden death of a helpless animal), readers expect some dramatic transformation. Instead, we see the narrator shaping into the sort of man his father is. Old Horse's death shows him that suppressed emotion is the way to act like a grownup.

The narrator does have his moment of excitement when he reacts to the death of Old Horse by cursing Gilly and cursing Tony and running as fast as he can, but this is an exception. His ordinary life is defined in the fourth paragraph, in which he explains that "nothing ever [happened] in summer." His life is boring at the beginning of the story and by the last line he is already looking forward to burying the events of the day, pretending like they are ended. Perhaps it would be possible to truly "end" them, but the fact that he is telling this story indicates that what happened before and after Old Horse's death continues. If the narrator seems unchanged, he is at least more aware of what goes unsaid at his house than he was before. Gilly may take a chance by letting a curse word slip out, but the narrator, who curses less often, understands that suppressing the emotion behind cursing can sometimes be as potent as cursing itself.

It is difficult for writers to include children in their stories without critics assuming that they are writing coming of age stories: just about anything that happens to children in literature can be considered potent enough to redirect the course of their lives. Ortiz's style, though, gives fair weight to all of the characters, raising the question of who might be most affected. Reading it as the narrator's story,

"The End of Old Horse" is a story about a boy's induction into the stoic Indian posture that his father recognizes, mocks, but adopts when faced with uncomfortable circumstances. If it's Gilly's story, it is a story of a boy who is so outraged about the death of an innocent animal, and so hurt to believe that his role model might be responsible that he can no longer abide by his parents' rules about obscene language. Seen as a story about Tony, it tells of a young man who is careless and causes his dog's death, driving him into isolation. A lesser writer would be lucky to make one of these interpretations viable, not to mention all three.

Source: David Kelly, Critical Essay on "The End of Old Horse," in *Short Stories for Students*, Thomson Gale, 2006.

Dennis R. Hoilman

In the following essay, Hoilman discusses Ortiz's writing career.

Simon J. Ortiz stands out among major Native American writers such as N. Scott Momaday, Leslie Marmon Silko, Gerald Vizenor, James Welch, Paula Gunn Allen, and Louise Erdrich in that, unlike these writers, he was not raised in a bi- or multicultural home with English as his first language. Rather, Ortiz grew up in a traditional Native American home—speaking, understanding, perceiving, and feeling in the Acoma language. As he says in *Woven Stone* (1992), "if there is anything that has sustained me through my years of writing it is that fact."

Ortiz is best known for his several books of poetry, chiefly on such Native American ideas as the importance of identification with a sacred place, the sense of the poet as the equivalent of the traditional storyteller, and the struggle for cultural survival. The theme of the journey recurs frequently in his verse, as the titles of his early collections of poetry indicate: *Going for the Rain* (1976), *A Good Journey* (1977), and *A Poem Is a Journey* (1981).

Simon Joseph Ortiz was born in Albuquerque, New Mexico, on 27 May 1941 and raised in McCartys—the "Deetseyamah" of several of his poems. The village of McCartys is located approximately fifty miles west of Albuquerque on the Acoma Indian Reservation. Ortiz's family belongs to the *Dyaamih hanoh* Eagle clan or, literally, Eagle people—a tightly knit clan that fosters close family and kin relationships as well as a communal outlook and sense of responsibility. Ortiz's parents, Joe L. Ortiz and Mamie Toribio Ortiz, attended St. Catherine's Indian School in Santa Fe and spoke English quite fluently, but the Acoma

> " For Simon J. Ortiz, memory and the storytelling inspired by memory provide his people with a sense of continuity. "

language—*Aacqumeh dzehni* was spoken in the home. Ortiz, whose father worked as a laborer for the Santa Fe Railroad, was brought up in frugal, difficult circumstances. Ortiz's father and other relatives abused alcohol, a habit that—as Ortiz describes in *Woven Stone* "caused family tension, arguments, distrust, fear, pain, all of the trauma of alcoholism." Ortiz continues, "Alcoholism I had known all my life. As a child I was traumatically afraid of the behavior of my father and others under the influence of alcohol. I just didn't understand it, yet I knew its fearsome, destructive impact first hand." Ortiz, whose own life and career also suffered because of alcoholism, later referred to his family as "dysfunctional," and alcoholism constitutes another theme that runs throughout his writing.

Ortiz attended the McCartys Day School, operated by the Bureau of Indian Affairs. At McCartys, as he later said, the policy was to "brainwash" the children and turn them into white people. He especially liked reading because of his interest in stories. He had been hearing them all his life—some were traditional stories of mythic heroes, while others evolved from current gossip about the Aacqumeh (Acoma) community in which he lived. All of these stories, however, interested the young Ortiz greatly, because—although unbeknownst to him at the time—they tied him into the communal body of his people and his heritage. As Ortiz elaborates in *Woven Stone*,

> Consequently, when I learned to read and write, I believe I felt those stories continued somehow in the new language and use of the new language and they would never be lost, forgotten, and finally gone. They would always continue.

He says that his poetry attempts to "instill that sense of continuity" and to connect directly to its primary source in the oral tradition as he knew it in childhood.

Except for an interruption during the fifth grade—when the family moved temporarily to Skull Valley, Arizona—Ortiz was able to remain in McCartys Day School through the sixth grade; McCartys provided him with a strong connection to his people. While in school in Skull Valley, he began to write poetry and song lyrics influenced by country and western singers, such as Jimmy Rodgers and Hank Williams. His first poem—written for Mother's Day—was also published in the school newspaper.

For part of junior high, from 1953 to 1954, Ortiz was sent to St. Catherine's Indian School in Santa Fe, and in one of his poems he writes about leaving his home and family to attend the school. He describes traveling with his parents to Santa Fe and how, when the three of them arrived at the school, he fainted:

> I just fainted, that's all, into the subtle chasm that opens
> and you lose all desire and control, and I fell, very slowly,
> it seemed. I found myself being carried out by my father to
> some steps in front of the boys [sic] recreation hall. He talked with
> me for a long time, slowly and gently, and I felt him tremble
> and stifle his sobs several times. He told me not to worry
> and to be strong and brave.
> I wonder if I have been. That was the first time I ever went
> away from home.

Next, from 1954 to 1956, Ortiz was sent to Albuquerque Indian School, which was closer to home. He went to high school in Grants, New Mexico, at an integrated public school with a mostly "Mericano" student body. He proved to be an outstanding student, winning many honors, both academic and athletic: Boys State, class officer, cocaptain of the football team, allstate in sports, Mr. Grants High, and Senior Honor Boy.

During his high school years he began to think of himself as a writer. He was reading widely, and he came to believe that "as an Acoma person I also had something important, unique, and special to say." In his nascent fiction—in high school he wrote more prose than poetry—the characters were poor, struggling, hardworking, enduring, and caring, but they were not specifically Native American or Indian or Acoma. Ortiz thought of himself as an Acoma person, but his "views and concepts in large part were those of the dominant society," he wrote in *Woven Stone*. "I loved my family, people, community, yet I was also swayed by powerful influences of the outside and even yearned and sought for those 'Mericano ways.'"

By the time of his high school graduation, then, Ortiz knew that he wanted to be a writer, but he had no idea how to proceed. He went to work in the Kerr-McGee uranium mines near Acoma, and the men he worked with, mostly working-class whites, served as the models for characters in his stories and poems. At this period in his life, he also developed a political consciousness, becoming aware of racial and ethnic discrimination, and, as he shows in *Woven Stone*, growing angry at the injustice:

> Like other colonized youth, I had been quietly seething for many years.... I recall the anger at my parents and grandparents, blaming them for not warning us and not protecting us from American life and its people, and I was upset at Acoma leadership for not fighting harder to hold our land and water.

During the early 1960s Ortiz began abusing alcohol. A few of his favorite writers—Dylan Thomas, Ernest Hemingway, Thomas Wolfe, and Malcolm Lowry—had been heavy drinkers, and Ortiz was undeterred by any thought that "alcohol might have done them in. I believed in their greatness and in drinking as a part of that." Eventually, he spent time in the Veterans Administration hospital in Ft. Lyons, Colorado, for treatment of his alcoholism.

After a year in the uranium mines, Ortiz enrolled in Fort Lewis College in 1962, planning to be an organic chemist. He soon discovered that he had little affinity for chemistry and in 1963 left college to enlist in the U.S. Army. While in basic training in Louisiana, he encountered overt racism for the first time and suffered the humiliations of having to use the "Colored Only" drinking fountains and restrooms. After serving three years in the army, Ortiz returned to the University of New Mexico, from 1966 through 1968. For one year, beginning in 1968, he attended the University of Iowa, where he was a Fellow in the International Writing Program. Although he considers himself first and foremost a writer, Ortiz has enjoyed a varied career. He has been a teacher—chiefly of creative writing and Native American literature—at the following institutions: San Diego State University and the Institute of American Indian Arts in 1974; Navajo Community College in Tsaile, Arizona, from 1975 to 1977; the College of Marin in Kentfield, California, from 1976 to 1979; the University of New Mexico in Albuquerque from 1979 to 1981; Sinte Gleska College in Rosebud, South

Dakota, from 1985 to 1986; and at Lewis and Clark College in Portland, Oregon, in 1990. He served as official tribal interpreter and lieutenant governor of the Acoma Pueblo community and worked as a consulting editor for Acoma Pueblo Press. He has also been a journalist, public relations director, and newspaper editor. He has had four marriages, each ending in divorce: to Agnes Goodluck, from 1967 to 1971; to Joy Harjo, from 1971 to 1974; to Roxanne Dunbar, from 1976 to 1980; and to Marlene Foster, from 1981 to 1984. He has three children—a son and two daughters: Raho Nez, Rainy Dawn, and Sara Marie.

Ortiz has received many awards and honors. In 1969 the National Endowment for the Arts (NEA) honored him for his work in journalism with a Discovery Award; in 1981 the NEA also awarded him a fellowship. In 1980 he and other poets were recognized at the White House Salute to American Poetry and Poets. His *From Sand Creek: Rising in This Heart Which Is Our America* (1981), a book of largely political verse, won the Pushcart Prize in 1981, and in 1989 the New Mexico Humanities Council recognized him for his contributions to literature with a Humanities Award. In 1993 he received a Lifetime Achievement Award for literature at the third annual "Returning the Gift" Festival of Native American Writers and Storytellers.

In his first major book of poems, *Going for the Rain*, Ortiz explores the theme of the journey in the context of a traditional Acoma ceremonial journey to the home of the Shiwana, or Cloud People. Shiwana are the deities who bring the rain necessary for survival in the arid, western New Mexico climate of Acoma—also known as the Sky City for its location at the top of a high mesa. Yet, as he says in *Woven Stone*, the book is also structured "in the narrative form of an actual journey on the heeyaanih, the road of life, and its experience." In the prologue to *Going for the Rain*, he compares the traditional journey to the Cloud People's home for rain to his journey—his search for inspiring words with which to heal his people. The traditional journey involves four distinct stages: preparation, leaving, returning, and the coming of the rain itself. Each stage is played out in the successive sections that divide the book.

In the first stage, known as preparation, the poet-persona makes prayers, sings songs, and considers what is important to him—his home, children, language, and "the self that he is." In the thirteen poems of the first section, Ortiz deals with themes analogous to the physical and spiritual preparations needed before the journey itself can begin. Several of the verses—"Forming Child," "Four Poems for a Child Son," "The Expectant Father," "To Insure Survival"—concern both the birth, in 1973, of his first daughter, Rainy Dawn, and the idea of language, a topic that he examines in all his writings. In a poem titled "Language," he listens to the sounds that Rainy Dawn makes as an infant, connecting her human sounds to sounds in nature—"the wind searching hillside ledge." For him the natural language of the infant is akin to a "language of movements—sights—/ possibilities and impossibilities—/ pure existence." The child,

> upon hearing a sound hears the poem
> of hearing—original motion of it
> is complete—sanctified—the sphere
> of who he or she is who is hearing
> the poetry. . . .

Language is primarily oral, something that is heard. Just to hear language is to hear a poem, according to Ortiz's lyric. Language as verse completes and sanctifies a person; hearing a poem thus establishes identity and a sense of self. At the end of "Language," he concludes that language is central to the self, expressing the core of one's being:

> All language comes forth
> outward from the center. Hits
> the curve of your being. Fits
> —"chiseled" occurs to me
> . . . .
> into thoughts of sound itself,
> the energy it is
> and the motion inherent in it.

According to Ortiz, language provides identity and continuity—not only for the self but also for a culture.

The second section of *Going for the Rain*, titled "Leaving," consists of twenty-four poems depicting Ortiz's travels. These travels include some short trips to places such as Spider Springs, Gallup, and Albuquerque in New Mexico, to Many Farms on the Navajo Reservation in Arizona, and others to the West Coast, the South, and New York City. While most of the poems in "Leaving," concern the alienation that a traveler sometimes experiences in an unfamiliar place, a few also delve into a traveler's sense of wonder at the diversity and beauty encountered on a trip. Significantly, in the poem titled "Many Farms Notes" and dated spring 1973, Ortiz, in response to a question regarding the main theme of his verse, replies, "To put it as simply as possible, / I say it this way: to recognize / the relationships I share with everything."

The twenty-six poems of the third section, titled "Returning," relate as well to his travels, but—as the title suggests—focus, in addition, on the poet's return to Acoma; these poems represent his gifts and blessings to his people. For example, "Leaving America" is set in the Kansas City bus depot, where the persona—surely Ortiz himself since the poems are autobiographical—meets another Indian, Roy, who is from Arizona and also returning home. "Just got paid," Roy says,

> laid off by the Rock Island Line.
> Going home.
> It's got red and brown land,
> sage, and when it rains,
> it smells like piñon
> and pretty girls at a Squaw Dance,

to which Ortiz replies "I know." As the title "Leaving America" evokes, the journey home bespeaks a cultural journey: Ortiz goes from the alienating American culture of white people back to the land and traditions of the Indian people—who, he suggests, are not "American."

"The Rain Falls" is the title of the fourth section of *Going for the Rain*. Like the rain that the journey to the Shiwana has engendered, the twenty-five poems of "The Rain Falls" constitute the fruits of the poetic journey that Ortiz has now completed. Launching the fourth section and bearing the dedication "for Joy" (Ortiz's first wife), the poem "Earth Woman" shows how woman embodies the earth itself:

> How gentle
> her movements, her hands,
> soft wind,
> warm rain,
> the moving pain
> of pleasure
> we share.

In the second poem, "Spreading Wings of Wind," about a plane ride from Rough Rock to Phoenix, Ortiz reminds himself that he belongs to a community—the Eagle Clan into which he was born:

> I must remember
> that I am only one part
> among many parts,
> not a singular eagle
> or one mountain.

The lyric ends by addressing non-Indians with a question, "What the hell are you doing to this land? / My grandfather hunted here, prayed, / dreamt. . . ." In "Four Deetseyamah Poems," a title that alludes to the Acoma name of McCartys, Ortiz finds himself absorbed into the land:

> when I have needed
> to envision my home, when loneliness

for myself has overcome me,
the Mountain has occurred.
Now, I see it sharing its being
with me, praying.

Storytelling, identity, and the journey are bound up in his work. As Andrew Wiget points out in the *Dictionary of Native American Literature* (1994), Ortiz's journey in all directions establishes Acu, "the point of origin as well as the destination of what otherwise appear to be pointless wanderings—as the geographical as well as spiritual center of the storytelling person's identity. . . ."

Ortiz's next book of verse, *A Good Journey*, encompasses more than fifty poems, mostly narrative, based on the oral tradition—especially "the oral voice of stories, song, history, and contemporary experience," as he elaborates in *Woven Stone*. The poems chronicle the writer's experiences and the people he has met in his travels, which took place in the late 1960s and early 1970s. Some lyrics have precise dates, while others mention the event motivating a particular poem. Many of the lyrics are about his children or are addressed to them; indeed, he titles the second of the five sections, "Notes to My Child." In the preface he quotes from an interview in which he was asked why he writes:

> Because Indians always tell a story. The only way to continue is to tell a story. . . . Your children will not survive unless you tell something about them—how they were born, how they came to this certain place, how they continued.

Ortiz goes on to explain that he writes for his children, wife, mother, father, and grandparents "and then reverse order that way so that I may have a good journey on my way back home." He suggests that the "good journey" of the title is the journey of return—these poems bring him back to his origins and identity within the Acoma community and culture.

Perhaps the growing political awareness of Ortiz's verse at this point also indicates that poetry returns him home. As in *Going for the Rain*, the poems in *A Good Journey* are personal and autobiographical, yet—unlike in the earlier book—they also display his response to history and to the dominant culture of white Americans. For example, in the fifth poem of the book, "A San Diego Poem: January-February 1973"—about an airplane flight to California—Ortiz discloses his resentment of Catholicism:

> I look below at the countless houses,
> row after row, veiled by tinted smog.
> I feel the beginnings of apprehension.

Where am I? I recall the institutional prayers
of my Catholic youth but don't dare recite them.
The prayers of my native selfhood
have been strangled in my throat.

The poem concludes when the persona arrives at Los Angeles International Airport and tries to find his way through the tunnels of its "innards":

> I am under L.A. International Airport,
> on the West Coast, someplace called America.
> I am somewhat educated, I can read and use a
>   compass;
> yet the knowledge of where I am is useless.
> . . . .
> America has obliterated my sense of
>   comprehension.
> Without this comprehension, I am emptied
> of any substance. America has finally caught me.
> I meld into the walls of that tunnel
> and become the silent burial. There are no echoes.

In "Blessings," which concerns a civil rights fund-raising function in 1969, he writes that Native Americans are not hungry for money or for "carefully written proposals." Rather,

> We are hungry for the good earth,
> the deserts and mountains growing corn.
> We are hungry for the conviction
> that you are our brothers and sisters
> who are willing to share our love. . . .

Storytelling as a theme also informs *A Good Journey*: the first section of the book is titled "Telling," and several of the poems stress the importance of the oral tradition. In dedicating *A Good Journey* to his children, Raho Nez and Rainy Dawn, Ortiz says:

> The stories and poems come forth
> and I am only the voice telling them.
> They are the true source themselves.
> The words are the vision
> by which we see out and in and around.

Stories are, in the words of his dedication, "the true source"—not just of themselves but of everything in one's consciousness, because they shape the consciousness of who people are and of what the world is. According to him, words are the eyes through which people see and know themselves—as well as the world outside and around them. In "I Tell You Now," the final poem in *A Good Journey*, Ortiz addresses an Indian woman he has seen on the street:

> I really have no words to match your stride.
> . . . .
> Even the sheaf of written stories
> I am carrying under my arm to the printers
> because as I watch you, the stories
> which I did work carefully at lack the depth
> and the meaning of your walk.

He then acknowledges the political ideas that he has incorporated with increasing frequency in his writing:

> Oh I guess the words are adequate enough—
> they point out American depredations,
> the stealing of our land and language,
> how our children linger hungry and hurt
> on street corners like the ones I just passed,
> but then I get the feeling that these
> words of my youth are mere diatribes.
> They remain useless and flat when what I really
>   wish
> is to listen to you and then have you listen to me.
> I've been wanting to tell you for a long time.
> I tell you now.

He implies that political diatribes are lifeless and flat, because they do not entail stories. "I Tell You Now" ends with a series of stories that Ortiz has been wanting to tell,

> because I want you to know
> and in that way
> have you come to know me now.

He shows that through stories people come together—not just Ortiz and the Indian woman to whom he is ostensibly speaking in "I Tell You Now," but also all Native American people and, indeed, his readers.

A third significant component to *A Good Journey* besides the two themes of travel and storytelling—is the character of Coyote, a combination of culture hero and trickster in the oral tradition. Coyote is prominently featured "in the origin and all the way / through" the stories in the oral tradition and the history of the people. Often Ortiz identifies himself with Coyote—the trickster, the trouble-maker, the constant victim of his own pranks. Yet, Coyote is also ancient, present at the creation of the world, and he is not only a source of disorder and sorrow but also brings good things to the people. In *A Good Journey*, Ortiz occasionally shows Coyote in the role of ragged wanderer—a lonely outsider—such as in "Two Coyote Ones"; while the lyric begins in the first person, suggesting Ortiz as the wandering persona, it ends with the assertion that the poem was really told in Coyote's voice.

At this early stage in his career as a writer, Ortiz was writing short fiction as well as poetry. Five of his short stories appear in Kenneth Rosen's 1974 anthology *The Man to Send Rain Clouds: Contemporary Stories by American Indians*, including four of his best: "The San Francisco Indians," "Kaiser and the War," "The Killing of a State Cop," and "The End of Old Horse." "The San Francisco Indians" captures with irony an old Indian man's encounter with members of a hippie "tribe" in San Francisco. The

hippies seek a "genuine Indian" to show them how to conduct a peyote ceremony—a rite about which the old man knows nothing. Both "Kaiser and the War" and "The Killing of a State Cop" depict the difficulties that confront Native American veterans when they return to the reservation. "The End of Old Horse" recounts, simply yet profoundly, a young boy's first encounter with the futility of death—in this case the death of a dog named "Horse."

In 1978 Ortiz published four additional short stories in *The Howbah Indians*, a collection that takes its title from that of the first story. "Howbah," as the narrator of the story explains, means "you all Indians—like you Oklahoma folks say: yo'all." Eagle, an army veteran who served in Korea, returns to the reservation and buys a gas station. He puts up a sign that is "a couple of hundred yards long," "like it was a high board fence." In red letters on a bright yellow background, so they can be discerned from ten miles away, the sign reads "Welcome Howbah Indians." The sign makes the Indians proud of Eagle. After a couple of years, however, Eagle loses his way and is found dead in a dry rainwash. "He had what looked like bruises from falling on his face or a stone, but the government police from the Bureau of Indian Affairs never bothered very much." Because the Indians still remember the sign, laughing and laughing "for the important memory and fact that it is," the futility of Eagle's aspirations becomes somewhat muted. As it turns out, the narrator of "Howbah Indians" has awakened suddenly one night, the memory of the sign having entered his sleep. "I felt good for remembering," he says, "and I wrote it down on a notepad. *Howbah Indians.*" The irony of the sign seems to escape the narrator, who does not recognize the fact that the "welcome" that "you all Indians" will receive will be the same quashed aspirations and the same end that "welcomed" Eagle. The story strongly implies that Eagle was murdered because he dared to aspire to a position of ownership, and because he dared to welcome all Indians to his station. Apparently, someone tried to teach Eagle a lesson—that Indians are not welcome and should stay in their place.

For *Fight Back: For the Sake of the People, For the Sake of the Land* (1980), Ortiz set the story, told in both lyric and narrative forms, in the context of the uranium boom of the 1960s. The focus of the book is on the injustice, discrimination, and bigotry that befell Indians as the "boom" flourished on land stolen from the Acoma people. In "What I Mean," a poem from *Fight Back*, he writes:

> We didn't talk much.
> Some people say Indians are just like that,

shy and reserved and polite,
but that's mostly crap. Lots of times
we were just plain scared
and we kept our mouths shut.
I mean Grants and Milan and the mines
between Haystack and Ambrosia Lake,
all that area used to be Indian land—
Acoma land—but it was surveyed
by the government and stolen
at the turn of the century
and there was plenty to say
but we didn't say it.

The book is divided into two sections—titled, respectively, "Too Many Sacrifices" and "No More Sacrifices." The first section features eighteen poems, mostly about people and incidents that he remembers from working in the mines and in the processing mills around Grants and Milan, towns in the vicinity of Acoma. The second section embodies a lengthy work—a piece mixing prose with poetry and titled "Our Homeland, A National Sacrifice Area"—and a concluding lyric called "A New Story." In the prose sections of *Fight Back*, he recounts the history of the land that surrounds Acoma, from the time that white people arrived on the land until the present. The interspersed poems make up his more personal responses to the prose story that he tells. The story recounts four hundred years of exploitation and injustice, and how the mining and processing industry has depleted and contaminated the water upon which Acoma depends. As he describes in *Fight Back*, Ortiz feels that

> Only when we are not afraid to fight against the destroyers, thieves, liars, exploiters who profit handsomely off the land and people will we know what love and compassion are. Only when the people of this nation, not just Indian people, fight for what is just and good for all life, will we know life and its continuance.

Ortiz sets his next book, *From Sand Creek*, in the Veterans Administration Hospital in Ft. Lyons, Colorado, where he underwent treatment for alcoholism in 1974 and 1975. The book takes its title from the site of Colonel John M. Chivington's massacre of more than a hundred peaceful Cheyenne and Arapaho people on 29 November 1864; the Sand Creek massacre is one of the most infamous episodes in the history of the conflict between the white man and the Indian. *From Sand Creek* consists of brief prose comments, often only a single sentence, on roughly one page and somewhat longer poems—though never longer than a single page—on the facing page. As he notes in the preface, Ortiz analyzes himself in *From Sand Creek* "as an American, which is hemispheric, a U.S. citizen, which is national, and as an Indian, which is

spiritual and human." He juxtaposes history with his own experience, presented as fragmentary, traumatic, and confined largely to Colorado in the vicinity of the site of the massacre. Many of the poems center on his experiences in the hospital or in the nearby town of La Junta, alluding to fellow patients such as Toby, Billy, Nez, W., the Texan, Dusty, the Colonel, Danny, Larry, and the Oklahoma Boy. In other poems the speaker imagines the scene of the massacre: "It almost seemed magical / that they had so much blood. / It just kept pouring, / like rivers, / like endless floods from the sky." He frames *From Sand Creek* with poems of hope and reconciliation, particularly his hope that "we will all learn something from each other. We must. We are all with and within each other." The opening poem suggests that instead of dwelling on the victimization and the guilt of the massacre, the "burden of steel and mad death," one must now look to the "flowers and new grass and a spring wind rising from Sand Creek." America, as the concluding poem says, must "not be vengeful but wealthy with love and compassion and knowledge." *From Sand Creek* is Ortiz's most cryptic, most difficult work.

In 1992 the University of Arizona Press published *Woven Stone*, which brings together *Going for the Rain*, *A Good Journey*, and *Fight Back*. *Woven Stone* includes an excellent autobiographical introduction by Ortiz, in which he discusses the events and issues that have influenced his life and poetry.

In *After and Before the Lightning* (1994), a collection of 133 short poems, with interspersed prose passages, Ortiz reflects on the events of the winter of 1985–1986, which he spent working among the Lakota people and teaching at Sinte Gleska College on the Rosebud Sioux Indian Reservation in South Dakota. He dates the poems, beginning 18 November and ending 21 March—a span of time denoting the season, as he says in his preface, between the last thunder and lightning in the fall and the first thunder and lightning in the spring. He divides the collection into four approximately equal sections: "The Landscape: Prairie, Time, and Galaxy," "Common Trails: Every Day," "Buffalo Dawn Coming," and "Near and Evident Signs of Spring."

After and Before the Lightning, like Ortiz's other works, develops the theme of the interrelatedness between people and the land, and—especially—his experiences driving on Highway 18 between the towns of Okreek and Mission, with the wind and snow fiercer than anything he had known at Acoma. As he writes in "Driving, the Snowy Wind," dated 19 November,

> The snowy wind is fierce,
> insistent, unrelenting,
> picking up dry snow
> off the hills, turning the hills
> into churning clouds and the sky,
> blending everything
> into one cold surging,
> exhaling, forceful breath.

In the preface to *After and Before the Lightning*, he explains the origin of these poems:

> I've felt I have never been very good at facing reality nor at dealing with it. And when I lived in South Dakota . . . I needed a way to deal with the reality of my life and the reality in which I lived. The winter prairie surrounded me totally; it was absolutely present in every moment. . . . The reality of a South Dakota winter demanded to be dealt with. So I was compelled the write the poetry in *After and Before the Lightning*.

The book concludes with "Lightning IV," a poem that encompasses the themes found not only in *After and Before the Lightning* but also in Ortiz's work as a whole: memory, life as a journey, man's relationship with the land, the significance of place, and the stories that sustain a people.

> Why we should keep riding
> toward the storm, we don't know.
> . . . .
> It is perhaps way past questioning,
> past the moment when it's too late.
> Our only certainty, when the horizon
> is no longer clear, is our memory
> of how the journey has been till now.
> . . . .
> How completely we feel the tremoring
> and shuddering pulse of the land now
> as we welcome the rain-heart-lightning
> into our trembling yearning selves.

For Simon J. Ortiz, memory and the storytelling inspired by memory provide his people with a sense of continuity. Together, memory and storytelling comprise a blueprint for the survival of Native American culture.

Source: Dennis R. Hoilman, "Simon J. Ortiz," in *Dictionary of Literary Biography*, Vol. 256, *Twentieth-Century American Western Writers, Third Series*, edited by Richard H. Cracroft, The Gale Group, 2002, pp. 239–47.

Matt Pifer

In the following review, Pifer praises the Men on the Moon *collection for its "lingering sense . . . that stories, our own personal histories, tie us to and teach us about our cultural importance and our political relevance."*

The twenty-six short stories collected in *Men on the Moon* illustrate the sense Simon Ortiz has of the subtleties and power inherent in language, a sense he developed, in part, from the tradition of storytelling so deeply rooted in the culture of his Acoma people, and from decades of communicating these narratives in short stories, essays, and, perhaps most famously, poems, many of which have been gathered in *Woven Stone*. Ortiz's stories are testaments to quiet lives balanced between extremes, which, as these dichotomies break down, leave the reader always conscious of the thin line between survival and death, freedom and repression, joy and anger. The characters, then, for better or worse, are often left facing a confused world wherein salvation is decided upon the edge of a quick wit, belligerence, ignorance, anger, or simply a good laugh.

These stories echo in both content and language the oral storytelling tradition, and thus offer a location, an intellectual pivot upon which political action can be promoted and maintained—a space of cultural recognition and, thus, cultural resistance. Driven by this political subtext, Ortiz's collection suggests that place is inextricably bound to a sense of identity, and that this act of defining, resisting dominant stereotypes, and so surviving, is a political action, is a way for Ortiz and other Native Americans to resist their own cultural and economic demise. For example, in the title story "Men on the Moon," Grandfather Faustin, an archetype who recurs in the stories, is given a television and witnesses one of the later Apollo missions to the moon. Faced with this technology, the advanced search for "knowledge," Faustin perhaps rediscovers the importance of dreams and stories in explaining life and uncovering how things are kept in relation.

This sense of ancestral perseverance surfaces throughout the collection, acting as an imaginative focal point, often in the subtle images which are lingering reminders to the characters of something they have lost or forgotten. These images, these textual voices, are a call to action, to remembrance. In "Woman Singing" the ancestral voice emerges from the song of a migrant worker who has been forced to sleep with Wheeler, the "potato boss," in order to survive, as Clyde, a fellow worker, realizes one terrible night: Clyde "tried to think of the song he had heard her singing. The People singing, he thought. Yes, the woman singing. The mountains, the living land, the women strong, the men strong, the children strong." The voice reverberating with this ancestral song pulls Clyde back to memories of his "People," and his identity is recast, made visible and powerful, by its relationship with the land, the women, the children, all of whom are strong and alive - surviving.

These major themes, ancestry and its emergence and persistence in the land, become frames, the prevailing context, for understanding and experiencing the quiet lives in Ortiz's stories, lives at once full of humor and anger and love and hate, all of which are vested in the rise and fall, the dirt and trees of the landscape. The lingering sense of this collection is that stories, our own personal histories, tie us to and teach us about our cultural importance and our political relevance.

Source: Matt Pifer, Review of *Men on the Moon*, in *World Literature Today*, Vol. 74, No. 1, Winter 2000, p. 215.

Bowker Magazine Group

In the following review, the reviewer praises "Ortiz's poetic gift and his intimate knowledge of oral storytelling."

Ortiz (*After and Before the Lightning*) is best known as a foremost contemporary Native American poet; his short fiction, written with a poetic emphasis on dense, potent language, is collected here for the first time. These 26 stories—penned between the late '60s and the early '80s—demonstrate the diversity of Native experience in modern America. Speaking in homage to, and solidarity with, his own Acoma Pueblo heritage, the author depicts American Indians in a wide range of social and geographic settings, from reservations to urban landscape. Many tales are melancholy, as they trace the fates of maligned, misunderstood and often visionary characters. In the title story, an aged Pueblo man watches television for the first time, sees astronauts walk on the moon and senses a sudden, irreversible loss of mystery. A young war widow takes a job at an Indian boarding school and must say goodbye to family and friends in the short "Home Country." Another tale, set in Oklahoma, juxtaposes generations in another way, as two brothers listen to an old drunk tell the story of Tecumseh's war; they know that Indians today need a new vision of themselves, another story that can build a powerful Indian identity. A sense of gentleness and wonder pervades the piece in which a father builds his son his first kite and watches the boy's exhilaration. The language of these rich narratives reflect both Ortiz's poetic gift and his intimate knowledge of oral storytelling.

Source: Bowker Magazine Group, Review of *Men on the Moon*, in *Publishers Weekly*, Vol. 246, No. 32, August 9, 1999, p. 345.

American Library Association

In the following review, the reviewer praises Ortiz for weaving "the tragic with the transcendent, the absurd with the cosmic."

Native American poet Ortiz's short stories seem more spoken than written, but there is nothing casual about their structure or intent. Having grown up in the Acoma Pueblo in New Mexico, Ortiz is acutely sensitive to the spiritual conflict between Indian and white cultures, and this ongoing strife is the underlying theme in each of his dramatic, sometimes humorous tales. In the unforgettable title story, for instance, a grown daughter and her son give her father his first television on the day the second Apollo mission blasts off for the moon. Faustin peers into the box and asks his grandson why these men want to go there. To learn "how everything was made in the beginning," he answers. "Hasn't anyone ever told them?" Faustin asks, both amused and alarmed at the white man's powerful machines, monomaniacal determination, and deep ignorance. Each of Ortiz's powerfully tender stories weaves the tragic with the transcendent, the absurd with the cosmic, whether it focuses on work or family, happiness or heartache, the laws of nature or of society, loyalty or love.

Source: American Library Association, Review of *Men on the Moon*, in *Booklist*, Vol. 95, No. 22, August 1999, p. 2028.

Sources

Pifer, Matt, Review of *Men on the Moon: Collected Short Stories*, in *World Literature Today*, Vol. 74, No. 1, Winter 2000, pp. 215–16.

Review of *Men on the Moon: Collected Short Stories*, in *Publishers Weekly*, Vol. 246, No. 32, August 9, 1999, p. 345.

Further Reading

Bruchac, Joseph, "The Story Never Ends: An Interview with Simon Oritz," in *Survival This Way*, University of Arizona Press, 1987, pp. 211–29.
  Bruchac focuses on the tension between tradition and Western culture in Ortiz's work.

Ortiz, Simon J., "The Historical Matrix towards a National Indian Literature: Cultural Authenticity in Nationalism," in *Critical Perspectives on Native American Fiction*, edited by Richard F. Fleck, Three Continents Press, 1993, pp. 64–68; originally published in *MELUS*, Summer 1981.

The title of Ortiz's essay makes it sound difficult to understand, but he approaches his subject with the same personal tone that he uses in his fiction, drawing from famous examples to make his point that the oral traditions and literary traditions of many tribes converge.

Sando, Joe S., *Pueblo Profiles: Cultural Identity through Centuries of Change*, Clear Light Books, 1999.

Sando, a member of the Jemez Pueblo, is an historian and archivist at the Indian Pueblo Cultural Center in New Mexico. His book highlights the major events in the history of the Pueblo tribes and also discusses the state of Pueblo life at the end of the twentieth century.

Wiget, Andrew, *Simon Ortiz*, Boise State University Western Writers Series, No. 74, Boise State University, 1986.

What is most interesting about this early 50-page overview of Ortiz's work is the way that Wiget places him as a Western, but not specifically Indian, writer.

An End to Dreams

Stephen Vincent Benét
1932

Stephen Vincent Benét is one of America's most popular short story authors. His *The Devil and Daniel Webster* is considered a classic, and his "An End to Dreams" appeared in *Pictoral Review* and won the O. Henry Award in 1932. Benét refused to follow the literary trends of his era, presenting instead in his work a more positive view of the American character in its historical moment. In his study of Benét in the *Dictionary of Literary Biography*, Joel Roache claims that Benét's vision of the human ability "to transcend its limitations" has assured that his short stories will enjoy a "secure reputation."

"An End to Dreams" focuses on the life of James Rimington as he dreams about it, while anesthetized in a hospital. As he lies in a hospital bed after a serious operation, James dreams about his personal and professional past. In his dream, he imagines that ambition prompted him to reject his small-town values, along with his childhood sweetheart, in order to gain power and wealth through the single-minded pursuit of corporate success. This success then alienated him from those he cared about and cost him any sense of peace. Just at the moment he dreams about dying alone in the hospital, he awakens, and the reader learns his life has taken a very different path. Benét's complex portrait of James, as he is portrayed in his dream and upon waking, presents a compelling exploration of the consequences of the pursuit of the American dream.

Stephen Vincent Benét   Photograph by Pirie MacDonald.
The Library of Congress

Author Biography

Stephen Vincent Benét was born on July 22, 1898 in Bethlehem, Pennsylvania. He felt a strong military influence during his childhood from his father, J. Walker Benét, who was an army colonel, and his mother, Frances Neill Benét, who descended from a Kentucky military family. Colonel J. Walker Benét was a great reader, especially of poetry, which helped shape his son's own love for reading and later writing. When Stephen was ten years old, he was sent to the Hitchcock Military Academy where he was quite unhappy. He was often abused by his school mates for his love of reading and dislike of athletics.

Benét was seventeen when his first book, *Five Men and Pompey*, a collection of verse, was published. During World War I, Benét worked in Washington, D.C., as a clerk, since, due to his bad eyesight, he was unable to serve in the military. He later attended Yale and received a master's degree. Instead of writing a thesis for his diploma, he submitted a volume of poems called *Heavens and Earth* (1920). His poetry received awards at Yale, including the first John Masefield Poetry Prize and the Ten Eyck prize. Benét published his first novel, *The Beginning of Wisdom* in 1921.

Benét continued his studies, this time in France, where he met Rosemary Carr, the woman he later married. Carr was a writer and journalist and together they lived a bohemian lifestyle until 1923 when they returned to the United States. During the 1920s Benét continued to write, and with the publication of *Tiger Joy* in 1925, his literary reputation was firmly established.

In 1926, Benét went back to France where he started to write *John Brown's Body*, an epic poem about the Civil War. Benét had always been fascinated with Civil War stories and had read through his father's old *Rebellion Records*. *John Brown's Body* received acclaim from critics and won Benét his first Pulitzer Prize in 1929.

In 1929, Benét was elected to the National Institute of Arts and Letters and in 1932 he won the O. Henry Award for the short story, "An End to Dreams." His popular short story "The Devil and Daniel Webster" was published in 1937 and was later made into a play, an opera, and a film.

Benét was a great advocate of America's entry into World War II as evidenced by a speech he wrote for President Roosevelt. He also worked as a screenwriter in Hollywood and wrote a series of radio scripts, including *Listen to the People* (1941) and *They Burned the Books* (1942). Benét was plagued with bad vision throughout his life, and he also suffered from arthritis and mental illness. He died of a heart attack in New York City, on March 13, 1943. In 1944, Benét was awarded his second Pulitzer Prize posthumously for his epic poem *Western Star*.

Plot Summary

The last thing James Rimington remembers in "An End to Dreams" is being given general anesthesia before an operation. As the story begins, he is looking up at himself in a mirror that appears to be held by a nurse. When he contemplates how strange that is, he is filled with terror. He then calms himself by deciding that he is alive "and over the worst." James recognizes that he needs a lot of sleep in order to recuperate before returning to work.

The next several passages contain scenes that slip through James's mind as he dreams. He wonders about how to fix a business deal and later about how he came to be so successful. Thinking back to when he was nine, Rimington remembers how ashamed he was of the patch on the jacket that he wore to school every day and how his classmates made fun of him by calling him "Patches." Their taunts roused him to anger, but some of the school boys overpowered him as their friends continued to mock him.

James dreams about being rescued by eight-year-old Elsa Mercer, which further humiliated him. Next, he dreams about his poverty and about Toby Beach, who although "fat and placid," had friends because his father was rich and had bought him a pony. James realizes, "If you had a pony and your father owned the bank, they wouldn't laugh at you." After that incident, young James determines, "I'm going to be rich" and then the children would want to play with him.

James dreams about coming home without the patched jacket that he had thrown away and about his mother talking to him about the reality of their situation. In defiance, he insisted to himself, "you could stop being poor if you wanted to enough." James understands how hard his mother worked but then insists that he became successful through hard work, which proves to him that all one needs is ambition. He wonders over how many people turned up for his mother's funeral in Bladesburg, his hometown, but decides that was due to the fact that she lived all of her life there. After the funeral, the townspeople had shown him the improvements they had made to the town but he secretly scorns their "small-town" mentality.

James's dream thoughts turn to how he looked as a teenager, and he smiles at the memory. Many evenings he would spend time with Elsa on her porch. He remembers working at the local bank and wonders how it has survived the recent "hard weather." In James's dream, Mr. Beach had turned down an idea James had for the bank, insisting "we're here to serve our own folks, not the Easterners." James thinks about how his plan had been "the first stepping stone" of his success.

He and Elsa had professed their love to each other and complained about not having enough money to get married. James does not regret his relationship with Elsa since it had prompted him to go to New York where he earned his fortune. Mr. Beach had warned him about getting involved with John Q. Dixon in New York because the man had the reputation of being "a pirate." Beach offered him a position as assistant cashier, suggesting that he would eventually move higher up in the bank, which would have given James the opportunity to marry Elsa.

He had considered the offer, imagining what life would be like as he slowly moved up from assistant cashier to "perhaps" owner at fifty. The townspeople would then have respect for him, no longer calling him "Patches." But he rejected this path, even while admitting that going to New York would mean that he could not continue to send his mother money. He also knew that even though he had promised, he would never come back to Elsa.

His dream memory jumps to his success in New York, where he was called "the quiet earthquake." James appears to have used Dixon's own tricks against him as the latter asked, "how much do you expect me to settle for, Jim?" Dixon suggested here that James had become as corrupt as he was. James catalogues the things he acquired as a result: expensive homes and a yacht where he could impress guests who came to find out how to gain similar success. There were also many "hollow" women who, he concludes, "had no importance" because the only thing that mattered to him was the work and the power it afforded.

In the dream, Elsa had in the meantime married Toby Beach with whom she had children. As James lies in bed, he weighs his choices. Even though he insists, "he had bought life on his own terms," he appears to regret his decisions, especially since he lost Elsa in the process. He tries to convince himself that what was important was work and power and averts his gaze from the mirror.

When he hears doctors talking in hushed tones, he looks through the mirror in an effort to discover what they are talking about. He gets annoyed when he decides they are not focusing on him. When he tries to get their attention, he finds that he is unable to speak. He tries to think who he could contact to help him but realizes that he has no friends. Eventually, he thinks about Elsa and conjures an image of her. As she tends her garden, he tries to make her think of him. She stops for a moment, with a concerned look flashing across her face, but returns to her work, for "the feebly burning lamp that had to do with James Rimington winked out." Her family is her main concern now.

His dream consciousness returns to the hospital where he seems to hear his doctor refer to a "sudden collapse" and call for oxygen as he concludes that men such as James do not have much to live for. James interprets this to mean that he is dying. After hearing one of the voices suggest that a mirror be used to see if he is still breathing, James looks at it and discovers that it is blank. Then all goes dark.

The scene jumps to a middle-aged woman sitting in a chair, who the reader discovers is Elsa

Rimington. James wakes up in the hospital confused, asking her if they are married. She confirms that they have been for thirty years. When he asks if he remembers his patched coat, she tells him how he kept wearing it, convincing the other children that it brought him luck. She tells him that the doctor is sure that he will be fine and that his children "are just crazy" to see him. James looks up at the ceiling and sees a spot of sun shining like a mirror and begins to tell her what he "saw," but he appears to realize that it has all been a dream. The story closes as James, filled with a sense of peace, takes Elsa's hand.

Characters

Toby Beach

Toby is a popular classmate of James, even though the boy is "fat and placid." He teaches James that "if you had a pony and your father owned the bank, they wouldn't laugh at you." Toby's father offers James a job at his bank that, in his dream, he rejects. In reality, though, James becomes a successful banker after accepting the position.

John Q. Dixon

In James's dream, one afternoon John Q. Dixon gets stuck in Bladesburg while traveling to New York City. James finds the courage to talk to the man, who is considered to be a "pirate" by the New York press. Dixon is James's hero, and he models himself after the man whom he believes has succeeded in realizing the American dream. Dixon is the epitome of the soulless robber baron of the early part of the twentieth century. His eyes can "look through a man" as he sizes him up to see what he can gain from him. James's association with Dixon corrupts him, however, to the point where James has become as much of a pirate as his mentor.

Elsa Mercer

In her childhood, Elsa is strong and kind. This "pig-tailed avenger" rescues James from the taunts of his classmates. James has a vision of her in his dream that seems to coincide with her true nature. In the dream, her patience becomes evident when she understands James's need to go to New York to seek his fortune and insists that she will wait for him. But James never returns to her in his dream. He admits that she gives him the courage to speak to John Q. Dixon that afternoon in Bladesburg.

Elsa exhibits this same level of support after James wakes from his dream. She is at his side,

praising him for his ingenuity when as a child his classmates made fun of his patched coat. She claims that he is the best patient at the hospital and tells him that their children and his sister are "just crazy" to see him. It is obvious that she provides him with the peace he experiences at the end of the story.

James Rimington

Benét presents two versions of James, one in the dream and the other in reality. Perhaps Benét is suggesting that James is a combination of both versions. The dream James is ruled by his monomaniacal drive to escape the grinding poverty of his childhood. Humiliated by his family's circumstances, which force him to wear a patched jacket, James recognizes that "when you were poor, people laughed at you." He also learns that money will buy friends as evidenced by his classmates swarming around the son of the local banker.

Lacking compassion, he views poverty as a weakness, insisting "you could stop being poor if you wanted to enough" and so regards his mother, who has worn herself out with work, with disdain. Beach has provided a way out of his poverty in Bladesburg, but the job does not offer James the level of success he craves. Beach admits that the plan James brings to him is "a brilliant scheme" but insists that they "can't touch it" because they are there "to serve our own folks, not the Easterners." James's response is to mock the older man's decent business practices.

When he thinks about leaving for the city, James recognizes that he would not be able to send his mother any money for a long time since "Dixon paid his clever young men starvation wages at first." He also acknowledges that he will never return for Elsa either, but his selfish pursuit of his dreams presses him to leave.

In his dream, James relocates to New York and becomes hardened by his drive for success and is nicknamed "the quiet earthquake." He thinks back to the days when he played the mandolin for Elsa, considering himself a foolish boy then. He has disciplined himself to focus only on work and his drive for success. In New York, he has become a "pirate" like his mentor John Dixon, who told him "when a man's tired making money he's tired of life." When James eventually defeats him, Dixon admits that he learned well his advice to "always squeeze the shorts" and looks at the younger man with "passionless comprehension." Success has made the dream James rigid and demanding, and as a result friendless.

At the hospital, the dream James becomes angry when he thinks that the doctors are not taking good care of him and insists that he should be their first priority. This James, however, is not strong enough to buy himself life, and thus he dies.

The true James emerges at the end of the story. We only learn a few details about him through Elsa that reflect his character. Apparently, he was strong enough to deflect criticism regarding his poverty when he convinced his classmates that his patched jacket brings him luck. This James turns into "a solid man. A settled, small-town citizen" who is loved by his wife and family and who has found ultimate peace in his situation.

Benét complicates our vision of James, however, by his juxtaposition of the two versions. The author suggests that James has dual impulses: to get out of his small town and pursue a selfish dream of power and wealth, and to become a "decent" citizen of his small town, living a quiet, settled life with his family. This duality creates a more complex and so more realistic vision of James's character.

Mrs. Rimington

James's selfless mother always looks "bewildered." James concludes that her inability to focus on and complete a task results from her being the sole caretaker to her five children. She is well-respected in their hometown, as evidenced by the kind words all say about her at her funeral.

Themes

The American Dream

Benét explores the destructive aspects of the American dream and suggests an altered version. In his dream, James follows the traditional plot of the dream, which involves rising from poverty to the top of the corporate world, amassing wealth and power along the way. He envisions, however, the destructive consequences of this achievement since it necessitated moving away from his family and the woman he loved.

In his dream, James imagines himself as hardened by his immersion in the corporate world of New York City. He becomes as corrupt as his idol, John Q. Dixon, beating the tycoon at his own game. When he returns for his mother's funeral, he scoffs at the small-town values of his hometown, with its decent, hard-working members like his mother, and

Topics for Further Study

- Read F. Scott Fitzgerald's *The Great Gatsby* and compare its treatment of the American dream to that of "An End to Dreams."

- Imagine a screen version of the story. How would you depict James's dream and the transition into reality?

- Investigate Freud's theories on dreams. Is James's dream an illustration of these theories? Explain how they are or are not.

- Compare and contrast the subject of success in "An End to Dreams" and "The Devil and Daniel Webster."

had not "cracked a smile" when given a tour of the new buildings. James's success has caused him to alienate and isolate himself from others except the "women of various ages and different looks . . . light and hollow as figures made of pasteboard" who "had no importance." As he lies dying in his hospital bed, he can think of no one who would come to his side. James recognizes the wrong path he has taken when he admits that he was "meant to grow up and marry Elsa and do all sorts of things." At that moment, his corporate "dream" dies. The doctor holds the mirror up to his face and finds there is no breath as darkness falls.

Benét's alternate vision of the American Dream involves a more gradual and less steep path to success. When James wakes from his dream, he finds that he is successful on a smaller scale as provider for his family and has been married to Elsa for thirty years. He has channeled his ambition in a different direction. Elsa reminds him that when his classmates teased him about his patched jacket, he convinced them that it helped him shoot marbles more accurately. As a result, "by the end of the year, every boy in school wanted a patch." James learned to make the best of his situation in his hometown and so determined to find a more comfortable version of the American dream.

Subconscious Desires

According to Sigmund Freud (1856–1939), founder of modern psychoanalysis, there are different levels of consciousness, one on the surface and the other beneath and often hidden from the conscious mind. The subconscious harbors desires that people do not recognize consciously. Often, these suppressed desires emerge in the form of dreams. Benét's story of James's dream focuses on material wealth, professional importance, and corporate success. Perhaps these dream subjects represent suppressed desires in James. In Benét's words, the dream emerges as James experiences a "shaken point of consciousness," which occurs when James believes he is coming out of anesthesia.

James's detailed reconstruction of his past suggests that he is unfulfilled on some level. While he is attended lovingly by his wife at the end of the story, he admits to a sense of defeat when he realizes that his vision of his success is only a dream. Even the title, "An End to Dreams," suggests that James's vision of his corporate rise was a suppressed desire. Benét's depiction of these dual levels of consciousness paints a more complex portrait of his main character.

Style

Foreshadowing

Benét uses foreshadowing to good effect in the story as he drops hints that Rimington is not what he appears to be. When he looks in the mirror as he is lying on the hospital bed, he admits that his face "seemed like the face of an utter stranger." He is in a "shaken point of consciousness" when he first stars at the mirror. As he looks at his reflection, "the lines began to smooth away, the heavy cheeks grew younger . . . as if he gazed at one of those magic tricks of the camera." A magic trick is being performed by his psyche, which has been suppressing his dreams of success in New York City. At the end of the story readers learn that his subconscious has manufactured this version of James through a dream. Another moment of foreshadowing occurs when he notes that his mother's only desire was "to have her children grow up decent small-town citizens," which is exactly what the real James has become.

Symbolism

Benét uses the mirror as a symbol of James's subconscious, which enables the author to present a dual vision of his main character as well as the ironic twist at the end of the story. Before he is completely conscious, James sees his reflection in what appears to be a mirror that he assumes a nurse is holding over his head. This mirror allows him to examine his past as it presents him with a look at what might have been. Sometimes it clouds, suggesting that the visions are false, as when James wonders what would have happened if he had "stayed in Bladesburg, worn the patched coat." When it clears, he continues his dreams of wealth and power.

Historical Context

The Jazz Age

American society went through a period of dramatic change in the aftermath of World War I. Traditional beliefs in God, country, and humanity were shaken as Americans faced the devastation of a war of this magnitude. The resulting feelings of confusion and dislocation led to a questioning and often a rejection of conventional morality and beliefs. In the 1920s, Americans recognized that an old order had been replaced by a new, freer society, one that adopted innovative fashions in clothing, behavior, and the arts. F. Scott Fitzgerald named this decade the "Jazz Age," which along with the "Roaring Twenties" came to express the cultural revolution that was then taking place.

Despite this era of being one of Prohibition (sale and consumption of alcohol was prohibited by the Eighteenth Amendment to the U.S. Constitution, which became law in 1919), Americans experimented with expressions of personal and social freedom in dress, sexuality, and lifestyle. Women cut their hair short and wore shapeless "flapper" dresses that gave then an androgynous air. Premarital sex began to lose its stigma, and exciting developments in musical styles pulled whites into predominantly black neighborhoods. The pursuit of pleasure, especially as related to the accumulation of wealth, became a primary goal, overturning traditional notions of hard work, social conformity, and respectability. Literary historian Margot Norris notes that during this age, "the aesthetics of glamour produced by material and social extravagance" were "simulated and stimulated by the celluloid images of the burgeoning movie industry."

Literature in the 1920s

Literature in the 1920s in America was dominated by a group of American writers that felt a

Compare & Contrast

- **1925–1935:** After the devastation of World War I, some Americans turn to a pursuit of happiness through the acquisition of wealth. Their extravagant and unchecked spending habits contribute to the economic crisis at the end of the 1920s.

  Today: After a decade of unprecedented and unrealistic spikes in the stock market, the Dow dropped considerably in the first years of the twenty-first century. As a result, many who amassed fortunes from employment in the technology sector, found themselves jobless. The market slowly recovered during 2004, but some economists worry that the slow economy will drive it down again.

- **1925–1935:** After a decade of buying on credit in the 1920s, Americans find themselves in the grips of a severe economic depression in the 1930s.

  Today: Economic policies, like unemployment compensation, are in place that would prevent the country from falling into a severe depression that would devastate the lives of American citizens as it did in the 1930s. However, suggested changes in Social Security may reduce benefits for Americans.

growing sense of disillusionment after World War I. As a result, many left the United States and lived in Europe. T. S. Eliot and Ezra Pound initially relocated to London, while Fitzgerald and Ernest Hemingway traveled to Paris, which appeared to offer them a much freer society than America or England did. During this period, Paris became a chosen destination for these expatriates, who congregated in literary salons (gatherings in private homes or apartments of artists and writers), restaurants, and bars to discuss their work in the context of the new age. Gertrude Stein, who hosted one such salon, announced: "you are all a lost generation," a line Hemingway used as an epigraph for *The Sun Also Rises*. Stein, an author herself, supported and publicized artists and writers in this movement. In addition to Hemingway's work, Fitzgerald's *The Great Gatsby* came to be seen as a penetrating portrait of this lost generation.

The characters in works by these authors reflected their growing sense of disillusionment along with the new ideas in psychology, anthropology, and philosophy that had become popular in the early part of the twentieth century. Freudianism, for example, which may have contributed to more open sexual expression during the Jazz Age, began to be studied by these writers, as they explored the psyche of their characters and recorded their often-subjective points of view of themselves and their world. Hemingway's men and women faced a meaningless world with courage and dignity, exhibiting grace under pressure, while Fitzgerald's characters sought the redemptive power of love in a world driven by materialism.

The Great Depression

The Great Depression held America in its grips during the 1930s. The depression was a severe worldwide economic crisis that occurred in the United States after the stock market crash of 1929. The impact on Americans was staggering. In 1933, the worst year, unemployment rose to 16 million, about one third of the available labor force. During the early years, men and women searched eagerly and diligently for any type of work. However, after several months of no sustained employment, they became discouraged and often gave up. President Franklin Delano Roosevelt's New Deal policies, which offered the country substantial economic relief, helped mitigate the effects of the depression, but the recovery was not complete until the government channeled money into the war effort in the early 1940s.

Offices of J. P. Morgan and Company opposite the columned façade of the New York Stock Exchange on Wall Street, New York, New York, 1930 © Hulton-Deutsch Collection/Corbis

Critical Overview

Although Stephen Vincent Benét gained popularity for his poetry and stories during his lifetime, little scholarly attention has been paid to his work. Some of his works, however, including his epic poem about the Civil War, *John Brown's Body*, and his short story "The Devil and Daniel Webster" are considered minor classics. He was awarded two Pulitzer Prizes: one for *John Brown's Body* and the other for *Western Star*, a long poem about American pioneers. "An End to Dreams" won the O. Henry Award in 1932.

Benét's work seems to lack originality and be old fashioned in its unabashed patriotism. Henry W. Wells, in his article on Benét for *College English*, argues that he "suffers from an inescapably romantic and youthful disposition for extremes of sentiment." Yet he also claims that Benét should be remembered and read for his inspired historical reflections. Wells insists that his two Pulitzer prize-winning works are "noble and refreshing contributions to American literature" from "one of the most enlightened poets of our times."

Basil Davenport, in his introduction to Benét's *Selected Prose and Poetry*, echoes Wells's assertion when he suggests, "There is no one to touch Benét in the variety and skill of his treatment of American themes." He also asserts that "The Devil and Daniel Webster," is a "legend so perfect that it seems to have been always a part of our folklore." In his article for *Modern Language Notes*, Gordon Bigelow (in a review of a book by Charles A. Fenton) writes, "Benét's best work in prose or verse usually came when he was able to exploit imaginatively the myth and fact of the American past." In his study of Benét, Joseph Wood Krutch, considers his work to be "solid" and insists that "it uses American material in a way which is not only interesting but tending at the same time to make the American past more dignified, more meaningful and more comprehensible to the imagination."

R. L. Duffus wrote in the *New York Times*, "Whether he wrote in solid prose or in measured lines he was a poet. He had the kind of imagination that sees meaning . . . and relations[hips]" that others miss. In his study of Benét in the *Dictionary of Literary Biography*, Joel Roache claims that Benét's vision of the human ability to "transcend its limitations" will assure for his short stories "a modest but secure reputation for at least several more generations."

Criticism

Wendy Perkins

Perkins is a professor of American and English literature and film. In this essay, Perkins examines Benét's mix of modernist and realist elements in the story.

Modernism, one of the most fruitful periods in American letters, emerged in the decade that followed World War I (1914–18). Modernist authors such as Ernest Hemingway and F. Scott Fitzgerald became part of what Gertrude Stein called, the "lost generation"—the generation who saw, often firsthand, the horrors of war and who struggled to survive despite a sense of lost values and ideals.

The 1920s became an age of confusion, redefinition, and experimentation. The spirit of the Roaring Twenties, or the Jazz Age as Fitzgerald called this period, was reflected in modernist themes. On the surface, the characters in many of the literary works of this decade live in the rarified atmosphere of the upper class. They drink, party, have sexual adventures, but underneath the glamorous surface emerges the meaninglessness at the heart of their existence. This meaninglessness was compounded in the 1930s when the Great Depression hit and so many Americans lost their wealth. The modernists reflected the *zeitgeist* (a German word for "spirit") of their age—a time when, in the aftermath of World War I, many Americans lost faith in traditional institutions such as the government, social norms, religion, and even the worth of family relationships.

Each modernist writer focused on different ways to cope with this loss: some of their characters try to drown a sense of emptiness in the fast-paced life of the 1920s, some in sexual relationships, and some in personal notions of courage. All ultimately have difficulty sustaining any sense of fulfillment and completion in the modern age.

Not all writers in the 1920s and 1930s dramatized the tenets of modernism in their works. Many, such as Zora Neale Hurston and Willa Cather, continued the tradition of realism, the dominant literary mode of the end of the nineteenth century. Realism focuses on the commonplace and the everyday, giving readers an impression that what is being presented is an accurate portrait of ordinary experience. Some incorporated the old with the new, combining elements of both schools. One such writer was Stephen Vincent Benét. In his award winning short story "An End to Dreams," Benét adroitly combines modernist subjects with realist sensibilities as he explores one man's pursuit of the American dream.

James Rimington could walk into any story by F. Scott Fitzgerald and be at home. Like Jay Gatsby, James is devoted to the American dream, to the belief that anyone can achieve financial success. Humiliated by the "grinding" poverty of his youth, which forced him to wear a patched jacket, James vows not to let anything stand in his way as he strives to gain wealth and the power it affords. After seeing a rich classmate gain popularity, James concludes, "if you had a pony and your father owned the bank, they wouldn't laugh at you." He believes that "you could stop being poor if you wanted to enough."

He is unable to recognize the decency of the residents in his small town, including his mother, who works selflessly for her family, and the value of their slow-paced but fulfilling lives. He turns down a job offer from the president of the local bank, which promised advancement but not the kind that would satisfy James. His ambition drives

> **His ambition drives him to abandon the girl he loves and move to New York City where he becomes as corrupt as the 'pirate' John Q. Dixon, eventually beating the powerful tycoon at his own game."**

him to abandon the girl he loves and move to New York City where he becomes as corrupt as the "pirate" John Q. Dixon, eventually beating the powerful tycoon at his own game.

James ends up like many modernists characters. His single-minded pursuit of wealth has thrown him into a world of "the books and the pictures, the charities and the gifts" because "one was not interested enough." He had plenty of women, but they were "light and hollow as figures made of pasteboard; they had no importance." All he had was his work and the power it gained him, but ultimately those were not enough to save him. Money could not buy him health, and as he lies apparently dying in his hospital bed, reviewing his life, he cannot find one person to help him, not one person who cares about his fate.

If the story had ended here, it would be an apt illustration of modernist themes with its focus on the meaninglessness in the materialism and superficiality of the American dream. But this ending would not fit Benét's own sensibilities. When James awakes from his dream of what might have been, he becomes a realist hero: he has made a nobler choice for the direction of his life. He is rewarded for that choice by the loving attention his family offers him, the immediate attention his wife Elsa expresses to him in the hospital. She refuses to leave his side and his children and sister are "just crazy" to see him.

Realist literature centers on conduct and the consequences of actions, especially on the dynamics of cause and effect relationships. While realist writers incorporated the idea of individuality from the Romantics, they focused on the ability to choose, which involved deliberation, weighing

What Do I Read Next?

- "The Devil and Daniel Webster" (1937), one of Benét's most famous stories, focuses on the battle of good and evil in the soul of a Yankee farmer.

- F. Scott Fitzgerald's novel *The Great Gatsby* (1925) shares many of the same themes as Fitzgerald's short story "Winter Dreams."

- *The Sun Also Rises* (1926), by Ernest Hemingway, one of Fitzgerald's "lost generation" compatriots, focuses on a group of disillusioned Americans living in Paris after World War I.

- *Discontented America: The United States in the 1920s* (1989), written by David J. Goldberg and published as part of the American Moment series, presents an overview of this decade and focuses specifically on how World War I affected American society.

alternative actions through a consideration of consequences. A responsible choice produces a moral hero, and as such, a definition of self. A classic illustration of this point can be found in Mark Twain's novel *Huckleberry Finn*. Huck's decision to "go to hell" on behalf of Jim the runaway slave makes him a realist hero. In the southern states before the American Civil War, Huck makes the moral and risky choice of helping Jim escape against the socially approved evil of slavery.

James weighs his alternatives in the story, deliberating about whether to stay in his hometown and marry Elsa or strike out for success and glory in New York City. By the end, James has made a responsible choice, rejecting the shallow pursuit of wealth and power and opting for the quiet but fulfilling small-town life with the comforts of human connection in his family. Benét's own sensibilities are evident here in his depiction of the extremes of the two choices: one offering a materially successful but emotionally empty existence, while the other offers the joys of family life.

Benét's vision of the American dream is illustrated in James's choice. Basil Davenport, in his introduction to Benét's *Selected Prose and Poetry*, writes that the attitude Benét expresses in his work is that life is "too good to waste in being rich and proper." Commenting on Benét's continuing popularity in America, David H. Webster concludes in his review of Benét's *Selected Prose and Poetry* (1960) that Benét is "significant in the sixties partly just because he rejected some of the attitudes common in the twenties and thirties."

In "An End to Dreams," Benét gives James a clear choice that is not available in modernist works. Relationships do not work out so smoothly in Fitzgerald's and Hemingway's worlds. They are destroyed by the pressures of the post-war age. Benét's ending appears to ignore those pressures in its celebration of family values and commitment. Yet the story presents a more complex vision of human desire. Ironically, through the depiction of his realist hero, Benét employs a modernist technique as he focuses on James's subconscious.

Influenced by the theories of Sigmund Freud, modernists explored the psychology of their characters, often attempting to convey both subconscious and conscious motivations. To accurately reflect these levels of consciousness, modernists employed stream-of-consciousness narratives (disjointed reflections of the conscious mind) and replaced traditional omniscient narrators with subjective points of view limited by the narrow, sometimes distorted vision of reality of a given character.

While James's narrative is not strictly stream of consciousness, it is subjective and fragmented as it jumps back and forth in time. Benét explores in a Freudian way James's subconscious desire for wealth and power that is so strong that it causes him to dream about an alternate world based on a moment in his past when he had to choose his path. Benét thus creates a realist text with an ironic modernist twist in its Freudian suggestion of dual layers of consciousness.

"An End to Dreams" echoes and at the same time overturns the modernist focus on spiritual stagnation, yet Benét complicates the issue in his presentation of James's dual worlds, suggesting Freud's contention that dreams reveal the dreamer's subconscious desires. At the end of the story, after James awakes from his dream and finds Elsa at his side, he is "at peace," but in that final moment, he knows "the measure of his victory and defeat." His choice to stay in his hometown can be viewed as a defeat since it denied his ambition, his dreams of glory. Despite the fact that he is at peace, his dream and sense of defeat suggest that he has some regret about the choice he has made.

Benét's adept combination of modernist themes and technique with realist sensibilities creates a compelling portrait of one man's ambivalent attraction to the American dream. In his examination of James's conflicting desires, he illustrates the complex nature of that dream.

Source: Wendy Perkins, Critical Essay on "An End to Dreams," in *Short Stories for Students*, Thomson Gale, 2006.

Sheldon Goldfarb

Goldfarb has a Ph.D. in English and has published two books on the Victorian author William Makepeace Thackeray. In the following essay, Goldfarb discusses the stark choice between two competing lifestyles depicted in "An End to Dreams."

In Stephen Vincent Benét's most famous story, "The Devil and Daniel Webster," Daniel Webster is able to convince a jury of damned souls that, despite promising his soul to the Devil in return for material prosperity, Jabez Stone should not have to surrender his soul after all, even though he did indeed receive ten years of prosperity. Avoiding the fact that Jabez Stone is breaching his contract, Webster focuses on the fact that there is good and bad in everyone and in all of American history, and without that good and bad together there could be nothing new.

Similarly, in his story "Johnny Pye and the Fool-Killer," Benét has his hero argue that there can be no progress unless people do foolish things. And in his story "Doc Mellhorn and the Pearly Gates," the central character is frustrated in Heaven because there are no sick people there on whom to practise medicine. He ends up going to Hell for a while in order to have a chance to practise his chosen profession, there being plenty of sick people there.

What emerges in all these stories is a sense of dualism, a sense of a need for good and bad. To live in Heaven without a chance to visit Hell once in a while would be stultifying. To be unable to do foolish or even evil things once in a while would mean an end to progress. What Benét argues for in these fairly well-known stories of his is for a mix of good and evil, a mix of ambition and morality, of adventure and staying home. Thus in "Johnny Pye and the Fool-Killer," Johnny Pye gets a chance to run away from home and take up with a snake-oil salesman, a money-obsessed merchant, and a band of soldiers before returning home to become a postmaster and marry his childhood sweetheart.

> Instead of a chance to have it all, James Rimington, the hero of 'Dreams,' is forced to choose. He has no possibility of pursuing both ambition and home-town values; he must choose one or the other."

It is different in Benét's less well-known story, "An End to Dreams." Instead of a chance to have it all, James Rimington, the hero of "Dreams," is forced to choose. He has no possibility of pursuing both ambition and home-town values; he must choose one or the other. As he says rather unhappily, "Of course you made a decision and took one path out of two. That was what life was for." In this story there seems no hope of duality.

In some ways, "An End to Dreams" is much like "The Devil and Daniel Webster" and "Johnny Pye and the Fool-Killer." All three stories tell of a suffering central character. There is Jabez Stone in "Daniel Webster," for whom nothing seems to go right. There is Johnny Pye in his story, who is abused by his adoptive parents. And then there is James Rimington in "Dreams," who is teased and bullied by the other schoolchildren because he is poor and wears patches on his clothes. "Patches," they call him. Like Johnny Pye, James Rimington decides to run away from home. And like Jabez Stone, he makes a deal with a devilish sort of figure. Not the literal Devil as in "The Devil and Daniel Webster," but a shady financier named John Q. Dixon. He is warned that Dixon is "crooked," and in order to become rich like him he has to cut his ties with his mother, his sweetheart, and his whole hometown; but he goes ahead, or so it seems, and as the story draws to a close it appears that he has done exactly what Jabez Stone did: sold his soul for material prosperity.

At the very end, though, in the little coda to the story, it turns out that all of James Rimington's life as a successful businessman was just a dream. Actually, he did not choose to leave his sweetheart and his hometown. His sweetheart, Elsa, is his wife of thirty years, and she is by his side in the hospital when he wakes up from an operation. All of his life as a hard-edged, powerful businessman seems to have been a dream induced by anesthetic during that operation. At first this seems like a good thing. Most of the story consists of James Rimington reviewing his apparent life as a prosperous businessman and not seeming to like it. It may have given him money and power, houses and women, but the women were "light and hollow" and they passed away with no importance in his life; and when he fears he is dying in the hospital there is no one to care about him. He frantically reviews who there might be. He seems not even to have any friends. The only people he can think of are his employees and his servants, and he knows they will not care about him dying. Even his sister would think first of their mother, not of him.

Thus when he wakes up from the operation and finds that he is alive and well in his old hometown with Elsa at his side, he is relieved. The last words of the story say he is "at peace." And yet the very same sentence says that he knew "the measure of his victory and defeat," an odd thing to say if choosing to stay with Elsa in the small town was entirely the right thing to do. Why is it a defeat as well as a victory? Moreover, the use of the word "defeat" reminds the reader of the earlier description of James Rimington the successful businessman as having "bleak, undefeated eyes." As a businessman, James Rimington did not suffer defeat; his life may have been bleak, but it was a life of triumphs. In contrast, James Rimington as the man who stayed in his hometown has in some way been defeated.

It is as if at one level Benét is pushing the reader to think that it is better to renounce the "crooked" world of the John Q. Dixons, as if it is best not to follow the path of ambition, while at the same time the story suggests some dissatisfaction with such a renunciation. In this context, it is interesting to consider the story's title. What are the dreams that are supposed to be ending in this story? On a literal level, the one dream there seems to be is the one about James Rimington pursuing a shady financial career; that is the dream he wakes from at the end of the story. Since that dream ends so badly, with James Rimington dying all alone, uncared for in a hospital bed, one might expect it to be referred to as a nightmare. But the story is not called "Escape from a Nightmare" or even "An End to Bad Dreams." It is "An End to Dreams."

Now, the word "dreams" usually has a positive connotation, and looking closely at what the word might be referring to in this story, the reader is likely to think of dreams of success and ambition. Is that what is ending for James Rimington? But is it an altogether good thing to give up one's dreams and ambitions? Perhaps not. And perhaps that is why at the end of the story James Rimington feels defeat as well as victory.

Joel Roache, in an article analyzing Benét's works in general, says that in Benét's stories the conflicts "are too easily resolved." That may be true of Benét's other stories, but it does not seem true at all of "An End to Dreams." Here the conflict between big city ambition and small town values remains totally unresolved. The life of ambition seems empty and bleak, but life in a small town, where James Rimington has taken a job in the local bank, seems lacking in achievement. He could have done so much more; in his dream he did do more—but at a price. As he himself says, "You can buy anything there is . . . but you have to pay for it." In this story it seems that the price of success is giving up the comforts of a wife and family. It seems a high price to pay, and yet not to pay it seems a problem. As James Rimington says, speaking as the successful businessman from the middle of the bad dream, staying in the small town and working in the bank, becoming a "settled small-town citizen," would have meant "thirty years of rolling a stone uphill."

The stone reference is an allusion to the ancient Greek myth of Sisyphus. Sisyphus is condemned by the gods to an eternity of rolling a stone up a hill, only to see it roll back down to the bottom as soon as he gets it to the top. The myth is a symbol of futility, and that is how James Rimington sees life as a small-town banker married to Elsa. Of course, that is James Rimington the big-city businessman speaking, and perhaps his view is not to be trusted, but his view is there in the story competing with the view that small-town ways are best.

The two competing views remain unreconciled in this story. Indeed, the choice between them is so stark and absolute that at times there seem to be two James Rimingtons in the story, the one who went off to become a businessman and the one who stayed home. In the middle of the dream, James Rimington thinks, "Suppose you'd stayed in Bladesburg, worn the patched coat? Would you still be James Rimington?" Near the end of the dream, when the dying businessman tries to contact Elsa telepathically, he thinks, "If he could only make her think of him—of him, not merely James Rimington . . ." It is as if there is a "him" separate from James Rimington, a core personality perhaps beneath the successful businessman or a small-town boy different from the businessman.

In any case, what the story presents is two paths so different that to pursue either is to call one's identity into question. To become James Rimington the successful businessman is almost to become a different person from the little boy who lived in Bladesburg and who might have grown up to work in the local bank. Thus in the end the story leaves us with two irreconcilable options, neither of which seems altogether appealing.

Robert Combs, in an article on "The Devil and Daniel Webster, says that the Faustian bargain of selling one's soul to the Devil for material prosperity is Benét's "great theme." It is certainly the theme of "The Devil and Daniel Webster" in a quite literal way. It also is the theme in a figurative sense of "An End to Dreams." But whereas in "Daniel Webster" it is possible to sell one's soul and somehow get it back, in "An End to Dreams" there is no such possibility.

In "Daniel Webster" and some of the other stories, the world Benét depicts is one in which a person can do some foolish or questionable things and still return to a life of virtue. In "An End to Dreams" there seems to be a brief yearning for such a situation, when the dying James Rimington thinks, "It couldn't be true. James Rimington couldn't be there dying. James Rimington was a boy in a patched coat who meant to grow up and marry Elsa and do all sorts of things."

The trouble is that the boy cannot marry Elsa and also do all sorts of things if those things are supposed to include big city success in the financial world. In this story, the boy can grow up to do one or the other, but not both. It is a sad conclusion, sadder than that in "The Devil and Daniel Webster."

Benét is more optimistic in "Daniel Webster," as he is in "Johnny Pye" and "Doc Mellhorn." In those stories Benét is able to create resolutions, but perhaps they are too easy resolutions as Joel Roache says. As an author Benét had his own choice to make, between suggesting that the pursuit of ambition could be reconciled with family and small-town values and suggesting that there could be no reconciliation between these approaches to life. It is a choice between a perhaps too easy resolution on the one hand and dissatisfaction on the other. In "An End to Dreams," he opted for dissatisfaction.

Source: Sheldon Goldfarb, Critical Essay on "An End to Dreams," in *Short Stories for Students*, Thomson Gale, 2006.

David Garrett Izzo

In the following essay, Izzo discusses Benét's writing career.

Stephen Vincent Benét is best known as the author of the classic Civil War verse epic *John Brown's Body* (1928) and the much-anthologized short story "The Devil and Daniel Webster" (1936). Yet, Benét, once one of the most popular writers in America, wrote many more stories, novels, poems, and dramas. The fact that Benét wrote plays has largely been forgotten, even though millions of Americans heard his radio plays in the late 1930s and early 1940s. Benét's poems and prose emphasize the spoken word and, in fact, many of his short stories have been adapted as plays by other writers because of their inherent stageability.

Stephen Vincent Benét was born on 22 July 1898 in Bethlehem, Pennsylvania, to Colonel James Walker Benét and Frances Neill Benét. His father, as a military man, took Stephen and his older siblings, William Rose and Laura—who also became writers—across the country to military posts in Watervliet, New York; Benecia, California; Rock Island, Illinois; and Augusta, Georgia. These varied experiences gave Benét a colorful childhood that was augmented by a lively imagination and the doting attentions of his parents and his brother and sister.

Benét's family was a ready and willing audience for his stories, and his parents were open-minded and progressive. In his *Stephen Vincent Benét: The Life and Times of an American Man of Letters, 1898–1943* (1958), Charles A. Fenton quotes Benét as saying of his father, "I cannot agree with those who say that the military mind is narrow and insensitive. . . . [Father] could write any fixed form of verse, was interested in everything. . . . He represented integrity—and a sense of humor." Moreover, family friend and poet Leonard Bacon writes of James Walker Benét in his *Semi-Centennial, Some of the Life and Part of the Opinions of Leonard Bacon* (1939): "He knew more about English poetry than most poets and all professors. . . . Such a man deserved to have all three of his children become poets." In 1915 William Rose Benét helped his younger brother to get his first book published. *Five Men and Pompey: A Series of Dramatic Portraits*, while certainly verse, is verse drama in the form of six first-person orations by Roman figures. Benét's inclination toward the dramatic and dramatic monologues served him well for the rest of his writing career.

When Benét entered Yale in 1915, he was already considered a wunderkind by such notables as

" In time Benét may
well once more be thought of
as a great writer, not just
a 'patriotic' writer."

F. Scott Fitzgerald, who thought Benét's poetry better than that of his good friend and Princeton classmate John Peale Bishop, whom he considered an accomplished poet. Fenton quotes critic Malcolm Cowley as remembering that "Benét was the bright star not only of Yale but of all the Eastern colleges." At Yale, Benét concentrated on getting published in the Yale literary magazines and enjoying his friendships with fellow writers Thornton Wilder, poets H. Phelps Putnam and John Chipman Farrar (who cofounded, with Stanley M. Rinehart Jr., the publishing firm of Farrar and Rinehart in 1929), novelist Hervey Allen, and playwright Phillip Barry. Tappan Wilder, the nephew of Thornton Wilder, recalls his uncle telling him about the Yale days when he and Benét read their plays to each other. In November 1919 Wilder and Benét, along with Richard Bassett, John F. Carter, Arthur Dallin, Norman Fitts, Ramon Guthrie, William Hanway, Quincy Porter, and Roger Sessions, founded a little literary magazine, titled *The S4N* (which stood for "space for name"), that lasted four years. They called it an "idea exchange."

At Yale, Benét and his classmate Wilder met with and saw a recital by poet Vachel Lindsay, who wrote poems meant to be dramatized. Lindsay did so powerfully and with a profound impact on the two undergraduates. In his diary (now at the Beinecke Library, Yale University) Wilder wrote about meeting the poet in his entry of 18 March 1918: "Wednesday aft. met Mr. Nicholas Vachel Lindsay at the [Elizabethan] club and Dr. Seymour asked me to dinner that evening to meet him. . . . Steve [Benét] came in afterward at table: [drawing of table] Afterward Mr. Lindsay read Congo, Gen. Booth enters Heaven, Lincoln and many others! He reads dramatically with shreeks, intonings and chantings." Lindsay died in 1931, but Wilder and Benét never forgot Lindsay's impact. Wilder based the hero of his 1935 novel, *Heaven's My Destination*, on Lindsay, and in his 1936 collection, *Burning City*, Benét

published his poetic ode to Lindsay, "Do You Remember Springfield?" For Benét, Lindsay proved that poetry could be potent dramatic oratory, and critics frequently compared Benét's poems to those of Lindsay. Many of Benét's poems were written as dramatic monologues with an eye toward potential performance.

Farrar, Benét's classmate, recalls in his 1943 memoir, "For the Record," that at Yale his friend's "first play . . . was a farce concerning the Greek Gods and heroes called *Poor Old Medusa*. It was produced under Monty [Montillion] Woolley's direction along with a satire . . . by Philip Barry and a war number of mine, in the ballroom of the Taft Hotel at New Haven before the 'Pump and Slipper Dance' in the spring of 1919. It was . . . pungent and certainly, before that exacting audience, successful." Woolley, who later became a stage and screen actor, was a Yale professor. In the same year he and Benét also collaborated on an acting version of Christopher Marlowe's play *Tamburlaine the Great* (1590). Later, in 1924, Farrar and Benét cowrote two plays, including a longer version of the "war number." Benét received a master's degree from Yale in 1920 and received a traveling fellowship for 1920-1921. Benét went to Paris, as did so many of his contemporaries, and there he wrote his first novel, *The Beginning of Wisdom*, published by the firm of Henry Holt and Company in 1921. This novel earned immediate recognition. Bishop praised it in a tripartite review in *Vanity Fair*, republished in *The Collected Essays of John Peale Bishop* (1948) titled, "Three Brilliant Young Novelists (*The Beautiful and the Damned* by F. Scott Fitzgerald; *The Beginning of Wisdom* by Stephen Vincent Benét; *Three Soldiers* by John Dos Passos)":

> *The Beginning of Wisdom* is a picaresque novel of a young man who successively encounters God, country and Yale. . . . [Benét] has so rare a skill with color, so unlimited an invention of metaphor, such humorous delight . . . so brave a fantasy. . . .

While in Paris, Benét met Rosemary Carr, the Paris correspondent for the *Chicago Tribune*. Returning to New York, they married on 26 November 1921. The Benéts had three children: Stephanie, born in 1924; Thomas Carr, born in 1926; and Rachel, born in 1931. In the 1920s Benét earned a living as a writer, mainly from his short stories and novels. He continued to write poetry but more for love than money. In 1922 and 1923 Benét published two long narrative poems that owed much to Lindsay: "The Ballad of William Sycamore," in the *New Republic*, and "King David" in *The*

Nation, which magazine awarded it the prize as best poem of 1923. (Both poems were also published in book form in limited editions in 1923.) The former poem is about an American frontiersman and the latter portrays the biblical king of Israel. Both are dramatic narratives, as was the earlier *Five Men and Pompey*, but the later poems are more mature, particularly "King David." Benét's biographer Charles A. Fenton writes that at this time Benét was making the "perilous and by no means automatic transition from natural aptitude to acquired craft. . . . He had something to say and the will to say it properly."

In 1924 Benét and his friend Farrar collaborated on two Broadway plays. The first was a long version of Farrar's "war number" from their Yale days, called *Nerves;* the second was *That Awful Mrs. Eaton*. The two friends wrote these plays, their first as professional dramatists, virtually simultaneously. In "For the Record" Farrar recalls that during the rehearsals of *Nerves;* they managed to convince a then-unknown actor, Humphrey Bogart, that he could be a natural on the stage. Bogart did, of course, become a stage and screen star, receiving his first good review for his performance in this play. *Nerves* is a World War I melodrama about an American officer who in training camp is falsely labeled as being a coward but who later proves his courage in battle and ultimately wins the girl. *That Awful Mrs. Eaton* is about the wife of John Henry Eaton, President Andrew Jackson's Secretary of War. Margaret O'Neill Eaton, the daughter of a tavern keeper, is looked down upon by the wives of the Washington establishment. (In the play Eaton is the Secretary of the Navy and his wife is a former tavernkeeper.) Jackson champions her attributes and she ultimately wins over her detractors by hosting a successful party at the White House. *Nerves* opened on 1 September 1924 and *That Awful Mrs. Eaton* on 24 September 1924. Reviews for both ranged from poor to mixed. Critics recognized youthful talent but also faulted the young writers for trying to say and do too much. One reviewer said *That Awful Mrs. Eaton* was "overstuffed." Benét later considered these plays as object lessons teaching him what not to do. His future screenplays, librettos, and radio scripts emphasized a lean rather than an "overstuffed" approach.

In 1925 and 1926 Benét continued to produce prose fiction, and his short stories were being published regularly in popular magazines. During 1927 Benét benefitted from a Guggenheim Fellowship, which gave him an income just for writing so that he did not have to worry about writing for an income. He once again turned to verse and composed his American Civil War epic *John Brown's Body*. This book-length poem was published in 1928 and was an instant success, achieving both critical praise and public popularity. The book was a best-seller, an unheard-of situation for a volume of verse, and it won a Pulitzer Prize in poetry in 1929. Benét was now famous. *That Awful Mrs. Eaton* earned him enough cash to invest in stocks. In October of 1929 he lost nearly everything in the stock-market crash that started the Great Depression. Relief from his financial troubles came from Hollywood, where the acclaim for *That Awful Mrs. Eaton* had reached.

The most esteemed American moviemaker of the silent era, D. W. (David Wark) Griffith decided it was time to do his first "talkie," and he asked Benét to write the screenplay for the cinema biography *Abraham Lincoln*. Benét traveled to Hollywood and quickly learned that screenwriting was a frustrating process that required on-the-fly rewrites to accommodate the day-to-day changes that evolved as Griffith directed the movie. Often, Griffith was not sure of what he wanted for a scene until it was actually being shot, and Benét would write dialogue on the spot. The task was arduous and frustrating for Benét, who also recorded his dismay at the backstage intrigue typical of Hollywood. Benét wrote to his agent Carl Brandt, "Nowhere have I seen such shining waste, stupidity and conceit as in the business and managing end of this industry. Since arriving, I have written four versions of *Abraham Lincoln*, including a good one, playable in the required time. That, of course, is out. Seven people, including myself, are now working in conferences on a 5th one. . . . If I don't get out of here soon I'm going crazy." Nonetheless, the motion picture was made and released by United Artists in 1930 to generally good reviews. Benét, however, while learning the motion picture business and sharpening his skills as a dramatist, never worked in Hollywood again. Although he worked on two further movies, he remained in New York. The Hollywood scene was too unreal for Benét, who was concerned about the bitter reality of business failures and mass unemployment caused by the Great Depression.

Benét began to write prose and poetry with an eye on current events. In the early 1930s he was a supporter of President Franklin Delano Roosevelt and the New Deal. In the mid-to-late 1930s he was one of the first American writers to realize the threat that fascism in Europe and Japan posed to world peace.

In 1937, perhaps inspired by his children, Benét wrote a libretto aimed at young audiences. He adapted Washington Irving's short story "The Legend of Sleepy Hollow" (1820) as the libretto for a light opera composed by another old Yale friend, Douglas Moore. They called it *The Headless Horseman*, and it was written specifically for the theater department of Bronxville High School in New York City, where Moore's children were students. The school staged the operetta on 17 March 1937. This production was followed by a radio performance broadcast on NBC on 22 April 1937, and a published version appeared later that year.

On 24 October 1936 Benét's most famous short story was published in *The Saturday Evening Post*, the best-selling weekly magazine in the United States. Published separately in book form the following year, *The Devil and Daniel Webster* struck a chord with millions of readers. The story of the great lawyer and orator who saves a man who had sold his soul to the devil resonated with readers who were still mired in the Great Depression and were troubled by the rise of fascism in Europe. Webster has to convince a judge and jury of scoundrels, handpicked by the devil from the souls of the damned, to nullify the contract signed by Jabez Stone, a farmer driven by a run of bad luck to make a deal with the mysterious stranger who calls himself Mr. Scratch. As a political parable, the story can be read with Jabez Stone representing the average American down on his luck; the judge and jury representing the fascists; Mr. Scratch, the forces of evil; and Daniel Webster, as the United States, coming to the rescue. No short story has ever had the national impact of *The Devil and Daniel Webster*. It was almost inevitable that the story would be adapted to the stage and then the movies.

Benét could now find support for new artistic ventures. Moore had wanted to do a bigger opera with Benét after their collaboration on *The Headless Horseman*. Benét's formidable popularity opened doors and *The Devil and Daniel Webster* was the logical choice for a new opera. In the short story Webster's summation to the judge and jury is described by its effect on the listeners:

> He painted a picture . . . and to each one of that jury he spoke of things long forgotten. For his voice could search the heart, and that was his gift and his strength. And to one, his voice was like the forest and its secrecy, and to another like the sea and the storms of the sea; and one heard the cry of his lost nation in it, and another saw a little harmless scene he hadn't remembered for years. But each saw something. And

when Dan'l Webster finished he didn't know whether or not he'd saved Jabez Stone. But he knew he'd done a miracle. For the glitter was gone from the eyes of judge and jury, and, for the moment, they were men again, and knew they were men.

In the operatic version Webster's effect has to be conveyed through Webster's words themselves. In Benét's libretto, Webster's closing speech is longer and must accommodate Moore's music, but it is no less effective, as the closing lines show:

> WEBSTER: Do you know him? He is your brother. Will you take the law of the oppressor and bind him down?
>
> It is not for him that I speak. It is for all of you.
>
> There is a sadness in being a man, but it is a proud thing too.
>
> There is failure and despair on the journey—the endless journey of mankind.
>
> We are tricked and trapped—we stumble into the pit—but out of the pit we rise again.
>
> . . . .
>
> I see you, mighty, shining, liberty, liberty! I see free men walking and talking under a star!
>
> God save the United States and the men who have made her free!
>
> The defense rests.
>
> JURY: [*Exultantly*] We were men—we were free— we were men—we have not forgotten—our children shall follow and be free.

Benét was quite aware that in 1939 Webster's words were also a warning that fascism in Europe and Asia were threats to freedom everywhere. The opera was staged through the auspices of the American Lyric Theater under the direction of the legendary John Houseman of the Mercury Theater. Benét's reputation and winning personality attracted famous names to work with Houseman, who later said in his autobiography, *Run-Through* (1972), "My collaborators were men whose work I admired: Fritz Reinder was our conductor; Eugene Loring, creator of Aaron Copland's *Billy the Kid*, was my choreographer. Even more important—and the main reason for doing the production in the first place— was the presence of [set designer] Robert Edmund Jones. . . . For years he had been an illustrious figure in the American theater; histories of the contemporary stage were filled with his designs."

The opera premiered 18 May 1939 on Broadway, in the Martin Beck Theater, to great acclaim. Renowned *New York Times* theater critic Brooks Atkinson wrote on 6 May 1939 that "*The Devil and Daniel Webster* represents some of the finest and most painstaking work of the season." The expense of the production prevented a long Broadway run, but the opera was produced many times by United Service Organization (USO) troupes during World War II and was an annual feature for many years at the Old Sturbridge Festival in Massachusetts.

Benét fashioned another adaptation of the story, this time for a movie version, co-writing the screenplay with Dan Totheroh. The movie was released by RKO Pictures in 1941 and was also well received. Unfathomably, however, RKO changed the title. Instead of using the title of what is one of the best-known stories ever written in America—ensuring instant public recognition—the studio called the movie *All That Money Can Buy*. In the motion-picture version, Walter Huston, who had portrayed Lincoln in the Griffith epic, played Mr. Scratch, receiving an Oscar nomination for Best Actor in a Leading Role, and Edward Arnold played Daniel Webster. In 1943 the script was included in *Twenty Best Film Plays*, edited by John Gassner and Dudley Nichols, as one of the twenty greatest screenplays since the "talkies" began in 1927.

During the late 1930s Benét, as were many other Americans, was alarmed at the growth of fascism in Asia and Europe. Benét took seriously his role as national spokesperson and began to write poems and stories as warnings to the American people. Among these were "Into Egypt" and "The Last of the Legions," collected in *Tales Before Midnight* (1939), and "The Blood of the Martyrs" and "By the Waters of Babylon," collected in *Thirteen O'Clock: Stories of Several Worlds* (1937). "By the Waters of Babylon," is credited by historians of science-fiction as the first tale written about a future world of survivors after an apocalyptic war. Benét wished to reach more Americans and realized that radio was the way to accomplish that. In those pre-television days radio had devoted audiences just as television does now. Benét's good friend Archibald MacLeish had written three plays for radio, and he encouraged Benét to do the same. Benét was a natural writer for radio: his mastery of the short story suited the need for compactness with an impact; his reputation as a man of conscience and a patriot who loved his country was exactly right for a United States facing the threat of fascism.

Benét wrote tirelessly for the cause of democracy before and during the war and either accepted no payment or directed that payment be sent to the USO. Benét's scripts were broadcast over national radio and were heard by millions. Many of them were subsequently published in pamphlet form and collected in *We Stand United, and Other Radio Scripts* (1945). The first was *We Stand United*, read by Raymond Massey at an America United Rally in Carnegie Hall sponsored by the Council for Democracy, broadcast on CBS Radio on 6 November 1940 and published in pamphlet form that same year. Its impact became a front-page story nationwide. *Listen to the People* was broadcast over NBC Radio on Independence Day 1941. Three days later *Life* magazine published the script. Biographer Fenton notes: "The response was extraordinary. Letters and telegrams came to him [Benét], and to *Life* and NBC, from every part of the nation: 'Your poems thrilled me,' Arthur Train wrote him, 'It is superb and inspiring and will have a tremendous effect throughout the nation. Congratulations!'" More scripts followed: *Thanksgiving Day—1941* (broadcast 19 November 1941), *They Burned the Books* (broadcast 11 May 1942), *A Time to Reap* (broadcast 26 November 1942), *A Child Is Born* (broadcast 21 December 1942), and *Dear Adolf*, the last a six-part series based on actual letters written to Adolf Hitler from representative Americans—a farmer, a businessman, a worker, a housewife and mother, a soldier, and a foreign-born American—broadcast on NBC Radio on successive Sunday afternoons from 21 June 1942 to 2 August 1942, with the exception of 19 July. *New York Times* writer John K. Hutchens wrote about *Dear Adolf*, in an article published 5 July 1942:

> Mr. Benét could not have chosen a better time or a greater subject . . . and it would seem that some of his colleagues among the first-rank writers might follow his lead—the 'names' who wrote so passionately a little while ago, and should not be silent now. . . . if they have their doubts about [radio's] value as an artistic medium, let them ponder on the success with which Mr. Benét, long established as a poet and short story writer before he turned to radio, adjusted himself to the new field. Not all of them are so well equipped as he, lacking the poet's gift of sharp, exact words and the singing phrase. But they might have a try at it.

Although frail health from a weak heart barred Benét from active military service, he worked as a soldier of democracy through his words. On 13 March 1943 he died of a heart attack in his wife's arms. He was only forty-four years old. Had he lived longer, Benét might well have written in his maturity works that would have superseded his last patriotic works, which came to limit his literary reputation and obscure his other artistic successes.

As a dramatist Benét is chiefly remembered only for the movie and opera versions of *The Devil and Daniel Webster*. Yet, from 1940 to 1944, his radio plays were listened to by millions of Americans. His other work remained enormously popular in anthologies throughout the 1950s, and many of his poems and stories were adapted for stage and screen or set to music because of their inherent dramatic qualities. For example, in 1953 actor-director Charles Laughton adapted *John Brown's Body* for the stage, where it had a successful Broadway run and a national tour. In 1954 M-G-M released a successful adaptation of Benét's short story "The Sobbin' Women," the musical *Seven Brides for Seven Brothers*, which in turn spawned a stage musical and a television series.

In a one-man play *The American World of Stephen Vincent Benét*, written and performed by David Garrett Izzo for Benét's one-hundredth birthday celebration on 24 July 1998 in his birthplace of Bethlehem, Pennsylvania, Benét's ghost speaks to the audience and recites from his work. Contemporary audiences enthusiastically responded to Benét's words. Cynthia Gordon of the *Easton* (Pa.) *Express Times* wrote of the play on 25 July 1998 that it "has created a remarkably moving portrait of one of the literary greats of the century. The warm, well-balanced qualities of Benét shone." Ultimately, the audience responded to the life and especially the words of Stephen Vincent Benét, which remain as resonant as when first written. Everything he wrote is imbued with dramatic qualities meant to be seen and heard. Audiences knowing little, if anything, about Benét, came to listen without prejudice and left wanting to know more about the man and his words. In 1999 Penguin Classics published the first Benét anthology in thirty years, *The Devil and Daniel Webster and Other Writings*. In time Benét may well once more be thought of as a great writer, not just a "patriotic" writer.

Source: David Garrett Izzo, "Stephen Vincent Benét," in *Dictionary of Literary Biography*, Vol. 249, *Twentieth-Century American Dramatists, Third Series*, edited by Christopher Wheatley, The Gale Group, 2001, pp. 12–20.

Joseph Wood Krutch

In the following review of Selected Works of Stephen Vincent Benét, *Krutch asserts that "our contemporary literature and our national consciousness are both very much the better" for Benét's works.*

The best of Mr. Benét's work, or at least those of his pieces which most completely come off and reach nearest to perfection, are those short prose pieces collected [in *Selected Works of Stephen Vincent Benét*] under the general title "Stories of American History." They are not merely local color stories and they are not merely pieces of folklore, or at least they are not at all examples of that sort of writing, at once precious and condescending, which literary folklorists are most likely to produce. For one thing the stories are, I assume, mostly created rather than merely retold. What is more important they seem to me to achieve exactly the effect which they are intended to achieve; they take American scenes and American men out of the realm of mere history or mere folklore and naturalize them in the world of the imagination. Or to put it concretely, they make it evident that Daniel Webster has as much right as Dr. Faustus ever had to hold converse with the devil.

One volume of the [*Selected Works*] is devoted to prose tales of which by no means all are in the manner just described. Eight of them, called "Tales of Our Time," seem strangely out of place for they are mildly moralized stories of the jazz age, good enough and quite competent, but scarcely distinguishable from hundreds written by dozens of other writers. The seven classified as "Fantasies and Prophecies" range all the way from the, to me, rather obvious "Doc Mellhorn and the Pearly Gates" to "The Last of the Legions," which is almost as good as the best of the American stories, and "The King of the Cats," which is probably one of the three best stories about a feline ever written—the other two being Wodehouse's tale of the missionary-bishop's Tom who went Bohemian in Chelsea and the other Saki's breath-taking anecdote about the cat who was unfortunately taught to talk. But the best are certainly in the "Stories of American History," among which should be singled out not only "The Devil and Daniel Webster," but also "Jacob and the Indians," as well as the finest of them all, "Johnny Pye and the Fool-Killer." "A Tooth for Paul Revere" is just a shade too quaint; "Freedom's a Hard-Bought Thing" just a shade too consciously heroic.

Mr. Benét has written a considerable body of interesting prose and verse and he has succeeded in interesting a great many people in it. Is *John Brown's Body* the American epic, or at least the nearest thing to it so far? Is Mr. Benét genuinely inspired by the strong American muse whose diverse heart so many have tried to understand? How much has he done to make it clear not only that enough men have died here, but that their deaths are memorable?

The safest answer as well as probably the justest is to refuse any reply to questions put in such grandiose terms. But if, instead, one asks simply whether this is solid work and whether it uses American material in a way which is not only interesting but tending at the same time to make the American past more dignified, more meaningful and more comprehensible to the imagination, then the answer is unmistakably affirmative. Our contemporary literature and our national consciousness are both very much the better for Mr. Benét's *Selected Works*.

Source: Joseph Wood Krutch, "Stephen V. Benet and the American Past," in *New York Herald Tribune Books*, June 21, 1942, p. 1.

Sources

Benét, Stephen Vincent, "The Devil and Daniel Webster," in *Selected Works of Stephen Vincent Benét*, Vol. 2, Farrar & Rinehart, 1942, pp. 33, 42–43; originally published in the *Saturday Evening Post*, October 24, 1936.

——, "Doc Mellhorn and the Pearly Gates," in *Selected Works of Stephen Vincent Benét*, Vol. 2, Farrar & Rinehart, 1942, pp. 418–20; originally published in the *Saturday Evening Post*, December 24, 1938.

——, "An End to Dreams," in *First-Prize Stories, 1919–1960*, Hanover House, 1960, pp. 224–25, 228, 229–33; originally published in *Pictorial Review*, February 1932.

——, "Johnny Pye and the Fool-Killer," in *Selected Works of Stephen Vincent Benét*, Vol. 2, Farrar & Rinehart, 1942, pp. 90–91, 92–97, 108; originally published in the *Saturday Evening Post*, September 18, 1937.

Bigelow, Gordon, Review of *Stephen Vincent Benét: The Life and Times of an American Man of Letters, 1898–1943*, in *Modern Language Notes*, Vol. 75, No. 1, January 1960, pp. 60–62.

Combs, Robert, "Waking from Nightmares: Stephen Vincent Benét's Faustian America," in *Stephen Vincent Benét: Essays on His Life and Work*, edited by David Garrett Izzo and Lincoln Konkle, McFarland, 2003, p. 163.

Davenport, Basil, "Introduction," in *Selected Works of Stephen Vincent Benét*, Holt, 1966, pp. iv–xii.

Duffus, R. L., "A Benét Anthology, and Three Novels," in the *New York Times*, November 28, 1943, p. 6.

Hemingway, Ernest, epigraph, in *The Sun Also Rises*, Scribner, 1926.

Krutch, Joseph Wood, "Stephen V. Benét and the American Past," in *New York Herald Tribune Books*, June 21, 1942, p. 1.

Norris, Margot, "Modernist Eruptions," in *The Columbia History of the American Novel*, edited by Emory Elliot, Columbia University Press, 1991, pp. 311–30.

Roache, Joel, "Stephen Vincent Benét," in *Dictionary of Literary Biography*, Vol. 102, *American Short-Story Writers, 1910–1945, Second Series*, edited by Bobby Ellen Kimbel, Gale Research, 1991, pp. 11–19.

Webster, David H., Review, in *College Composition and Communication*, Vol. 12, No. 2, May 1961, p. 125.

Wells, Henry W., "Stephen Vincent Benét," in *College English*, Vol. 5, No. 1, October 1943, pp. 8–13.

Further Reading

Berman, Ronald, *Fitzgerald, Hemingway, and the Twenties*, University of Alabama Press, 2001.
  Berman presents a penetrating analysis of the literary world in the 1920s.

Fenton, Charles A., ed., *Selected Letters of Stephen Vincent Benét*, Yale University Press, 1960.
  This collection of Benét's letters catalogues his responses to the political and social climate during his lifetime as well as his theories on writing.

Griffith, John, "Stephen Vincent Benét," in *Dictionary of Literary Biography*, Vol. 48, *American Poets, 1880–1945, Second Series*, Gale Research, 1986, pp. 9–19.
  For those interested in a study of Benét's poetry, Griffith presents a comprehensive examination of his major poems.

Stroud, Parry, *Stephen Vincent Benét*, Twayne, 1962.
  This biographical study also includes analyses of Benét's main works.

Fleur

Louise Erdrich

1986

One of the most important Native American authors writing in the United States as of 2005, Louise Erdrich is famous for her unique storytelling technique that draws from her knowledge of Chippewa (or Ojibwa) life and legend. Although Erdrich is a poet and nonfiction writer as well, her most prominent work involves episodes from the lives of several Chippewa families whose roots are in the Turtle Mountain Reservation in North Dakota. These richly drawn characters, whose lives intertwine across generations, have filled five novels and many short stories. In her individual style that alternates between a variety of first-person narrative voices, Erdrich captures the essence of these characters and their viewpoints as they tell the stories of their lives.

Erdrich draws much of her material from the stories of her Chippewa mother, and one of the first characters she developed out of these childhood tales was Fleur Pillager, the subject of Erdrich's 1986 short story "Fleur." In this story about sexuality and female power, a seemingly timid and insecure narrator describes the time Fleur spends in the small town of Argus, North Dakota. After Fleur is raped by the men who work with her in a butcher's shop, she is avenged by their mysterious deaths inside a frozen meat locker. Although "Fleur" was adapted and included as the second chapter of Erdrich's 1988 novel *Tracks*, the subject of this entry is the original short story, as published in *Esquire* magazine in August of 1986. As of 2005, it was available in short story collections, including *Esquire's Big Book of Fiction* (2002), edited by Adrienne Miller.

Author Biography

Born in 1954 in Little Falls, Minnesota, Louise Erdrich was the eldest of seven children. Her mother, a Native American of the Chippewa tribe, was the daughter of Turtle Mountain Reservation Tribal Chairman Patrick Gourneau, and her father was of German descent. Both of her parents taught at the Bureau of Indian Affairs boarding school in Wahpeton, North Dakota, near the Turtle Mountain Reservation. Erdrich grew up in Wahpeton, and in 1972 she entered the first co-educational class of Dartmouth College in New Hampshire, on scholarship.

The year Erdrich began at Dartmouth, her future husband and collaborator Michael Dorris was appointed head of the Native American studies department. Erdrich began to write short stories and poems and held a variety of minimum-wage jobs, and after graduation she taught in the North Dakota Arts Council's Poetry in the Schools program. Erdrich earned a master's degree in creative writing at Johns Hopkins University and then edited a Boston Indian Council newspaper before returning to Dartmouth as a writer-in-residence in 1981. Marrying Dorris shortly after she began to teach there, Erdrich became the mother of his three adopted children and had three more children with him. Dorris assisted Erdrich greatly in the writing and promotion of *Love Medicine* (1984); in fact, all of their works during the years of their marriage were collaborative efforts. After the success of her first novel, Erdrich received a Guggenheim fellowship and continued to publish short stories, including "Fleur," which originated in a long manuscript of her mother's stories that Erdrich wrote during her student days.

"Fleur" was incorporated into Erdrich's 1988 novel *Tracks*, the third work in her saga dealing with twentieth-century Chippewa life. Erdrich continued to publish writings throughout the 1990s, including prominent and successful novels and short stories, a nonfictional account of her experience as a mother, some children's literature, and poetry. Although she co-wrote fictional and nonfictional works with Dorris through the early 1990s, Erdrich began to have serious family problems, including a son's death, and she separated from her husband in 1995. Two years later, Dorris killed himself, an event that likely influenced Erdrich's 1999 novel *The Antelope Wife*. In the early 2000s, Erdrich published many works of fiction, including *Last Report on the Miracles at Little No Horse* (2001),

Louise Erdrich   Photograph by Eric Miller. AP/Wide World Photos

Range Eternal (2002, for children), *The Master Butchers Singing Club* (2002), *The Game of Silence* (2002), *Four Souls* (2004), and *The Painted Dream* (2005).

Plot Summary

"Fleur" begins by stating that Fleur Pillager was only a girl when she drowned in Lake Turcot, which is located in Native American reservation in North Dakota. Two men dive in and save her and, not long afterward, both disappear. Fleur falls in the lake again when she is twenty, but no one is willing to touch her. One man bends towards her when she washes onshore, and Fleur curses him, telling him that he will die instead of her. He drowns shortly thereafter in a bathtub. Men stay away from Fleur, believing that she is dangerous and that the water monster Misshepeshu wants her for himself.

Because she practices what the narrator calls "evil" ways, Fleur is unpopular on the reservation, and some gather to throw her out. In the summer of 1920, she leaves on her own accord for the town of Argus. Noticing a steeple, she walks straight to the church and asks the priest for work. He sends her to a butcher shop where Fleur works with the owner's wife Fritzie, hauling packages of meat to a locker. Fleur gives the men a new topic of conversation, particularly when she begins playing cards with them.

Pulling up a chair without being invited, she asks if she can join their game of cards. Fleur borrows eight cents from the narrator Pauline and begins to win. The men unsuccessfully try to rattle her, and Tor discovers that she is unable to bluff, but Fleur continues to win. Fleur finally picks up Pauline, who is hiding in the walls, and puts her to bed. The game continues night after night, and each time Fleur wins exactly one dollar. The men are soon "lit with suspense" and ask Pete to join the game. Lily is confounded by Fleur and suspects that she may be cheating for low stakes.

In August, when Fleur has won thirty dollars, Pete and Fritzie leave for Minnesota. With Pete out of the way, Lily raises the stakes in an attempt to shake Fleur. After a long night of going up and down, Fleur wins the entire pot and then leaves the game. The men begin drinking whiskey straight from the bottle and go outside to hide in wait for Fleur. Lily attempts to grab her, but she douses him with a bucket of hog slops and runs into the yard. Lily falls into the sow's pen, and the sow attacks him. He beats its head against a post and eventually escapes to chase Fleur to the smokehouse with the other men. They catch Fleur, who cries out Pauline's name, but Pauline cannot bring herself to help.

The next morning, the weather begins to turn into a violent storm and the men take shelter in the meat locker. Pauline goes to the doors and slams down the iron bar to lock them inside. The winds pick up and send Pauline flying through the air, and Argus is thoroughly wrecked by the storm. Because everyone is occupied with digging out from the storm, days pass before the townspeople notice that three men are missing. Kozka's Meats has been nearly destroyed, although Fritzie and Pete come home to find that the back rooms where they live are undisturbed. They dig out the meat locker to discover the three men and Lily's dog frozen to death.

Pauline says as a kind of summary, from an unspecified period of time in the future, that "Power travels in bloodlines, handed out before birth," which implies that Fleur was responsible for the deaths of the men. She says that now she is about the only one who visits Fleur, who lives on Lake Turcot and may have married the water spirit Misshepeshu or taken up with white men or "windigos"

(evil demons), unless she has "killed them all." Fleur has had a child, but no one knows for sure who fathered it. Pauline emphasizes that old men talk about the story over and over but, in the end, "only know that they don't know anything."

Characters

Tor Grunewald

One of the men who works at Kozka's Meats, Tor is involved in the card games with Fleur and dies in the meat locker with Lily and Dutch. He a "short and scrappy" man married to a woman that does not appear in the story except to say that she received a blow to the head during the storm.

Jean Hat

Jean is run over by a cart after saving Fleur from drowning in Lake Turcot.

Dutch James

Pauline's stepfather, Dutch works at Kozka's Meats and dies in the meat locker the night after he rapes Fleur with Tor and Lily. He brings Pauline's mother from the reservation and marries her, but she dies after a year, and he forces Pauline to drop out of school in order to take her mother's place in the butcher shop. He smokes cigars and, when he gets angry, veins bulge in his forehead.

Fritzie Kozka

Pete's wife, Fritzie is "a string-thin blonde who chain-smoked and handled the razor-sharp knives with nerveless precision." She works with Fleur but is not as strong as she, so Fleur is responsible for much of the heavy lifting. Fritzie keeps close tabs on her husband, refusing to tolerate any talking behind her back. A practical business owner, she refuses to let the town break through the meat locker in order to discover whether the men are inside because it would spoil the frozen meats, her and Pete's major investment.

Pete Kozka

The owner of the butcher shop, Pete is a soft spoken man who keeps his thoughts to himself because of his wife's influence. The only book he reads is the New Testament, and he always carries the lens of a cow's eye for good luck. Pete hires Fleur because of her strength and seems to bear no ill will towards her, which is why, Pauline implies, his and Fritzie's living space is spared by the storm.

George Many Women

George Many Women bends over to look at Fleur when she washes up on the shore of Lake Turcot. Fleur curses him, saying he will take her place, so he refuses to go outside, but Fleur's magic seems to work nevertheless because he soon drowns in a bathtub.

Misshepeshu

The "waterman, the monster" Misshepeshu is a "love-hungry" devil that lives in Lake Turcot and yearns for young girls like Fleur. Chippewa mothers warn their daughters that he may appear handsome to them, with "green eyes, copper skin, a mouth tender as a child's," but when they fall in his arms "he sprouts horns, fangs, claws, fins." Once he changes shape, he appears somewhat like a merman, with joined feet and brass scales, until he pulls the girls under, at which point he "takes the body of a lion or a fat brown worm." Erdrich implies in "Fleur," and makes more explicit during Eli Kashpaw's courting of Fleur in *Tracks*, that the form-shifting, magical Misshepeshu is associated with Fleur's sexuality and sexual power.

Pauline

Pauline is Dutch's stepdaughter and the narrator of the story. She blends into the walls, or "melt[s] back to nothing" as though she is a part of the furniture, and she knows about everything that goes on at Kozka's Meats, including Fleur's rape. A "skinny, big-nosed girl with staring eyes," Pauline is captivated by Fleur but has mixed feelings about her, ranging from fear to admiration to disdain. She is also somewhat jealous of Fleur's good looks and powers because by contrast Pauline is quite homely, with a dress that hangs loose and a curved back like an old woman's. A timid and insecure girl, she cannot bring herself to come to Fleur's aid when she is raped, and she seems to feel somewhat regretful about this. It may be a reason why she locks the men inside the meat locker during the storm, murdering them, although Pauline seems to imply that she felt compelled to do this because of Fleur's magic.

Whether to believe Pauline about this motive is one of the cruxes of the story. Erdrich's novel *Tracks* suggests much more explicitly that Pauline is not a reliable narrator. She is eager to stress that she has a minimal impact on the story, but she is the one who actually locks the men in the meat locker. Regardless of whether Pauline murdered the men of her own volition or whether she is a reliable narrator, she retains a close connection with Fleur after the storm in Argus, as though she is drawn to her and repelled by her at the same time.

Fleur Pillager

The intriguing subject of Erdrich's story, the daring Fleur Pillager is a Chippewa woman with magical powers. Chippewa men are attracted to her good looks, but they fear her because she has power from spirits and natural forces. She has "wide and flat" cheeks and a strong, muscular upper body, but her hips are "fishlike, slippery, narrow" and she has "sly brown eyes." She wears a green dress that, during the August night at the climax of the story, looks like a transparent "skin of lakeweed." The men at Kozka's Meats do not notice her very white, "strong and curved" teeth nor the fact that her fifth toes are missing, and they vastly underestimate her.

Fleur's reasons for moving to Argus are unclear; she may simply want a change from her home on Lake Turcot, or she may fear that people on the reservation will try to get rid of her. In any case, she works hard and with great strength, and she is able to cheat the men at cards (possibly using some kind of supernatural powers). The men, particularly Lily, are infuriated by her confidence and boldness, perhaps more than by the possibility that she cheats at cards. The women seem to respect Fleur, and Fleur takes to Pauline and appears to protect her. Pauline, however, has complex feelings about Fleur that must be deciphered in the subtext of what Pauline says.

Pauline claims that Fleur is "haywire, out of control," and that she "messed with evil, laughed at the old women's advice, and dressed like a man." She goes on to claim that Fleur practices ancient Chippewa medicine and charms, and she emphasizes that Fleur is responsible for summoning the storm that kills the three men who raped her. Pauline also suggests that Fleur magically compelled her to lock the men in the meat locker. It is not clear that all of these things are true or that Fleur is singlehandedly responsible for all that happens. In one sense, Fleur is a victim who is raped by three brutal men. In any case, as she is presented by the narrator, Fleur possesses magical power related to her femininity, which no one fully understands.

Lily Veddar

Lily is a fat man "with snake's cold pale eyes and precious skin, smooth and lily-white, which is how he got his name." He works at Kozka's Meats and likes to play cards with his "stumpy mean little bull" dog on his lap. The main actor in the rape and the events leading up to it, Lily attempts to bait

Topics For Further Study

- Research Native American history in the late-nineteenth and early-twentieth centuries. What did Native American communities go through in the adjustment to reservation life? How did U.S. government policy towards Native Americans change, and what were the effects of these policies? How did the experience of Chippewa tribes in North Dakota fare in comparison to other tribes across the country?

- Fleur and Pauline appear in a variety of Erdrich's works, as do their relatives and descendents. Assign a group of classmates to each read a novel from Erdrich's saga that begins with *Love Medicine* (1984) and continues through *The Painted Dream* (2005). Then, have a group discussion about what happens to these characters, how they relate to one another, and how "Fleur" is important to Erdrich's saga as a whole.

- Research the history of violence against women in the early twentieth century. How was violence against women reported and documented? What organized attempts were there to combat it? What was the status of the Women's Rights Movement? How would you characterize male attitudes towards women during this period?

- Research the history of North Dakota and the Great Plains, paying particular attention to Chippewa history. What kinds of immigrant groups came to this part of the country during the nineteenth and early-twentieth centuries? Where did the Chippewa migrate, when did they do so, and how were reservation boundaries chosen? How did the disappearance of the buffalo affect life on the Great Plains? What is life like now on North Dakotan Chippewa reservations such as Turtle Mountain?

Fleur by raising the stakes in the card game. During the chase, Lily falls into the sow's pen and has a dirty and vicious fight with it in which he crawls around in the mud and is bitten in the shoulder. Erdrich implies during this description that Lily is a pig himself.

Themes

Female Power

One of the most important themes in Erdrich's story is that of female power. The situation at Kozka's Meats is somewhat like a battle between the sexes, in which Fleur, Pauline, and Fritzie have their own methods of dealing with a brutish, dangerous group of men. Daring and fearless Fleur is the most overt wielder of female power, as Pauline emphasizes throughout the story. Fleur seems to draw this power from ancient Chippewa spirits, medicines, and charms, as well as her sexuality. This may be a reason why the men rape her, to

maintain what they perceive as their rightful control over her, because they are sexist and masochistic. In the end, they realize they cannot understand or control her.

The fact that Pauline locks the three men in the meat locker indicates that she too has power, the ability to remain out of sight and then take revenge at the right moment. Unlike Fleur, Pauline is meek and insecure, unable to stand up for herself or for Fleur at the crucial time. Nevertheless, Fleur and Pauline connect, both in Argus and after Fleur leaves Argus. They have two different kinds of female power, one direct and confrontational, the other indirect and secretive. Fritzie, able to control her husband and censor him effectively, illustrates a third kind of female power, which is that of a wife over her husband.

Except for Pete, who is under Fritzie's strict control to the point where he can talk about nothing but agriculture, the male workers attempt to make a show of their own power. They disdain women, then find themselves outwitted by Fleur and

---

rape her to prove their dominance over her. Erdrich strongly suggests, however, that women have the real power at the same time that they can be abused by men (raped like Fleur, forced to keep out of sight within the walls like Pauline, or overworked like Fritzie). In fact, despite the fact that they are butchers, the men are continually compared to the meat and livestock, while the women are the ones sharpening knives, carrying packets, and boiling heads. The long passage describing Lily's fight with the sow makes it clear that he is like a pig himself, and the final image of the men frozen in the meat locker suggests that these men have been reduced to the level of carcasses.

Sexuality

Erdrich frequently refers to Fleur's sexuality and her good looks, beginning with her description of Fleur's drowning. Fleur's interactions with the waterman/spirit can be understood, in part, as a metaphor for her sexual development; Misshepeshu is a "love-hungry," sexual creature connected to Fleur's own sexual powers. Fleur is characterized as androgynous and fishlike: "her hands large, chapped, muscular, Fleur's shoulders were broad as beams, her hips fishlike, slippery, narrow." Fleur's daring personality, which fascinates and infuriates the men at the butcher shop, exudes from her sexuality, particularly during the night when she is raped. She wears a tight, transparent dress and gives the men a "wolfish" grin when she wins the card game; in response the men try to convince themselves of their power over her by violating her sexually. Fleur returns to Lake Turcot where she has a child and is visited only by Pauline (although, apparently, some say she has relations with white men or Chippewa spirits). Though she has a child, she is not married, and she lives independently, apart from male control. The men who attempt to take possession of her, either by saving her or raping her, die.

Racism and Sexism

The men at Kozka's Meats resent Fleur because she is capable, strong, beats them at cards (thus spoiling their chief source of pleasure), and because she is a Native American. Tor calls her a "squaw," or a Native American woman, as an insult, and the men believe that they should be superior to her intellectually and physically simply because of their male gender. Erdrich's story dramatizes white racism and male sexist beliefs, especially as these apply to Great Plains Native Americans. "Fleur" enacts the racism and sexism

common in the 1920s that resulted in severe abuse and injustice.

Style

Magic Realism

Pioneered by post–World War II Latin American writers such as Jorge Luis Borges and Gabriel García Márquez, magic realism is a literary technique in which supernatural elements appear within an otherwise realistic narrative. Magic, spiritual powers, and inexplicable paranormal events all may be elements in a story employing this technique, which tends to challenge the reader's perception of ordinary reality.

Erdrich uses magic realism when she implies that Fleur has special powers that enable her to swim with the water spirit Misshepeshu, drown and still live, and summon a storm to kill men who attack her. Events that can be explained logically, the narrator invests with magical interpretation. Fleur is infused with magical power from the spiritual world. In this story that takes on the quality of myth, Erdrich is able to locate the essence of Fleur's significance in the ambiguity of her sexuality, in male attraction to and fear of female power. Erdrich presents the magical as real, without restricting herself to verisimilitude.

First-Person Narrative Perspective

Observant, unobtrusive Pauline is a mysterious person, who tells this story filtered by the lens of superstition and myth. She deliberately shapes the story as she reports it, on the one hand saying she sees more than others because she is "invisible," and on the other, admitting that there are some things one cannot say. For example, Pauline states that Fleur studied evil ways "we shouldn't talk about," which implies that Pauline censors or alters as she narrates.

Pauline's bias in favor of Fleur becomes particularly important as the story comes to its climax, when she stresses that Fleur is responsible for the deaths of the three men. In fact, the events of the story suggest that Pauline herself is responsible for their deaths. By the end of the story, when Pauline states that the old men chattering about the story "don't know anything" about what really happened, the reader senses that Pauline knows what happened herself and that she chooses not to tell all of it. Erdrich's use of such a first-person limited perspective allows her to add intrigue and mystery to

Compare & Contrast

- **1910s:** Chippewa cope with poverty, lack of adequate hunting space, depression, and loss of land. There is little or no organized resistance to the American government, although Chippewa leaders and activists interact with government agents from the Bureau of Indian Affairs.

  1980s: The militant American Indian Movement, founded by three Chippewa in 1968 to address disenfranchisement, poverty, and treaty rights of Native Americans, continues to carry out some activism, including taking over a camp in the Black Hills of South Dakota between 1981 and 1984. The movement is in decline, however, due to Federal Bureau of Investigation actions against it and the Indian Self-Determination and Educational Assistance Act of 1975, which helps to alleviate many of its concerns.

  Today: Chippewa continue to struggle with poverty. Most have only the minimum education, and nearly fifty percent are unemployed, for a variety of reasons. The Turtle Mountain Reservation in North Dakota has experienced a longstanding plague of corruption in the tribal council, and the effects of a casino it operates on its land have not been altogether positive.

- **1910s:** North Dakota reaches the end of a population boom as poverty, low farm prices, and bank failures loom on the horizon.

  1980s: The North Dakotan economy suffers from a rise in oil prices and a severe drought beginning in 1987.

  Today: Although the North Dakotan economy has picked up since the 1980s, much of the state continues to be plagued by drought.

- **1910s:** German-Russian and Norwegian immigrants and white-owned businesses buy up Chippewa land.

  1980s: Reservation boundaries are stable, although many consider Turtle Mountain Reservation crowded.

  Today: The Turtle Mountain Reservation continues to be crowded, and some land has been developed for a hotel and casino.

---

the story and question whether it is ever possible to really know what happened in such a situation.

Historical Context

North Dakota in the Early Twentieth Century

West of Minnesota, on the southern border of Canada, and within the large area of the central United States known as the Great Plains, North Dakota has an arid climate with extreme temperatures and a rural economy. Sparsely populated until the late-nineteenth century, the state has a history of groups of Native Americans and immigrants competing for land. Anglo-American and Canadian settlers moved to North Dakota in the mid-nineteenth century to farm and participate in the fur trade, but many moved away in the late-nineteenth century, and Norwegian and German-Russian immigrants began to replace them. By 1910 North Dakota had an uncommonly large percentage of foreign-born residents, and its two main immigrant groups tended not to mix.

North Dakota experienced a population boom between 1898 and 1915, when railroads had been completed, connecting the region with the West. In politics, Republican Progressives instituted reforms and made a number of businesses public enterprises in order to stand up to the Minneapolis-St. Paul grain traders. They were accused of mismanagement, pro-German sympathies, and socialism, however, and they were removed from office in the recall election of 1921. In 1913, the year the events of "Fleur" take place, people were beginning to suffer in small towns, farms, and on Native American reservations, which were particularly hard-hit by disease, drought, and lack of food. Sioux, Chippewa, and other tribal lands had been greatly reduced by this time, to some of the least fertile areas of the state, and Native Americans continued to die after the disappearance of buffalo herds and the onset of disease and malnutrition in the late nineteenth century.

Chippewa

The Chippewa, otherwise known as Ojibwa or Anishinabe, first came in contact with French colonial fur traders in the sixteenth century, in the Great Lakes region. Traditional Chippewa lifestyles varied according to region, but most Chippewa were hunters and not farmers, a tradition that continued into the twentieth century. Many Chippewa became involved in the French fur trade after contact with Europeans, which led to alliances with the French. Like other Plains Native Americans, they were gradually driven off their indigenous land by expanding Americans of European decent. In addition to killing Chippewa in conflicts such as the French and Indian War and the War of 1812, these Americans forced Chippewa tribes into undesirable areas, depleted the plains of animals for them to hunt, and spread disease. Chippewa tribes were also involved in a series of disputes with the Sioux, whom they drove south as they made their way to Minnesota, North Dakota, and Ontario.

After the buffalo were nearly exterminated and many Native Americans faced malnutrition, the American government passed the Dawes Severalty Act of 1887. Forcing Native Americans to give up tribal lands for individual land grants, this policy led to the transfer of nearly sixty percent of Native American land to whites by the time it was repealed in 1934. Because of disease, inadequate hunting space, malnutrition, and the loss of land to whites, the suffering of the North Dakota Chippewa persisted into the early twentieth century. Untold numbers died, lived in poverty, and/or suffered from depression as they were forced to change their way of life.

Critical Overview

Louise Erdrich has been a popular novelist and a critical success since the publication of her first novel *Love Medicine* in 1984. "Fleur," which was in draft form during Erdrich's college days, gained early praise from Erdrich's professor and future husband Michael Dorris. As Ruth Rosenberg quotes Dorris in her entry on Erdrich for the *Dictionary of Literary Biography*, Vol. 152: "['Fleur'] was alternately hilarious and terribly sad, a building swirl of impressions that clung to the imagination with incredible power." Critics tended to agree; the story was selected by editor Sharon Ravenel as a distinguished short story of the year, and in 1987 it was a first-place winner in the O. Henry Awards. The story was then incorporated into Erdrich's successful 1988 novel *Tracks*.

In her essay "The Short Stories of Louise Erdrich's Novels," Suzanne Ferguson compares the original story version of "Fleur" to chapter 2 of *Tracks*, writing that the story version "explicates and foregrounds the conflict between masculine/white and feminine/Indian forces." Ferguson goes on to assert that the central focus of the story is not Fleur but Pauline, who, she argues, is actually responsible for allowing Fleur to be raped "out of weakness— and possibly envy of Fleur's strength and attractiveness," and then avenges her "on behalf, perhaps, of women in general." Other critics discuss the characters of Fleur and Pauline across the entire novel *Tracks*, focusing on various themes, including feminism, displacement, Native American history, and the issue of narration. Barbara Hoffert in her *Library Journal* review of the novel calls it a "splendid" work by a writer "whose prose is as sharp, glittering, and to the point as cut glass."

Criticism

Scott Trudell

Trudell is an independent scholar with a bachelor's degree in English literature. In the following essay, Trudell discusses female relationships, female sexuality, and female power in Erdrich's work, focusing on her short story "Fleur."

Fleur Pillager is a symbol of female sexuality and mystique throughout Erdrich's Chippewa saga. She draws the great practitioner of old Chippewa ways, Eli Kashpaw, to court her; she is rumored to have sexual relations with the water spirit Misshepeshu; she retains some form of magical and sexual power from the spirits; and her daughter Lulu becomes a great matriarch of the Turtle Mountain Reservation, having eight children all by different fathers. Fleur's sexuality refuses to conform to white American notions of an attractive woman.

Men surveying damage done by tornado, similar in time and place to the tornado mentioned in "Fleur" Corbis-Bettmann

Even her name, which combines the French word for "flower" with the English word that means taking spoils by force, seems to be a contradiction within early twentieth-century American society, incorporating both the male model of ruthlessness with the female model of beauty and frailty.

"Fleur," a story that had been in Erdrich's mind and in draft form on paper for many years, is the first chronological appearance of this fascinating and nonconformist character. It describes Fleur's connection to traditional Chippewa ideas about sexuality, it suggests that she wields a magical power over men, and it explores the nature of her strengths and vulnerabilities. One purpose of this essay, therefore, is to explore ideas about femininity that Fleur expresses and represents as they are developed in this story that introduces her.

As much as it is about Fleur and her Chippewa sexuality, however, "Fleur" is also about the narrator Pauline, who becomes another of Erdrich's most important figures in the Chippewa saga. After giving birth to the other matriarch of the Turtle Mountain Reservation, Marie Lazarre Kashpaw, Pauline abandons her and transforms into a sadistic, half-crazy nun. Later (as related in *Love Medicine*), she becomes locked in a vicious battle with her daughter, although Marie does not know that Pauline, now Sister Leopolda, is actually her mother. Like Fleur, the development of Pauline's guilt-ridden, timid, obsessively Christian sexuality (or repression of her sexuality) has its roots in the story of her experience in Argus, where she is shown to be almost the direct opposite of Fleur at the same time as the two young women share a mysterious bond. This essay highlights Pauline's role in the story and in some of the central themes of Erdrich's saga, therefore, paying particular attention to the relationship between Fleur and Pauline.

Because it tells of the beginning of this relationship, "Fleur" is, in a way, an origin or source of Erdrich's profound and longstanding exploration of competing ideas of female power and sexuality. In *Tracks*, Pauline and Fleur fight a kind of battle between Christianity and Chippewa mysticism that is full of sexual overtones. In *Love Medicine*, the daughters of Pauline and Fleur carry on an intense, lifelong conflict that is as much about their own sexualities and sources of power as it is about the fact that they are in love with the same man. In the end, however, they have a reconciliation of sorts that emphasizes the feminine bond between the nagging, jealous, industrious Marie and the sensual, manipulative, and seductive Lulu.

This bond can perhaps best be described as a bond of power. Despite the rampant sexism and violence against them, by both white and Native American men, it is important to note that, in "Fleur" and throughout Erdrich's saga, the women actually run the show. Although men rape Fleur and demean Pauline, the two Chippewa women (and both are Chippewa despite Pauline's later denial of her half-Chippewa heritage) laugh last in Argus. Their victory over the men, in which they reduce Lily to a pig in the mud and freeze all three men in the meat locker like the animals they are, is best understood as a triumph of female power. Even Fritzie participates in this drama, bringing Pete away from the struggle just like she brings him away from the lewd masochistic table talk: by her wifely control over his speech and actions. Fritzie also reveals herself to have power over men by refusing to allow the meat locker to be broken open in the search for Tor, Lily, and Dutch. Indeed, it is significant that Fritzie, not Pete, makes the decision that protecting their "investment" is more important than the possibility (if a very small one) of saving the men's lives.

Each of these three women has developed her own avenue to power, and for all of them this power is somehow related to sexuality. For Fritzie, her power is a function of her exclusive control over her husband as a sexual object; he is not allowed to discuss other women or even read anything but the Bible. Accordingly, she sees the frozen, locked up meats—an overt metaphor for men and male sexuality since they are being punished for their rape of Fleur—as her investment and postpones the opening of the locker that has become their grave.

The fact that Fleur's power is sexual is even more overt, beginning with her association of Misshepeshu, Fleur's water spirit and possible husband. Fleur's mysterious communion with the waterman is developed throughout *Tracks*, but it begins in the first paragraphs of "Fleur," when Misshepeshu is described as a "devil ... love-hungry with desire and maddened for the touch of young girls, the strong and daring especially, the ones like Fleur." This sexual creature is associated with Fleur's magical powers and "ways we shouldn't talk about," and he is subtly invoked again at the height of Fleur's sexual desirability, on the night the men rape her. That night, described as "drenched" in a tight-fitting green dress that "wrapped her like a transparent sheet," a "skin of lakeweed," Fleur stands in steam and paddles skulls in a vat, her sexual power drawn from wetness, the lake, and Misshepeshu. Fleur's power does not seem to diminish because the men

> " Their victory over the men, in which they reduce Lily to a pig in the mud and freeze all three men in the meat locker like the animals they are, is best understood as a triumph of female power."

rape her; even if she has nothing to do with their deaths, she escapes with their money and, as is clear from the subsequent events in *Tracks*, continues to wield power over men, including Eli Kashpaw.

Pauline, on the other hand, at first seems to have no power at all, let alone sexual power. She is completely ignored by men and observes them while being invisible to them. She disappears by becoming "part of the walls" of Kozka's Meats. Unlike Fleur's dress, Pauline's "dress hung loose," her "back was already curved, an old woman's," and the men "never saw [her]." Pauline's only power seems to be that she "knew everything, what the men said when no one was around, and what they did to Fleur," and it is from this knowledge that she gains the power to kill the men, including her stepfather.

There are two key aspects to Pauline's character and her revenge over the three men that are crucial to understanding the nature of her power over others. First, there is the fact that Pauline is an almost omniscient narrator. Pauline is able to manipulate the reader's understanding of Fleur and of the story by framing the events to make it appear that Fleur has killed the men with her magical or spiritual powers, when in fact Pauline is the one who locks them in the meat locker. Because she is able to lurk at the periphery without drawing the attention, interest, or violence of the men that Pauline is able to maintain control over the narrative and discover how to kill the men.

Second, the power Pauline assumes is based on her feelings for Fleur and these feelings seem, at least in part, sexual. Pauline gains the courage and motivation to kill the men because she wants

What Do I Read Next?

- Erdrich's *Tracks* (1988), which focuses on the lives of the Nanapush and Kashpaw families between 1912 and 1924, is the ideal work to read after "Fleur." In it, the reader will discover what happens to Fleur and how the story of her experience in Argus fits into her life on the Turtle Mountain Reservation.

- *A Yellow Raft in Blue Water* (1987), by Erdrich's estranged and late husband Michael Dorris, is a compelling novel about three generations of Native American women.

- *Harpers Anthology of 20th Century Native American Poetry* (1988), edited by Duane Niatum, is an excellent collection of Native American poetry.

- Erdrich's *Four Souls* (2004) is the sequel to *Tracks*, following Fleur Pillager's dramatic quest for justice after she leaves the Turtle Mountain Reservation for Minneapolis in 1919.

to avenge Fleur's rape and because she feels very strongly about Fleur herself. Pauline feels a complex host of emotions towards Fleur, from guilt that she did not help Fleur when she was raped, to admiration for her boldness, to jealousy of her charms and powers, to sexual attraction to her. Pauline's emphasis on Fleur's good looks, intrigue with the stories of Fleur's connection to Chippewa spirits that she has denied in herself, and fascination with Fleur's great powers to the point that Pauline blames her for the deaths of the men she has killed herself, all suggest her attraction to Fleur, though she would never admit this to herself.

In "Fleur," therefore, Erdrich develops one of the central points that will resonate throughout her saga: that women establish their power by using their sexuality and communion with other women. Pauline's mix of jealousy, fear, and attraction to Fleur, like their daughters' intense lifelong battle, culminates in a kind of reconciliation and mutual understanding. While the rest of her family dislikes and despises Pauline, Fleur retains a certain closeness towards her that, as Erdrich reveals in "Fleur," comes from their bond of female power. Whether it is Fleur's aggressive and outward sexual power or Pauline's introverted and repressed homosexual desire, this communal female power, a formidable force that underlies Erdrich's entire saga of Chippewa life, is drawn from female sexuality.

Source: Scott Trudell, Critical Essay on "Fleur," in *Short Stories for Students*, Thomson Gale, 2006.

Suzanne Ferguson

In the following essay excerpt, Ferguson explores the difference in the interpretation of "Fleur" when it is read as a short story rather than as part of a novel.

In much recent short story theory, attempts are made to identify formal characteristics peculiar to the genre of "short story," or, in a variation of that attempt, to identify elements in a story that influence the reader to believe s/he is coming to the conclusion, or at least foreseeing the end of a "story" (see, especially, the work of Susan Lohafer), thus implying a conception of reading that attends to formal signals of a "whole" fictional work. In 1982, Suzanne Hunter Brown, who has since carried her psychological/cognitive investigations further, experimented with reading a chapter of Hardy's *Tess of the D'Urbervilles* as if it were an independent story, showing how different elements emerged with different importance when read as elements of a short story rather than a novel. She concluded, as I do in "Defining the Short Story, Impressionism and Form" and as have other critics such as Karl-Heinz Stierle and Mary Rohrberger, that in the short story, the reader is more likely to focus on theme and symbol, which allow us to process the text as a meaningful construct, rather than on verisimilitude, which allows the reader to "live" vicariously through a novel. This is not to say that verisimilitude is unimportant in the short story, but rather that we experience it differently in a fiction we expect to be short because we are attending more carefully to its potential for creating themes. Also importantly, more interpretive "capital" is likely to be located in the individual words and phrases of the short story text than of the novel, where according to Brown the reader generally attends more to and recalls whole scenes.

Similar attempts have been made to theorize special generic characteristics of the story "sequence" or story "cycle," analyzing volumes of stories presented by their authors as having special interrelationships, with their multiple representations of themes that are progressively or recursively developed. Yet what of the novel that has appeared, wholly or partly, as independent stories in magazines? When the stories were published, they were read *as* short stories—yet because we now know them to be "chunks" of novels, we cease to consider them as separate works.

Louise Erdrich's novels are among those that have frequently been preceded by story publication, and indeed narrative situations in which individual story-tellers narrate their own or others' "stories" are typical of the Erdrich novel and have been frequently remarked by her critics. The stories that make up Erdrich's novels rub against each other, juxtaposing different narrative voices, time frames, and styles, creating productive dissonances of signification and feeling. Yet despite being what one critic calls "collection[s] of interlocking narratives," her novels are not generally similar to those collections that are identified as "cycles" or "sequences," like *Winesburg, Ohio*, *Dubliners*, *Go Down Moses*, *The Golden Apples*, or the like, precisely because the "stories" have become "chapters," and the intermittently reappearing narrators achieve independent, important lives as characters in their own narratives as well as in those of the other character/narrators. Neither are the "short stories" *interpolated* into a "master" narrative like the "stories" told by characters in *The Confidence Man* or *Absalom, Absalom!* Rather, they are the episodes of that narrative.

In this paper, I want to return to "framing" some of Erdrich's stories as short stories, in order to explore their construction of meanings in that genre, comparing them with their novelistic counterparts, in a sense "defamiliarizing" them to explore the interpretive differences that emerge when they are read as stories rather than parts of novels, and speculating on the generic and interpretive implications of Erdrich's "new" kind of story-sequence novel. I will discuss the four stories that have so far been singled out for *Best American Short Stories* or *Prize Stories, the O. Henry Awards:* "Saint Marie" and "Scales," Chapters 2 and 11 of *Love Medicine;* and "Fleur" and "Snares," Chapters 2 and 5 of *Tracks*. The stories range in length from 4,200 words ("Snares") to about 6,000 ("Fleur")—an "average" length for short stories. All four are "told" in first person, as if to a reader/listener, in a generally "oral" style that does not intrinsically distinguish any particular audience. . . .

"Fleur"

A 6,000-word narrative that became Chapter 2 of *Tracks,* "Fleur" was published as a story in

> **"** As a chapter, the narrative is crucial to establishing Fleur's centrality to *Tracks,* and it is Pauline's role as a *narrator* rather than as a *character-agent* that is most essential there.**"**

Esquire in 1986. In *Tracks,* it is the narrative of the young Pauline Puyat, later to become the sadistic Sister Leopolda. She is one of the two primary narrators of the novel, balancing Old Nanapush, the adoptive uncle of its protagonist Fleur Pillager and a major trickster figure in the unfolding saga. In Chapter 1 of *Tracks,* Nanapush relates the sad history of his and Fleur's tribe during the last years of the 19th century and the first of the 20th, especially the epidemic and famine of the winter of 1912. Pauline's narrative of Fleur in Chapter 2 is thus the primary introduction of Fleur's character in an action, a retrospective exposition showing why she is thought to have supernatural powers, and in particular the power to destroy men. As a short story, "Fleur" is also ostensibly—for its narrator—a sort of traditional exemplum of the man-destroying woman. Indeed, the narrator (she has no name in the story) *tells* us that Fleur "almost destroyed th[e] town" of Argus, North Dakota. However, the story *shows* that the men of the Argus butcher shop essentially destroy themselves—morally by raping Fleur, and physically by shutting themselves into an ice-filled meat locker during a tornado, where the narrator, not Fleur, entraps them. The "story," "Fleur," explicates and foregrounds the conflict between masculine/white and feminine/Indian forces, while the "chapter" establishes one possibly demented or dishonest narrator's view of a complex and powerful protagonist who becomes important to us not only as representative of the struggle of the traditional native American values against the materialistic ravages of modern Euro-American culture, but of what we might see as universal human values of love and family ties as well as female nature and power.

The changes in the novel version are not to Fleur's character but in connections made with other characters and other episodes. In the novel, one of the men trapped in the locker lives (albeit ravaged by gangrene), and a second child is introduced: Pauline's younger cousin Russell Kashpaw, who along with Pauline helps trap the men in the locker, and who becomes a significant figure in *The Beet Queen* and *The Bingo Palace*. The deliberateness of the men's closing out the children in the storm is explicit in the novel, where in the story the shutting out of the narrator might be inadvertent and never realized by the men, to whom she has been essentially "invisible" even in their presence.

Although identical from story to novel, the spectacular scene of an enormous sow's attacking Fleur's primary enemy, Lily Veddar, who has pursued Fleur into the sow's pen when she went to feed the animal after winning all the men's money in a poker game, takes on more powerful significance in the story, providing a memorable "objective correlative" for the violence of the struggle between the female and male forces of the story. The actual rape of Fleur which follows is represented only as the cries the narrator hears and is too afraid to answer with some protective action, while the fight of Lily with the sow is "shown" in graphic, indeed virtuosic detail. Next day, when the tornado appears, it seems to the girl an incarnation of the sow: "a fat snout that nosed along the earth and sniffled, jabbed, picked at things, sucked them up, blew them apart, rooted around as if it was following a certain scent . . .," suggesting that the real sow was somehow possessed when it attacked Lily and that the same demonic spirit now activates the winds. Yet tornadoes are common enough on the Great Plains, and the oppressive heat and humidity on the night of the card game and its aftermath, the rape, are clear indications not only of a naturalistic explanation of why the men behave so irrationally but how they know to take shelter in the locker when the storm approaches.

The "point" of the short story is located in the character of the unnamed narrator rather than of Fleur, for after all she has said about how Fleur destroys men (and almost the town), it is the narrator herself, the barely visible, anonymous narrator, who barricades the men in the locker and doesn't reveal their whereabouts after the storm. Thus, aided by the men's selfishness and indifference to her plight and perhaps by their shame at having raped Fleur, it is *she* who kills the men, although Fleur (who has already left town, most likely before the storm) is held responsible by the community. This nameless narrator, a figure for the alienated, self-less female child, tells us in the end only the "facts" of how the men were found, not admitting her guilt, then or later, when she returns to the reservation to "live a quiet life."

The *real* story of the narrator's tacit league with Fleur against the men is embedded in the folk-tale-like narration of Fleur's supernatural powers as the lover of the lake spirit, Misshepeshu, powers validated by the narrator's appeal to the authority of her grandmother. The narrator reports in seemingly free indirect style the grandmother's opinion of the strange deaths of the men who saved Fleur from her "first drowning" early in life: "it went to show, . . . [i]t figured to her, all right. By saving Fleur Pillager, those two men had lost themselves." The narrator's alliance with the other Indians—especially the mothers—in relating the story of Fleur's early drownings and the relationship with Misshepeshu—who may have fathered a child Fleur bore later—is shown in her consistent use of the first person plural in this expository part of the story, although she uses the singular for her narrative of what happened in Argus. At the beginning of the story she is the voice of the emerging modern, Americanized Indian community which estranges Fleur, the traditional Indian, whose independence and spirituality they cannot tolerate. The short story is less *about* its title character, a powerful traditional woman (possibly a witch), than about the nameless, nondescript, adolescent female narrator who out of weakness—and possibly envy of Fleur's strength and attractiveness—allows Fleur to be raped then avenges her on behalf, perhaps, of women in general. As a chapter, the narrative is crucial to establishing Fleur's centrality to *Tracks,* and it is Pauline's role as a *narrator* rather than as a *character-agent* that is most essential there.

Source: Suzanne Ferguson, "The Short Stories of Louise Erdrich's Novels," in *Studies in Short Fiction*, Vol. 33, No. 4, Fall 1996, pp. 541–55.

Patricia Angley

In the following essay excerpt, Angley discusses Fleur in terms of how she embodies the beliefs of the Chippewa and of her own clan—the bear clan.

Just as the bear's tracks disappear from the Chippewa homelands during the opening decades of the twentieth century, the traditional ways of the Native Americans are being erased by the encroachment of white technology and greed. The environment that supports an ancient way of life is on the verge of destruction, and this environment, this land, is what Fleur fights to save. Even though her fight is in some ways a hopeless one, the struggle transforms and strengthens Fleur. Fleur's choices ensure the continuation of the Pillager clan and its powers, however marginalized they may appear to be in Erdrich's other three novels. In the *The Sacred Hoop: Recovering the Feminine in American Indian Traditions*, Paula Gunn Allen states:

> Indians endure—both in the sense of living through something so complete in its destructiveness that the mere presence of survivors is a testament to the human will to survive and in the sense of duration and longevity. Tribal systems have been operating in the "new world" for several hundred thousand years. It is unlikely that a few hundred years of colonization will see their undoing. (2)

Fleur, like the Indians Allen refers to, endures and does so in the strongest sense of the word. Fleur is earthy, slippery and transformative, cunning, magical and powerful—the embodiment of a way of life that will not be eliminated. Through Fleur as envisioned in these stories that Nanapush and Pauline narrate, Erdrich creates new Chippewa stories as she re-vises the old ones. Erdrich puts down linguistic tracks that symbolize both the presence and the loss of a culture whose myths, history, and religion are reflected in the oral tradition.

Earthy. As I mentioned earlier, the Pillager clan is known as the bear clan. In Chippewa mythology, the bear *manito* (supernatural spirit) represents a wide range of:

> sentiments, expressing some awe and also some love. For the bear was considered quasi-human, in anatomy, erect carriage, cradling of young with the forearms . . . shows of intelligence, inclination to moderate conduct despite great physical strength. (Landes, *Ojibwa Religion* 27)

Nanapush describes Fleur by saying, "All she had was raw power, and the names of the dead that filled her" (Erdrich, *Tracks*). Likewise, Pauline observes ". . . we followed the tracks of her bare feet and saw where they changed, where the claws sprang out, the pad broadened and pressed into the dirt. By night we heard her chuffing cough, the bear cough."

Slippery and transformative. While Fleur's identification as bear-like or wolf-like strongly links her to the earth and while the bear and the wolf make tracks, or leave their imprint on the earth like Fleur does, she is also tied just as strongly with water as is the entire Pillager clan. In fact, as Van Dyke notes in "Questions Of The Spirit: Bloodlines In Louise Erdrich's Chippewa Landscape": "Fleur Pillager is an exemplification of traditional Chippewa

> " The myth of the bear moving between worlds is an apt description of Fleur who moves between the material and corporeal, the ancient and the modern, the ordinary and the extraordinary, the Chippewa world and the white world."

power, and she owes her power to her spirit guardian, Misshepeshu, the water spirit man" (15). Pauline's description of Fleur reflects Fleur's "fishness" when she says, "shoulders were broad and curved as a yoke, her hips fishlike, slippery, narrow. An old green dress clung to her waist, . . ." Nanapush notes Fleur's affinity for the water monster when he describes Fleur's power over Misshepeshu. He reveals that Fleur's return from Argus was welcomed because "we didn't like to think how she did this—she kept the lake thing controlled." In the eyes of both narrators, Fleur is powerful. She is also transformative: a bear one minute, a wolf or a fish the next.

Cunning, magical and powerful. Fleur has the Pillager grin which is described as wolf-like. Her teeth are "strong and sharp and very white." Her eyes are described as sly and brown. When describing Fleur after Fleur has defeated the white men in Argus at the poker table and after Fleur supposedly caused the storm that destroyed much of the town, Pauline makes an important statement about the nature of Fleur's power:

> Power travels in the bloodlines, handed down before birth. It comes down through the hands, which in the Pillagers are strong and knotted, big, spidery and rough, with sensitive fingertips good at dealing cards. It comes through the eyes, too, belligerent, darkest brown, the eyes of those in the bear clan, impolite as they gaze directly at a person. (Erdrich, *Tracks*)

Few would doubt the magical, shaman-like power of Fleur Pillager, and because fewer women than men attain this rank, Fleur seems to be even more extraordinary. As Landes says, "The fact that certain women do not try any masculine pursuits, throws into stronger relief the fact that other women do make these techniques their own in greater or smaller part" (*The Ojibwa Woman* 177).

Erdrich refers to *Tracks* in an interview with Hertha Wong. She discusses her vision of the quartet of novels as comprising the four elements: air (*The Beet Queen*), water (*Love Medicine*), earth (*Tracks*), and the fourth (recently published as *The Bingo Palace*) will most likely be fire. The fourth novel will follow *The Beet Queen* chronologically. Therefore, *Tracks*, the first in terms of chronology, is earth. In Native American tales, earth is often associated with the feminine, with mother. In "Adoptive Mothers and Thrown-Away Children in the Novels of Louise Erdrich," Wong notes that "[m]other is not merely one's biological parent; she is all one's relations (male and female, human and animal, individual and tribal); and she is connected to the earth" (177). Also, the bear often represents the transformative power of the Great Mother in Native American myth, and Fleur is a member of the bear clan. Discussing why she chose the number four for her novel sequence, Erdrich notes:

> It's the number of completion in Ojibway mythology. There are different myths, but one of them is the bear coming through different worlds, breaking through from one world into the next, from the next world into the next world. The number of incompletion is three and the number of completion is four, so four is a *good* number. (211)

The myth of the bear moving between worlds is an apt description of Fleur who moves between the material and corporeal, the ancient and the modern, the ordinary and the extraordinary, the Chippewa world and the white world. Fleur's strength is tested repeatedly in the novel, especially when she loses her second born, a son, in childbirth. Her inability to save him seems to indicate that Fleur, as Sidner Larson says, "is beaten down" (11), and perhaps she is, at least temporarily. Nevertheless, Fleur does not give in passively to fate; she mourns her loss and continues her fight to survive as she faces even more loss.

By the end of the novel, the Pillager land is lost to the logging company; although, Fleur has a moment of great irony when she saws the tree trunks so that with the right amount of wind, they will all fall over (in a circle). It is no accident that the wind comes up just as the loggers begin their destruction of her forest. In "Woman Looking: Revis(ion)ing Pauline's Subject Position in Louise Erdrich's *Tracks*," Daniel Cornell discusses Fleur's loss of power against the Euroamerican institutions,

a loss he argues that Nanapush predicts. Cornell says "Fleur has no where to go where she will not already be positioned as 'other,' both as a woman and as an American Indian" (62). And, finally, she loses Lulu, her only surviving child, but this loss is by Fleur's own-choice. Fleur sees no other way to prepare Lulu for survival in the white man's world except to send her away to the government school. Wong's view of Fleur's decision to send Lulu away is that "abandoning one's child is not an act of selfishness; it is an act of despair or an act of desperate mercy" ("Adoptive Mothers" 186). Perhaps the greatest love is that which recognizes its inability to "own" another person. Thus, at the end of the novel, Fleur packs her few possessions. Nanapush says:

> When she buckled herself into the traces of the greenwood cart I said, "Stay with us." I got no answer. There was none that I expected. An extra set of moccasins and a thin charred pair of patent leather shoes were slung over one shoulder . . . . She looked around at me, her face alight, and then she set out. (Erdrich, *Tracks*)

Fleur is gone, but not defeated. Fluer's power to transform her losses into strengths is hinted at in the *The Beet Queen*, but in *The Bingo Palace* Fleur triumphs over those forces which had seemingly beaten her down.

Fleur chooses to continue a nomadic existence living off of what she can barter (peddle). She moves between both worlds, her own and the white world. She appears briefly in *The Beet Queen*. It is eight years after she walked away from her forest. She uses her medicine to save the life of Karl Adare who has shattered his feet jumping off of a freight train. While Fleur works to break Karl's fever, his vision is of a bear. "A bear rose between the fire and the reeds. In the deepest part of the night, the biggest animal of all came through in a crash of sparks and wheels" (Erdrich, *The Beet Queen*). The next morning Karl's fever has disappeared. This section from *The Beet Queen* supports my view of Fleur as undefeated, as enduring.

Fleur also resurfaces in *The Bingo Palace*. Her great-grandson, Lipsha, goes to Fleur's home in the remote woods to ask her for a "special" love medicine. Lipsha is caught between two worlds, and in order to "find" himself he has to acknowledge the power of the traditions which Fleur has not forgotten. Fleur is waiting for Lipsha.

> We think about the Pillager woman, Fleur, who was always half spirit anyway. A foot on the death road, a quick shuffle backwards, her dance wearies us. Yet, some of us wish she'd come out of the woods. We

don't fear her anymore—like death, she is an old friend who has been waiting quietly, a patient companion. We know she's dawdling, hanging back as long as she can, waiting for another to take her place, . . . This time she's waiting for a young one, a successor, someone to carry on her knowledge, . . . (*Bingo Palace*)

Wong notes that ". . . Native American women long have been associated with the continuance of tribal tradition, both through childbearing and through transmission of cultural values in stories" (174). Fleur is responsible for passing on the tribal spiritual beliefs to her heirs, to Lipsha.

The Bingo Palace reveals that rather than allowing her spiritual beliefs and her "will" to be destroyed by the white man's interference in Chippewa life, Fleur fights. She eventually wins the Pillager land back by getting into a "cosmic" card game with former Indian Agent, Jewett Parker Tatro, who had purchased the Pillager land from the logging company. Dressed in stark white and accompanied by a white boy, Fleur sets her trap. "Fleur was never one to take an uncalculated piece of revenge. She was never one to answer injustice with a fair exchange. She gave back twofold" (*Bingo Palace*). Fleur is not a victim at the end of *Tracks*. She is waiting for an opportunity to subvert the power of the white man, and when she subverts Jewett Parker Tatro in *The Bingo Palace*, she moves back onto the Pillager land. Therefore, in this four-novel sequence, Fleur's allegiance to the ancient ways continues to empower her bloodline, and Fleur derives much of her power from that which is natural and feminine in her spiritual beliefs.

Paula Gunn Allen discusses the feminine in Native American culture, which Fleur draws upon for her strength. Allen's chapter, "Grandmother of the Sun: Ritual Gynocracy in Native America" from her book *The Sacred Hoop* is revealing. Looking at ancient Native American myths, Allen shows that Woman is at the center of everything (11). Also, in her introduction to this book, Allen states, "Traditional tribal lifestyles are more often gynocratic than not, and they are never patriarchal" (2). A little further on, Allen argues:

> In tribal gynocratic systems a multitude of personality and character types can function positively within the social order because the systems are focused on social responsibility rather than on privilege and on realities of the human constitution rather than on denial-based social fictions to which human beings are compelled to conform by powerful individuals within the society. (3)

Allen's description of the power structure of patriarchy reveals a Western world view. Many feminist authors have posited that patriarchy has evolved from men's deep-seeded fear of women. Certainly, the men who played poker with Fleur and the loggers who encroached upon Pillager land represent patriarchy, and in the end, they have reason to fear Fleur.

Allen's chapter on gynocracy contains mythic tales similar to the Chippewa tales about Misshepeshu who is supposedly Fleur's spirit lover. Allen quotes a portion of a translation of Fr. Noel Dumarest, a nineteenth-century priest, who transcribed the following Keres creation myth.

> In his account [Fr. Dumarest's], when the "Indian sister" made stars, she could not get them to shine, so "she consulted Spider, the creator." He characterized the goddess-sisters as living "with Spider Woman, their mother, at *shipapu*, under the waters of the lake, in the second world." (16)

The similarity between *shipapu* and Misshepeshu is obvious, and Fleur's immersions in Matchimanito Lake are directly related to spiritual renewal and empowerment. In the Chippewa language *maci manito* means evil spirit (Van Dyke 18). In the Keres myth, the powerful women creators live at *shipapu*, while in the Chippewa myths, the water monster is male and he is often evil. Despite their differences, these two myths reveal the power of ritual birth or renewal which is symbolized by water. Fleur can be seen as a representative of a feminine view of humankind that deconstructs and embodies oppositions such as good and evil, material and corporeal, feminine and masculine. This fluidity reflected in Erdrich's characterization of Fleur is reminiscent of the Great Mother figure in many Native American belief systems who represents the cycles of the natural world which are both creative and destructive.

Another mythic connection is the significance of the white scarf that Fleur wraps around her shaven head in *Tracks*. In *The Beet Queen* and *The Bingo Palace* white is also a color associated with Fleur. White is the color of snow (frozen water) which is symbolic of the harsh reality of the Chippewa way of life on the northern plains. Winter with its chilling cold and snow is an element or a force that Fleur and the other characters in the book learn to respect. Several times in the novel, Fleur nearly loses her life to both of these elements. Water can mean both a real and a symbolic rebirth, just as snow can mean both a real and a symbolic death. In fact, in *Tracks* Pauline is described as *windigo* (insane), a term which has its origins in Chippewa mythology where it means "giant cannibalistic skeleton of ice" (Landes, *Ojibwa Religion*

12–13). Winter, then, plays heavily into the lives and imaginations of the characters in *Tracks*. Another mythic parallel that can be found in Allen's chapters is that in Keres myth *Shipap* (notice the similarity to *shipapu* and Misshepeshu) is the female center of the earth, and the "color of Shipap is white" (19). Ojibway artist Norval Morriseau says of Misshepeshu, ". . . the true water god, the white one in colour, . . ." (qtd. in Van Dyke 19). With her white scarf and her white suit, Fleur represents the Great Mother—earth, water, fire, and air—who is central to Native American spirituality and myth and who has both feminine and masculine traits.

Source: Patricia Angley, "Fleur Pillager: Feminine, Mythic, and Natural Representations in Louise Erdrich's *Tracks*," in *Constructions and Confrontations: Changing Representations of Women and Feminism, East and West*, edited by Cristina Bacchilega and Cornelia N. Moore, Literary Studies East and West, No. 12, University of Hawai'i, 1996, pp. 159–69.

Ruth Rosenberg

In the following essay, Rosenberg discusses Erdrich's writing career.

The families Louise Erdrich first introduced in a short story, "The World's Greatest Fishermen" (1982)—the Kashpaws, the Lamartines, the Pillagers, and the Morrisseys—have also appeared in four of her novels. The focus of each changes as previously silent characters speak, revealing their secrets. Three generations interact in the Turtle Mountain Reservation of North Dakota and the nearby town of Argus. Erdrich claims she has no control over whose voice will emerge or what part of the past will be disclosed. Thus the story keeps growing, its truths changing as each new narrator adds an additional perspective. Readers discover a community of unpredictable people by overhearing their gossip, puzzling out their relationships through subtle clues. Despite their tragedies, they are exuberantly funny. Erdrich also possesses the gift of depicting spirits as vibrant presences, not transcendent beings. These forces emanate from stones, pulse from drums, rustle in the leaves of trees, can be summoned by medicines, or flow through fingertips. The forces under a lake, the power within a pipe, and the ancestors' dancing in the northern lights control the destinies of these people.

Louise Karen Erdrich was born on 6 July 1954 in Little Falls, Minnesota, the eldest of seven children. Her mother, Rita Joanne Gourneau Erdrich, had been born on the Turtle Mountain Chippewa Reservation, of which Patrick Gourneau, Erdrich's grandfather, had been tribal chairman. Her father, Ralph Louis Erdrich, of German descent, taught at the Bureau of Indian Affairs boarding school, where her mother also taught. The family lived in faculty housing at the edge of the small town of Wahpeton, North Dakota, three hundred miles away from the Turtle Mountain Reservation. Some aspects of her paternal grandmother, Mary Erdrich Korll, appear in *The Beet Queen* (1986) as well as in the poetry sequences called "The Butcher's Wife" in *Jacklight* (1984) and *Baptism of Desire* (1989). Her great uncle, Ben Gourneau, inspired some of the details for the characterization of Eli Kashpaw. Her mother had told her many of the stories in *Tracks* (1988), the first written but third published of her novels.

In a 1991 *Writer's Digest* interview, collected in *Conversations with Louise Erdich and Michael Dorris* (1993), Erdrich credits a childhood without movies or television for her narrative impulse:

> The people in our families made everything into a story. They love to tell a good story. People just sit and the stories start coming, one after another. You just sort of grab the tail of the last person's story: it reminds you of something and you keep going on. I suppose that when you grow up constantly hearing the stories rise, break and fall, it gets into you somehow.

Erdrich's tetralogy is comprised of chapters narrated by different speakers. The events, spanning a century, assume the form of a traditional Chippewa story cycle. As Erdrich explained to Malcolm Jones of the *St. Petersburg Times* in 1985:

> This reflects a traditional Chippewa motif in storytelling, which is a cycle of stories having to do with a central mythological figure, a culture hero. One tells a story about an incident that leads to another incident that leads to another in the life of this particular figure. Night after night, or day after day, it's a storytelling cyle.

Erdrich told Joseph Bruchac in *Survival This Way: Interviews with American Indian Poets* (1987) that she idolized her grandfather: "He is funny, he's charming, he's interesting." She respected his being able to live with dignity in two cultures—maintaining the old religion, speaking "the old language," doing pipe services for ordinations, knowledgeable about the ways of the animals. But he also attended mass, "gave Tricia Nixon an Anishinabe name, for publicity," and danced in powwows. In a 1986 interview with Nora Frenkiel of the *Baltimore Sun* she recalled how "he searched his fields for old stones used in tomahawks, and remade the entire beadwork." But above all, she says, "My grandfather was a great storyteller." Although none of her fiction is autobiographical, she has given her character Nector Kashpaw some of her grandfather's attributes. Nector's devoted wife, Marie, bears some resemblance to her grandmother, Mary Gourneau, who married at age fourteen.

Erdrich's father made the Depression era so vivid for her that she was able to fictionalize his accounts in *The Beet Queen*. She got the idea for the novel from his anecdote about his first airplane ride, which inspired a plot based on Adelaide's flight. He also gave her the idea for one of her poetry sequences, as she told Jan George in 1985: "My father is a terrific storyteller and made his relatives and the characters in the towns where he grew up almost mythic. I owe 'Step-and-a-Half-Waleski' in *Jacklight* completely to him. There really was a woman like her in his childhood." Erdrich's father also introduced her to William Shakespeare, playing and replaying records of *Macbeth* and *King Lear*. He encouraged her and her sisters to write by occasionally paying them a nickel for their stories. Her sisters Heidi and Lise are also published authors. When Erdrich was judging the entries for a volume of best American short stories, she regretted that the rules prevented her from accepting Lise's submission.

Except for a few years in a parochial school, Saint John's, in Wahpeton, Erdrich attended public school. One small detail that surfaced later in her fiction was her election to the B# piano club while she was taking music lessons with her teacher Sister Anita. Wallace Pfef in *The Beet Queen* is described as being a supporter of the B# piano club. Another incident, which she uses in *The Bingo Palace* (1994), had actually happened to her when she was fourteen. One May night she took her sleeping bag out to the football field and awoke at dawn with a skunk curled up on top of her. In a 1993 essay in the *Georgia Review* she wrote how she envied skunks their fearlessness. She wrote in the January 1985 *Ms.* that performing on the piano in public "terrified me to the point of nausea or paralysis."

In 1972 she entered Dartmouth College on scholarships as part of its first coeducational class. That same year her future husband, Michael Dorris, had been appointed head of the Native American studies department. Their first collaboration was published in an Indian magazine, a children's story that he wrote and she illustrated. Dorris said in *The Broken Cord* (1989) that "her bold, quirky drawings" were "better than my text."

Her first publications were in Dartmouth literary magazines. One of her teachers, A. B. Paulsen,

> **She considers it her favorite because it gave her such difficulty, and she wishes she had had more time with it."**

considered her a poet of unusually high talent. She finally felt credentialed when *Ms.* accepted one of her poems; an American Academy of Poets Prize in 1975 was further validation. After graduation she worked as poet in the schools for the State Arts Council of North Dakota, teaching "children, convicts, rehabilitation patients, high-school hoods and recovering alcoholics." The following summer James Wright, a Dartmouth history professor, invited her to serve as consultant on a documentary he was filming on Northern Plains Indians for Nebraska Public Television.

A variety of minimum-wage jobs followed, many of which found their way into her fiction later. Many of her characters are waitresses, as she had been, either "on the night shift in an all-night family diner" or "on the breakfast shift as a short-order cook." She prides herself on still being able to crack four eggs one-handed. She also weighed trucks on the interstate and worked as flagger on a construction site—both jobs she gave to characters. She weeded beets, picked cucumbers, delivered newspapers, sold popcorn, and worked as an ad manager and as a bookstore distributor of small-press publications. The scenes in *Love Medicine* (1984) set in the elder-care center gain verisimilitude from her having worked in one.

In 1979 a fellowship at Johns Hopkins University enabled Erdrich to move to Maryland and concentrate on her writing. In a small apartment she worked on the poems she submitted as her thesis. After receiving her master's degree in 1980 she became editor of the Boston Indian Council newspaper, *The Circle*. In Massachusetts she wrote a textbook, *Imagination* (1981), for Merrill while waitressing at a pastry shop.

An invitation to read at Dartmouth led to her meeting Dorris again. As he wrote later in *The Broken Cord*, her reading left him "dazed, stunned."

Her poems were "vivid stories, tight and condensed as black holes in space." They had time only to exchange addresses because he was leaving for New Zealand and she for the MacDowell Colony in New Hampshire. Their correspondence became an exchange of manuscripts, each writing long editorial comments on the other's drafts. After working at Yaddo, Erdrich was invited to serve as writer in residence at Dartmouth. Her arrival on campus in January 1981 coincided with Dorris's return. On 10 October 1981 they were married in a civil ceremony in the backyard of the house Dorris had shared with his three adopted children. Erdrich's mother had sewn the wedding gown and mailed it to Cornish, New Hampshire, from North Dakota.

To pay for repairs on their farmhouse the couple collaborated, under the pseudonym Milou North, on stories published in the British magazine *Woman*. Erdrich told the *Washington Post* in October 1988 that their first fictions were "not terribly deep, but they were uplifting. Always about a young woman under stress who resolved her crisis affirmatively."

Their next collaboration won the Nelson Algren Award, a five-thousand-dollar prize from *Chicago* magazine. Dorris's aunt Virginia Burkhardt had sent them the announcement of the contest early in January; the deadline was 15 January. In a single day Erdrich drafted the story of a family reunion "with events, but no conversation or details." As she finished each page at the kitchen table, she took it into the living room for Dorris's suggestions. After they mailed off "The World's Greatest Fishermen" they spent so much time discussing the revisions they would make when it returned that they had enough material for a novel. It became the opening chapter of *Love Medicine*. Two other chapters, "The Red Convertible" and "Scales," had already been published. When Anne Tyler selected "Scales" for *The Best American Short Stories 1983* she wrote of Dot Nanapush, "You think you won't care much about a gigantic, belligerent, pregnant woman who weighs trucks for a living? Just wait. By the time you see her violently knitting her orange and hot-pink baby clothes you'll care passionately."

For a year and a half the couple imagined scenarios for their characters, who, in the course of many conversations, became as familiar as relatives. The "Saint Marie" chapter gave them some problems. Dorris felt that it was not working in the nun's voice and suggested it be told by the novitiate. Erdrich went out for a long walk. "The next day," Dorris told Shelby Grantham of *Dartmouth Alumni Magazine* in 1985, "there was a new draft on my desk. We had no other words about it—it just appeared there. And it was absolutely right." Henry Abrams, who selected it for the 1985 O. Henry Awards, agreed.

When they sent *Love Medicine* to publishers it received polite responses but no offers. Dorris finally managed to place the manuscript with Holt by printing up stationery with the letterhead Michael Dorris Agency and promoting it himself. The novel became an immediate best-seller. The American Academy of Arts and Letters gave the thirty-year-old novelist the Sue Kaufman Prize for Best First Fiction, and distinguished writers acclaimed her achievement. Philip Roth praised her "originality, authority, tenderness, and pitiless wild wit." Toni Morrison wrote that "the beauty of *Love Medicine* saves us from being devastated by its power." Ursula K. Le Guin called Erdrich "a true artist and probably a major one," while the *Chicago Tribune* called her "the first novelist of her generation to have achieved front-rank writerly stardom."

The author who had seldom seen television was wooed by producers who saw possibilities in *Love Medicine* as a television serial; movie rights were also optioned. A measure of its worldwide appeal was its translation into eighteen languages. Native Americans wrote her thousands of letters, some of them asking how she could have known things that had actually happened to them. She appreciated their endorsement, especially those who told her she was the first writer who knew how Indians really talked. She acknowledged this at the New York Historical Society when the National Book Critics Circle honored her as the year's best novelist. It was the Chippewa who deserved the recognition, she said: "I accept this award in the spirit of the people who speak through the book." In 1984 she also won the Virginia Scully Award for Best Book Dealing with Western Indians and in 1985 the American Book Award from the Before Columbus Foundation.

A wide readership responded to promotions by the Book-of-the-Month Club and the Quality Paperback Book Club. An academic audience, the Great Lakes Colleges Association, conferred upon her its prize for Best First Work of Fiction. In 1985 she received a Guggenheim Fellowship.

In August 1985 Dorris went on sabbatical to research *The Broken Cord* while Erdrich worked on *The Beet Queen*, based on her father's people. The family moved to Northfield, Minnesota, to a six-bedroom Victorian house a block away from Carleton College.

Erdrich submits her work to continual revision. The first longhand drafts are passed back and forth between the couple for interlinear comments. Then Dorris triple-spaces the manuscript on his word processor, using a different font for each successive version. The final manuscript is spread out on a long table and read aloud page by page. They do not send it out until they have achieved consensus on every word. Therefore they were surprised to find themselves still prompted to further revision after *The Beet Queen* seemed ready to send to the publisher. In a 1986 interview in the *North Dakota Quarterly* Erdrich said, "Right after Christmas, we started rewriting it from page 206 on. In a month, we rewrote pages 206 to 393, and made a whole new ending. The last 15 pages are completely new."

Some reviewers objected to the carefully reworked ending. Michiko Kakutani in the 20 August 1986 *New York Times* lamented its artifice in reassembling all the characters at a parade. Dorothy Wickenden in the 6 October *New Republic* wrote that "the coming together of all the characters and themes at the beet festival—complete with Dot's dramatic reliving of her grandmother's flight—is a contrivance." Josh Rubin in the 15 January 1987 *New York Review of Books* deplored the outlandish coincidences "in the novel's final set piece, which blatantly arranges the intersection of the redemptive return of wastrel Karl, the black-comic demise of Cousin Sita, and the rigged election of sullen Dot Adare as the 1972 Beet Queen of Argus, North Dakota."

The carefully contextualized conclusion arose from a spiderweb image in a mother's dream in the center of the novel. She notices "in the fine moonlight floss of her baby's hair, a tiny white spider making its nest. It was a delicate thing, close to transparent . . . throwing out invisible strings." The novel was spun out of that central metaphor. Erdrich's daughter Pallas, whose "passion is spiders" and who was delighted that one "spun a delicate web in an eave above her bed," inspired that passage.

The passages between the chapters lyrically describing the characters' dreams are the "invisible strings" making the episodes coherent. When the Bantam paperback edition failed to include these, Erdrich's lawyer, Charles Rembar, offered to share the expense of recalling the fifty thousand copies already in print. When they declined Erdrich changed to another publisher. HarperCollins paid an unprecedented six hundred thousand dollars for the paperback rights. From its third week after publication *The Beet Queen* was on *The New York Times* best-seller list. It was featured by the Book-of-the-Month Club as an alternate selection, was named by *Publishers Weekly* as one of the "Best Books," and was nominated for the National Book Critics Circle Award. It was published in England and translated into Danish, Norwegian, Finnish, Swedish, German, and French.

Erdrich's technical virtuosity impressed many critics. In the 15 January 1987 *New York Review of Books* Rubin wrote that her storytelling was so compelling that her authorial strategems "don't undermine the story's forward momentum and emotional conviction." Robert Bly in the 31 August *New York Times Book Review* expressed "amazement and gratitude at this splendid, feisty talent, capable of bizarre comedy, ordinary Midwestern facts and vigorous tragedy." Russell Banks in the 1 November 1986 *Nation* applauded the "exquisite ironies" wrought from "a Bruegel-like realism" and the elegant orchestration of the multiple voices that "blend, as in a chorus, without ever losing their remarkable individuality. Erdrich has been able to give each of her characters their own tone, diction, pitch and rhythm, without letting go of her own."

For her third novel Erdrich returned to her student manuscript, *Tracks*, portions of which had already been published as short stories. "Fleur" had been doubly honored. In 1986 it was cited by Sharon Ravenel as a distinguished short story of the year, and in 1987 it was chosen by William Abrahams as the first-place winner of the *Prize Stories: The O. Henry Awards*. In *The Broken Cord* Dorris described its impact on him a decade before at Dartmouth: "Louise read a section of what she described as a novel-in-progress: the tale of a Chippewa woman who bested a group of men in a card game in a butcher shop and their fury over the loss. It was alternately hilarious and terribly sad, a building swirl of impressions that clung to the imagination with incredible power." Erdrich said that rereading it led her to the realization "that it was now part of what the novel could be, and it eventually became the second chapter in the book." Dorris saw in the emerging trilogy three of the four natural elements. As the first novel had been governed by images of water, the second had reiterated references to air. The third would be dominated by images of earth, as the fourth would be by fire. The plot of *Tracks* is a conflict over the land. The Anishinabe are threatened by surveyors preparing for allotment as well as by loggers. Since it moved back into tribal history to events between 1912 and 1924 Dorris considered it a prequel to the other two novels. Alternately narrated by Nanapush and Pauline (who becomes Sister Leopolda in *The Beet Queen*), its silent auditor is the child Lulu (the matriarch of *Love Medicine*). The already-published short story "Snares," which had been selected for *The Best American Short Stories 1988*, became the fifth chapter.

Erdrich was reluctant to let this book, scheduled for publication in September 1988, go. She considers it her favorite because it gave her such difficulty, and she wishes she had had more time with it. In spite of her feeling that it was still incomplete, *Tracks* was widely praised, was adopted in college courses, and immediately ascended the best-seller lists. *Studies in American Indian Literatures* devoted two issues to it. Among the many topics discussed, that of dealing with ritual materials, of trying to transform an oral tradition into a written one, suggests why she felt *Tracks* posed such problems.

Erdrich uses the double-voiced narration again in her next book, *Baptism of Desire*. The Trickster voice is apparent in the "Potchikoo" cycle, while the convent voice can be heard in the Catholic poems. The two antithetical belief systems energize her poetry.

In 1990 Erdrich and Dorris collaborated on a travel book later printed in a limited edition. *Route Two* resulted from their family visits to relatives across the continent. They plotted their next project, the novel *The Crown of Columbus* (1991), on their drive through Saskatchewan described in *Route Two*. They had been intrigued by Columbus's multiple identities in the public mind for a decade, researching the complex personality of the man credited with "discovering" Native Americans. Erdrich undertook the task of reading every book that Columbus had mentioned in his diaries. Like the protagonist, Vivian Twostar, she worked in Dartmouth's Baker Library. At the time Erdrich was pregnant with their third daughter, Aza, as Vivian was with her baby, Violet.

The second narrator, Roger Williams, is writing an epic poem about Columbus. Erdrich described him in a 1991 *Mother Jones* article on the couple as "terribly self-important," and Dorris added that he is "a very fastidious, self-protective, established English professor." His joining the quest for the missing pages of Columbus's diary jolts him out of his academic isolation into the disorder of the everyday. As another of their pseudonymous publications Erdrich and Dorris submitted the poem about Columbus under the name Roger Williams to the periodical *Caliban*, admitting they were jealous of their invented author since he got printed with his first submission. The French publishers of the book wanted Williams's poem displaced to an appendix. However, Erdrich and Dorris defended its position within the text, since everything in the poem is paralleled in the novel and it therefore assumes structural importance.

Erdrich enjoyed the opportunity to write about literate characters in an academic setting, which allowed her to exercise her gift for parody. Her penchant for playing with forms made *The New York Times Book Review* writer uncomfortable. The book, he wrote, mixes too many genres: "domestic comedy, paperback thriller, novel of character, love story." Carla Freccero disagreed in the 17 October 1991 *Women's Review of Books*: "What has appeared to some critics as a helter-skelter fragmentary novel catering to popular tastes is in fact a highly structured, complex, symbolic rewriting of American history, framed by four parallel discoveries and four returns." With a first printing of 150,000 copies; excerpts in *Redbook*, *Mother Jones*, and *Caliban*; movie rights sold to Cinecom; and a two-hundred-thousand-dollar advertising campaign and author tours, the book became a resounding commercial success, and it was chosen as a Book-of-the-Month Club alternate.

In 1993 Erdrich was invited to serve as the guest editor of *The Best American Short Stories 1993*. Pam Lambert in the 15 November 1993 *People Weekly* noted that Erdrich fortified herself for the task of selecting from the 120 entries with "a case of licorice. 'I like the red better, but you feel more professional eating black.'" Reviewers praised the collection assembled by Erdrich, calling it "remarkably rich." Her criteria had been "intellectual pleasure" as well as "texture, place, aroma, succulence, and stiff particularity," she wrote in her introduction.

In November 1993 Holt issued an augmented version of *Love Medicine*. Erdrich's editor there, Marian Wood, justified the expanded edition because the series of which it forms a part is "organic," and its growth had to be accommodated. The four inserted chapters set up *The Bingo Palace*. Serving as transitions to this fourth novel are the chapters "The Island," "Resurrection," "The Tomahawk Factory," and "Lyman's Luck." Erdrich's explanation, in the 14 October *New York Times*, of the augmented edition is interesting for what it reveals about her methods of composition:

> When I started working on my new book, *The Bingo Palace*, I started sifting through these notebooks I have of handwritten manuscripts and notes of everything I'd done before. It's basically like a big compost pile. The notebooks not only suggested the shape for the new book, but they suggested that there were parts of *Love Medicine* that I had forgotten. . . . I felt that these voices needed to be included.

Those voices—Lulu, Marie, and Lyman—give readers the background knowledge needed to understand Lipsha's accession to the Pillager powers in *The Bingo Palace*. Lulu tells how Lipsha's father, Gerry, was conceived by the medicine man, Moses Nanapush, who was Fleur's cousin—the only male Pillager who survived the epidemic depicted in *Tracks*. Marie tells of the ancestral pipe to be inherited by Lipsha, which, when its stem is joined to its bowl, connects heaven and earth. Lyman speaks of the profound mourning for his brother, Henry Lamartine, Jr., which will be resolved by his performance of the grass dance. The business acumen he inherited from Nector Kashpaw, which leads him to found not only a tomahawk factory but also a bingo palace, leads finally to tribal recognition of his paternity. The epic ends with a reconciliation of sons with fathers after the rivalry between Lipsha and Lyman is healed during a joint vision quest. Not only are the old ceremonies restored but even the old language, as Gerry tells his son where to find him in Anishinabec. Gerry is the fictionalized counterpart of the Chippewa hero Leonard Peltier, wrongly imprisoned for eighteen years. His martyrdom inspires the union of all tribal people in protest.

Erdrich had been working on a story cycle called "Tales of Burning Love," scheduled for publication in 1995, when *The Bingo Palace* came to her during a blizzard. She interrupted her work on the story cycle to draft the novel in six weeks. Then an invitation came to write an introduction for a captivity narrative that had long been a family favorite. She reminisced about the history of a boy who in 1789 was adopted by the Ojibwa:

> [T]he darkly bound narrative of the captivity of John Tanner stood upright on a shelf in my grandparents' Turtle Mountain Reservation home. It belonged to my grandfather Patrick Gourneau, and I first read it on the sun-soaked back steps of his house, just beyond the shade of the spreading woods where Tanner once joined an ill-fated early nineteenth-century Cree party. The story of Shaw-shaw-wa-be-na-se, or The Falcon, was a family touchstone especially cherished by my sister, Lise. Erdrich is also considering a book about the kindly Father Damien. In preparation she is

studying the lives of the saints and the history of the Jesuit missionaries as well as researching Catholic devotions. As she told Bruchac, "You never change once you're raised a Catholic. You've got that symbolism, that guilt."

Erdrich is also planning a book about Mustache Maude, a female cattle rustler, "a North Dakota maverick" about whom she had published a short story in *Frontiers*. "The story was, as early work often is, an experiment in voice and form," Erdrich explained to an interviewer.

Erdrich has compiled a book of nature essays, selected from the many she has published in magazines, called *The Bluejay's Dance* (1995). The conceit of dancing away the threat of death is an apt metaphor for survival humor. She writes of a baby bluejay that had escaped a swooping hawk by fluffing its feathers and dancing a "manic, successful jig—cocky, exuberant, entirely a bluff, a joke." All of Erdrich's life-affirming exuberance is in that image.

Source: Ruth Rosenberg, "Louise Erdrich," in *Dictionary of Literary Biography*, Vol. 152, *American Novelists Since World War II, Fourth Series*, edited by James Giles and Wanda Giles, Gale Research, 1995, pp. 42–50.

Jennifer Sergi

In the following essay, Sergi examines Erdrich's storytelling style in Tracks, *especially as it relates to Chippewa traditions.*

Without stories there is no articulation of experience: people would be unable to understand and celebrate the experiences of self, community, and world. And so cultures value the tellers of stories. The storyteller takes what he or she tells from experience—his or her own or that reported by others—and in turn makes it the experience of those who are listening to the tale (WB, 87). The storyteller relies on memory (his or hers and his or her listener's) and creates a chain of tradition that passes on a happening from generation to generation.

Louise Erdrich is just such a storyteller. In her third novel, *Tracks* (1988), she not only chronicles the story of the Chippewas' struggle to preserve their land and culture; she also gives us the story of these stories and their tellers as well. She is telling this novel "the Indian way." The "artistry of the Indian 'word sender' characterizes reality: peoples, landscapes, seasons, tonalizes, lightens, spiritualizes, brightens, and darkens human experience, all the while working with the reality that is" (KL, 223). This reality is shown to readers by two

> "The stories are circular and continuous and serpentlike. By telling tribal stories, singing old songs, Nanapush gives his culture a chance for continuation...."

storytellers who alternate chapters, in separate, very distinct voices: Pauline, a young mixed-blood who is confused and psychologically damaged by her unbalanced commitment to Catholic martyrdom and Chippewa tradition; and Nanapush, a wise old tribal leader gifted in the ancient art of storytelling. It is through Nanapush that Erdrich captures the act of Indian storytelling. It is written down, but Erdrich wishes to record and preserve not just the memories, intertwined closely with personal history and a sense of loss, but a cultural tradition, one that is oral, performed, formulaic, and perpetuated by the storyteller, who learns the rhythms and melodies—the craft—and expands, ornaments, and varies the tradition his or her own way, Thus Erdrich's Native American, and more specifically Chippewa, "tracks" are evident in her narratives, if not as those of the one who experienced it, then as those of the one who reports it.

How this oral tradition and history is being recorded is important, therefore, and "tracing the connective threads between the cultural past and its expression in the present" becomes a primary focus of scholars as well as novelists (KL, 2). How are translators and Native American artists, like Erdrich, bringing the oral and mythic traditions of their ancestors into print for native and non-native readers? Erdrich does this in a number of ways in *Tracks:* 1) she captures the form and purpose of oral storytelling; 2) she includes the contents of Chippewa myth and legend; and 3) she preserves these cultural traditions in a voice that harks back to the old as it creates anew.

Kenneth Lincoln, a Native American literature scholar, is also exploring the nature of the transition from orality to writing, and within his definition of

Indian storytelling he describes the "story-backed old man giv[ing] the child eyes and voices, narratives that touch and are carried for life: words incarnate, flesh-and-blood ties, an embodied imagination. And the tribal backbone extends through ancestors who carry history in their bodies" (KL, 222). The fictional prototype of this "story-backed old man" is Erdrich's narrator, Nanapush. Nanapush is telling the story to his adopted granddaughter Lulu: "My girl, I saw the passing of times you will never know." He knows the old ways: "I guided the last buffalo hunt. I saw the last bear shot. I trapped the last beaver with a pelt of more than two years' growth. I spoke aloud the words of the government treaty, and refused to sign the settlement papers that would take away our woods and lake." He also tells Lulu how she fits into this history: "You were born on the day we shot the last bear."

Moreover, much as in Indian storytelling, it is not only what Nanapush has to say and to whom, but also the way in which he says it that is important. Nanapush's narrative style points to the novel's roots in Chippewa oral tradition. Erdrich is sensitive to the immediate difference between the printed word and the spoken, and she effects an accommodation between her printed text and her narrator's delivery. The stylistic devices of repetition and parallelism, employed as early as page 2 of the novel, work to create tension, balance, and symmetry in the words of Nanapush. His words suggest the rhythms of speech: at key moments in the narrative, readers sense a whispered statement, an abrupt phrase, a long pause. Before he tells the story of how Margaret loses her braids, for instance, he leads in with: "I can only tell it step by step." Erdrich also continually and skillfully reminds us of his audience and the intimacy attached to their relationship: "This is where you come in, my girl, so listen." Lulu sometimes grows tired of the long story, and in his own style Nanapush manages to reprimand the youngster and, in the process, remind her of her roots and her role in this storytelling tradition: "I made her sit down and listen, just the way you are sitting now. Your mother always showed the proper respect to me. Even when I bored her, she made a good effort at pretending some interest."

Erdrich's narrator not only serves to remind us of the importance of the ancient art of storytelling to a tribe, but his name also recalls the novel's debt to Chippewa mythic tradition. In Chippewa woodland myth Nanapush is the trickster-transformer who "wanders in mythic time and space between tribal experiences and dreams" (GV, 3). He is a teacher and healer and upholder of ancient and living traditions; but he is also human. He is sometimes prone to violence and overactive appetites. This paradoxical character is part of Chippewa creation and ceremonial stories. In my research of Chippewa tradition, myth, and legend the stories about the trickster vary, as does the spelling of his name (most likely because of phonetic transcription from oral tradition), but there are several similarities in all of them to Erdrich's Nanapush. (I must pause here to make a distinction. Chippewa is a comparatively modern and English term for the tribe; an older term is Ojibway. The name for these people in the language itself is Anishinaabe. Erdrich uses both Chippewa and Anishinaabe in the novel; all three were found in my research.) In most of the translations he possesses magic and wit. He plays tricks and is the victim of tricks. He is fond of and is good at hunting. He travels in a birchbark canoe, and the Anishinaabe honor and respect him. In chapter 3 of *Tracks* Nanapush tells us part of the origin of his name: "My father said, 'Nanapush. That's what you'll be called. Because it's got to do with trickery and living in the bush. Because it's got to do with something a girl can't resist. The first Nanapush stole fire. You will steal hearts.'" Erdrich's Old Nanapush, then, serves a triple purpose in reminding readers of *Tracks* of the importance of tribal tradition, mythic condition, and storytelling.

Along with this trickster figure, there is other evidence in the novel that Erdrich is interested in preserving and presenting Chippewa cultural tradition to her audience. I cannot know for sure if Erdrich heard these stories as a child, read the accounts and research of Chippewa myth, tradition, legend, and religion, or discussed them as a member of an academic community. However, I do know they are incorporated, integrated, and an important part of her novel. So, like the creation figure Nanapush and her storyteller Nanapush, Erdrich imagines and desires her own variation of the mythic stories for the enjoyment and knowledge of her modern reading audience.

The setting of her novel is the fictional Matchimanito Lake. It may not be a real geographic location, but Matchi Manito is an evil manito in modern Ojibwa myth (CV, 82). The name of the lake is not the only reminder of Chippewa myth in *Tracks*. There is talk of windigos and manitous, burying the dead in trees, dreamcatchers, Jeesekeewinini (medicine man), and "Anishinabe characters, the old gods," as Nanapush refers to them. In chapter 6 Pauline gives us a description of "the heaven of the Chippewa," where Fleur goes to gamble for the life of her child. The gambling

crowd "play for drunkenness, or sorrow, or loss of mind. They play for ease, they play for penitence, and sometimes for living souls."

Gerald Vizenor, a mixed-blood member of the Minnesota Chippewa tribe as well as a teacher and scholar, records a number of the oral creation stories in his book *The People Named the Chippewa: Narrative Histories*. In his prologue Vizenor recounts a story told by Odinigun, an elder from the White Earth Reservation, telling of Naanabozho's gambling in "the land of darkness." In this story Naanabozho must play the great gambler for "the destinies of the trickster and tribal people of the woodland." The tone and, of course, the setting of these two stories are similar; the stakes and energies are high. The outcomes are very different, however: Fleur's baby dies, while Naanabozho succeeds in not losing his tribes' spirit to the land of darkness.

One of the most prevalent and important "signs" of Chippewa myth in *Tracks* is Misshepeshu, the water monster. In the novel Misshepeshu's origin is tied to the arrival of the Pillager clan on Matchimanito Lake. The monster was thought to be responsible for Fleur's powers and the demise of her enemies. Pauline describes him in chapter 2:

> He's a devil, that one, love hungry with desire and maddened for the touch of young girls, the strong and daring especially, the ones like Fleur.
>
> Our mothers warn us that we'll think he's handsome, for he appears with green eyes, copper skin, a mouth tender as a child's. But if you fall into his arms, he sprouts horns, fangs, claws, fins. His feet are joined as one and his skin, brass scales, rings to the tough. . . . He holds you under. Then he takes the body of a lion, a fat brown worm, or a familiar man. . . . He's a thing of dry foam, a thing of death by drowning, the death a Chippewa cannot survive.

Erdrich's description of the lake monster is very similar to that given by Christopher Vecsey, another scholar interested in recording Chippewa oral myth. According to his account of this Chippewa myth, the Underwater Manito is "associated with both the lion and the serpent" (CV, 74). It inspired both awe and terror, as well as reverence, and was thought to be responsible for both malicious and good deeds: "It could cause rapids and stormy waters; it often sank canoes and drowned Indians." In some tales, however, it "fed and sheltered those who fell through the ice."

Erdrich uses this dialectical being throughout *Tracks*. When Fleur returns to Matchimanito from Argus, the townspeople attribute good fishing and no lost boats to Fleur's ability to "keep the lake thing controlled." Her special connection to Misshepeshu is even thought to be sexual, and the paternity of Lulu is questioned: "Lulu's eyes blazed bright as his, . . . eyes hollow and gold." Just before Pauline takes her vows and becomes Sister Leopolda, she tells the story (in chapter 8) of her entanglement with the lake monster. For Pauline, who has just recovered from self-inflicted burns, the lake monster represents the devil. She is delusional and very confused about her religious faith and her Chippewa traditional beliefs: "Christ had hidden out of frailty, overcome by the glitter of copper scales, appalled at the creature's unwinding length and luxury. New devils require new gods." She makes a last visit to Matchi-manito Lake, "determined to wait for my tempter, the one who enslaved the ignorant, who damned them with belief." She tells her story of a sexual, violent encounter with the monster in which she strangles him with her rosary, but the thing "grew a human shape . . . the physical form of Napoleon Morrissey." She feels no guilt for murdering the father of her child, because "he had appeared . . . as the water thing, glass breastplate and burning iron rings." Pauline believed she "tamed the monster that night, sent [him] to the bottom of the lake and chained [him] there by [her] deed. . . . [She] was a poor and noble creature now, dressed in earth like Christ, in furs like Moses Pillager [the medicine man and Fleur's brother], draped in snow or simple air." This description symbolizes the utter confusion some Chippewa could feel because of the crisis in their belief system brought on by Christian influences. Of course Pauline is an extreme example of the pull between Catholic teachings and Chippewa traditions, but Erdrich uses the lake monster, the underwater manito Misshepeshu, in this case as a symbol of the crisis of identity for Pauline.

Misshepeshu serves several symbolic purposes for Erdrich: he is an example of native tradition and lore; he brings the crisis between Chippewa myth and Catholic teachings to a state of rupture in the novel; and the language used to describe him becomes symbolic of the storytelling itself. According to Nanapush:

> Talk is an old man's last vice. I opened my mouth and wore out the boy's ears, but that is not my fault. I shouldn't have been caused to live so long, shown so much of death, had to squeeze so many stories in the corners of my crain. They're all attached, and once I start there is no end to telling because they're hooked from one side to the other, mouth to tail.

The stories are circular and continuous and serpentlike. By telling tribal stories, singing old songs,

Nanapush gives his culture a chance for continuation: "During the year of my sickness, when I was the last one left, I saved myself by starting a story. . . . I got well by talking. Death could not get a word in edgewise, grew discouraged, and traveled on." He not only discouraged death, but he encouraged life and continued his name with his storytelling. When a priest comes to baptize Fleur's illegitimate child, Nanapush tells him the baby is his: "There were so many tales, so many possibilities, so many lies. The waters were so muddy I thought I'd give them another stir." He later saves this child with his talking. Nanapush knew "certain cure songs, words that throw the sick one into a dream . . . holding you motionless with talking." Lulu was "lulled with the sound of [his] voice" and cured of frostbite with Nanapush's ancient gift.

For Nanapush, being a talker was a form of survival; he used his words and his "brain as a weapon." This gave him his identity as a trickster and a leader. He learned to ask questions and tell stories "without limit or end." As much power as the spoken word has for Nanapush, he has learned to fear the printed words the white man brings to his land: "Nanapush is a name that loses power every time that it is written and stored in a government file." Still, when he is about to lose his land, he admits to Father Damien that he should have tried to "wield influence with this [new] method of leading others with a pen and piece of paper."

As Nanapush is exploring the dichotomous nature of the transition from orality to writing, so is Erdrich. Readers are learning of the Chippewas' oral tradition through a printed text. Erdrich shows this duality through Nanapush. Although he expresses his disgust with the "barbed pens" of the bureaucrats encroaching on his people, making them "a tribe of file cabinets and triplicates, a tribe of single-space documents, directives, policy. A tribe of pressed trees. A tribe of chicken-scratch that can be scattered by a wind, diminished to ashes by one struck match." Nanapush tells us that he saves his granddaughter and brings her to his home with papers and records from the church: "I became a bureaucrat myself . . . to draw you home." It is interesting that Erdrich chooses the word draw in this case, evoking an image of the pen rather than of the voice. She realizes the conflict, to which she in part contributes: the Indian "oral tradition of medicine, religion, history, and tribal ceremony bridged from living ritual performance into the marketplace of print" (KL, 82). Nevertheless, for Nanapush and the Native Americans, the last word must be survival. His stories preserve and pass along, tracing and trying to make sense of living history. Erdrich gives us these stories in print; through her language she gives poetic voice and historical witness to human events, which is what all cultures expect from their storytellers.

Source: Jennifer Sergi, "Storytelling: Tradition and Preservation in Louise Erdrich's *Tracks*," in *World Literature Today*, Vol. 66, No. 2, Spring 1992, pp. 279–82.

Thomas M. Disch

In the following review, Disch praises Erdrich for being able to "communicate what is unique and terrific about Indian culture and character without piety or scolding."

Louise Erdrich is the first novelist of her generation—she was 30 when her first novel, *Love Medicine*, appeared in 1984—to have achieved front-rank writerly stardom. While her peers were writing just those novels that the young are expected to write, chronicling their first dates and drug busts, Erdrich lighted out into the territory of Literature, working on a scale, and with an artistry, that simply dwarfs her contemporaries. One must reach for names like Balzac and Faulkner to suggest the sweep of her three interlocking novels, which already constitute a comedie humaine of some 800-plus pages, a North Dakota of the imagination that, like Faulkner's Yoknapatawpha County, unites the archetypal and the arcane, heartland America and borderline schizophrenia.

Tracks, the third novel of this world-in-progress, is chronologically the earliest, being set from 1812 to 1924, and its main characters are members of Chippewa families, weakened by starvation, decimated by plagues and being slowly bulldozed from their treaty lands by the white men, whose tawdry triumph was chronicled in Erdrich's *The Beet Queen* (1986). There's no question on which side of the racial divide the author's sympathies lie (Erdrich is herself of German-American and Chippewa descent); the Chippewas of *Tracks* and *Love Medicine* are noble and anything but savages. But her novels never slip into the tendentious tone of the minority spokesperson; Erdrich never preaches, never even appears to be much concerned about the ways in which her Indian characters are being given a raw deal. The injustices of history are simply part of the landscape she paints.

Tracks is about survival. It begins in 1912, after two epidemics—the "spotted sickness" and consumption—have wiped out whole families in the densely packed reservations/prison camps of North Dakota. The story is narrated alternately by two survivors of those plagues: Nanapush, an old man whose many bereavements have dulled neither his sense of humor nor his sexual appetite, and the ineffably demented Pauline, an orphaned waif who blossoms into the kind of monster you love to hate. (Readers of *Love Medicine* already have encountered her as the older but ever-malevolent Sister Leopolda.) The tale these two narrators tell centers around the love of Fleur Pillager and Eli Kashpaw (both of whom had cameo roles in the earlier novels); but "love" doesn't quite convey what passes between this pair, while "passion" calls to mind the guff of conventional bodice-ripping fiction. The love that Erdrich celebrates is simply the fuel of the process of survival.

Yet it may be that the secret of Erdrich's success is the way she spins the straw of conventional women's romance novels into the gold of literature. Fleur Pillager's curriculum vitae is an erotic daydream, a fantasy of feminist revenge and the story of a mother's perfect (and ultimately misunderstood) love, while the man she loves with such tender fury is a darkly handsome huntsman who more than one once does her wrong and more than once is forgiven. Joan Crawford would have killed for the role. But the thing is, Erdrich is serious, as in Serious Literature; and as she takes each one of these old chestnuts from the fire of her imagination, it is fresh and tasty.

One reason for this may be that she is able to write about erotic matters convincingly from a male point of view; her male characters never have the unreal shimmer of wish-fulfillment that so often sets the TILT light to flashing when Sex A is writing about the sex life of Sex B. And one reason for this clarity of gender may be that her novels have been, by her own report, an enterprise she shares with her husband, Michael Dorris. However she does it, or they do it, the scene in which Eli Kashpaw and the nymphet Sophie Morrissey are bewitched into having sex verges on the Wagnerian in its delectable suggestiveness. (It's also a good example of how pornography cannot be legislated out of existence without gutting literature, for the Sophie-Eli scene could not be published under new anti-child pornography codes proposed by various states.)

A rarer virtue still, Erdrich can communicate what is unique and terrific about Indian culture and character without piety or scolding. She is no schoolmarm wrapping your knuckles for saying "Indian" instead of "Native American." She doesn't re-fry old legends. She doesn't explain. She gets us inside her character's skins by tailoring them so artfully they slip right on.

None of the above explains why Louise Erdrich's books, though written in prose that Ph.D. candidates can purr over, are sure-fire best-sellers. The reason is (as usual in such cases) that she knows how to plot. With almost each new chapter, her readers will be amazed, confounded or enlightened by some new swerve of the story. Those who can't do this sort of thing are prone to dismiss it as 'mere' cleverness; those who can do it—like Larry (*Lonesome Dove*) McMurtry or Robert (*The Secret of Santa Vittoria*) Crichton—enthrall vast audiences, sell millions of copies and still carry off literary prizes. Louise Erdrich can do it in spades, for not only are each of her novels cannily and precisely plotted, but, as their several strands interconnect, there are further "Oh-hos" and "Eurekas" for the attentive reader. Thus, readers of *Tracks* will discover that one of the romantic couples in *Love Medicine* actually was committing incest. They'll find out more about the dead man Lulu discovered in the woods, and his murderer, and who their daughter was. For this reason I urge readers who've not yet read *Love Medicine* to do so before they begin *Tracks*. (There are also connections with *The Beet Queen,* but they aren't as crucial.) Readers who have read *Love Medicine* will need no urging. Louise Erdrich is like one of the those rumored drugs that are instantly and forever addictive. Fortunately in her case you can just say yes.

Source: Thomas M. Disch, "Enthralling Tale: Louise Erdrich's World of Love and Survival," in *Chicago Tribune*, September 4, 1988, Books sec., p. 1.

Barbara Hoffert

In the following review, Hoffert calls Erdrich's writing "sharp, glittering, and to the point as cut glass."

In her splendid new work, Erdrich retrieves characters from her first novel, *Love Medicine,* to depict the escalating conflict between two Chippewa families, a conflict begun when hapless Eli Kashpaw—who has passionately pursued the fiery, elemental Fleur Pillager—is made to betray her with young Sophie Morrissey through the magic of the vengeful Pauline. That simple summary belies the richness and complexity of the tale,

told in turn to Fleur's estranged daughter by her "grandfather," the wily Nanapush, and by Pauline, a woman of mixed blood and mixed beliefs soon to become the obsessive Sister Leopolda. As the community is eroded from without—by white man's venality—and from within, even Fleur must realize that "power goes under and gutters out." Not so for Erdrich, whose prose is as sharp, glittering, and to the point as cut glass. Highly recommended.

Source: Barbara Hoffert, Review of *Tracks*, in *Library Journal*, Vol. 113, No. 14, September 1, 1988, p. 182.

Sources

Erdrich, Louise, "Fleur," in *Esquire's Big Book of Fiction*, edited by Adrienne Miller, Context Books, 2002, pp. 358–72.

Ferguson, Suzanne, "The Short Stories of Louise Erdrich's Novels," in *Studies in Short Fiction*, Vol. 33, No. 4, Fall 1996, pp. 541–55.

Hoffert, Barbara, Review of *Tracks*, in *Library Journal*, Vol. 113, No. 14, September 1, 1988, p. 182.

Rosenberg, Ruth, "Louise Erdrich," in *Dictionary of Literary Biography*, Vol. 152, *American Novelists Since World War II, Fourth Series*, edited by James Giles and Wanda Giles, Gale Research, 1995, pp. 42–50.

Further Reading

Peterson, Nancy, "History, Postmodernism, and Louise Erdrich's *Tracks*," in *PMLA*, Vol. 109, No. 5, October 1994, pp. 982–94.

Discussing *Tracks* from the standpoint of postmodern theory, Peterson argues that Erdrich has difficulty bringing Native American history into an epoch in which history and narrative are self-referential and not representational.

Stookey, Lorena Laura, *Louise Erdrich: A Critical Companion*, Greenwood Press, 1999.

Stookey's useful companion to Erdrich's novels clarifies and analyzes the relationships and characters in the author's fictional world.

Williams, Terry Tempest, "Facing the World without Land to Call Home: *Tracks* by Louise Erdrich," in *Los Angeles Times*, September 11, 1988, Book Review Section, p. 2.

Williams's review praises the detail of Erdrich's novel.

The Good Shopkeeper

Samrat Upadhyay

1999

Samrat Upadhyay's short story has won many distinctions. It was honored by being published in *Best American Short Stories* (1999) and is often singled out by book reviewers as an excellent example of Upadhyay's best writing.

The story focuses on Pramod, who is both a young husband and a new father. At the moment that the story begins, Pramod is troubled by the recent loss of his job. Although he is a good accountant and an excellent and respected employee, the large company has replaced him with another accountant who has computer skills. The modern world has, in other words, pushed Pramod to the side. Pramod is humiliated by this experience as he must present himself to his well-financed brother-in-law and plead for help. As time passes and Pramod cannot find a job, he tumbles into a depressive state. The only escape from his worries is an affair with a nondescript woman, whom Pramod meets while sitting in a park. The woman constantly reminds Pramod that he worries too much about life and that he should take life as it comes. Later, when Pramod demonstrates that he wants to beat up everyone who has humiliated him, this same woman brings Pramod back to his senses.

In part, this story is about the false importance people attach to material things and to the artificial significance that prestigious jobs may temporarily bring them. The tumble down into obscurity can happen with one simple decision made by a large, non-caring corporation; at least that is what

happens in this story. One lesson implied here may be that people must learn to be self-reliant and create their sense of self-worth from within. Although life appears to be filled with complexities, it is in simplicity that one often finds the answers.

Author Biography

Samrat Upadhyay was born in Kathmandu, Nepal, but has spent almost as much of his life in the United States as he has in his native country. His parents were civil servants and saw to it that their son was well versed in English. When he was twenty-one, Upadhyay won a scholarship to the College of Wooster in Ohio, where he earned a bachelor's degree. He had first thought that he would major in business but found that he was not particularly drawn to that subject, so he switched to English because of his love of literature. He soon enjoyed high praise from his professors for his command of the English language, so when he was considering graduate school, he decided to pursue a creative writing degree at Ohio University. He followed this up with a doctorate from the University of Hawaii.

Upadhyay was at the University of Hawaii when he wrote and published his short story "The Good Shopkeeper," which he has stated launched his career as a writer. It was only the second short story of his to be published, and it appeared in the university's literary magazine *Manoa*. Since then, Upadhyay has published several more short stories, most of which have been collected in his *Arresting God in Kathmandu*. This collection has brought Upadhyay awards and high praise. His next publication was the novel *The Guru of Love*.

Besides his writing, which he practices every morning for three hours before his family awakens, Upadhyay is also a teacher. He has taught English in Nepal and in Saudi Arabia. Later, he taught creative writing at Baldwin-Wallace College in Ohio. In addition to his teaching assignments, Upadhyay has been an editor for *Travellers' Nepal* and for *Hawaii Review*.

In 1993, Upadhyay returned briefly to Nepal. It was there that he married his wife, Babita. As of 2005, the couple had one child, Shahzadi. As of 2005, Upadhyay teaches creative writing on the graduate level at Indiana University in Bloomington.

Plot Summary

The story opens with Pramod announcing that he has lost his job. His wife, Radhika, cries when he tells her. Then Pramod scolds her; he does not like to tell her things because she does not think "with a cool mind." But Radhika is not passive. She responds that she has a right to be emotional. It is not fair, after working for this company for three years that they let her husband go. Pramod reports that the company had no choice. They were out of money.

When his wife asks why they singled Pramod out and why they did not fire someone else, Pramod makes clear that others have more technical skills. Radhika, on the other hand, reminds her husband that other people also know "many influential people." Not to be undone, Pramod tells his wife he will go visit Shambhuda the next day.

In the morning, Pramod sets out to meet with Shambhuda. Along the way, the narrator comments on events that Pramod would normally not see: people on their way to work, others going to the temple, monkeys ready to snatch bags of food from unsuspecting people. He sees a former employer, Ram Mohan, and almost tries to avoid him until Pramod remembers how kind the old man is. Ram Mohan scorns the company that has fired Pramod.

Pramod meets with Shambhuda, who with both a confident and a lackadaisical manner tells Pramod not to worry. He will see what he can do. Then he dismisses Pramod. Just before leaving, Pramod notices all the figurines of the gods that decorate Shambhuda's house and wonders if these gods cause Shambhuda to be a success.

As time passes, everyone learns that Pramod is out of work. They are all supportive of him, but Pramod comes to hate their empathy, sensing that some of them might even be gloating at his misfortune. He dislikes his own reactions to their comments and especially dislikes the feelings he gets when he is around his wife's relatives who are better off than his family.

A month passes and still no job for Pramod. His wife suggests that they borrow money from her family, which Pramod dislikes to do. She also suggests that they sell their land in the south and buy some kind of shop, maybe "a general store or a stationery outlet." Pramod does not like this idea for several reasons. He does not believe that the land would bring much money. But he is also humiliated by the idea of being a shopkeeper. After being an accountant, he does not like the thought of having to cater to other people, especially people he does not like or who, in his view, are beneath him. At night, Pramod turns away from his wife in bed and instead fantasizes about being a man of influence. He even goes so far as to imagine himself in a big office, supervisor of a big international company, with his brother-in-law Shambhuda a mere office boy who begs for money from him.

At this point, a small and plump woman approaches Pramod while he is sitting on a park bench. She works as a domestic, cleaning other people's houses. Pramod, at first, thinks the woman is rude to talk to him. She is beneath him in status. The woman is married, but her husband lives in another town, she tells Pramod. As Pramod talks to her, he reflects on how low he has fallen since he lost his job: now he is sitting in the park in the middle of the morning, talking to a cleaning woman.

The woman tells Pramod that he thinks too much. Though Pramod feels superior to this woman, who is only referred to as the housemaid, he is attracted, at least superficially, to her simple outlook on life. She offers him a respite from his worries. So when she asks him to come to her apartment, he follows her as if he has no choice. He also has sex with her as if fate had directed it and he must comply. In other words, when he is with her he does not think. He only reacts to the circumstances. When he goes home after that first night, Pramod feels renewed. His lifted spirits make his wife ask if he has found a job, thinking that is the reason for his feeling better. But Pramod yells at her, stating that there is no job and suggests that no one, including Radhika's brother Shambhuda, can help.

The story jumps ahead, with Pramod and the housemaid walking through the marketplace on the way to her apartment when they run into Ram Mohan. Pramod is embarrassed to be seen with the woman and pretends not to be with her. Later, she questions why he was so afraid. As time passes, Pramod spends more time with the housemaid, sometimes even staying overnight with her. Thoroughly discouraged, Pramod does nothing to find work. When he visits his wife's relatives, he is moody and defensive. The men make fun of him, stating that they are the fools for working so hard, while Pramod spends the whole day without any worries. Shambhuda comes to Pramod's defense. He tells the other men to stop mocking Pramod. They all have had their troubles in the past, Shambhuda reminds them. Then Shabhuda mentions having rescued one of the men after that man had embezzled some money. Tempers flare, and one of

the men accuses Shambhuda of having murdered a police inspector. The women enter the room and calm the men. Then Radhika returns and goes directly to Pramod and accuses him of having started the fight. Pramod tells her, "You are a fool," and then he leaves the house.

In the next scene, Pramod has returned to the housemaid's apartment. The narrator states that Pramod has gone there because he wants to be anesthetized. He later asks the housemaid if she worries that her husband might show up. The woman asks Pramod, in turn, what he would do if this should happen. Pramod says that he would beat him up. Then he pretends to throw Karate punches and kicks, pretending to beat up everyone who has recently angered him, including Shambhuda. The woman laughs and asks him: "What good will it do . . . to beat up the whole world?"

Something snaps inside Pramod, making him realize his own foolishness. He tells the housemaid that he must return home, despite the fact that she has prepared him a dinner. En route Pramod stops at the temple, and once he enters his house, his mood is changed. He plays with his baby and sings to it, then surprises Radhika with a proposal of starting up a shop. That night "he started to think." And what he thought about pleased him. Maybe he would make a good shopkeeper after all.

Characters

Housemaid

The housemaid is not given a proper name. She is the woman whom Pramod meets in the park and with whom he has an affair. The housemaid tells Pramod that he thinks too much and offers him a temporary escape from his troubles. She also helps him to look at life differently. She expresses a simple acceptance of life as it comes to her, enjoying every moment instead of wasting time worrying about the details and possible consequences. Eventually Pramod realizes that this woman is only a temporary fix to his problems, and he stops seeing her. But she has comforted him during his depression over losing his job.

Kamalkanth

Kamalkanth is one of two men who often appear at Shambhuda's house at the same time when Pramod visits his brother-in-law. Kamalkanth is described as a poorly dressed man, and it is suggested that Shambhuda pays him under the table for special business services. After Pramod bumps into the men several times, Pramod notices that Kamalkanth sneers and snickers under his breath, suggesting that he and his friend are laughing at Pramod and his predicament.

Ram Mohan

Ram Mohan, a former employer of Pramod, sympathizes with Pramod about the loss of his job. Pramod times his morning walk so that he can avoid passing Ram Mohan; Pramod is embarrassed by Ram Mohan's goodness and consideration. Although Ram Mohan is sympathetic to his crisis, Pramod grows tired of hearing Ram Mohan tell him that something will come his way soon. Ram Mohan also makes Pramod self-conscious when Ram Mohan sees Pramod with the housemaid.

Pramod

Pramod, the protagonist, is an accountant who has just lost his job. Pramod knows a fellow accountant who is computer literate is still employed with the same company. Pramod has been so comfortable in his job, and he does not know how to find another one. Humiliated, he decides to seek help from his wife's relative. It embarrasses him when people ask him how he is doing, because he has no prospects and has no positive news. In this interim, he takes up with a woman whom he considers beneath him socially, and she encourages him to re-evaluate his life. He has been worrying too much about appearances, and through the housemaid, he learns to see life more simply.

Pramod's evolution from an arrogant man who has lost his job and temporarily lost his identity, to a more modest figure is the basic focus of this short story. As Pramod confronts his professional changes, the story takes on the drama of a psychological study of someone in crisis. Pramod's changes are subtle, but the results of those changes are personally dramatic for this character. He must strip himself of his ego in order to accept a possible path toward recreating his professional identity.

Radhika

Radhika, Pramod's wife, prods Pramod a bit when he begins to sulk about having lost his job, and she also tries to inspire him. When that does not work, she appears to fall into the background as Pramod is absent from their apartment. However, her anger comes to the forefront while she and Pramod are visiting Radhika's family. When the men tease that maybe Pramod has a better definition of life (one without a job and one with a

mistress), Radhika must admit to herself that all is not well in her relationship with Pramod. She yells at Pramod at this point and blames him for setting off a fight between her brother and other male relatives. In the end, it is Radhika's idea that gives Pramod hope for the future. She is dependent on her husband and his choices, but their property may serve him as he finds a new way to make a living.

Shambhuda

Shambhuda, an influential brother-in-law of Pramod and brother to Pramod's wife, is involved in the construction business and obviously makes a lot of money. He has a bulging stomach, which he displays immodestly, when he is first introduced in the story. He promises to help Pramod to find a job, but he never comes through with anything substantial. Except for one moment when he defends Pramod at a family party, there is little evidence to suggest that he has any particular commitment to his brother-in-law.

Themes

Humility

As Upadhyay's short story "The Good Shopkeeper" opens, the protagonist Pramod is just beginning his downslide from arrogance into humility. He has assumed he was sitting on top of the world with his great job as an accountant for a large corporation. He was making a good salary and proving to his wife's family (who enjoyed a better economic status than his family) that he was on equal footing with them. But corporations have no heart, this story implies. So when a more qualified young man appears with more technologically advanced skills, Pramod finds himself a victim of progress. He finds that he must take advantage of his wife's connections and humble himself in front of his brother-in-law. And when that does not work, Pramod fantasizes about having money, working in a fancy office, and in his dream it is his brother-in-law who must grovel to Pramod. But his fantasies satisfy Pramod only temporarily. So he seeks another diversion. He has an affair with a housemaid, a married woman whom he sees as socially beneath him, allowing him at least a few moments of arrogance. At this point, Pramod has still not learned how to be humble. Instead, he continues to try to find ways to make himself feel superior. This appetite for feeing superior keeps him from considering becoming a shopkeeper. Only when he is

Topics For Further Study

- Research Hinduism and the caste system, then see if what you have learned helps you find more meaning in this story. Also, find definitions for all foreign words you note in the text and see if knowing those definitions helps readers understand the passages in which they occur.

- Plan a trip to Nepal for your class. Decide how long the trip will last, what parts of the country you will visit, which festivals you will witness, and what special monuments of interest you will see. Be as detailed as possible, choosing the airlines you will use to get there as well as where you will stay and how you will travel through the country. Create a budget for this adventure as accurately as possible. Also make sure to check with the U.S. State Department to find out if there are any travel restrictions.

- The protagonist Pramod has a fantasy during the course of this short story. In that fantasy, he imagines himself sitting in a large office with his brother-in-law coming in to ask him for a favor. Reread the section of the story in which Pramod describes what he looks like and how his brother-in-law appears. Then draw a cartoon impression of that scene.

- Choose one of the minor characters in Upadhyay's short story and write a letter to Pramod. In this letter, describe your feelings for him and what he is doing with his life as he struggles to redefine himself. You might chose to be Pramod's wife, in which case you may want to let Pramod know that you are aware of the affair he is having with the housemaid. Or you could select Pramod's brother-in-law and explain to Pramod why you are having trouble finding him a job. Whichever character you choose, make sure that the letter fits in with the clues that the story provides.

---

knocked off this artificial pedestal created by ego does he come to realize that his position in society is not important. Pramod realizes, finally, that his family matters most. So it does not matter what kind of job he holds. What matters is that he does not lose his wife by having an affair with another woman and that he does take care of his family economically, even if he must work as a shopkeeper. Once Pramod is humbled by his situation, in other words, he realizes what is truly important to him.

Simplicity

At the beginning of this story, material wealth is a measure of self-worth. Pramod is proud of what he can afford. But as his possessions accumulate his life becomes more complex. The more he owns, the more he worries about maintaining his position. So when he loses his job, everything in his life begins to unravel. He worries so much he cannot see the life that is passing in front of him. He becomes blind to his love for his wife and his child. On a whim, he acquiesces to a sexual relationship when a woman approaches him. Ironically, some good comes from this affair: Pramod learns the lesson of simplicity. The woman quotes her husband as saying that city people spend all their time worrying. The woman believes that one should live moment to moment and not worry about consequences until they appear. In other words, she enjoys what she has in front of her without worrying about the possibilities that it might be taken away. She lives in a simple apartment, eats simple food, and works at a job that she does not have to worry about when she comes home. Although her life is not perfect, some of her philosophy about simplicity tempers Pramod's outlook. Rather than losing his house, his wife, and his child while he holds out for a more respectable job to be arranged for him, he needs to pursue the potential in a simple job that will provide simply and adequately for him and his family.

Modern Impersonality

Modern culture is impersonal in this short story. Pramod's loss of job is the prime example.

When he tells family and friends about his loss, they empathize with him and wonder how such a thing could happen. Pramod was a hardworking and loyal employee. He had worked for the company for three years. But the employer, an international company, is focused on money as everyone else is. Loyalty to its employees does not increase the profitability of that company. What the company demands is efficiency, which relates directly with profit. So when another man appears who is a good accountant and has current computer skills, the company demands that Pramod be replaced. Even within the family, Pramod confronts modern impersonality. His brother-in-law, although he promises to find a job for Pramod and assures him that everything will be all right, does not come through for him. Despite being part of the family, Shambhuda is a businessman who is driven by profit. The story suggests that Shambhuda might have even murdered someone in order to protect his profits. Although it is never disclosed why Shambhuda does not find a job for Pramod, the suggestion is that in this world even family cannot be relied upon to help a relative in difficult financial times. Eventually Pramod gets over his depression, he finally realizes that he has to find his own way in order to survive. Thus he realizes that being a shopkeeper may not be such a bad thing. Even though a shopkeeper does not have the same social status as a corporate accountant, Pramod hopes to be self-sufficient when he has his own business.

Style

Limited Third-Person Point of View

Upadhyay uses limited third-person point of view. The narrator tells the story with apparent objectivity, observing the protagonist and his actions. The narrator is privy to only the protagonist's thoughts. Cues are given regarding what the other characters think, but mostly these characters are depicted according to how Pramod thinks. What goes through the minds of the other characters is suggested rather than revealed explicitly. Most of the story is colored by Pramod's interpretation.

Conflict

Conflict exists between Pramod and his wife, as well as between him and other family members who are themselves in conflict, but most of the conflict takes place in the protagonist's own psyche. Pramod has a certain image of himself based on his past work. He has become comfortable and even somewhat arrogant about his professional rank. So when he loses his job, he also loses his identity. The conflict is a psychological one therefore. Pramod must create a new self-image. Resolving this conflict proves to be more of a challenge than Pramod might have guessed. At first he thinks he will receive help. He prays; he visits his in-laws. As time passes and his frustrations mount, he has conflicts with everyone who tries to communicate with him. The only one who does not appear to cause conflict is the housemaid, who offers Pramod an escape from the pressing need to find work. With the housemaid Pramod can almost forget who he is. He uses her like someone else might use a drug. Eventually, however, Pramod realizes that he must solve his own problems. He must do this by relying on himself, taking a risk, and trying something new.

Character Development

Protagonists in well-written short stories generally go through some form of dramatic change. If the main character does not develop, the character is said to be flat. The change conveys the point of the story; without significant transformation the story may seem to lack meaning. In this short story, the protagonist Pramod goes through a noteworthy evolution. In the beginning of the story, Pramod has just found out that he has lost his job. He is stunned by this announcement, but he has not fully felt the full impact of the loss. He assumes that he will find another job, hopefully one similar to the one that he just lost. As time goes by, however, he understands how much his job has defined his life. It brought money and prestige to him and his wife. In losing his job, Pramod also feels that he has lost his position in his society. As even more time passes, Pramod becomes depressed. He does not even want to feel the love of his wife or his child. He finds numbed solace in the bed of a stranger, a woman with whom he has no intentions of developing an emotional attachment. He uses her to help him forget. It finally dawns on Pramod what he really wants. He realizes that he must change his whole perspective on life. He must become self-reliant.

Historical Context

Nepal Overview

About the size of Arkansas, Nepal is north of India and just south of China. It is a land-locked country with a dramatic landscape of the

Himalayan Mountains to the north, bringing frigid weather in the winter, to the flat river plains of the Ganges in the south with subtropical weather. Mount Everest (over 29,000 feet), the world's tallest mountain, is found in Nepal as are eight of the ten highest mountains of the world. It is also a country of famine, polluted water, and rapid deforestation due to a lack of any other fuel alternatives. In the early 2000s, more than 27 million people call Nepal their home and a wide majority of these people are Hindu, making Nepal the only official Hindu state in the world. The ethnicity of the Nepalese people is a mixture of Indo-Aryans from India and Mongoloids from China and Tibet. Buddhism is the other major religion in the country, with Nepal proud to claim that Buddha was born here.

The capital is Kathmandu, which lies in the eastern portion of the country. Like the rest of the country, Kathmandu has both scenic wonders and filth and wear and tear. The country tries to maintain its heritage while coping with twenty-first-century challenges brought by a growing population and economic difficulties. More than 700,000 people live in the capital city.

Brief Political History of Nepal

Recorded history of Nepal goes back at least to 700 B.C. when the Kiratis people lived in the Nepal Valley. This was the approximate period of the Buddha's birth, and Buddhism flourished in the area. By 200 A.D., however, Buddhism had given way to Hinduism, which continues to be the major religion of the area. In more recent history, warriors from India invaded the area, and when British forces controlled major portions of India in the eighteenth century, Nepal lost part of its territory to British India. However, the country was never controlled by a foreign government. Nepal maintained its independence while enjoying good relationships both with Britain and later with India when that country reestablished its independence in the mid-twentieth century.

Nepal, the only Hindu monarchy in the world, was ruled by an inherited monarch until 1951, when a cabinet system of government was begun. Eight years later, the country held its first elections. However, in 1960, the reigning monarch, King Mahendra, dissolved the parliament, and ever since there has been little political stability in the country. In 2001, Nepal made headlines in newspapers all over the world when the crowned Prince Dipendra murdered ten of his family members, including his parents, King Birenda and Queen Aishwarya, then

took his own life. It has been assumed that the issue that spurred these killings was the prince's inability to convince his parents to allow him to marry a woman he loved. The new king, Gyanendra, in 2002, attempted to secure his own power by dissolving the current prime minister and his cabinet for incompetence. But with these acts as well as a growing insurgency by Nepalese people influenced by the political theories of the Maoists, Nepal continues to suffer from political insecurities. Voting rights have been promised by 2005. However, the insurgents are growing stronger and more active. Warnings have been issued by the U.S. government, suggesting that tourists be very cautious while visiting Nepal today.

Famous Authors of Nepal

Modern literature in Nepal often begins in the early nineteenth century with poetry of such artists as Shuwananda Das, Radha Ballav Arjjyal, and Shakti Ballav Arjjyal, whose poems are devoted to the brave acts of soldiers and kings. During the later part of the nineteenth century and into the twentieth century, there was a turn in subject matter as writers focused more on stories of mythology. One of the most well known writers of that time was Bhanu Bhakta Aacharya, who wrote *Ramayan, Badhu Shiksha* and *Ram Gita*. As the twentieth century progressed, topics for writers changed again and under Western influence, English words began to be incorporated in literary pieces. Works became more personal and topics such as sex and family dynamics were explored.

Nepalese Culture

The culture of Nepal is often described as caught between two ages, the sixteenth century and the twenty-first. While the Nepalese value their heritage and traditions, they are increasingly more in contact with Western consumer society and the urge toward capitalism is changing Nepalese lifestyle. Their arts and festivals remain shaped by the past. The music of Nepal, for example, is handed down through religious ceremony. Many of the songs are sung during religious ceremonies. The most popular (as well as most traditional) instruments are drums and wind instruments. Vijaya Dashami, a national festival held in early fall, honors the family. It is a time for music and lavish meals. Another major festival, Maha Shivatri, honors the Hindu god Shiva. Thousands of pilgrims travel to Kathmandu to the temple of Pashupatinath

A statue of Shiva, a popular pilgrimage spot during the Khumb Mela religious festival, India
© Janez Skok/Corbis

during this festival, where they bathe and fast. Pramod visits this temple soon after learning that he has lost his job.

Critical Overview

Upadhyay's "The Good Shopkeeper" was chosen for the *Best American Short Stories, 1999*, and subsequently was published in the 2001 collection *Arresting God in Kathmandu*, which won the Whiting Award for best emerging writers. Some critics, however, have pointed out some flaws. For instance, Kavitha Rao, writing for *Far Eastern Economic Review* found that Upadhyay's collection "has very little to distinguish it from other writers from South Asia," except for the fact that Upadhyay's tales are set in Nepal. But despite this criticism, Rao singled out "The Good Shopkeeper" as Upadhyay's "most successful story."

Writing for the *Village Voice*, S. Shankar also singled out "The Good Shopkeeper" in this critic's review of *Arresting God in Kathmandu*. Shankar found this one to be the "best story" in the

collection. Shankar states, "The insights into Pramod's world that Upadhyay offers through his story are subtle and satisfying," then goes on to praise Upadhyay's "fine sense of place."

Writing for *Publishers Weekly*, Jeff Zaleski praised Upadhyay for his subtleties: "there are no lush descriptions or forays into spirituality" in these short stories, Zaleski writes. Unlike other exotic stories written about lands far from the shorelines of the United States, Zaleski found Upadhyay's writing refreshing. He found the author's writing to be assured and anchored in "small yet potent epiphanies."

Alix Wilber, writing for the *Seattle Times*, was not so impressed. The writing is a little too bland for Wilber, who stated that the stories included in the collection *Arresting God in Kathmandu* are "minimalist in form language." Although Wilber found Upadhyay's stories to be interesting and his writing to be "fluent," the writing was, nonetheless," too unaccented to be interesting on its own."

Other critics have found more to praise in Upadhyay's writing. One is Ronny Noor, who reviewed Upadhyay's collection for *World Literature Today*. Noor concluded his article with these words: "These beautiful stories . . . are full of tender grace, woven in words that are not only perfectly set like beads in a necklace but also flow smoothly from sentence to flawless sentence without a bump."

Criticism

Joyce Hart

Hart is the author of several books. In the following essay, Hart examines the roles of the two female minor characters in Upadhyay's short story.

Samrat Upadhyay's short story "The Good Shopkeeper" focuses mainly on the evolution of protagonist Pramod as he sorts through his options upon losing his job. Although the female characters, Pramod's wife, Radhika, and the unnamed woman with whom Pramod has an affair, are given little space in this story, their significance and their effect upon the protagonist is profound. It might even be true that these two female characters prevent Pramod from being lost in a downward spiraling depression.

Radhika appears first of the two female characters in "The Good Shopkeeper." Although

Pramod reprimands her at the opening of the story, it is Radhika who offers the solution to his dilemma, even though it takes the entire length of the story, which covers more than a month, for Pramod to recognize and accept her advice. In the beginning, Pramod accuses Radhika of being too emotional, and he tells her this is why he is reluctant to share information with her. Her emotions, Pramod tells her, are what keep Radhika from thinking clearly. Pramod, of course, believes that he, as an accountant, always thinks in a clear, rational manner. He is, after all, a man who works with numbers all day. What could be more rational than that?

Having just lost his job and along with it, his self-image, Pramod invests in thinking clearly as the only way that he is going to successfully work his way through this crisis. And who can argue with that? On his first day of unemployment, he asserts that his own performance is not to blame for his losing his job. He recognizes that his company has run out of money and has no other choice but to let him go. "It is not their fault," Pramod tells his wife.

In response, Pramod's wife asks: "So only you should suffer?" This is a reasonable question. In a company that really cares about its employees, could not everyone come together and give up a little, instead of one person having to give up all? Although this idea makes sense, Pramod finds a flaw in his wife's supposition. He acknowledges that the person who has replaced him on the job is more technically skilled than he is. So in conclusion, it makes more sense (at least economically if not socially) that Pramod is the one who is let go. Then Radhika finds a flaw in Pramod's argument. She adds that there is one more important factor in Pramod's release that her husband might have overlooked. The man who has replaced him has more influential social connections than Pramod. Her statement implies that connections matter more than qualifications.

So Radhika's suggestion prompts Pramod to seek his own connections through his wealthy and influential brother-in-law, Shambhuda. If this connection were to work for Pramod, help would be coming from Radhika's side of the family, through his wife. But as it turns out, Shambhuda does next to nothing for Pramod. He lifts Pramod's mood from time to time, telling him that things will get better, but no job prospects ever appear. Even though Shambhuda does not find a new job for Pramod, Radhika is the one who pushes Pramod out the door and into the streets to look for another

> " The simplicity of this woman is ridiculous, Pramod thinks. At first, he even feels like laughing at her. But instead, he follows her home and engages in sexual intercourse with her."

job. She provides the impetus that Pramod needs. Even her existence along with their child heighten his need to secure an income for their household.

When Pramod realizes that finding another job, especially one as prestigious as the one he has just lost, is going to be harder than he realized, he becomes physically ill. The pressure gets to him. He pays his next month's rent out of savings, but as that month passes by, he must turn to Radhika once again. It is Radhika's family who lends him and his wife the money to manage their mounting bills. The loan gives them more time, but it also makes Pramod feel belittled. He wants to be a good provider for his family and does not want his wife's family to think otherwise. But he has no choice. Radhika understands her husband's disposition and tells him not to worry. "She was still tying to maintain an optimistic attitude," the narrator informs the readers. But this optimism is something that Pramod "no longer shared." Slowly but surely, Pramod slips out of his rational mode and plunges deeper into worry and frustration, emotions that contribute to his depression.

Now Radhika is the one to think more effectively. She conceives a logical plan that might save them: They should sell the land they own in the south and buy a shop. The money they make from the sale could afford them a well-stocked store that the two of them could work; and with a little bit of luck, they could be back on the road to success. Pramod's first reaction to this plan is defensive. His ego, in particular, is completely stunned. How in the world could he go from being an accountant at a large corporation to being a small-time shopkeeper? The idea is absurd. "I am an accountant, do you understand? I have worked for many big people," Pramod snaps at his wife. He later regrets

What Do I Read Next?

- Upadhyay's short story "The Good Shopkeeper" was first published in the literary magazine *Manoa* in 1999. However, in 2001, this same story was also published in a collection of Upadhyay's short stories called *Arresting God in Kathmandu*. This is Upadhyay's first book published in English, which went on to win the Whiting Award. A common theme runs through these stories: Upadhyay explores the changes that Nepalese face and the effects of those changes on their private lives.

- In 2003, Upadhyay published his first English novel, *The Guru of Love*. In this story, a math teacher living in Nepal has an illicit affair with a young girl. But this is more than a love story. The setting of Nepal is significant as it reveals weaknesses of the government and the strength of the Nepalese people as they try to bridge their ancient traditions with the ever-changing influences from outside.

- Kamila Shamsie's novel *Salt and Saffron* (2002) provides another version of what it is like to live in a country torn by sudden changes. This novel is set in the United States, but myths and histories of ancestors form the frame of reference for the protagonist as she manages her life. Thus the novel provides a Pakistani perspective on America.

- Award-winning author Jhumpa Lahiri published a collection of short stories called *Interpreter of Maladies* (1999). These stories focus on changes that people face in relationships and in a new land. Her characters generally are people from India, adjusting to their new lives in the United States.

- *Reading "Lolita" in Tehran: A Memoir in Books* (2003) is written by Azar Nafisi, who was a professor in a Tehran university. She resigned because of the stifling politics. After her resignation she called together a group of women who met in secret to discuss the several well-known novels in Western literature. This book is her account of those meetings.

---

his rash comments to her. But even in a more rational mood, as he lies awake at night, his pride and emotionality still overrule his rational thinking. He comes up with reasons why being a shopkeeper would not work, but none of them is actually viable. He believes that he would have trouble dealing with customers whom he dislikes. He thinks the land they own is worthless. In truth, he is totally humiliated by the whole idea. A shopkeeper is a role that Pramod believes to be below him.

Pramod literally turns his back on his wife as they lie together in bed, and metaphorically he does so by becoming sexually involved with another woman. This woman, identified only as a housemaid, is his respite from having to think. She tells him upon their first meeting that he thinks too much. She sees right through him. From the very first time they meet, she catches him in a lie. She asks where he works. This is a simple question, but it galls Pramod that she immediately touches upon such a sore topic. He tells her he works in an office. She prods on: Is it a holiday, she asks simply, realizing that most office workers would not be spending the morning in the park. She also notices how worried Pramod looks. "In this city I see so many worried people," she tells Pramod. "They walk around not looking at anyone, always thinking, always worrying. This problem, that problem." She compares her life, which she classifies as poor, to those who have much more than she does. She says, "For us poor people. Life is what God gives us." In other words, she takes what is handed to her and deals with it in the best way she can. Rich people assume they create their circumstances; they worry about protecting what they have and plan or connive how they can get more. By contrast, the housemaid suggests, poor people enjoy life more because they are resigned to their fate. They assume they are not responsible for their circumstances. Ironically their poorer living conditions free them to enjoy the present moment more, whereas rich people are so preoccupied with their wealth, that pleasures slip by unnoticed as they compete for more possessions.

The simplicity of this woman is ridiculous, Pramod thinks. At first, he even feels like laughing at her. But instead, he follows her home and engages in sexual intercourse with her. As this woman takes up more and more of his time, Pramod becomes more and more disconnected from his former self. He stops looking for a job and even refuses to go home to his family one night. But one day, after having spent an uncomfortable afternoon with his wife's family, Pramod goes to see the woman, then senses something has again changed inside of him. He lies down in her bed and instead of being sexually aroused, "he felt like a patient, ready to be anesthetized so that his insides could be removed." At this point, Pramod has grown tired of his emotions. He wants to be numb. When he acts out a scene of wanting to fight with everyone who has caused him to wallow in his emotions, the woman asks: "What good will it do . . . to beat up the whole world?"

This question throws Pramod off guard. He stops in mid-motion and ponders it. Then he gets up, kisses the woman on the cheek, and tells her that it is time for him to go home. Pramod realizes finally, through the woman's simple clarity, that he has indeed been wasting time and effort. He has been fighting the wrong battle. Instead of fighting his depressive emotions, he has been fighting all the meaningless situations that have surrounded him since he lost his job. He has taken out his emotions, in other words, on everyone around him. But now it is time to get back on track. And when Pramod realizes this, he goes straight home to the people in his life who hold the most significance. He is gleeful and takes time to notice his child. The story ends much where it began. But at the climax of this story, Pramod is a different man. He has evolved, thanks to the gentle pressures and simple insights of the two female characters of this story.

Source: Joyce Hart, Critical Essay on "The Good Shopkeeper," in *Short Stories for Students*, Thomson Gale, 2006.

Bryan Aubrey

Aubrey holds a Ph.D. in English and has published many articles on contemporary literature. In this essay, Aubrey discusses the moment of quiet epiphany in which the protagonist moves from fear and despair to acceptance and wisdom.

> " Somehow, through pathways unknown, he manages to reconnect with the flow of life, dropping his preconceived ideas about the way things ought to be and accepting with good grace the way they are."

In a *San Francisco Chronicle* review of Upadhyay's collection of stories, *Arresting God in Kathmandu*, in which "The Good Shopkeeper" appears, Tamara Straus describes the theme of the story as "the escapism of love." No doubt this is true in a certain sense, but the story is more than a testament to the therapeutic effects of an extramarital affair. It is one of those stories in which much is hidden and unsaid, a quality that makes it, in spite of the simple clarity of the prose, rather mysterious, as mysterious as life itself. It raises questions that must have occurred to many people at some point in their lives. How do transformations happen? How does a person move, when all seems lost, from a condition of rigidity, fear, and despair, to acceptance and wisdom? For this is indeed what happens to Pramod, the protagonist, in a moment of quiet epiphany that is all the more moving for the understated way in which it is presented. Upadhyay is not an author who beats his reader over the head with an explicit moral or message.

Although for the Western reader the Nepalese setting is exotic and some of the local customs unfamiliar, the basic situation in the story is easy to understand. Anyone who has endured long-term unemployment, or had a friend or family member endure it, will attest to the fact that such a situation can sap a person's confidence and self-esteem, lower his/her status in the eyes of family and friends, and even undermine his/her will to live. In a sense, a person needs as many skills and resources to cope with unemployment as s/he does to handle a job.

It quickly becomes clear that Pramod lacks such skills. He is himself a somewhat ordinary man. There is nothing special about him. With his wife and baby and his job as an accountant with a firm in the city, he is a conventional middle-class Everyman. The misfortune he meets is not his fault. It could happen to anyone, as he himself points out. And like most people in such a situation, once he has gotten over the initial shock, he tries to be optimistic about the prospects of finding a new job, saying that he will end up with something even better than before. This of course is what people say to themselves, and others say to them, in order to mask their fear that it might in fact not be so.

Pramod does everything he can to remedy the situation, especially badgering his influential, if corrupt, brother-in-law, to help him. But when nothing happens, his confidence sags. He starts avoiding people, and he has to borrow from his wife's family, who as the situation drags on, cease to treat him with respect. This wounds his pride. Pramod is very conscious of social position and class. He is aware, for example, that his wife's family is better off than his own, and he resents having to ask Shambhuda for help. When his wife comes up with a practical suggestion, that he sell their land in the south and set up a general store or a stationery outlet, he dismisses it out of hand. Being a shopkeeper is beneath him, he insists. His peremptory dismissal of his wife's suggestion shows how attached he is to his self-image as a middle-class accountant. He has his perceived position and role in the social hierarchy, and he refuses to let go of it. But since his job search continues to be fruitless, what is he to do?

Immediately after Pramod loses his job, he seems inclined, in a vague sort of way, and perhaps without being fully conscious of it, to turn to religion. Early in the morning, he goes to the temple, and even stands in line for tika from the Hindu priest in the shrine. *Tika* (also known as *bindi*) is a red dot, traditionally made from the red flower kum kum, that is applied to the forehead between and slightly above the eyes. It is thought to awaken a person's connection to the divine. Usually *tika* is worn by married women, but priests and other men who are on a spiritual path wear it also.

It is clear that obtaining *tika* is something Pramod does not usually do. He does not appear to be a particularly religious man, although religion seems to play a prominent role in his society. But on this occasion, when his life has been suddenly upset, he turns to religion, perhaps for hope and security. This is not at all uncommon for those who suddenly find themselves in a very difficult situation or who have suffered some trauma. They seek reassurance that everything will be all right.

Religious belief and practice confront Pramod again at Shambhuda's home, where Shambhuda is performing a *puja* (a devotional ceremony to the gods), which he does every morning. While Pramod waits, he gazes at the religious pictures on the wall. He is especially drawn to one that depicts Lord Shiva, one of the three most important gods in the Hindu pantheon, with the snake god, Nag, around his neck. Pramod is aware that Shambhuda is a successful businessman, and after their conversation, in which Shambhuda promises to help him, Pramod again looks at the religious pictures and wonders "if they had anything to do with Shambhuda's prosperity and quiet confidence in life." The question of whether the gods assist those who are devoted to them, or who at least follow the prescribed rituals, hovers in the background of the story. Although Pramod does not seem to consciously pursue the matter, he does take walks to the temple every morning before sunrise, and he gains solace from the temple lights, which remain lit until dawn.

After Pramod has been unemployed for quite some time, a new element is introduced into the story. This is his meeting with the servant woman in the city park, which introduces a sharp contrast of values into Pramod's rather enclosed world of family and friends. It is framed by the contrast between city and country, a literary theme as old as literature itself, used by writers from Virgil to Shakespeare. The idea is that life in the city is materialistic and corrupt. In ruthlessly pursuing their personal ambitions and self-interest and in jockeying for power over others, city-dwellers have lost touch with the simple and pure values of life that are preserved in the country. The idea is expressed by the servant woman, who remains unnamed throughout the story: "In this city I see so many worried people. They walk around not looking at anyone, always thinking, always worrying. This problem, that problem." She fears that if she stays too long in the city, she will become like everyone else. Her negative view of city life is certainly confirmed at the family game of flush that Pramod watches later in the story. The men all make cruel digs at each other, and it appears that crimes such as embezzlement, bribery, and even murder are part of the family's way of doing business.

The servant woman's approach to life is completely different from the habitual complexity of the city dweller. "I don't think that much," she says. "What is there to think about? For us poor people, life is what God gives us." Pramod reacts smugly to her comments, secure in his belief that he is more

Dunbar Square in Nepal © Tibor Bognar/Corbis

knowledgeable and sophisticated than this simple village woman. He does not stop to consider that perhaps her phrase "life is what God gives us," with its implication that the village people are content with their lot and do not argue about what comes their way in life, might have something to teach him. At the moment he is too concerned with feeling superior, and this shows once again his strong attachment to conventional social hierarchies. Pramod, in fact, can fairly be called a snob. He is shocked that the servant woman has the nerve to ask him where he works, since she is obviously from a much lower class than he is. Even talking to her is a sign of how far he has fallen, he thinks. However, this does not mean he is above going back to her apartment and having sex with her, although this takes place after he has once more reassured himself of his superiority to this woman: "he knew a lot more than she did," although he does not tell her this (no doubt he congratulates himself on his tact).

It should also be pointed out that above the bed on which they engage in sex is an another religious icon, this time a poster of a smiling Lord Krishna, one of the most beloved divinities in Hindu mythology. Once again, religion seems to hover suggestively at the margins of the story.

As the extramarital affair continues, Pramod's state of mind deteriorates, and he seems ready to walk away from his responsibilities as husband and father. A reproach from his wife, who blames him for creating the acrimony that surfaces during the game of flush, sends him out of the house, contemplating suicide. But he ends up going nowhere near the pond at the center of the city in which he thought he might have the courage to drown himself. Instead, he finds himself drawn to his lover's room. This scene is notable for the absolute contrast in mood and attitude between Pramod, who at first is so worried and depressed that all he can do is fall asleep, and the woman, who has about her an air of complete unconcern. When he asks if she is afraid that her husband may make a surprise visit to the room, she replies that she never thinks about it. It is not in her nature to do so, she adds as he questions her further. When she asks him what he would do in that situation, all his anger and aggression against the world boils up to the surface. He jumps up and makes a series of mock karate kicks as he imagines confounding all his enemies. When he has tired himself out, she says to him, "What good will it do . . . to beat up the whole world?" In response, he raises a finger "as if to say, *Wait*." But he says nothing at first. Instead, he smiles, kisses her on the cheek, and announces that he is going home to his wife.

Just what is going on here? This is in fact the crucial moment to which the whole story has been building. When Pramod raises his finger, it seems as if he is about to argue with the woman. But he does not argue. Instead, her words seem to trigger a new realization in his mind. In that moment, all his absurd macho posturing, his grievances against the world, his defiance and his despair, all fall away. His excessive concern about social status, and his rigid self-image, which so limited his ideas about what occupation he should pursue, likewise crumble away into nothing. In this moment of epiphany, his mind is at last free to embrace something new.

It is clear that after he leaves the woman, he is a changed man. Back at home, he plays with the baby and surprises his wife by indicating that he is willing to accept her idea, put to him a long time ago, that he should sell their land in the south and become a shopkeeper. The solution to his problem was there all along but he could not see it. But now, having freed himself of stubbornness, pride, and snobbery, he embraces the idea willingly, even with a sense of humor. He no longer resists the opportunity that life is presenting to him. Perhaps he may recall the words of the housemaid when they first met, that "life is what God gives us."

How does this profound change happen? Pramod offers no explanation. Somehow, through pathways unknown, he manages to reconnect with the flow of life, dropping his preconceived ideas about the way things ought to be and accepting with good grace the way they are. Did the gods who watch silently from the walls play a role in helping him? Was the housemaid in truth a messenger from God, appearing in his life for a certain purpose and departing only when that purpose was accomplished? Wisely, the author leaves the reader with the mystery and does not try to explain it.

Source: Bryan Aubrey, Critical Essay on "The Good Shopkeeper," in *Short Stories for Students*, Thomson Gale, 2006.

Bonnie Weinreich

Weinreich has a bachelor's degree in English and has worked as a staff reporter for a daily newspaper. In this essay, Weinreich considers the universal theme of the conflict between fate and free will, as demonstrated in "The Good Shopkeeper," and how the American perspective, as exemplified by Ralph Waldo Emerson in his essay

"Self-Reliance," provides insight into the protagonist Pramod.

"The Good Shopkeeper" considers the quandary every human faces: Does a person have control over his or her destiny (free will), or does some unseen force or fate control a person's life (fatalism)? Samrat Upadhyay chooses to examine this question by throwing his protagonist, Pramod, a blow that upends his world-he is fired from his job. For most readers, this is a concrete dilemma, one they can envision or perhaps have experienced. Along with Pramod's job goes his self-esteem, his position in the community, and his relationship with his family. The author is a native of Nepal, and the setting he employs may seem exotic to the American reader, but the way he carries Pramod through his challenges crosses national, religious, and ethnic boundaries. How Pramod evolves from a lost soul, who views his bad luck as out of his control and others' responsibility to fix, to a person who looks within for the response to his predicament is the thread that holds "The Good Shopkeeper" together.

In his writings Ralph Waldo Emerson (1803–1882), the noted nineteenth-century American philosopher, considers the consequences of hewing to standards set by others or breaking stride with what society mandates one of the essential parts of the human condition, and this alternative is at the center of the conflict for Pramod. Emerson's essay, "Self-Reliance," serves as a blueprint to follow as the reader watches Pramod grow toward independence and all quotations here come from this essay by Emerson.

Americans are conditioned culturally to believe they have control over their lives; it is fundamental to their approach to problem solving, and Emerson is among the standard bearers for this philosophy. In contrast, the Hindu sensibility is attuned to acceptance of fate, and in the first part of "The Good Shopkeeper," Pramod reacts to his situation with characteristic resignation. Initially, Pramod is not a sympathetic character. He spends a lot of time and energy looking to others to solve his problems. He is whiny and obnoxious, arrogant and irresponsible. He is mired in a useless routine shaped by social hierarchy. Emerson says, "Society everywhere is in conspiracy against the manhood of every one of its members." Yet Pramod, thinking his brother-in-law Shambhuda is superior because he is rich and powerful and therefore in a position to alleviate his financial problems, visits Shambhuda so often looking for help that "it took him longer and longer to give Pramod an audience." The use of "audience" here clearly sets the tone for these meetings—Pramod is the supplicant; the rich relative, Shambhuda, is his superior.

Emerson would take issue with Pramod's approach to faith as well. Everyday Pramod visits a nearby temple before daylight, afterward visiting "people of influence, people who could maneuver him into a job without the rigors of an examination or an interview. He tried to keep his faith that something would turn up." When he falls on hard times, Pramod, who is not known to be a religious man, apparently hopes for some kind of divine intervention. While left waiting for Shambhuda to finish a telephone conversation, Pramod observes a picture gallery of the gods lining Shambhuda's wall and wonders if the gods are responsible for his prosperity. For Pramod, even Shambhuda's success seems due to outside forces. For Emerson, an ordained minister who eventually left his church, "Prayer that craves a particular commodity, anything less than all good, is vicious. . . . But prayer as a means to effect a private end is meanness and theft."

Readers may identify with Pramod's bereft feelings in facing his job loss, but these sympathies give way when he ignores his family and has an affair with a housemaid he chances to meet in the park. The maid reinforces his fatalism two ways. First, she gives Pramod someone to lord over, feeding his arrogance that he is better than the maid simply because he is an accountant. He sees her as simple, yet she initiates the affair. Second, the maid articulates the idea that poor people, at least, have no power over their lives when she says, "For us poor people, life is what God gives us." Being a maid is a low position in any society, and the author further diminishes her status by not giving her a name. Pramod's liaison with her allows him to escape from the trials of his situation and the nagging of his worried wife. For his part, Pramod "didn't know what he thought of her, except there was an inevitability to all this." And as he has sexual relations with her, he thinks, "The act had an inevitability that he could not control." Again Pramod sees himself as a leaf in the wind, buffeted about by circumstances beyond his control. The American reader has trouble with this attitude; few believe one has no control over engaging in an affair. This attitude contradicts the concept of free will, of Emerson's vision of self-reliance: "He who knows that power is inborn, that he is weak because he has looked for good out of him and elsewhere, and so perceiving, throws himself unhesitatingly on his thought, instantly rights himself . . . [and] works miracles."

> "Because, in part, of its universal relevance, 'The Good Shopkeeper' is the most successful story in *Arresting God in Kathmandu*, the collection in which it appears. Readers everywhere can identify with beleaguered Pramod as he makes all the wrong choices before finding the strength to change."

It takes a family fight, a startling revelation (that Shambhuda is a suspected murderer), and some wise words from the maid to illuminate for Pramod the reality that he counts on others who are neither reliable nor worthy of the respect he has been giving them. It is important to note that, again, Upadhyay makes the women in Pramod's life powerful: Setting up shop is his wife's idea, which he rejects initially as beneath him. When he accepts the possibility of becoming a shopkeeper, he comes out of his depression, regains his self-respect, and fantasizes that as a shopkeeper he can ignore Shambhuda, and his wife will serve tea to the maid. The notion that his wife would be subservient to his mistress may offend or amuse some American readers, but it is a concept explored in another of Upadhyay's stories. It is hard to imagine an American woman finding herself in such an arrangement.

In revealing that Shambhuda may be a murderer or may have arranged a murder, Upadhyay brings the powerful down. In presenting the maid as a positive influence on Pramod, he elevates the poor and humble. Through these characterizations particularly, the author shows that position or wealth does not determine a person's character. However, Pramod's somewhat self-deluding fantasies make the reader wonder if he has learned his lesson, since he seems to be maintaining a bit of arrogance as he considers how he will treat the people who come into his shop.

Emerson closes "Self-Reliance" by saying, "Nothing can bring you peace but yourself. Nothing can bring you peace but the triumph of principles." Upadhyay guides Pramod, and the reader, through the process of self-discovery until he comes to this realization. What remains is for Pramod to allow principles to guide his actions, and Upadhyay leaves unanswered the question of whether Pramod will do so. The reader can believe, that based on his development in the story, Pramod is likely to continue on that path. That he plans to ignore the powerful Shambhuda is a step in the right direction.

Because, in part, of its universal relevance, "The Good Shopkeeper" is the most successful story in *Arresting God in Kathmandu*, the collection in which it appears. Readers everywhere can identify with beleaguered Pramod as he makes all the wrong choices before finding the strength to change.

Emerson says:

> There is a time in every man's education when he arrives at the conviction that envy is ignorance, that imitation is suicide. . . . The power which resides in him is new in nature, and none but he knows what that is which he can do, nor does he know until he has tried.

Source: Bonnie Weinreich, Critical Essay on "The Good Shopkeeper," in *Short Stories for Students*, Thomson Gale, 2006.

Sources

Noor, Ronny, Review of *Arresting God in Kathmandu*, in *World Literature Today*, Vol. 76, No. 1, Winter 2002, pp. 139–40.

Rao, Kavitha, "Another Place," Review of *Arresting God in Kathmandu*, in *Far Eastern Economic Review*, Vol. 164, No. 31, August 9, 2001, p. 50.

Richardson, Robert D., Jr., ed., *Ralph Waldo Emerson, Selected Essays, Lectures, and Poems*, Bantam Books, 1990, pp. 149, 151, 165, 171.

Shankar, S., "Getting Bourgie in Kathmandu," Review of *Arresting God in Kathmandu*, in *Village Voice*, Vol. 46, No. 34, August 28, 2001, p. 69.

Straus, Tamara, Review of *Arresting God in Kathmandu*, in *San Francisco Chronicle*, August 26, 2001.

Wilber, Alix, "*Kathmandu* Is Rare Peek inside Nepal," Review of *Arresting God in Kathmandu*, in *Seattle Times*, September 23, 2001, p. J12.

Zaleski, Jeff, Review of *Arresting God in Kathmandu*, in *Publishers Weekly*, Vol. 248, No. 31, July 30, 2001, p. 62.

Further Reading

Khadka, Rajendra, *Travellers' Tales Nepal*, Travellers' Tales Guides, 1997.
>   Caught between India and China and closed to the rest of the world until the 1950s, Nepal has been a place of great mystery for Westerners. This is a collection of stories by people who have visited Nepal.

Onesto, Li, *Dispatches from the People's War in Nepal*, Pluto Press, 2005.
>   Onesto chronicles some events occurring in Nepal. The Nepalese people have been in a long-standing war for liberation. By asking hard questions, Onesto records current events through the people who matter the most in these circumstances: those who are fighting this war.

Oshoe, Palden Choedak, *The Nepal Cookbook*, Snow Lion Productions, 1996.
>   For a different take on Nepal, readers might be interested in cooking and tasting some of the dishes for which Nepal is known. Some recipes contain a mixture of ghee, garlic, chili, and cumin.

Whelpton, John, *A History of Nepal*, Cambridge University Press, 2005.
>   Whelpton, a historian and linguist who teaches in Hong Kong, has traveled extensively through Nepal and provides a reflective history of that country.

Greatness Strikes Where It Pleases

Lars Gustafsson
1981

"Greatness Strikes Where It Pleases" by Swedish writer Lars Gustafsson, was first published in Sweden in 1981. Translated into English in 1986, it appeared in *Stories of Happy People* (Norton, 1986; in print). It can also be found in *You've Got to Read This: Contemporary Writers Introduce Stories That Held Them in Awe*, edited by Ron Hansen (New York, 1994).

"Greatness Strikes Where It Pleases" is the story of a severely mentally retarded boy who is sent to an institution for the retarded, where he grows to manhood. The story covers a period from the 1930s to the late 1970s. Although set in Europe (possibly in Sweden, the country of Gustafsson's birth, although no specific country is identified), the story might equally well have been set in the United States. In a few short pages, it reveals a great deal about the inner life of a mentally retarded person and also much about the attitudes taken by society to the mentally retarded. On one level, it is a story of loneliness, isolation, and neglect, but on another level, it affirms the uniqueness and the dignity of the mentally retarded man, who against all odds creates an imaginative life for himself that allows him to feel in harmony with the larger forces at work in nature and the universe.

Author Biography

Novelist, poet, and essayist Lars Gustafsson was born in Västerås, Sweden, on May 17, 1936.

Lars Gustafsson   Photograph by James Andanson. © Andanson
James/Corbis SYGMA

He recalls in his notebooks that he felt isolated in his early school years, since he was already thinking about the serious issues in human life and society. He wanted to be a poet from the age of fourteen. Leaving Västerås in 1955, he studied philosophy, aesthetics, sociology, and literature at the University of Uppsala, and in 1957, he received a scholarship to study at Magdalene College of Oxford University. This was also the year in which his first published prose work appeared. This was *Vägvila: Ett mysteriespel på prosa: Till det förflutna och minnet av vindar* (*Rest at the Roadside: A Mystery Play in Prose: To the Past and the Memory of Winds*). His first novel, *Poeten Brumbergs sista dagar och död: En romantisk berättelse* (*The Poet Brumberg's Final Days and Death: A Romantic Story*) followed in 1959. His first poetry collection was published in 1962.

After Gustafsson received his Filosofie Licentiat degree from the University of Uppsala in 1960, he became editor, and from 1965 to 1972 editor-in-chief, of the Swedish literary journal, *Bonniers Litterära Magasin*. In 1962, he married Madeleine Lagerberg, with whom he had two children. During the 1960s he published four collections of poetry, three novels, and five collections of essays. Selections from three of the poetry volumes

appeared in translation in *The Stillness of the World before Bach: New Selected Poems* (1988). The critical essays established Gustafsson's reputation in Europe as an intellectual who grappled with political and philosophical issues.

During the 1970s, Gustafsson traveled extensively throughout the world, and he also wrote five novels, which further enhanced his reputation in Sweden. One of these, *Tennisspelarna: En berättelse* (1977) became the first of his novels to be translated into English, as *The Tennis Players* (1983). In 1978, he received a Ph.D. in philosophy from the University of Uppsala.

In 1981, Gustafsson converted to Judaism, having rejected during the 1970s the Lutheranism in which he was raised. In the same year he published the collection of short stories, *Berättelser om lyckliga människor*, in which the story, "Greatness Strikes Where It Pleases" first appeared. The collection was translated by Yvonne L. Sandström and John Weinstock as *Stories of Happy People*, and published by New Directions (New York) in 1986.

Gustafsson emigrated to the United States in 1982 and lived in Austin, Texas, where he became adjunct professor of Germanic Studies at the University of Texas. His first marriage having ended in divorce, he remarried, to Dena Alexandra Chasnoff, and he became an American citizen in 1983.

Two of his novels during the 1980s have been translated into English. These are *Sorgemusik för frimurare* (1983), translated as *Funeral Music for Freemasons* (1987); and *Bernard Foys tredje rockad* (1986), translated as *Bernard Foy's Third Castling* (1988). The novel *En kakelsättares eftermiddag* (1991) was translated as *A Tiler's Afternoon* (1993).

Gustafsson has as of 2005 written eighteen novels, and his work has been translated into fifteen languages. He has won many awards, including the Prix Européen de l'essai Charles Veillon (1983), the Swedish Academy's Bellman Prize (1990), and the Swedish Pilot Prize (1996).

Plot Summary

"Greatness Strikes Where It Pleases" begins in the 1930s, when the mentally retarded boy is living with his family on a small farm by the woods. He has a brother and sister, older by two and three years respectively. They practice with their tools in the woodshed, making wood cars and boats, but the retarded boy is horrified by tools such as chisels, saws and axes, because he cannot learn how to handle them correctly. He also has difficulty in remembering the names of the tools. There are other tools in the shed, including a mallet that is too heavy to lift and a hanging ice saw that he is forbidden to touch. Sometimes the boy is beaten because his parents are afraid he will badly hurt himself; they want him to keep away from the tools. Sometimes his brother and sister tease him, sending him to the barn to fetch objects that do not exist. He is unsure about what things exist and what do not.

For this boy, better than tools are mushrooms that grow in the woods behind the barn. He enjoys their different shapes and smells and the way they feel when he touches them. But his parents do not allow him to go to the woods where the mushrooms grow.

He starts school in 1939, at the age of seven. World War II has just begun. The teacher at the one-room school is kind and helpful as the boy tries to learn to read. He can tell the letters apart, but he cannot make sense of words. During recess, he walks around by himself, apart from the other children. He does not understand why he is at school, and he remains there for only one week. After this one attempt to educate him, his parents send him away to an institution for retarded boys. At the institution, he misses the life he has known on the farm. He amuses himself by picking a spider "apart, leg by leg," and feeding paper to the fat boy in the bed next to him, whose habit is to eat little paper balls. The retarded boy is comforted by the patterns he observes in the wallpaper. Out of the criss-crossing lines he is able to make shapes like trees.

The following spring, in 1940, he is sent home because the institution is to be used for other purposes. After he has been home for a week, he almost drowns in a brook. He is rescued by his brother and then beaten by his parents for his carelessness.

In the spring of 1945, when he is about thirteen and living again at the institution, he becomes sexually aware and learns how to masturbate. This discovery makes him happy, because he realizes that his body holds secrets that he may be able to discover. It is "the happiest spring of his life."

During this period, he is allowed to observe other boys working in the wood shop. A new teacher is kind to him, allows him "to sort pieces of wood in the lumber room," and gives him other small tasks to perform. He is confused by the boisterousness of the other boys, but the teacher knows how to quiet things down without being abusive toward the boys. The teacher becomes the center of the boy's world.

The boy does not get on so well with the female aides. They tell him he is in the way and cause him some anxiety with their attitudes that veer between disgust and maternal feelings. There is a high turnover of staff, so the boy never really gets to know any of the aides.

After a couple of years, the wood shop teacher leaves, and many of the boys are moved to a different institution. Only the more severely retarded, including the boy, remain.

In 1952, a truck loaded with wheat overturns on the road near the institution. For weeks the boys find wheat in the ditches and hedges and play with it. They regard it as "a mysterious gift" from outside.

This is the last memorable thing that happens in the boy's life for some while. As he becomes an adult, he lives for mealtimes, and by the age of thirty he has become grotesquely fat. He is allowed to help in the apple orchard across the road, although he is not much use there. In 1956, a motorized cultivator arrives, which frightens him. He rushes back to the home, where he is left alone.

One of his peculiarities that amuses the men who work in the garden is that he is afraid of birds. If a bird such as a sparrow flies up suddenly from a bush or from a new-plowed field, he is terrified. Even as an adult, he runs babbling into the kitchen on such occasions.

At the end of the 1950s, the man's parents die. Nobody tries to explain this to him, and he does not know exactly when or in what order they die. He is just aware that he has not seen them for a few years, and he misses them in a vague kind of way.

In September, 1977, the retarded man sits in the dayroom in the new home, sixty miles from the previous one, which was torn down in 1963. He sits in his favorite spot by the window, looking out onto an asphalt yard with a wilted flowerbed and three parking places. It is a still day. He sits there for hours, moving his chair a few inches every hour so that it always remains in the patch of sunlight. In some mysterious way, he is in harmony with the entire cosmos. In the shadows cast by the leaves against the wall, he sees the mushrooms that he used to love as a child. He lets his imagination roam over those shapes, recreating many mushrooms, each one different from the others, and allowing them all to grow in fantastic and unique ways. He appreciates how mysterious life is and has a sense of its greatness, a greatness which includes himself.

Characters

The Boy

As a young child, the unnamed boy is active and curious. He loves to play in the woods, and he is especially drawn to the mushrooms that grow there. His senses are very much alive, and he discerns the way things and people smell. Although he is teased by his brother and sister, he does not seem to be unhappy. When he is sent to the home for the mentally retarded, he misses the sights and sounds of life with his family on the farm. The boy's difficulty is that he has intellectual disabilities that make it very hard for him to learn. At home, he cannot master how to use the tools in the woodshed and sometimes hurts himself trying. His language skills are also poor. He cannot connect words to things and feels that words belong to other people, not to him. At his first and only week in school, he cannot learn how to read and does not know how to make friends.

At the institution, he is not the most severely disabled of the residents. Although not able to communicate with words, he is able to wash and feed himself. He also still exhibits curiosity, observing the activities in the wood shop and being amused, and sometimes frightened, at the antics of the other boys. He responds well when a new teacher at the home treats him with dignity and keeps him busy with chores. When left to his own devices, he shows he has an active imagination, creating meaningful patterns as he stares at wallpaper, and later, when he is an adult, at the shadows of leaves against the wall.

As an adult, he suffers from institutional neglect. Left alone, without any meaningful activities, he gets fat, and his mind appears to stagnate.

The New Teacher

The new teacher is a young, quiet man who is employed by the institution to teach in the wood shop. He remains patient and calm and knows how to maintain discipline without being harsh. He treats the boys well.

Themes

Loneliness and Neglect

The mentally retarded boy, who is unable to speak and communicate his needs in a normal way, has to endure the loneliness of someone who does not fit into the expectations and norms of society.

He is at the mercy of others who order his world for him in a way that suits them, and in a way that leaves him powerless. The people who are in charge of him hold keys that he does not possess—the use of language, for example—and, as he knows, they want things from him. They want him to behave in a certain way, to respond to them in a certain way, but he never does understand what that way might be. Since humans normally organize and make sense of their world through language, he is at an enormous disadvantage, because words are a mystery to him. For this boy, language seems like an arbitrary thing, something invented by the strong, and he knows very well that he is not one of the strong.

As a child, the unnamed boy seems to be a stranger or an outsider even in his own family. His brother and sister fool him into going to look for objects that do not exist and laugh heartily as his expense when he cannot find them. He feels cut off from his siblings because they are allowed to use the tools in the woodshed and he is not. When he first attends school, he is similarly isolated. He does not mix with the other children and does not enjoy the noise they make as they play. He cuts a solitary figure. Things do not change much when he is sent to an institution for the mentally retarded. He is not allowed in the wood shop because he cannot be trusted with the tools, and the other boys sometimes laugh at him. Few people show him any understanding. The exception is the kind teacher who treats him as a human being and looks directly into his eyes as he speaks to him. During this period, when the boy is thirteen, and continuing until he is about eighteen, there seems to be a genuine possibility of what the narrator calls "an awakening." But when the teacher leaves and the wood shop closes, the opportunity for development is lost, and the pattern of the boy's life for the next quarter of a century is set. There is no longer anything in his environment to stimulate his interest. He is fed and clothed at the Home, but no other attempt is made to give him meaningful activity: "His senses were asleep: there was nothing that made enough of a claim on them." Although sometimes he is treated with kindness, as when the aides try to comfort him when he is frightened by birds, he also has to endure humiliation and lack of respect, as when the foreman, who probably means no harm, laughs at his efforts to rake leaves in the apple orchard. Progressively becoming more and more isolated, the boy, who has now grown into a man, is left to while his life away getting fat and sitting around the Home in a chair, gazing out at the yard.

From Disharmony to Harmony

For most of his life, and in most ways, the boy lacks meaningful connection to his environment. He lives in a world that does not make any sense to him. This is partly because he cannot learn to read or write or communicate verbally, which means that he cannot comprehend why things happen as they do. He is especially uncomfortable with machines, the objects that the human world has manufactured, which operate in unfamiliar ways and have power to injure him. To this boy, the world behaves in unpredictable ways. When a bird flies up suddenly from a bush and terrifies him, it is only "one of the thousand ways in which the world would turn *unreliable*."

However, he is able to enjoy his senses. As a child, he savors the smell and the feel of mushrooms and other plants that grow wild. He feels a kinship with them, even though he has no names for them. This experience of being connected to the world stays with him as the years go by. He frequently reverts to it or tries to recreate it, as a way of imposing order, familiarity, and meaning on an otherwise strange and incomprehensible world. During the only week he ever spends at a normal school, when he tries copying letters, they turn out looking like mushrooms.

Later, when he is sent to the institution, he gazes at the patterns on the wallpaper until the patterns resemble trees. Like mushrooms, trees were things he could respond to even when he was very young. When the wind blew through the big ash trees outside the schoolhouse, he thought to himself, "*The trees are so happy ... when the wind comes. That gives them something to do.*"

When he reaches manhood, he appears to others to be a fat, mentally retarded man with a vacant mind who lounges for hours in a chair by the window doing nothing. But the reality is somewhat different. As he gazes at the shadows cast on the wall by the leaves in the yard, he is once more able to revert to his love of mushrooms and the feeling of friendship that he felt in their presence. Over the years, in his imagination, he creates an almost infinite number of different mushroom shapes from the shadows, each one of which is unique. In his own way he understands the greatness and the mystery of life as it unfolds over long stretches of time. And as he moves his chair every hour to stay in the sun, he unconsciously aligns his own life with the life of the entire cosmos. Out of harmony with the human world, he silently places himself in harmony with something so much greater and more permanent.

Topics for Further Study

- Research current definitions of mental retardation. Is the condition solely related to intellectual abilities or are other factors involved? What are some of the causes of the condition? Is there any way of preventing it?

- Research the Americans with Disabilities Act of 1990. What are its main provisions? What type of disabilities does it cover?

- From your reading of the story, describe some of the good things about the care the protagonist receives at the institution and some of the bad things. What conclusions do you draw from the story about the needs of the mentally retarded?

- Reread the first three pages of the story, which describe the boy's childhood up to the age of seven. Now write a paragraph that describes a few of your own remembered experiences of being a very young child. Try to recapture how you really felt and how you saw things at that time. Are there any similarities between the boy's experience and your own?

Style

Point of View

The story is told in the third person by a narrator who has insight into how the retarded boy and later man experiences the world. The narrator is a mature and sophisticated adult; when he needs to he uses complex sentence structures (one sentence contains 132 words), and the last six paragraphs are written in a heightened, lyrical style that enables him to convey his vision of the connection between the mentally retarded man and the infinity of the cosmos. This is a reality that the man cannot know for himself, except by some unconscious instinct.

However, although the adult narrator has greater intelligence and verbal range than his subject, he uses several techniques that bring the reader closer to the experience of the retarded individual. First, the story contains no dialogue, which has the effect of conveying the locked-in nature of the boy's experience; he cannot communicate with the rest of the human world. Second, in spite of his more sophisticated consciousness, the narrator's style is predominantly simple, which conveys the childlike nature of the boy's experience. Monosyllabic phrases such as "The House, large, white, behind trees and a fence," and "a wind came through the big ash trees" suggest a child's perceptions, expressed in language a child might use. Third, metaphor (the comparison of one thing to another dissimilar thing in such a way as to bring out a similarity between them) is employed to convey how the boy experiences ordinary things in a special way. The ice axe is "a cruel giant with dragon's teeth"; and the knot he ties his shoelaces with is a "small, evil animal that the lace passed through." Fourth, in order to bring the reader closer to the boy's experience, the narrator sometimes employs the second-person form, as in, "water you inhale deeply has a strange way of stinging," and "the joiner's saws . . . that clattered so merrily when you released the tension." Finally, the boy is unnamed throughout. He is referred to only as "he." This namelessness conveys the way society depersonalizes him. He is a category—a mentally retarded male—rather than a living person with a personality and with likes and dislikes, interests and needs.

Historical Context

Treatment of the Mentally Retarded

Societal attitudes about mental retardation changed considerably over the course of the twentieth century. In the United States in the early part of the century, individuals with mental retardation were generally sent away to schools for the feeble-minded, where standards of care varied widely. These were usually large institutions, each accommodating more than one thousand children and adults. Most of the institutions were in rural areas. They often had gardens and a fully operational farm. The male inmates worked on the farm, operating the heavy machinery and tending to the animals. Females did domestic chores such as laundry. Those who were only mildly retarded cared for the more severe cases and also for the young children. Some inmates returned to their families for holidays.

Social trends in the early twentieth century, however, did not favor enlightened treatment of the mentally retarded. Instead of the retarded being viewed as harmless children who needed to be taken care of, there was a growing perception that they posed a potential threat to society. It was claimed by society opinion-makers that because of their weak powers of reasoning, the mentally retarded were more likely than others to indulge in criminal activity or immoral sexual behavior. In his book *Inventing the Feeble Mind: A History of Mental Retardation in the United States*, James W. Trent Jr. comments on the period 1900–1920, noting "the increasing insistence . . . that mental defectives, in their amorality and fecundity, were not only linked with social vices but indeed were the most prominent and persistent cause of those vices."

Along with the virtual criminalization of mental retardation, came the eugenics movement, which sought to sterilize those considered unfit to have children. The eugenics movement arose out of a scientific interest in heredity and the belief in the necessity of creating superior human stock. Eugenics attracted support from many of the leading minds of the day, including Theodore Roosevelt, Woodrow Wilson, Andrew Carnegie, and many other progressive thinkers. The goal was to use knowledge of heredity to prevent the birth of mental defectives. Eugenicists believed that by cultivating good human stock, many problems that had plagued humanity, such as poverty and crime, as well as mental retardation, could be eradicated. Soon the list included vices such as prostitution, venereal disease, illegitimate births, and drunkenness. Particularly targeted were the mildly retarded, known at the time as morons, since unlike "idiots" (those with the lowest intelligence), they could pass for normal in everyday society and were therefore more dangerous. It was also argued that mental retardation was a permanent condition and that retarded persons could not be educated.

In 1907, the state of Indiana passed the first sterilization law in the United States. Although it focused on criminals and rapists, it also included the mentally retarded. By 1917, eleven more states had followed. After World War I, fifteen more states permitted sterilization in some circumstances. In the 1927 case *Buck v. Bell*, Supreme Court justice Oliver Wendell Holmes, in upholding a sterilization law, declared "Three generations of imbeciles are enough."

The eugenics movement flourished not only in the United States but also in Nazi Germany in the 1930s and 1940s, where 400,000 people were sterilized. Involuntary sterilization also took place in

Compare & Contrast

- **1920–1940s:** In the United States, people can be confined involuntarily in an institution for the mentally retarded on the basis of a note from a physician or psychologist. In some states, the person concerned has no right to a lawyer or a court hearing. This arrangement results in the commitment to institutions of many who are not retarded but whose behavior is regarded as problematic.

  Today: People with mental retardation are guaranteed full civil rights under the Americans with Disabilities Act of 1990. This act protects access to jobs, transportation, and public places such as movie theaters, restaurants, and stores. Children and adults with mental retardation cannot be denied access to private day care on the basis of their disability.

- **1961:** President John F. Kennedy creates the President's Panel on Mental Retardation. The president calls upon Americans to address the needs of mentally retarded people and their desire to be included in the everyday life of the community.

  Today: In 2003, the President's Committee on Mental Retardation is renamed the President's Committee for People with Intellectual Disabilities. In renaming the committee, the terms "mental retardation" and "intellectual disabilities" are considered synonyms. The committee continues to address the needs of the same people as in the past, but under a more acceptable name. The new term attempts to remove negative attitudes and encourage positive images of people with intellectual disabilities.

- **1968:** The first Special Olympic Games is held at Soldier Field, Chicago, Illinois, inspired by Eunice Kennedy Shriver and underwritten by the Kennedy Foundation. The Games feature 1,000 athletes with intellectual disabilities from 26 states and Canada competing in athletics, floor hockey, and aquatics.

  Today: The 2003 Special Olympics World Summer Games are held in Dublin, Ireland. These are the first Summer Games ever held outside the United States. It is the world's largest sporting event for 2003, featuring 7,000 athletes from more than 150 countries participating in 21 sports.

- **1970s:** In the United States, the death penalty is reinstated in 1976, and execution of the mentally retarded is permitted.

  Today: In 2002, in line with international norms, the Supreme Court rules that the death penalty for mentally retarded persons is "cruel and unusual punishment" and therefore violates the Eighth Amendment to the Constitution. This opinion results in reprieves for many death row inmates, since it is estimated that as many as 10 percent suffer from mental retardation.

Sweden (where "Greatness Strikes Where It Pleases" may be set). Between 1926, when a law permitting sterilization was passed, and continuing until the 1970s, up to 60,000 women were sterilized, for reasons that included mental retardation.

In the United States in the years leading up to World War II, the institutionalization of the mentally retarded increased. Many people were committed involuntarily by court order, and they were committed for life. In 1926, there were 43,000 mentally retarded people at state institutions, and this number increased to 81,000 in 1936.

During this period, and persisting right up to the 1950s and in some cases beyond, mental retardation was regarded as a shameful thing. Few families would want to admit that one of their members suffered from the condition. According to Trent, "To have a defective in the family was to be associated with vice, immorality, failure, bad blood, and stupidity."

After World War II, when the full horrors of the Nazi embrace of eugenics became widely known, support for sterilization in the United States faded. It also became known that many previously

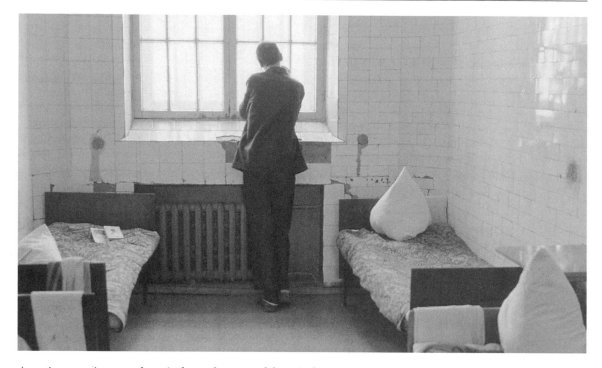

A patient staring out the window of a mental hospital   © Peter Turnley/Corbis

institutionalized mentally retarded individuals had served successfully in the U.S. armed forces during the war.

During the 1960s, there were a number of scandals about how the mentally retarded were being treated in institutions. A notorious photo essay in *Look* magazine in 1966 showed neglect, filth, and boredom in state schools for the retarded. In 1967, a visitor to the Sonoma State Hospital in California saw, as reported by Trent, "wards of naked adults sleeping on cement floors often in their own excrement or wandering in open dayrooms." Many were so heavily medicated they were in a daze. In 1972, in another public scandal, two homes for the retarded in New York were the subject of a television expose, which showed conditions, as Trent puts it, "not unlike Nazi death camps."

During this period also, there was a gradual change in public attitudes toward the mentally retarded. People began to realize that such individuals could live outside the institution and lead productive lives. In the 1970s, a public policy of deinstitutionalization led to thousands of retarded people being integrated into their communities, in public schools, and in the workplace. The emphasis was on normalization and inclusion rather than segregation.

Critical Overview

Although Gustafsson's work is not as widely known in the English-speaking world as his admirers might like it to be, the translation of his short story collection *Stories of Happy People* did receive some positive reviews when published in 1986. In *Studies in Short Fiction*, Daniel P. Deneau selected "Greatness Strikes Where It Pleases" as one of the two memorable stories in the collection. He described it as "an absorbing account" of a mentally retarded person, in which, at the end, "in lyrical prose we learn of his feeling of oneness with the universe and his understanding of the great mystery of which mankind is a part." Deneau quotes Gustafsson's statement that "Nobody really knows what a human being is," and comments that in all his stories, including "Greatness Strikes Where It Pleases," "[Gustafsson] quietly illustrates mysteries rather than certainties."

In the September 7, 1986, *New York Times Book Review*, Eric O. Johannesson noted that the book was a collection of "10 delightful and significant narratives." Although he does not mention "Greatness Strikes Where It Pleases" directly, his general comments can be applied to it. According to Johannesson, the book "celebrates possibilities.

In their efforts to cope with particular situations, Mr. Gustafsson's characters are generously granted sudden insights, epiphanies or sorts." In a fictional world that "seems inherently valueless, value is conferred by a shift of point of view, of perspective. Thus new possibilities are offered. It is a joyous, life-enhancing philosophy."

Charles Baxter, in his introduction to the story in the anthology, *You've Got to Read This: Contemporary Writers Introduce Stories That Held Them in Awe*, describes it as "something of a miracle: it induces in the reader a bit of a trance, and in this trance it convincingly portrays its subject as mysteriously exceptional, godlike." Baxter also has praise for Gustafsson's "very tricky maneuver," in which the protagonist's manner of perceiving the world "must come to us through words and a literary language that the boy and subsequently the man do not possess." Baxter praises the narrator for not taking pity on the mentally retarded character and for granting him "*nobility*, free from condescension." However, in illustrating how the narrator accomplishes this, Baxter misreads the entire paragraph beginning "In a world that had no center, he reigned like a quiet monarch," which in fact describes the young teacher at the institution rather than the protagonist.

Criticism

Bryan Aubrey

Aubrey holds a Ph.D. in English and has published many articles on contemporary literature. In this essay, Aubrey discusses how Gustafsson gives the mentally retarded man a dignity that belies his intellectual deficiencies and how the story compares with other literary works that include mentally retarded characters.

Gustafsson's "Greatness Strikes Where It Pleases" says a great deal in a short space about mental retardation and how it was regarded in the mid-twentieth century. It deserves a place alongside other short stories of the century, such as Jack London's "Told in the Drooling Ward" (1914) and Eudora Welty's "Lily Daw and the Three Ladies" (1941), both of which treat the subject of mental retardation with humor and understanding.

The boy in Gustafsson's story is recognized by his family as being retarded when he is still very young. He does not learn as quickly as his brother and sister, and his language skills lag behind the

> **"** Instead, artfully combining images of motion and stillness, and alternating between the vast and the minute--from the galaxy to the unborn fetus-- he invests the severely retarded, obese man with a massive dignity, a greatness even, by placing him in harmony with the great rhythms of the cosmos and with its inscrutable mysteries and purposes."

norm. But his parents seem to have little idea of what to do with him. They beat him so that he will not go to the woodshed and hurt himself, and they also ban him from the woods behind the barn, which is the only place he feels at home. They no doubt feel protective of his welfare, but like other parents of a mentally retarded child, they must decide what to do with him. This boy is given only a week at a normal school. When he cannot learn anything in that time he is, one presumes, declared impossible to educate—a not uncommon attitude at the time. Not knowing what else to do with him, and perhaps feeling the stigma often attached to those who had a retarded person in the family, his parents send him to an institution. For the better part of the century, institutionalization of the retarded was the norm. It was considered better for the general welfare if they were herded together, isolated from society's embarrassed and disapproving gaze.

The home in the story takes in boys of all levels of mental retardation. Some are severe cases, such as the fat boy who makes little paper balls out of anything he can find and eats them. Some of the boys cannot feed themselves properly; most of them move around slowly, and "some were so deep

What Do I Read Next?

- Gustafsson's short novel *Funeral Music for Freemasons* (1983; English translation, 1987) tells the story of what has happened to three people who knew each other at the University of Uppsala in the 1950s. One is a poet who later works as a tour guide in Africa; another tries but fails to establish a career as an opera singer; and the third becomes a successful nuclear physicist at Harvard.

- William Faulkner's *The Sound and the Fury* (1929), besides being considered one of the most important American novels of the twentieth century, is interesting because of its treatment of Benjy Compson, a severely mentally retarded individual who narrates the opening section. Benjy cannot talk and is eventually sent to an asylum. The novel as a whole traces the decline of an aristocratic Southern family from 1910 to 1928.

- John Steinbeck's *Of Mice and Men* (1937) is a somber tale about two laborers, George and Lennie, who dream of creating a better life for themselves as farmers in California. Lennie is mentally retarded. He possesses great physical strength and is devoted to George but, because of his simple mind, he is helpless to exert any influence on the tragic course of events.

- The *New York Times Book Review* commented on the similarities between some of Gustafsson's stories and those of the Danish writer, Isak Dinesen. Dinesen's *Winter's Tales* (reissue ed., 1993) contains some of her best work, in which fairy tale and myth coexist with a deep understanding of human nature.

---

in their own worlds that nothing could have disturbed them." The protagonist is himself considered one of the "hopeless ones," but that is only after an encouraging period in his life comes to an end. The shining light in this story is the unnamed teacher who arrives at the home when the boy is about thirteen years old. The fact that there is a teacher at all shows that the home does make some effort to educate its residents, unlike some of the worst institutions in Europe and the United States that during the twentieth century had the responsibility of caring of some of society's most vulnerable citizens. In the story, the boys who are only mildly retarded are given practical training in the wood shop, and their new teacher makes every effort to involve the unnamed protagonist, who is more severely retarded, in useful activity. He is allowed to sort pieces of wood, sweep floors, and empty pails of wood shavings. The teacher treats him like a human being, and the boy responds. He is made to feel that he really exists, even though he still lacks language skills, and the other boys laugh at him.

The real tragedy in the boy's life comes after the teacher leaves. No one thereafter takes much notice of him, and as a result of his neglect, he "slip[s] away," into his interior world, isolated from meaningful human contact. As an adult he is allowed to get fat, and apart from his supervised and unrewarding trips to the apple orchard, he appears to spend most of his time, for many years, sitting in a chair in the dayroom gazing out of the window.

It is here that the story takes an almost mystical turn. The arc of the retarded man's life has appeared to be plunging downward. His parents are dead. He has no friends. No one thinks about him. He has nothing to do. As the narrator puts it, he is "quite empty," and this condition has endured for ten years. But then comes the astonishing reversal. The emptiness turns out to be an illusion. Hidden to the undiscerning eye is a fullness in this man's life that belies his apparent isolation. Far from being empty, his mind is in fact intricately at work, constructing meaning and delight for himself in the mushroom patterns he creates from the ever-changing shadows of the leaves on the wall. These images reconnect him to nature, reminding him of the kinship he felt with mushrooms in those long ago days in the woods, before society labeled him as a mental defective and packed him off to an institution. As he sits and watches, and with an ingenuity that no observer would suspect, he allows his self-created mushroom-shapes to grow, to live and to die in a natural cycle that makes him feel in harmony with nature's infinite variety, with the entire stream of time and space, of which he knows himself, all "mysterious and great," to be a part.

No one had ever written about a mentally retarded person in this way before. The stories by London and Welty, although they empathize with the retarded, are more naturalistic in vein. London creates an entertaining adventure around Tom, his first-person narrator, who is a twenty-eight-year-old "feeb," that is, a resident of a home for the feeble-minded, in California. The twist is that Tom, who works as an attendant and helps to feed the more severely retarded (the "droolers" of the title), is a lot smarter than many of the so-called normal people who run the institution. In Welty's story, three respectable ladies in Mississippi, horrified by the emerging sexuality of the mildly retarded Lily Daw, conspire to have her sent to the Ellisville Institute for the Feeble-Minded. The story is a satire which exposes the fear that people had at the time—the story was published in 1941—of the supposed rampant, immoral sexuality of the mentally retarded.

Gustafsson's purpose is quite different. He does not try to pretend that the boy is more intelligent than he appears or poke fun at or criticize those who have charge of his life. Instead, artfully combining images of motion and stillness, and alternating between the vast and the minute—from the galaxy to the unborn fetus—he invests the severely retarded, obese man with a massive dignity, a greatness even, by placing him in harmony with the great rhythms of the cosmos and with its inscrutable mysteries and purposes. By moving his chair, so slowly, so awkwardly, with such difficulty, to ensure that he always stays in the sliver of sunlight that illumines the floor of the dayroom, he becomes, in spite of his big, cumbersome body, a tiny part of the eternal cosmic dance.

Perhaps the only work of literature that comes anywhere near a resemblance to this extraordinary tour de force is William Wordsworth's poem "The Idiot Boy," from his *Lyrical Ballads* (1798). In this ballad, a woman named Betty Foy sends Johnny,

her retarded young son, out on a pony at night to fetch the doctor to aid a sick neighbor. Johnny, not grasping what is expected of him, fails to summon the doctor and instead spends the entire night out under the stars, worrying the life out his mother. But the "idiot boy" is the real hero of the poem. In his simplicity, he possesses a spontaneity and oneness with nature that eludes the adults in the poem, who are weighed down by their worries and concerns. Several times Wordsworth uses the word "glory" in association with Johnny, which, like Gustafsson's use of the word "great" in connection with his protagonist, is not a word that most people would immediately associate with the mentally retarded. But in the penultimate stanza of "The Idiot Boy," for example, Betty asks Johnny what he did all night, to which he responds, "The cocks did crow to-whoo, to-whoo, / And the sun did shine so cold." The narrator comments in the following line, "Thus answered Johnny in his glory." Like Johnny, the retarded man in "Greatness Strikes Where It Pleases" has an inner life that cannot be appreciated by those who assess human worth only in terms of narrowly defined notions of intelligence. As he sits alone at his window, he is a part of what Shakespeare, in *The Winter's Tale*, called "great creating nature" (IV, iv, 89), which has a place and a purpose for everything under the sun, including those who, through no fault of their own, are left in isolation to spin their dreams and seek their connection to the great whole.

Source: Bryan Aubrey, Critical Essay on "Greatness Strikes Where It Pleases," in *Short Stories for Students*, Thomson Gale, 2006.

Ia Dübois

In the following essay, Dübois discusses Gustafsson's writing career.

Lars Gustafsson is one of the most prolific Swedish writers since August Strindberg. Since the late 1950s he has produced a voluminous flow of poetry, novels, short stories, critical essays, and editorials. He is also one of the few Swedish writers who has gained international recognition with literary awards such as the Prix International Charles Veillon des Essais in 1983, the Heinrich Steffens Preis in 1986, Una Vita per la Litteratura in 1989, a John Simon Guggenheim Memorial Foundation Fellowship for poetry in 1994, and several others. His major works have been translated into fifteen languages, and Harold Bloom includes Gustafsson in *The Western Canon: The Books and School of the Ages* (1994). While the problem of identity has been the defining theme of Gustafsson's writings,

"On the other hand, realism embraces his poetry as much as the enigmatic is omnipresent in it."

his social criticism has often vexed the Swedish cultural elite. As a result he is seen as a controversial writer in Sweden rather than as one embraced by the establishment. Recurring references to his native province of Västmanland in his works have led Swedish critics to characterize Gustafsson as a "lokalpoet" (provincial poet). In contrast, international critics view him as a philosopher and even a "universalgenie" (universal genius), as one reviewer wrote in the German newspaper *Kieler Nachtrichten* on 28 October 1993. In 1996, when Gustafsson received the Pilot Prize in Sweden for his writings, the jury defined him eloquently as a "diktarfilosof, fantast, encyklopedist, hemmastadd främling på varje breddgrad från Västmanlands slussar till Texas vidder" (a poet philosopher, a dreamer, an encyclopedist, a stranger familiar with every latitude from the locks of Västmanland to the Texas plains).

In *The Public Dialogue in Sweden: Current Issues of Social, Esthetic and Moral Debate* (1964), Gustafsson writes: "People have spoken of the vacuum which Christianity has left behind, how a language which was meant to express the drama of the inner life ceased to be public property when the corresponding articles of faith also ceased to be.... They have said that it is a job for the modern author to supply us with such a language." Acutely aware of what he saw as a profound spiritual crisis in society—a crisis paralleled within the individual—he set out to find that lost language. His writings describe this search, which he conducts on two fronts: outwardly, in the form of social criticism, and inwardly, in the form of a probing quest for individual self-awareness. Gustafsson's discussions of philosophical and existential questions, with frequent mention of such authorities as Heraclitus, René Descartes, Søren Kierkegaard, Friedrich Nietzsche, and Ludwig Wittgenstein, especially displays his analytical-philosophical erudition. He shares the desire of these philosophers to identify and define human reality further and to explore the "tillstånd mellan tillstånden" (in-between stage), the dimension between the soul and the world, for answers to the enigma of human existence.

Lars Erik Einar Gustafsson was born on 17 May 1936 in Västerås, Sweden, to Einar H. Gustafsson, a merchant, and Lotten M. Carlsson Gustafsson. In *Ett minnespalats: Vertikala memoarer* (A Palace of Memories: Vertical Memoirs, 1994) he reminisces about walks to a park with his father, recalling how the smoke from his father's cigarette and the smell of his wet wartime uniform conveyed a sense of comfort and security to the young Gustafsson. On the other hand, he mentions his mother in the memoir only in relation to parental arguments, a fact that is interesting because of the elusive role that women play later in his works. His personal notebooks, donated to the University of Uppsala, reveal the author as an outsider who, as a teenager, was already thinking as an adult. The pain of isolation during these early school years—combined with his memories of yellow light reflected on his grandmother's kitchen floor, of the smell of wet wool, of the images of murky river water in his native city, and of the nature of the surrounding province—imbue Gustafsson's novels of the 1960s and 1970s.

In 1955 Gustafsson left Västerås to study philosophy, aesthetics, sociology, and the history of literature at the University of Uppsala. During the Uppsala years he often debated about the function of metapoetry in Swedish literature of the 1950s with Göran Printz-Påhlson, a contemporary Swedish poet and literary critic. He also helped establish the literary journal *Siesta* in 1956, where he debuted as a poet in the same year with "Gestaltlös sångare" (Singer without a Figure). In 1957 Gustafsson received a scholarship to study with Gilbert Ryle at Magdalene College of Oxford University, where the analytic and linguistic philosophy of Ryle and Wittgenstein became an integral part of Gustafsson's literary pursuit and the focal point of his continued academic research. He received his Filosofie Licentiat degree—a predoctoral degree—from the University of Uppsala in 1960. In 1978 he received a Ph.D. in theoretical philosophy, also from the University of Uppsala. His dissertation, *Språk och lögn: En essä om språkfilosofisk extremism i nittonde århundradet* (Language and Lie: An Essay on Extreme Linguistic Philosophy in the Nineteenth Century), was published that same year.

Vägvila: Ett mysteriespel på prosa: Till det förflutna och minnet av vindar (Rest at the Roadside: A Mystery Play in Prose: To the Past and the

Memory of Winds, 1957) was Gustafsson's first published work of prose. Yet, he considers *Poeten Brumbergs sista dagar och död: En romantisk berättelse* (The Poet Brumberg's Final Days and Death: A Romatic Story, 1959) his first novel—a romantic novel-within-a-novel, in which the narrator finds Jacob Brumberg's diary and a draft to a novel called "The Prince." This work exemplifies the romantic trend in Swedish literature of the 1950s; in *Tre Romantiska Berättelser: Studier i Eyvind Johnsons* Romantisk berättelse *och* Tidens gång, *Lars Gustafssons* Poeten Brumbergs sista dagar och död *och Svens Delbrancs* Kastrater (1999), Leif Dahlberg underscores certain intertextual references in Gustafsson's book, such as Friedrich von Schlegel's *Lucinde* (1799), Rainer Maria Rilke's *Duineser Elegien* (1923; translated as *Duino Elegies*, 1939), and James Joyce's *Ulysses* (1922). The erudition and affinity for philosophy, mythology, and metaphysics that characterized Gustafsson's works for the next three decades already appear in *Poeten Brumbergs sista dagar och död*. Increasingly known in literary circles at this time, he also began developing a reputation as a novice who challenges established authors.

Gustafsson's career solidified during the 1960s with the publication of four poetry volumes, three novels, and five collections of critical essays. In the novel *Bröderna: En allegorisk berättelse* (The Brothers: An Allegorical Story, 1960) identity conflicts and a childhood trauma appear for the first time. Here they are presented through the mythological motif of twins. In the three novels that he wrote during the 1960s, including *Bröderna, Följeslagarna: En äventyrsberättelse* (The Companions: An Adventure Story, 1962), and *Den egentliga berättelsen om Herr Arenander: Anteckningar* (The Real Story about Mr. Arenander: Notes, 1966), loneliness is a common theme. Gustafsson's memories from childhood, such as the reflection of yellow light on his grandmother's kitchen floor and the red schoolhouse where he was the student of an abusive teacher, permeate all three works. The autobiographical aspect of the novels are further underscored through their various depictions of a young boy growing up in Västmanland; of a college student and his adventurous journey through Europe to find out who he really is; and, finally, of Mr. Arenander, who—sharing the memories of the young boy and the college student—personifies the culmination of identity conflicts and of existential loneliness.

Since Gustafsson was involved in debates about poetics in the 1950s and published his first poem in 1956, his verse reflects the traditional style and motifs that critics have defined as emblematic of this time. His first poetry collection came out in 1962. *Ballongfararna* (The Balloonists) was followed by *En förmiddag i Sverige* (A Morning in Sweden, 1963), *En resa till jordens medelpunkt och andra dikter* (Journey to the Center of the Earth and Other Poems, 1966), and by *Bröderna Wright uppsöker Kitty Hawk och andra dikter* (The Wright Brothers Look for Kitty Hawk and Other Poems, 1968). Selections from these three volumes appeared in translation in *The Stillness of the World before Bach: New Selected Poems* (1988). In accordance with the realist trend of "nyenkelhet" (new simplicity), as practiced by Swedish writers in the 1960s, Gustafsson's verse style is direct and to the point. On the other hand, realism embraces his poetry as much as the enigmatic is omnipresent in it. His desire to make visible what is invisible motivates recurring existential questions also in these verse collections; his use of Jules Verne's science-fiction classic *Voyages au centre de la Terre* (1864; translated as *Journey to the Center of the Earth*, 1872); and their references to explorations of the North Pole—whether by balloonists or by seafarers or through alchemy and mysticism. In his foreword to *Ur bild i bild: Samlade dikter 1950–1980* (1982), Gustafsson describes the calling he felt to be a poet, at the age of fourteen: "Poesins demon eller ängel måste ha gripit mig om strupen sommaren 1950" (The demon or angel of poetry must have grabbed me by the throat in the summer of 1950). Thus, he is foremost a poet whose lyricism also informs his prose.

The 1960s were eventful and productive years for Gustafsson. In 1962 he married Madeleine Lagerberg, with whom he has two children, Joen and Lotten. Hired in the early 1960s by *Bonniers Litterära Magasin*— a journal put out by Albert Bonniers Publishers in Stockholm—he worked by day as an editor and wrote his poetry and novels at night. Gustafsson served as editor in chief of the magazine from 1966 to 1972. Through his work at Bonnier he became friendly with prominent Scandinavian and international authors and literary organizations—such as Gruppe 47 (Group 47), an association of German-speaking writers that presented his poems in translation at a reading in Sweden in 1964. Ultimately enhancing his international career, this event catalyzed Gustafsson to immerse himself in German cultural life. Since that presentation he has returned to Germany frequently to read from his own works, to write, and to lecture. Gustafsson's years at *Bonniers Litterära Magasin* were also controversial—largely because of certain social upheavals, both in Sweden and abroad. In 1965 he published Göran Sonnevi's poem "Om kriget i Vietnam" (On the War in Vietnam), which in effect demarcated a new period of political and "factional" writing in the country; "factional" is a term, prevalent in Sweden in the 1960s, that reflects a combination of the words "facts" and "fictional." Gustafsson's efforts to transform the traditional and conservative journal into a progressive and liberal medium in line with its time reaped much criticism, from both within and without the house of Bonnier.

While Gustafsson's novels and poetry evince existential and psychological questions in the personal sphere, his essay collections verify his public position as a European intellectual with a particular focus on the political and the philosophical. He takes his responsibility as an intellectual seriously, asserting in the 7 July 1980 issue of *Svenska Dagbladet* that "De intellektuellas uppgift i ett samhälle är att bidra till dess självkännedom" (The intellectuals' task in society is to contribute to its self-awareness). In *The Public Dialogue in Sweden* he suggests that the "nihilism of values" in contemporary Swedish society reflected the ongoing philosophical debates of the 1940s and 1950s. Gustafsson's interest in exploring diverse events and personae in the arts and sciences is quite evident in *Förberedelser till flykt och andra berättelser* (Preparations for Flight and Other Stories, 1967), a work that he calls a turning point in his career as a writer.

In a postscript to the 1976 edition of *Förberedelser till flykt och andra berättelser*, Gustafsson remarks that although the book was largely forgotten soon after it was first published, stories from it were later translated and received acclaim in other countries. For Gustafsson this book captures the emptiness and coldness he was experiencing at the time of its writing—conditions that he tried to depict by experimenting with different literary techniques. "Besökaren" (The Visitor), a story from the collection, describes an angel who, on a cold winter night, sees a lonely man on a country road. The angel tries to reach into the man to undo the enigma his life embodies but finds only coldness and emptiness—then leaves in horror while the man struggles toward the warmth of a yellow light shining from his house. *Förberedelser till flykt och andra berättelser* especially foreshadows Gustafsson's works of the 1970s. The juxtaposition of warmth with coldness seen in "Besökaren" reappears as a theme in the poetry collection *Varma rum och kalla* (1972; translated as *Warm Rooms and Cold*, 1975). The idea of a void sensed within an individual—a feeling that, as Gustafsson describes, results from an oppressive power system and its public lies—also recurs in his verse. These motifs dominate the five novels he wrote in the 1970s.

While Gustafsson and some critics view *Förberedelser till flykt och andra berättelser* as a transitional work, others rather see the epic poem *Kärleksförklaring till en sefardisk dam* (Declaration of Love to a Sephardic Lady, 1970; selections translated in *The Stillness of the World before Bach*) as a turning point in his writings. The poem starts with reminiscences of cold winter days in early childhood and, typical of a Gustafsson text, progresses to reflections on world literature and history. Yet, the verse is foremost an affectionate declaration to a "dam, krinna, flicka" (lady, woman, girl) who has the power to turn the speaker's coldness and bitterness into mourning and fatigue. She is his true inner self, his "anima," a metaphysical motif that Gustafsson employs in his verses of the 1970s and 1980s. Most strikingly, at the time of composing *Kärleksförklaring till en sefardisk dam* Gustafsson began to compare his writings to "ett sorgearbete" (a grief work).

The female characters in Gustafsson's works are rarely women of flesh and blood. Instead, they are creatures from mythology—such as Circe, Eurydice, and Medusa—or the persona's anima or a seductive, redheaded woman who appears in his life for a fleeting moment. In *Kärleksförklaring till en sefardisk dam* the object of the speaker's love relates to memories of women who have offered him a sense of warmth and security: "Först i tui- eller tre års åldern, / förväxlade jag dig med en mormor Emma, / . . . Nästa gång jag åter såg dig var du en sefardisk dam" / (First, two or three years old, / I confused you with a grandmother Emma, / . . . Next time I saw you, you were a Sephardic lady). The Sephardic lady does not stay a muse in this poem yet personifies the speaker's anima, which Carl Gustav Jung defined as the archetype of the human soul: "Du är min anima, och jag känner dig inte" (You are my Anima, and I don't know you). A metaphysical symbol, she also represents Gustafsson's inner quest. While the poem calls up incidents from the speaker's past— and displays images from Gustafsson's novels and poems of the 1960s—it also signals a more direct link to Gustafsson's life through the mention of certain persons, places, and events. At the same time Gustafsson portrays the persona as a European intellectual and thus contrasts it with himself, a poet from provincial Västmanland.

On 16 September 1970, around the time that Gustafsson wrote *Kärleksförklaring till en sefardisk dam*, Jerome Hollander—then the American ambassador to Sweden—gave a talk about the Vietnam War at the cathedral in Västerås. The event drew protest and resulted in an incident of police brutality. This politicization of the religious sphere of the cathedral outraged Gustafsson, who five days later requested, in a letter to the Bishop of Västerås, that his membership in the Lutheran State Church be withdrawn. (Until recently in Sweden, citizens were Lutherans automatically at birth; in 1996 the Swedish government began the process of separating itself from the Church and made the separation official in 2000.) In 1981 Gustafsson converted to Judaism, eleven years after the Sephardic lady in *Kärleksförklaring till en sefardisk dam* occasioned the first reference to Judaism in his work.

Gustafsson spent most of the 1970s writing a "pentalogy," the five works of fiction that cemented his reputation as one of the most important Swedish novelists: *Herr Gustafsson själv* (Mr. Gustafsson Himself, 1971), *Yllet* (The Wool, 1973), *Familjefesten* (The Family Reunion, 1975), *Sigismund: Ur en polsk barockfurstes minnen* (1976; translated as *Sigismund: From the Memories of a Baroque Polish Prince*, 1985), and *En biodlares död* (1978; translated as *The Death of a Beekeeper*, 1981). All of these works were later collected and republished as *Sprickorna i muren* (The Cracks in the Wall, 1984) with a postscript by the author. The novels share a protagonist named Lars—whose life echoes Gustafsson's own—and feature the recurring phrase "Vi börjar om från början. Vi ger oss inte." (We'll start all over. We won't give in.) The first novel, *Herr Gustafsson själv*, opens with familiar images of a lonely childhood and of disturbances at school. On an airplane to Berlin the protagonist, Lars, meets redheaded Hanna von Wallenstein, a philosophy professor. With Wallenstein's help, Lars embarks on a quest into his past and his soul, commencing his "grief work." In *Herr Gustafsson själv* Gustafsson also makes repeated references to Hector Berlioz's *Symphonie Fantastique* (1830), instilling in the novel a sense of the fantastic in both its form and content.

Herr Gustafsson själv represented the author's attempt to establish his authenticity as a writer, which he did by presenting the protagonist with his own name and biographical facts, thus confusing the boundaries between autobiography and fiction. Many critics viewed his experimentation as self-sublimation. The polemic aspect of the novel—Gustafsson's criticism of the "public lie" that

infiltrates society and further separates the individual from the government—was seen as a sign of the writer's own search for power. In contrast Gustafsson has asserted more than once that the novel is not about himself but rather about the 1960s. Understandably, his autobiographical style and prominent position as editor in chief of *Bonniers Litterära Magasin* made him an easy target for criticism. For example, Lars Bäckström, his former friend and colleague, wrote that

> "Herr G" i romanen visade sig ha för mycket gemensamt med den LG som är en etablerad maktfigur, kritiker i *Expressen*, förlagsman och multinationell författarföretagare inom Bonnierkonglomeratet. Från en sådan position kan man väl uträtta åtskilligt av värde men man saknar motivation, ja, det är emot ens intresse att skärskåda sig själv.

> ("Mr. G" in the novel turned out to have too much in common with the LG who is an established power figure, critic at the daily *Expressen*, editor and multinational author-entrepreneur within the Bonnier publishing conglomerate. In such a position one could do a great deal, but one lacks motivation, yes, it counters one's own interests, to scrutinize oneself.)

During his years with *Bonniers Litterära Magasin*, Gustafsson endured many attacks for giving the journal a new liberal slant and responded publicly to diatribes from the press. In 1972, having received a one-year fellowship from the Deutscher Akademischer Austausch Dienst in Germany, he resigned from his position and left with his family to write in Berlin, where he worked on most of his next three novels—*Yllet*, *Familjefesten*, and *Sigismund*.

If *Herr Gustafsson själv* is Gustafsson's most controversial novel, *Yllet* is his most emblematic because of his use of the smell of wet wool to describe the stagnation of Swedish society. Wool has an ambiguous role in the novel, as the protagonist of *Yllet* suggests: "Ylle har två egenskaper förstår ni. Det skyddar mot kyla, mot vinter och blåst. Men det sluter inne också" (You see, wool has two characteristics. It protects against cold, against winter and wind. But it also confines). Unlike Gustafsson's previous works of the 1970s, *Yllet* focuses much more on descriptions of nature in Västmanland and of life in the small town of Trummelsberg. The main character, Lars Hedin—born, like Gustafsson, in 1936—has left his career as a university academic to become a math teacher in a junior high school. He becomes increasingly frustrated and disappointed by the petty politics of the school and the community that supports it. Hedin finds relief from his suffocating existence in his efforts to rescue a brilliant student from being expelled because of misbehavior. In the course of helping the teenager, Hedin becomes romantically involved with his girlfriend. The novel is thus both a fierce criticism of the alienating bureaucracy in Sweden and a sensual yet doomed love story.

Gustafsson continued his social criticism in *Familjefesten*, in which social power is no longer merely symbolic but woven into the actual plot of the novel. In the context of a family reunion in the Västmanland countryside, the bureaucrat Lars Troäng reminisces about the government power games that he tried to stop by leaking information to the news media. Surprisingly, instead of the expected scandal, his leaks are suppressed by the media and he is viewed as paranoid. *Familjefesten* constitutes an "action novel" based on certain Swedish political scandals of the 1960s, such as the so-called IB-Affair—an incident of espionage that the secret police in Stockholm mishandled in the early 1960s. The novel both emphasizes Gustafsson's efforts to make visible the infiltration of public lies in society and reflects the topic of the dissertation—language and lies—that he was also writing at the time.

Although *Yllet* and *En biodlares död* have been more popular in Sweden and other countries, Gustafsson writes in the postscript to *Sprickorna i muren* that *Familjefesten* is the darkest of the five novels, while *Sigismund* is the best. *Sigismund* was written during years in Germany, where much of the plot is also set. Although *En resa till jordens medelpunkt och andra dikter*, his poetry volume of ten years earlier, had already evidenced his affinity for Verne, the novel occasioned Gustafsson's first attempt to introduce an element of science fiction into his prose. He makes science fiction thematic in two of the four individual stories in *Sigismund*: in one story about an intergalactic war and in another story about Sigismund, the king of Poland and Sweden in the seventeenth century. King Sigismund role-plays with someone called Mr. Gustafsson, an author writing in Berlin, and a third character, the woman painter Laura G., enhances the complexity of one of the stories as the female version of Mr. Gustafsson. The encouraging outlook "You can, if you want to" emanates from the interaction of these personages. Lies and secrets are conquered as the king awakes in his sarcophagus and Laura G. is allowed to descend into and explore Hell.

Gustafsson introduces psychological and philosophical aspects into the novel to create a light and hopeful conclusion to his exploration of the public lie. The interaction between King Sigismund and Mr. Gustafsson is played out as a philosophical Heraclitean concept of sleep and dream to emphasize the possibility of change and departure. Gustafsson invokes Heraclitus in the postscript to *Sprickorna i muren* to explain his intentions:

> En man tänder om natten ett ljus, har hans ögonljus utsläckts. Levande berör han den döde i römnen; vaken berör han den sovande.

> (A man lights a lamp for himself in the night, when the light of his own eyes is extinguished. The living man touches the dead in his sleep; the waking man touches the sleeper.)

This interrelation between sleep and dream recurs in Gustafsson's later poetry and prose, particularly in the novel *Bernard Foys tredje rockad* (1986; translated as *Bernard Foy's Third Castling*, 1988). Furthermore, the presence of Laura G. as a female counterpart to the author continues the idea of the anima that Gustafsson introduced in *Kärleksförklaring till en sefardisk dam*.

En biodlares död, the fifth and final novel of the *Sprickorna i muren* series, is one of Gustafsson's greatest works. Written while Gustafsson was Thord Gray Professor of Literature and Philosophy at the University of Texas at Austin in 1974, the novel is his best received work and has been translated into thirteen languages, including Japanese and Hebrew. Set once again in Västmanland, *En biodlares död* is told in the form of entries from a diary belonging to Lars Westin, a reclusive retired teacher who has died of cancer; before his death he supported himself by raising bees in seclusion. Pain—specifically, the euphoric feeling of freedom from pain—is the theme of the novel, which also focuses in part on existential questions and on Jewish mysticism. Moreover, as he once asserted, Gustafsson based *En biodlares död* both on the story of his own decisions regarding religion in Sweden and on the biblical story of Job.

While in Gustafsson's previous works, the narrative voice has been closely linked to the author himself, in *En biodlares död* the narrative "I" dissolves in extreme pain, concluding, "Jag. jag. jag. jag, . . . efter bara fyra gånger ett meningslöst ord" (I, I, I, I, . . . after only four times already a senseless word). Critics who had previously expressed irritation at the self-referential tendencies in Gustafsson's earlier writings received *En biodlares död* with respect and admiration. Åke Janzon wrote in his review in *Svenska Daglbladet* (27 January 1978) that "Lars Gustafsson undervisar inte längre, han lyssnar. Jag tror inte han någonsin nått närmare människan själv än i denna fina och sinnrika bok" (Lars Gustafsson does not teach anymore, he listens. I don't think he has ever come closer to the human self than in this fine, ingenious book).

What was regarded as fantastic and egocentric in Gustafsson's prior works of fiction are transformed in *En biodlares död* into aspects of metaphysical and religious thought. Gustafsson has compared the progression of the novels—and their increasing awareness of the self in society—to the stages of Hell, Purgatory, and Paradise in Dante's *La Commedia* (The Divine Comedy, 1306–1321). The protagonists' discovery of their frailties and fears in the first two novels corresponds to the descent into Hell, while the next two novels reflect Purgatory through the alienation of the main characters from the government and through the influence of dreams and the unconscious on them. Finally, Gustafsson renders Paradise in the fifth novel when Lars Westin, the protagonist of *En biodlares död*, finds comfort and release through spirituality.

While Gustafsson was working on *Sprickorna i muren*, he published a lighthearted novel, *Tennisspelarna: En berättelse* (1977; translated as *The Tennis Players*, 1983). The book is derived from his experiences as a visiting professor at the University of Texas and includes a variety of entertaining stories. In a scene describing an early morning tennis match, for example, the movement of the ball arouses philosophical-mathematical speculations between the players. In another of the narrative strands Gustafsson creates an intriguing mystery based on August Strindberg and his writing of *Inferno* (1897). *Tennisspelarna* was also the first of Gustafsson's novels to be translated into English. Reviewing the book for *The New Yorker* (2 January 1984), John Updike concluded that "It is farce, but underplayed, and swiftly over, leaving a certain resonance of the personal; the conjunction of sunstruck Texas realities with the intellectual murk of fin-de-siècle Northern Europe . . . is of course one the author lived through." Indeed, the intermingling of Strindberg's *Inferno*, Kurt Gödel's mathematical theories, and Nietzsche's philosophical constructs in the novel displays an erudition characteristic of Gustafsson.

Toward the end of the 1970s Gustafsson was at his peak as a poet, novelist, essayist, and intellectual. By then he had established a reputation as a brilliant cultural commentator in Sweden and Germany as well as in France and Italy, countries in which translations of *Den egentliga berättelsen om Herr Arenander* and *Familjefesten* had recently appeared. Although the Västmanland province

remained his point of departure, his worldview became more global through travel experiences. His extensive travels in Africa, Asia, Europe, and the United States during this decade resulted in more prose works: *Världsdelar: Reseskildringar* (Continents: Travel Accounts, 1975), *Kinesisk höst* (Chinese Autumn, 1978), and *Afrikanskt försök: En essä om villkoren* (African Effort: An Essay about the Conditions, 1980). In 1977 Gustafsson also published a new collection of poetry, *Sonetter* (Sonnets), embodying thirty sonnets and three sestinas. While critics admired the didactic quality of the verses, they also questioned his skill as a writer of sonnets.

Nonetheless, also during this time, critics often castigated him for displays of carelessness and arrogance in his works of nonfiction. Critics especially received his postdoctorate essay collections such as *Språk och lögn, Konfrontationer: Stycken om konst, litteratur och politik* (Confrontations: Texts About Art, Literature, and Politics, 1979), and *Filosofier: Essäer* (Philosophies: Essays, 1979) with much ambivalence, casting into question his reputation for keen cultural commentary. Thus, although they lauded him for his creative use of fantasy and erudition, they simultaneously found fault with his cavalier attitude toward facts and with his continued tendency to view himself and his opinions as pivotal in social and cultural matters. As Åke Lundquist wrote in *Dagens Nyheter* (18 January 1985) in his review of *Frihet och fruktan: 22 brev* (Freedom and Fear: 22 Letters, 1985)—which Gustafsson cowrote with Per Ahlmark—"Lars Gustafssons debattmetod är auktoritär. I sina åsikter tycks han mig ofta ta miste. Han uttrycker sig arrogant och hånfullt, det är lätt att tycka illa om honom" (Lars Gustafsson's method of debate is authoritarian. His opinions are often based on misinformation. He expresses himself with arrogance and disdain, it is easy to dislike him). On the other hand, while critics questioned Gustafsson's reputation as an intellectual and a social critic, they continued to laud his poetry, particularly *Artesiska brunnar cartesianska drömmar: Tjugotvå lärodikter* (Artesian Wells Cartesian Dreams: Twenty-two Didactic Poems, 1980), excerpts from which were translated in *The Stillness of the World before Bach*. The collection harks back to his earlier poetry and incorporates themes and metaphors such as the natural life of Västmanland, the idea of the anima, the image of turbots frozen with open eyes in the ice, and the philosopher Heraclitus.

In the 1980s Gustafsson went through significant changes in his personal life. In 1981 he converted to Orthodox Judaism. Then in 1982, after divorcing Madeleine Gustafsson, he married Dena Alexandra Chasnoff, a native of Texas. Raised in the Orthodox Judaic tradition, Chasnoff was a main reason behind Gustafsson's decision to convert. In 1983 the couple settled in Austin, where Gustafsson became an adjunct professor at the University of Texas, teaching philosophy, the history of ideas, and literature on a part-time basis. He and his wife have two children, Benjamin and Karin Julia, whom he has mentioned intermittently in recent writings.

Gustafsson's style of writing was also changing at this time. Two novels that appeared in the 1980s, *Sorgemusik för frimurare* (1983; translated as *Funeral Music for Freemasons*, 1987) and *Bernard Foys tredje rockad*, especially signal this development. The linear narrative prevalent in most of his novels of the 1960s and 1970s grows fragmented in the 1980s and assumes postmodern contours. He employed this fragmented technique previously in *Sprickorna i muren*, which follows five distinct protagonists who have the same name, Lars; through the novels in that series Gustafsson suggests that these main characters represent different aspects of one person and could thus be fused into a single character. Furthermore, in both *Sorgemusik för frimurare* and *Bernard Foys tredje rockad* the action is spread over various continents—Europe, Africa, and the United States—and thus emphasizes Gustafsson's new global outlook.

Sorgemusik för frimurare relates the story of three different people—Jan, Ann-Marie, and Hasse—who have known each other since they were students at the University of Uppsala in the 1950s. Jan was an aspiring poet in college but later gave up his literary career when he left Sweden to work as a tour guide in Senegal, Africa. Ann-Marie, Jan's girlfriend at the University of Uppsala, aspired toward a career as an opera singer; her world was the music of Wolfgang Amadeus Mozart, whose *Masonic Funeral March* (1785) is reflected in the title of the novel. After university Ann-Marie leads a lonely life, however, and she never quite succeeds on stage. Hasse, in contrast, becomes a successful nuclear physicist at Harvard and travels the globe to present his research and negotiate business enterprises. He is married and lives in Austin, Texas. Both of the characters who were once aspiring artists face endings: Jan dies from cancer shortly after his return to Sweden after a long period in Africa, while Ann-Marie resigns from her position in the theater to exist merely as a receptionist at a business concern. Hasse, the entrepreneur scientist living in the United States, is the only successful person.

Sorgemusik för frimurare combines elements from Gustafsson's previous works yet hints at his new life in the United States. The character of Jan, who has Gustafsson's birth date, also has much in common with earlier protagonists. For example, like Lars Herdin in *Yllet*, Jan is unable to resist the cancer of bureaucracy and of society and the figurative death that they bring. Like Lars Westin in *En biodlares död*, Jan is also an outsider keen on exploring the existence of a metaphysical presence. Linked romantically to both Jan and Hasse, Ann-Marie recalls the elusive woman who signifies anima in Gustafsson's works. Furthermore, she is often associated with yellow light, the metaphor that Gustafsson uses to describe moments of harmony and peace in his poetry and prose. The novel ends with a scene in which Hasse is playing tennis in the United States. Although he appears as a peripheral character in the novel, there are hints throughout that he is indeed the main protagonist. Hasse voices the same loss of self as the earlier characters, yet handles the loss in a more constructive way than the others. In spite of his strength he is a transitional figure: he still has one foot in his bourgeois past in Sweden, and he admits that his shadow—his past in Sweden—is stronger than his new self in the United States. Critics have postulated that Hasse, the successful individual, is Gustafsson's idea of a happy person. More accurately, he is a confused and resigned individual who misses his shadow and his playful games with symbols in his youth. In this context *Sorgemusik för frimurare* can be seen as a precursor to the individuation that occurs in *Bernard Foys tredje rockad*.

Bernard Foys tredje rockad is Gustafsson's most postmodern work. The development of three different plots within the novel creates fragmented situations, which—like symbols—are imbued with meaning. The French critic Roland Barthes defined such fragmentation as the ludic technique, the literary game that, according to him, is necessary to break the mirror effect of literature based on reality. For Barthes, the ludic technique makes language visible as a character in the room: the situations become scenes that give the reader more than conventional psychological analysis. This approach matches perfectly both Gustafsson's literary style and his affinity for games, an inclination he probably inherited from Einar, his game-loving father.

Bernard Foys tredje rockad is divided into three sections: "Oktobers månads tak är lågt" (October's

Roof Hangs Low), "När blomblad ännu föll om våren" (When Petals Still Fell in the Spring), and "Den mogna åldern" (The Age of Maturity). The first part is a detective story, in which an American rabbi, Bernard Foy, becomes involuntarily drawn into an international espionage ring. In the second section an aging poet named Bernard Foy confesses that he wrote the previous detective story. The old poet has composed the heroic adventure to amuse himself and to avoid writing the promised sequel to his autobiography, which should have been completed a couple of decades earlier. When the poet declares that the successful publication of the first volume of his autobiography, "När blomblad ännu föll om våren," should have been followed by "Den mogna åldern" and "Oktobers månads tak är lågt," Gustafsson is actually combining the poet's reality with the simulated reality and topography of the novel at hand.

Gustafsson alerts the reader to the existence of a metanovel yet negates such an existence by frustrating the reader's expectations: the chronology of the section titles in the novel do not parallel that of Foy's proposed autobiographical work. A separate reality emerges from the titles of the poet's autobiographical project and those of the sections in the actual novel. A third, in-between stage of reality appears, underscoring the close relationship between the novel and Gustafsson's own body of work as a whole and to its autobiographical components. The title "Oktobers månads tak är lågt" and its narrative about the American rabbi points symbolically to the author's own situation as a Jew residing in Texas. The title "När blomblad ännu föll om våren" evokes childhood metaphorically: as Foy the poet spends most of his time reminiscing about his past, he regresses to a stage of infantile dependency. This situation—a Swedish poet or artist dying, whether literally or metaphorically, in his native land—also recalls Jan and Ann-Marie in *Sorgemusik för frimurare*. Finally, although the title of the final section of the novel, "Den mogna åldern," implies a narrative about an individual at a mature age, Gustafsson depicts a teenaged Foy. The teenager behaves with the insights, intellect, and perspective of a mature adult, however, rather than with the emotional despair of a youth who has just lost both of his parents. In many ways Foy as a youth exemplifies the typical Gustafsson protagonist, who suffers in isolation: the teenager hides in the dark heating ducts underneath his town in order to compose the opus that will help him overcome the pain of losing his father—a scenario familiar from *Herr Gustafsson själv*, in which the

narrator states that his writing is a "grief work." The unfolding story of *Bernard Foys tredje rockad* conveys how such pain and grief are overcome.

If the three sections of *Bernard Foys tredje rockad* are read in reverse order, they reflect indeed on Gustafsson's literary career as a whole: in the beginning the teenager withdraws into himself and into an underworld to create; then, as a member of the Swedish cultural establishment, the poet—who had been regarded previously as godly by idolizing admirers—withdraws from society after suffering a stroke; and finally, the rabbi, whose courage and intellect help prevent an international nuclear disaster, represents a new culture and genealogy. Withdrawal and isolation, emotional as well as social, has characterized his main characters since Gustafsson's first literary work appeared in 1957. Expressions of anxiety and coldness are present in each work: there are examples of autism and images of Greenland ice in *Bröderna* that reappear in the first two sections of *Bernard Foys tredje rockad*. In *Herr Gustafsson själv* coldness surrounds and exists within the protagonist, and he finds solace only in memories of yellow light and in the act of speaking: ". . . talandet är moderlighet och skydd. Det är min värme, min enda form. Min vagga" (. . . the act of speaking is maternal and protective. It is my warmth, my only form. My cradle). In reverse order, the closure that Rabbi Bernard Foy represents can then be seen as a result of a long discourse that was initiated as a grief work by someone who found solace in the Jewish faith.

William Fovet, in an article for *Horisont* (1987), has emphasized the multidimensional aspect of *Bernard Foys tredje rockad*, defining the text as "ett *öppet* kenst verk" (an *open* piece of art), a cosmos in itself. This perspective seems natural to an author who admires the complexity of works such as Douglas Hofstadter's *Gödel Escher Bach* (1979), in which the worlds of mathematics, visual art, and music are tied together. Gustafsson has claimed that *Bernard Foys tredje rockad* was written as an effort to transfer mathematical-musical compositions into the structure of a novel. The work also represents his attempt to create a fiction within a fiction. These innovations helped the novel attain a significant place in literary criticism and in literary history. Important as a milestone in Gustafsson's writings, *Bernard Foys tredje rockad* was also published the year that the writer celebrated his fiftieth birthday. At this juncture his life was peaceful and harmonious, as opposed to the identity conflicts and alienation that ruled before, and the novel can therefore be viewed as ending a significant period of Gustafsson's voluminous productivity. When asked whether or not *Bernard Foys tredje rockad* indeed symbolize a kind of closure, Gustafsson affirmed that he had to find "ett nytt språk" (a new language) for his future works.

In 1988 Gustafsson published *Fyra poeter: Gustaf Adolf Fredenlund, Bernard Foy, Ehrmine Wikström, Jan Bohman* (Four poets: Gustaf Adolf Fredenlund, Bernard Foy, Ehrmine Wikström, Jan Bohman), a collection of poetry in which he continues the plays on identity featured in his previous two novels. The four fictive poets personify different age groups and different styles of writing; Foy and Bohman are obviously the poet-protagonists from the two previous novels. Yet, although the reader perceives Gustafsson's influence in *Fyra poeter* through certain references to topics raised in earlier works, an additional understanding of aging and of the passage of time also emerges. Such understanding is heightened in his next collection, *Förberedelser för vintersäsongen: Elegier och andra dikter* (Preparations for the Winter Season: Elegies and Other Poems, 1990). The first part of the volume exhibits thoughtful and nostalgic memories of the past as well as reflections on the present. The juxtaposition of past and present is particularly evident in "Austin, Texas," in which the poet compares his own childhood to that of his young son, Benjamin. The poem makes Gustafsson's situation as an expatriate poignantly clear: that which is natural to the son will always be foreign to the man who grew up in a different culture and climate. Another memorable lyric is "Elegi över den gamla mexikanska kvinnan och hennes döda barn" (translated as "Elegy for the Old Mexican Woman and Her Dead Child" in the 8 October 1990 issue of *The New Yorker*), which Gustafsson wrote in memory of a Mexican woman who had been carrying a dead fetus in her womb for sixty years. The image of this woman still connected to her dead child is analogous to the grief work that the poet expressed in his writings. *Förberedelser för vintersäsongen* brought him two distinguished awards in Sweden: the Bellman Prize of the Royal Swedish Academy in 1990 and the Poetry Prize of the Swedish Broadcasting Corporation in 1993.

Gustafsson's new understanding manifests itself further in the novel *En kakelsättares eftermiddag* (1991; translated as *A Tiler's Afternoon*, 1993), which he refers to as a supplement to *En biodlares död*. Like the earlier narrative, *En kakelsättares eftermiddag* deals with loneliness and human misfortune. The life of the main character, however, has little in common with Gustaffson's own biography.

In *En kakelsättares eftermiddag* Torsten Bergman is a retired tiler who lives alone in a decrepit house in which the basement, with all his tools and piles of saved tiles, is flooded with murky water. He receives a call to help a former colleague set tiles in a house under construction. When he arrives, no one is there to confirm his job or offer information, and a mystery begins to emerge as Bergman searches the building. The nameplate of a tenant, Sophie Karlsson, intrigues him; he imagines her both as a woman painter, Sophie K., who is a seductive, red-headed woman dressed in black velvet, and as his former teacher from elementary school. Elusive and absent, Sophie nevertheless has a presence in the text that is reminiscent of how Gustafsson characterizes women in his earlier works. The mysteries of the plot and his conversations with Stig, a colleague, provide the backdrop for Torsten's soliloquies about his past and his misfortunes, which—as in the myth of Sisyphus—impel Torsten to start anew repeatedly. Published simultaneously in Sweden and in Germany, *En kakelsättares eftermiddag* was soon translated into seven languages. While Swedish critics focused on the relation of the novel to Gustafsson's previous works and on its elements of social criticism, critics in France and Italy applauded its philosophical theme.

In 1993, the same year Gustafsson was awarded a John Simon Guggenheim Memorial Foundation Fellowship for poetry, his fifteenth novel was published. *Historien med hunden: Ur en texansk konkursdomares dagböcker och brev* (translated as *The Tale of a Dog: From the Diaries and Letters of a Texan Bankruptcy Judge*, 1998) has been called a *roman noir*— French for "dark novel"—because of its dominant existential theme. Gustafsson considers *Historien med hunden* the third part of a trilogy that began with *En biodlares död*, also recounted in the form of diary entries, and *En kakelsättares eftermiddag*. Apart from the character of Jan van der Rouwers, a Dutch philosopher-semanticist, *Historien med hunden* consists of distinctly Texan personalities. Gustafsson's familiarity with the city of Austin and with life in Texas is evident; he describes places and incidents with the same ease and sensitivity as he did in the earlier narratives that were set in Västerås. Good versus evil constitutes the central theme of *Historien med hunden*, in which two murders set the plot in motion. Erwin Caldwell, a judge, commits the first crime when he kills a stray dog that has been irritating him for some time; Caldwell also empties his trash on his neighbor's well-manicured lawn. The other murder is of van der Rouwers, a professor whose body is found floating in the Texas Colorado River at the Tom Miller Dam. The judge's crime and the subsequent discovery of the professor's anti-Semitic views from pieces he wrote in Belgium during World War II are reminiscent of Gustafsson's affinity for games and for philosophical explorations of identity and ethics.

By the time of the appearance of *Historien med hunden*, Gustafsson had been living in Texas for ten years. For reviewers of *Historien med hunden*, the passage of time and the impressive number of Gustafsson's publications cast his career in a new light. The novel drew quite positive responses, suggesting that critics had abandoned their diatribes against the writer. Magnus Eriksson, for example, writes in his review in *Svenska Dagbladet* on 26 August 1993: "Som vanligt präglas det hela av en oemotståndlig blanding av förströddhet, skarpsinne och infallsrikedom. . . . Som läsare kan man endast tacka för en utsökt roman och önska Herr Gustafsson välkommen hem" (The whole thing is as usual an irresistible mixture of distraction, acumen, and ingenuity. . . . As a reader, one can only express gratitude for an excellent novel and wish Mr. Gustafsson welcome home). The cynicism of past reviewers receded once Gustafsson stopped reflecting on his own life in his writing. Critics also appreciated the novelty of an American setting.

In the 1990s Gustafsson's works largely concern aging and death, perhaps because of personal tragedies and losses involving people close to him. Tomas Tranströmer, an internationally acclaimed poet and Gustafsson's friend, suffered a stroke in 1990; another friend, the esteemed writer Sven Delblanc, died from cancer in 1992; and Yvonne Sandström, Gustafsson's old schoolmate and frequent translator of his works, died in 1994. Most significantly, Gustafsson lost his father Einar, who died at age eighty-six in 1993. These losses inevitably reminded him of human frailty, and thoughts of the past and people from his past pervaded his poetry and prose at this time. One work of nonfiction, *Ett minnespalats*, consists of stories about people and events that have had a significant impact on his life and writings. *Ett minnespalats* features a sensitive and humorous eulogy that he composed for his father in the form of a chapter, "Agenten" (The Agent). In the poetry collection *Stenkista* (Caisson, 1994), Gustafsson compares the burdens of his life to the heaviness and sturdiness of a caisson. The stones that weigh the caisson down symbolize the experiences of his life:. . .

(When I was very young
I didn't really exist anywhere.

Now, with all these stones aboard,
and there are more every year, dead friends,

dead relatives, dead expectations,
not to mention the great weights of unfinished
   business,

which soon will be visible over the surface
everything rests rather firmly.

[*To plant a caisson. That is heavy.*])

The perspective of an aging man prevails throughout the book, which also includes a poem that divides the narrator's life into decades, "Mina Decennier" (My Decades), as well as another that pays tribute to Delblanc, "Sven Delblanc 1931–1992." In addition, two rhymed poems, "Skåpets sånges" (Songs of the Cupboard) and "Envei," remind the reader of Gustafsson's stylistic playfulness and the origins of his style in the traditional poetry of the 1950s.

Gustafsson's sixteenth novel, *Tjänarinnan: En kärleksroman* (The Maid: A Love Story, 1996), features a prodigal son's return to Sweden. Dick Olsson, a bachelor living in Austin, Texas, and working as a successful consultant of computer images, learns of his mother's death in Stockholm. He has Eleonore, a Colombian and the maid of the title, take care of his house while he is away attending to his loss. Receiving a less than favorable response from critics, the novel lacks the complexity that distinguishes most of the author's earlier works. *Tjänarinnan* is still important, however, for Gustafsson's portrayal of an aging man who tries to come to terms with his loneliness and his past. The descriptions of Olsson's existential loneliness, of his thoughts about his dead mother, and of how to fit his attendance at her funeral in Stockholm into his already busy calendar make this book emblematic of Gustafsson's position at that time as an aging, successful, and busy author.

In the novel *Windy berättar: om sitt liv, om de försvunna och om dem som ännu finns kvar* (1999; Windy Tells: About Her Life, about Those Who Are Gone and Those Who Remain), Gustafsson introduces a young female narrator for the first time. Through a soliloquy delivered by Windy, a hairdresser, the plot develops in the time it takes for her to cut the hair of a University of Texas professor. She tells him about her life and her customers, most of whom are professors or students at the university. The novel recalls Gustafsson's previous book, *Historien med hunden*, in that Windy refers to its major events, such as a certain murder and the boat house fire, and to a main character, Judge Caldwell. Like *En kakelsättares eftermiddag*,

Windy berättar is also an existential and philosophical work. While Torsten Bergmann, the protagonist of the earlier novel, struggled fruitlessly to complete a job or to succeed at something, Windy's life story follows her endless struggle to overcome hardships and to support her two daughters as a single mother. Furthermore, Gustafsson's increasing familiarity with the landscape of Texas is evident through his detailed descriptions of nature—which, as passages from his previous books display, also resembles his native Västmanland.

He returns to Västmanland in the short mystery novel, *Blom och den andra magentan* (Blom and the Second Magenta, 2001). The plot concerns a rare stamp: a one-cent British Guiana stamp was colored magenta by mistake in the mid nineteenth century. In 1856 a Swedish captain affixed the stamp to a postcard that he sent to his brother, who was living in the small community of Väster Våla. Someone has now learned about the stamp—the only one like it left in the world—and thinks it might still be hidden in an old nearby estate that remains largely intact. This entertaining thriller, in which an eccentric Stockholm police detective—who is a former theologian—arrives on the scene to solve the mystery, reaffirms Lars Gustafsson's affinity for intellectual games. Despite the general characterization of his writings as "grief work," *Blom och den andra magentan* attests to, if not also underscores, his pleasure in the act of creating.

Source: Ia Dübois, "Lars Gustafsson," in *Dictionary of Literary Biography*, Vol. 257, *Twentieth-Century Swedish Writers After World War II*, edited by Ann-Charlotte Gavel Adams, The Gale Group, 2002, pp. 115–30.

Charles Baxter

In the following essay, Baxter says "Greatness Strikes Where It Pleases" is "experienced in nearly frozen narrative events of almost pure feeling."

He had been invited to introduce a story and was pulling down books from the shelves to reread a few of the old obscure favorites. They had to be obscure, he thought, or there was no point in introducing one of them. The books were scattered on the floor, and he had to be careful to avoid tripping over them or kicking one of them into the corner. Some of the stories, once reread, no longer seemed quite so appropriate for the occasion, however. Conrad Aiken's "The Woman-Hater" still had its shockingly beautiful paragraph two pages from the end, when the college kid is kissed by a woman he doesn't know and wakes up like Sleeping Beauty, but the rest of the story seemed too drab,

too perfunctorily written. Aiken's "Silent Snow, Secret Snow," about a boy's descent into schizophrenia, was still perfect in its evocation of a child's mental vertigo but was, it seemed, constantly anthologized. Evan Connell's "Arcturus" was too long for inclusion in an anthology, as was Isak Dinesen's "Sorrow-acre." Kipling's " 'They' " could effectively give anyone the shivers. All the same, it seemed, upon reexamination, too tricky by half and culturally unpleasant in the way Kipling could sometimes be. Anyone introducing such a story might feel an urge to apologize for it—a bad way to start. Katherine Anne Porter's "Noon Wine" was bulletproof but, like "Arcturus," too long and hardly obscure. He didn't know enough about some writers and their traditions, Yasunari Kawabata's or Bessie Head's, for example, to introduce one of their stories. And he didn't feel like introducing writers who needed no introduction, at least from him: Chekhov or Alice Munro or Italo Calvino. Dozens of others.

Sighing happily, he took down Lars Gustafsson's *Stories of Happy People* and reread "Greatness Strikes Where It Pleases." Probably it was the story he had wanted to introduce all along.

This story, translated by Yvonne L. Sandstroem and John Weinstock, is part of a book first published in Sweden in 1981 whose concern is that most complex and elusive fictional subject, happiness. Happiness is fundamentally antidramatic. For the most part, it resists conflict altogether, having passed beyond it or finessed it. In this sense it is distinct from the emotions of triumph or contentment. There are probably no stories in Paradise, and there are very few stories *about* Paradise. In America we secretly tend to think of happiness as rather dull and banal, middle class, unworthy of our attention, possessed by the likes of Ozzie and Harriet. Gustafsson's protagonists in this book, by contrast, approach happiness warily and treat it as the utterly mysterious condition that it is.

In one story we follow Nietzsche, floating in and out of excruciating migraines in his pension room on the shore of Lago Maggiore, discovering that he himself is part of a great truth, a wildly humorous and very clever joke in which he is the perfect thing that makes the world not-perfect. In another, we follow two obsessed lovers; in a third, an old Swedish industrial engineer who discovers in the quotations from Chairman Mao a catalyst for remembering a truth buried in his memory and almost obliterated by historical trauma. Whatever happiness Gustafsson's protagonists find, it always has the virtue of a pleasing complexity, like a very oddly shaped crystal.

The subject of, and virtually only character in, "Greatness Strikes Where It Pleases" is what we would call a retarded person, a sort of boy who grows to be a sort of man. The story has no interest in the pathos of this situation, none whatever. It is hardly interested in this character as a *person* at all: his actions and decisions are virtually irrelevant to the story's progress, which is genuine but minimal. All the same, the story is something of a miracle: it induces in the reader a bit of a trance, and in this trance it convincingly portrays its subject as mysteriously exceptional, godlike.

"Greatness Strikes Where It Pleases" is one of the few stories I know of where time virtually stands still throughout the entire story. Or rather it is experienced in nearly frozen narrative events of almost pure feeling. The story has eliminated transitions: one moment the boy is with his parents; at the next moment he is in a home; then he is a man. Man and boy are virtually the same. Nothing leads to anything else. Nothing has to. Instead, one scene *yields* to another, as dough in the oven yields to the heat to become bread, or as the front of a crowd changes direction because of some pressure from the rear. Everything within the story—grass, mushrooms, wood saws—is defamiliarized, an object for endless contemplation.

The protagonist (he has no name) has almost no words, does not own the words that are used against him, but recognizes that the strong, unlike him, *do* own the words and use them to punish others, including himself, and to order the business of the world. Gustafsson's story is involved in a very tricky maneuver here, because all this must come to us through words and a literary language that the boy and subsequently the man do not possess. The words of the story must induce a feeling for his perceptions even though the perceptions do not come to him in exactly this form.

"He had no words for the world, and birds' suddenly flying up was one of the thousand ways in which the world would turn *unreliable*." That's the horror. But the story is dominated by pleasures, slow-seeming ones. *"The trees are so happy, he thought, when the wind comes. That gives them something to do."*

We all have intuitions that we don't exactly have the words for, especially when we're children. These intuitions probably have the form of shaped sensory perceptions of emotions that have what amounts to a distinct outline. Henry James, in his

> **"** Light floods through everything, and we enter something like the mind of the infinite, which is still the mind of a retarded boy, shockingly apart from the rest of us, hugely beautiful, and great.**"**

preface to *What Maisie Knew,* argues that fiction, or at least *his* kind of fiction, shouldn't be stuck with only the language that the characters themselves possess. By a certain sleight-of-hand, the writer gives to the character the language that the character deserves, a language that honors the character's intuitions. Our feelings can be sophisticated even when our language is not.

The narrator of "Greatness Strikes Where It Pleases," as I've said, never takes pity on the subject of the story. What he does is much odder. He gives him instead the benefit of his intelligent and informed fascination and curiosity. He engages in a thought experiment in which the young man is granted *nobility,* free from condescension. This character gradually becomes an ambassador from and then a monarch of a country that the rest of us know almost nothing about but can still perceive. It is the country of contemplation-without-thought.

> In a world that had no center, he reigned like a quiet monarch, too self-evident ever to feel that his own order was being threatened, too rich to demand anything from the poor, an envoy in chaos serving an order so noble that it was also able to accept the necessity of disorder.

That's beautiful. And in its simple complexity— there *is* such a condition—it gives an inkling of the almost stationary beauty of the story's conclusion, where Gustaffsson's protagonist begins to take on the mind of a mushroom, which is also the mind of God.

Sitting in his chair, so fat he spills out over the edges, this nameless character ends in an exalted, ethereal state, both weighed down and lifted up, that cannot truly be shared by anyone capable of reading this story. The boy who has been excluded from everything wordly, worldly, and human has now attained a state that you, the reader, can only read about but never have in quite the way he has it.

The final six paragraphs of this story are remarkable and hair-raising. The story has stopped progressing, in its unusual manner. Instead, and at some distance from you, it turns, very very slowly, like a wheel in the sky. The chords are slow and sustained, and they are in no hurry to get anywhere because they have already arrived at their destination. It is like the music of Thomas Tallis or what we know of the conversation of angels. Light floods through everything, and we enter something like the mind of the infinite, which is still the mind of a retarded boy, shockingly apart from the rest of us, hugely beautiful, and great.

Source: Charles Baxter, "Introduction to 'Greatness Strikes Where It Pleases,'" in *You've Got to Read This: Contemporary Writers Introduce Stories That Held Them in Awe,* edited by Ron Hansen and Jim Shepard, HarperCollins, 1994, pp. 258–60.

Daniel P. Deneau

In the following mixed review of Stories of Happy People, *Deneau asserts that Gustafsson "quietly illustrates mysteries rather than certainties" in his stories.*

The versatile Lars Gustafsson (1936–)—sometimes poet, novelist, playwright, editor, critic, philisopher, teacher—is said to be well known in Sweden and other European countries; and surely he must be appreciated by New Directions, which has issued translations of three Gustafsson novels and now offers his *Stories of Happy People,* a collection of ten pieces of short fiction, two previously translated into English. Neither Gustafsson's title nor his epigraphs (suggesting "adaptation" and "groping") seem particularly accurate or ironical.

It is unfortunate that the selections are presented without any introduction, footnotes, or even dates. Several commentators have suggested that there have been significant changes in Gustafsson's novels and poetry through the years, and readers of *Stories* must wonder if the selections are arranged in the order of composition or original publication. My guess is that the first five stories are "early"; certainly they are episodic, inconclusive, and even enigmatic, the latter not because of complexity but because of Gustafsson's apparent unwillingness to struggle for some degree of coherence. The final sentence of the second story, an episodic account of "The Four Railroads of Iserlohn," is an appropriate verdict: "Here ends our impossible story." Similar

comments appear late in the third and fourth stories: "On his way to the bus stop, he realized that he was either at the beginning or at the end of a very powerful story." The last five selections, however, are not punctuated in a similar way, and they do have more shape and focus than their predecessors.

For one reason or another, additional generalizations are not easy to formulate. Given Gustafsson's academic background (D.Phil., Uppsala, 1961 or 1962), a reader should not be surprised by allusions to Dante, Bach, Pascal, Mallarmé, Malthus, Ibsen, Sartre, Bergman, and even I. A. Richards and Cleanth Brooks; nor should one be surprised by a sprinkling of reflective or "philosophical" comments. Sometimes these seem weighty, but generally they are as clear and apt as the following: "What struck him more and more often was the narcissistic aspect of this whole fitness craze. . . . essentially they were nothing but a blind, uncertain, narcissistic generation preoccupied with the last and, in its own way, the most fragile of all the continents of hope: your own body." Several of the stories deal with travelers to China, Germany, Greece, and the United States; the stories have some cosmopolitan flavor but present only glimpses of modern Sweden. Gustafsson seems conscious of changes which have occurred from decade to decade in the twentieth century, and he may show some nostalgia for the Sweden of his youth. Certainly one suspects that the stories contain bits, perhaps more than bits, of autobiography: for instance, the longest story in the volume, "What Does Not Kill Us, Tends to Make Us Stronger" (one of those forgettable titles), deals with the career of "Lars," a Swedish teacher at the University of Texas, a university where Gustafsson himself served as a visiting professor (the same university is the setting for *The Tennis Player*). Let us hope that the male-female relationships in the volume are imaginary, for all of them seem impermanent or troubled. Here and there one receives glimpses of topics which concern Gustafsson in his longer works. For instance, writing in the "Translator's Introduction" to Gustafsson's *Foray into Swedish Poetry* (essays on fifteen poets), Robert T. Rovinsky indicates that as a critic "one of Gustafsson's main concerns is for what he calls . . . 'the very mysteriousness of human existence.'" The same might be said of Gustafsson's the short story writer. "Nobody really knows what a human being is" he repeats, and in all of his stories he quietly illustrates mysteries rather than certainties.

Only two of the stories, the seventh and ninth, actually seem memorable, perhaps because the unusual protagonists make a significant degree of mysteriousness seem inevitable. In the sixth story, "The Fugitives Discover That They Know Nothing," two sophisticated people meet by chance in Athens, engage in a brief affair, and then simply walk away from one another: ". . . they had come close to something great, ... Greatness Arrived. And they were unable to receive it." (Why? What Greatness? I have no idea.) The seventh story, "Greatness Strikes Where It Pleases," is an absorbing account, extending from childhood to middle age, of a mentally retarded male, though one may read a number of pages before becoming aware of the way the protagonist's childishness will be evaluated by society. At the end the unnamed protagonist is a huge and shapeless form sitting in the sunlight, but in lyrical prose we learn of his feeling of oneness with the universe and his understanding of the great mystery of which mankind is a part. The somewhat similar ninth story, "The Bird in the Breast," tells of a woman who, different from childhood, gradually withdraws farther and farther into a private world, where there is an extraordinary drama as death approaches.

Source: Daniel P. Deneau, Review of *Stories of Happy People*, in *Studies in Short Fiction*, Vol. 27, No. 3, Summer 1987, pp. 316–18.

Sources

Baxter, Charles, "Introduction to 'Greatness Strikes Where It Pleases,'" in *You've Got to Read This: Contemporary Writers Introduce Stories That Held Them in Awe*, edited by Ron Hansen, Perennial, 1994, pp. 258–60.

Deneau, Daniel, P., Review of *Stories of Happy People*, in *Studies in Short Fiction*, Vol. 27, No. 3, Summer 1987, pp. 316–18.

Gustafsson, Lars, "Greatness Strikes Where It Pleases," translated by Y. Sandstroem and J. Weinstock, in *Stories of Happy People*, New Directions, 1986, pp. 91–103.

Johannesson, Eric O., Review of *Stories of Happy People*, in *New York Times Book Review*, September 7, 1986, p. 18.

London, Jack, "Told in the Drooling Ward," in *Short Stories of Jack London*, edited by Earle Labor, Robert C. Leitz III, and I. Milo Shepard, Macmillan, 1990, pp. 494–501.

Shakespeare, William, *The Winter's Tale*, edited by J. H. P. Pafford, Arden Edition, Methuen, 1963, p. 93.

Trent, James R., Jr., *Inventing the Feeble Mind: A History of Mental Retardation in the United States*, University of California Press, 1994.

Welty, Eudora, "Lily Daw and the Three Ladies," in *The Collected Stories of Eudora Welty*, Harcourt Brace Jovanovich, 1980, pp. 3–11.

Wordsworth, William, "The Idiot Boy," in *Lyrical Ballads*, edited with introduction, notes, and appendices by R. L. Brett and A. R. Jones, Methuen, 1971, pp. 86–101.

Further Reading

Black, Edwin, *War against the Weak: Eugenics and America's Campaign to Create a Master Race*, Four Walls Eight Windows, 2003.
> Investigative journalist Black tells the story of America's experiment with eugenics during the twentieth century and how it influenced Hitler and the Third Reich in Germany. Black argues that after World War II, eugenics was reborn as human genetics. He claims that confronting the history of eugenics is essential to understanding the implications of the Human Genome Project and twenty-first-century genetic engineering.

Noll, Steven, and James W. Trent Jr., eds., *Mental Retardation in America: A Historical Reader*, New York University Press, 2004.
> Exploring historical issues, as well as current public policy concerns, this book covers various topics that include representations of the mentally disabled as social burdens and social menaces, Freudian inspired ideas of adjustment and adaptation, the relationship between community care and institutional treatment, historical events which upheld the policy of eugenic sterilization, the disability rights movement, and the passage of the Americans with Disabilities Act in 1990.

Shorter, Edward, *The Kennedy Family and the Story of Mental Retardation*, Temple University Press, 2000.
> Using some Kennedy family records that have not previously been seen by historians, Shorter presents the story of how the Kennedy family played a major role in educating Americans about mental retardation.

Zigler, Edward, and Robert M. Hodapp, *Understanding Mental Retardation*, Cambridge University Press, 1986.
> This is a guide to current research and theory about mental retardation. Topics addressed include issues of definition, classification, and prevalence; motivation and personality factors; intervention in the lives of retarded persons; the possibility of "miracle cures"; and the problems of institutionalization and mainstreaming.

Islands

Aleksandar Hemon

1998

When Aleksandar Hemon traveled to Chicago from his native Bosnia in 1992 on a brief cultural visa, he did not expect to become a prominent and successful writer in English within six years. This is what he did, however, immigrating to the United States as a refugee when war broke out in Bosnia-Herzegovina (one of the former Yugoslavian states) and mastering the English language. Hemon began to write semi-autobiographical short stories characterized by a frank and immediate voice, often dealing with political themes, including the war in the former Yugoslavia and with Yugoslavian history. Sophisticated and striking, his stories brought him nearly immediate recognition as an important and gifted writer.

One of these stories, entitled "Islands," is steeped in the rich history of 1970s Yugoslavia, before the dictator Marshal Tito died and the region fell into instability and civil war. In it, a young boy from Sarajevo, Bosnia, travels to a Croatian island with his parents in order to vacation at his Uncle Julius's house. Deeply affected by his uncle's stories about Joseph Stalin's Soviet labor camps of the 1940s, the young narrator becomes self-conscious about his place in politics and society. "Islands" is composed of thirty-three short scenes that comment on themes ranging from memory and childhood trauma to self-consciousness and the concept of authority. Originally published in the spring 1998 edition of *Ploughshares*, the story was reprinted as the opening tale of Hemon's debut collection of short fiction, *The Question of Bruno* (2000).

Author Biography

Aleksandar Hemon is a Bosnian who was born in Sarajevo, the capitol of what is now Bosnia-Herzegovina, in 1964. He was interested in soccer and spying as a child, among other things, and later he worked as a journalist. In 1990, he received a bachelor's degree from the University of Sarajevo, and in 1992 he came to Chicago as part of a government-sponsored journalist exchange program. He had only a basic command of English and intended to stay for only a short time, but when war erupted in his country he applied to stay in the United States as a refugee. His application was successful, and Hemon held a series of part-time jobs while improving his English, including a kitchen worker, a bicycle messenger, and a fund-raiser for Greenpeace.

Hemon began writing in English within three years of his arrival in the United States, and he earned a master's degree from Northwestern University in 1995. "Islands" was originally published in the spring 1998 edition of *Ploughshares*, and it was included in Hemon's collection of short fiction, *The Question of Bruno* (2000). His short stories have also been published in magazines, including the *New Yorker*, *Esquire*, and *Triquarterly*, and "Islands" was included in *Best American Short Stories 1999*. In 2002, Hemon published his first novel *Nowhere Man*, which follows Josef Pronek, the protagonist of a story in *The Question of Bruno*, through his adolescence and his move to Chicago as war is breaking out in Bosnia. Critically acclaimed, the novel has been compared to the work of Vladimir Nabokov, the famous Russian emigré to the United States, and praised for its imaginative treatment of political and psychological themes. Hemon has received numerous awards for his writings, and in 2004 he was awarded a MacArthur Fellowship.

Plot Summary

Scenes 1–5

"Islands" begins with the young unnamed narrator driving with his family from Sarajevo to the coast, where they take a ship to the island of Mljet, which is part of the neighboring state of Croatia. On the ship, the narrator loses his hat in the wind and, realizing he will never see it again, sobs himself to sleep. The family is greeted on Mljet by Uncle Julius, whose lack of teeth disturbs the

Aleksandar Hemon   Photograph by Sophie Bassouls. © Bassouls Sophie/Corbis SYGMA

narrator. While they walk back to the house, Uncle Julius explains that Mljet used to be overrun by snakes until someone brought a group of young mongooses to the island. Now the mongooses have killed all the snakes and overrun the island themselves.

Scenes 6–12

At the house, Aunt Lyudmila gives the narrator a slobbery kiss. He walks upstairs to a room with a picture of the Yugoslav dictator Josip Tito and an image of the island. Later that night, the narrator wakes up and finds the adults talking and drinking wine outside. He overhears Uncle Julius saying that his grandfather was a beekeeper, and the narrator tells them he is thirsty. Aunt Lyudmila offers him a cup of water, but he refuses because he sees a slug in the water tank.

Scenes 13–17

Uncle Julius tells a story about the time he spent at the Arkhangelsk labor camp in northern Russia, where Stalin began to send young children as punishment for missing school. They were abused and died frequently, but Uncle Julius met one named Vanyka who managed to survive. When

Uncle Julius was sent to Siberia to be a gravedig-ger, he saw Vanyka again, begging to die, and he gave him a piece of bread. Vanyka told him what happened after he got drunk and shouted, "Thank you, Stalin, for my happy childhood!" The guards abused him and moved him to another camp, but Vanyka continued to speak out, steal from the weak, and find men who would protect him in ex-change for sex. He began to kill as well and was sent to an island for the worst criminals, from which he fled with two other criminals. Vanyka killed and ate the two other men, but guards eventually caught him and put him in solitary confinement. He had been trying to kill himself, but the guards would not let him die. The narrator asks what happened to Vanyka, but Uncle Julius simply says, dismis-sively, he "was killed."

Scenes 18–26

Each morning on Mljet, the narrator wakes up, eats an unappetizing breakfast, walks down a path while frightened of mongooses, and arrives at the gravel beach. His parents allow him to swim, and he sees jellyfish and once a school of what look like "miniature swordfish." One day, while walk-ing up the path at sunset, the narrator and his par-ents see a man allow his German shepherd to kill a mongoose. Sometimes Uncle Julius takes the nar-rator to his apiary, which is a place where bees are raised for their honey. The narrator holds a flam-ing rag on a stick to repel the bees but runs away out of fear.

Scenes 27–33

One day, Uncle Julius takes the narrator and his parents to the island in the middle of one of Mljet's lakes. The narrator almost falls out of the boat, but Uncle Julius catches him. Uncle Julius says the island used to be a haven for pirates who took hostages for ransom, then was a German prison, and now houses a hotel that rarely has any tourists. They walk to the restaurant and Uncle Julius tells a story about his student days in Moscow, when he saw the "oldest man in the world." Uncle Julius explains that the man made him realize that everyone becomes like a child in old age and that there is no point to life because "nothing will change." The narrator and his parents take a ship to the mainland and the narrator sleeps on the way to Sarajevo. They find their plants with-ered and the cat starving because their neighbor who was supposed to feed them has died of a heart attack, and the cat looks at the narrator with "irre-versible hatred."

Characters

Father

The narrator's father makes no individual ap-pearances in the story but is grouped together with his mother. They are not neglectful parents, which is clear from the narrator's description of how spe-cific they are in their rules about when and for how long he can swim, but their son tends not to notice them. He describes them as "sprightly," or lively and animated, although it is difficult to tell whether they are truly enjoying the trip.

German Tourists

The narrator encounters a number of older German tourists on his trip to Mljet, who tend to be somewhat oblivious. They are foreign sightseers who see this Slavic island region as outsiders, with apparently no real comprehension. They are sun-burned, take numerous pictures, and one of them vomits over the side of the ship.

Uncle Julius

A Mljet native who deeply affects the narra-tor, Uncle Julius is a mysterious and somewhat disturbing old man. The story of his life is never spelled out, but the reader is able to piece together some key details of his years in Russia based on the stories he tells. He is from the Ukraine, which was a part of the former U.S.S.R., and he spent his student days in Moscow, where he studied biology. It is unclear how or why he became a prisoner in Stalin's labor camps, but by 1943 he was in the camp at Arkangelsk, Russia, where he met Vanyka for the first time. After this, Uncle Julius was trans-ferred to different camps (for how long or how many he is unsure), but he ended up as a grave-digger in Siberia. Somehow he made his way to Mljet, where he is married to Aunt Lyudmila and keeps bees in the tradition of his Ukrainian family.

With his soft lips "like slugs," his stink of "rot and decay," his bulging eyes, his "peculiar, tran-quil smile," and his stained gums missing their teeth, Uncle Julius cuts a rather fearsome figure to a young boy. The most frightening aspects of his character, however, are his horrific stories, which he says the narrator "should know." Someone, likely Aunt Lyudmila, says ominously that the nar-rator "won't be able to sleep ever again" if he hears Uncle Julius's stories, and the last story in which Uncle Julius tells the narrator "You might as well stop living now, my son," is particularly disturb-ing. In fact, Hemon seems to emphasize that the main subject of "Islands" is the impression that

Uncle Julius makes on the young narrator, implying that it affected him for many years afterwards.

Aunt Lyudmila

Aunt Lyudmila is Uncle Julius's wife. The narrator says her face is like "a loaf of bread with a small tubby potato in the middle" and that her calves, ankles, and bare feet are bruised, swollen, and warped. This must be because she has been subject to very hard work throughout her life, with the implication that she is a tough and stolid woman. It is unclear how or when she met Uncle Julius. The narrator does not seem to like her because of the slobbery kiss she gives him and her failure to notice or object to the slug in the water tank.

Mother

The narrator's mother has slightly more presence in the narrative than does his father. She is the one who tends to speak to the narrator and take care of him, and he suggests that he is close to her early in the story when he hides his face in her skirt. Nevertheless, she is grouped with her husband as a rather abstract authority figure to whom the narrator generally pays little attention.

Narrator

A sensitive and perceptive nine-year-old boy who remains unnamed is the narrator and protagonist of Hemon's story. As he begins his island voyage, he wears a round straw hat painted with the seven dwarves from *Snow White*, but it blows away in the wind. He enjoys swimming and playing in the sand, but he is unenthusiastic about the trip to Mljet. A generally obedient boy, he is impressionable and curious. The main subject of the story is the narrator's experience as he listens to Uncle Julius's stories and his perceptions of his uncle's general attitude towards him. Uncle Julius is not necessarily trying to scare or traumatize the narrator, but he does seem to be imparting some type of lesson.

Because Hemon's collection *The Question of Bruno* is autobiographical, from the perspective of an older Bosnian man living in the United States, and because the story is organized in brief scenes like islands of memory, there is the sense that the narrator is an adult thinking back to his childhood. However, the narrative perspective is that of an observant child who is still forming his opinion about the world. He seems unsure quite how all of the pieces of the story fit together, but he seems to recognize that they are significant to his youth and development. This is perhaps why he speaks about

waking up without knowing "where I was or who I was" and feeling "present in my own body" when he dives into the sea; he is forming an understanding of his place in his family and society.

Joseph Stalin

As brutal or more brutal than Adolf Hitler, Joseph Stalin (1879–1953) was the ruthless communist dictator who headed the Union of Soviet Socialist Republics (U.S.S.R.) between 1924 and 1953. Stalin attempted to industrialize the Soviet Union by destroying millions whom he thought stood in his way: farmers, intellectuals, religious people, political dissenters, and those who were undesirables for whatever reason. Under his command, more than 10 million people perished in labor camps that dotted Siberia.

Comrade Tito

Marshal Josip Broz Tito (1892–1980) was the communist president of the former Yugoslavia (a country consisting of six republics that was created in 1945) from 1953 until his death in 1980. A war hero and longtime Communist Party member, he unified the country imitating Stalin's government and policies but then broke away from the international Communist Party after a rift with Stalin.

Vanyka

The subject of Uncle Julius's story about the time he spent in Soviet labor camps, Vanyka is a resourceful and desperate blonde boy with blue eyes whose life is destroyed by Stalin's regime. He is only twelve when he is sent to Arkhangelsk camp either because he was "repeatedly late for school or missed several days with no excuse." Unlike most of the other children at the camp, he manages to survive by "lending himself" which means he offers himself sexually to criminals, as well as by stealing food and bribing guards.

Because of Vanyka's habit of speaking his mind, the guards beat him mercilessly and abuse him. He begins to kill and do "bad, bad things." He learns how to survive, but he continues to speak out so the authorities send him to a sort of pirates' island on which criminals are allowed to rob and kill each other. Vanyka attempts to escape, killing and eating three people in the process, but guards catch him and put him in solitary confinement, torturing him. He tries to kill himself and, when Uncle Julius meets him for the second time, all he wants is to die, but the guards keep him alive so he suffers more. The narrator is deeply affected by Vanyka's story and asks what happened to him, but

Uncle Julius simply says dismissively that he was killed, frightening his nephew even more.

Themes

Memory

Partly because it is the first story in an autobiographical collection of fiction from the perspective of a Bosnian immigrant to the United States, there is the sense that "Islands" is a journey into childhood memory from the standpoint of an adult. The story's short scenes are like islands of memory that combine to form an array of impressions about the family trip to Mljet. They contain specific observations and piece together the overall impression or significance of the trip. For example, with the frame of reference of a little boy, the narrator describes "a Popsicle-yellow lizard, as big as a new pencil, on the stone wall behind Uncle Julius's back," with its "unblinking marble eye."

Hemon seems to be commenting, therefore, on the nature of memory and the process of extracting significance from past experience. He implies that the memory selects certain details to retain vividly, and these chosen parts act as beacons or signposts to what was significant or moving about an experience. These memories combine in complex and subtle ways; the narrator may remember the German shepherd's gums so vividly, for example, because they remind him of Uncle Julius's toothless gums, and he may remember his cat's "irreversible hatred" in such stark terms because he may feel that he has been neglected himself. Hemon implies that the memory categorizes and stores what is important to it in this sort of coded manner, particularly childhood memories when revisited or re-envisioned in adulthood.

Childhood Trauma

One of the key themes of "Islands" is the significance of the events of the story to the narrator's later life, particularly the trauma he feels during the vacation. Although he experiences a number of potentially traumatizing events, such as when he loses his hat or sees a German shepherd kill a mongoose, the narrator is most significantly troubled by the stories and general persona of his Uncle Julius.

Uncle Julius is not necessarily a malicious man, but he does seem to think it is a good idea for the narrator to hear some bone-chilling stories,

as evidenced when he says "he should know" in reference to the story about Vanyka. If, as is likely, "Islands" is told from the point of view of an adult looking back on his childhood, these tales would have stayed in the narrator's memory for a long time and hold significance for him. Because they are filled with such a threatening vision of the world, however, they are emotionally disturbing and appear to become longstanding childhood trauma.

Self-Consciousness

The narrator of Hemon's story frequently talks about his sense of himself, usually in physical terms such as his awareness of his own body. When he is swimming, for example, the narrator notes that "the shock of coldness would make me feel present in my own body," and when he is walking along the path to Uncle Julius's house he notes that "the sudden coolness made me conscious of how hot my shoulders felt." Perhaps the most important of these moments comes after Uncle Julius tells the story of Vanyka. After sleeping, the narrator wakes up "and didn't know where I was or who I was" and then gets up "out of my nonbeing." Although all of these moments are understandable and even common, they imply that the narrator is experiencing a period of self-consciousness, questioning his identity and his place in the world.

Authority

"Islands," a story about a child's relationship with adult family members, includes a lengthy passage about the dictatorship of Joseph Stalin. In this way, the story takes on the theme of power and influence over others. Uncle Julius seems to influence the narrator, and this resonates, in certain ways, with his horrific description of power and authority during Stalin's regime. It is clear that the narrator identifies with Vanyka, although their situations contrast sharply; he attempts to imagine what it would be like to have one's childhood and happiness taken away by a brutal and tyrannical system of authority. Interestingly, the narrator seems to have little tension or confrontation with his own parents (although they do have strict rules about swimming, for example), so Uncle Julius seems to inspire him to think about authority in a new way. Hemon is careful to bring up the theme of authority at the final moment of the story, in which the narrator views what he considers the "irreversible hatred" of a cat that has been neglected and (though accidentally) tortured by those who hold power over it.

Topics For Further Study

- Research the history of the Bosnian Civil War between 1992 and 1995. What were its key causes? What parties and factions were involved? Describe the ethnically motivated violence and discuss why it could be considered genocide. What has happened to those accused of war crimes? Discuss the United Nations response, the nature of the peace settlement, and the outcome of the war.

- Think of a family vacation you took when you were in elementary school, or a period of time spent with a relative that made an impression on you. What are your most vivid memories of it? Write down a series of memories and then form them into a series of short storytelling scenes. What was important about the episodes you chose? What are your lasting impressions? What do they say about your relationship with your family or your relative?

- Read another story in *The Question of Bruno*, such as "A Coin" or "The Sorge Spy Ring," and compare it to "Islands." Describe the common features of the stories' narrative voices, technical styles, and storytelling structures. Describe their key differences. How do their themes relate, and how does a knowledge of another of Hemon's stories add to your appreciation of "Islands?"

- Do research on the Soviet labor and prison camps of the 1930s and 1940s. Who was sent to the camps, and why? What was life like inside them? How did the camps differ (how would a camp in Arkhangelsk have differed from one in Siberia, for example), and how did they change during Stalin's long reign? How did the camps affect Soviet life and the perception, domestically and internationally, of communist governments?

Style

Short Scenes

The fact that "Islands" is made up of thirty-three short scenes is crucial to its storytelling format. Although they combine to form a chronological narrative, these scenes are like brief glimpses into specific moments of the narrator's childhood, or individual islands of memory that can seem somewhat distinct. In fact, some of the scenes focus on specific details that do not at first seem to correspond to the main point and progression of the story, such as the narrator's vivid description of the fish that he sees while swimming. All of the scenes are important either in developing the sense of place or developing the plot, but Hemon's emphasis on their distance from each other reinforces the sense that the narrator is searching through his clumps of significant memories to find the story. The format of the story, therefore, may be intended to imitate the way that the mind accesses its childhood memories. It is also significant in drawing attention to the idea of islands and isolation, ideas that frequently recur in the narrative and underscore the setting of the story as well as some of its content.

First-Person Childhood Perspective

Hemon is adept at developing a believable first-person narrative voice that speaks and thinks like a nine-year-old boy. Although there is the suggestion, given its place in the larger collection, that "Islands" is being told from the standpoint of an adult looking back on a childhood experience, Hemon is nevertheless careful to enter the narrator's childhood mind in his telling. The narrator's language and the nature of his observations reflect the curiosity, attention to detail, and impressionability of a nine-year-old. Hemon is thereby able to allow his readers to enter the world of a child and bring to life the true significance of the trip to Mljet.

Historical Context

Bosnia-Herzegovina

Given the autobiographical nature of Hemon's short story collection, and based on details from the story, "Islands" is likely set in the 1970s, a decade of relative prosperity in what is in 2005 Bosnia-Herzegovina. Hemon wrote the story in the 1990s, having recently emigrated from Bosnia to the United States. In order to understand the history of Bosnia-Herzegovina in the 1970s and the 1990s, however, it is necessary to have some knowledge of its long and turbulent history.

Bosnia-Herzegovina is one of the six major Balkan states that comprised the former Yugoslavia. It has many of its cultural roots in the Islamic tradition, because of the Ottoman Turkish domination between the fourteenth and nineteenth centuries. By 1908, however, the Austro-Hungarian Empire had officially annexed Bosnia-Herzegovina and attempted to use it as a buffer between the largely Catholic Croatia and the largely Eastern Orthodox Serbia. Ethnic tensions ran high throughout World War I and II, with a Serb-dominated coalition government in place until civil conflicts broke out during World War II. Communists led by Marshal Josip Broz Tito prevailed and set up the Federal Republic of Yugoslavia.

Tito was the communist dictator of the country for nearly five decades, and his style of leadership cannot be described simply as totalitarian, nor can his government be described simply as communist. A war hero revered in Yugoslavia and throughout the world, Tito brought stability and unity to the nation and instituted reforms that allowed the economy to prosper by the 1970s. He defied Stalin with pro-Yugoslavian policies, which led to a rift with the Soviet Union and Western aid to his country. However, throughout his rule, Tito retained control by suppressing nationalist tendencies and forcibly promoting Yugoslav unity.

By the 1970s, minority groups had dispersed into various republics, so Bosnia-Herzegovina was by no means simply a Muslim-dominated area. As evidenced in "Islands," it would be customary for Bosnians living in Sarajevo, as well as Germans and other tourists, to travel to the Croatian island of Mljet. After Tito's sudden death in 1980, however, nationalist tendencies that had been suppressed for years began to emerge in different regions of Yugoslavia. Slovenia and Croatia declared independence in 1990 and 1991, followed by Bosnia-Herzegovina in December of 1991. A number of conflicts began to break out at this point, and coalitions broke apart because of ethnic tensions and nationalistic aspirations. Bosnia was deep in civil war by 1992, with Bosnian Muslims besieged in Sarajevo by Serbian forces and Bosnian Muslims fighting with Bosnian Croats who desired to be a part of a greater Croatia. The situation in Sarajevo reached the point of ethnic cleansing, with Bosnian Muslims starving and dying in great numbers. The United Nations did little to help the situation, but the war in Bosnia-Herzegovina came to an end in 1995 with United Nations troops securing the peace.

Writers in English as a Second Language

Hemon has been compared to two influential European writers who wrote in English as a second language: Joseph Conrad and Vladimir Nabokov. Conrad, the author of *Heart of Darkness* and numerous other famous works, was Polish and learned English only as an adult living in Britain and working as maritime merchant. Nabokov, the sardonic and sophisticated author of novels, including *Lolita*, learned English at an early age but, unlike Conrad, began his writing career in his native language. He became a famous U.S. writer in the post–World War II period, and his writings particularly influenced Hemon. Like Hemon, Nabokov and Conrad were linguistic prodigies who explored the process of forging works in a language not native to them.

Critical Overview

Hemon's first short story collection was extremely well-reviewed in the press; as Richard Eder writes of the book in the *New York Times Book Review*: "Several of the shorter pieces are so good as to make the reader feel certain of having discovered not just an extraordinary story but an extraordinary writer: one who seems not simply gifted but necessary." Other reviewers were equally positive, and the collection received a significant amount of attention. Perhaps, in part, because of the continued crisis in the former Yugoslavia, reviewers tended to pay particular attention to Hemon's treatment of history and politics, praising his insights about Bosnian culture.

Although critics were almost entirely positive and the collection was nominated for a number of awards, some dissenting opinions emerged, including a *National Review* article, in which Stephen

Schwartz writes, "In *The Question of Bruno*, Hemon has produced a first volume of narratives that is, in its essential part, a pure and simple imitation of the outstanding Yugoslav author Danilo Kis." Many critics would disagree with this contention, although some gave Hemon mixed reviews.

Sybil S. Steinberg, who calls Hemon's stories "expertly wrought," mentions "Islands" specifically in her *Publishers Weekly* review, writing that "History . . . erupts" into the narrative. One of the most thorough discussions of the story, however, appears in Daniel Orozco's *San Francisco Chronicle* review of the collection. After claiming that the story "is emblematic of Hemon's startling vision," Orozco writes, "This is a funny and horrifying child's perspective on a dread vacation. . . . this darkly comic story suddenly shifts into even darker territory, with the brutalities of Stalin's regime casting a deep, disquieting pall."

Criticism

Scott Trudell

Trudell is an independent scholar with a bachelor's degree in English literature. In the following essay, Trudell discusses the narrator's loss of innocence in "Islands," particularly how this loss is articulated in his identification with the Soviet prisoner Vanyka.

Uncle Julius scares and traumatizes his nine-year-old nephew in a variety of ways during the short scenes that make up Hemon's story, "Islands." His toothless and smelly body, his description of the snakes and mongooses on Mljet, his characterization of the death of his grandfather, his comments about the former pirate island now sporting a hotel, and his story about the oldest man in the world during which he tells his nephew, "You might as well stop living now," are all frightening for a nine-year-old boy. Perhaps the aspect of the visit that has the greatest impact on the narrator, however, is Uncle Julius's story about Vanyka, the boy whose life is destroyed by the horrific series of circumstances to which he is subjected in the northern Russia.

In fact, "Islands" is balanced between the story of the nine-year-old protagonist on a trip to the Croatian island of Mljet to visit his Uncle Julius, and the story of the boy Vanyka and his experience with the brutal Soviet penal system of the 1940s. These stories describe vastly different circumstances in

Harbor of Dubrovnik in Croatia, formerly part of Yugoslavia Photograph by Susan D. Rock. Reproduced by permission

vastly different societies; in fact, they are like individual islands that do not seem to connect. Like the other islands in Hemon's story, however—Mljet, the pirate's island within Mljet, the prison island to which Vanyka is sent, and the short scenes of island memories themselves—these apparently distinct stories are actually related quite closely. Indeed, one of the central points of interest in "Islands" is how the two glimpses of childhood contrast, and what this says about the societies in which the boys were raised.

Uncle Julius, who seems to want to make an impression on his nephew, tells the story of Vanyka for his benefit, saying ominously that "he should know" the story. The fact that he asks how old the narrator is immediately before doing so suggests that Uncle Julius is imparting a cautionary tale in which Vanyka is meant to serve as a double for the narrator. Since they are nearly the same age, Uncle Julius implies, his nephew should learn something from Vanyka's experience. The essence of this lesson seems to be that the narrator must lose his innocence and recognize the horrible realities of the world.

For his part, the narrator clearly identifies with Vanyka and shows interest in his fate. Since no one

> "Vanyka's childhood trauma brings out the narrator's own loss of innocence, instead of minimizing it or overshadowing it, mainly because his story calls attention to the brutal ways in which authority and society force children to grow up."

else dares say anything when Uncle Julius falls silent, it is a sign of great curiosity that the narrator brings himself to ask, "So what happened to him?" Although the narrator does not mention Vankya for the rest of the story, the unfortunate prisoner's horror story seems to linger on in the narrator's fearful and confused thoughts.

For example, Vanyka's story seems related to the narrator's drama of self-perception. It is immediately after Vanyka's story that the narrator wakes up without knowing "where [he] was or who [he] was." Getting up "out of [his] nonbeing," the narrator is quite self-conscious, and his identity confusion continues throughout the story. Being cold is the only thing that seems to give him some sense of himself; when he dives into the freezing water he feels "present in [his] own body," and the coolness of the path to the house makes him "conscious of how hot [his] shoulders felt." Since the only other extreme cold in the story is that of Arkhangelsk and Siberia, Hemon may be suggesting that Vanyka's story also provides the narrator with a sense of his identity.

Perhaps, more importantly, however, the narrator identifies with Vanyka and is influenced by his story because both boys undergo a loss of innocence. Vanyka attracted the attention of Uncle Julius because he was able to survive the brutal environment of the camp, but, more importantly, because he shouted out ironically, "Thank you, Stalin, for my happy childhood!" Circumstances have

tortured Vanyka and robbed him of his joy and his health, but the most striking thing is that it all happened to him when he was less than fifteen years old, simply because he missed several days of school. Before he went to the camp Vanyka was at the stage of his life that Uncle Julius describes as "knowing nothing, remembering nothing," and within a short period of time he decided that he wanted to die because his life was worse than death.

The narrator is not injured, tortured or imprisoned, but he does experience a loss of innocence. Hemon, who throughout the story is interested in themes of birth, aging, and losing one's childhood, is careful to emphasize in the first sentence the "yolky" sun (an image signifying birth and innocence) and the naive, happy childishness of the narrator. Continually asking if they are there yet during the journey, the narrator innocently wears his straw hat painted with the seven dwarves until the wind suddenly snatches it from his head and he realizes he "would never, ever see it again." Although this could be written off as a funny and seemingly harmless detail, it makes the narrator sob himself to sleep and foreshadows the more shocking losses that follow.

Uncle Julius's intimidating presence wears down his nephew's innocence at every turn. The narrator is frightened or troubled by snakes, mongooses, slugs, Stalin, the futility of life, the lack of a sense of self, undergoing a process of sharp maturation and disillusionment. Instead of the bright yellow, yolky sun, the narrator is confronted with "smoldering soggy eggs" like a fried, melted childhood. This process climaxes when Uncle Julius tells him there is no point in living because "nothing will change," and when his starving cat in Sarajevo looks at him with "irreversible hatred." Here at the end of the story, the narrator seems to have aged years.

Vanyka's childhood trauma brings out the narrator's own loss of innocence, instead of minimizing it or overshadowing it, mainly because his story calls attention to the brutal ways in which authority and society force children to grow up. In fact, one of the most crucial aspects of the narrator's maturation process is clear only when, as in Vanyka's story, the political context is made explicit. This is the way that communism, the government, and society at large play a key role in a child's loss of innocence. Vanyka's loss of childhood is so explicitly related to Stalin and the Soviet labor camps that his experience causes the reader to consider whether the narrator's maturation process may also be affected by Yugoslav communist society.

Upon closer examination, it becomes clear that Hemon is, in fact, commenting on Marshal Tito's communist government and its treatment of Yugoslavian youth. The first clear signal of this is the fact that, in scene 1, the narrator sings communist songs for the entire journey to Mljet about "mournful mothers looking through graves for their dead sons." Communism is thus initially associated with the "yolky" sun and the youthful innocence of the narrator before he begins to experience doubt and fear. Hemon is then careful to emphasize that there is a picture of Tito in the narrator's bedroom "smiling, black-and-white," as well as one in the abandoned island hotel.

After Vanyka's story, however, the narrator begins to be disillusioned with life and human nature, particularly with communism and other systems of power and authority. It begins to be clear, for example, that the mongooses are similar to the communists who took over Russia in the sense that they have merely replaced one exploitative system (the Czarist reign signified by snakes) with another. This seems to reinforce Uncle Julius's comment that vermin follow "one pest after another, like revolutions," implying that the communist revolutions in Russia were simply methods of rearranging systems of power and oppression. The German shepherd that kills the mongoose underscores this point by signifying yet another disillusioning shift of power. Interestingly, the dog's "pink-and-brown gums" and "saliva" are sharply reminiscent of Uncle Julius's toothless pink, stained gums and his slobbery kiss. By the end of the story, the narrator himself (having matured and lost his innocence) is the authority figure that, though unwittingly, tortures and starves his cat so that it responds with "irreversible hatred."

Forms of authority and kinds of oppression combine, therefore, until the narrator seems to concede Uncle Julius's point that "Life is nothing if not a succession of evils" perpetrated by those in power. Although the narrator does not necessarily come to believe wholeheartedly in this conclusion, it is clear that it has made a lasting impression on him. He even comes to a point where he must decide whether Uncle Julius is right that he "might as well stop living now" and, like Vanyka, give up on anything except the hope of death. Hemon is able to articulate the great trauma of this experience only by doubling the narrator with Vanyka. It is through the juxtaposition of their stories that Hemon is able to communicate the great tragedy of a young boy's loss of innocence.

Source: Scott Trudell, Critical Essay on "Islands," in *Short Stories for Students*, Thomson Gale, 2006.

What Do I Read Next?

- Hemon's critically acclaimed novel *Nowhere Man* (2002) follows the early life and emigration to the United States of Josef Pronek, the protagonist of the longest story of *The Question of Bruno*.

- In Vladimir Nabokov's intriguing novel *The Real Life of Sebastian Knight* (1941), the narrator searches for the essence of his half-brother but ends up raising more questions than he answers.

- *In Our Time* (1925) is Ernest Hemingway's striking collection of early short stories, largely about a young man's experience growing up in the Michigan woods.

- Viktor Meier's *Yugoslavia: A History of its Demise* (1999) provides an overview of the history of the former Yugoslavian states in order to analyze the devastating wars and ethnic conflicts that shook the region during the 1990s.

Michele Levy

In the following review, Levy describes The Question of Bruno *as "an intertextual, postmodern metafiction that problematizes history and identity."*

The first work by Aleksandar Hemon, a Bosnian Serb who writes in English and now lives in Chicago, *The Question of Bruno* is an intertextual, postmodern metafiction that problematizes history and identity. Its subtly linked tales embody traces of Kafka and Conrad, earlier writers-in-exile who likewise probed these issues. Many "stories" mingle here, of a Napoleonic soldier, a German spy, Yugoslavia, Western Europe, the Soviet Union, World Wars I and II, a Bosnian exile, and even the United States, whose blindness to history counters that exile's history-consciousness. Spies figure prominently as well, underscoring how history masks identity and ideology obscures truth for the good of the system, feeding "history" new villains.

Through family members, whether real or fictional, Hemons, Hemuns, Franco-Ukrainian,

Yugoslavian President Josip Broz Tito (left) shaking hands with Soviet Premier Nikita Khrushchev
© Bettmann/Corbis

Ukraino-Bosniacs, or Bosnian Serbs divorced from their Ukrainian roots, Hemon critiques "ethnic purity" and explodes "family" myths, as in the infamous family reunion, the Hemoniad. Placing a relative at the scene of the Archduke Ferdinand's assassination, the narrator of "The Accordion" confesses to "doctoring" history, but adds: "Parts of it [this story], however, washed against my shores, having floated on a sea of history books, dotted with islands of black-and-white photographs. A considerable part reached me after it passed through tunnels and mazes of the family memories and legends." Thus does Hemon critique the nature of history.

Erased fictional and historical boundaries, as when characters meet real historical figures, contextualize the work's center, the Bosnian War. In "Blind Josef Pronek & Dead Souls" that conflict catches a young Sarajevan blues musician and writer, as it did Hemon, on an American tour. Repeatedly asking Pronek why it happened, Americans answer his confused silence with, "Thousands of years of hatred," an apparently well-meaning generalization that negates all possibility of, and responsibility for, real understanding. When even his girlfriend's father reiterates, "Thousands of years of hatred, I guess." the question of Bruno arises.

Immediately after both parents declare the Bosnian War "mind-boggling," the dotty grandmother, bearing the tattoo of a concentration-camp survivor, asks, "Where is Bruno?" She searches for him desperately, questioning even Pronek, calling out at last, "Come here, Bruno! Eat with us! We have everything now!" Linking Bosnia to the Holocaust, Hemon constructs the missing Bruno as the human cost of both.

In the last story, "Imitation of Life," the exile-narrator returns to Sarajevo. Waking to Nazi flags "after a night of unsettling dreams," he flees to the train station. But wounded German soldiers dot the tracks, and Nazis remove a hanged man from above his head. Once again Hemon weds the Third Reich and past and present Bosnia to the randomness of death, the quest for identity, and the impossibility of fully escaping one's personal and tribal history.

Finally, Hemon's layered collection challenges us to confront history, wherein ideology fights truth, society the individual. Subverting official "stories," his forms reiterate that while Might too often makes Right, rendering the impotent expendable, art can uncover hidden "histories" and so redeem lives and sufferings concealed by societal masks.

Source: Michele Levy, Review of *The Question of Bruno*, in *World Literature Today*, Vol. 75, No. 2, Spring 2001, p. 332.

Bowker Magazine Group

In the following review, the reviewer praises The Question of Bruno *for being "generously endowed with pathos, humor and irony."*

Much like his protagonist in the novella *Blind Jozef Pronek & Dead Souls*, the cornerstone of this collection of eight stories, Hemon came to the U.S. as a tourist, but had to stay as a refugee when his native Yugoslavia splintered apart. The expertly wrought stories he has written since movingly set his characters' personal memories side by side with history's accidents, the guilt of exile sharing space with the horrors of war, in both straightforward narratives and border-erasing experiments. The constant themes of war and exile mingle most affectingly in "A Coin," in which a Sarajevan's letters detailing the day-to-day terror of the Yugoslavian conflict—what it's like to run the gauntlet of Sniper's Alley or to be unable to bury your dead safely—reach an uneasy emigre in the U.S. who feels eerily isolated from current events and the tides of history. History likewise erupts in "Islands," when a favorite uncle interrupts a family vacation to relate his boyhood experiences in Stalin's labor camps to a narrator not much older than he was then. Elsewhere, history footnotes fiction, as in the experimental "The Sorge Spy Ring," which juxtaposes a wryly compiled case file of an actual Soviet agent with a boy's fantasy of his father's spying for the U.S.S.R. Although Hemon's satiric vision of the U.S. in "Blind Jozef" (a shorter version was published in the *New Yorker*) is less fresh than that of his Titoist childhood, its portrait of a Bosnian writer marking time in a grungy, postmodern Chicago is wryly uncompromising. Generously endowed with pathos, humor and irony, and written in an off-balance, intoxicating English, this collection announces a talent reminiscent of the young Josef Skvorecky.

Source: Bowker Magazine Group, Review of *The Question of Bruno*, in *Publishers Weekly*, Vol. 247, No. 20, May 15, 2000, pp. 87–88.

Mirela Roncevic

In the following review, Roncevic calls Hemon "a rare talent who deserves our attention."

Hemon left his native Bosnia just before the outbreak of the civil war, settled in Chicago, and soon after began rigorously studying English. Unsurprisingly, his debut has been compared to the fiction of Conrad and Nabokov—icons who proved that the risky business of writing in an adopted language can produce admirable results. But Conrad's crowded, premeditated sentences and Nabokov's rhythmical and metaphorical prose are quite different from Hemon's clearheaded fiction, which centers on the unique political tensions of Tito's Yugoslavia. Hemon's writing is sensible, with a hint of satire, and is heavily based on wistful description rather than farfetched dialog. Although dissimilar in format, the seven stories here echo the same nostalgic voice and the theme of dealing with the sudden eruption of childhood memories and the "shifting identities" of a weary immigrant. This kind of fiction doesn't betray itself, but the author's bold experimentation with form easily outsmarts the reader. "The Life and Work of Alphonse Kauders" is actually highly suggestive of Donald Barthelme's clever symbolism, while "A Coin" reveals that Hemon can tell a war story in the tradition of Tim O'Brien, combining magical realism with raw truth. This is the work of a rare talent who deserves our attention.

Source: Mirela Roncevic, Review of *The Question of Bruno*, in *Library Journal*, Vol. 125, No. 12, July 1, 2000, p. 144.

Daniel Davies

In the following review, Davies praises the language in "Islands" for being "beautiful and terrifying in its precision," and compares Hemon's "allegorical power" to that of Albert Camus.

The prospect of writing fiction would make most people nervous. Have I got anything to say? If so, can I say it well? Or will my efforts be laughed out of literary agents' in-trays? So imagine attempting to write in somebody else's language. Of course, many authors have done this in the past. Joseph Conrad penned all his masterpieces in English (his third language), which was the second language of Vladimir Nabokov. Samuel Beckett had a penchant for writing in French, as did T S Eliot. But these are great names in modern literature—and only underline the difficulty of writing in a non-native tongue.

Now we have Aleksandar Hemon, half-Ukrainian, half-Serb. Born in Sarajevo in 1964, he uprooted to Chicago in 1992. Although a published author in his own language, he has been writing in English since only 1995. In his first book in his adopted tongue, *The Question of Bruno,* he gives us seven short stories and a novella. Even if you didn't know that English was his second language, there are plenty of sentences to arouse your suspicions. For example: "He walked up a dilapidated sinuous road exuding heat." This, to me, reads like a translation, and makes me wonder about Hemon's process. Did he think of the sentence in his first language and busy himself with English dictionaries to write it down in his second?

But if some of the language is stilted and clumsy, much of its starting in its virtuosity. In the same story, the narrator describes a dying mongoose: "There was a hole in its chest—the dog seemed to have bitten off a part of it—and I saw the heart, like a tiny tomato, pulsating, as if hiccupping, slower and slower." this is both beautiful and terrifying in its precision, and one can sense Hemon's satisfaction in the central simile.

Both these sentences come from the opening story, "Islands", a boy's vision of a family trip to the island of Mljet that culminates in his uncle's recollections of life in one of Stalin's labour camps. At a time when so much new fiction in English centres around the metropolitan adventures of trendy twenty/thirty somethings in London/New York, Hemon's stories turn over a very different side of life—full of fear, isolation, brutality, and bloodshed. In "Islands"—and with an allegorical power reminiscent of Camus—Hemon uses the struggle between snakes and mongooses to gesture towards the ethnic in his homeland.

Yet the collection is far from relentlessly grisly. Hemon is a playful and experimental writer, whose favourite trick is to intertwine fact and fiction. He is fascinated by the intersection of individual perspective with the impersonal, seismic movement of history. In "The Accordion", Archduke Franz Ferdinand, on his fateful trip to Sarajevo, spots a musician in the crowd, holding an accordion. The accordion player is the narrator's great-grandfather, who is destined to die in the war that is triggered by the assassin's bullet. This mixing of the imaginative and the historical also gives a clue to Hemon's ambition. The question of Bruno is partly a history of Europe during the past century.

Time and again, however, he strikes a more autobiographical note. "Blind Joseph Pronek and Dead Souls", a superb 78-page novella, tells the story of a young Bosnian writer who emigrates to Chicago. The story explores a recurring theme in the collection: exile. The protogonist, Pronek, is a cross between E Annie Proulx's Quoyle and Saul Bellow's Herzog: hapless, erudite, and likeable. America, through his defamiliarising gaze, is not a pretty sight—a country plagued by jingoism and hubris. But it is also a story of great humour and wit. Hemon has some fun with language, contrasting the Americans' slang with Pronek's clumsy attempts at idiomatic English.

The importance of language to one's relation to the world—and to one's self-image—is perhaps the collection's dominant theme. In "Exchange of Pleasant Words", the narrator speaks with great feeling about the immigrant existence: "we have to live these half-lives of people who cannot forget what they used to be and who are afraid of being addressed in a foreign language, no longer able to utter anything meaningful." It could be, of course, that part of Hemon's purpose in writing *The question of Bruno* was to find meaning in his new life in America. Irrespective of whether he has succeeded, this is a collection of grace, intelligence, and originality.

Source: Daniel Davies, "The Half Lives of Immigrants," in *Lancet,* Vol. 356, No. 9245, December 2, 2000, p. 1937.

Sources

Eder, Richard, "An Expatriate at War," in *New York Times Book Review,* July 30, 2000, p. 12.

Hemon, Aleksandar, "Islands," in *The Question of Bruno*, Vintage International, 2001, pp. 1–21; originally published in *Ploughshares*, Vol. 24, No. 1, Spring 1998, pp. 12–25.

Orozco, Daniel, "Funny, Startling Stories of War and Loneliness," in *San Francisco Chronicle*, June 4, 2000.

Schwartz, Stephen, "A Theft of Style," in *National Review*, Vol. 52, No. 20, October 23, 2000, pp. 79–81.

Steinberg, Sybil S., Review of *The Question of Bruno*, in *Publishers Weekly*, Vol. 247, No. 20, May 15, 2000, pp. 87–88.

Further Reading

Hemon, Aleksandar, "The Book of My Life," in the *New Yorker*, Vol. 76, No. 40, December 25, 2000–January 1, 2001, p. 94.
    Hemon's autobiographical article for the *New Yorker* discusses his relationship with his literary mentor and his attitudes towards Serbian nationalism.

Radzinsky, Edvard, *Stalin: The First In-depth Biography Based on Explosive New Documents from Russia's Secret Archives*, Doubleday, 1996.
    Radzinsky's intimate and compelling biography of Stalin provides the key context for Uncle Julius's stories about the Soviet labor camps during the 1930s and 1940s.

Rawicz, Slavomir, *The Long Walk*, Globe Pequot Press, 1997.
    Rawicz's memoir recounts his escape from a Stalin labor camp in Siberia and how, along with several other prisoners, he walked south all the way to India. This remarkable eye-witness account depicts the horrible treatment of political prisoners, and its description of the topography crossed gives a clear idea of how remote Siberia is from Europe and from India.

Utterson, David, Review of *The Question of Bruno*, in *Times Literary Supplement*, No. 5067, May 12, 2000, p. 23.
    Utterson's positive review provides a good example of the British reaction to Hemon's collection.

Mowgli's Brothers

Rudyard Kipling
1894

"Mowgli's Brothers" was first published in May of 1894 as one of seven stories included in Rudyard Kipling's collection *The Jungle Book*. Several years after first outlining the traits and personality of his character Mowgli, Kipling published *The Jungle Book*, which was considered "the literary event" of 1894. Kipling is known for his colorful depictions of characters, both human and animal, and for setting, most often the jungles of India, and his predilection for delivering a moral or lesson. "Mowgli's Brothers" is no exception. It is the story of the orphaned boy, Mowgli, who is adopted by a pack of wolves and must learn how to live in the jungle with the pack. The tale is rich in self-exploration and the search for personal identity.

The story exemplifies the struggle between Mowgli's learned traits as a wolf and his innate traits as a man. The two mutually exclusive identities create great difficulty for Mowgli as he attempts to be both what he is by birth and what he has become in the jungle. Through his attention to the Law of the Jungle, Mowgli is proven a worthy member of the pack. Yet, through his innate human faculties, he possesses a power that is enviable among the jungle creatures. In the polar characteristics of Mowgli's complex identity as wolf and man, Kipling constructs a didactic framework from which he delivers lessons and morals.

Author Biography

Joseph Rudyard Kipling, a turn of the nineteenth-century author, was one of Britain's most distinguished writers of novels and short stories. A prolific writer, Kipling achieved recognition quickly, and his works left an impressive mark on the literary world of short fiction and children's literature.

Kipling was born December 30, 1865 in Bombay, India, the first child of John Lockwood Kipling and his wife Alice. Except for a short trip to England in 1868 for the birth of his sister, Kipling lived in India most of his first five years. Kipling's sister appeared to be stillborn, with a black eye and a broken arm, but was revived by the doctor. This event earned her the nickname *Trixie*, for her father's description of her as a "tricksy baby."

During the latter half of his stay in India, Rudyard was considered a tiny despot. He was a rowdy, vocal, and slightly unruly child. He spoke to the servants in their native tongue, loved his ayah (Indian maid or nurse), and was sincerely happy surrounded by India's exotic riches. However, the pleasure he found in India was short-lived, as his parents sought to save their children from the fever-ridden climate and wanted them to acquire English educations. Thus, in 1871, Rudyard and Trixie were sent to be educated at a foster home in Southsea, Hampshire. Rudyard was incredibly forlorn and the experiences of these early years undeniably shaped his writings.

In 1878, Kipling attended a boarding school known as the United Services College at Westward Ho in north Devon. Over the next four years, Rudyard became a voracious reader and his writing skills blossomed. At sixteen, Kipling returned to his parents in Lahore, India and began working for the newspapers, the *Civil and Military Gazette* and the *Pioneer*. Alongside his journalism, Kipling wrote many poems and short stories. These writings were later collected and published, winning him early fame.

During his years with the *Pioneer*, Kipling was able to do a great deal of traveling. In 1889, he went through Asia and the United States, visiting Burma, Singapore, Hong Kong, Japan, San Francisco, and New York City. By 1890, Kipling made his way to England where he befriended Wolcott Balestair, an American literary agent living in London. The two worked together briefly before Wolcott's untimely death from typhus in 1891.

In 1892, Rudyard married Wolcott's sister, Carrie Balestair, and the two embarked on a round-the-world voyage. During this trip, Kipling outlined

Rudyard Kipling   © Underwood & Underwood/Corbis

"Mowgli's Brothers" and, upon completion of the trip, the couple settled in Brattleboro, Vermont. In Brattleboro, the Kiplings had their first two children, Josephine and Elsie. It is also there that Kipling wrote his most famous work, *The Jungle Book*.

The Kiplings returned to England in 1896, due to a family quarrel, and they quickly had their third child, John. In 1899, during a visit to United States, the family fell ill with pneumonia and Josephine died. During these years, some of Kipling's most famous works were published. He gained world recognition for *The Jungle Book*, *The Second Jungle Book*, *Kim*, *Stalky & Co.*, and *Just So Stories*.

Although he was content throughout most of his life, Josephine's death had a profound impact upon Kipling. The loss was devastating, and in the wake of his increasing popularity, it was difficult for Kipling to escape tourists and devotees. In 1902 he moved, seeking seclusion, to a home in Sussex where he spent all of his remaining years. However, Kipling continued to write and travel. His works earned him great accolades, including knighthood and the poet laureateship of England, most of which he refused. He did, however, accept one award, the Nobel Prize for Literature in 1907.

As his works depict, Kipling was feverishly passionate about travel and dedicated to his children.

Media Adaptations

- The stories of Mowgli from *The Jungle Book* have been adapted for the screen. Most notable is Disney's 1967 animated feature staring Phil Harris as the voice of Baloo and Bruce Reitherman as the feral man-cub, Mowgli.

- In addition to the animated feature, Disney produced a second adaptation in 1994, called *Rudyard Kipling's "The Jungle Book."* Stephen Sommers directed Disney's return to the tales of Mowgli, setting aside animation in favor of live action.

- In 1942, Zoltan Korda directed a rough rendition of *The Jungle Book*, starring the young Indian actor, Sabu. The movie does not follow the text exactly, but the movie's Technicolor and exotic setting are effective.

All of his popular works were filled with lessons to children and inspired adults, giving newfound meaning to the genre of children's literature. On January 18, 1936, Rudyard Kipling died of peritonitis caused by a hemorrhaging gastric ulcer. His work continued to be praised into the early 2000s, its morals and the metaphors of his tales, fables, and novels proving to be timeless.

Plot Summary

The story opens with the presentation of Mother and Father Wolf and the family's necessity for food. Father Wolf is readying himself to begin hunting to feed his mate and cubs when the jackal, Tabaqui, enters their den looking for scraps. Tabaqui finds a bone and is satisfied. After eating the bone, the devious jackal compliments the wolves' children to their faces, which is considered unlucky. Both Mother and Father Wolf are uncomfortable, and Tabaqui revels in his mischief. Amidst the tension, Tabaqui delivers the news that the lame tiger, Shere Kahn, plans to shift his hunting patterns to the wolves' hills. This news angers Father Wolf who knows that the tiger will disrupt the patterns of local game, making his hunt increasingly difficult. The exchange so frustrates Father Wolf that he throws Tabaqui out of his den.

After sending Tabaqui out of their cave, Mother and Father Wolf hear the tiger below in the brush. Father Wolf is angered because the tiger's noise will surely scare away his family's dinner. Mother Wolf realizes that Shere Kahn is not hunting game, but man. The wolves are anxious as they listen to the tiger because the Law of the Jungle forbids killing man, except under certain circumstances. They hear the tiger spring to attack, but none of the villagers is caught. The tiger lands in the fire, burning his paws and scaring the villagers away. The wolves are pleased, but they hear something coming towards their den. Father Wolf poises himself for attack, and just as the creature is about to arrive, Father Wolf leaps to attack. Checking mid-jump, Father Wolf realizes the creature is a small "man-cub." Father brings the boy into the den and the boy pushes his way in between the wolf cubs looking for warmth. Next, Shere Kahn and Tabaqui arrive, blocking the entrance to the wolves' cave and demanding the man-cub. Father Wolf does not comply, and the tiger roars with anger. Mother Wolf leaps forward, threatening and insulting the lame tiger. Shere Kahn, although filled with fury, leaves the den, proclaiming that eventually he will get the man-cub. Shere Kahn knows that tall cubs, man or beast, must be presented to the pack at Council Rock. The tiger believes the pack will reject the man-cub, and he will be able to finally eat the boy.

The wolves decide they must keep the man-cub, and Mother Wolf names him Mowgli the Frog because he is small and hairless. After some time, Mother and Father Wolf decide that it is time to present their cubs to the pack at Council Rock. At the Council Rock, the cubs are all brought before the pack. Akela, the leader, instructs everyone to, "Look well—look well, O Wolves!" If there is a dispute over the right of a cub to be accepted into the pack, then the cub must be spoken for by two members of the pack other than his mother and father. Mother Wolf pushes Mowgli into the middle of the pack to be accepted or rejected. There is a great disturbance, fueled by Shere Kahn's desire to eat the boy. Yet, in the end, two extended members of the back, Baloo the Bear and Bagheera the Panther, speak for Mowgli. Baloo agrees to teach the boy the Law of the Jungle, and Bagheera buys the pack with a freshly killed bull. With this, Mowgli enters the wolf pack.

After Mowgli's first appearance at Council Rock, the story leaps forward by a decade. With the help of his family, Baloo, and Bagheera, Mowgli now understands the Law of the Jungle. He knows what to eat, how to kill, and how to enjoy the jungle. He understands that Shere Kahn is not to be trusted. Mother Wolf tells him that one day he must kill Shere Kahn.

Akela is aging, and Shere Kahn sees the changing of leadership as an opportunity to turn the pack against Mowgli. He plants the seed of envy amongst the young wolves by reminding them that no animal in the jungle can look Mowgli between the eyes. The tiger challenges the wolves by proclaiming that Mowgli is too powerful, too much like man, and that he does not belong in the jungle. Shere Kahn convinces part of the pack to plot against Akela. Once Akela misses a kill, the Law of the Jungle allows the pack to challenge the leader one-by-one until someone kills the leader, taking his position. With the change of tide, Shere Kahn believes he will finally be allowed to eat Mowgli.

Bagheera is aware of Shere Kahn's devious plan. He informs Mowgli and counsels the boy. The panther tells Mowgli to steal fire from the village and then, at Council Rock when the pack is set to challenge Akela, wield the fire and save the aging leader from the tiger's cabal. Mowgli follows Bagheera's advice. At his final appearance at Council Rock, Mowgli listens to Shere Kahn's attempts to incite his followers to overthrow Akela. Clearly his only motivation is his desire to eat Mowgli. With a large portion of the pack against him, Mowgli begins to understand that he must leave the jungle and return to a human existence. Yet, in a final act of gratitude, Mowgli silences Shere Kahn and his wolves. He ignites a dead branch with the fire he has stolen from the villagers, frightening all the beasts. Mowgli exerts the power of fire, burning Shere Kahn and sending him howling into the jungle. After disposing of the tiger, Mowgli demands that Akela be allowed to live, and he banishes the mutinous members of the pack. With this final show of power, Mowgli knows he must forever leave the jungle and enter an unknown future in the village. He says farewell to his foster family and walks down the hillside toward the village.

Characters

Akela

Akela is the stoic leader of the wolf pack. He is also called The Lone Wolf. At Council Rock, Akela shows no change in emotion as the families present their cubs to the pack. Even when Mother Wolf pushes Mowgli into the moonlight, Akela proclaims, "Look Well, O Wolves!" Akela proves himself a fair leader even when his pack wishes to banish Mowgli. He stands by the man-cub as part of the pack because Mowgli has proven himself. Akela has great respect for the Law of the Jungle and rules his wolves with integrity and justice. Mowgli, recognizing Akela's good and faithful nature, saves Akela from certain death at their final meeting at Council Rock.

Bagheera

Bagheera, a cunning, terrifying black panther, is known both as a smooth talker and a wild, reckless assailant of the jungle. At the first Council Rock, as the pack circles hoping to kill Mowgli, Bagheera offers a recently killed bull to the pack in exchange for the child's life. This, coupled with Baloo's offer to teach the boy the Law of the Jungle, saves Mowgli's life. Bagheera plays an important role in Mowgli's development. Bagheera lived among men as a young panther and, thus, knows the character of man, and he recognizes them in Mowgli. Most pervasive and devastating to Mowgli's future in the pack is his ability to stare down any animal in the jungle, even the fierce Bagheera. Bagheera's explanation of Mowgli's place among men and his power over the animals helps guide Mowgli in his final appearance at Council Rock. Bagheera is Mowgli's mentor, his most trusted guide as Mowgli makes his final maneuvers before leaving the jungle.

Baloo

Baloo, a quiet, brown bear, is responsible for teaching wolf cubs the Law of the Jungle. Although a famous character from other stories, Baloo is only briefly mentioned in "Mowgli's Brothers." At the first meeting at Council Rock, Baloo speaks for the man-cub and promises to teach him the ways of the pack. Baloo and Bagheera the panther are responsible for saving Mowgli from the wolves at this first meeting at Council Rock.

Father Wolf

Father Wolf is Mowgli's surrogate father in "Mowgli's Brothers." Father Wolf nearly kills Mowgli as he rustles out of the bushes, fleeing from a tiger. Father Wolf checks his lunge, just as the boy ambles out. Mother Wolf and Father Wolf decide to raise the boy alongside their cubs and, when the time is right, bring Mowgli before the pack at Council Rock.

Mother Wolf

Mother Wolf is Mowgli's surrogate mother in "Mowgli's Brothers." She is also called Raksha, The Demon, because of her prowess as a hunter and devoted mother. Mother Wolf is responsible for naming Mowgli and convincing Father Wolf to raise him with their other cubs. At Council Rock when it appears the pack may not accept Mowgli, Mother Wolf shows devotion to her man-cub as she prepares to fight to the death to protect him from Shere Kahn and the naysaying members of the pack. She is deeply devoted to and proud of Mowgli and incredibly saddened by his decision to leave the jungle.

Mowgli

Mowgli, the main character of "Mowgli's Brothers," is first named by Mother Wolf as Mowgli the Frog when he wanders into their den after a narrow escape from the tiger, Shere Kahn. Although a human, Mowgli, with the help of Baloo the Bear and Bagheera the Panther, is accepted at Council Rock by the pack as one of their own. Because of his innate human traits, Mowgli is able to stare down and intimidate the animals of the jungle. Mowgli does not recognize this as an enviable skill; he simply finds it amusing that the animals will lower their eyes when he stares at them. Unfortunately, this creates a division among the animals—those who are friendly with Mowgli and those who are envious of Mowgli. Eventually, Mowgli recognizes that his inclusion in the pack is disrupting the Laws of the Jungle and that many wish to banish him from the jungle. Yet before his departure, Mowgli takes it upon himself to right several wrongs, punishing Shere Kahn and the wolves that turned against him and saving Akela from an unjust death. His self-realization as a man and the division among the pack members lead Mowgli to his voluntary exile from the jungle and his return to the world of man.

Shere Kahn

Shere Kahn is the tiger responsible for scaring a human family who, in their retreat from the tiger, abandon their young son. The young child, Mowgli, wanders into a wolves' den. Shere Kahn looks eagerly for the easy meal, but it is to no avail because Mother and Father Wolf refuse to give the boy up. Shere Kahn, also referred to as The Big One, Lungri, and The Lame One (due to his lame paw), is most noted for disrupting the Laws of the Jungle. Because of his lame paw, Shere Kahn preys too frequently upon man and domestic cattle. Shere

Kahn's choices disturb regular movements of game and have even brought men into the jungle, bearing torches and guns. Later, when Mowgli is brought to Council Rock, the pack's decision to accept the man-cub angers Shere Kahn who vows to avenge his lost meal and someday eat him. However, his plans are foiled because Mowgli grows up with great prowess, and his skill becomes the envy of the jungle. Eventually, Mowgli is the avenger, burning Shere Kahn's brow and sending him howling into the jungle.

Tabaqui

Tabaqui is a mangy, untrustworthy jackal referred to as The Dish Licker. He is Shere Kahn's sidekick. Tabaqui directs Shere Kahn to Mother and Father Wolf's den as the tiger searches for his lost meal, the child later named Mowgli. In the den, Tabaqui comments about the Wolf's cubs, making them both very uncomfortable. Eventually, because of Tabaqui's deviousness and Shere Kahn's tyrannical requests, Mother and Father Wolf scorn them both, driving them from their den.

Themes

Nature versus Nurture

The nature part of the story pertains to Mowgli's innate classification as a human. His body is human, hairless and upright. The nurture part of the story pertains to his learned traits and characteristics. His extended foster family teaches him everything he must know to be a wolf. He hunts when he is hungry; he sleeps in a cave with his family. Mowgli understands and lives by the Law of the Jungle. Mowgli's identity grows based on both his innate nature and the conditioning he receives from his surrogate family. Although he never breaks the Law of the Jungle, he continues to develop his prowess as a human being. This fact is evident in his ability to stare down any animal in the jungle. In addition, Mowgli grows as a human even though he follows the jungle code. He understands and recognizes himself as being like the villagers even though he feels as if he could live as a wolf for all of his days.

Experience and Knowledge

Mowgli develops an understanding of the jungle based on his experience. Interacting with the jungle and the teachings of Baloo, Bagheera, his family, and the pack shape his experience and

Topics For Further Study

- When he returns to his family and the village after being away in the jungle for a decade Mowgli is not prepared for human lifestyle. How would you expect Mowgli to interact with his father? What would be some possible arguments Mowgli might face living in a house as opposed to a cave? Are there any lessons that would cross over or possibly even benefit his human family?

- British imperialism played an important role in Kipling's writing and life. The social codes he felt compelled to follow were directly related to his fevered defense and support of spreading justice. However, it is apparent his wishes were not fulfilled as many Indians suffered great injustice and dehumanization. Research another example of imperialism during the last two centuries, explaining the impact on literature and politics.

- Charles Darwin was a British naturalist who lived during the nineteenth century. In his work *On the Origin of Species*, Darwin constructs a scientific theory of evolution, concluding that variations within a species occur at random and that survival of each organism is dependant upon that organism's ability to adapt to an environment. In light of this theory, examine Mowgli as an evolutionary human organism. Is Mowgli still human? Is he a wolf? Has he undergone a specialization that sets him apart from all humans and all animals, thus creating a new organism? If he is not a new organism, what can be made of his adaptation to the jungle environment?

---

develop his knowledge of the jungle. In this regard, Mowgli is an example of empiricism. With his accumulation of knowledge through experience, Mowgli is able to develop the skills necessary for survival and pleasure in the jungle. Experience provides him with knowledge, both of the jungle and of himself as a wolf.

Reason and Knowledge

Mowgli develops his knowledge of humans through his reasoning faculty. It is from within that Mowgli is able to grasp his identity as a human. He is able to see the similarity between himself and the villagers, but it is his deduction that leads him to the knowledge of his inborn nature. Reason compels Mowgli to grasp the universals that mandate his power over the animals. Even Mowgli's dear friend and mentor, Bagheera, the most feared animal in the jungle, cannot withstand the stare of the boy. Mowgli does not learn the power of the stare. He grows to understand it through the rationalist process of deductive reasoning. This power, in turn, helps Mowgli to understand the determined laws that dictate his nature as a human being.

Abandonment

In "Mowgli's Brothers," Mowgli faces abandonment twice: first, he loses his family in the tiger attack, and, second, at the end of the story, he is cast out by the pack. Both events are compensated by victories. When Mowgli loses his family, he is embraced, protected, and accepted by a team of foster parents: Mother and Father Wolf, Akela, Baloo, and Bagheera. His extended family loves him deeply, but they are also aware and leery of his power. The boy's strength as a human being lessens his vulnerability. This circumstance mitigates the trauma of his separation from his birth family. In the other instance, when most of the pack wishes to banish Mowgli, he defeats his enemy, the lame tiger, Shere Kahn. Mowgli overcomes the banishment by singeing the tiger, sending him fleeing into the jungle, and by exercising his will over the pack to save Akela and get rid of his saboteurs.

Laws and Codes

Kipling's story is based on laws and codes. He constructs a strict Law of the Jungle that mimics the strictness of the code Mowgli's foster family makes

Mowgli follow as a youth. Within a framework of codes, Kipling creates the complicated title character. With the Law of Jungle and the Law of Man, Mowgli faces two systems that are intended to dictate his decisions. However, these codes clash, so Mowgli is pulled in opposite directions.

Discrimination and Envy

Kipling explores both discrimination and envy in "Mowgli's Brothers." In the beginning of the story, Mowgli is treated differently than the other wolf cubs because his appearance is different than theirs. Because Mowgli is a member of another specie and looks different, and the wolf pack wants nothing to do with him. He is different. He cannot be accepted as a member because he does not look like the group. Luckily, Baloo and Bagheera are able to save Mowgli from certain death. Later, as the boy grows and learns, discrimination and envy become linked. Mowgli learns the Law of the Jungle, and it directs his decisions. At the same time, because he is human, he is able stare down the animals. While Mowgli sees this trait as humorous, the animals see it as proof that he is superior to them. The animals see his stare as proof that he is wise beyond their comprehension. Shere Kahn and the wolves are jealous of Mowgli's stare, so they work together to banish Mowgli from the pack. Their envy of Mowgli's apparent power causes them to want to drive Mowgli from the jungle.

Mowgli as a Jungian Archetype

Psychologist Carl Jung used the term archetype in connection with his description of the unconscious. He argued that the unconscious is composed of two parts: the personal, consisting of an individual's own memories and repressed information; and the universal or archetypal, consisting of those patterns and symbolic elements that all human beings inherit from a shared racial past. The content an individual shares with all other members of the race Jung called the collective unconscious. The archetype is prototypical or original material. This content surfaces in literature in the form of the recurrent story, myth, or character type. It causes strong emotional response because it is universally relevant. Literary criticism can apply the term archetype to a given story or character that illustrates a paradigm or recurrent pattern.

Mowgli's story echoes the myth of Romulus and Remus, the twin boys who were taken from their mother and thrown into the Tiber River. The brothers were discovered by a female wolf, who suckled them. In this myth, Romulus grew up to become the founder of Rome. The character of Mowgli and his story repeat some features of the Romulus myth. Mowgli, a human child, is reared among wolves and then leaves the animal kingdom to return to human civilization. In this sense, then, one might say that Mowgli is archetypal. In terms of Jung's idea of the collective unconscious, one might interpret the end of Mowgli's story, his departure from the jungle and return to the village, as a reenactment of a memory stored in the vague recesses of the unconscious of a time when human beings stood upright and "left" the animal kingdom. Something distinguished these very early human-like beings from the animals around them (perhaps their ability to stare down the animals), and this difference caused them to separate from jungle existence. The remembered moment is itself a construction or distillation of a developmental process that occurred during the development of the human race. That extremely slow process is compressed and dramatized succinctly in Mowgli's departure from the wolf pack.

Style

Beast Fable

"Mowgli's Brothers," as well as the other short stories in Kipling's collection, is a beast fable, a story in which the characters are animals with human faculties. Kipling's fable teaches lessons. The fable is effective in "Mowgli's Brothers" because it creates a world beyond human civilization, the jungle, which is governed by a different set of rules. The animals are expected to follow the Law of the Jungle. Within the fable, animals are able to reason and speak within a set of laws similar to man's laws but still outside them. The fable form allows the mutually exclusive laws of man and beast to be dramatized. Even if the Law of the Jungle is similar to the Law of Man, the distinction between animals and humans makes clear the differences between their codes. Thus, the fable, which puts forth these two codes, provides the stage for Mowgli's conflict of identity.

Point of View and Narrative Voice

Kipling uses the third person in "Mowgli's Brothers." The third-person narrative defines the contrasting laws without bias. However, the narrative is sometimes emotional. The narrator describes lawbreakers, like Shere Kahn and Tabaqui, negatively. These characters are unattractive, while

Compare & Contrast

- **Late Nineteenth Century:** Kipling and other British imperialists staunchly believe in the benefits of colonization and its positive effect on economy, justice, and public health worldwide.

  Today: Historians and modern politicians alike are quick to note that imperialism, regardless of the era, has a dire impact on indigenous cultures.

- **Late Nineteenth Century:** Conservatism dictates the social code under which men and women interact. Women and men are expected to remain reserved under all social circumstances.

  Today: Men and women alike are believed to be empowered with creativity and are encouraged to show their individuality and to think "outside the box." Television shows featuring extreme behavior and achievement are popular.

- **Late Nineteenth Century:** Strict adherence to code and law is imperative to being a good, upstanding citizen. There is little flexibility in conservatism and the Victorian order must be upheld at all costs.

  Today: Adherence to the law is presented as essential for the proper functioning of society, but this is balanced with an awareness of the weaknesses of the legal system. In addition, in the United States, the more conservative Republican party and the more liberal Democratic party vie for political control of the country, so the country may alternate between a period of greater conservatism and a period of greater liberalism.

kindly characters, such as Bagheera, are described in positive terms. This helps to create the tone needed to develop the plot and conflict between the characters.

Historical Context

Born in India in 1865, Kipling was a product of late nineteenth-century British imperialism, an expansionist policy that justified the economic benefits to be had in conquering undeveloped lands with a language of paternalism and benevolence. In 1899, Kipling's poem, "White Man's Burden" (which was in fact addressed to Americans as they took control of the Philippines) revealed the racism inherent in imperialism and, historically, did much to tarnish Kipling's reputation.

The purpose of British imperialism in the second half of the nineteenth century was to find a solution to longstanding economic depression in England. The answer seemed to lie in the previously untapped natural and cultivated resources of other countries. Many people shared Kipling's belief that the British were racially superior and that this supposed superiority obliged the British to impose their culture, government, and education system on other countries. The propaganda of the day, openly attacked in Joseph Conrad's novel *Heart of Darkness* (1902), claimed that the dark races in non-industrialized regions of the Earth would be given the lamp of progress. In truth indigenous cultures were destroyed, natives were often virtually enslaved, and local resources were exploited. However this situation was not initially the perception back home. By the last quarter of the nineteenth century, the British Empire controlled one-fourth of the inhabited land on the Earth. In 1877, Queen Victoria was proclaimed Empress of India. When she celebrated her fiftieth and her sixtieth anniversaries as queen (in 1887 and 1897), Victoria was heralded as the greatest of monarchs.

Kipling believed in imperialism; he believed in the responsibility and duty of spreading British laws and their administration and enforcement. In stories, like "Mowgli's Brothers," the effect of British imperialism on Kipling's storytelling is

Movie still of the 1942 film version of "The Jungle Book," starring Sabu The Kobal Collection. Reproduced by permission

evident. He created stories and characters that are ruled by laws. While creating entertaining plots, Kipling used these rules to create tension, cause conflict, and provide a means for expressing lessons and morals.

Critical Overview

Unlike many authors, Kipling received praise early in his career and consistently throughout his life. In 1894 when it first appeared in print, *The Jungle Book*, however, received both praise and criticism. Some viewed the publication as one of the greatest literary events of the year. Several publications lauded Kipling's work. For example, according to Harry Ricketts in his biography of Kipling, the *Athenaeum* gave its praise: "our sincere thanks to Mr. Kipling for the hour of pure and unadulterated enjoyment which he has given us, and many another reader, by this inimitable 'Jungle Book.'"

Yet Kipling and *The Jungle Book* were criticized, too. According to Ricketts, the American Henry James wrote to English writer, Edmund Gosse:

He sends me too [James told Gosse] his jungle book which I have read with extreme admiration. But *how*

it closes his doors & sets his limit! The rise to 'higher types' that one hoped for—I mean the care for life in a finer way—is the rise to the mongoose & the care for the wolf. The *violence* of it all, the almost exclusive preoccupation with fighting & killing, is also singularly characteristic.

The Jungle Book was intended for children, not adults. Yet it was full of warring creatures, savage beasts, and conflict resolved by force and fire. But despite the more brutal elements, the morals of the stories remained central, and the book was propelled into the spotlight, for both juvenile and adult readers.

Even though some authors expressed criticism, Kipling's importance was acknowledged by some of his peers. Mark Twain, for example, according to Ricketts, stated that Kipling as "the only living person not head of a nation, whose voice is heard around the world the moment wit drops a remark." Other authors, both British and American, agreed; Kipling was held in high regard, both as a writer and a public figure.

In 1927 several enthusiasts founded the Kipling Society. The literary society, which still existed as of 2006, published a quarterly magazine, *The Kipling Journal*, containing literary criticism, historical information, and biographical information.

In fact, Kipling's fiction and his message were interesting enough to stimulate much detailed, academic discussion. M. Flint states in his article in *Studia Neophilogica*, "Mowgli's cognitive development can be seen in the way his focalization of the world, while remaining restricted, ultimately allows him to realize that the code of signification, the paradigms, of the animal world are no longer adequate to explain and understand his own world. . . ." Flint's analysis of Mowgli dissects the character's struggle with his own identity amidst the contrasting codes of man and beast. Beyond Mowgli, this struggle connects to the search for identify and community in a context large enough to confront the individual with difference and exclusion.

Criticism

Anthony Martinelli

Martinelli is a Seattle-based freelance writer and editor. In this essay, Martinelli examines the identity of the main character, Mowgli, through rational and empirical philosophical doctrines.

In "Mowgli's Brothers," Rudyard Kipling tells the tale of his celebrated "man-cub," who is rescued from certain death as an infant and raised by a pack of wolves. Although a human being, Mowgli effectively becomes a "wolf cub" in nearly every other respect and grows to adopt the Law of the Jungle as his code of behavior. However, through his innate ability to reason, Mowgli soon recognizes the existence of the Law of Man as a distinct code of behavior, a recognition that immediately gives rise to a conflict between codes, sending Mowgli into an existential crisis. Mowgli is, essentially, a character trapped between the Law of the Jungle and the Law of Man. Mowgli's struggle to resolve this crisis represents the tension between the opposed philosophical doctrines, empiricism and rationalism. Mowgli makes choices, defines his being, and is an existentialist as he exercises his will outside the structure of a particular dogma, making Mowgli a prototypical existentialist.

The Law of the Jungle, as explained explicitly in the story, is the set of rules that dictates the education, movements, and interactions of different groups of animals within the jungle and animals' relationships to humans outside the jungle. While an important part of the communication between the beasts in the jungle is each animal's need for food, the most important code pertains to killing

> " In this momentary separation from the Law of Man and the Law of the Jungle, Mowgli is a unique creation: he is an existentialist."

man. The Law of the Jungle greatly limits an animal's right to kill man because frequent hunting of humans brings "the arrival of white men on elephants, with guns and hundreds of brown men with gongs and rockets and torches" and disrupts the balance of the jungle.

The Law of the Jungle also imposes rules that are particular to classifications of animals. On a wider scale, cubs are taught the Law of the Jungle through experiences within the jungle. With the help of elders and friendly beasts, such as Baloo the Bear, Mowgli develops his understanding of the Law of the Jungle and is able to build his position in the jungle through experience. Through this empirically gained identity, Mowgli is able to adhere to the Law of the Jungle and see himself as part of the pack.

An analysis of Mowgli's position as "Mowgli the Wolf" and his realization of "self" through his interactions with the jungle creates an empirically determined identity. As a philosophical doctrine, empiricism is defined by the contention that all knowledge of matters of fact (e.g. the jungle or the village) distinct and separate from the relation of concepts (e.g. mathematics or philosophy) is based upon experience. In short, all knowledge, outside purely conceptual relations, has its source in what is experienced, not what is simply imagined or thought. John Locke, often considered the father of British empiricism, argued in *An Essay Concerning Human Understanding* that in experience "all our Knowledge is founded; and from that it ultimately derives itself." Therefore, Mowgli's knowledge of the jungle and of what it means to be a wolf comes from the empirical data that bombard his senses through his interactions with the jungle.

The Law of Man does not necessarily contradict the code followed in the jungle, but it certainly

What Do I Read Next?

- *The Second Jungle Book*, the second and final installment, was published in 1895. Much like *The Jungle Book*, the second consists of poems and short stories about the jungle, animals, and, most important, the man-cub Mowgli.

- *Captains Courageous*, published serially in *McClure's Magazine* in 1897, is the story of Harvey Cheyne, the pampered son of a millionaire, who falls overboard from an ocean liner. He is rescued by a fishing vessel where he must work, initially against his will, to hold his place aboard the boat. Like Mowgli, Harvey is inadvertently thrust into a completely foreign world where he is forced to adapt in order to survive.

- *Stalky & Co* (1899), based upon Kipling's experience at the United World College Westward Ho!, is a collection of short school stories. Kipling appears as the main character, Beetle, who learns lessons about imperialism, warfare, and becoming a man of service.

- *Kim*, published serially in *McClure's Magazine* in 1901, is often called Kipling's finest work. This is the story of an orphan born in colonial India who is torn between his love of India's culture and vitality and the demands of British imperialism.

- Kipling's *Just-So Stories* (1902) is a well-known collection of short stories giving imaginative answers to questions like "How did the whale get his throat?" and "Who invented the alphabet?"

- *Heart of Darkness* (1902), by Joseph Conrad, is a complicated adult novel. It is the tale of Marlow, a seaman, who makes a journey up the Congo River. In part the novel is Conrad's attack on imperialism and the abuses of Leopold II who regarded Congo as his personal resource.

- *Anne of Green Gables* (1908), by Canadian author L. M. Montgomery, is a children's classic from Kipling's era. *Anne of Green Gables* captures the hopes and struggles of childhood and is considered Montgomery's most famous work.

- *Peter Pan* (1911), by J. M. Barrie, is another children's classic from Kipling's era. Similar to "Mowgli's Brothers," the story of Peter Pan contrasts good and evil and is intended to teach lessons and morals.

- Volume 2 of *The Letters of Rudyard Kipling* (1995) covers the years between 1890 and 1899. This was a pivotal time in Kipling's life when he first becomes a celebrity and when he lost his beloved daughter to pneumonia.

---

occurs exclusively and separately from the Law of the Jungle. Man, after all, exists outside the jungle, just as beasts exist outside the village. In the story, the codes of man, unlike the codes of the jungle, are revealed through negation and rational deduction. The Law of Man is not explained in the text like that of the Law of the Jungle; instead it must be understood through the way Kipling and other British people lived during the Victorian period. It is reasonable to assume that the codes humans follow in Kipling's stories are the same codes that dictate human interactions in his era. A code of man, for instance, can be deduced as follows: when beasts from the jungle kill man with too great a frequency, the Law of Man dictates that the jungle should be torched and that animals should be killed or driven deeper into the woods. The code followed by man is, in the broad sense, about self-preservation.

The Law of Man during this late-Victorian era is primarily commanded by rules established by courts and by ethical and moral codes outlined by the church. The courts mandate that certain crimes, such as murder, are illegal. These types of actions are in opposition to the Law of Man and are, thus, punishable. The church defines moral human behavior with rigid statements about family values and individual obligation to God: fathers are expected to provide for their children and wives;

mothers are expected to raise their children and support their husbands; and all of mankind is expected to respect God and his creations. Although there is little interaction with humans in the story, Mowgli does come into contact with one group of humans when he is attempting to acquire fire. It is Mowgli's first exposure to a nuclear family, and he comments, "they are very like me." The description of the family, although brief, suggests the importance of family and its place in the code of man.

Mowgli does not live under the Law of Man, yet it is apparent to the inhabitants of the jungle that he is different. It is not his sheer physical appearance that dictates this determination; it is something additional, something in Mowgli. During a conversation with the panther Bagheera, Mowgli has his first revelation. Bagheera, like Mowgli, spent his earliest years outside his inborn identity; men raised Bagheera, just as beasts raised Mowgli. Everyone in the jungle fears "Bagheera—all except Mowgli." Kipling writes:

> "Oh, *thou* art a man's cub," said the Black Panther, very tenderly; "and even as I returned to my Jungle, so thou must go back to men at last,—to the men who are thy brothers,—if thou art not killed in the Council."
>
> "But why—but why should any wish to kill me?" said Mowgli.
>
> "Look at me," said Bagheera; and Mowgli looked at him steadily between the eyes. The big panther turned his head away in half a minute.
>
> "*That* is why," he said shifting his paw on the leaves. "Not even I can look thee between the eye and I was born among men, and I love thee, Little Brother. The others they hate thee because their eyes cannot meet thine—because thou art wise—because thou hast pulled thorns from their feet—because thou art man."
>
> "I did not know these things," said Mowgli sullenly. . . .

In this exchange, Kipling presents the rational, innate beings of Mowgli and Bagheera: Mowgli's innate being, regardless of the wolf identity he has gained through experience, is that of man; Bagheera's innate being, regardless of the understanding of man he gained through his captivity, is that of the beast. The Black Panther, although feared in the jungle and aware of the code of man because of his upbringing, is still unable to withstand the power of the stare of "Mowgli the Man."

An analysis of Mowgli the man through his revelation near the end of the story creates an identity founded upon rationalism. Rationalism states that all knowledge can be obtained from reasonable deduction, from thought alone, independent of that which is experienced. Benedictus Spinoza, a seventeenth-century rationalist, argued in *Tractatus Theologico-Politicus* that "the natural light of reason does not demand anything which it is itself unable to supply." Essentially, Spinoza states that everything people know is determined by and springs forth from universal laws and exists and acts in a certain and determinate way. Thus, Spinoza would see Mowgli's return to the Law of Man as a self-determined necessity—Mowgli is man, he is not beast—it is mandated by universal laws that he returns to the Law of Man.

During his final visit to Council Rock, Mowgli finds himself in a difficult situation. Here both Mowgli and Akela are to make a last stand before the pack. Mowgli is to be banished from the jungle, and old Akela's position as leader is to be challenged by the pack because he missed a kill. Both situations arise from Shere Kahn's hatred of Mowgli and from his manipulation of the wolf pack. Both Mowgli and Akela can expect death as the outcome of their situations. However, because he is privy to Shere Kahn's devious intention, Mowgli has other plans. Upon his arrival at Council Rock, "more than half the Pack yelled: 'A man! a man! What has a man to do with us? Let him go to his own place.'" Shere Kahn responds, "No, give him to me. He is a man and none of us can look him between the eyes." Akela then outlines Mowgli's empirically understood identity as a wolf by saying, "He [Mowgli] has eaten our food. He has slept with us. He has driven game for us. He has broken no word of the Law of the Jungle." The argument within the pack, between Shere Kahn and Bagheera, exemplifies Mowgli's conflict. He is both man and wolf; he is a construct of two mutually exclusive beings.

At this moment Mowgli begins to accept his future as man. He proclaims to his naysayers, "Ye have told me so often tonight that I am a man (and indeed I would have been a wolf with you to my life's end), that I feel your words are true. So I do not call ye brothers any more, but *sag* [dogs], as man should." Interestingly, though, Mowgli is neither man nor wolf in this instance; instead, he takes on a separate being in the revelation that his being is based on neither the empirically gained knowledge of wolf nor the rationally gained knowledge of man. Here Mowgli is not of a particular system; he is separate from the codes of the jungle and the codes of man; he is distinct and separate from any one dogma. In this momentary separation from the Law of Man and the Law of the Jungle, Mowgli is a unique creation: he is an existentialist.

Existentialism has its roots in the first half of the twentieth century, an era much later than Kipling's. Existentialism is in opposition to empiricism and rationalism. For the empiricist or rationalist, knowledge gained through experience or reason can be obtained by any contemplative observer. However, the existentialist view of the problem of being is separate from and must take precedence over the philosophical investigation of knowledge, its acquisition, and its relation to being. For the existentialist, being cannot be an object of simple inquiry. Being is only *revealed* to the individual. It is not mandated or determined by laws or natures; it cannot be acquired through experience or through reason. Mowgli's existence at Council Rock is basic: he is present at that moment in a volatile world. He understands his being in terms of the moment of his existence, not in terms of his significance as abstraction. This is apparent because Mowgli makes decisions in terms of their impact on that particular existence. As he stands at Council Rock, naked and longhaired like a wild animal but wielding flame like a powerful man, Mowgli is aware of his freedom of choice, but he is ignorant of his future. At Council Rock, after sending Shere Kahn whimpering into the jungle with a singed brow, Mowgli demands of the pack that wants to banish him that "Akela goes free to live as he pleases. Ye will *not* kill him, because that is not my will. Nor do I think that ye will sit here any longer, lolling out your tongues as though ye were somebodies, instead of dogs who I drive out—thus! Go!" Here Mowgli is not bound by a code or by a predetermined duty to save Akela but is compelled to assume the responsibility of making choices.

In these final moments between the Law of the Jungle and the Law of Man, Mowgli anticipates a philosophical trend that followed Kipling's time. Perhaps it is unintentional on the author's part, but Mowgli is a character of great complexity, so much so that Mowgli's pursuit of being connects the philosophy of Kipling's predecessors and the great thinkers who followed his era.

Source: Anthony Martinelli, Critical Essay on "Mowgli's Brothers," in *Short Stories for Students*, Thomson Gale, 2006.

Donald Gray

In the following essay, Gray discusses Kipling's writing career.

It is easy to underestimate the variety, complexity, and subtlety of Rudyard Kipling's writing. He became an extraordinarily popular writer in the 1890s with short stories and poems enlivened by strange and interesting settings, a brisk narrative economy, and the fresh energy of the voices that told his tales, sometimes in working-class dialects and usually in the smart, confident tone of someone who affected to know how the world really worked. Readers and critics who esteemed the refined melancholy and stylistic elaborations of the fin de siècle often thought his effects coarse and common. The loose colloquial forms and development of his tales and fables came to seem obvious and old-fashioned to early-twentieth-century readers learning to enjoy the compression and elliptical styles of James Joyce, Katherine Mansfield, and Virginia Woolf and the rhetorical intensity of D. H. Lawrence. Kipling's popularity itself sometimes made him suspect to readers who had learned from literary modernism that popularity was necessarily purchased by undignified concessions to vulgar tastes and conventional expectations.

The themes of Kipling's short stories have also been criticized by contemporaries and increasingly by later critics and readers as simple-minded and even pernicious. He often seems to honor white men and Western technology as agents of a desirable dominion over less-progressive peoples and parts of the world. He has been read as the eulogist of an oligarchy of effective administrators, soldiers, engineers, doctors, and an occasional journalist who belong, formally or informally, to a club almost always closed to women. Such men are also almost always British, bred in the schools and ethical code of a professional middle class in which they learned how to obey the law that work be honorable and honest while making up their own rules for getting the job done.

These assessments are just but incomplete. From the beginning, especially in his short stories, Kipling wrote as powerfully, and more often, of the waste and cost of the work of empire as he did of its efficiencies. He was always aware of the impermanence of dominion, the inevitable decline and succession of empires. He knew that Western perspectives—sometimes he even seemed to recognize that masculine perspectives—were inescapably limited. There is much in the world that a European male simply cannot comprehend, and much that he comprehends quite differently from the equally valid understanding of someone who organizes experience by the interests and values of another culture or a different gender. The mystery of the world and the burden of human fallibility and mortality can sometimes baffle attempts to do orderly work in the world and tell coherent and conclusive stories about it.

In his best short stories, early and late, Kipling found ways to play these uncertainties and contingencies against his desire for order and his trust in the kinds of men and work he thought could create and sustain it. He wrote fiction that moved not only by the conventions of realism but also by those of fable, ghost stories, and science fiction, and sometimes he incorporated one of these fantastic modes into a realistic story in order to show the instability or surprise in what is taken to be real life. The many voices of his fiction—of Americans, Indians, women, an Irish soldier and a cockney sailor, animals, and machines—sometimes testify to what is common and fundamental in experience and sometimes remind readers that they are always hearing only one version of the story. Especially in his later stories Kipling liked to suggest what the story left out or to take in matter that the story left unexplained. He could be as confident, sureminded, and repetitive in his narrative practices as some readers since the 1890s have judged him to be. He could also use his considerable craft as a short-story writer, a talent that he learned to take seriously and to enlarge as he matured, to complicate and call into question the structure of belief and practice by which he wanted to order the world.

In his fragmentary autobiography, *Something of Myself for My Friends Known and Unknown* (1937), Kipling wrote, "Everything in my working life has been dealt to me in such a manner that I had just to play it as it came." Certainly one of the most powerful cards dealt to Kipling was his birth and experience in India, and as a young man he played it masterfully. His father, John Lockwood Kipling, had worked as a sculptor during the construction of the Victoria and Albert Museum in London in the 1860s. He traveled to India in 1865 as professor of sculptural history at the University of Bombay. His mother, Alice Macdonald Kipling, had also moved in the company of artists in London. His family was affectionate and talented, giving support and encouragement that Kipling was later to depend on as "the family square."

When Kipling was not yet six years old he was sent away with his younger sister, Alice, to begin his education in England. They were lodged at Southsea with a religiously evangelical family who held strict views about the upbringing of children. Kipling perhaps exaggerated the meanness of this period when he recalled it in his autobiography and the short story "Baa, Baa Black Sheep" (1888). He remembered himself as the black sheep. His energy and curiosity about books and almost everything else consistently brought punishments at home, and

> **He was always aware of the impermanence of dominion, the inevitable decline and succession of empires."**

undiagnosed problems with his eyesight created difficulties at school. When he was eleven his mother returned to England, probably summoned by a friend who had discovered his predicament. She placed him in the United Services College, a school organized to prepare the sons of military officers and colonial administrators for similar careers.

Kipling flourished in his new school. Here the code of the boys and the rules of the masters created a discipline that was masculine and institutional, with clear premises and hierarchies and consistent administration. He read widely, learned Latin well enough to amuse himself as an adult by translating and imitating Horace, and wrote for the school paper. He formed the close friendships memorialized in his school novel *Stalky & Co.* (1899) and became what he admired the rest of his life, a capable, knowledgeable, eminent member of a group of like-minded males. At Southsea he learned, as he wrote in "Baa, Baa Black Sheep," that "when young lips have drunk deep of the bitter waters of Hate, Suspicion, and Despair, all the Love in the world will not wholly take away that knowledge; though it may turn darkened eyes for a while to the light, and teach Faith where no Faith was." At the United Services College he learned to balance his dark knowledge that one day the apparently secure world will collapse into confusion with the satisfaction of freely accepting a set of rules that give hard work its reasons and rewards.

At the end of 1882 Kipling returned to India to work as subeditor (the editor was the only other staff member) of the *Civil and Military Gazette*, a daily newspaper in Lahore. He wrote, edited, and translated scraps of news: "Wrote in course of year 230 columns matter," he noted in his diary in 1884. As a reporter he traveled to public events and the courts of native rulers, and he spent his evenings at home in the "family square" or at clubs where, he wrote in his autobiography, he met "none except picked men at their definite tasks." In 1885 he wrote the first two stories he thought worthy of inclusion in later editions of his works for a family magazine subsequently issued as a Christmas number by the newspaper. Then he began to write stories for the newspaper that had to fit into columns of two thousand words. When in 1887 he moved to a bigger paper as a reporter and editor of its supplement, the *Week's News*, he immediately contracted to supply fiction to the supplement.

The matter of his stories was India, usually the events of the offices, garrisons, and bungalows of the British in India, occasionally the character and customs of India itself as it could be known by an Englishman. The teller of the stories was often someone like Kipling—a detached observer, a retailer of the tales he heard in railway carriages and at the club. When he collected some of the stories he wrote for the *Civil and Military Gazette* as *Plain Tales from the Hills* in 1888 for an Indian publisher, they were widely read and discussed by the British in India, although the one thousand copies the publisher sent to England were little noticed. Kipling followed this mixed success in the same year by collecting some of the stories he had written for the *Week's News* in six volumes of the Indian Railway Library, published by the proprietors of his newspaper. He retained the titles of these volumes when he later combined them in two volumes of his collected works: *Soldiers Three*, *The Story of the Gadsbys*, and *In Black and White* in one volume (1892) and *Wee Willie Winkie*, *Under the Deodars*, and *The Phantom 'Rickshaw and Other Stories* in the other (1892). After serving what he called a seven-year apprenticeship in India, he left in 1889, sailing east to visit China, Japan, and California, then traveling across the United States to sail for England.

Kipling arrived in London in the fall of 1889, three months short of his twenty-fourth birthday. By the end of the next year he was famous. All through 1890 he wrote about India in new stories and poems—among them some of his best known, including "Gunga Din," "Danny Deever," and "Mandalay"—that appeared monthly, sometimes weekly in British and American periodicals. He collaborated on one novel, *The Naulahka: A Story of West and East* (1892), with Wolcott Balestier, and completed another, *The Light That Failed* (1891), that was also published in England and the United States in an American magazine. British and American publishers reprinted the stories of *Plain Tales from the Hills*, which went through three printings in six months in England, and the volumes of the Indian Railway Library. At the end of 1890 Kipling

put his new stories together with some unpublished fiction and a dozen stories from Indian newspapers to make his first substantial volume of short stories first published outside India, *Life's Handicap: Being Stories of Mine Own People* (1891).

At the end of this first phase in his career, Kipling had seen into print more than one hundred short stories, more than half the number written for adults that he finally admitted into authorized editions of his work. Often composed to meet the deadlines and space requirements of newspapers, many of these stories nonetheless hold together to compose a body of writing marked by complicated themes and ambitious practices. In these stories he found his hero, the competent man (and, only occasionally, woman) of deeds rather than talk who did the real work of the world. He made India into a place that expressed his abiding sense of reality as a finally incomprehensible mystery within which humans constructed different codes of belief and conduct, some more honorable and availing than others but none essentially more true than others. He became known for a kind of literary realism within which he could register the costs as well as the material and moral benefits of the work people do. But his laconic style of anecdote occasionally turned his stories into something like parables, and he began to experiment with stories that left the conventions of realism entirely to move into fable.

Private Terence Mulvaney, described in "The Three Musketeers" (1887)—collected in *Plain Tales from the Hills*—as one of "the worst men in the regiment as far as genial blackguardism goes," fairly represents the hero of Kipling's early stories. Mulvaney gets drunk, gets into fights, flirts with other peoples' wives, and finally loses his corporal's stripes. But when it comes down to it, Mulvaney is capable, a brave and effective soldier. He leads a group of naked men in "The Taking of Lungtunphem" (1887), collected in *Plain Tales from the Hills*, and helps to turn an ambush into a vividly described victory in "With the Main Guard" (1888), collected in *Soldiers Three*. In "The God from the Machine" (1888), another story in *Soldiers Three*, he prevents the inappropriate elopement of the colonel's daughter. In "The Incarnation of Krishna Mulvaney" (1888), collected in *The Courting of Dinah Shadd and Other Stories* (1890), he destroys a scheme in which a contractor is cheating his coolie workers and then, after a farcical sequence created by his drunkenness, impersonates the Hindu deity Krishna and extorts 434 rupees and a gold necklace from a priest. After he marries and leaves the army, there is no place for Mulvaney in

England. He returns to India in "The Big Drunk Draf" (1888), gathered in *Soldiers Three*, as a civilian, "a great and terrible fall." Even out of uniform, he helps to discipline an unruly regiment of men waiting to go home by advising its young officer to tie one of the men spread-eagle to tent pegs and leave him out one frosty night. "You look to that little orf'cer bhoy. He has bowils. 'Tis not ivry child that wud chuck the Rig'lations to Flanders an' stretch Peg Barney on a wink from a brokin' an' dilapidated ould carkiss like mesilf."

Competence and effectiveness in these stories often require a bending of regulations or a neglect of protocol. When in "Thrown Away" (1888), a story in *Plain Tales from the Hills*, a sheltered boy breaks under the strain of his work and shoots himself in the head, a major and the teller of the story organize the lie that he died of cholera to protect his honor and the sensibilities of his mother. "The tale had credence as long as was necessary; for everyone forgot about The Boy before a fortnight was over. Many people, however, found time to say that the Major had behaved scandalously in not bringing in the body for a Regimental funeral." Strickland, a police officer who appears in several stories and later in Kipling's novel *Kim* (1901), uses his intimate knowledge of native ways to disguise himself in order to defeat an accusation of adultery against an innocent woman in "The Bronckhorst Divorce Case" (1888) and to be near and finally to win the woman who becomes his wife in "Miss Youghal's *Sais*" (1887), both collected in *Plain Tales from the Hills*. The narrator of the latter story refers to Strickland's "crowning achievement" of "spending eleven days as *faquir* or priest in the gardens of Baba Atal at Amristar, and there picking up the threads of the great Nasiban Murder Case. But people said, justly enough, 'Why on earth can't Strickland sit in his office and write up his diary, and recruit, and keep quiet, instead of showing up the incapacity of his seniors?'"

Even competent men can be defeated by the reality of British India and of India itself. Bureaucratic rigidity in "In the Pride of His Youth" (1887), a story in *Plain Tales from the Hills*, frustrates Dicky Hatt, who works "like a horse" to save money to bring his wife and child out from England. But "pay in India is a matter of age, not merit, you see, and if their particular boy wished to work like two boys, Business forbid they should stop him." By the time Dicky is given a salary that will enable him to pay the cost of passage, his child is dead and his wife has divorced him. He quits at age twenty-three: "I'm tired of work. I'm an old man now."

Other careers are destroyed, and sometimes made, because of tedium. Her gender deprives Mrs. Hauksbee, a clever, manipulative woman who appears in half a dozen stories, of a field in which she can openly exercise her intelligence and ambition. Out of boredom she incites callow young men to waste their time by riding miles to flirt with her and tries to become influential by intriguing to make the careers of cheats and fools. In "At the Pit's Mouth" (1888), collected in *Under the Deodars*, another woman, named only the Man's Wife, relieves her boredom by manufacturing "some semblance of intrigue to cloak even her most commonplace actions." She conducts an affair in a cemetery until her lover, the Tertium Quid, becomes depressed by the presence of shallow graves filling with water. When he is killed in an accident, she goes to bed for three days, "which were rainy; so she missed attending the funeral of the Tertium Quid, who was lowered into eighteen inches of water, instead of the twelve to which he had first objected." The condition of people at Simla, the hill town to which British administrators and their families retreat in the hot weather, and in the married quarters of garrisons is presented at its extreme in "A Wayside Comedy" (1888), collected in *Under the Deodars*. Each of the five men and women isolated in the "rat-pit" of a remote station is in some way unfaithful to friend and spouse. By the end of the story everyone knows about and has been hurt by these betrayals, but all stay in their marriages and their jobs, visiting one another as before, singing to the banjo and laughing "the mirthless mirth of these men on the long white line of the Narkarr Road."

Beneath what the British do to one another in India lies what India does to them. Kipling's India is violent and dangerous, only lightly marked by British rule. One of his first published stories— "The Strange Ride of Morrowbie Jukes" (1885), collected in *The Phantom 'Rickshaw*—describes a grotesque community of Hindus who have "had the misfortune to recover from trance or catalepsy" before their bodies were burned. They are dumped into a crater whose walls are unscalable cliffs, like the trap "the ant-lion sets for its prey," and left to scramble against one another in a brutal contest of survival. In "Dray Wara You Dee" (1888), included in *In Black and White*, one of several stories Kipling tells in the voice of a native, the speaker recounts how he has beheaded his wife because she was unfaithful and then cut off her breasts to advertise her crime. "Your Law!" he says. "What is your Law to me!"

When Englishmen cross into this India, even the most compassionate and competent are baffled. John Holden in "Without Benefit of Clergy" (1890), a story in *The Courting of Dinah Shadd*, buys a fourteen-year-old "Mussleman's daughter" from her mother, falls in love with her, fathers a son, and lives happily in a house in the native precincts of the city. "The delight of that life was too perfect to endure. Therefore it was taken away as many things are taken away in India—suddenly and without warning." His lover and son die of fever; the house is torn down; and Holden is called away to relieve a British colleague dying in the epidemic. Trejago, the hero of "Beyond the Pale" (1888), gathered in *Plain Tales from the Hills*, is undone because of his intimate knowledge of India. A young woman, Biesa, who has spoken to him from behind a grated window in an alley sends him a letter made of objects whose meaning he must interpret. "Trejago knew far too much about these things, as I have said. No Englishman should be able to translate object-letters." His translation begins an affair that lasts until one night, after an interval of three weeks, he knocks at the grating and the girl "held out her arms into the moonlight. Both hands had been cut off at the wrists, and the stumps were nearly healed." Trejago never discovers what has happened. "He cannot get Biesa—poor little Biesa—back again. He has lost her in the City where each man's house is as guarded and as unknowable as the grave; and the grating that opens into Amir Nath's Gully has been walled up."

India baffles the British even when they do not venture into its mysteries. "False Dawn" (1888), collected in *Plain Tales from the Hills*, tells of a midnight picnic in the ruined gardens of an old tomb during which Saumerez, a civil servant, intends to propose to Edith Copleigh. A dust storm blows up, and in the "roaring, whirling darkness" he proposes by mistake to Maud, her older sister. The narrator rides after the distressed Edith and, "ringed with the lightning and the storm," brings her back to correct the mistake, but the mistake cannot really be corrected. He ends his story "tired and limp, and a good deal ashamed of myself." He knows that this trivial tale carries a deep, sad lesson about the cost of trying to stage picnics and decorous courtships in the ruins and violent weather of this alien place. He also knows that from another perspective the story is even sadder. "There is a woman's version of this story, but it will never be written . . . unless Maud Copleigh cares to try."

Kipling's manner in these stories is that of a realist. He suggests that he tells the real story beneath the official narrative and superficial glamour of empire. Kipling fills the stories with the place-names of India, words from its languages, and the dialects, jargon, and shoptalk of British soldiers and administrators. Most often the narrator has heard his stories from someone else, but rather than diluting his authority, this enhances it: he knows all the stories, more about the British in India than anyone else. His tone, with a few lapses, is matter-of-fact. He wants to shock his readers, but he is not shocked, and some of his most devastating stories concern events that at home would be quite ordinary. For example, in "Bitters Neat" (1887), a story from the *Civil and Military Gazette* that Kipling did not put into *Plain Tales from the Hills* until an 1897 collected edition of his writing, a young woman falls in love with Surrey, an efficient yet dull man unaware of her infatuation. She refuses a proposal from another man, goes somewhat crazy, and is sent home. When Surrey learns why the young woman has gone, he is unstrung: "I didn't see, I didn't see. If I had *only* known." The narrator, who has known the whole story all along, spends no other words of pity or irony on Surrey. He drops directly to what he has also always known, what this story is really about—"the hopelessness and tangle of it—the waste and the muddle."

In some of these stories Kipling leaves realism to make his skepticism about certainty and permanence into parables about empire itself. The heroes of "The Man Who Would be King" (1888), competent men in the style of Terence Mulvaney, use their knowledge of India to disguise themselves to make a dangerous journey beyond the northern frontier. Then they use their training as soldiers to drill an army and organize the region into their kingdom. The region once had been conquered by Alexander, who introduced Masonic rituals, and the two Englishmen use their knowledge of Masonry to pass themselves off as gods. The ambitious Daniel Dravot has himself crowned king. "I won't make a Nation," he says, "I'll make an Empire. . . . Two hundred and fifty thousand men, ready to cut in on Russia's right flank when she tries for India! . . . Oh, it's big! It's big, I tell you. But there's so much to be done in every place." After Dravot is tricked and killed by suspicious priests, his partner, Peachy Carnahan, survives a crucifixion and is set free, maimed and mad, to make his way back to India, carrying Dravot's head and crown in a sack. When Carnahan dies in an asylum, the narrator, who has seen the contents of the sack, asks "'if he had anything upon him by chance when he died?' 'Not to my knowledge,' said the Superintendent. And there the matter rests." Like Alexander yesterday, like England tomorrow, another empire has come to nothing, this time leaving no trace at all.

The tactics of the stories of Kipling's first collections eventually extend his ironic sense of the contingency of systems to the premise of his own kind of realism, which is founded on the secular, materialistic creed that people can know the world, even if they cannot always command it. He plays with this creed in ghost stories in which he allows the inexplicable to stand unexplained. Is the apparition of "The Phantom 'Rickshaw" (1887) a hallucination, or is it retribution for the lover's heartless rejection of the woman whose ghost haunts his rides with his fiancée? The narrators of many of these stories occasionally admit that their compressed forms leave complicated questions unanswered and intricate characters unrealized. The narrator poses a conundrum to himself at the end of "The Bronckhorst Divorce Case": "What I want to know is, 'how do women like Mrs. Bronckhorst come to marry men like Bronckhorst?'" In "The Last of the Stories," a fantasy that Kipling wrote in 1888 but left unpublished until 1909, when it was collected in *Abaft the Funnel*, the narrator visits a hell populated by grotesque dolls who tell him that they suffer from his botched attempts to make them seem real. Even so, "'I've touched 'em raw. . . . I show you what they ought to be. You must find out for yourself how to make 'em so.'"

The one hundred stories of these first collections are told by a chorus of voices. Each voice contributes a piece to a mosaic that collectively represents a stable, comprehensible reality. But as the narrator acknowledges at the end of "False Dawn," another voice would tell a different story. Thus, each perspective offers not a piece of the whole but a singular, subjective version of it. In "To be Filed for Reference," the last story in *Plain Tales from the Hills*, police officer Strickland and the narrator study a manuscript left by McIntosh Jellaludin, a drunken Scot who changed his religion, went to live with a native woman, and descended into India. Neither Strickland nor the narrator can make any sense of the manuscript, but Kipling gives it the title of his own never-finished novel of native life, "The Book of Mother Maturin." There are stories that Kipling as a Western realist can neither understand nor write. Writing of the tales of Gobind, a Hindu holy man he invents for the preface of *Life's Handicap*, he says his "tales were true, but not one in twenty could be printed in an English book, because the English do not think as natives do." Kipling then introduces his own stories, "collected

from all places, and all sorts of people." He adds, "The most remarkable stories are, of course those which do not appear—for obvious reasons."

In the two decades after the publication of his first collections of short stories Kipling consolidated and enlarged his fame. After traveling to South Africa, Australia, and (for the last time) India, he married Carrie Balestier, an American, in 1892 and moved to Brattleboro, Vermont. There he began to write the children's stories of *The Jungle Book* (1894) and *The Second Jungle Book* (1895), in which the boy Mowgli learns the law of the jungle and becomes leader of its creatures before marrying and settling on the boundary of the forest, a master of the two cultures, the wild and the civilized. Kipling's novel *"Captains Courageous": A Story of the Grand Banks*, was published in 1897, and he followed the great success of *Barrack-Room Ballads and Other Verses* (1892) with collections of poems in 1896 and 1903 and in the United States the first collected edition of his verse in 1907. He visited President Grover Cleveland in the White House and met Theodore Roosevelt, whose energy he admired. He picked up the notion, which he still seemed to hold when he wrote his autobiography at the end of his life, that the United States was in decline, its hardy stock devastated in the Civil War and replaced by less vigorous immigrants. A rancorous dispute with his brother-in-law, which ended in court, precipitated Kipling's return to England in 1896.

Back in England, Kipling rose from fame and affluence to eminence. When he visited Scotland Andrew Carnegie offered him his house; he spent his winters in South Africa in a house provided by Cecil Rhodes. The editorial page of the *Times* was open to him whenever he wanted to address his contemporaries in verse on public issues, as he did when he warned them of the obligations and costs of empire in "Recessional" (1897) and "The White Man's Burden" (1899). He witnessed some of the Boer War (1899–1902), during which he contributed to and helped to edit a newspaper for the troops. He received honorary degrees from Cambridge and Oxford but refused a knighthood in 1899 and declined to stand as a Conservative for Parliament. In 1907 he became the first British writer to be awarded the Nobel Prize for Literature.

Kipling continued to write for children and young adults; his efforts include his school novel *Stalky & Co.; Just So Stories: For Little Children* (1902), a collection of fables about animal origins; and *Puck of Pook's Hill* (1906) and *Rewards and Fairies* (1910), fanciful retellings of stories from

British history. He wrote about India again in *Kim*, probably his most successful novel.

Now at home in England, Kipling bought Bateman's, a seventeenth-century house in Sussex, and knit himself into the life of a member of a high professional caste. He explored the countryside in the automobiles he enthusiastically acquired; prosecuted a steady commerce with magazine editors, publishers, and literary agents in Britain, the United States, and Canada; and enjoyed his fraternity with other leading men in their professions at London clubs and public dinners. Two more collections of short stories published before 1900, *Many Inventions* (1893) and *The Day's Work* (1898), include stories about India, but increasingly in the stories collected in the two volumes published in the first decade of the twentieth century, *Traffics and Discoveries* (1904) and *Actions and Reactions* (1909), Kipling reflected the experience and opinions of a man making himself comfortable not in the outposts but at the center of empire.

In the short stories of these collections Kipling sometimes attacked the complacency and enervation of the comfortable English at home. In a few stories published in the 1890s—for example, "Love-o-Woman," told by Mulvaney and first published in *Many Inventions*—he continues to try to shock people at home by retailing the self-destructive appetites for drink and women that can be set loose out on the margins. He urged the support of a large volunteer army in the tractlike fantasy "The Army of a Dream" (1904), collected in *Traffics and Discoveries*. In "One View of the Question" (1890), a story in *Many Inventions*, he reversed his usual perspective so that an Indian visitor to London could conclude that "the fountain-head of power is putrid with long standing still" and predict, with a smugness that Kipling surely intended as cautionary, that "the Sahibs die out at the third generation in our land." That prediction seems already to be coming true in "A Deal in Cotton" (1902), collected in *Actions and Reactions*, in which the narrator revisits Strickland, now retired to a seaside resort in the west of England, and hears of how Strickland's son, helpless with fever, was made to look good in his African post by the contrivance of his Indian servant.

When Kipling looks from England at the work of the empire at this stage of his career, however, he usually tends to remember not war and waste but the benefits whites bring to natives. "William the Conqueror" (1895), gathered in *The Day's Work*, opens with the observation, "famine was sore in the land, and white men were needed."

Scott, a civil servant, and William, the oddly but revealingly named sister of a British officer in the police, alleviate the disaster in a heroic bout of work that also turns out to be their courtship. A third-generation Anglo-Indian in "A Tomb of His Ancestors" (1897), another story in *The Day's Work*, uses the natives' belief that he is the reincarnation of his grandfather, an administrator of fabled effectiveness, to complete a successful vaccination campaign. In "Little Foxes" (1909) in *Actions and Reactions*, British administrators in Africa settle land disputes during ingeniously organized fox hunts: "One gets at the truth in a hunting-field a heap quicker than in your law courts." Generally in these stories, white people do good for natives, and the British do more good than anyone. Certainly they do more than the engaging American who thinks of war as a game and tries to sell the gun he has invented to the Boers in "A Captive" (1902), collected in *Traffics and Discoveries;* more than the Boers with their dishonorable guerrilla tactics in "A Sahib's War" (1901), also in *Traffics and Discoveries;* and more than the Jewish shipowners cleverly outwitted in "Bread Upon the Waters" (1896), collected in *The Day's Work*.

A set of fables in these four collections epitomizes some of these themes and the convictions they express. Kipling loved modern machinery—the railways and steamships of the old century, the motorcars, wireless, and airplanes of the new. When he installed a turbine in an old mill on his Sussex property, he wrote a fable—"Below the Mill Dam" (1902), collected in *Traffics and Discoveries;*—in which the Waters and the Spirit of the Mill discuss the innovation. All approve except an old English rat, who is discovered by the electric lights turned on by the turbine and killed. Yet Kipling was deeply hostile to political innovation. When in "A Walking Delegate" (1894), a story in *The Day's Work*, a Kansas horse brings socialist views to a Vermont stable—"'As usual,' he said, with an underhung sneer—'bowin' your heads before the Oppressor, that comes to spend his leisure gloatin' over you'"—he is argued down and beaten by the other horses. "'There's jest two kind o' horse in the United States—them ez can an' will do their work after bein' properly broke an' handled, an' them as won't.'" A wax moth that insinuates itself into "The Mother Hive" (1908), included in *Actions and Reactions*, so subverts the work of the hive that it produces a batch of Oddities who destroy it with theories that honeycombs should be built of democratic circles and that bees can live on the honey of the hive without producing more.

As the plates and rivets of "The Ship That Found Itself" (1895), gathered in *The Day's Work*, tell one another during its first Atlantic run, each must learn its place in the hierarchy of the Design, "how to lock down and lock up on one another." Then "the talking of the separate pieces ceases and melts into one voice, which is the soul of the ship." Waste in these fables is not a natural condition within which humans build more or less adequate shelters of work and rule. Instead, Kipling here imagines existences governed by design and law that creatures, to their ruin or profit, choose to resist or accept.

As his convictions settled in the two decades before World War I, Kipling's narrative practices became expansive and adventurous. No longer constrained by the limitations of space imposed on his early stories, he constructed elaborate plots, sometimes around nothing more than a practical joke. He began his practice of prefacing and concluding his stories with verses that sometimes enforced, sometimes complicated, their themes. He told some stories in several voices, giving them the feel, obliqueness, and surprise of conversation. If the stories of the *Jungle Books* and *Just So Stories* are included, he wrote as many fables as realistic short stories in these years. He even toyed with science fiction. At the end of "With the Night Mail: A Story of 2000 A.D. " (1905), a fantasy about airplanes and a world benevolently regulated by the Aerial Board of Control that was collected in *Actions and Reactions*, his invention spills over into appendices of mock news stories, a book review, and advertisements for used dirigibles and aerial chauffeurs ("Must be member of the Church of England, and make himself useful in the garden"). The best measure of the development of Kipling's talent as a short-story writer in these years is that the four collections published between 1893 and 1909 contain five or six of his most accomplished and interesting stories, and none is like any of the others.

For example, "The Bridge-Builders" (1893), collected in *The Day's Work*, begins as a typical Kipling story celebrating capable men doing good work in India despite the heat, disease, and interference of remote and ignorant superiors. Trying to protect their uncompleted bridge from a flood, the British engineer Findlayson and his lascar overseer Peroo are swept in their boat into the river, out of realism and into fable. In a trance of weariness smoothed with opium, they witness the gods debate the plea of the river to destroy the bridge that obstructs her. "Be certain that is only for a little," Krishna says, and then tells the gods that except for Brahma, the principle of life, they themselves are

only for a time: "The fire-carriages shout the names of new Gods that are *not* the old under new names." When morning comes the bridge still stands. Findlayson and Peroo are rescued by a westernized Indian in his steam launch on his way to the temple "to sanctify some new idol." The realistic part of the story honors Findlayson's work in careful descriptions of it; the fable both subverts and sanctifies it. Although it too will ultimately be washed away, Findlayson's work, like the "fire-carriages" of the railway, speaks the name of gods. The bridge is an idol rightly to be worshipped, an authentic contemporary expression of reverence for Brahma.

" 'They' " (1904), a story in *Traffics and Discoveries*, is to an early Kipling ghost story such as "The Phantom 'Rickshaw" what "The Bridge-Builders" is to some of Kipling's early realistic anecdotes about good work in India. The narrator clatters in his motorcar through a magically beautiful southern English landscape to find by accident a lovely Elizabethan house behind a lawn full of topiary yew cut as knights and ladies. Gradually it comes to him that the children he entertains with his motorcar are ghosts summoned by the need of the gracious blind woman who lives alone in the house. Kipling's young daughter Josephine, born in 1892, had died during his visit to the United States in 1899, and his loss underwrites the poignancy of the narrator's decision not to return to the house. Kipling prefaced " 'They' " with a poem in which the Virgin Mary releases children from heaven so that their spirits will comfort people on earth. The ghostliness in this story is not a realist's playful reminder that he cannot know everything. It is rather a possibility of belief, an earthly paradise, from which the narrator is shut out because of his commitment to the valuable, practical work that makes and purchases motorcars.

Each of these four collections of short stories includes one or two stories governed by the physical action of farce. The deft timing of "My Sunday at Home" (1895), a story in *The Day's Work*, tops its principal plot, in which an American doctor mistakenly administers a purgative to a perfectly healthy workingman, with a final scene in which the enraged victim is approached by yet another doctor intent on doing him good. Kipling then caps the story with a lightly ironic comment on "man who is immortal and master of his fate." Included in *Actions and Reactions*, "The Puzzler" (1906), named for a densely branched tree, is more ambitiously metaphorical. A group of important men—politicians and government ministers—set a monkey loose in the tree to test its impenetrability.

One of the puzzles of the story is how to catch the monkey after it has escaped into a house. Another puzzle is how to get an idea about the governing of colonies through the dense thicket of British government at home. The solution to the first puzzle also solves the second: bonded by the fun of their adventure in catching the monkey and facing down the indignant residents of the house, the important men work together to get the idea through, "a little chipped at the edges."

"Mrs. Bathurst" (1904), collected in *Traffics and Discoveries* and perhaps Kipling's finest short story, begins with its tellers reminiscing about a farcical episode of their youths, turns into something like a ghost story, and ends as a commentary about the difficulty of catching reality in the frame of narrative. Vickers, a naval warrant officer, is haunted by a sequence he sees in a "cinematograph" shown in a carnival at Cape Town. Night after night he takes Pyecroft, the principal teller of the story, to watch a woman step out of a train in Paddington Station and walk toward the camera, looking "out straight at us . . . till she melted out of the picture—like—like a shadow jumpin' over a candle, an' as she went I 'eard Dawson in the tickey seats be'ind sing out, 'Christ! there's Mrs. B!' " Two other people help Pyecroft tell the story. One, like Pyecroft, has known Ada Bathhurst as the generous proprietor of a small hotel near Auckland. The other knows what happened to Vickers. None of them know what Mrs. Bathhurst was doing in London—"She's lookin' for me," Vickers says—or what Vickers has done to be haunted by her, or what he tells the captain of his ship before he is sent upcountry alone on a detail, or why he deserts, or who is with him when he is found with another person on a railway track in a teak forest, both "burned to charcoal" by lightning. The artful ramble of the story, as its several tellers exchange information and opinions that end without resolving its plot, testifies both to the ambition of realistic narrative to take in everything and to the futility of that ambition. By this time Kipling has learned to accommodate his own skepticism about ascertaining fact within the structure of a story that defeats its drive for closure. Ten years earlier, in the preface to *Life's Handicap*, he marked the limit of his craft by referring to stories he could not tell. In "Mrs. Bathurst" he makes the same point not by withholding the story but by trying, and failing, to tell it.

Three collections of Kipling's short stories were published in the last twenty years of his life: *A Diversity of Creatures* (1917), *Debits and Credits* (1926), and *Limits and Renewals* (1932). He was now a wealthy man: except for *Thy Servant a Dog,*

Told by Boots (1930), three sketches about the faithfulness of dogs told by one of them, his new books sold only modestly, but editions of his children's stories, anthologies of his stories and poems, editions of his collected works, and the *Inclusive Editions* of his poems (first published in 1919) brought him a large annual income. One of his biographers, C. E. Carrington, estimates that in his lifetime Kipling earned more than $4 million, mostly from his writing and the rest from investments its income purchased.

During his cousin Stanley Baldwin's terms as prime minister in the 1920s, Kipling's advice to the Conservative party acquired a quasi-official status, and when he visited Scotland he stayed at Balmoral with the king. He suffered a stomach disease that he incorrectly feared was cancer, and his wife carefully guarded his privacy at Bateman's. But when he believed the world was going wrong, he used his public presence to try to set it right. With his friend H. Rider Haggard he founded a short-lived Liberty League to oppose socialism. He bitterly regretted the 1921 treaty that set Ireland on its way toward independence of England, and he resigned from the Rhodes Trust in 1925 because he thought its policies encouraged the growth of a commonwealth of autonomous nations to replace an empire ruled by white men from home.

In the short stories of his last three collections, Kipling's conviction that at least some of the time right-minded people know exactly what to do coexists with his persistent sense of the uncertainties of knowing and doing. A set of stories about the consequences of World War I shows this mix of skepticism and sometimes belligerent certainty. Like many of his contemporaries, Kipling at first welcomed the war as an occasion to renew and test courage and honor. He enlisted his talent and name in a series of pamphlets and newspaper articles about the army in France and the work of the navy. When his only son, John, was reported missing in action in France in 1915—his body was never found—Kipling responded in part in the manly code in which he had been schooled: "it's something to have bred a man." (Interestingly, he used a woman's voice to express his grief in the 1916 ballad "My Boy Jack.") He soon undertook to edit a history of his son's regiment, *The Irish Guards in the Great War* (1923), and to serve on the Imperial War Graves Commission, which established and supervised military cemeteries outside England.

Before his son's death Kipling wrote three short stories that express a simple morality about the war. In "Swept and Garnished" (1915), collected in *A Diversity of Creatures*, the house of a tidy German woman is haunted by the ghosts of children killed by German shells and bombs. In "Sea Constables" (1915), included in *Debits and Credits*, one of Kipling's competent, affluent gentlemen serving as a volunteer forces a neutral vessel trying to run the blockade into a remote port, where he lets its captain die of pneumonia unattended. After a child in an English village is killed by a bomb dropped from a German airplane in "Mary Postgate" (1915), a story in *A Diversity of Creatures*, a middle-aged spinster finds the injured German pilot in her garden. Already grieving over a young friend killed while training to be a pilot, she lets the German die, takes a hot bath, and comes down looking "quite handsome."

However, in some of the stories he wrote after the war, Kipling considers that it is not so easy to watch men die. All these stories are about the psychic damage of war and how friends or small communities protect or cure its victims. When the narrator discovers Masonic Lodge Faith and Works 5837 E.C. in "'In the Interest of the Brethren'" (1918), collected in *Debits and Credits*, this creation of merchants and professional men provides food, lodging, and the comforts of ritual to young men on leave from the war. In two later stories, "The Janeites" (1924) and "A Madonna of the Trenches" (1924), both collected in *Debits and Credits*, the members of the lodge do what they can to hold together men who might never be able to leave the war behind. During the war Brother Strangwick in "A Madonna of the Trenches" saw an apparition of his recently deceased aunt in a trench. Shocked out of his certainties about life and death, he now refuses to get married and get on with life. Brother Humberstall, who tells most of "The Janeites," returns to the front after the explosion of an ammunition dump "knocked all 'is Gunnery instruction clean out of 'im." He is kept going by officers who induct him into a select society of initiates in the details of Jane Austen's fiction. None of the officers survives the collapse of the front at Sommes, and back home after the war Humberstall fills his days by shuffling through his memories of the war and by trying to play his Janeite game with his sister. Strangwick and Humberstall tell their stories at the lodge, presumably not for the first time, to sympathetic men who listen to them and send them home, only temporarily relieved of their burdens.

In other stories about the trauma of the war, friends conspire not just to sustain but to cure the victims. For example, the several tellers of a story in *Limits and Renewals*, "Fairy-Kist" (1927)—some of them members of Lodge 5837 who also meet occasionally with other successful men as an Eclectic *but* Comprehensive Fraternity—not only solve the mystery of a dead body much more neatly than the tellers of "Mrs. Bathhurst" manage to do, they also diagnose and make harmless the obsession of a man who, "wounded and gassed and gangrened in the War," goes around England planting flowers. In "The Woman in His Life" (1928), collected in *Limits and Renewals*, a servant, once his orderly, helps a man who was a sapper in the war recover from the lethargy and hallucinations of his delayed reaction to the horrors of his experience beneath no-man's-land in France. In another story from the volume, "The Tender Achilles" (1929), a group of colleagues, one of them a member of Lodge 5837, combine to return to his important research a scientist unstrung by memories of his inevitable failures as a surgeon in field hospitals during the war: "Everything that a man's brain automatically shoves into the background was out before the footlights, and dancing Hell's fox-trot, with drums and horns." Unlike Strangwick and Humberstall, the men saved in these stories belong to the same mercantile and professional classes as the men who do most of the saving. Kipling here does not put at permanent risk the caste on which he often depended in his later stories to do the real work of making order.

In other stories in these three final collections, such men manage triumphs as complete as those in "Fairy-Kist" and "The Tender Achilles." Returning to the scientific fantasy of a world run by the technicians of the Aerial Board of Control in "As Easy as A.B.C." (1912), included in *A Diversity of Creatures*, Kipling describes how these powerful masters of machines and electricity effortlessly and bloodlessly suppress a revolt in Chicago of malcontents who want to bring back the days of crowds, sensational journalism, and democracy. In "The Honours of War" (1914), collected in *A Diversity of Creatures*, Kipling returned to Stalky, the hero of his school novel, to tell how grown-up, hearty army men discipline the unrest of subalterns, just as back in India in their own young manhoods they once gave Elliot-Hacker a bath on his veranda, and "his lady-love saw it and broke off the engagement, which was what the Mess intended, she being an Eurasian." In "Unprofessional" (1930), included in *Limits and Renewals*, a group of doctors and scientists, "tried and proved beneath glaring and hostile moons in No Man's Land," marry biology and astrology to cure a cancer and hold off death long enough for one of them to marry the woman they have cured.

On the other hand, at the end of "Unprofessional" two of the successful team, from opposite ends of the middle classes, recall the unrelieved sorrows of their marriages to drunken wives. In this story and others Kipling allows pain to be felt beneath or beyond the resolutions of his plots. A woman in a story in *Debits and Credits*, "The Wish House" (1924), whose fantasy is solidly rendered in the dialect and details of working-class life, cures the cancer of her faithless lover by wishing it to herself. She is troubled only by the worry that he will marry before she dies. "But the pain do count, don't ye think, Liz?" she says on her deathbed. "The pain *do* count to keep 'Arry—where I want 'im. Say it can't be wasted, like." In "The Gardener" (1925), gathered in *Debits and Credits*, an unmarried woman visiting the grave of a man she has always called her nephew in a military cemetery in France is guided to it by a gardener who might be Christ and who in any event pleases her by speaking her secret and referring to her son. But the story leaves unexplained and unresolved a curious episode in which she fails to comfort, and even inadvertently insults, another woman who lives without relief in the troubles of her secret: she must invent subterfuges to give herself reasons to visit the grave of a man who never acknowledged her as his lover when he was living. A story collected in *Debits and Credits*, "The Eye of Allah" (1920), one of several historical fantasies Kipling wrote in the last phase of his career, elevates the difficulties that create such incomplete resolutions into a social and cultural dilemma. A thirteenth-century abbot knows that the prototype of a microscope one of his monks has brought back from the Moors in Spain will lead to the cure of disease. He also knows that its revelation of a hellish world of bacteria in a drop of water will lead to persecution for magic and blasphemy. After a collegial conversation in which some of his monks freely exchange opinions about the significance of this technological advance, the abbot puts on the ring of his authority and smashes the instrument. His act, decisive but unsatisfying, preserves his community, but it also helps to preserve a backward and rigidly dogmatic church that requires such sacrifices.

Two similar, well-managed stories demonstrate how in these stories at the end of his career Kipling sometimes drove toward clear resolutions and sometimes drifted to what he had always known as "the hopelessness and tangle of it." Both stories work out elaborate hoaxes, of which Kipling was always fond. Caught in a speed trap in a small village, a couple of journalists, a member of Parliament, and the proprietor of a music hall combine their talents to revenge themselves in "The Village That Voted the Earth Was Flat" (1913), collected in *A Diversity of Creatures*. Kipling calls on his exuberant invention and his close knowledge of politics and popular media to describe how the conspirators concoct newspaper stories, commission a music-hall song, and arrange a question in Parliament to convince the public of the lie that the villagers of Huckley are fools who have voted their belief in a flat earth. In this story Kipling exercises his scorn at the ease with which popular opinion can be created by the instruments of politics and popular culture, while at the same time he maneuvers an absolute triumph of sound men who know their jobs over officious incompetents who have risen to an authority and status beyond their talents.

The hoax of "Dayspring Mishandled" (1924), included in *Limits and Renewals*, is also sponsored by revenge. Castorley, who has risen from writing for a fiction syndicate in the 1890s to become an expert on Geoffrey Chaucer, says something insensitive (it remains unrevealed) about a paralyzed woman Manallace cares for and loves. Manallace, who writes historical novels "in a style that exactly met, but never exceeded, every expectation," spends years fabricating and arranging for the discovery of the manuscript of a supposedly lost tale by Chaucer. Castorley falls into the trap, but before he publishes the book that Manallace lies in wait to ambush, he dies, perhaps of kidney disease, perhaps at the hands of the physician to whom Lady Castorley turns her eyes as her husband's coffin crawls into the crematorium. Here the joke does not clap shut, as it does in the Huckley hoax. Like Manallace's clever machine of vengeance, the plot pulls up short before a deep trouble that cannot be comprehended by farce, then tumbles into other troubles that were there all along—not just the mystery of Lady Castorley and the possible malignity of her lover but also the unspecified cruelty of her husband and the unexamined affection of Manallace for the sad woman who may never have loved him.

The writer of Kipling's obituary in the 25 January 1936 *Times Literary Supplement*, trying to figure out "Rudyard Kipling's Place in English Literature," acknowledged that by the time of his death "many had lost interest in him and many others had been repelled." What repels mid- and late-twentieth-century readers is most often the politics of Kipling's endorsement of empire. George

Orwell, writing a few years after Kipling's death, judged his colonial politics not only repellent but ignorant in his neglect of the economic basis of empire. But Orwell also thought that because of what he left out as well as what he included, Kipling accurately described the life and attitudes of British colonial administrators and soldiers, providing "not only the best but about the only literary picture we have" of late-nineteenth-century Anglo-India. Lionel Trilling, who found Kipling unreadable after his own adoption of liberal politics, nonetheless remarked the "anthropological view" that Kipling learned in India: "the perception that another man's idea of virtue and honor may be different from one's own but quite to be respected." Noel Annan has argued that this awareness of the relativity and individual integrity of cultural institutions and authority assures Kipling's place in the history of ideas. This view has made Kipling interesting to an increasing number of literary and cultural critics and historians who go to his writing not just for a picture of the lives of colonialists but also for a sensitive register of the tensions and contradictions in their exercise of dominion over ways of knowing that Kipling at least sometimes thought of as valid and valuable.

Other commentators who have sustained or revived interest in Kipling's writing since his death have not troubled so much with his politics but instead honored his craft. Despite his disappointment in Kipling's fiction after *Traffics and Discoveries*, Edmund Wilson presented to formalist literary critics a Kipling who was attractive because of his themes of loneliness and isolation and his accounts of a perilous fortitude. J. M. S. Tompkins has written of the sophisticated use of irony by which Kipling maintains his equilibrium on the edge; Bonamy Dobrée of Kipling's modulation in and out of the fabulist forms in which he tended to express his certainties; and Elliot K. L. Gilbert of the tactics that mediate between Kipling's notion of "the irrationality of the universe and man's need to find some order in it." These fundamentally existentialist ideas about how Kipling's craft fashioned order in and against the void are consistent with the interests and language of late-twentieth-century literary criticism. Sandra Kemp, for example, writes of how Kipling's recognition that identity, like everything else, is constructed and contingent informs self-consciously fictional narratives in which he tries out a repertory of identities, no longer resisting the void but rather inhabiting it as a condition that enables him to explore the exhilarating possibilities of otherness.

One reason to attend to Kipling's craft is that such attention makes clear the continuity and development of his talent during the nearly half century in which he wrote short stories. He now is probably best known outside academic literary criticism as the author of the *Jungle Books* and *Just So Stories*, and perhaps after that as a writer of short stories, poems, and a novel, *Kim*, about the British in India. Recent attention to his colonial politics, although it makes him freshly interesting, also helps to fix him in the moment of his first fame at the turn of the century, as if he wrote little that matters after 1901 or what he wrote has little to do with the books that made him famous. But Kipling's practice was always various, and it grew more supple as he graduated to long forms. He continually experimented with voices and points of view. The connected narratives of *The Story of the Gadsbys* are told entirely in the dialogue of quick, fluid scenes that read like scripts for short films. The comic effects of Mulvaney's dialect point up the ravages of the losses he describes in the same way that the working-class dialect in "The Wish House" plays against and makes poignant the fantastic event that is the hinge of the plot. Kipling learned to move in the same story from one set of conventions and expectations to another and so to reproduce his sense of a reality in which the meaning of things would not settle and stay fixed. He also learned in stories such as "Mrs. Bathhurst" to let the voices mix with one another to tell their tales in pieces and layers and so to express his skepticism that the whole story could ever be told.

As a young man Kipling sometimes deprecated his calling. Throughout his life he spoke of his "Daemon," who brought the words from somewhere beneath his will. "When your Daemon is in charge, do not try to think consciously," he wrote in his autobiography. "Drift, wait, and obey." At the end of his life, however, Kipling proudly owned the craft that deliberately selected and refined the welter of experience. In the chapter on "Working Tools" in his autobiography he mentions first as instruments of the "Higher Editing" a pot of India ink and a brush. He advises that writers "consider faithfully every paragraph, sentence and word, blacking out where requisite," repeating the process after letting the manuscript "lie by to drain as long as possible," and then repeating it again after reading the words aloud. He habitually read his writing aloud, testing the "weights, colours, perfumes, and attributes of words in relation to other words. . . . There is no line of my verse or prose which has not been mouthed till the tongue has made all smooth."

In "Proofs of Holy Writ" (1934), the last short story by Kipling published in his lifetime (it was collected in volume thirty-four of *The Sussex Edition of the Complete Works of Rudyard Kipling*), he compared his method of composition to that of William Shakespeare. Shakespeare, with occasional help from an outclassed Ben Jonson, has agreed to help the translators of the King James Bible with the rhythms of their sentences:

> "Quiet man!" said he. I wait on my Demon! . . . How shall this open? 'Arise.' No! 'Rise.' Yes. And we'll have no weak coupling. 'Tis a call to a City! 'Rise—shine.' . . . Nor yet any schoolmaster's 'because.' . . . 'And the glory of God!' No! 'God's' over-short. We need the long roll here. '*And the glory of the Lord is risen on thee.*'"

Kipling started out by presenting himself as a clever young man who wrote "penny farthing tales" in which he pretended to transmit the words of men he met at the club and in railway carriages. He ended by imagining how a craft such as his can find words and a sound that will wake the lessons of a great prophet.

Source: Donald Gray, "Rudyard Kipling," in *Dictionary of Literary Biography*, Vol. 156, *British Short-Fiction Writers, 1880–1914: The Romantic Tradition*, edited by William F. Naufftus, Gale Research, 1996, pp. 181–99.

Carole Scott

In the following essay, Scott explores the whys and hows of Kipling's creation of a "testing ground" and a "code of behavior" for his protagonists.

Kipling's obsession with the mastery of rules, laws, and codes of behavior dominates his work as it did his life. He wrote a charter for his children that identified in detail their "rights" to the Dudwell River near Bateman's; he created a Jungle society with a code "as perfect as time and custom can make it" (*The Second Jungle Book*); and he knew how to manipulate the rules to hasten his son's classification into active military service in World War I. Anyone at all familiar with Kipling's childhood will readily understand these concerns. The shock of being moved at the age of five from a pampered life with his family in India to the care of a harsh foster mother in Southsea, England, must have been traumatic enough. To be rescued after five long years from this "House of Desolation" only to be sent away again in less than a year to public school, a place of strict, often physical, discipline and institutionalized bullying, reinforced Kipling's sense that the world was a dangerous and uncertain place. These early experiences shaped his vision of the world and taught hint how to survive:

one must understand the system of order, master its code of rules, and apply them relentlessly.

Many writers, especially writers for children, have created unforgettable imaginary realms with their own sometimes fantastic rules; the entrances to such "otherworlds" are often surprising—a mirror, a wardrobe, a rabbit hole—dramatizing the borders of these magical realms and emphasizing their distinctness from the "real" world from which the children have come. It is not surprising, considering the drastic and painful changes to which little Rudyard had been subjected, that the grown Kipling would similarly plunge his young fictional protagonists into parallel worlds with new rules and new modes of survival, and that these otherworlds would be decidedly nonutopian. To Kipling, life was brutal, and his books for young people express this clearly, too clearly perhaps for modern tastes. For just as we find it hard to understand why a proud and loving father would push a seventeen-year-old into battle long before it was necessary, we wonder at his fascination with rules and laws, and why they are associated with such a high degree of violence. We are concerned that he expresses not only casual tolerance, but even encouragement, of behavior and attitudes that we consider unnecessarily brutal and cruel, even sadistic, especially in books for young people. Kipling exalts the harshest side of the manly code, especially the enthusiastic approval of physical punishment and violence and the stalwart indifference to pain, while encouraging the suppression of softer "feminine" feelings that he thought made men vulnerable. Published within a span of five years (1894–99), each of the three works I have selected for analysis, the Mowgli stories (which I shall be treating as one work), *Captains Courageous,* and *Stalky & Co.,* features a testing ground for the protagonist, a combat zone with its own set of laws, code of behavior, mode of being, and appropriate style of language.

The sense that Kipling's harsh code goes too far is not just a modern reaction. Despite his many admirers, there has always been an undercurrent of criticism, even revulsion (particularly in the period between the two World Wars) against the sentiments he expresses. When Martin Seymour-Smith in 1989 describes Kipling's publicly expressed philosophy of life as "cheap, shoddy, unworthy and impractical" and his public utterances revealing of a man "grotesque, merciless and insensitive," he follows in the tradition of Richard Buchanan who, in 1900, declared that Kipling was "on the side of all that is ignorant, selfish, base and brutal in the instincts of humanity" and that "the vulgarity, the brutality, the savagery, reeks on every page." Max Beerbohm's well-known caricatures of Kipling, which began in 1901 and continued for almost thirty years, express a similar opinion.

However, in spite of the criticism, there is no doubt that Kipling's exaltation of the ideals of warfare and its opportunities for manly conduct and heroism was widely shared in his time; it is not often that a new writer achieves popularity as fast as he did. Indeed, his successful expression of the exultant warrior mentality in his books for young people makes them of special cultural significance, for they helped to shape the minds of the young men who were later to die in the mud of Flanders fields. The books teach the ways to achieve success and self-esteem in later life, creating a picture of manliness, courage, and obedience to a clearly enunciated code of behavior from which one may not deviate for any reason. It is not surprising that the young men encouraged to display these traits would advance cheerfully to be mown down by the relentless German machine guns, and would even show their gallant sportsmanship by kicking footballs before them as they went, steadfastly "playing the game." John Kipling naturally falls into this metaphor when he writes his father from the war zone, "Remember our C.O. was 7 months on a "Brigade" staff & what he doesn't know about the game isn't worth knowing." (Gilbert 213).

The rules of war are very different from the rules of games, but Kipling and his contemporaries were not at all clear on this issue; tragically, it took the Great War and its spokesmen, Wilfred Owen, Siegfried Sassoon, and Rupert Brooke, to change the popular vision of the time. For the metaphor of war as game, which Kipling endorsed but by no means invented, had been nurtured by such poets as John Masefield and Sir Henry John Newbolt, whose "Vitaï Lampada" (1898) became a public school favorite. Beginning with the image of a school cricket match, Newbolt's poem ends with the later depiction of the boys at war. I reproduce the first and last verses:

> There's a breathless hush in the Close tonight—
> Ten to make and the match to win—
> A bumping pitch and a blinding light,
> An hour to play and the last man in.
> And it's not for the sake of a ribboned coat,
> Or the selfish hope of a season's fame,
> But his Captain's hand on his shoulder smote—
> Play up! play up! and play the game!
> . . . .
> The sand of the desert is sodden red—
> Red with the wreck of a square that broke;
> The Gatling's jammed and the Colonel dead,

"These early experiences shaped his vision of the world and taught hint how to survive: one must understand the system of order, master its code of rules, and apply them relentlessly."

> And the regiment blind with dust and smoke;
> The river of death has brimmed its banks,
> And England's far, and Honor a name;
> But the voice of a schoolboy rallies the ranks:
> Play up! play up! and play the game!

While it is true that moving onto the playing field or the battlefield involves entering into a distinct arena, where there are opposing teams and winners and losers, carrying the metaphor further is frightening. It is noteworthy that Newbolt's lifelong friend Douglas Haig was the general most responsible for the squandering of life, because he stubbornly persisted in relying on the soldiers' courage and fortitude instead of realizing that these qualities were meaningless in the face of the "stuttering rifles' rapid rattle."

In *The Great War and Modern Memory,* Paul Fussell discusses in detail the common attitude to war in the decades prior to 1914. He particularly notes the sense that when ordinary men moved into battle they took on the dimension of heroes, and points out how the elevated diction of warfare, very different from the language of everyday life, contributed to this perception. Thus the enemy is "the foe," the dead on the battlefield are "the fallen," to die is to "perish," warfare is "strife," and a soldier is a "warrior." The vision that war is glorious and transforms its participants into figures of mythical proportion is aptly illustrated in the mid-century incident that led to Tennyson's "Charge of the Light Brigade." "Someone had blundered," the poem tells us; but the stupidity and bungling that sent close to six hundred men to their deaths for absolutely no purpose is passed over lightly. Instead, the poem focuses upon the glorious bravery of the men of the Light Brigade, and how valiantly and honorably (though futilely) they gave their lives, ennobled by their sacrifice and enshrined in the hearts of posterity for time immemorial. It was not surprising that young men reared on the glowing illusion that "laying down one's life" or "making the supreme sacrifice" for family and country was a beautiful and somehow sanctified act should flock to the recruiting stations at the declaration of war. Thomas Babington Macaulay's "Horatius," written a few years before Tennyson's poem, put it well:

> . . . how could man die better
> than facing fearful odds
> For the ashes of his fathers
> And the temples of his Gods.

No wars are pretty, but the gulf that lay between rhetoric and reality in the Great War was especially striking.

In this context, Kipling's fictional realms, the "otherworlds" he created as arenas of conflict or combat zones, are more understandable. They are definitely men's worlds; most of the players are male, and the few women we encounter are, like Harvey's mother or the fishermen's womenfolk in *Captains Courageous,* safe on land outside the field of combat. At home the women are soft, nurturing, and emotional. They fear, they weep, they suffer vicariously for their menfolk. Harvey's mother breaks down completely, incapable of any kind of action, when she thinks he is drowned; the passion with which Kipling describes how the entire railroad system conspires to speed her to her recovered son is sentimental to the point of excess. Messua, too, is pictured as vulnerable, suffering for her maternal love and kindness to Mowgli when the villagers stone her; incapable of self-preservation, she must depend on her adopted son for protection. The only self-sufficient female is Raksha, but of course she is a wolf! The men, on the other hand, display no such soft emotions; they are fierce, courageous, hard, even cruel; they exult in pain and they exult in winning. But to escape from the female world and female feelings, they must move over the boundary into another world.

In both the Mowgli stories and *Captains Courageous* we find the main character clearly crossing over from his ordinary world into a completely different one. Mowgli has somehow strayed from the sphere of humankind, and when he walks into Raksha's lair he has entered the Jungle world where animals talk and have created a social structure and history, and where he must learn to survive on their terms. Harvey tumbles from his old life in the luxury liner headlong into another realm. Saved from drowning in the ocean, he is literally reborn into the microcosm of the fishing boat named the *We're Here,* where he takes the place of a young man lost at sea just a few days before. He has shed his old identity as he has his wad of money, and must take on new habits, new behavior, and a new perspective on his place in society, playing the part of a man in a man's world, subject to the common code that ensures the survival of the floating community. In *Stalky & Co.,* although we receive some description, especially regarding M'Turk, about the homes from which they have come, there is no account of the boys' arrival at the school. The boundary over which they have stepped is not dramatized, although it is clear that it exists, for their excursions into the surrounding countryside are carefully prescribed, and being out of bounds is punishable. The incident where the Head banishes himself from this sequestered world to preserve it from the danger of diphtheria outside emphasizes its separateness.

The Law of the Jungle in the Mowgli stories is described by Kipling as preeminent and "as old and as true as the sky" with a code that is absolute, seemingly immutable, and unquestionable. The reader is never told how or by whom it was established, or how it might be changed. Driven by a supposedly ageless and eternal vision imbued with a rational wisdom that accepts and incorporates the apparent vagaries of animal behavior and provides a clear pattern fair to each, the law defines each creature's hierarchy, its rights and obligations, and the rules of interaction with its own kind and with other species. Thus the tiger can claim one night of the year when he is entitled to kill Man; a mother wolf has the right to a portion of any wolf's kill for her litter; the jackal may run with the tiger and take what he leaves; and the elephant who lives a hundred years and more has the responsibility to proclaim the Water Truce. Only the Bandar-log, the Yahoos of the Jungle, are outside the law and are consequently viewed with contempt by all of the other animals. While time moves on and the players change, the principles and rules remain; the law has "arranged for almost every kind of accident that may befall the Jungle People, till now its code is as perfect as time and custom can make it." Because it is clearly understandable and dependable, it governs even out-of-the-ordinary situations, like the time of drought, or Mowgli's kidnapping by the Bandar-log and his incarceration among the snakes of the ruined city, when the Master-words of the Jungle ensure safe passage.

The notion of the supremacy of the law, driven by a Darwinian belief in the perfectibility that "time and custom" will unquestionably bring about, suggests a supreme power whose vision is realized in this exact code. Whether this supreme power is divine, or a reflection of the Victorian imperialistic sense of responsibility for bringing light and civilization to benighted areas of the world, is not important here; in fact, the sense of mission characteristic of both is clearly expressed in Mowgli's need to "let in the Jungle" in an attempt to cleanse the nearby village where superstition and greed has led to behavior that violates the morals of the Jungle Law. Because he is so clever and learns the Jungle Law better than the animals, Mowgli becomes invincible. He achieves individual power by following the law and interpreting it with human intelligence, illustrating that the individual is the expression of this deeper power rather than a free agent who can operate outside it.

Those of us who were introduced to the Mowgli stories in childhood probably accept without question that the Jungle in this context is an appropriate source of values. We still delight in Mother Wolf's claiming of the naked man cub, protecting him against the villainous Shere Khan, and watching benignly as he suckles with her own brood. Like Mowgli we feel the joys of companionship with the other wolves and his sense of belonging as he learns to claim, "We be of one blood, ye and I"; and we know his loneliness when he is thrust out of this idyllic existence because of his growing manhood. We share his sense of increasing competence as he learns the rules and becomes Master of the Jungle, and his distaste for the moral turpitude of the village.

When we think a little more objectively, however, the notion of finding codes of behavior in the Jungle, a place usually used as a metaphor for savagery and lawlessness, seems contradictory and strange. And when we analyze these codes more carefully, we find that a great many of them regulate the ordered hierarchy of power, particularly power over killing and ownership of the kill. When you wish someone well you wish him "good hunting," and Chil the Kite's function as the scavenger of the dead is cheerfully acknowledged: "almost everybody in the Jungle comes to [Chil] in the end." Moments of great accomplishment are similarly violent: Mowgli laughs when he sets fire to Shere Khan's coat, and later, having killed him, dances in triumph upon his skin pegged out on the Council Rock. "Letting in the Jungle" features Mowgli's relentless revenge against humankind, and the story is followed by "Mowgli's Song Against People," which celebrates the obliteration of a village. The nature of the language as well as the splendid rhythms of the death chants and songs gives a legendary quality to this long tale of hunting, killing, and revenge. The violence is continuous, but the everyday tone encourages us to accept it as the way things are, where winning means survival. " 'When tomorrow comes we will kill for tomorrow,' said Mowgli, quoting a Jungle saying; and again 'When I am dead it is time to sing the Death Song. Good Hunting Kaa!.' " There are really only two occasions where death seems frightening. The first is in "Kaa's Hunting," where Kaa tells Mowgli "what follows is not well that thou shouldst see" and we are left with the image of the mesmeric Dance of the Hunger of Kaa that will lead to the death of many of the Bandar-log, unable to resist in their hypnotized state; the second is in "The King's Ankus" where men kill not for food, but for greed. Somehow the killing on these two occasions seems unsporting and not played by the appropriate rules.

Source: Carole Scott, "Kipling's Combat Zones: Training Grounds in the Mowgli Stories, *Captains Courageous* and *Stalky & Co.*," in *Children's Literature*, Vol. 20, 1992, pp. 53–68.

Roger Lancelyn Green

In the following essay, Green traces the setting of Kipling's Jungle Book *stories to actual places in India while in search of the elements of Mowgli's life that may have been inspired by actual events.*

[Roger Lancelyn Green's name requires no introduction for anyone familiar with Kipling studies. It is enough to say that he is a distinguished man of letters, a writer of a catholic and readable array of books, a leading authority on Kipling and his period, and in his leisure was Editor of this *Journal* for twenty-three years, from 1957 to 1979.

In 1975 he published a collection of light but learned essays, entitled "*Holmes, This is Amazing*": they were straight-faced but "unorthodox" investigations into the quasi-factual background of some literary episodes relating to Sherlock Holmes, Allan Quatermain, Lord Greystroke (better known as Tarzan of the Apes), and others. One of the others was Mowgli, whose history was discussed in a piece entitled "Mowgli's Jungle."

Perhaps on account of the Editor's modesty, it never appeared in the *Kipling Journal*. It is certainly overdue, and we have pleasure in reprinting it now, with the author's approval. Readers will see at once that Mowgli is treated as a real person—this being of course consistent with the investigative position adopted in the other essays in the volume in which "Mowgli's Jungle" first appeared.—*Ed.*]

It was seven o'clock of a very warm evening in the Seeonee. hills when Father Wolf woke up from his day's rest.

" When it became necessary to disguise the location of Mowgli's adventures it may well have been Sahi who gave Kipling the idea of using Seeonee, and who supplied him with any necessary information about the district--which Kipling had never visited, and knew only from descriptions."

This first sentence of "Mowgli's Brothers," the first narrative in *The Jungle Book*, seems straightforward enough, and should set Mowgli's jungle adventures in the neighbourhood of Seeonee, near the Waingunga River, not far from Khaniwara in Madhya Pradesh (the old Central Provinces).

But there are several curious complications in the setting of Mowgli's adventures that have never been explained; and it seems almost as if their true site was being carefully concealed. Certainly Kipling changed his mind about the locality of Mowgli's jungle after he had written "In the Rukh" and the first draft of "Mowgli's Brothers."

When "In the Rukh" was reprinted, with illustrations, in the American *McClure's Magazine* in June 1896, Kipling added a prefatory footnote:

> This tale, published in "Many Inventions" (D. Appleton & Co.), 1893, was the first written of the Mowgli stories, though it deals with the closing chapters of his career—namely his introduction to white men, his marriage and civilization, all of which took place, we may infer, some two or three years after he had finally broken away from his friends in the jungle (*vide* "The Spring Running," *Second Jungle Book*). Those who know the geography of India will see that it is a far cry from Seeonee to a Northern forest reserve; but though many curious things must have befallen Mowgli, we have no certain record of his adventures during those wanderings. There are, however, legends.—*Rudyard Kipling.*

Kipling did not, unfortunately, tell any of these legends; indeed, some of Mowgli's remarks in this story seem to have puzzled him, for he added two more notes. "A woman, an old woman, beloved, saw me playing by night with my brethren in the crops," says Mowgli; and Kipling comments, rather improbably:

> The scornful allusion here is clearly to Buldeo the Shikarri, who . . . interfered with Mowgli when the latter was skinning Shere Khan. It is not easy to understand the reference to "playing by night with my brethren," unless, indeed, Mowgli while among the villagers had stolen out to gambol with Grey Brother, and was under suspicion of wizardry before the fight with Shere Khan.—R.K.

And after Mowgli's confession that "From village to village I went, . . . a herder of cattle, a tender of buffaloes, a tracker of game," his biographer notes:

> It is to be observed that Mowgli here makes no reference to the circumstances of The Spring Running; but evidently he wandered far among men after his return to Messua's hut (*vide Second Jungle Book*).—R.K.

Kipling himself did not make any mention of Mowgli's later jungle adventures when, so it seems, he had decided not to tell any more of them after " 'Tiger! Tiger!' " for he concluded this with the statement that

> Mowgli went away and hunted with the four cubs in the Jungle from that day on. But he was not always alone, because years afterward he became a man and married. But that is a story for grown-ups.

The story referred to is, of course, "In the Rukh," written before any of the others, which tells how Mowgli as a grown man, but still accompanied by the four wolves, took service under Gisborne of the Department of Woods and Forests, and married the daughter of his butler, Abdul Gafur.

The site of Gisborne's *rukh* is uncertain—since cartographers have failed to identify the Kanye river which flowed through it; but it was presumably over a hundred miles south of the Changamanga Reserve, itself about fifty miles south-west of Lahore, on the edge of the Rechna Doab. For Mowgli tells Gisborne that he came "from over there," pointing "towards the north."

Unless Mowgli had wandered many hundreds of miles up into the forests of the Doon in the north of India, near Simla, "north" seems to be a deliberate blind—or else a simple mistake on Kipling's part. It would certainly be impossible if Mowgli really came from Seeonee in Central India: but there is good evidence that the whole setting in and near Seeonee was a conscious attempt to disguise the real location of Mowgli's earlier life in the jungle.

Kipling tells us in the Preface to *The Jungle Book* that

the adventures of Mowgli were collected at various times and in various places from a multitude of informants, most of whom desire to preserve the strictest anonymity,

and he only mentions one of the *Bandar-log*, "an esteemed resident of the upper slopes of Jakko" near Simla, who presumably supplied reformation about the attempt to abduct Mowgli, described in "Kaa's Hunting"; and

Sahi, a savant of infinite research and industry, a member of the recently disbanded Seeonee pack,

who, however, is only credited with "valuable data on people, manners and customs."

When it became necessary to disguise the location of Mowgli's adventures it may well have been Sahi who gave Kipling the idea of using Seeonee, and who supplied him with any necessary information about the district—which Kipling had never visited, and knew only from descriptions.

The moment at which Kipling suddenly found himself compelled to change the situation of Mowgli's home jungle to Seeonee came between the writing of the first and second drafts of "Mowgli's Brothers." The first draft begins:

It was about seven o'clock of a very warm evening among the Aravulli hills when the Father Wolf woke up from his day's sleep.

A little further on we are told that

the wolves were talking in their own language, but the way in which animals talk is very much the same as the way in which the men round them talk. So these wolves spoke like the Mewari herdsmen whose goats they stole.

When Shere Khan is first mentioned we are told that he was

the Tiger who lived near a branch of the Bunas river twenty miles away,

and Tabaqui explains that Shere Khan

"is coming here to hunt for man, and he will lie up at the Bunas in his own country."

During the 'Over-looking' at the Council Rock the Lone Wolf, Akela, tells the Pack the advantages of having a man's cub as one of their number—among them that the local villagers will believe that they are all demons and leave them alone:

"Many years ago, before I could kill, so my father told me, a grey pack that hunted below the Abu hills kept with them a man's cub and till that man's cub died no villager stirred from his hut at night—no, not though the pack killed the goats at his doorstep. They believed that he was a demon . . ."

And finally, Bagheera tells Mowgli that

"I was born among men, and it was among men that my mother died—in the cages of the palace at Oodeypore, a week's hunting from here."

Now the Aravulli Hills, Mount Abu and the Bunas River are all within a fifty mile radius of Oodeypore (now usually spelt Udaipur) in the district of Mewar in the State of Rajputana; nearby also is Bhurtpur where Hathi and his sons sacked the fields—and Udaipur is also much too far from Seeonee for there to be any likelihood of Bagheera travelling over a thousand miles after his escape from the King's Cages which still stand at the foot of the hill below the Palace.

There is also the matter of the Cold Lairs. Of course there are many ruined cities decaying in the jungles throughout India—but there does not seem to be one reasonably near the Seeonee district. On the other hand, not seventy miles from Udaipur and much nearer to the Aravulli Hills stands Chitor (usually known as Chitorgarh to distinguish it from the modern town that has only sprung up at its foot during the last few years: it was still only a village when I visited it in 1968, a growing town in 1971)—and Chitor fulfils every requirement for the original Cold Lairs.

Some king had built it long ago on a little hill. You could still trace the stone causeways that led up to the ruined gates . . . A great roofless palace crowned the hill, and the marble of the courtyards and the fountains was split, and stained with red and green, and the very cobble-stones in the courtyard where the king's elephants used to live had been thrust up and apart by grasses and young trees. From the palace you could see the rows and rows of roofless houses that made up the city looking like empty honeycombs filled with blackness . . .

There too you may find the

terrace above the red sandstone reservoirs that were half-full of rainwater. There was a ruined summerhouse of white marble in the centre of the terrace . . .

A much less ruined summer-house stands on the terrace above the reservoir by the Gau Mukh, the "Cow's Mouth" (which plays such an important part in Nicholas Tarvin's adventures not many years after Mowgli's, as narrated in *The Naulahka*), and from beneath the summer-house a passage is said still to run to a distant treasure-chamber underground—undoubtedly that inhabited by the White Cobra in "The King's Ankus"—though today's explorer is not permitted to enter it.

Chitor has been cleared of the trees and creepers which were destroying it, and there are fewer and fewer of the *Bandar-log*, the Monkey People, to be seen there. But Mowgli's adventures must have taken place about a hundred years ago [*written in 1975*]—and even when Kipling visited the site in 1887, as described in "Letters of Marque," the place was still completely overgrown, with the outer walls crumbling, the buildings infested with snakes, and apparently a crocodile in one at least of the reservoirs.

During the last hundred years a great deal of the country between Chitor and Udaipur, and below the slopes of the Aravulli Hills that sweep round them to the west and north, has been cleared of jungle and cultivated. But patches still remain wild—and in one of these (though rather near to the modern road) rises

> a hilltop covered with stones and boulders where a hundred wolves could hide,

or, as the original manuscript has it,

> the great mound of splintered rocks all mixed up with scrub and thorn brushes—

that must surely be the Council Rock.

Only the gorge below the Bee Rocks defies identification. But I was unable to follow the Bunas River up into the heights of the Aravulli Hills near Mount Abu—and it may well be there. (There *is* a gorge frequented by wild bees near Seeonee, but this seems hardly sufficient to suggest that even one of Mowgli's adventures took place there.)

Kipling gives us no indication as to the date of Mowgli's birth. He was seventeen years old at the time of the Spring Running when he left the jungle, and we may assume that he was twenty at least when Gisborne found him in the *rukh* and he joined the Forestry Service. If we consider that the four wolves who still accompanied him were, as is implied, the very same who had been cubs in the Home Cave when Father Wolf rescued him at the age of two from Shere Khan and brought him to Mother Wolf, they had already exceeded the normal life-span of wolves in a completely natural state—and were still flourishing at about the age of twenty when Müller nearly shot one of them by mistake as it guarded Mowgli's eldest child.

If, as is generally agreed, Müller, "head of the woods and forests of all India," is the Inspector-General of Forests whose real name was Ribbentrop, and whom Kipling met in Lahore in 1883, we may assume that his meeting with Mowgli in Gisborne's *rukh* had recently taken place. And this being so, Mowgli must have been born about 1860.

Why Kipling needed to disguise the setting of all his earlier adventures we shall probably never know. But is it not possible that by 1894 when the *Jungle Book* adventures were being written, Mowgli had become an important person in India, and did not want to be identified with the hero of these stories? "In the Rukh" had already appeared in April 1893 in *Many Invetions*, and Mowgli would have been just in time to persuade Kipling to alter the setting from Mewar to Seeonee, and remove other references that might have identified him too closely, before the publication of "Mowgli's Brothers" in its revised version in January 1894.

With his unique background and abilities Mowgli might well have achieved a position of great importance under the British Raj, or perhaps at the court of the Maharajah of Udaipur, by the time he was thirty-four . . . 'But that is another story.'

Source: Roger Lancelyn Green, "Mowgli's Jungle," in *Kipling Journal*, Vol. 57, No. 227, September 1983, pp. 29–35.

Anonymous

In the following obituary published originally in Times Literary Supplement *on January 25, 1936, the anonymous author assesses Kipling's place in literature and his time.*

Rudyard Kipling was a national institution . . . and regarded as such by all the world. His fame had been long established and his literary activity slight for many years. It was also the case that many had lost interest in him and many others had been repelled. Seldom had a famous national institution been the object of more hostile criticism; some of it, indeed, unfair and marred by lack of understanding, yet some of it damaging enough. There are veterans who were hostile from the first; there are today many thousands of young enthusiasts: but broadly speaking the vocal sections of two generations have been at variance regarding him. Now the time has come for a reckoning; not a final reckoning, for posterity will have its say, but for the verdict of this age, comprising the old and the young, sitting as the jury. The critic writing at the moment must try to assist the jury to find that verdict, not as advocate for or against—they have both been heard at length but, so far as he can and dare, as judge summing up. Conscious of his own limitations and mindful of the disasters of many who have assumed the role, he may also attempt a harder task: that of prophecy. Kipling in life and work alike was downright and decided, without hesitation as to goal or the road that led to it. Let us treat him as he would have chosen to be treated, without timidity or hedging. Let us venture not only to decide what shall be the verdict of our time upon him but to predict boldly what shall be his place in the annals of our letters.

We have to envisage him both as poet and writer of fiction, and in the former aspect our task is, it may be admitted, a difficult one. On the prose side the case is very different. There is, we believe, no heavy risk in the prophecy that Rudyard Kipling will live and be admired as one of the most virile and skilful of English masters of the short story; that if that art, in which we are weak, shows with us no great development in future, he will remain, in years to come, as he now is, unique; that if it goes forward and gives birth to new triumphs, he will still rank among the greatest of the pioneers.

The pioneer has always a special meed of honour, and that honour is Kipling's for more reasons than one. He won it alike for matter and manner. He was definitely the man of the hour, a milestone on the path of letters like Bryon and Chateaubriand. He appeared at a moment when literature in this country was being sicklied o'er, not with the pale cast of thought but with the unnatural bloom of cosmetics. We can realize now more fully than was realized then that fine and enduring work was being done in the aesthetic nineties, outside the school of the aesthetes, even outside that of the two giants who had no relationship to that school, George Meredith and Thomas Hardy. Yet the general atmosphere was stale and scented, artistically as well as literally *fin-de-siècle*. There was an extraordinary preoccupation with the artificial, a delight, by no means assumed on the part of many of the 'yellow' world, in 'bought red mouths', 'parched flowers', pallid women, 'delicate' sins.

Before the nineties opened there had spread bruit of a young writer out in India who knew little of this world of opera-cloaks and gold-headed canes and scorned what he did know. Kipling was, as his acute French observer, M. André Chevrillon, remarked, English *'d'une façon simple, violente et, de plus, tres nouvelle'*; the world which he entered so violently, which he did more than any other to destroy, being, on the contrary, the pale and unsatisfying reflection of a phase in French literature. Kipling was indeed English, but in those early days he was the mouthpiece of classes and types that were not themselves vocal and had long lacked a chronicler. India, with its heat and dust, its diversities of creed and caste was suddenly brought to the door of the stay-at-home Englishman. He learned with a thrill how the more adventurous of his race, from private soldiers to governors of

> " He sees the savage in man and that it is not far below the surface, and he is disposed to question the benefits of civilization."

provinces, lived; how they fought and organized and ruled. For this precocious genius had not only observed and recorded for him a great number of interesting and astonishing facts and occurrences; he had also put at his disposal a marvellous power of catching an atmosphere, of summing up an impression of the scenes upon which the writer had looked. This was life indeed, exclaimed the reader in his armchair; this was life as it should be lived, this young seer in India was revealing the highest destiny of the Englishman. Soon it appeared that life could be lived elsewhere than in India. It could be lived in America, in Africa, in the ports of the world, at sea, whether in crack cargo-boats, rusty tramps or the fishing smacks on the Grand Bank, in the cab of a steam-engine; even, for those who knew how, in an unconventional public school. The same vigour, the same brilliant technique, the same power of making mechanism romantic marked each new effort and bound together the spell he had put upon the English public.

And then there came another phase. The worshipper of dangerous living, of physical excitement, of noise, some detractors averred, became entranced with the peaceful beauties and with the traditions of the English countryside, and touched upon them with as much originality as he had all the rest. Such are the broad lines of his literary career.

Rudyard Kipling is first of all master of the *conte*. He attempted full-length novels, achieving in *The Light that Failed* and *Captains Courageous* romances to which no adjective higher than 'successful' can be applied: in *The Naulahka* written in collaboration with his brother-in-law, not even that; and in *Kim* his one masterpiece in that province. But in the short story he has had few English rivals, even if we take the best work of others to match against his, and from his take any of forty or fifty which it is hard to separate from the point of view of merit. The short story was suited to his peculiar gifts of compression, of clarity, of characterization that needs no building up but is completed and fixed in a flash. In his stories he has used almost every kind of matter, though the love of the sexes plays a very much smaller part than with most writers. War, adventure of every type, machinery pure and simple, have been his familiar subjects. He has employed the grotesque, the horrible, and very often the eerie in his plots, looking with anxious but never credulous eyes at what may be distinguished or imagined 'at the end of the passage', in the half-world betwixt fact and dream. Nor has he neglected that form of short story which is almost an allegory, among which the Mowgli tales of *The Jungle Book* stand highest. In a great number of the early stories, in those of Mowgli above all, we seem to detect a form of idealism with as little historical justification as that of Rousseau. He sees the savage in man and that it is not far below the surface, and he is disposed to question the benefits of civilization.

The sentiment was perhaps with him no more than a phase, but those who study him closely can have little doubt that it existed. They will assuredly not regret the fact. For in the Mowgli stories Kipling achieved a rare feat: he invented a new form of expression. And these tales have a charm, a beauty, a boldness of imagination that we have not often seen equalled in our time. The animals are not, as are those of Kipling's numerous imitators in this vein, creatures with men's minds in the bodies of beasts. The sentiments of beasts may be inaccurately described; that we cannot tell, though we may suspect that their intelligence is exaggerated; but the whole affair is managed with such marvellous dexterity that we are convinced and willingly surrender to him our judgment. Can an animal find enjoyment in the thrill of danger, as many human beings can? Hear his answer and see if you can state the contrary opinion with equal plausibility?

> To move down so cunningly that never a leaf stirred; to wade knee-deep in the roaring shallows that drown all noise from behind; to drink, looking backward over one shoulder, every muscle ready for the first desperate bound of keen terror; to roll on the sandy margin, and return, wet-muzzled and well plumped out, to the admiring herd, was a thing that all tall-antlered young bucks took a delight in, precisely because they knew that at any moment Bagheera or Shere Khan might leap upon them and bear them down.

That word plausibility, in fact, gives us the key to one of the chief secrets of his popularity. It also explains a certain impatience felt by those who

caught him out. For, excellently documented as he was, he was not always correct—could hardly be so, seeing how wide was his range. But, right or wrong, he was always equally assured, cocksure said the less friendly of his critics. And yet, these slips apart, his plausibility is amazing. The finest of the stories, such as 'On Greenhow Hill', 'The Return of Imray', 'The Strange Ride of Morrowbie Jukes', 'the Man who would be King', 'Without Benefit of Clergy', 'the Mark of the Beast',—have the verisimilitude of chronicles. Let us say that chronicles they are indeed, the chronicles of an epoch of British administration in India, infused with the imagination of a great writer of fiction.

The poetry is another matter. Poetry demands a standard even higher than prose; that is to say, an infelicitous expression, a piece of loose thinking are in it more painfully apparent and bring their own condemnation more swiftly. In his early work in verse Kipling did not fly high. *Departmental Ditties* may have won him his earliest fame, but these popular ballads, parodies, society verses, satires, clever and witty as they are, do not warrant the bestowal of the title of poet. The elevation of Mr. Potiphar Gubbins, the transfer to Quetta of Jack Barrett, may take their place somewhere below the satiric verse of Marvell and above that of Churchill; the rest, if they live, will live because they are Kipling's. Yet on the last page of that volume came a poem, *'L'Envoi',* which few probably noticed, which a bold prophet might have seen as a cloud no bigger than a man's hand. Till that cloud has sailed up we continue in the arid heat of dexterity, of rhetoric, of admonition, of a sententiousness often grating. We are warmed and made happy by wit and humour, we recognize a master of metre, rhythm and onomatopoeia in a line like

> The heave and the halt and the hurl and the crash of the comber wind-hounded.

But almost always we are either pulled up with a jar by a phrase which is definitely inappropriate, definitively no poetry; or, if we escape that, subsequent reflection seems to indicate a flaw in taste, a thought of which the expression begins well but is not sustained at the level of its early dignity and beauty. But the cloud was drawing nigher and swelling in size. There may be difference of opinions whether the later stories of the English countryside are the equals of the more brilliant exotic predecessors. There can be little doubt that in the lovely songs, strewn among them, buttercups and daisies amid rich green grass, Kipling reached his highest as a poet. The passionate patriotism which had often previously run riot, shocking and offending the weaker brethren, is here even more intense, but purified, purged of that note of brawling.

> Under their feet in the grasses
> My clinging magic runs.
> They shall return as strangers,
> They shall remain as sons.
>
> Scent of smoke in the evening.
> Smell of rain in the night,
> The hours, the days and the seasons,
> Order their souls aright.

In these songs, with their simplicity, their kindly and gracious philosophy, he reveals at last that lyric sweetness whereof we had had promise in 'L'Envoi', and himself as not merely a satirist or humorist or master of the banjo ballad, but a lyric poet.

> Cities and Thrones and Powers,
> Stand in Time's eye,
> Almost as long as flowers,
> Which daily die:
> But, as new buds put forth
> To glad new men
> Out of the spent and unconsidered Earth,
> The Cities rise again.
>
> This season's Daffodil,
> She never hears,
> What change, what chance, what chill,
> Cut down last year's;
> But with bold countenance,
> And knowledge small,
> Esteems her seven days' continuance
> To be perpetual.

(Even in reading these lines we pause. Is there not something school-boyish in the irony of that 'almost as long'?)

Yet let us make no mistake. More of Kipling will go down to posterity than the fastidious literary critic is prepared to pass. The flaws are those of a great and original craftsman; in the most faulty productions there is power; one feels everywhere in them the grip of a strong hand. Often that which is not poetry is life itself. Take a poem such as 'If'; not poetry at all, some critics may declare. It may not be, yet it has been an inspiration to many thousands and those not the most ingenuous or limited in their appreciation of poetical merit. Its moral maxims are as clean-cut and forcible as those of Pope or Edward Young. Almost all the patriotic verse, though it may grate often upon the ears of those whom Kipling called, with rather less than strict fairness but a large measure of truth,

> Brittle intellectuals who crack beneath a strain,

and sometimes upon any critical ears, represents at least one side of England. 'Wordswoth,' wrote Lowell, 'never lets us long forget the deeply rooted stock from which he sprang—*vien ben da lui.*' The

words may be applied with equal justice to Kipling. At his worst as at his best, the love of England breeds in him a passionate intensity and sincerity which ennoble even the verse marred by the shouting of party warfare or by extreme patriotic dogmatism, as by technical faults of like nature.

What verdict England of the future will pass upon England of the last years of Victoria and Edward VII, is uncertain, but it is incontestable that the age will always rank as one of the greatest in our history—great materially and great in national temper. And may one not dare to foresee that when, long hence, that age and its characteristics and products are called to mind, the name of Rudyard Kipling will come first to men's mouths when they talk of its most typical representatives? Is it not likely that then the lesser work will take its place with the greater, as all part of and symbolic of the country which he loved and celebrated?

It were not easy to imagine two writers more widely separated than Rudyard Kipling and Maurice Barrès, but their names are linked by the fact that as contemporaries, born within a few years of one another, each set up a philosophy of nationalism and each was assailed from a point of view in which the political mingled with the artistic. Each might have taken as motto the words of Disraeli: 'Now a nation is a work of art and a work of time;' and each tripped not seldom in the snares which arrogance sets for the feet of the nationalist. Hear them each, Barrès on his beloved Hill of Sion-Vaudemont:

> *Où sont les dames de Lorraine, sœurs, filles et femmes des Croisés, qui s'en venaient prier à Sion pendant que les hommes d'armes, là-bas, combattaient l'infidèle, et celles-là surtout qui, le lendemain de la bataille de Nicopolis, ignorantes encore, mais épouvantées par les rumeurs, montèrent ici intercéder pour des vivants qui étaient déjà des morts? Où la sainte princesse Philippe de Gueldre, à qui Notre-Dame de Sio découvrit, durant le temps de son sommeil, les desseins ambitieux des ennemis de la Lorraine? . . .*

and Kipling on his Sussex Downs:

> See you the dimpled track that runs,
> All hollow through the wheat?
> O that was where they hauled the guns
> That smote King Philip's fleet.
>
> See you our stilly woods of oak,
> And the dread ditch beside?
> O that was where the Saxons broke,
> On the day that Harold died.

While Barrès, a mystic, heard 'the hushed and timid voices' of the gods of his ancestors at those spiritual points where, it seemed to him, the crust of the material world was thin and the poetry of great deeds and great lives came through it as in a vapour, Kipling, more realistically, conjured up upon the Downs his ancestors, themselves. *Puck of Pook's Hill, Rewards and Fairies,* have in them the very marrow of England. For them, at least, we may prophesy with assurance that death will not come quickly. In these entrancing volumes, in many another tale of the stamp of 'An Habitation Enforced', there is far more than merely the exquisite art of telling a story; there is the recreation of history, the essence of a nation's beginning and early development. The figures of De Aquila and Sir Richard Dalyngridge are not only great characters of fiction but pendants to the works of great historians. 'And so was England born.' The work of Kipling, as of Barrès, at its greatest moments is a flower of national art. It was fitting that the former should have known and loved and been honoured of France; and that the latter, though he said hard words of England, should have been the guest of our fleet in time of war and lauded its traditions to his countrymen.

We have hinted that the young men have less pleasure in the work of Kipling than those who reached manhood at any time between the publication of *Departmental Ditties* and that of *Kim,* though there is some doubt as to how far the young writers represent their generation in this. In any case there is in it nothing uncommon or prejudicial to his eventual fame. At Wordsworth's death, when subscriptions were being collected for a memorial to him Macaulay declared to Arnold that ten years earlier more money could been raised to do him honor in Cambridge alone than was now raised all through the country. Thirty years later Arnold was bewailing that the diminution of Wordsworth's popularity was continuing, that, effaced first by Scott and Byron, he was now completely effaced by Tennyson. The selected poems of Wordsworth, which Arnold was then editing, to which the essay quoted was a preface, ran through thirteen editions between 1879 and the close of the century, and there have been many others. That which is popular today may be outmoded to-morrow, but if it has the stuff of life in it, it will assuredly not be dead the day after. Yet, where Kipling is concerned, it is improbable that there will ever be unanimity of opinion.

He was a man of strong prejudices, strong political views, with little tenderness for the opinions of others, and—though to lesser extent than now—he may always divide men into camps. So much granted, there will be, we are convinced, in years to come a general agreement upon the high merit of a great part of this man's work. The perfervid admirers will come to admit that there is dross—dross,

why he threw it up in a heap about him as he worked, till at times we could scarce see him over the top of it! Those of the type of mind which is antagonized by a loud-voiced patriotism and Toryism will allow those English songs and stories which we last considered to be free from that offence, and will perhaps even pardon it elsewhere for the vigour and skill with which it is presented. Both will proclaim him a magician in the art of the short story, who raised it to a higher station in our literature than it had known before his coming. As novelist they will call him author of one, but one only, of the finest romances of his time. As a poet he will be remembered for a mass of vigorous, pithy, if faulty, work of the second order; for a patriotic hymn that had become part of every national ceremony; last, not least, as the singer of English country beauties and traditions. And if, amid the work he leaves behind him, those juries of the future contrive, to catch a glimpse of the man himself, as his own time knew him, they must add to their verdict a rider that this was a great man as well as a great writer; and honourable and fearless and good.

Source: Anonymous, "Rudyard Kipling's Place in English Literature," in *Kipling: The Critical Heritage*, edited by Roger Lancelyn Green, Barnes & Noble, 1971, pp. 384–93.

Sources

Flint, M., "Kipling's Mowgli and Human Focalization," in *Studia Neophilologica*, Vol. LXV, No. 1, 1993, p. 78.

Kipling, Rudyard, "Mowgli's Brothers," in *The Jungle Books*, Vol. 1, Doubleday, 1948.

Locke, John, "Book II—Of Ideas," in *An Essay Concerning Human Understanding*, edited by Peter H. Nidditch, Oxford University Press, 1975, p. 105.

Spinoza, Benedictus, "Theologico-Political Treatise: Chapter IV: *Of the Divine Law*," in *The Chief Works of Benedict de Spinoza*, translated by R. H. M. Elwes, Dover, 1951, p. 61.

Further Reading

Bauer, Helen Pike, *Rudyard Kipling: A Study in Short Fiction*, Twayne, 1994.
> Bauer explores the themes and morals of Kipling's short fiction. The book includes essays on the Mowgli tales and other short works.

Cain, Peter, and Tony Hopkins, *British Imperialism, 1688–2000*, 2d ed., Longman, 2001.
> Critic R. D. Long calls this book "the standard work on British Imperialism and may remain so for the foreseeable future."

Gilmour, David, *The Long Recessional: The Imperial Life of Rudyard Kipling*, Farrar, 2003.
    Gilmour focuses on Kipling's political life and his pessimistic approach to the colonization that made him a rare human and British imperialist.

Mallett, Phillip, *Rudyard Kipling: A Literary Life*, Palgrave Macmillan, 2003.
    Mallett studies the influences on Kipling's work, including his family, his laureate status, and his relation to the literary world.

Orel, Harold, *A Kipling Chronology*, G. K. Hall, 1990.
    Orel provides an excellent reference outlining Kipling's life and career in a timeline with short, insightful descriptions of all major events in his life.

Orel, Harold, ed., *Critical Essays on Rudyard Kipling*, G. K. Hall, 1989.
    This collection of essays establishes the complexity of Kipling, his characters, and his contribution to British and children's literature. The collection contains essays dedicated to poetry, short fiction, and other writings.

The Pearl

John Steinbeck

1947

In *The Log from "The Sea of Cortez"* Steinbeck writes that he heard a story about a Mexican boy finding a huge pearl and thinking that he would never have to work again. Soon, however, so many people tried to take the pearl from him that he threw it back into the sea. The story so struck his imagination that he created his own version of it in his celebrated novella *The Pearl*. Steinbeck changed the boy into the adult Kino, and gave him a family, and created a compelling story of oppression, rebellion, and greed.

After Kino finds the largest and most beautiful pearl he has ever seen, he is convinced that it will ensure him and his family a promising future. He will be able to have enough money to cure his son Coyotito from the poison of a scorpion's bite, to marry Coyotito's mother, and to provide his son with an education, which he knows will help him to escape the bonds of the oppression under which his people suffer. Kino does not count, however, on the power of the pearl to inspire the worst as well as the best in human nature.

Author Biography

John Steinbeck Jr. was born in Salinas, California, on February 27, 1902. His father John served as the county treasurer in Salinas. His mother Olive was a school teacher and helped inspire her son's passion for reading. In the summers during his youth, Steinbeck worked on nearby ranches as a hired hand. This work cultivated his love for the earth, which emerges in so many of his works.

After high school, Steinbeck attended Stanford University between 1920 and 1926, where he studied marine biology but did not earn a degree. After moving to New York, he determined to make a career out of writing. He worked briefly as a reporter for the *American* before deciding to return to California.

For the next couple of years, he took on odd jobs to support himself while he wrote. He worked as a painter, fruit picker, and surveyor, among other professions. Steinbeck wrote his first novel in 1929, *Cup of Gold*, which was not well received. His next two novels, *The Pastures of Heaven*, published in 1932, and *To a God Unknown*, published the next year, were also unsuccessful.

In 1930, Steinbeck and his first wife, Carol Henning, moved to Pacific Grove where he gathered material for his first successful novel, *Tortilla Flat*, a humorous story about Mexican Americans. It earned Steinbeck the California Commonwealth Club's Gold Medal for best novel by a California author. The 1937 novel *Of Mice and Men* established his literary reputation as one of America's finest novelists. Steinbeck's most celebrated work, *The Grapes of Wrath*, published in 1939, earned him the Pulitzer Prize. The book was later made into a film by John Ford and became one of the American Film Institute's top 100 classic films.

During World War II, Steinbeck wrote war propaganda and worked briefly as a war correspondent for the *New York Herald Tribune*. Some of his dispatches were later collected and published with the title, *Once There Was a War*. He wrote the screenplay for Alfred Hitchcock's film *Lifeboat* in 1944. After the war, he wrote two more successful works, *Cannery Row* (1945), and *The Pearl* (1947).

In his later years, he tried to reclaim his waning status as a major American novelist with works such as *Burning Bright* (1950), *East of Eden* (1952), and *The Winter of Our Discontent* (1961). None of these novels, however, gained Steinbeck the praise his earlier works received. Yet, in 1962, Steinbeck was awarded the Nobel Prize for Literature. He died December 20, 1968, in New York City and at his request his ashes were buried in the Garden of Memories Cemetery in Salinas.

John Steinbeck National Archives and Records Administration

Plot Summary

Chapter 1

The Pearl begins as Kino, a Mexican pearl diver in the village of La Paz on the gulf of California, awakes before morning. His wife Juana and child Coyotito lie nearby in their brush house. Kino contentedly listens to the waves on the beach and declares "it was very good." His ancestors had passed their songs down from generation to generation to Kino, who this morning has the "Song of Family" in his mind. Juana rises and makes breakfast for the family, as she does every morning, and sings part of the Family Song.

Suddenly Kino sees a scorpion crawling down one of the ropes that holds the baby's cradle, and a new song, a "Song of Evil," enters his head. He lunges at it but is too late and the scorpion stings Coyotito. Juana immediately tries to suck out the poison from the wound, but the area begins to swell. She and Kino take the baby to the doctor in town, along with many neighbors who have come to watch, but because they have no money, he will not see them. Filled with shame and rage, Kino smashes his fist against the doctor's gate.

Media Adaptations

- *La Perla*, a Mexican and American production of *The Pearl* was released in 1947. Steinbeck worked on the screenplay and the film was directed by Emilio Fernandez.

- In 2001, Hollywood released another version of *The Pearl*, starring Richard Harris and Lukas Haas. This film was directed by Alfredo Zacharias.

- An audio version of *The Pearl*, produced by Penguin and read by Hector Elizondo, is available through Audio Books.

Chapter 2

After Kino and his family return to their fishing village, Juana places a seaweed poultice on the baby's wound and prays that Kino will find a pearl that would pay for the doctor. That afternoon when Kino goes diving, he finds the largest pearl he has ever seen, "The Pearl of the World," "as large as a sea-gull's egg" and as "perfect as the moon," and he howls with joy.

Chapter 3

Soon the entire town knows of the pearl, speculating on what it is worth. All suddenly are interested in Kino as the pearl "stirred up something infinitely black and evil in the town." Kino had become "curiously every man's enemy," but he and Juana are oblivious to the town's dark thoughts. They dream of what they can do with the money they will gain when they sell the pearl, deciding that they will be able to get married and buy new clothes and get their son an education, which will grant him freedom.

Kino, however, begins to hear the "Evil Song" as he thinks others will try to steal the pearl from him and so he makes "a hard skin for himself against the world." When the doctor hears the news, he reminisces of his past life in Paris and decides that he will take Coyotito as a patient and so get his hands on some of the money from the pearl. He comes to the brush house and warns Kino and Juana that the

poison may still be inside their son but that he can help. After the doctor forces Coyotito to swallow what he insists is medicine to drive the poison out, Coyotito becomes ill. Soon, however, he appears to recover and the doctor demands payment. Kino determines to sell the pearl the next day. That night, though, someone comes to the hut to try to steal the it. Kino scares him away but not before he is hit in the head. Juana warns that the pearl is a "sin" and will destroy them, but Kino insists it is their only chance to send Coyotito to school.

Chapter 4

The townspeople follow Kino into town on his journey to meet with the pearl buyers and speculate about what they would buy with the money he will earn for it. The first buyer offers only 1000 pesos, claiming that the pearl is "fool's gold" and has little value. When Kino refuses the offer and insists that it is worth 50,000 pesos, the buyer calls others in to make bids, but they also determine the pearl to be worthless. Kino declares that he is being cheated and vows to journey to the capital to sell it even though he is afraid to go there. His neighbors are unsure about whether Kino has been cheated or whether he is being greedy. That evening when Kino is again attacked by robbers outside his brush house, Juana pleads with him to destroy the pearl, but he refuses, insisting that he "is a man" and so can handle any trouble they may face.

Chapter 5

In the middle of the night Juana arises and takes the pearl to the water, ready to throw it in. Kino, however, stops her just in time, grabs the pearl and beats her in an animalistic rage. On his way back to the brush house, he is sickened by what he has done. On the trail assassins attack him, but this time he kills one of the men. Juana realizes that at this point, "the old life was gone forever." Realizing that he will be accused of murder, Kino decides that they must flee and turns to his brother Juan Tomas and his wife for help. Kino admits, "This pearl has become my soul. . . . If I give it up I shall lose my soul."

Chapter 6

Kino and his family travel up the coast but soon realize that trackers are following them. In an effort to lose them, they head into the mountains. At one point, Kino considers turning himself in to save his family, but Juana convinces him that the trackers would kill all of them to get the pearl. The family stops near caves to rest, but the trackers eventually catch up with them. Under the cover of darkness, Kino tries to jump one of the men while the other two are sleeping. He is able to kill all three, but a random rifle shot during the struggle hits Coyotito, killing him.

Kino and Juana return to La Paz, devastated at the loss of their son, appearing as if "removed from human experience." Hearing the Song of the Family ringing in his ears like "a battle cry," Kino grasps the pearl, which has become "gray and ulcerous" with "evil faces" peering from it. When he tries to give it to Juana, she insists, "no you." Kino then throws it with all of his might into the green water, and it disappears.

Characters

Coyotito

Coyotito, Kino and Juana's infant son, is the catalyst for his parents' obsession with the pearl. Both of his parents want the pearl to help pay for his recovery from the scorpion sting and for his education, so that he will not be limited by the same oppression under which his parents have suffered.

Doctor

The doctor is part of the system that oppresses Kino and his family. The villagers know "his cruelty, his avarice, his appetites," his laziness, and his incompetence. His sense of superiority prompts him to regard Kino and his neighbors as animals and so determines that he need not treat them. Only after he learns of Kino's pearl does he offer help so that he may be able to get his hands on it and regain the luxurious life he has enjoyed in Paris. To that end, he deceives Kino and Juana about Coyotito's illness and his own powers as a healer.

Juan Tomas

Kino's brother Juan Tomas provides Kino with shelter and wise counsel.

Juana

Juana is a dutiful wife who rises every morning to make breakfast for her family. She exhibits a fierce, instinctual need to protect her child as evidenced by her clearheaded response to the scorpion's sting and her insistence that they take him to the doctor, knowing that there is little chance that the doctor will see him yet ready to face the resulting shame. Coyotito is Juana's first baby and so he is "nearly everything there was in [her] world."

Her strength and endurance, however, are her most dominant qualities. Kino "wondered often at the iron in his patient, fragile wife" who "could arch her back in child pain with hardly a cry" and "stand fatigue and hunger almost better than Kino himself." He notes that "in the canoe she was like a strong man." Although patient with and obedient to her husband, she tries to convince him to throw away the pearl when she recognizes the danger it brings.

Her endurance is displayed after Kino beats her. As he stands over her with his teeth bared, she stares as him "with wide unfrightened eyes." She accepts that he had been driven over the edge of reason and decided "she would not resist or even protest." As a result, Kino's rage disappears and is replaced by disgust for what he has done to her.

Juana shows a great and patient understanding of her husband. After he beats her, she feels no anger toward him, recognizing that as a man "he was half insane and half god." She knows that he will "drive his strength against a mountain and plunge his strength against the sea" and that he would inevitably be destroyed by both. Although puzzled by the differences she recognizes between men and women, she "knew them and accepted them and needed them" because as an Indian woman "she could not live without a man." She then determines to follow him, hoping that her reason, caution, and "sense of preservation could cut through Kino's manness and save them all." Juana endures the pain of her injuries as she escapes with Kino and Coyotito.

Her ability to defy her husband by attempting to throw the pearl in the sea while admitting that she could not survive without him reveals her great courage. She is driven by her need to "rescue something of the old peace, of the time before the pearl." Yet after Kino kills his attacker, she shows her resilience when she immediately admits that the past was gone, "and there was no retrieving it. And knowing this, she abandoned the past instantly. There was nothing to do but to save themselves." The death of her child appears to break her, however. As she walks back to the village at the end of the story, "her wide eyes stared inward on herself" and she "was as remote and as removed as Heaven."

Kino

Even though he lives in poverty, Kino is content at the beginning of the story because he is surrounded by the family he loves. It is only after his child's life is threatened by the scorpion bite that Kino determines that he will rebel against the system that oppresses him.

His obsession with the pearl is prompted by his desire for respect and power, but most importantly for the education of his child. He wants to be able to marry Juana, to buy a rifle that can "[break] down the barriers," to dress his family in nice clothes, and finally to enable his son to free himself and his people from subjugation.

Kino's fierce desire to provide for and protect his family reduces him to a primal state. Ironically that desire to provide for them causes him to viciously attack Juana. Later, after he kills his attacker, the narrator concludes that Kino is "an animal now, for hiding, for attacking, and he lived only to preserve himself and his family." This primal nature enables him to escape his trackers, at least initially. The narrator notes that "some ancient thing stirred in Kino. . . . some animal thing was moving in him so that he was cautious and wary and dangerous." At the end of the story, he appears broken as he retains his primal state. He, along with Juana, appears "removed from human experience." He "carried fear with him" and "he was as dangerous as a rising storm."

Themes

Greed

The story has been applauded as a parable that warns of the effects of greed. A parable is a story that is chiefly intended to convey a moral or truth. After Kino finds the pearl, he learns how far others will go, including committing murder, to gain wealth and the power that it brings. All those who hear about the pearl, even his neighbors "suddenly became related to [it], and [it] went into the dreams, the speculations, the schemes, the plans, the futures, the wishes, the needs, the lusts, the hungers, of everyone." And since Kino stood in their way, "he became curiously every man's enemy." Kino recognizes this desire in himself, not for wealth, but for the power the pearl can grant him. He says the pearl is his soul.

Environmental and Biological Determinism

Steinbeck incorporates naturalistic elements in the story through his focus on environmental and biological determinism. Determinism is a way of understanding what causes humans to experience what they do. The assumption is that there are forces (such as race, economic class, environment, and chance) at work that determine the outcome of

Topics for Further Study

- Read Steinbeck's short story "The Chrysanthemums" and compare the main character in it to Juana. Both are strong women but they deal with their husbands in different ways. What do these differences say about their character and their culture? What similarities do you find in both women?

- Stephen Crane's "The Open Boat" is a naturalistic story that focuses on the environmental forces that control human destiny. Compare and contrast these forces with those forces that control Kino and his family.

- Research the history of the Mexican Indians who lived in the La Paz region. How did they become marginalized in Mexican society? What are their lives like today?

- Consider an alternate ending for the story. What would have happened to the family if Coyotito had lived? Do you see any possibility that Kino could achieve his dreams given the constraints of his world? Explain.

He is connected to his ancestors through their songs, which he often hears in his head. The frequency of the Family Song and the Enemy Song suggests his strong link to those ancestors as well as to his environment. Kino experiences a combination of rage and fear as he confronts his oppressors, showing strength as well as an intuitive assessment of the reality of his position. He is a proud man who feels shame when he stirs up the courage to challenge that position and is rebuffed.

Like Juana, he is a responsible parent who strives to provide the best life possible for his child. This commitment gives him the courage to rebel against the status quo by calling on the doctor, by refusing to accept the offer from the pearl buyers, and by fleeing the village after he murders one of his attackers. His loyalty is also expressed toward his neighbors when it does not even occur to him to take one of their boats during his escape.

human events, regardless of human intention and effort to shape events otherwise. Kino's fate is sealed by these forces, which prevent him from escaping the limitations of his world. The most obvious determinants are his social and economic status.

Kino knows that "other forces were set up to destroy" his plan to provide his family with an opportunity to escape oppression. He believes though that these forces are created by the gods, who "do not love men's plans," who "do not love success unless it comes by accident," and who "take their revenge on a man if he be successful through his own efforts." This deterministic view maintains that the individual is powerless to shape his circumstances or to rise above them. Perhaps it is the gods or fate but some arbitrary force beyond the self controls everything.

Since Kino is an Indian and has no education, he does not know how to fight against the ruling class who exploit him in an effort to keep him in his place. He cannot read the medicine packet that the doctor uses to "treat" Coyotito, he does not have the knowledge to judge the real value of the pearl, and he does not know how to find someone who will give him a fair price. He is poor because he is a member of an oppressed race, and so he must live in dangerous conditions where scorpions can pose a risk.

Another dangerous and immediate environmental factor is posed by the greedy men who want to steal his pearl. Kino is almost killed by these attackers until he kills one in self defense. Their greed illustrates the biological forces with which Kino must also grapple.

At least initially, both Kino and Juana are committed to their dreams. Juana becomes "a lioness" when her baby is stung by the scorpion, which ironically triggers the path to his destruction. Her fierce sense of protection prompts her to convince Kino to go to the doctor and later to find the biggest pearl he can catch so that they will have the money to cure their child.

After Kino finds the pearl, his own biology takes over as he becomes filled with a hatred that "raged and flamed in back of his eyes, and fear too, for the hundreds of years of subjugation were cut deep in him." That rage, coupled with his own instinct to provide the best for his family, urges him on even as murderers wait outside his brush house to attack him. These urges become obsessions as his brain "burns" in dreams of his son's future. Even after Juana warns him of the dangers of keeping the pearl, Kino insists he will not give it up,

claiming "this is our one chance. . . . Our son must go to school. He must break out of the pot that holds us in."

His obsession with the pearl prompts him to violently attack Juana when she tries to throw it back into the sea. His brain, "red hot with anger," reverts to a primal state as he punches and kicks her with "his teeth bared" and hissing "like a snake." These dual forces, Kino's environment and his own biology conspire against him: his burning desire for a better life for his family and the oppression of the ruling class that forces him into subjugation ultimately shape his destiny.

Style

Parable

A parable is a story designed to illustrate a lesson or moral. Steinbeck notes at the beginning of *The Pearl* that the story of Kino and the pearl has been told so often, "it has taken root in every man's mind" and "heart." He characterizes the story as a parable when he explains that "there are only good and bad things and black and white things and good and evil things and no in-between anywhere."

On one level, the story can be viewed as an allegory of good and evil, with Kino and his family representing good, and those who try to steal the pearl from him as evil. In this reading, the lesson or moral focuses on how the pearl inspires greed. However, there are some "in-between things" that suggest a more complex reflection of reality, especially in Steinbeck's exploration of the interplay of oppression and rebellion.

Symbolism

The dominant symbol in the novel is the pearl. Initially it is "the Pearl of the World," "as large as a sea gull's egg" and as "perfect as the moon"; it represents a bright future for Kino and his family. Kino sees the pearl as providing the "music of promise and delight" with its "guarantee of the future, of comfort, of security." It promised "a poultice against illness and a wall against insult. It closed a door on hunger." As it inspires greed in the hearts of others, however, and Kino is forced to face the consequences of that greed, the pearl transforms into a "gray and ulcerous" object with "evil faces" peering from it."

The scorpion becomes a symbol of this transformation. Like the scorpion's sting, the pearl

Compare
&
Contrast

- **1940s:** World War II results from the rise of totalitarian regimes in Germany, Italy, and Japan. More than two hundred countries band together to fight against the militaristic expansion of these totalitarian regimes.

  Today: The United States, with the help of coalition forces, invades Iraq in 2003, acting upon information that Iraq supposedly poses a threat and has weapons of mass destruction. During 2004, several coalition allies pull out of Iraq, and the supposed weapons of mass destruction are not found. More than one thousand U.S. military persons are killed in the ongoing U.S. occupation; tens of thousands of Iraqis are killed.

- **1940s:** Poor Mexicans who cannot make enough money to survive in their homeland emigrate to the United States in search of better jobs.

  Today: Mexicans continue to cross the border. U.S. officials try to guard national borders, especially after terrorist attacks on September 11, 2001, but the federal government also discusses ways to allow Mexicans in the United States to find temporary employment.

- **1940s:** Steinbeck uses naturalism and the form of the parable in *The Pearl*. Important literary styles are realism, naturalism, modernism.

  Today: Two popular literary forms are psychological realism and autobiography, which may be confessional, humorous, or historical. Historical mysteries are popular as proven by the bestseller, *The Da Vinci Code*.

---

infects those who come into contact with it because it stimulates their greed. They turn into predators symbolized by the story's nighttime setting, when "mice crept about on the ground and the little night hawks hunted them silently." The darkness is filled with a "poisonous air." At the beginning of the story, the attacks that Kino must fend off are symbolized by the two roosters near his house, who "bowed and feinted at each other with squared wings and neck feathers ruffed out."

Historical Context

Pearl Diving in La Paz

La Paz (meaning "peace" in Spanish) is in the Mexican state of Southern Baja California on the Sea of Cortez. For several centuries, the area was famous for its pearl diving and was known as "The City of Pearls." The oyster beds, however, became diseased and died out in the middle of the twentieth century.

In the mid 1900s, approximately 800 divers would submerge themselves in the waters off La Paz at depths of up to 12 fathoms. Divers had to tear the oysters by hand from their beds, a process that often left their hands with deep cuts and gashes. The number of divers decreased to about 200 by the end of the century as the oyster population declined and divers lost their lives due to accidents and shark attacks.

Naturalism

Naturalism is a literary movement that emerged in the late nineteenth and early twentieth centuries in France, England, and the United States. Writers included in this group, such as Emile Zola, Thomas Hardy, and the Americans Stephen Crane and Theodore Dreiser, write about biological and/or environmental determinism that prevents their characters from achieving the goals they seek. These characters' plans for the future and their choices (the exercise of their free will) are all swamped by forces beyond their control. For example, in *The Red Badge of Courage* Crane depicts how one Civil War soldier is overwhelmed by the U.S. political and military conflict. Zola's and Dreiser's work include this type of environmental

A huge pearl is the focus of John Steinbeck's "The Pearl" © Tom Stewart/Corbis

determinism coupled with an exploration of the influences of heredity in their portraits of ordinary men and women engaged in a relentless and brutal struggle for survival.

World War II

The world witnessed a decade of aggression in the 1930s that culminated in the 1939 onset of World War II. This war resulted from the rise of totalitarian regimes in Germany, Italy, and Japan. These militaristic regimes gained control, in part, as a result of a global economic depression and from the conditions created by the peace settlements following World War I, called the Treaty of Versailles. The dictatorships established in these three countries were committed to territorial expansion. In Germany Hitler strengthened the army during the late 1930s. In 1936 Benito Mussolini's Italian troops took Ethiopia. From 1936 to 1939 Spain was engaged in civil war involving Francisco Franco's fascist army, aided by Germany and Italy. In March 1938 Germany annexed Austria and in March 1939 occupied Czechoslovakia. Italy took Albania in April 1939. One week after Nazi Germany and the U.S.S.R. signed the Treaty of Nonaggression, on September 1, 1939, Germany invaded Poland. On September 3, 1939, Britain and France declared war on Germany after a U–boat sank the British ship *Athenia* off the coast of Ireland. Another British ship, *Courageous*, was sunk on September 19. All the members of the British Commonwealth, except Ireland, soon joined Britain and France in their declaration of war against Germany.

On December 7, 1941, Japan attacked the U.S. military base in Pearl Harbor, Hawaii. As a result of the four-hour attack, approximately 2,400 Americans died and 1300 were wounded. Three days later, Germany and Italy declared war on the United States. The total number of European casualties by the end of the war was approximately 40,000,000. More than 400,000 Americans died.

Critical Overview

"The Pearl of the World" first appeared in *The Women's Home Companion* in 1945. The 1947 revised version, *The Pearl,* gained immediate critical and popular attention. During the following years, the novella was attacked by some, such as Warren French in his article on Steinbeck, as being too "sentimental." Many readers, however, continued throughout the twentieth century to praise the story's themes and construction.

Ernest E. Karsten Jr., in his 1965 article on *The Pearl*, praises its "combination of simple story, strongly established symbolism, social commentary, and important themes," and argues that Steinbeck's "beautiful writing makes this a literary work that may well become a classic and certainly as fine an introduction to the genre as could be found."

In his 1947 review of the novella for the *New York Times*, Carlos Baker writes that the novella "fits as neatly into the list of Steinbeck's books as the last gem in a carefully matched necklace." Orville Prescott, in his review for the same paper, commends Steinbeck's "artful simplicity exactly suitable to his theme" and insists that it is "the best book which Mr. Steinbeck has written since "The Red Pony" and *The Grapes of Wrath*." Prescott especially praises the characterizations in the book, noting that Kino's "devotion to his family and his courage in the face of death are deeply moving" and that these traits give the novella "a universally human quality, for they are the virtues which men everywhere have always admired above all others."

Criticism

Wendy Perkins

Perkins is a professor of American and English literature and film. In this essay, Perkins explores the interplay of oppression and rebellion in the novella.

In *The Grapes of Wrath* (1939), John Steinbeck chronicles a family's hard journey from the Oklahoma Dust Bowl to the migrant camps of California. His portrayal of the plight of the Joads and that of other migrant workers is a poignant examination of oppression and the drive to rebel against it. In *The Pearl*, Steinbeck returns to these themes in his story of a Mexican pearl diver and his family. This novella, however, written after the devastation of World War II, takes a darker, more pessimistic vision of the spirit of rebellion. Richard Astro, in his review of the book, notes that in Steinbeck's post-war works, including *The Pearl*, his "organismal view of life, his belief that men can work together to fashion a better, more productive, and more meaningful life, seemed less and less applicable to the world he saw around him." Through his depiction of Kino and his family's experiences with the pearl, Steinbeck celebrates the spirit of rebellion but also acknowledges the dark forces that can eventually crush it.

Orville Prescott, in his 1947 review of *The Pearl* for the *New York Times*, argues that the novella is "permeated with the special sort of impotent and sullen bitterness which only an oppressed and subject people know." Prescott notes that Steinbeck has often turned his attention to the oppressed. "His admiration for them seems to have been a conscious protest against the decadence and cruelty and stupidity which have been so prevalent in this century among so-called civilized people." Kino and his family suffer the cruelty of so-called civilized people because their race is different from that of the ruling class.

The members of Kino's family, as well those of his community, have been denied basic human rights; they have been marginalized and disenfranchised. The money they earn from diving for pearls is not enough to adequately feed, shelter, and educate themselves and their families. Even though Kino determines that life is "good" when he awakens surrounded by his family and "the little splash of morning waves on the beach," the tentative nature of this good life becomes immediately evident when a scorpion stings his child. He and his family are forced to live in a brush house, where scorpions can come and go as freely as the members of his family, posing a constant danger to their lives.

When the inevitable happens, and a member of the community faces death from a scorpion sting, medical attention is denied because there is no money to pay the doctor. Kino must face this reality after Coyotito is stung. The neighbors marvel at Juana's call for the doctor, knowing that "the doctor never came to the cluster of brush houses" for "he had more than he could do to take care of the rich people who lived in the stone and plaster houses of the town." Yet Juana rebels against this limitation for Coyotito's sake, for her first baby. Juana's eyes "as cold as the eyes of a lioness," inspire Kino to join her in her fight against the rules of oppression.

When Kino approaches the doctor's gate, however, he hesitates: "This doctor was not of his people. This doctor was of a race which for nearly four hundred years had beaten and starved and robbed and despised Kino's race, and frightened it too." He admits that "as always when he came near to one of this race, [he] felt weak and afraid and angry at the same time" since "all of the doctor's race spoke to all of Kino's race as though they were simple animals." The doctor proves Kino's assertion when he complains that he will not see Coyotito, insisting, "I am a doctor, not a veterinary."

Another consequence of this type of oppression is the disruption of the community, which provides an effective way to suppress any rebellion within that community. Disruption can be seen in the behavior of the doctor's servant who refuses to speak to Kino in their native language. Allegiance to the ruling class and betrayal of the individual members of the community emerges again when many of Kino's neighbors are ready to take the word of the pearl dealers over Kino's regarding the value of the pearl. This behavior leads to an acceptance of the status quo rather than a rebellion against it.

One of the most powerful tools of oppression is the denial of an education. The Indian pearl divers have no money to buy themselves an education and so do not have the knowledge necessary to successfully rebel against authority. This is evident in their passive response to the pearl dealers and in Kino's frustrated dependence on the doctor who exploits Kino's lack of education when he insists that the baby will die without his intervention.

Kino recognizes that education empowers individuals and that the only way he can experience that empowerment is by selling his pearl. When the doctor gives Coyotito "medicine" that he claims will cure the child, Kino recognizes that he is trapped by his ignorance "as his people were always trapped, and would be until, as he had said, they could be sure that the things in the books were really in the books."

The pearl becomes so crucial to him because he understands that the money will grant him respect, when he can afford to marry Juana, and power, when he can purchase a rifle and give his son an education. If his son can learn to read and write, Kino insists, "these things will make us free because he will know–he will know and through him we will know."

The possibility of being able to give this gift to his son causes Kino to rebel against his oppressors. He develops "a hard skin for himself" as he stands up to the pearl dealers. Although he admits being "afraid of strangers and of strange places" and "terrified of that monster of strangeness they called the capital," he determines to go and get the best deal for the pearl. Juana understands that he has "defied not the pearl buyers, but the whole structure, the whole way of life," and she is afraid for him.

Kino, though, will not back down, and so risks his life to fend off those who try to steal the pearl from him. Even when Juana pleads with him to

> " Kino, though, will not back down, and so risks his life to fend off those who try to steal the pearl from him."

destroy the pearl, claiming that it has an evil force within it, he refuses, fueled by his dream "that Coyotito could read, that one of his own people could tell him the truth of things." After killing one of his attackers, Kino refuses to turn himself in to the authorities, knowing that his dream would then be destroyed.

He struggles mightily to hold onto the pearl and at the same time protect his family from the trackers. He insists that his community will offer support, that his friends will protect him, but Kino's brother recognizes the power of authority to destroy allegiances when he suggests that his friends will help him "only so long as they are not in danger or discomfort from it."

Kino's rebellious spirit challenges but cannot change the system. Unable to fight off the forces that try to oppress him, he loses his son along with his dreams of a better life for his family. The loss of the pearl at the end of the story suggests his loss of hope for the future and a loss in his belief that he can control his life and destiny.

In *East of Eden*, Steinbeck offers his response to oppressive political systems that try to crush the human spirit, declaring that he believes that the "free, exploring mind of the individual human is the most valuable thing in the world." And so, he insists that he would fight for "the freedom of the mind to take any direction it wishes, undirected" and fight against "an idea, religion or government which limits or destroys the individual" for "if the glory can be killed, we are lost." Steinbeck illustrates the tragic consequences of the loss of that freedom of the spirit in *The Pearl*, expressing a profound sympathy for the individual and the community that suffers under such an oppressive system.

Source: Wendy Perkins, Critical Essay on "The Pearl," in *Short Stories for Students*, Thomson Gale, 2006.

What Do I Read Next?

- Stephen Crane's short story "The Open Boat" (1898) depicts the desperation of four shipwrecked seamen who are controlled by the whims of the sea.

- *The Awakening* (1899) is Kate Chopin's feminist novel of a young married woman who confronts the conflicting demands of housewife and artist and inevitably suffers the consequences of trying to establish herself as an independent spirit in a world governed by strict codes of conduct.

- In *The Log from the Sea of Cortez*, Steinbeck relates the folk tale that inspired his writing of *The Pearl*.

- Steinbeck's *The Grapes of Wrath* (1939) focuses on a group of people forced to leave their homes during the Great Depression and travel to California where they struggle to survive as migrant workers.

Harry Morris

In the following essay, Morris examines "The Pearl" alongside early English allegories and finds "the continuing tradition of true allegory and the modern writer's strong links with the past."

John Steinbeck has never been very far away from the allegorical method. Some of his earliest work—and among that, his best—shows involvement with elements of allegory. *The Grapes of Wrath* (1939) employs as a framework the journey, the most common of allegorical devices:

> Go thou to *Everyman*,
> And show him in my name
> A pilgrimage he must on him take
> Which he in no wise may escape.

Eight years later, Steinbeck displayed his perfect familiarity with *Everyman* by using a passage from the morality play as an epigraph for his own most complete allegory of the life-journey, *The Wayward Bus* (1947). *In Dubious Battle* (1936) has some things in common with the medieval psychomachia, the debate, the poetry of warfare between body and soul, between head and heart. The title itself comes from the opening book of *Paradise Lost* (I.104), where, shortly following, Milton presents his own great allegory of sin and death (II.648–814). Some episodes in *The Pastures of Heaven* (1932) and some stories in *The Long Valley* (1938) move into allegory frequently, although in the early fiction allegorical materials are so completely absorbed into the techniques of realism as to be almost undetectable.

But beginning in 1945 and through the years immediately following World War II, following the realistic works that belong to that war, Steinbeck wrote a series of novels that he proclaimed openly to be allegorical. In addition to the already mentioned *Wayward Bus* (1947) were *Burning Bright* (1950) and *East of Eden* (1952). Preceding these three was *The Pearl*. Peter Lisca, in *The Wide World of John Steinbeck* (1958), cites letters which Steinbeck wrote to Pascal Covici to show that *The Pearl* was completed by early February 1945. *Woman's Home Companion* in its December issue of the same year was the first publisher, presenting the short novel under the title *The Pearl of the World*. An earlier letter to Covici indicates that while the story was still in progress Steinbeck called it *The Pearl of La Paz*. When it was issued in book form in 1947 to coincide with its release as a motion picture by RKO, it had become simply *The Pearl*. A rehearsal of these variations in the title should not be considered pedantry, for nothing more clearly indicates the allegorical nature of the work as it developed in Steinbeck's mind from the beginning. Although the city of La Paz may be named appropriately in the title since the setting for the action is in and around the place, the Spanish word provides a neat additional bit of symbolism, if in some aspects ironic. In its working title, the novel tells the story of The Pearl of Peace. When this title was changed to *The Pearl of the World* for magazine publication, although the irony was partially lost, the allegorical implications were still present. But Steinbeck had apparently no fears that the nature of the tale would be mistaken when he reduced the title to merely *The Pearl,* for he could rely still upon the epigraph to warn his readers:

> If this story is a parable, perhaps everyone takes his own meaning from it and reads his own life into it.

Status of Allegory

But why should a critic labor to put the stamp of allegory on a modern novel? For also two hundred years now such a mark has been almost equivalent to a seal of literary oblivion. Shakespeare, the greatest writer in the English language, had eschewed allegory. One of the next best, Chaucer, turned an early hand to translating *The Romance of the Rose,* but after a few more false starts, found his genius in narrative and satire and produced his two masterpieces, *Troilus and Criseyde* and *The Canterburry Tales.* But it was Coleridge who downgraded allegory in a series of critical pronouncements and then became the master and model of a hundred and fifty years of literary criticism. His influence has been such that I have heard one of America's foremost poets and one of the major figures in what has long been called the "New Criticism" say, "I simply cannot read Spenser," by which he meant he could not abide allegory. Steinbeck's *Pearl* has come also under this interdict. When first published, it was reviewed by Maxwell Geismar, who wrote, ". . . the quality that has marked Steinbeck's work as a whole is . . . the sense of black and white things and good and bad things— that is to say, the sense of a fabulist or a propagandist rather than the insight of an artist?" The fabulist as Geismar describes him is neither more nor less than the allegorist. We see how far distaste for allegory has come. The writer who employs the mode is read out of the ranks of the artist; the fabulist lacks insight.

It is doubtful that Coleridge ever intended his sometime-mentioned disapproval of allegory to be taken as strong aversion. His lecture on Spenser seemed to equate allegory with a one-to-one relationship between story and underlying meaning:

> No one can appreciate Spenser without some reflection on the nature of allegorical writing. The mere etymological meaning of the word, allegory,—to talk of one thing and thereby convey another,—is too wide. The true sense is this,—the employment of one set of agents and images to convey in disguise a moral meaning.

The unfortunate suggestion that moral meanings have to be disguised is also present. But the more famous and more severe disavowal is in Coleridge's *Statesman's Manual:*

> Now an allegory is but a translation of abstract notions into a picture-language which is itself nothing but an abstraction from objects of the senses; the principal being more worthless even than its phantom proxy, both alike unsubstantial, and the former shapeless to boot.

But elsewhere Coleridge found exceptions to his general censure: the allegory of Cupid and Psyche, the Sin and Death episode in *Paradise Lost,* and the first part of *Pilgrim's Progress.*

> **"** Much has been made of the *leitmotif* of music in *The Pearl:* the song of the family, the song of the enemy, etc. **"**

Nevertheless, Coleridge had done almost irreparable damage. Only recently have there been signs that allegory has been given a false character. Rosemond Tuve has shown that the first mistake is to imagine that medieval and Renaissance allegory could ever be comprehended as a one-to-one relationship of story and second meaning. Allegory in Spenser's hand is as rich in its multiplicity of meaning as is symbolism, the most highly admired literary device both of Coleridge and of modern criticism. Parable in the New Testament and medieval commentary on the Old Testament gave rise to the rich legacy that we call the fourfold manner of Scriptural interpretation, of which Dante wrote, "although [three of] these mystical meanings are called by various names, they may all be called in general allegorical, since they differ from the literal." No literary figure can ever quite ignore that Christ chose to talk in parables; none can ever forget that *The Divine Comedy* is one of the most complex allegories ever written. Great allegory, even in its purest forms—in so medieval a work as the anonymous *Pearl* of the fourteenth century— carries all the exciting allusiveness of the most complex symbolism. Our own age is rediscovering this fact, and much fine literature is being produced in the allegorical mode, from the serious attempts of Steinbeck already mentioned and including such important novels as Orwell's *Animal Farm,* Faulkner's *A Fable,* and Katherine Anne Porter's *Ship of Fools* all the way to the intellectualized comic strips of Schulz and Walt Kelly. Of course, allegory has never been completely dead in the modern novel, for in their ways Conrad's *Heart of Darkness,* Mann's *Magic Mountain,* and Joyce's *Ulysses* carry an allegorical burden. It has become fashionable to call them mythopoeic—reworkings of old or inventions of new myths—but the myths themselves are true allegories.

Steinbeck's Method

In reading *The Pearl,* we encounter the work of a professed parabolist, and we must assert, and so reject Geismar's explicit objections to *The Pearl,* that the fable is an art form and that the fabulist as artist has never lacked insight. We cannot evaluate Steinbeck's performance with the criteria employed for judgment of the realistic novel. We cannot condemn *The Pearl* because as Geismar says it is all black and white, all good and bad. Such was Steinbeck's intention:

> And because the story has been told so often, it has taken root in every man's mind. And as with all retold tales that are in people's hearts, there are only good and bad things and black and white things and good and evil things and no in-between anywhere.

Writing about its composition, Steinbeck said elsewhere, "I tried to write it as folklore, to give it that set-aside, raised-up feeling that all folk stories have." He was telling us again that *The Pearl* is not totally in the realistic tradition.

But Steinbeck knew that the modern fabulist could write neither a medieval *Pearl* nor a classical Aesopian Fox and Grapes story. It was essential to overlay his primary media of parable and folklore with a coat of realism, and this was one of his chief problems. Realism as a technique requires two basic elements: credible people and situations on the one hand and recognizable evocation of the world of nature and of things on the other. Steinbeck succeeds brilliantly in the second of these tasks but perhaps does not come off quite so well in the first. In supplying realistic detail, he is a master, trained by his long and productive journeyman days at work on the proletarian novels of the thirties and the war pieces of the early forties. His description of the natural world is so handled as to do double and treble duty in enrichment of both symbolism and allegory. Many critics have observed Steinbeck's use of animal imagery that pervades this novel with the realistic detail that is also one of its strengths:

> Kino awakened in the near dark. The stars shone and the day had drawn only a pale wash of light in the lower sky to the east. The roosters had been crowing for some time, and the early pigs were already beginning their ceaseless turning of twigs and bits of wood to see whether anything to eat had been overlooked. Outside the brush house in the tuna clump, a covey of little birds chittered and flurried their wings.

Kino is identified symbolically with low animal orders: he must rise early and he must root in the earth for sustenance; but the simple, pastoral life has the beauty of the stars, the dawn, and the singing, happy birds. Yet provided also is a realistic description of village life on the fringe of La Paz. Finally, we should observe that the allegory too has begun. The first sentence—"Kino awakened in the near dark"—is a statement of multiple allegorical significance. Kino is what modern sociologists are fond of calling a primitive. As such, he comes from a society that is in its infancy; or, to paraphrase Steinbeck, it is in the dark or the near-dark intellectually, politically, theologically, and sociologically. But the third sentence tells us that the roosters have been crowing for some time, and we are to understand that Kino has heard the cock of progress crow. He will begin to question the institutions that have kept him primitive: medicine, the church, the pearl industry, the government. The allegory operates then locally, dealing at first with one person, Kino, and then with his people, the Mexican peasants of Lower California. But the allegory works also universally, and Kino is Everyman. The darkness in which he awakes is one of the spirit. The cock crow is one of warning that the spirit must awake to its own dangers. The allegorical journey has often been called the way into the dark night of the soul, in which the darkness stands for despair or hopelessness. We cannot describe Kino or his people as in despair, for they have never known any life other than the one they lead; neither are they in hopelessness, for they are not aware that there is anything for which to hope. In a social parable, then, the darkness is injustice and helplessness in the face of it; in the allegory of the spirit, darkness concerns the opacity of the moral substance in man.

The social element is developed rapidly through the episode of Coyotito's scorpion bite and the doctor's refusal to treat a child whose father cannot pay a substantial fee. Kino's helplessness is conveyed by the fist he crushes into a split and bleeding mass against the doctor's gate. This theme of helplessness reaches its peak in the pearl-selling attempt. When Kino says to his incredulous brother, Juan Thomás, that perhaps all three buyers set a price amongst themselves before Kino's arrival, Juan Thomás answers, "If that is so, then all of us have been cheated all of our lives." And of course they have been.

Kino is, then, in the near dark; and, as his misfortunes develop, he descends deeper and deeper into the dark night of the soul. The journey that the soul makes as well as the journey that the living Kino makes—in terms of the good and evil that invest the one and the oppression and freedom that come to the other—provides the allegorical statement of the novel.

Difficulties of the Method

In the attempt to achieve believable situations, create three-dimensional characters, Steinbeck met greater difficulties that he did not entirely overcome. The germ-anecdote out of which he constructed his story gave him little more than the bare elements of myth:

An event which happened at La Paz in recent years is typical of such places. An Indian boy by accident found a pearl of great size, an unbelievable pearl. He knew its value was so great that he need never work again. In his one pearl he had the ability to be drunk as long as he wished, to marry any one of a number of girls, and to make many more a little happy too. In his great pearl lay salvation, for he could in advance purchase masses sufficient to pop him out of Purgatory like a squeezed watermelon seed. In addition he could shift a number of dead relatives a little nearer Paradise. He went to La Paz with his pearl in his hand and his future clear into eternity in his heart. He took his pearl to a broker and was offered so little that he grew angry, for he knew he was cheated. Then he carried his pearl to another broker and was offered the same amount. After a few more visits he came to know that he could not sell his pearl for more. He took it to the beach and hid it under a stone, and that night he was clubbed into unconsciousness and his clothing was searched. The next night he slept at the house of a friend and his friend and he were injured and bound and the whole house searched. Then he went inland to lose his pursuers and he was waylaid and tortured. But he was very angry now and he knew what he must do. Hurt as he was he crept back to La Paz in the night and he skulked like a hunted fox to the beach and took out his pearl from under the stone. Then he cursed it and threw it as far as he could into the channel. He was a free man again with his soul in danger and his food and shelter insecure. And he laughed a great deal about it.

Steinbeck recorded this sketch in *The Sea of Cortez* (1941), where he noted also how difficult it would be for anyone to believe:

This seems to be a true story, but it is so much like a parable that it almost can't be true. The Indian boy is too heroic, too wise. He knows too much and acts on his knowledge. In every way, he goes contrary to human direction. The story is probably true, but we don't believe it; it is far too reasonable to be true.

We see in Steinbeck's source all the major elements of his expanded version: the Mexican peasant, the discovered pearl, the belief that the pearl will make the finder free, the corrupt brokers, the attacks, the flight, the return, and the disposal of the pearl. But there are also additions and alterations. The episodes of the doctor and the priest are added; the motives for retaining the pearl are changed. While the additions add perhaps some realism at the same time that they increase the impact of the allegory, the alterations tend to diminish the realistic aspects of the hero. Kino becomes almost unbelievably sophisticated. The boy wants only to be drunk forever; Kino wants his son educated. The boy wants to buy prayers for his own soul and for the souls of his relatives in Purgatory; Kino distrusts the priest who asks that the church be remembered when the pearl is sold, closes his fist only more tightly about the pearl, determined instead to buy a rifle. The boy's desires are primitive; they are consonant with his origins and his intellect, crafty and wise as he may be. Kino's wants are sophisticated; he sees in the pearl not the objects that can be bought, but beyond. Coyotito's education will make the Indians free, a social, political, and economic sophistication; new clothes and a church wedding will give Kino and Juana position and respectability, again a social sophistication; the rifle will give Kino power, an intellectual sophistication. With the rifle all other things were possible: "It was the rifle that broke down the barriers. This was an impossibility, and if he could think of having a rifle whole horizons were burst and he could rush on." Later, ironically, all that the rifle gives to Kino is the power to destroy human life; and in this irony, the symbolic import of the pearl-rifle fusion gives to the allegory the very complication that Geismar (and even Steinbeck himself) says is lacking. The pearl is not clearly good or evil, black or white.

Diminished Realism

In these alterations, employed perhaps to add reality to a fable, Steinbeck has diminished realism. Narrative detail alone supplies this element. The opening of chapter three, like the beginning paragraph of the book, is descriptive:

A town is a thing like a colonial animal. A town has a nervous system and a head and shoulders and feet. A town is a thing separate from all other towns, so that there are no two towns alike. And a town has a whole emotion.

Animal imagery again dominates the human scene, but this passage is only the first half of a statement that is concluded midway through the chapter:

Out in the estuary a tight woven school of small fishes glittered and broke water to escape a school of great fishes that drove in to eat them. And in the houses the people could hear the swish of the small ones and the bouncing splash of the great ones as the slaughter went on. . . . And the night mice crept about on the ground and the little night hawks hunted them silently.

Symbol, allegory, and realistic detail are again woven satisfactorily together. The large fish and the hawks symbolize the doctor, the priest, the brokers, and the man behind the brokers, in fact all enemies of the village people from time prehistoric. Allegorically these predatory animals are all the snares that beset the journeying soul and the hungering body. Realistically these scenes can be observed in any coastal town where water, foul, and animal ecology provide these specific denizens.

Somewhere in every chapter Steinbeck adds a similar touch: the tidepool description that opens chapter two, the pearl-buyer with his sleight-of-hand coin manipulation midway in chapter four, the great wind passages at the end of chapter five, and the wasteland imagery a third of the way into chapter six. All these passages operate symbolically as well as realistically, and some of them work even allegorically.

Interpretation of the Allegory

One of the major charges against allegory is obscurantism. Why does the author not say what he means outright? Is it not too easy to derive two or more entirely separate and frequently contradictory meanings from a single allegory? These are the terms in which Coleridge first objected. Being told what a poet intended by his allegory, he responded,

> Apollo be praised! not a thought like it would ever enter of its own accord into any mortal mind; and what is an additional good feature, when put there, it will not stay, having the very opposite quality that snakes have—they come out of their holes into open view at the sound of sweet music, while the allegoric meaning slinks off at the very first notes, and lurks in murkiest oblivion—and utter invisibility.

Such is the reaction to *The Pearl* of Warren French in *John Steinbeck* (1961), who finds Kino's disposal of the pearl capable of contradictory interpretations: it may be seen as "noble renunciation," but it can also be read as "defeatism." *The Pearl* is most commonly understood as a rejection of materialism. Peter Lisca accepts the theme of anti-materialism but suggests a second layer of allegory which creates a "pattern of man's search for his soul." Others think *The Pearl,* like many another Steinbeck novel, to be a search for values, something like Odysseus' ten-year wanderings in the Homeric epic.

I often wonder at the ability of the anti-allegorists to read any piece of literature. Like Coleridge, allegory-haters are usually symbolism-lovers. How do they find any more certainty in the meaning of the evasive symbol than in "obscure" allegory? How do they respond to the "negative capability" of Shakespeare and Keats? What is their

reaction first to Christ's parables or Dante's *Paradiso* and then to the mountains of commentary on both that indicate there is very little certainty in any interpretation? We might say to them (since allegory deals almost always with the ways toward faith) that their faith is weak and urge that they ask in order to be given, seek in order to find, and knock in order to have opened.

But even the interpreters who have dealt with and accepted the allegory of *The Pearl* have been disturbingly vague. What are the results of Kino's particular search, we ask? What is the nature of Kino's soul? its disposition? in grace? in reprobation? What set of values did he arrive at? What is the precise nature of the materialism which he rejected?

Let us consider the general implications of any allegorical journey. Either it chronicles the transition of the soul from its captivity in the body and this mortality to liberation in Paradise and eternal life, or it records simply man's passing from a state of sin to one of grace. Quite often both these things happen at the same time. In *The Divine Comedy,* for example, Dante the pilgrim passes from this world into the existence of the afterworld; yet the entire journey is also one man's moral regeneration from error to rectitude, an object lesson that instructs the traveler in the nature of sin and the terrors of its punishment as opposed to the beatitude of salvation and the glories of its rewards.

But one thing always remains at the end of an allegorical journey. The traveler of the literal journey is still alive, still mortal, still in this world, and still to make the true journey from the corruption of this earth to the crystal bowers of heaven or sulphurous pits of hell that is undergone only after death.

Kino's Journeys

Kino's flight may be seen as a double journey, with a third still to be made. The journey is one half spiritual—the route to salvation of the soul—and one half physical—the way to freedom from bodily want. The second half is obvious; it is the theme of most of the early Steinbeck works; it is delineated in the list of things Kino will buy with the pearl. The first half may not be obvious, since for a long time now critics have been calling Steinbeck's writing non-teleological, by which they mean it does not concern itself with end-products, with what might be, what should be, or what could be, but only with what is. Especially is he unconcerned with eschatology. This view has long seemed to me mistaken. An allegorist with no teleology, no eschatology is almost a contradiction in terms. How this view of Steinbeck came into being is easy to see. His early novels such as *In Dubious Battle* and *The Grapes of Wrath* are a-Christian. No set of characters ever swore by Christ's name or cried out their disbelief in the church more often than those in *In Dubious Battle*. Mac says to Jim Nolan, "You got no vices, have you. And you're not a Christer either." But these are early works. In Steinbeck's latest novel, *The Winter of Our Discontent* (1961), the central character, Ethan Allen Hawley, is a regular member of the Episcopal Church; his problems are oriented about morality in a Christian framework, and much of the incidental symbolism is sacramental. Perhaps we have witnessed in Steinbeck himself an orthodox conversion, which, once witnessed, gives us cause to look for signs of it in previous writings. *The Pearl* is one of the first in which I detect a change; Juan Chicoy's bargains with the Virgin of Guadalupe in *The Wayward Bus* may be reluctant religion, but they represent at least a willingness to sit at the arbitration table with what used to be the enemy. *East of Eden,* in my view, among other things is an allegory of redemption through grace.

One of Kino's journeys then is the search for salvation. The forces that necessitate the literal journey, the flight, are cloaked in mystery and darkness:

> "I was attacked in the dark," said Kino. "And in the fight I have killed a man."
>
> "Who?" asked Juan Thomás quickly.
>
> "I do not know. It is all darkness—all darkness and shape of darkness."
>
> "It is the pearl," said Juan Thomás. "There is a devil in this pearl. You should have sold it and passed on the devil."

We are reminded of the formlessness of Milton's allegorical Death. Juan Thomás, torn like Kino by desires for a better life but concerned for his brother's safety, both blesses the journey and argues against it:

> "Go with God," he said, and it was like a death.
>
> "You will not give up the pearl?"
>
> "This pearl has become my soul," said Kino.
>
> "If I give it up I shall lose my soul."

Already almost overburdened with multiple symbolic equivalences—it stands for greed, for beauty, for materialism, for freedom from want, for evil, for good, for effete society, degenerate religion, and unethical medicine, for the strength and virtue of primitive societies—the pearl, with these words of Kino, stands also for Kino's soul.

The Indian boy of the germ-story had quite falsely identified his hold on the pearl with a firm grasp on salvation, a salvation absolutely assured while he still went about enveloped in flesh and mortality: "he could in advance purchase masses sufficient to pop him out of Purgatory like a squeezed watermelon seed." Kino also holds the pearl in his hand and equates it with freedom from want and then, mystically, also with freedom from damnation: "If I give it up I shall lose my soul." But he too has mistaken the pearl. The chances are very much more likely that with freedom from want his soul will be all the more in danger from sin. The Indian boy becomes free only when he throws the pearl away, only when he is "again with his soul in danger and his food and shelter insecure." The full significance of Kino's throwing the pearl back into the sea now becomes clear: the act represents his willingness to accept the third journey, the journey still to be made, the journey that Dante had still to make even after rising out of Hell to Purgatory and Paradise, the journey that any fictional character has still to make after his dream-vision allegory is over. Kino, Dante, Everyman have been given nothing more than instruction. They must apply their new knowledge and win their way to eternal salvation, which can come only with their actual deaths.

Kino's Triumph

It is difficult to understand how Warren French can interpret the "gesture [of flinging the pearl back into the sea] . . . as defeatism," how French can say that Kino "slips back not just half a step, but toboggans to the very bottom of the heap, for his boat smashed, his baby dead, and the pearl cast into the sea, he has less when the story is over than he had when it started." Kino is not defeated. He has in a sense triumphed over his enemy, over the chief of the pearl buyers, who neither gets the pearl nor kills Kino to keep him from talking. Kino has rid himself of his pursuers; he has a clear road to the cities of the north, to the capital, where indeed he may be cheated again, but where he has infinitely more opportunity to escape his destiny as a hut-dwelling peasant on the edge of La Paz. He has proved that he cannot be cheated nor destroyed. But his real triumph, his real gain, the heights to which he has risen rather than the depths to which he has slipped back is the immense knowledge that he has gained about good and evil. This knowledge is the tool that he needs to help him on the final journey, the inescapable journey that everyman must take.

Bahia de la Ventanas, a beach at Hotel Las Arenas, southeast of La Paz where John Steinbeck's "The Pearl" is set   Photograph by Dave G. Houser. © Dave G. Houser/Corbis

A final note should be added concerning some parallels between Steinbeck's novel and the anonymous fourteenth century. *Pearl*. The Pearl Poet tells the story, in dream-vision and allegory, of the personal grief of a loving father who has lost his daughter, a child dead before she had lived "two years in our land." As the poem opens, the narrator returns to a place where a "pearl of great price" has dropped from his hand to the ground. He falls asleep over the spot; a young maiden appears whose garments are covered with pearls; and the narrator speaks to the girl, now identified with the pearl he has lost and whom he believes to be his daughter in heaven, grown in stature and wisdom:

> O Pearl, quoth I, in pearls bedight,
> Art thou my pearl that I have 'plain'd?

She lectures him about the ways to salvation. He struggles to cross a stream that separates him from her and from the heavenly city—the new Jerusalem—which is her abode. The effort awakens him, and he rises from the ground with new spiritual strength.

Steinbeck's familiarity with medieval English literature is easy to document. His general interest in allegory indicates a steeping in the tradition. The epigraph to *The Wayward Bus* establishes his close

reading of *Everyman;* and two quotations from Old English in *The Winter of Our Discontent* (one of them significantly from the poetic *Genesis* in the Junius MS., 11. 897–899) show not only wide reading but also study in the original Anglo-Saxon.

The importance of the medieval *Pearl* for a reading of Steinbeck's novel is centered in the role of the children in each. Coyotito can, in several ways, be identified with Kino's "pearl of great value." The pearl from the sea is only a means by which Coyotito will be given an education. For the doctor, who at first refused to treat Coyotito, the child becomes his means to the pearl, i.e. the child is the pearl to him. But more important than these tenuous relationships is the fact that with the death of Coyotito the pearl no longer has any significance. The moment the pursuer with the rifle fires, Kino kills him. Kino then kills the two trackers who led the assassin to him and who were unshakable. This act gives Kino and his family unhindered passage to the cities of the north, where either the pearl might be sold or a new life begun. But the chance shot has killed Coyotito, and though Kino and Juana are now free, they return to the village near La Paz and throw the pearl back into the sea. Thus the sole act that has altered Kino's determination to keep the pearl which has become his soul is the death of his child; and, as I read the allegory, Kino and Juana turn from the waterside with new spiritual strength, regenerated even as the father in the medieval *Pearl*.

Much has been made of the *leitmotif* of music in *The Pearl:* the song of the family, the song of the enemy, etc. The suggestion for this musical background, interlaced as it is with Steinbeck's chief themes (cleaning of the soul, new wealth, complete well-being) may have come from the second stanza of the medieval poem:

Oft have I watched, wishing for that wealth
That was wont for a while to make nought of my
    sin,
And exalt my fortune and my entire well-being—
. . . .
Yet never imagined I so sweet a song
As a quiet hour let steal to me;
Indeed many drifted to me there.

And, finally, the medieval *Pearl* ends on the same note of renunciation that is the crux of Steinbeck's fable:

Upon this hill this destiny I grasped,
Prostrate in sorrow for my pearl.
And afterward to God I gave it up.
(modernizations of *The Pearl* by Sister Mary
    Vincent Hillmann)

However, I do not think that anything overmuch should be made of these similarities. Possibly the mere title of Steinbeck's allegory brought memories to his mind of the fourteenth century poem. He may have gone back to look at it again, but he may have satisfied himself with distant evocations only. For myself, whatever likenesses I find between the two works serve only to emphasize the continuing tradition of true allegory and the modern writer's strong links with the past.

Source: Harry Morris, "'The Pearl': Realism and Allegory," in *English Journal*, Vol. 52, No. 7, October 1963, pp. 487–95, 505.

Sources

Astro, Richard, "John Steinbeck," in *Dictionary of Literary Biography*, Vol. 9, *American Novelists, 1910–1945*, Gale Research, 1981, pp. 43–68.

Baker, Carlos, "Steinbeck at the Top of His Form," in the *New York Times*, November 30, 1947, pp. BR4, 52.

French, Warren, "John Steinbeck," in *Twayne's United States Authors Series Online*, G. K. Hall, 1999.

Karsten, Ernest E., Jr., "Thematic Structure in *The Pearl*," in *English Journal*, Vol. 54, No. 1, January 1965, pp. 1–7.

Prescott, Orville, "Books of the Times," in the *New York Times*, November 24, 1947, p. 21.

Steinbeck, John, *East of Eden*, Penguin, 1992.

———, *The Pearl*, in *The Short Novels of John Steinbeck*, Viking, 1953, pp. 471–527.

Further Reading

Mitchell, Marilyn H., "Steinbeck's Strong Women: Feminine Identity in the Short Stories," in *John Steinbeck: A Study of the Short Fiction*, edited by R. S. Hughes, Twayne, 1989, pp. 154–66.
    Mitchell looks at strong women in Steinbeck's fiction.

Owens, Lois, *John Steinbeck's Re-Vision of America*, University of Georgia Press, 1985.
    Owens analyzes the changes in Steinbeck's vision of America over the course of his literary career.

Timmerman, John, "Steinbeck's Environmental Ethic: Humanity and Harmony with the Land," in *Steinbeck and the Environment: Interdisciplinary Approaches*, edited by Susan F. Beegel, Susan Shillinglaw, and Wesley N. Tiffney Jr., University of Alabama Press, 1997, pp. 310–22.
    Timmerman examines Steinbeck's vision of the environment and people's relationship to it.

Tuttleton, James W., "Steinbeck Remembered," in the *New Criterion*, Vol. 13, No. 7, March 1995, pp. 22–28.
    Tuttleton presents a comprehensive overview of Steinbeck's career and reputation.

Rosa

Cynthia Ozick

1983

"Rosa" by Cynthia Ozick was first published in the *New Yorker* in 1983. However, its protagonist, Rosa Lublin, was introduced three years earlier in "The Shawl," a much shorter story also published in the *New Yorker*. The two stories were re-released together as a book in 1989 entitled *The Shawl*. "Rosa" also appeared in the anthology *Prize Stories 1984*, a collection of O. Henry Prize winners.

While "The Shawl" tells the painful story of how Rosa's infant daughter is brutally killed by a Nazi guard in a concentration camp, "Rosa" revisits the protagonist 30 years later, who is still devastated by her daughter's death. Living a meager, isolated existence in a "hotel" for the elderly, financed by Stella her resentful niece, Rosa is unable to let go of her daughter and the past.

"Rosa" dramatizes the lasting impact of the Holocaust on a unique, complex character who is not entirely sympathetic. While obviously the far-reaching effects of the Holocaust is a major theme in this story, Ozick also deals with themes of alienation and denial and explores how American culture devalues and isolates the elderly.

Author Biography

Cynthia Ozick was born April 17, 1928, in New York City, the second child of Russian immigrants William and Celia Ozick. Her parents owned and operated a drugstore in the Bronx, where Cynthia worked delivering prescriptions. Her father was a Jewish scholar, and her uncle was a well-respected Hebrew poet who first introduced her to the world of literature.

During her early school years in the Pelham Bay section of the Bronx, Cynthia endured anti-Semitic attacks and slurs, especially when she refused to sing Christmas carols with the rest of her class. She escaped into reading, getting books from her older brother and from a traveling library that came by her parents' drugstore. Her school life took a more positive turn when she entered Hunter College High School in Manhattan, where Ozick's academic excellence was more appreciated. After high school, she went on to graduate cum laude from New York University in 1949. She then earned a master's degree from Ohio State University, writing her master's thesis on the works of Henry James, a writer who influences her own work.

In 1952 Ozick married lawyer Bernard Hallote and worked briefly for Filene's Department Store as an advertising copywriter. In 1966, the year after Ozick gave birth to her daughter Rachel, Ozick's first novel, *Trust,* was published to positive reviews. Ozick followed *Trust* with three collections of short fiction: *The Pagan Rabbi and Other Stories, Bloodshed and Three Novellas,* and *Levitation: Five Fictions,* which were all critically acclaimed, firmly establishing Ozick as an important voice in contemporary literature.

In 1983 Ozick published both her second novel, *The Cannibal Galaxy* and a collection of essays entitled *Art and Ardor.* In that same year, "Rosa" appeared in *The New Yorker,* winning an O. Henry Prize for short fiction. Subsequently, she published three more novels—*The Messiah of Stockholm* (1987), *The Puttermesser Papers* (1997), and *Heir to the Glimmering World* (2004)—as well as three collections of essays: *Metaphor and Memory* (1989), *Fame and Folly* (1996), and *Quarrel and Quandary* (2000). *The Shawl,* a book composed of the two short stories "The Shawl" and "Rosa," was released in 1989.

Over her career Cynthia Ozick's work has been awarded numerous honors, including the O. Henry Prize for short fiction (in 1975, 1981, 1984, and 1992), a National Endowment for the Arts fellowship (1968), the American Academy of Arts Award for literature (1973), and a Guggenheim Fellowship (1982). Much of her fiction centers on Jewish culture and issues, and she has received awards from many Jewish literary organizations. In 1972 she was awarded the B'nai Brith Jewish Heritage

Cynthia Ozick Photograph by Louis Lanzano. AP/Wide World Photos

Award; in 1977, National Jewish Book Award for fiction; in 1984, the Distinguished Service in Jewish Letters Award.

Plot Summary

The story "Rosa" is set in 1977, the same year in which it was written. "Rosa" is written in the third person limited point of view, but the reader is allowed only Rosa's viewpoint on events; letters in the story are, of course, written in first person. Because Rosa's mental state is unstable, her perceptions are not always the most reliable.

Cynthia Ozick begins "Rosa" by describing the current state of Rosa Lublin's meager existence. Having destroyed her own antique shop in New York City ("It was a mad thing to do") Rosa is now living in a shabby "hotel" for the elderly in Miami, Florida. Her resentful and critical niece Stella, still living in New York, supports her. Rosa sees no one, goes out only when absolutely necessary, and barely eats enough to stay alive. She spends most of her time composing letters to her daughter Magda, who was killed as an infant by a Nazi guard in a concentration camp, 35 years ago.

As the story begins, Rosa reluctantly sets off to the laundromat ("After a while, Rosa had no choice"). While watching her clothes swirl about in the washer, she is approached by the flirtatious older man, Simon Persky. Like Rosa, he is from Warsaw, Poland, but Rosa is quick to tell him, "My Warsaw isn't your Warsaw." Undeterred, Persky helps her fold her laundry and insists on taking her to a diner for a hot cup of tea and a Danish. There he tells her that he is a retired businessman who once owned a button factory and that his wife is in a mental institution. Rosa tells him how she destroyed her antique shop, "Part with a big hammer . . . part with a piece of construction metal I picked up from the gutter." When Perksy encourages her to tell more about her life, she gets up to go. She says she has no life, because "Thieves took it."

When Rosa arrives back at her hotel, a package and two letters are waiting for her. The first letter is from Stella, who writes to tell Rosa that she has sent her Magda's shawl in a separate package. The tattered shawl in which Rosa swaddled baby Magda is all that she has left of her daughter, and now she treats it as a sacred relic. Stella's letter describes with disdain how Rosa worships the shawl: "You'll open the box and take it out and cry, and you'll kiss it like a crazy person." Assuming the package she has received contains the shawl, she begins to tidy up her room in preparation: "Everything had to be nice when the box was opened."

Before reading the second letter, Rosa inventories her laundry and discovers she is missing one pair of underpants. At first, she is ashamed of her own carelessness: "Degrading. Lost bloomers— dropped God knows where." Then she latches onto the idea that Persky picked up the underwear but was too embarrassed to hand them to her. Finally, she decides that Persky has stolen them.

After reaching this questionable conclusion, Rosa opens the second letter, which is from Dr. James Tree, a university researcher who is conducting a study on repressed animation in Holocaust survivors. It is not the first such letter Rosa has received. The impersonal, clinical tone outrages her, so she lights a match and burns the letter.

Next, Rosa writes her own letter, a long letter in Polish to her daughter Magda. Rosa has invented an entire life for her daughter, whom she now imagines to be a professor of Greek philosophy at Columbia University. In the letter she tells Magda that her niece Stella suffers from dementia, and to humor her, Rosa agrees that Magda is dead. Rosa writes that Stella believes Magda's father was a Nazi who forced himself on her, but Rosa insists Magda's father was the son of a family friend, to whom Rosa was engaged. "No lies come out of me to you," she writes.

Rosa finishes the letter to Magda and then prepares herself to open the box containing Magda's shawl. She puts on a nice dress, fixes her hair, even puts on some lipstick, but then when she sits down on the bed to open the box, she is lost in a reverie of concentration camp memories. After hours spent reliving past horrors, she finally leaves her room in search of her lost underpants.

Rosa wanders Miami at night, looking for her underwear in a host of unlikely places: on the street, at a newsstand, and then finally, at the beach. She goes through a gate and onto the private beach of a fancy hotel, where she stumbles upon two men having sex. She tries to leave the beach, but she is locked in, a trespasser. She reacts to the barbed wire fence surrounding the beach. Desperate, she asks the men for help, but they laugh at her. Finally, she escapes by making her way through the hotel kitchen. Once in the lobby, she demands to see the manager, whom she chastises for the barbed wire on the fence. When the manager asks her to leave and not disturb "important guests" who are visiting the hotel, Rosa leaps to the conclusion that Dr. James Tree is staying at the hotel: "I see you got Tree! You got a whole bunch of Trees!"

When Rosa returns to her hotel, she discovers Simon Persky there, waiting for her. He invites himself up to her room for a cup of tea. During their conversation, Persky asks if Rosa lost her family in the Holocaust. Rosa says there are just three left: Rosa herself, Stella, and one more. She offers him the box with Magda's shawl as "evidence." But the box contains not the shawl, but the study on repressed animation sent by the persistent Dr. Tree. Enraged, Rosa hurls the book at the ceiling. Persky leaves, promising to return the next day.

The next day Rosa receives the package containing the shawl and takes it up to her room. When she handles the shawl, a vision of her daughter at sixteen springs to life. Rosa picks up her pen and writes another letter to Magda. But when the phone rings with a call from Simon Persky, the vision vanishes.

Characters

Finkelstein

Finkelstein is the manager of the Hotel Marie Louise. Rosa is trapped on the hotel's private beach when she inadvertently trespasses. After she escapes, she rages at Finkelstein for having barbed wire around the perimeter of the hotel beach.

Rosa Lublin

The title character of the story, Rosa Lublin—who reflexively gives her name as Lublin, Rosa—is a 58-year-old Holocaust survivor now living in Miami, Florida. Rosa lost her only child, a baby daughter named Magda, when a Nazi guard threw the baby against an electrified fence. Rosa's life stopped at this moment; she tells Simon Persky: "Before is a dream. After is a joke. Only during stays." For Rosa, the Holocaust has never really ended.

Rosa is full of contradictions. She is Jewish and yet anti-Semitic; she has contempt for Persky yet fixes her hair and worries about a hole in her dress while she is with him. She finds her lost underpants rolled in a towel but tells her niece Stella, "A man stole my underwear." She seems determined to live as little as possible. Repeatedly, when she is told to get on with her life, she replies, "Thieves took it."

It becomes clear as the story progresses that Rosa is mentally unstable, especially during the nighttime search for her lost underwear. Her musings on their whereabouts progress from questionable to absurd, for example, when she concludes that the underwear "thief" may have buried them on the beach.

Magda

Though Rosa's daughter has been dead for more than 30 years when this story takes place, Magda figures as an important character in the story because to Rosa, she is still very much alive. Rosa writes her long letters telling of her life before the Holocaust and describing life in the Warsaw ghetto. When Rosa embraces the shawl that once held baby Magda, a vision of Magda springs to life before her.

Through Rosa's letters Stella suspects Magda was fathered by a Nazi who forced himself on Rosa. Though Rosa denies this vehemently in her letter to Magda, later when she is gazing upon the vision of Magda, the reader learns, "she was always a little suspicious of Magda, because of that other strain, whatever it was, that ran in her." In "The Shawl," the story that precedes "Rosa," Stella has a different word for it: "Aryan." When writing Magda, Rosa uses endearments such as "my yellow

lioness," "yellow blossom," and "yellow flower." The yellow suggests the yellow Star of David, which Nazis forced Jews to wear on their clothing. The name, Magda, suggests Mary Magdalen (the reformed prostitute Jesus healed of evil spirits [Luke 8:2]), and it also suggests magdalen, which is a reformatory for wayward women or prostitutes. In her name, baby Magda may embody Rosa's memory of the traumatic rape by a Nazi.

Simon Persky

Simon Persky is a flirtatious, 71-year-old man who "picks up" Rosa at the laundromat. Though he has had his share of tragedy—his wife now lives in a mental institution—his philosophy of life seems to be the antithesis of Rosa's: he is determined to enjoy the moment and help Rosa do the same. Persky is undeterred by Rosa's strange outbursts—"If there's one thing I know to understand, it's mental episodes," he says—and persistently chips away at her defenses.

Persky is a well-off retired businessman who once owned a factory that manufactured buttons and other notions. Button metaphors recur in the story. For instance, when Persky offers to take Rosa to a library to get some books, Rosa is touched: "He almost understood what she was: no ordinary button."

Stella

Stella is Rosa's niece living in New York, who supports Rosa financially (repeatedly reminding her, "I'm not a millionaire"). Stella was in the concentration camp with Rosa and her baby daughter when the baby was killed. It is obvious that Rosa resents Stella for having survived: "Stella was alive, why not Magda?"

Unlike Rosa, Stella is determined to leave her Holocaust experience in the past. About Stella, Rosa writes in one of her letters to Magda: "Every vestige of former existence is an insult to her." Stella finds Rosa's obsession with Magda and her shawl exasperating and will only let her have the shawl periodically. In her exchanges with Rosa, Stella is not only impatient but cold and unfeeling. Rosa refers to her as the "Angel of Death," to whom she attributes almost every negative experience of her life: "It comes from Stella, everything!"

Despite Stella's attempts to deny the past, there are signs that she is not succeeding. Now 49, Stella is still searching for a husband, taking night classes in hopes of finding a man to marry. As Rosa writes to Magda, "Because [Stella] fears the past, she distrusts the future ... as a result she has nothing."

Dr. James Tree

Dr. Tree is a university researcher and Ph.D. who is conducting a study on the metaphysical aspects of "Repressed Animation" in Holocaust survivors. He contacts Rosa requesting that she meet with him at her home as part of his research: "I should like to observe survivor syndroming within the natural setting."

The language Dr. Tree uses in his letters to Rosa is impersonal and clinical. Earnestly oblivious to his own insensitivity, he even sends Rosa a copy of a study on repressed animation, with the recommendation: "Of special interest, perhaps, is Chapter Six, entitled 'Defensive Group Formation: The Way of the Baboons.'" He sees her not as a human being, but as a curiosity to be examined, a specimen, a supposedly lower form of life.

To Rosa Dr. Tree becomes the enemy, the symbolic representative of all the people who cannot—or will not—understand what she has been through, extending her oppression and leaving her alienated and isolated.

Themes

The Holocaust

"Rosa" gives a dramatic example of how the Holocaust not only took the lives of the millions of Jews who died in concentration camps, but also emotionally crippled millions of others who survived. While Rosa and Stella survived the camp physically, both are disabled emotionally, though they deal with it in very different ways. Rosa refuses to move on; Stella refuses to look back. Rosa tells Persky that Stella "wants to wipe out memory."

Conflict in approaches to dealing with the Holocaust has given rise to an important debate in the years since World War II (1939–1945). An extremist movement calling its members "Holocaust revisionists" claims that the annihilation of Jews in Nazi concentration camps either never happened at all or was vastly exaggerated. Denounced by historians, these "revisionists" have nonetheless made themselves heard, attempting, like Stella, to "wipe out memory."

Alienation

Rosa lives in almost complete isolation, partly because of her own efforts. Though she is supremely articulate in her native Polish, her English is still halting and broken, even after more than 30 years in the United States. "Why should I learn English?" she asks Persky. "I didn't ask for it, I got nothing to do with it." Through her own brand of anti-Semitism, she alienates herself from her own people, even those who have suffered the same tragedies. In a letter to Magda, she writes, "imagine confining *us* with teeming Mockowiczes and Rabinowiczes and Perskys and Finkelsteins, with all their bad-smelling grandfathers and their hordes of feeble children!" Finally, through her own mental illness, living in her fantasy world with visions of Magda, she further distances herself from reality and others.

Rosa's alienation is not entirely her own doing, however. In New York, she attempted to reach out to customers of her antique shop, to tell her story, but no one listened. "Whoever came, they were like deaf people," she says. Also, the impersonal university letters from Dr. Tree epitomize the kind of insensitivity that has convinced Rosa no one will ever understand.

Treatment of the Elderly in America

Like Rosa, the other elderly residents of the Miami hotel are isolated, shut off from their families and their former lives: "Everyone had left behind a real life. Here they had nothing." In letters they read "rumors of their grandchildren," but it all seems unreal. Rosa's visions of Magda are more substantial than the connection many of the residents experience with their living family members. These people are essentially forgotten.

This is all too typical of American attitudes toward the elderly; while other cultures value and revere the elderly, Americans tend to view them as burdens who have outlived their usefulness. One way or another, the younger people featured in the story are all fenced off from the elderly. The Cuban receptionist, for instance, works in a cage; the gay men on the beach are enclosed by a barbed-wire fence.

Idolatry

Idolatry, the worship of something or someone other than God, is a recurrent theme in Cynthia Ozick's work. Though Rosa writes in a letter to Magda, "I don't believe in God," she worships Magda's shawl with all the fervor and ritual of religion, giving it the status of a relic like medieval

Topics For Further Study

- In interviews, Cynthia Ozick has said that in principle, she is against making fiction out of the Holocaust, but felt compelled to write "The Shawl" and "Rosa." What might be the dangers of using the Holocaust or other historical events as a basis for fiction? What positive results might come from this fiction? Write about the pros and cons of creating art from history.

- The five stages of grief, as identified by psychiatrist Elisabeth Kubler-Ross, are denial and isolation, anger, bargaining, depression, and acceptance. In which of these stages is Rosa living? Can you find signs of the other stages throughout the story? Does she progress or regress through the process as the story continues?

- Rosa experiences "mental episodes," as Persky would call them, throughout the story. What events trigger these episodes and why? How does her fragile mental condition affect her ability to cope with her loss? Do some research on post-traumatic shock syndrome and then write an essay in which you explain its relevance to Rosa's mental state and those events that exacerbate it.

- A recurring theme in Ozick's work is idolatry, the worship of someone or something other than God. Rosa's idol is Magda's shawl. How did Hitler use idolatry to create the Holocaust? Can you find other examples of idols in society in the early 2000s?

Christians did objects associated with the life of Jesus. As Stella writes her, "You're like those people in the Middle Ages who worshiped a piece of the True Cross." Rosa makes special preparations for the opening of the box, putting on a nice dress, fixing her hair, tidying her room. Once opened and taken from the box, the shawl has the power to bring the dead back to life, conjuring the vision of Magda at age sixteen. In "The Shawl," the story which precedes "Rosa," baby Magda is somehow sustained by sucking on the shawl, even though Rosa is no longer capable of nursing her.

Sex and Shame

Rosa tells Magda in one of her letters, "I was forced by a German, it's true, and more than once." Though she denies that Magda is the result, late in the story when Magda's vision begins to fade, Rosa implores her, "Magda, my beloved, don't be ashamed! Butterfly, I am not ashamed of your presence."

When Rosa imagines that Persky has picked up her lost underpants, her first thought is one of disproportionate humiliation: "Oh, degrading. The shame. Pain in the loins. Burning." Later she wanders Miami at night in a futile search for the lost underwear, and her lost innocence. When Persky asks her what she lost, what she is looking for, she replies, "My life."

Style

Setting

The setting of Miami, Florida, figures prominently in this story. The incessant heat and humidity add to Rosa's suffering and make her even more reluctant to leave her room. "Where I put myself is in hell," Rosa writes to Stella early in the story. The frequent mentions of the intense, suffocating heat confirm this impression. The heat is described as "cooked honey dumped on their heads," and "burning molasses air"; the sun is "a murdering sunball." When Rosa burns the letter from Dr. Tree, she thinks, "The world is full of fire! Everything, everything is on fire! Florida is burning!"

In Florida, Rosa is surrounded almost entirely by other elderly people whose productive lives, like hers, are in the past. In the mirrors in the lobby, the elderly hotel guests see themselves as they used to be, not as they are now; they are arrested in time, just as Rosa's life remains centered on the moment of her daughter's death.

Metaphor

Metaphor is a technique which conveys a description of one thing in terms of another. Buttons, for instance, are a recurring metaphor in Ozick's story. Simon Persky tells Rosa he once owned a button factory. Later, Rosa reflects on how trivial Persky's life seems to her, "himself no more significant than a button." Then she extends this metaphor to the city's entire population: "All of Miami Beach, a box for useless buttons!" When Rosa flies into a rage after opening the package from Dr. Tree, she yells at Persky, "I'm not your button, Persky! I'm nobody's button." And finally, when the vision of Magda appears wearing a dress Rosa herself wore as a teenager, the buttons are so beautiful that "Persky could never have been acquainted with buttons like that." Attached to cloth, buttons function as fasteners, creating connection, holding separate parts together; collected in a box, buttons are useless, meaningless. Buttons become a metaphor for these elderly people, collected in Florida, but detached and without function or purpose.

Mirrors constitute another recurring metaphor in "Rosa." Rosa's antique shop, for instance, specialized in old mirrors, perfect for a character who spends her life gazing into the past. The mirrors in the lobby of Rosa's hotel reflect the past as well, showing the elderly guests what they want to see and nothing more.

Point of View

"Rosa" is written in third-person subjective point of view, which means the reader has access to Rosa's internal thoughts and feelings, but not those of others. Because Ozick moves from ordinary narration right into Rosa's thoughts without any distinguishing punctuation, readers get the feeling they are constantly inside Rosa's head. This feeling becomes especially important during Rosa's moments of dementia, blurring the line between what is imagined and what is real.

Though the bulk of the story is told in the third person point of view, much of what we learn about Rosa's background, and also about Stella, we learn from the long letters Rosa writes to Magda, which are of course written in the first person. There is a sharp contrast between the way Rosa writes and the way she speaks, because she writes in her native Polish. Letter-writing Rosa is articulate and well-educated;

Rosa's spoken English, however, "ain't no better than what any other refugee talks," as Persky says.

Unlike the usual prose written in the first person, the style of a letter is dictated in part by the recipient. Rosa's letters to Magda are rife with endearments, rhapsodic in their description of Warsaw and her former life, and somewhat arrogant. She expresses her opinions and views openly and lies boldly because she knows there is no real reader to contradict or chastise her. She can ignore reality and paint a picture of life as she wishes it to be.

On the other hand, Stella's two short letters to Rosa are caustic and critical, revealing the resentment she feels towards Rosa. She knows that though Rosa saved her life, Rosa would much prefer it if Stella had been the one to die, rather than Magda. She is jealous of the shawl, as if it were Magda herself. This is implied in her description of Rosa's ritual of worshiping the shawl ("What a scene, disgusting!") and also by her withholding the shawl, only allowing Rosa to have it periodically.

Finally, the letters written by Dr. Tree, in their highly clinical, emotionless language, portray him as unfeeling and arrogant. His repetitive use of the term "survivor," a label that could be attached to any living thing, plant or animal, reveals his attitude towards the recipient of his letter. Rosa notes this immediately when she reads it: "*Survivor.* Even when your bones get melted into the grains of the earth, still they'll forget *human being.*"

Irony

Irony appears in "Rosa" on many levels; some almost humorous, some tragic. First there is the irony that Rosa has survived the Holocaust and the camps only to be "confined" in Miami with many of the same people for whom she had so much contempt in her earlier life. She is confronted again by barbed wire and by a scientist who wishes her to consent to an "experiment," just as many Holocaust victims were used as experimental subjects.

Dr. Tree's letters ironically speak of "Repressed Animation," written by a man who has clearly repressed any human feeling or compassion towards the people he studies. He writes in the service of science, but he is unable to recognize the way he objectifies the subjects of his research. To further drive home the message that he sees Rosa on the level of any other laboratory animal, he refers her to a study entitled, "Defensive Group Formation: The Way of the Baboons."

Compare
&
Contrast

- **Early 1940s:** Central and eastern Europe is the largest center of the world's Jewish population by the start of World War II (1939–1940), with an estimated 9.5 million of the world's 16.7 million Jews (following historical shifts from Palestine to Babylon in ancient times, then to Spain in the eleventh century until the Inquisition, when the center began shifting to central and eastern Europe).

  Late 1970s: With about two-thirds of Europe's Jewish population wiped out by the Nazis during World War II and the Holocaust, the center of Jewish population has shifted to the United States and Israel. An estimated 5.7 million Jews live in the United States, and 3.2 million in Israel.

  Today: In 2000, the world's Jewish population is estimated at 13.2 million, of which only 1,583,000, or twelve percent, live in Europe. Most Jews live either in the United States or Israel. In most recent years, the worldwide Jewish population has risen slightly but still remains at a statistical zero-population growth.

- **Early 1940s:** The legal rights, property, homes, businesses, social freedoms, indeed all aspects of human community life for Jewish citizens is systemically taken away by the Nazi government (in Germany itself and in Nazi-occupied European states from France in the West to occupied Russia in the East) without legal or political opposition. The depth of this political powerlessness is ultimately expressed by the Holocaust, the government-sanctioned and -operated extermination of some 6 million European Jews, along with millions of others, such as Christian sympathizers, political dissenters, homosexuals, and physically or mentally handicapped persons.

  Late 1970s: The state of Israel, in the three decades since its founding as a sovereign nation by Jewish nationalists in 1948, has ascended to become a regional power through factors including the following: its powerful modern economy, its defeat of neighboring Arab countries in armed conflicts in 1967 and 1973, its strong economic and political alliances with the United States government and private constituencies, and its possession of nuclear weapons.

  1990s: The 1990s have seen a resurgence of Nazi ideology. Neo-Nazis uphold such beliefs as anti-Semitism and a hatred of foreigners. Neo-Nazi doctrine tends to draw young people in countries around the world to participate in these hate groups.

- **Early 1940s:** From 1943 to 1945 at the Auschwitz death camp, Dr. Josef Mengele performs hundreds of gruesome medical experiments on the camp's inmates. Ostensibly the goal of these experiments is genetic research aimed at creating a super-race of defect-free Aryans for the Reich. In truth, there is no scientific value to Mengele's experiments; using the pretext of science, they are in fact extraordinary instances of individual and group sadistic torture, mutilation, and murder. Operations are routinely performed without anesthesia, including amputations and transplants.

  Late 1970s: In November 1977, in Great Britain, the first successful in vitro fertilization is performed on Lesley Brown, a woman formerly unable to conceive due to blockage of her fallopian tubes. After months of careful monitoring, Brown delivers a healthy baby girl on July 25, 1978. The birth of Louise Brown not only gives hope to thousands of infertile couples, it also raises a host of questions regarding the ethical and moral implications of creating life in the laboratory. Issues such as surrogate mothers, the morality of discarding some embryos in favor of others, the possibility of sex selection and genetic engineering are all hotly debated long before the baby is even born.

  Today: In the early 2000s, in vitro fertilization is a fairly commonplace procedure that helps infertile couples worldwide.

Finally, though Stella clearly resents supporting Rosa and tries to keep all contact with her as brief as possible, she guarantees continued and regular contact by keeping Magda's shawl. She knows that as long as she keeps it, she and Rosa are connected by a bond much greater than the financial support she provides.

Historical Context

Cynthia Ozick's "Rosa" first appeared in the *New Yorker* in 1983. In 1979, a group calling itself the Institute for Historical Review (IHR) was founded by Willis Carto. Carto had also founded Liberty lobby, an anti-Jewish propaganda organization. Members of the IHR call themselves Holocaust revisionists. They claim that the Holocaust either never happened or has been greatly exaggerated by the Jewish people. The IHR and its claims have been denounced by historians, who cite the vast volume of documentation seized from the Nazis themselves, as well as firsthand accounts from survivors. Indeed, the Holocaust is one of the best documented events in history.

The establishment of the IHR occurred, ironically, just two years after the establishment of the Simon Wiesenthal Center, a Jewish human-rights organization dedicated to apprehending Nazi war criminals and keeping the memory of the Holocaust alive. In 1981 the center produced an Academy Award–winning documentary about the Holocaust entitled *Genocide*.

"The Shawl" and "Rosa" deal with the pivotal event of Rosa Lublin's life, the death of her infant daughter, who was thrown against an electrified fence by a Nazi guard. This brutal killing was drawn from an actual event Ozick read of in William Shirer's *The Rise and Fall of the Third Reich*.

Critical Overview

Since she published her first novel in 1966, Cynthia Ozick has garnered substantial critical acclaim for both her fiction and her essays. Many critics acknowledge that she is a gifted writer, and one of the most important voices in contemporary literature. John Sutherland, in the October 8, 2000, *New York Times Book Review*, calls her "the most accomplished and graceful literary stylist of our time."

Some critics believe, however, that Ozick's penchant for displaying her own prowess with words interferes with her message. Accusing her of "Parading her erudition like a peacock," Ilan Stavans, in the July 16, 1999 issue of *Times Literary Supplement*, notes that while Ozick's words are meticulously chosen, "their splendour can also get in her way, obstructing the plot, making it morose, dispensable." Bruce Bawer, in the *Wall Street Journal*, also mentions that Ozick can be "too preoccupied with intellectual matters for [her] own good,—or, to be specific, for the good of [her] fiction."

Whatever negative criticism Ozick has received, very little of it has been attached to the two stories featuring Rosa Lublin, "The Shawl" and "Rosa." Each story won an O. Henry Prize for short fiction when it was first published in the *New Yorker* (in 1980 and 1983 respectively). In his *The Wall Street Journal* review of the book *The Shawl* (which combines both stories in one volume), Bruce Bawer writes, "Ms. Ozick succeeds stunningly in bringing this tragic, demented woman to life." Critics were especially impressed by Ozick's sensitive handling of the difficult subject matter. Irving Halperin, in *Commonweal*, writes, "In a time when the memory of the Holocaust is being trivialized by slick fiction, talk shows, and TV 'documentaries' . . . Ms. Ozick's volume is a particularly welcome achievement of the moral imagination." Francine Prose in the September 10, 1989 *New York Times Book Review* says that Ozick "pulls off the rare trick of making art out of what we would rather not see."

Overall, these two stories featuring Rosa Lublin are considered some of Ozick's finest work. Both are often included as required reading for students studying the Holocaust.

Criticism

Laura Pryor

Pryor has a bachelor of arts degree from the University of Michigan and twenty years experience in professional and creative writing with special interest in fiction. In this essay, Pryor examines how the current life of the title character in "Rosa" mirrors her past Holocaust experience and the disparate methods the characters use to cope with that experience.

How does one deal with the Holocaust and its memory? This is the question that "Rosa" brings to mind, but does not necessarily answer. Rosa Lublin's niece Stella theorizes that there are three lives: before the Holocaust, during, and after. Rosa claims: "Before is a dream. After is a joke. Only during stays." Rosa's answer to dealing with the Holocaust is to carry it with her every day, to deny that there is a life after by living only in the past.

In fact, in moving to Miami Beach, Rosa has returned to a confined camp of sorts. Where the Warsaw ghetto segregated and confined Jews, Miami Beach confines the elderly. The few younger people Rosa encounters are segregated from the elderly by fences: the gay men at the beach, the receptionist in her "cage." Even the description of the elderly as "scarecrows, blown about under the murdering sunball with empty rib cages" brings to mind images of emaciated concentration camp prisoners.

The words and images Ozick uses to describe Miami Beach depict a place just this side of hell. The heat and humidity are oppressive, thick, and suffocating; the air is "molasses," the streets are a "furnace," the sun is "an executioner," bringing to mind more images of Holocaust atrocities. The heat serves to further confine Rosa in her dismal, grimy room, which she shares with "squads of dying flies." In coming to Miami, Rosa has moved back into the worst of her past.

As Rosa lives in the past, clinging to her memories of Magda, there are signs that she would actually like to move on but has no idea how to do it. First, there is the simple fact that she continues to live, however marginally. Second, it seems that she realizes her mistake in coming to Miami; she writes her niece, "Where I put myself is in hell," and she later suggests naively to Stella that she could return to New York and re-open her store. Finally, her attempts to get rid of the optimistic Persky seem half-hearted, and when she is with him she worries about her hair, her missing button, the fact that she is not wearing her nice shoes. Though these signs indicate some willingness to move forward, her isolation and misery have become such an ingrained way of life that she is not even fully aware of other options. When Persky comes into her dingy room and sets her table to eat the crullers he has brought, "to Rosa this made the corner of the room look new, as though she had never seen it before."

The incident on the private hotel beach gives Rosa a chance to rewrite her own history in some small way. When she is trapped on the beach behind barbed wire, she is forced to relive the past not just in her mind, but in reality. She pleads with the men on the beach to let her out, but they refuse. They are her persecutors, her jailers. This time, however, she makes her own escape, finding her way through the hotel kitchens and into the Eden-like lobby. After telling off the hotel manager, she marches out of the lobby, "Irradiated, triumphant, cleansed." When she returns to the hotel, Persky is waiting for her; the next morning, she requests that her phone be reconnected. She has taken one tentative step into the future. Even Magda seems to know that something is different: when Rosa opens the box containing Magda's shawl, this time, "For some reason it did not instantly restore Magda." In fact, when Rosa first looks at the shawl, she is "indifferent." For the first time, she is seeing the shawl for what it really is, "a colorless cloth."

The ever-patient Persky seems ideally suited to lead Rosa from the confinement of her own misery. She has a button missing; he is a manufacturer of buttons. She barely eats enough to stay alive; in both of their meetings he buys her food. As Rosa comes to realize, "he almost understood what she was: no ordinary button." Between the extremes of living in the past and denying it, Persky takes the middle road. Unlike Stella, he is sympathetic to Rosa's anguish, though he advises, "Sometimes a little forgetting is necessary."

Cynthia Ozick has made the emotional anguish of Holocaust survivors immediate and real by making Rosa a flawed, not entirely sympathetic character. Rosa is both an intellectual snob and an anti-Semite, despite all that she has suffered at the hands of anti-Semitism. It is exactly because she is not heroic or noble that the reader can relate intimately to her suffering. Her experiences are made even more immediate by Ozick's technique of shifting from narrative to Rosa's thoughts without punctuation. What is actually true and what is the product of Rosa's unstable mind? The lines are blurred.

While Rosa has lived the last 35 years in the past, Stella has spent the last 35 years trying to ignore it. Though Rosa describes her as pretty, Stella has been unable to find "the one thing she wanted more than anything: an American husband." Ozick does not reveal what Stella does for a living, though her constant reminders to Rosa that she is not a millionaire would indicate a lack of success in this area as well. As Rosa asks aloud to Stella's letter, "And you, Stella, *you* have a life?" It would appear that Stella's methods of dealing with her war-time

What Do I Read Next?

- Ozick's "The Shawl" (1989) tells the harrowing story of Magda's death at the hands of a Nazi guard and will give readers greater insight into the title character of "Rosa."

- *A Cynthia Ozick Reader* (1996) gives readers a wider sampling of Ozick's other work, including seven poems, eight essays, and seven fiction pieces.

- Technically a novel, Elie Wiesel's *Night* is an autobiographical account of Wiesel's experience at Auschwitz. Published in 1960, it is one of the most famous accounts written of the Holocaust.

- The novel *Washington Square* is a good introduction to Henry James. This novel is shorter and easier to read than some of his more famous, later works. The Modern Library Classics edition of this novel also includes an introduction by Cynthia Ozick. James was a major literary influence on Ozick, who wrote her master's thesis on his works while she attended Ohio State University.

- New Yorker Ruth Puttermesser is probably Ozick's most famous fictional character. A number of short stories featuring Puttermesser were combined to create a novel called *The Puttermessser Papers* (1997). It is one of Ozick's most highly acclaimed works.

experience have been as ineffective as Rosa's. In fact, by trying to blend in with other Americans and hide her own past, Stella does not even have her own heritage to rely on and draw strength from.

Like Rosa and Stella, other people have their own difficulties in dealing with the Holocaust. If Rosa is representative of one extreme (remembering to the point of obsession) and Stella represents the other (denying or ignoring the Holocaust entirely), then Ozick seems to advocate memory. Though hardly lovable, Rosa is a far more sympathetic character than the cold and critical Stella. The importance of remembering the Holocaust has been underscored in the late twentieth century and early 2000s by the rise of the Holocaust "revisionist" movement, an extreme group that denies the Holocaust ever really happened or if it did, it has been greatly exaggerated. Ozick's Rosa, stubbornly and proudly clinging to the past despite the urgings of those around her, is a defiant answer to these deniers. Though Persky advocates "a little forgetting," the more problematic question for Rosa, and for society in general, is how much forgetting is too much? At what point does forgetting become carelessness, leaving the door ajar for future persecution, for history to repeat itself? And to what extent does this forgetting devalue the suffering and

sacrifice of millions of Jews suffered and died at the hands of the Nazis?

"Rosa" and "The Shawl" not only raise these questions, they are in some small measure part of the answer. If writers and artists can create work that brings the suffering and horror of the Holocaust so sharply into focus, as these stories do while avoiding the temptation to create myth from history, they can help all people remember and understand.

Source: Laura Pryor, Critical Essay on "Rosa," in *Short Stories for Students*, Thomson Gale, 2006.

Joseph Alkana

In the following essay, Alkana explores how the form of "Rosa" and "The Shawl" issues "a challenge to conventional aesthetics, a challenge that also touches upon questions of history and theology."

For American Jewish writers, the Holocaust remains a compelling subject for fiction; and their work constitutes an ongoing reply to Theodor Adorno's famous claim "that it is barbaric to continue to write poetry after Auschwitz." The task of telling Holocaust stories has involved a recognition that beyond the fundamental value of presenting witness and survivor accounts, whether in nonfictional or fictional forms, there is value in telling more stories, particularly stories of life after Auschwitz. A work such as Art Spiegelman's *Maus* features a self-conscious narrative style that addresses this as an imperative while highlighting the sense that conventional literary forms may be inadequate to the task. Such anxiety is evident in the trajectory of American Jewish literary attitudes toward the Holocaust, and the career of Philip Roth exemplifies changing literary responses to the Holocaust.

The characteristic American Jewish response during the years following the Holocaust, when not omission, took the form of allusion in place of direct commentary. This strategy is evident in one of Roth's better known early pieces, "Defender of the Faith." In this story, the problematic status of allegiances and cohesion within a group of American Jewish soldiers is given added dramatic and moral weight by the Holocaust, the one principal event that is cited only obliquely and, at that, by a self-serving Jewish soldier in a manipulative plea for ethnic unity. Roth's work since that time has displayed more explicit and sustained interest in the Holocaust and its consequences. For example, he facilitated the American publication of Bruno Schulz and Jirí Weil, Jewish writers who remained in Europe during the Holocaust. And more recently, in *Operation Shylock,* Roth centered his reflections on identity around such related things as the Holocaust crimes trial of John Demjanjuk, an interview with Aharon Appelfeld, the Israeli writer of Holocaust novels, and the notion of "Diasporism," a bitterly comic reflection on the possibility of a Jewish to post-Holocaust Europe. Between the silences of "Defenders" and the articulations of *Shylock,* Roth offered a serious questioning of Holocaust literature in *The Ghost Writer,* which critiqued the American Jewish reception of Anne Frank's *Diary,* particularly its adaptation for the stage. The elevation to iconic status of Anne Frank by American Jews during the 1950s led Roth to suggest that through excessive sentimentality and a lack of historical consciousness Jews of that era not only failed to come to terms with the Holocaust—to the extent that such a thing is possible—but too often were relying on successes in the United States to justify their complacency after the Holocaust. Roth emblematically transforms Anne Frank into Anne Franklin as part of his satire on upper-middle-class materialism and a concomitant American exceptionalist ideology that reinforced the sense of the foreignness of the Holocaust.

> **The clearest attempt by an American fiction writer to move beyond these negative, though necessary, steps of rejecting sentimentalism and universalism and toward the development of a more complex post-Holocaust literary aesthetic is offered by Cynthia Ozick's *The Shawl*.**

Roth's satire of sentimentality about victimization and his insistence on the historical specificity of Holocaust suffering are two characteristics of much recent work on the Holocaust. The clearest attempt by an American fiction writer to move beyond these negative, though necessary, steps of rejecting sentimentalism and universalism and toward the development of a more complex post-Holocaust literary aesthetic is offered by Cynthia Ozick's *The Shawl.*

The Shawl is neither Ozick's first nor her most recent fictional reflection on the Holocaust. Earlier short pieces, such as "Bloodshed" and "The Pagan Rabbi," and her lengthy first novel, *Trust,* dramatize predicaments posed by the Holocaust and its consequences. Her most recent novels, *The Cannibal Galaxy* and *The Messiah of Stockholm,* directly treat the Holocaust as the central event in twentieth-century Jewish consciousness. *The Shawl,* a pair of related stories that appeared individually in 1980 and 1983 and were published together in 1989, resembles Ozick's other fiction insofar as it deals with a theme Ozick's crtics agree is one of her primary concerns, the tension between Jewish and non-Jewish cultures. But unlike her other writings on the Holocaust, the very form of the two stories that constitute *The Shawl* issues a challenge to conventional aesthetics, a challenge that also touches upon questions of history and of theology. The two stories of *The Shawl*, "The Shawl" and "Rosa," are presented in historical sequence: "The Shawl" describes in an elliptical, impressionistic manner the concentration camp captivity of Rosa, her perceptions of her niece, Stella, and the death of her infant daughter, Magda; "Rosa," set approximately four decades later in Miami Beach, tells of how Rosa feels radically isolated and remains preoccupied with her murdered daughter. The historical circumstances these two stories describe, the moments of crisis faced by the protagonist, and the language used to convey Rosa's character in the two stories are deeply interrelated, each feature serving to expand on and to complicate the others.

In the lengthier "Rosa," the reader is furnished with a character portrait that reveals the protagonist to be both alienated and alienating, someone who through bizarre and self-righteous judgments globally repels the sympathies of others. The early action of the story unfolds as a reflection of her character: we are introduced to Rosa Lublin, described in the first sentence as a "madwoman and a scavenger," a woman who for no apparent reason had destroyed her small used-furniture shop and moved from New York to Miami, thus becoming financially dependent on her niece. In a rare venture from her filthy room, which is cluttered with letters written in Polish to her dead daughter, whom she imagines "a professor of Greek philosophy at Columbia University," Rosa goes to a laundromat, where she meets a garrulous retired button manufacturer, Simon Persky. Rebuffing with sarcasm Persky's advances, Rosa indicates her alienation from Jewish culture and from humanity in general. Her wholesale rejection of people, even those who might be inclined to commiserate with her, may well be an understandable result of her Holocaust experiences, but it also marks her as someone with whom most people would prefer to sympathize from a distance.

By sculpting such a sharply edged protagonist, Ozick does more than create the premise for a story; she also takes a stance against a tendency that she along with other Jewish writers have found vexatious—universalism, the tendency to level human suffering under the general heading of an all-inclusive existential or theological quandary. As Ozick herself noted in an essay, when distinguishing between death camp victims,

> Those who suffered at Auschwitz suffered with an absolute equality, and the suffering of no one victimized group or individual weighs more in human anguish than that of any other victimized group or

individual. But note: Catholic Poland, for instance (language, culture, land), continues, while European Jewish civilization (language, culture, institutions) was wiped out utterly—and that, for Jewish history, is the different and still more central meaning of Auschwitz. (*Metaphor* 43)

Ozick here takes issue with the approach to Holocaust suffering that focuses on personal experience, an approach that all too readily can feed into a universalist interpretation, by choosing to highlight distinctions based on group histories. Ozick's own focus on group identity is inverted by Rosa, who continues to evade any self-definition that groups her with other Jews. Rosa thus rejects Persky's overtures, attempting to spoil his excitement at discovering that they both came from the same city by insisting, "'My Warsaw isn't your Warsaw.'" And Rosa substantiates this by proudly claiming that she knows no Yiddish, preferring instead the "most excellent literary Polish" with which she composes her letters to Magda. Rosa thereby sets herself apart as one who rejects a Yiddish-speaking Jewish identity in favor of kinship with a secularized Polish-Jewish community which "was wiped out utterly."

The remainder of "Rosa" dramatizes the difficulties created by her rejection of the living in favor of both a dead daughter and an inhospitable pre-Holocaust Polish culture. She spends her time holding off the persistent and pesky Persky, searching through the streets and the beach in a grotesquely comic manner for a pair of underwear she suspects him of stealing from her laundry and, finally, succumbing to his insistent sociality by inviting him up to her room over her newly reconnected telephone. Rosa's obsession with her underwear parallels her obsession with another garment, the shawl in which she had wrapped the infant Magda. Through much of "Rosa," she awaits the arrival of the shawl, promised to her by Stella, who accuses her of acting crazily: "You're like those people in the Middle Ages who worshiped a piece of the True Cross." Rosa's worshipful stance mirrors a fundamental predicament within Ozick's work, a dilemma she believes inevitably confronts the Jewish artist. Janet Handler Burstein summarizes the critical consensus when she observes, "Ozick's conviction that art is idolatrous for Jews announces itself in essay after essay." Ozick's vision of the Jewish artist's conflicted state parallels Rosa's obsession with her past, as indicated by the epithet with which Stella labels Rosa, "parablemaker." It is as a parable maker, one who keeps recalling the past but recalling it in an altered manner, that Rosa undertakes the problematic yet necessary task of Jewish authors who write about the Holocaust.

Although Rosa's rejection of her Jewish contemporaries and her strangely anachronistic assimilationist attitude may be troublesome from Ozick's perspective, Rosa's refusal to forget the past signifies her importance. Unlike the niece whom she ridicules for forgetfulness ("'Stella is self-indulgent. She wants to wipe out memory'") and American exceptionalism ("Stella Columbus! She thinks there's such a thing as the New World"), Rosa continually finds reminders in her surroundings: the stripes of a dress summon forth a camp uniform, and the clinically detached language of a midwestern professor researching Holocaust victims resembles dehumanizing Nazi rhetoric. When the environment fails to trigger associations, she deliberately sets out to remember. In a letter to Magda, she tells of physical privations in the Warsaw Ghetto and the loss of her secularized, urban Polish-Jewish identity, as expressed in the outrage of her family, who had affirmed Enlightenment ideals, at being treated like "these old Jew peasants worn out from their rituals and superstitions." But Rosa also fashions a new past for herself and Magda, one with which she rejects Stella's seemingly more accurate memory: "Your father was not a German.I was forced by a German, it's true, and more than once, but I was too sick to conceive. Stella has a naturally pornographic mind, she can't resist dreaming up a dirty sire for you, an S.S. man!" Rosa recalls being raped in a Nazi brothel, yet she detaches Magda from these memories, instead substituting the image of a Polish Gentile husband and father to Magda, "respectable, gentle, cultivated."

Rosa's invented lineage for Magda coupled with her monologues directed toward a fictive adult daughter denote her madness, yet they also link her to the writer's work. A writer's tendency toward obsession and madness motivates "Envy," and a more general connection between madness and the imagination may be found in "The Pagan Rabbi"; but, unlike these early Ozick stories, *The Shawl* specifies the Holocaust as the source of a disruptive yet recuperative imagination. Rosa's obstinate inventiveness certainly reflects a Holocaust survivor mentality insofar as it manifests an amalgam of guilt, shame, fear of not being believed, and an inability to accept powerlessness in the face of deadly force. As if to compensate for this powerlessness, Rosa invents, and this outrages Stella and elicits the label "parable-maker." It is the making of parables

about the Holocaust, the rules to guide or limit a post-Holocaust aesthetic, that *The Shawl* dramatizes and questions.

Ozick's critics have offered commentaries and insights on the symbolism and the ethical import of *The Shawl,* but they generally have displayed only passing interest in the aesthetic implications of juxtaposing its two stylistically dissimilar component pieces. In part this no doubt reflects the tendency in Ozick's own essays to diminish the significance of aesthetic issues in favor of the ethical. Critics have followed Ozick's lead when tracing the progress of her career from the Jamesian convolutions of her first novel, *Trust,* to her most recent works, which, despite Jamesian overtones (such as the similarly compulsive searches for manuscripts in *The Messiah of Stockholm* and "The Aspern Papers"), assert the primacy of the ethical. Alone among scholars writing on *The Shawl,* Joseph Lowin has focused on the relationship between the utterly disparate styles of its two stories, suggesting that the elaboration in "Rosa" on the sparse language of "The Shawl," which fills a mere seven pages, amounts to a midrashic commentary. Lowin's observation, however, would seem to contradict Ozick's own assertion, regarding the need to negotiate between traditional Jewish and Western Enlightenment aesthetic forms, that "Such a project cannot be answered with a proposal to 'compose *midrashim,*' by which is usually meant a literature of parable" (*Metaphor* 238). Midrashic parable, though perhaps not constitutive of *The Shawl* in the straightforward manner that Lowin suggests, does furnish the basis from which Ozick attempts to elaborate a way of telling post-Holocaust stories, of exploring the relationship between dominant Western fictional forms and this traditionally Jewish one.

The inclusion within the past decade of *midrash* among the arsenal of terms available to literary theorists has brought to the foreground the debate over definitions and descriptions of the methodologies of midrash. This debate, which like midrash itself does not lend itself to summary without loss, nevertheless yields several points useful to a discussion of the aesthetics and argument of *The Shawl.* Although it primarily concerns itself with the exegesis of sacred texts, midrashic activity frequently takes the form of fiction, especially didactic fiction. These fictions focus on textual gaps, which may be regarded in two ways. Midrash as textual exegesis attempts to render comprehensible fissured or otherwise perplexing biblical passages. A second, related function of midrash is that which brings about interpretations consistent with contemporary religious beliefs and circumstances. Thus the didactic or moralistic aspects of midrash work to cast contemporary intellectual and ethical dilemmas as extensions of tradition. This process of mediating the intellectual distances between sacred scripture and a present largely constituted by relationships with non-Jewish cultures locates for itself space within an otherwise canonically foreclosed past by identifying interpretive problems in sacred texts.

It is with the first sense of midrash in mind, the act of filling textual gaps, that Lowin discovers a midrashic quality in "Rosa," which elaborates and explains much of the earlier story. "The Shawl" provides little more than the most essential information for the construction of a narrative: the names of the three characters, descriptions without explanations of their deprivations, sketchy accounts of their journey on foot to a camp, Rosa's act of hiding the silent Magda in her shawl, and, finally, a depiction of how Magda, deprived of the shawl by Stella, comes out crying into the roll call area where a helmeted guard throws her against an electrified fence. The only dialogue reported is Stella's response to her study of Magda's face ("Aryan") and her explanation of why she took Magda's shawl ("I was cold"). The lack of explanation, the omissions in this brief story, recalls Daniel Boyarin's succinct description of midrashic exegesis: "The biblical narrative is gapped and dialogical. The role of the midrash is to fill in the gaps."

"Rosa" might be considered the equivalent of a supplementary or exegetic commentary on "The Shawl" were it not for the complexity of their relationship: "Rosa" delivers an account of a survivor's life that ultimately refutes the lesson learned from "The Shawl," seeking to displace it rather than merely elaborate on it. From the perspective suggested by the later story, "The Shawl" resembles less a primary and sacred text that needs to be interpreted than it does a potential obstacle to understanding. "The Shawl" describes how Rosa is brutalized, and to these events she reacts with a tangled set of inconsistent beliefs that include the importance of remembering history, the distortions of her own and Magda's histories, and a sense of alienation from others in her community. Rosa's feeling of alienation from other Jews did not begin with the Holocaust—"Her father, like her mother, mocked at Yiddish; there was not a particle of the ghetto left in him, not a grain of rot"—but her experiences would appear to have

reinforced it. By the conclusion of the second story, however, a shift in her attitude has appeared, one that induces Rosa to become more social and to diminish the imaginary role of her daughter in her life. The need for this final change in attitude, for this reconfiguration of "The Shawl" by "Rosa," becomes apparent when we observe that "The Shawl" *itself* appears to be a midrashic commentary on a biblical story, a midrashic commentary of the second type, one that seeks to reconcile the Bible with recent history.

The midrashic dimensions of "The Shawl" emerge upon a comparison with what Jewish commentators typically treat as the preeminent episode in Genesis, Abraham's binding of Isaac, an episode referred to among midrashic writers by the Hebrew word for *binding*, *Akedah*. The Akedah features a series of basic plot elements and symbols that are refracted through Ozick's reconfiguration in "The Shawl." The sparsely worded biblical account begins with God calling to Abraham and summoning him to travel to Moriah and, once there, to prepare Isaac for a burnt sacrifice. In contrast to, for example, his extended debate with God over the fate of Sodom and Gomorrah, Abraham responds without question to the instructions, and, accompanied by Isaac and two others, he travels for three days. He then takes Isaac alone to prepare an altar, and he binds Isaac as for a sacrifice. At this point, an angel intercedes, commanding Abraham to not harm Isaac. After Abraham sacrifices a ram, the story concludes with God's final iteration of the promise to Abraham that his descendants will be plentiful and have strength against their enemies.

The parallels between the two stories are sufficiently striking to make "The Shawl" seem like a female version of the Akedah. Each story features a parent of the same gender as the imperiled child traveling through unnamed territories, the biblical wilderness and the ironically equivalent wilderness of World War II Europe. And the children resemble each other in that both were conceived in unlikely circumstances: Isaac is born to the post-menopausal Sarah, and, as Rosa states in the second story, she thought she was "too sick to conceive." The children are greatly loved by their parents; the prominence of parental love is indicated in the Akedah by God's initial words to Abraham, in which Isaac is identified as the son "whom you love" (Genesis 22:2), coincidentally the first biblical use of the word *love*. Correspondingly, Rosa makes clear her devotion to Magda throughout both "Rosa," as her ongoing conversation with her daughter suggests, and "The Shawl," in which she hides the fifteen-month old at obvious peril to herself. In their journeys to the places where their children are threatened with death and burning, the protagonists are accompanied by companions of the same gender who are not actually present when the final actions occur. The protagonists' minimal speech is balanced against the surveillance over both sets of actors by largely silent powers with control over life and death. The binding of the two children, of Isaac in preparation for a sacrifice and of Magda with the shawl to keep her hidden and silent, furnishes each story with its name and serves as the single most prominent symbolic point at which the two stories converge.

But why should Ozick have chosen the Akedah as the occasion for a midrash? An answer to this question needs to take into account the attitude of God as it frequently has been explained by Jewish commentators. The Akedah typically has been understood to display God's abhorrence of human sacrifice and preference for spiritual dedication. In a direct commentary on the Akedah, Ozick uses this reading as the grounds for her interpretation of the episode, citing its insistence on "Judaism's first social task, so to speak. The story of Abraham and Isaac announces, in the voice of divinity itself, the end of human sacrifice forever. The binding of Isaac represents and introduces the supreme scriptural valuation of innocent life" (*Metaphor* 274).

Ozick thus interprets the Akedah as God's unambiguous rejection of human sacrifice, a rejection that reveals not merely some distinction from other deities—Ozick characteristically juxtaposes the Jewish deity against those of the Greeks—but an imperative that helps make the Akedah a defining episode. Her view of the ethical centrality of the Akedah harmonizes with the midrashic understanding that the Akedah refers not merely to Abraham but to the entire nation of Israel as well. In his remarks on the midrashic commentary *Genesis Rabbah,* Jacob Neusner summarizes the traditional attitude, asserting that "the testing of Abraham stands for the trials of Israel" (269). Abraham thus proves himself worthy of God's blessing, the promise to protect Abraham's descendants: "I will make your seed many, yes, many, like the stars of the heavens and like the sand that is on the shore at the sea; your seed shall inherit the gate of their enemies" (Genesis 22:17).

This final point creates the need for a midrash—not an exegetical midrash that seeks to bridge scriptural gaps but an attempt to resolve the tension between a biblical story and human history. The circumstances of death camp victims test God's promise to Abraham, and the deaths of children pose some of the most intense psychological and theological problems to writers on the Holocaust. Elie Wiesel's *Night,* itself largely organized around the relationship between a son and his father, presents perhaps the paradigmatic dramatic enactment of this situation when it tells of how three inmates implicated in an act of sabotage were publicly hanged. The two adult victims shouted, "'Long live liberty'" (61), and they quickly died, but the one child among them died slowly and silently. Wiesel recounts that he heard a man behind him repeatedly asking,

"Where is God now?"

And I heard a voice within me answer him:

"Where is He? Here He is—He is hanging there on this gallows. . . ." (62)

The question asked by Wiesel's fellow inmate is one implied by Ozick in "The Shawl." This question is accusatory, as is so much Holocaust writing, and in Ozick's story, which ultimately offers a different response than the one supplied by Wiesel, it takes the form of a midrashic problem because of the dramatic link between her story and that of Abraham and Isaac.

The differences between the Akedah and "The Shawl" signal Ozick's attempt to make salient the tension between sacred scripture and human history. The most consequential difference between the two stories is the nature of supreme power: in the Akedah, the power over life and death ultimately resides in God, while in the camps a human power prevails, and from this all other distinctions devolve. The sites are themselves infused with the characters of each type of power: Rosa marches to a slave labor camp, whereas Genesis identifies Abraham's destination as Mount Moriah, the future location of the Temple. The way by which the protagonists submit themselves to power reflects basic differences: although Rosa has the most limited range of choice, which she exercises in her attempt to preserve Magda, Abraham and, according to midrashic tradition, Isaac voluntarily submit to God's command. Moreover, the vastly differing conclusions characterize the two types of power: Abraham elicits words of blessing and the promise of life, while by contrast Magda dies, and Rosa, to maintain the secret of her motherhood and thus her own life, smothers a scream by stuffing the shawl into her mouth. The words of an angel direct

Abraham to spare Isaac's life, but the only sound accompanying Magda's murder by a silent guard is the incomprehensible chatter of the electric wires.

Despite the differing relationships between speech and silences (or incomprehensibility) in the two stories, silences structure the actions in both, the lapses of speech, not surprisingly, also denoting distinctive moral responses and responsibilities. Unlike Rosa's silence and secretive preservation of Magda, an enactment of her maternal devotion, Abraham's wordless acceptance of God's command signals a detachment from both his paternal bond and his relationship with Sarah, who presumably would challenge his intention. Abraham's withdrawal from his family leads Jacques Derrida to speculate that silence and secrecy are essential to our understanding of Abraham's action and *in*action: "He doesn't speak, he doesn't tell his secret to his loved ones. . . . Abraham is a witness of the absolute faith that cannot and must not witness before men. He must keep his secret." Abraham's commitment to secrecy and his silence most tellingly elides the "paradox, scandal and aporia" that Derrida locates between an ethics that would prioritize Abraham's ordinary allegiances to family and his devotion to a transcendent deity. From Derrida's perspective, the eruption of the paradoxical and the scandalous in the Akedah, which calls into question the function of morality and moral judgment, would seemingly highlight by contrast Rosa's silent preservation of Magda; for despite the question of Magda's paternity, Rosa's silence and actions coalesce in an unambiguous devotion to family that on its face comports with normative ethics. Yet when we juxtapose the silences of "The Shawl" against the speech of "Rosa," we may find, if not the aporia of the Akedah, both paradox and scandal; once again we encounter the unseemliness and impropriety of Holocaust fiction, particularly that which attempts to restore speech to the camps, a realm that its creators treated as secret.

The speech of "Rosa" fills many textual gaps left by "The Shawl," but speech also functions in its own right as an obsessional focus for Rosa, one that ultimately and ironically isolates her. Rosa treats her language as essential to her being. When she tells Persky, "My Warsaw isn't your Warsaw" and, again, "Your Warsaw isn't my Warsaw," her point is obviously less geographical or temporal than it is linguistic, cultural, and, in the final instance, constitutive of her identity. She took her cue from her parents, who eschewed Yiddish and instead "enunciated Polish in soft calm voices with the most precise

articulation." It is this memory of language that anchors Rosa in a family network, as she rhapsodizes in one of her letters to Magda: "A pleasure, the deepest pleasure, *home* bliss, to speak in our own language" (emphasis added). Now that her immediate family is gone and she lives in the United States, her Polish language remains as her home.

Rosa's sense of a linguistic home is challenged by the instrumentalist vision of language Persky reveals when conversing with Rosa in her room:

". . . this is very nice, cozy. You got a cozy place, Lublin."

"Cramped," Rosa said.

"I work from a different theory. For everything there's a bad way of describing, also a good way. You pick the good way, you get along better."

"I don't like to give myself lies," Rosa said.

"Life is short, we all got to lie."

To Persky's conventional sensibilities, what matters is getting along, and any epistemological or aesthetic orientation in language-use should at most be secondary. Hence, when describing his "loiterer" son, who is what Rosa wishes Magda to be, a philosopher, he bluntly opines, "Too much education makes fools." But Rosa the parable maker labels Persky's use of language "lies," and she resists the notion that one can find a "good way" to describe her experiences, metaphorically speaking to Persky of her three lives, "The life before, the life during, the life after." Persky, with the embarrassment of a Jew who had spent the Holocaust years in the United States, nevertheless echoes the ordinary advice give to one who has experienced loss: "it's over. . . . You went through it, now you owe yourself something." Persky here professes the wisdom of a button manufacturer, his belief that gaps exist to be spanned and veiled with cloth, an outlook he initially displays when professionally observing a missing button at Rosa's waist: "A shame. That kind's hard to match, as far as I'm concerned we stopped making them around a dozen years ago."

Despite his commonplace advice to the obsessed Rosa, Persky seems attracted to Rosa's display of a loss for which no compensation is available; if Persky cannot answer Rosa's demand for a wisdom or a language commensurate with her loss, then what he offers is relationship. Relationship is paramount to Rosa's idea of a "mother tongue" that connects her to a literary tradition ("For literature you need a mother tongue") and that also, and more significantly, forms the basis of her "home bliss," her bond not only to her parents but to the language that constitutes her own ongoing sense of motherhood and being. Her roomful of letters to Magda in a "lost and kidnapped Polish" would bond her with Stella as well, "but her niece had forgotten Polish." Rosa's fervor for her language isolates her and structures the devotional posture Stella criticizes as idolatrous; yet her fantasy of Magda as a professor at *Columbia* University, which approximates the epithet "Stella Columbus," brings these two relatives into at least a lexical relationship. The tension between Magda and Stella, a competition that began even before Stella took Magda's shawl in the camp, is suggestive of Rosa's inevitably fractured worldview.

The most basic of Rosa's contradictions is between her private idolatry and her public role as an idol breaker. Rosa's foremost public act, her moment of American fame, was, according to newspaper headlines, as the destroyer of her second-hand furniture store: "WOMAN AXES OWN BIZ." Rosa's bizarre action remains unexplained until late in the narrative when she recalls in a letter to Magda some of the humiliations and privations of everyday ghetto life, experiences she had tried to relate to uncomprehending or unsympathetic customers. As she ruefully remarks, even when she tried to pare down the enormity of her loss to some particular item, "no one understood." The customers "were in a hurry," too great a hurry to hear of her history and, presumably, too averse to the painful stories of an obsessed woman. Her destruction of the items within her shop would serve to enact her criticism of their misplaced attention; more pointedly yet, her destruction of her own store is a mute critique of the American iconization of business.

In her role as a destroyer of American icons, Rosa once more recalls Abraham, specifically the Abraham of midrashic stories who had to depart his homeland after smashing the idols in his father's shop. Rosa's rescue and subsequent emigration to the United States may not quite parallel Abraham's leave-taking from home nor his destination, but her willingness to mark herself as an outcast by wrecking things and images that others prize, but which she considers meaningless diversions, complicates Stella's accusation that Rosa is an idol worshipper. This complication serves to thematize a pair of related problems entailed by the worship of lifeless things (whether physical objects or language itself). First, the silence of idols demands explanatory speech, such as Abraham's provocative story to his father that the idols had destroyed one another or Rosa's own provocations,

her making of parables. And second, an isolating engagement with something that cannot reply, like the shawl, may displace dialogue with those who can. The dramatizations and structurings of silences, unanswered speech, and interpretive elaborations in *The Shawl* link it to another text that considers the Akedah: Erich Auerbach's comparison of Hebraic with Hellenic modes of literary representation in the opening chapter of *Mimesis.*

The relationship between the need for textual interpretation and the Akedah has been prominent to literary theorists since Auerbach chose the Akedah as his representative biblical text, a choice that seems as deliberate as Ozick's when we recall that he wrote *Mimesis* between 1942 and 1945 while at the Turkish State University at Istanbul. (In 1935 Auerbach had been forced to leave his professorship at the University of Marburg as a result of Aryanization policies and the Nuremberg laws.) Most relevant to the coincidental choice of biblical texts are questions about interpretation and the Akedah, and the relationship of Ozick's ideas about aesthetics with Auerbach's. In his comparison between the relative clarity of the Homeric and the biblical, which in its textual sparseness relies on a dense background of motivation and history, Auerbach insists that radically differing modes of interpretation, and thus cognition, are both assumed and demanded; and this insistence entails for Auerbach—as for Ozick—extensive ethical and political consequences.

These consequences result from the particular method by which the biblical works to intrude on its readers' lives: it attempts to propel itself, through mediating interpretive processes, into the historical realm. By contrast, the Homeric, characterized by a "procession of phenomena [that] takes place in the foreground," a "legendary" style, and static, unvarying characters, assumes a uniformity of explicative strategies and an ideal of hierarchical social stasis, the latter understood to reflect an immutable underlying order resistant to historical change. When confronted with the Homeric, the job of the critic is to analyze, for Homer presents "no teaching"; and because there is no underlying stratum, "he cannot be interpreted." The danger of the Homeric, with its implied rejection of historical complexity, leads Auerbach to ask his reader to "think of the history which we ourselves are witnessing; anyone who, for example, evaluates the behavior of individual men and groups of men at the time of the rise of National Socialism in Germany" will understand how ahistorical legend defies the complexities of history; Auerbach feels no need to elaborate on the problems that such simplifications entail. Although the more historically oriented Hebrew writings also lend themselves at times to such simplification, for the most part they demand a more complex interpretive mode, one outlined in Auerbach's essay "'Figura.'"

In "'Figura,'" first published in 1944, Auerbach conveys the sense of crisis over National Socialism that pervades *Mimesis.* "'Figura'" elaborates on the interpretive processes briefly described in the opening of *Mimesis,* and Auerbach here identifies interpretation as a site where history, ethics, and aesthetics intersect. Figural interpretation, unlike the "symbolic" interpretations be associates with "magic power," "must always be historical" (57). The historical dimension of figural interpretation derives from its method: "Figural interpretation establishes a connection between two events or persons, the first of which signifies not only itself but also the second, while the second encompasses or fulfills the first. The two poles of the figure are separate in time, but both, being real events or figures, are within time, within the stream of historical life" (53). As Geoffrey Green points out, Auerbach's insistence on historically oriented interpretation serves his refutation of Nazi mysticism and aestheticism in both a direct manner and in an indirect one as well. Auerbach painstakingly describes in "'Figura'" the development of the historicized figural method as a foundation for Christian interpretation and theology. Without commenting on the analogies with certain midrashic interpretative methods, he effectively tethers the Christian to the Jewish as he attempts to drive a theoretical wedge between Nazism and Christianity.

When Auerbach affixes Christian to Jewish interpretive traditions, we confront the distance of four decades that separates his from Ozick's work; the crisis of survival facing Auerbach, and thus the need to cultivate potential allies by stressing the cultural affinities of Christians and Jews while casting Nazism as essentially anti-Christian, no longer has relevance. Contemporary American Jewish writers accordingly tend to stress the complicity of Christianity with Nazism rather than seek distinctions. This sort of pointed assessment may be found in one of Ozick's essays, "Of Christian Heroism," which distinguishes between heroic rescuers of Holocaust victims, victimizers, the victims themselves, and the bystanders who, "taken together," she judges to be "culpable" (*Fame and Folly,* 201). Attention to such distinctions is typical of Ozick as an essayist who prizes clarity and moral judgment, yet Ozick's fiction reveals greater tension and

ambiguity, as in her presentation of Rosa as simultaneously an idolater and an iconoclast. This kind of ambiguity, which suggests a continuity between her reasoning and Auerbach's coupling of the Christian with the Jewish, pervades *The Shawl* from its opening pages.

The Shawl begins with an epigraph taken from Paul Celan's "Todesfuge": *"dein goldenes Haar Margarete / dein aschenes Haar Sulamith."* Celan's Holocaust poem uses these two phrases as a kind of refrain; he routinely returns to the distinction between the Jews and the Germans with his apostrophic lines, "your golden hair Margarete" and "your ashen hair Shulamith" (Celan 63). The distinction between Margarete and Shulamith, between the golden and the ashen, appears to be an odd one for Ozick to emphasize, for, while both Celan's poem and her story respond to the Holocaust, she blurs Celan's distinction. Blue-eyed Magda, whom Rosa addresses in her letters as "my gold," "my yellow lioness," is the subject of Rosa's and Stella's scrutiny during their forced march in "The Shawl"; and Stella, with an observation that sets Magda apart, calls her "Aryan," adjudicating Magda's status based on her presumptive paternity. Rosa obviously rejects Stella's desire to make the kind of exclusionary racial appraisal that replicates those of the Nazis, and her own steadfastness toward Magda points out a different irony, the fact that Judaic matrilineal law would lead both Jews and Nazis to recognize the golden, blue-eyed Magda as a Jew. Thus Celan's distinction between the golden and the ashen is effaced by Ozick in a move that suggests her valuing of categorical purity or distinctions operates, like Auerbach's, as a secondary element of some larger strategy.

Ozick's stories may offer a greater degree of aesthetic complexity than the stark dichotomy outlined in Celan's brief poem, yet this should not obscure her skepticism toward aestheticist demands, a skepticism as profound as Auerbach's. Auerbach's distrust of aestheticism pervades his historicist, philological methodology, while Ozick's repeatedly emerges in her essays. Her position is apparent, for example, in her 1970 criticism of contemporary fictional trends, as opposed to the tradition of the densely historical nineteenth-century novel whose ethical concerns she more clearly values: "Now it is the novel that has been aestheticized, poeticized, and thereby paganized. . . . The most flagrant point is this: the nineteenth-century novel has been declared dead" (*Art* 164). For both Ozick and Auerbach, the turn toward historical understanding is primary, and the story of the binding of Isaac provides the two with an occasion to raise questions about interpretation and to affirm an ethical imperative: a rejection of appeals to higher authorities and causes that diminish the quotidian world of human sociality and history. In a discussion of the Holocaust, Ozick declared "that Nazism was an *aesthetic* idea. . . . Let us have a beautiful and harmonious society, said the aesthetics of Nazism; let us get rid of this ugly dark spot, the Jew, the smear on the surface of our glorious dream. Do we not know the meaning of aesthetic gratification?" ("Roundtable" 280). The price of aesthetic consistency that Ozick raises in this question is the issue central to *The Shawl* and Ozick's Holocaust literary aesthetics.

Ozick's Holocaust literature has thematized invariably unsuccessful attempts at accommodating cultural fissures. Joseph Brill's "dual curriculum" in *The Cannibal Galaxy,* a juxtaposition of Jewish and European classics, and Lars Andemening's attempt in *The Messiah of Stockholm* to retrieve a manuscript lost during the Holocaust—gestures aimed at relieving the historical and cultural tensions either deepened or precipitated by the Holocaust—are, in Ozick's fictions, doomed. The midrashic dimensions of *The Shawl,* by contrast, convey inescapable and irreconcilable tensions. "The Shawl," with its retelling of the Akedah in a world where no angel arrives to save the child, presents a story understood by its protagonist as a model for human relations, a story that overshadows the original biblical promise of rescue and life. Rosa is left with nothing but contempt and anger toward the living, an alienation that by the conclusion of the second story begins to yield. "Rosa" thus attempts a midrashic displacement of "The Shawl," just as "The Shawl" had rewritten the Akedah; and, in so doing, "Rosa" restores the primacy of the Akedah. But this restoration does not blot out the memories of "The Shawl." Rather, as Rosa's mental image of Magda recedes yet does not disappear when she accepts Persky's visit at the conclusion, the memories of Holocaust deaths do not disappear, nor can they simply be assimilated into life afterwards.

This failure to assimilate Holocaust experiences into the everyday serves as a defense against Adorno's challenge to a post-Holocaust literary aesthetic. If fiction may properly operate in a kind of productive tension with history, then the central fantasy of "Rosa," her ongoing relationship with her dead daughter, may be understood to preserve the memory and experience that history or the well-meaning, therapeutic sociality of a Simon Persky could well occlude. The ending of *The Shawl* sees Rosa reunited with the magical shawl that brings with it the memory of Magda, allowing Magda briefly to live again within Rosa's altered memory. Rosa's defiance of her own history is hardly unique to Holocaust literature. In Jirí Weil's *Life With a Star,* the narrator routinely addresses his lover, a woman whose death was truimphantly announced over loudspeakers in Prague. And still more similar to *The Shawl* is Sandra Brand's account of survival that concludes, after her arrival in the United States, "For me, my child has remained alive. He is with me whenever I want him. . . . 'Bruno, you are the only child I have ever had,' I murmur fiercely to a little boy that only I can see. 'Nothing can come between us any more!'" The line of demarcation between the living and the dead appears in such accounts to soften momentarily, but the limits of language and literature to compensate for loss remain intact. In Primo Levi's words, "the injury cannot be healed."

If the promise of healing is compromised by the almost inevitable accompaniment of sentimentality—"to give myself lies," as Rosa might put it—nevertheless as a nonremedial intervention may plausibly constitute a central feature of a post-Holocaust aesthetic. In *The Shawl,* the preservation of invention and parable is maintained despite a wariness toward universalizing myth and the dangers of emotional appeals. Notwithstanding the ways that personal experience might be sacrificed by attention to common history, the most efficacious gesture remains the return to the historical and social realm advised by Auerbach and enacted with difficulty by Rosa. The return to the social and historical as well as the desire to preserve personal experience may furnish the clearest intellectual response to the Holocaust, but it is Rosa's posture of wariness that may prove most telling. Derrida's discussion of the Akedah, a discussion that more than once slides into the topic of the Holocaust, begins by referring to Kierkegaard's *Fear and Trembling;* Derrida observes that the trembling associated with the Akedah "suggests that violence is going to break out again" (54). The unpredictability of the Akedah is its salient feature here: the fantastic and unprecedented directive to Abraham with its implied threat comes against all rational expectation and without warning (as does the timely angelic intercession and appearance of the ram); similarly, it is not unreasonable to adduce from experience that the more general threat of political, possibly genocidal, violence may apparently diminish but persists in the world. For the traumatized Rosa, who, when faced with an uncooperative hotel manager, summons forth the accusation, "Finkelstein, you S. S., admit it!," the Holocaust remains a paradigmatic experience. Yet the excesses of her interpretations and responses to the world, her avoidances and distortions of reality, call into question the uses of rather than the need for her Holocaust. remembrances.

The issue facing Rosa is one that, in a somewhat attenuated form, faces those in the United States who attempt to memorialize the Holocaust: how does one build museums, commemorative structures, or archives without turning away from the present moment? In the case of narrative structures, a turning away from the present generally devolves into the kind of sentimentality and universalist interpretations that have accompanied Anne Frank's story. Obverse to these evasions are such moments as the confrontation in *Operation Shylock* between Roth's ghostly cousin Apter, a Holocaust survivor, with an extraordinarily difficult person: "Cousin Philip, I understood what I was up against. I said to her, 'Madam, which camp?' 'All of them!' she cried, and then she spat in my face." The fury she broadcasts, like Rosa's, may be understandable, but her unsocial behavior renders her less than the ideal victim, one who should be ennobled by suffering. The "useless violence" of the Holocaust analyzed by Primo Levi or what Emmanuel Levinas has termed "the paradigm of gratuitous suffering" (162) may not generate sympathetic victims receptive to Persky's prescription of conventionality; yet it is interesting to note how Persky's intercession dramatizes the interpersonal focus of Levinas, for whom the interpersonal in ethics has a philosophical and metaphysical priority.

The measured advocacy of the interpersonal realm offered in *The Shawl* comports with Ozick's characterization elsewhere of the Jewish "Lord of History" (*Metaphor* 253), yet it presents less a developed ethical or theological position than it does the grounds for an aesthetic tension. While Ozick the essayist is quite ready to argue forcefully in favor of or against artistic and social agendas, her fiction, particularly *The Shawl,* maintains greater equanimity. Such balance is, of course, not suggested by Rosa's definitions of her life in terms of dichotomies: either Magda or Stella, either the assimilationist view of her parents or the separation of Yiddish speaking or Zionist Jews, either full speech in her language or a partial, circumscribed, inadequate English. Like the logic of God's initial directive in the Akedah, which presents Abraham with a stark choice of allegiances, Rosa's logic has

remained exclusionary, reminiscent of those times the Holocaust has been sentimentalized or memorialized in opposition to a present historical moment. But Rosa's uneasy acquiescence to sociality, as suggested by her concluding decisions to restore her telephone and to invite Persky to her room in which the ghostly presence of Magda remains, reveals a departure from her either/or mentality, a departure for which fidelity to Holocaust experience does not necessarily overwhelm sociality. Like the angelic intercession of the Akedah, which preserves Abraham's metaphysical and familial allegiances. *The Shawl* maintains the two basic categories as defined by the moments of the two constituent stories. Yet the irreconcilable tensions of *The Shawl* reinforce Primo Levi's insistence that there are wounds without the promise of healing, experiences without the offer of positive significance. Those who seek such a positive significance reveal their own desire for a happy ending more than anything else, for unlike acts of martyrdom or victimizing, either of which reveals moral choice, there is no moral stance implicit in being a victim.

Source: Joseph Alkana, "'Do We Not Know the Meaning of Aesthethic Gratification?': Cynthia Ozick's 'The Shawl,' the Akedah, and the Ethics of Holocaust Literary Aesthetics," in *Modern Fiction Studies*, Vol. 43, No. 4, 1997, pp. 963–90.

Rachel Hadas

In the following review, Hadas praises how Ozick "sets before us a world of eloquent excursions and crisp choices."

Randall Jarrell once commented that the poems of the anthologist (and poet) Oscar Williams had the air of having been written on a typewriter by a typewriter. Update the technology, and you get a fair description of the ambience of Umberto Eco's large new book, *Foucault's Pendulum.* Described on the jacket as a novel, *Foucault's Pendulum,* which is really closer to a catalogue, compendium, or anatomy than it is to any form of fiction, often seems to have been written on a computer by a computer. Oscar Williams was presumably wounded by the comparison of his sensibility to a typewriter. Eco's response, I suspect, would be a knowing wink or a weary shrug, to the effect of "Yes—so?" Even if the book's slickly mechanical surface isn't the whole point, I seem to hear Eco saying, this text's texture is at least its *point d'appui*—certainly it's nothing to reproach me with.

Indeed. If intentionality still holds—if any effect, however disheartening, is laudable so long as it's what the author was aiming for—then presumably there's nothing wrong with the almost remorselessly contrived, anticlimactic air of the whole enterprise. *Almost* but not quite remorselessly; moving moments do occur in this colossal *jeu d'esprit,* but they are simply outweighed by the not very buoyant mass of Eco's encyclopedic erudition.

Schematically cluttered and chaotically schematic, *Foucault's Pendulum* is an exhausting, exhaustive, and vastly knowing book. A magpie's nest of arcana, a beaver-dam of bricolage, a Rosetta Stone of the conspiratorial and the occult—these and many other comparisons suggest themselves in lieu of plot summary. In fact there is no need to come up with evocations, for the book teems with self-description. Few novels are so packed with phrases each of which could serve as an epigraph to the whole. Here are three among many more:

> Whenever a poet or preacher, chief or wizard spouts gibberish, the human race spends centuries deciphering the message.

> I have come to believe that the whole world is an enigma, a harmless enigma that is made terrible by our own mad attempt to interpret it as though it had an underlying truth.

> There is no image that, combined with others, does not embody a mystery of the world.

But there's little fun to be had in unravelling work that is so unashamedly self-conscious to start with that it seems to have provided the reader with a figure at once explanatory and admonitory for connecting the dots. Merely follow through the connections, according to *Foucault's Pendulum,* and the resulting spiderweb of lines will inevitably mean something, will get you somewhere. The one heroic gesture in the novel is of the *gran rifiuto* variety: the dangerous admission that there is no meaning:

> I have understood. And the certainty that there is nothing to understand should be my peace, my triumph. But I am here, and They are looking for me, thinking I possess the revelation They sordidly desire.

The sinister They of the above passage could be construed as the fat collective spider in the web of meanings in which Eco's hapless heroes get caught. Alison Lurie has noted that deconstructionist critics often give the impression that their authors "are flies struggling in the sticky verbal strands of theoretical discourse."

Dubious or dangerous as they may be, the pleasures of knowing (and of being knowing), of laying bare preexisting but hitherto undeciphered connections, of wandering in a web of signs, are what *Foucault's Pendulum* is all about. These

> "Ozick's tributes to the power of the word are etched by the force of her own artistry. Even so, we may pay for the distilled poetic force of *The Shawl* in the coin of human sympathy."

actions are performed by its heroes, the editors Casaubon (one recalls the scholar of that name, and his unfinished *Key to All Mythologies,* in *Middlemarch*), Diotallevi, and Belbo; they are also mimetically performed by Eco's reader. As the editors become engulfed in their project, tracing a web whose filaments extend in time and space from Templars through Rosicrucians to the *Protocols of the Elders of Zion,* from the pyramids to the Eiffel Tower, and so on *ad nauseam,* so too the reader is drawn—ought one to write "strung"?—along.

When Eco bothers to write like a novelist, the narrative has its memorable moments, spiced with suspense or even feeling. Almost all these moments occur either very early or very late in the novel, at the point of entry into the maze or at the *cul de sac* of the labyrinth. The bulk of the book, detailing the serpentine meanderings of data, has a harsh, disembodiedly donnish humor but is disastrously deficient in human feeling. Eco only sporadically remembers to animate his characters at all in terms of any sentiment other than their consuming obsession with The Plan. Whether, then, we are looking for feeling between one character and another, between author and characters, or between author/characters and ourselves, most of *Foucault's Pendulum* will frustrate our naive request.

The Name of the Rose, Eco's 1983 novel, tempered its arcane excesses with memorable characters, a good suspenseful plot, and an overall thematic appropriateness of mode to matter. If Eco was liable to divagate into lengthy lectures, descriptions, and speculations, well, it seemed natural for William to instruct Adso in politics, or for Ubertino to discourse on theology. As well as continually educating the reader, all these voices (and there are many more in *The Name of the Rose* than

I mention here) throw a varied novelistic light on their own speakers, giving characters richness and depth. *The Name of the Rose* is Tolstoyan in its many-sidedness and humanity compared to *Foucault's Pendulum,* a book even longer, more packed with words, but where human talk is severely subordinated to reading, or deciphering, what has been encoded, word-processed, erased, hidden. This is a book not about voices but about writing; it might have been written to order as an illustration of the kind of poststructuralist emphasis on the *scriptible* discussed by Terry Eagleton in his *Literary Theory: An Introduction.* Eagleton writes:

> the 'living voice' is in fact quite as material as print . . . since spoken signs, like written ones, work only by a process of difference and division, speaking could be just as much said to be a form of writing as writing is a second-hand form of speaking.

> Just as Western philosophy has been 'phonocentric,' centered on the 'living voice' and deeply suspicious of script, so also it has been in a broader sense 'logocentric,' committed to a belief in some ultimate 'word,' presence, essence, truth or reality which will act as the foundation of all our thought, language and experience. It has yearned for the sign which will give meaning to all others—the 'transcendental signifier'—and for the anchoring, unquestionable meaning to which all our signs can be seen to point . . .

> That any such transcendent meaning is a fiction—though perhaps a necessary fiction—is one consequence of the theory of language I have outlined.

Perhaps *Foucault's Pendulum,* whether or not it is necessary, is itself a fictional consequence of deconstructionism: a curious, rebarbative, talky specimen of the Novel of Ideas.

In the absence of any transcendent sign, meaning refuses to stand still and be understood; restlessness prevails. I found I could bear to read *Foucault's Pendulum* only in short snatches, and preferably if I was in motion—pedaling away on the stationary bike at the health club, for example. People on either side of me were plugged into their Walkmans, but I, on a high cultural plateau, could read about Casaubon searching Belbo's computer files, or the secret role of the Rosicrucians in the writing of Shakespeare's plays. The passages that inspired me to dog-ear pages (pedaling all the while) never had anything to do with action; they were clever, paradoxical comments on the irresistible, frantic, doomed search for meaning.

In the midst of all this self-consciousness, an element of shoulder-shrugging, of not quite concealed indifference, came to predominate. Perhaps it was all those hours on the bike (though for the figure to be really apt the bike would have to be a treadmill) that prompted the image of a squirrel rapidly shuffling through a pile of leaves in search of a buried nut. I was the squirrel; so was any reader of *Foucault's Pendulum;* so were Casaubon and Belbo. The squirrel is well fed and glossy, if not positively overweight; its search is sheerly reflexive, instinctive on the one hand and increasingly halfhearted on the other. In the midst of its scrabbling, it slows down, pauses, and seems to forget what all the hustle and bustle was about. No real appetite impelled it anyway. No real hunger kept me reading this novel—habit, or reflex, had to take the place of appetite, and habit soon flagged. The nuggets I found were dwarfed by the enormous amount of verbal baggage the book carries around—baggage which began by being predictable and soon became something more aggressive, a series of insistent pokes from an incorrigible monologuer who knows perfectly well that his listeners long to escape. For deconstructionists, says Eagleton, literature "testifies to the impossibility of language's ever doing more than talk about its own failure, like some barroom bore." The innumerable decodings, rewritings, and revisions in *Foucault's Pendulum* come to have something of this deadly inevitability, as does the plot. If I had the courage of my postmodern impulses, if I could really give rein to discontinuity instead of merely pedalling at it, then I could read Eco's book every which way, back to front, upside down, and find designs everywhere. My expectations were too staid, and they were frustrated.

Cynthia Ozick's *The Shawl,* on the other hand, is a work (really a single work, though strictly speaking it consists of a story and a novella) that not only can but must be read at a sitting. I read it sitting still in an armchair at home, with tears running down my face. I didn't feel irked or overburdened by learned clutter; I felt pity, grief, and gratitude. Is Aristotle suddenly hovering in the vicinity? Ozick isn't precisely writing tragedy; for one thing, there are very funny moments in *The Shawl.* (Eco's shaggy-dog sarcasm is cut off from extremes of laughter and tears; it provokes a snicker.) What is classical is the elegant shape of this little novel, in which Ozick sets before us a world of eloquent excursions and crisp choices. Both "The Shawl" and its longer sequel, "Rosa," could be said to be located in hell, but it is a hell ordered by the writer's art. Ozick is everywhere sparing of detail—to luminous effect. As Rosa sees her child tossed at the barbed wire in the camp, the scene is rendered with meticulous cubism: urgent, inevitable, fragmented, and rapid at once.

Far off, very far, Magda leaned across her air-fed belly, reaching out with the rods of her arms. She was high up, elevated, riding someone's shoulder. But the shoulder that carried Magda was not coming toward Rosa and the shawl, it was drifting away, the speck of Magda moving more and more into the smoky distance. Above the shoulder, a helmet glinted. The light below tapped the helmet and sparkled it into a goblet. Below the helmet a black body like a domino and a pair of black boots hurled themselves in the direction of the electrified fence.

In these two stories there is only this one death, a death not even quite seen or described. There is one shawl, first the starving baby's pacifier, then, for the surviving mother, a talisman. Eco wold weave a dozen shawls into a shroud of Turin which he would then painstakingly and predictably expose as a fake. Nothing in the world of *The Shawl* is breathlessly catalogued, only to be tossed onto the scrapheap of history. The baby Magda has been tossed against the fence, but even this life and death are not lost on or for the hoarding survivor Rosa, who writes Magda, now a full-grown and beautiful ghost, long letters in Polish.

Letters are to *The Shawl* as The Plan is to *Foucault's Pendulum;* both works concern written records rather than lived lives, or texts rather than voices. Rosa's past suffering has almost destroyed her, whereas Casaubon and his friends can be said to have sought out their own suffering; but in both works a single character seems to embody the life force, urging the preoccupicd philosopher out of his or her obsession with the irrecoverable past. Nubile and warmhearted Lia, Casaubon's girlfriend and the mother of his child, disappears from Eco's novel for a long stretch; Cordelia-like, she seems to signify by her eclipse that the forces of evil are triumphing. Lia's odd analogue in *The Shawl* is Simon Persky, the kind old man who befriends Rosa in the laundromat, offers her tea, advises her not to live in the past. In Ozick's bright tragedy or dark comedy, it is Persky who may prevail; the ghost of Magda shyly flees this presence of the present. In Eco's compendium, Lia and the baby would appear to be the losers: Casaubon is, or thinks he is, doomed by The Plan.

In its miniature manner, *The Shawl* is as much a museum as Eco's hypertrophied catalogue. Ozick's central icon is the shawl itself, but surrounding this fetish are various kinds of writing: letters from the inimitable James W. Tree, Ph.D., of the Department of Clinical-Social Pathology, University of Kansas-Iowa; and finally Rosa's letters to Magda. Writing to her dead daughter is a daily ceremony for Rosa; it can be no accident that some of

Ozick's most beautiful and penetrating prose is devoted to the uncanny power of writing.

> What a curiosity it was to hold a pen—nothing but a small pointed stick, after all, oozing its hieroglyphic puddles: a pen that speaks, miraculously, Polish. A lock removed from the tongue. Otherwise the tongue is chained to the teeth and the palate. An immersion into the living language: all at once this cleanliness, this capacity, this power to make a history, to tell, to explain. To retrieve, to reprieve! To lie.

Eco too is eloquent on the mysterious luminosity of "the secret cipher [where] everything was the hieroglyph of something else." But because in *Foucault's Pendulum* he lacks or spurns the novelist's gift for grounding ideas in a human context, his weary *aperçus* remain disembodied and detachable as aphorisms. Ozick's tributes to the power of the word are etched by the force of her own artistry. Even so, we may pay for the distilled poetic force of *The Shawl* in the coin of human sympathy. Except for Persky, all the characters are tinged with a glow of hell-fire: the "sodomists" on the night beach, thc rcd-wigged hotel manager, "the black Cuban receptionist" who sits "maneuvering clayey sweat balls up from the naked place between her breasts with two fingers." Rosa, herself grotesque, sees grotesquerie everywhere, and nowhere more than in the ineffable epistles of James W. Tree, Ph.D., of the Department of Clinical-Social Pathology, University of Kansas-Iowa. Studying survivors, Dr. Tree hopes

> . . . that you would not object to joining our study by means of an in-depth interview to be conducted by me at, if it is not inconvenient, your home. I should like to observe survivor syndroming within the natural setting.

One wants to cheer Rosa's ritual response.

> With these university letters Rosa had a routine: she carried the scissors over to the toilet bowl and snipped little bits of paper and flushed. In the bowl going down, the paper squares whirled like wedding rice.

This particular letter, however, is singled out for special treatment; Rosa burns it, and then turns to what is in a way a corresponding ritual, writing

> the first letter of the day to her daughter, her healthy daughter . . . her daughter who was a professor of Greek philosophy at Columbia University . . .

This letter, which occasions Rosa's meditation on the power of the pen, also has a telling reference to Rosa's own mother's Polish, which was "very dense. You had to open it like a fan to get at all the meanings." *The Shawl* does in fact rather resemble a furled fan, all contained pattern, condensed suggestion, graceful potential. Eco, representing a different tradition of modernist fiction, gustily flaps his bulging catalogues. The opposing narrative strategies of these two works make their powers to move us, even to amuse us, vastly incommensurate: in sheer affective force, the light shawl outweighs the massy pendulum. There is, nevertheless, a way in which both works feel belated, nostalgic, postmodern, if one sense of postmodernism is that meaning is something that belongs to the past, something to which, in the absence of the original owner, we have only confused and disputed squatter's rights. Both Ozick and Eco show how fiercely possessive, how idolatrous we can become, clasping tatters to our chests like precious heirlooms, like maps of buried treasure, like shawls.

Source: Rachel Hadas, "Text and Stories," in *Partisan Review*, Summer 1991, pp. 579–85.

Bruce Bawer

In the following review, Bawer praises Ozick's portrayal of Rosa, saying she "succeeds stunninngly in bringing this tragic, demented woman to life."

"To be Jewish," Cynthia Ozick once told a *Paris Review* interviewer, "is to be a member of a civilization—a civilization with a long, long history, a history that is, in one way of viewing it, a procession of ideas." Few figures in American letters have struggled to swell the ranks of that procession as visibly as have Ms. Ozick and her fellow novelist Saul Bellow. For Ms. Ozick and Mr. Bellow are not only authors but intellectuals, intensely engaged with weighty social, moral and metaphysical questions.

Both could be justly faulted, however, for being rather too preoccupied with intellectual matters for their own good—or, to be specific, for the good of their fiction. Their characters almost invariably are highbrows, their narratives habitually crowded with heady abstractions. Both are better at making a reader think than at making him feel; both often appear to be more interested in philosophizing about a story than in bringing it to life. "I believe unashamedly," Ms. Ozick has said, "that writers are the most (maybe the only) interesting people." Not infrequently, alas, one has the impression that both writers find only themselves interesting.

Yet both have chosen, in newly published books of fiction, to treat a subject remote from their own experience: the life of Polish Holocaust survivor in America. In the hands of such cerebral, egotistic, and less-than-diffident writers, this might seem a treacherous topic. Fortunately, however,

Ms. Ozick and Mr. Bellow have approached their momentous common theme with considerable circumspection. As if to reflect this stance, both volumes are exceedingly modest in scale.

Ms. Ozick's book, *The Shawl*, consists of two related stories that were published in *The New Yorker* in the early '80s. The first, the taut, harrowing "The Shawl," depicts the incidents leading to the concentration-camp death of Rosa Lublin's baby, whom she has kept hidden in a shawl. In "Rosa" she appears 30 years later—solitary, mad and dwelling in a Miami residential hotel for the elderly. Ms. Ozick does a splendid job of conveying the hotel's atmosphere: It's less a place to live than a waiting room for death. And indeed, though her niece urges her to forget the past and go on with life, Rosa's constant refrain is that she doesn't have a life: "Thieves took it."

Yet Ms. Ozick succeeds stunningly in bringing this tragic, demented woman to life. One reason is that Ms. Ozick doesn't render Rosa as an unimpeachable icon of suffering; on the contrary, Rosa is an intellectual snob whose outrage over the Holocaust centers largely on the fact that it reduced her delicate, poetry-writing mother and her distinguished bank-director father ("who knew nearly the first half of the *Aeneid* by heart") to the level of "teeming Mockowiczes and Rabinowiczes and Perskys and Finkelsteins, with all their bad-smelling grandfathers and their hordes of feeble children!" Beautiful and harrowing, these stories are a masterly achievement.

Mr. Bellow's *The Bellarosa Connection* is, like *The Shawl*, concerned with survival and memory. The narrator heads the Mnemosyne Institute, a Philadelphia school for mnemonic techniques. "Memory is Life," he says, and the story he tells concerns his memories of his late friend Harry Fonstein. Fonstein was saved from the Holocaust through the capricious long-distance intervention of Billy Rose, the flamboyant Broadway producer, whose name he heard as "Bellarosa" and whom, after coming to America and making good, he vainly attempted to meet and thank.

A preposterous situation? Yes. And that's Mr. Bellow's point: How is one to find existence anything but absurd when an impulsive act by a ludicrous showbiz figure can mean the difference between life and death? Like Rosa's niece, the narrator counsels forgetting: "First those people murdered you, then they forced you to brood on their crimes .... Forget it. Go America. Work at your business." But Fonstein cannot forget.

This story is elegantly shaped and compellingly told. But Mr. Bellow shows the too little, tells too much. Fonstein and Rose barely exist except as excuses for him to touch upon pet themes and to pontificate about such things as "the ground bass of brutality, without which no human music is ever performed." Yes, he keeps Rose mostly offstage for a reason: He wants him to remain mythical, as concealed from us as from Fonstein. But the effectiveness of all this depends largely on whether the reader is as captivated as Mr. Bellow is by flashy gangsterish types like Rose.

Too much of this book, moreover, strikes one as artificial. Mr. Bellow's chief device for underscoring the memory theme—the Mnemosyne Institute—never seems anything but a slick contrivance. And the story itself sometimes feels overly schematic, its contours and denouement a bit too glibly reminiscent of previous Bellow fictions, especially *Seize the Day* and *Humboldt's Gift*. Though it is, then, in many ways, a testament to its author's deep intelligence and moral seriousness, *The Bellarosa Connection* ultimately lacks both the passion and the compassion of *The Shawl*.

Source: Bruce Bawer, "Change of Pace for a Pair of Heavyweights," in *Wall Street Journal*, September 29, 1989, Leisure & Arts sec., p. 1.

Sources

Bawer, Bruce, "Bookshelf: Change of Pace for a Pair of Heavyweights," in *Wall Street Journal*, September 29, 1989.

Halperin, Irving, Review of *The Shawl*, in Commonweal, December 15, 1989, pp. 711–12.

Ozick, Cynthia, "Rosa," in *The Shawl*, in Vintage International, 1990, pp. 14–70.

Prose, Francine, Review of *The Shawl*, in *New York Times Book Review*, September 10, 1989 .

Stavans, Ilan, Review of *The Puttermesser Papers*, in *Times Literary Supplement*, July 16, 1999.

Sutherland, John, Review of *Quarrel and Quandary*, in *New York Times Book Review*, October 8, 2000.

Further Reading

Frankl, Viktor E., *Man's Search for Meaning*, Simon and Schuster, 1984.

> Frankl took nine days in 1945 to write this little book, assuming it would be published anonymously. Instead, the book brought its author worldwide fame. Using his own experience in a Nazi labor camp, Frankl demonstrates his extraordinary theory that human experience holds meaning, even in its most miserable state, and that humans are capable at all times of finding beauty in their circumstances.

Grove, Andrew S., *Swimming Across: A Memoir*, Warner Books, 2001.

> Andris Grof (later Andrew Grove), born in Budapest, Hungary, survived in hiding during the Nazi occupation and escaped to the United States shortly before the Communist take over in 1956. The author subsequently became one of the founders of Intel and held the position of chairman in that U.S. company.

Levi, Primo, *Survival in Auschwitz: The Nazi Assault on Humanity*, Simon and Schuster, 1996.

> Levi pronounced himself lucky to be arrested and sent to Auschwitz in 1944. His late arrival made his survival until liberation more likely. This memoir by the Italian chemist includes the difficulties that confronted survivors immediately after liberation and the challenges they faced then in finding their way back home.

Shermer, Michael, *Denying History: Who Says the Holocaust Never Happened and Why Do They Say It*, University of California Press, 2002.

> An in-depth study of the Holocaust deniers, their motivations and their claims. Each claim is carefully examined and refuted.

Spiegelman, Art, *Maus—A Survivor's Tale: My Father Bleeds History*, Pantheon, 1986.

> A Pulitzer Prize–winning graphic novel (essentially a long comic book for mature readers) telling the story of Spiegelman's father and his persecution by the Nazis in World War II. In this tale, the Jews are mice, the Nazis cats, and the Americans are dogs.

A Silver Dish

Saul Bellow

1978

Saul Bellow's story "A Silver Dish" illustrates the skill of one of the greatest American authors of the twentieth century. The story spans a period from the middle of the Great Depression to the mid-1980s, showing the changes that time renders in both society and in one man's life. The main character, Woody Selbst, is one of Bellow's finest creations. A lonesome, successful businessman, Woody reminisces about the circumstances under which his father, a con man and thief, caused him to lose his scholarship to a seminary school, an act that redirected his entire life.

Bellow, the 1976 winner of the Nobel Prize for Literature, fills this long tale with acutely observed details and characters who are so unusual that they feel like they could only come from real life. Woven throughout the story are meditations about religion, death, and responsibility that one expects in Bellow's fiction. Long for a short story, "A Silver Dish" holds as much insight, humor, and wisdom as one may hope to find in a novel.

This story was first published in the *New Yorker* in 1978 and was subsequently published in Bellow's 1984 collection *Him with His Foot in His Mouth*, which as of 2006 is in print.

Author Biography

Saul Bellow is considered one of the greatest writers America has ever produced, having won every major writing award available, including the Nobel Prize for Literature. He was born on June 10, 1915, in Lachine, Quebec, Canada. His parents, who had recently emigrated from Russia, moved the family to Chicago in 1924. After high school, Bellow attended the University of Chicago for two years then graduated with honors from Northwestern University in 1937, taking degrees in sociology and anthropology. He went on to do some post-graduate work at the University of Wisconsin, but soon returned to Chicago, which is the city that he has been most closely associated with throughout his long lifetime.

For most of Bellow's life, he was a teacher. His first position was at Pestalozzi-Froebel Teachers College in Chicago, from 1938 to 1942. During World War II, he served with the Merchant Marines. With money from a Guggenheim fellowship, he traveled in Europe after the war. After a stint as an editor at *Encyclopedia Britannica*'s "Great Books" program from 1943–1946, he took positions at University of Minnesota (1946–1949; 1954–1959), and then the University of Chicago, where he became the Grunier Distinguished Professor in the university's acclaimed Committee on Social Thought, in 1962. Bellow's affiliation with the committee lasted for more than three decades, until 1993. He then went to Boston University and became a professor of English, a position that he held until his death in 2005.

Bellow was productive and his writings won high critical acclaim. After the publication of his first novel, *Dangling Man*, in 1944, he produced ten novels and a few collections of plays, short stories, and novellas. His essays are also widely regarded, particularly "The Old System," a report on Israel's Seven-Day War that he wrote in 1967 for *Newsweek*. In addition, he was a frequent magazine contributor and an editor of dozens of volumes of fiction. His works are celebrated around the world: a partial list of his awards includes the National Book Award (Bellow is the only person to win it three times, for *The Adventures of Augie March* in 1953, *Herzog* in 1964, and *Mr. Sammler's Planet* in 1970); the National Institute of Arts and Letters Award; the French Croix de Chevalier des Arts et Lettres; and, of course, the Nobel Prize for Literature in 1976. He was also a controversial figure: in 1970 he was booed off the stage at a reading in San Francisco by protestors who objected to his conservative views, and, after the publication of *To Jerusalem and Back*, about a trip to the Holy Land in 1976, critics characterized him as an opponent of Israel. Saul Bellow died at 89 on April

Saul Bellow   The Library of Congress

5, 2005, at Brookline, Massachusetts. He had had five wives, three sons, and with his fifth wife, one daughter, born when he was 84.

Plot Summary

Saul Bellow begins "A Silver Dish" by focusing on Woody Selbst, the protagonist, at age sixty. He is a successful businessman, the owner of a tile distribution company, living alone in an apartment on the top floor of his company warehouse. It is Sunday morning, and the bells are ringing in churches all around the South Chicago neighborhood where he lives. Woody reflects on the death of his father, Morris "Pop" Selbst, earlier in the week. He thinks of other people in his life: his mother, whose conversion to Catholicism hastened her husband's abandonment; his two weak-willed sisters, who are in their fifties and still living with their mother; his wife, from whom he has been separated for fifteen years, and Helen, his mistress; and Halina, the woman for whom his father left the family when Woody was fourteen and with whom his father lived for over forty years. He has a particular time of the week allotted for each of them. Sunday has always been his day to spend with Pop.

Media Adaptations

- Bellow was interviewed by Matteo Bellinelli on the video *Saul Bellow* (1994), released by Films for the Humanities & Sciences.

- An audio interview, *On Art, Literature, and American Life*, is available from Encyclopedia Americana/CBS News Audio Resource Library.

- A four-cassette video collection produced by Boston University, called *Conversations with Saul Bellow: Novelist, Author of Short Stories and Plays*, was released in 1987.

The church bells and thoughts of his father lead Woody to recall an incident that happened during the Great Depression, when Woody was seventeen. He was attending a seminary, with his tuition paid for by a rich patron, Mrs. Skoglund, a friend of his aunt and uncle. They all took an interest in him because he was Jewish and had converted to Christianity. One day, his father came to him and said that Halina had stolen money from her husband so that he, Morris, could pay a bookie and that he had to put the money back or the husband would beat Halina and possibly kill her. He wanted Woody to take him to Mrs. Skoglund's house, so that he could ask the wealthy woman for a loan. Woody knew that Mrs. Skoglund did not approve of Selbst and that there was a danger that she might quit paying his tuition if she thought that his father had too much influence on him, but out of loyalty to his father he agreed.

They traveled by trolley car from the south side of Chicago to the affluent suburb of Evanston, north of the city, during a blinding blizzard. At the Skoglund mansion, Woody talked their way in the door past the suspicious housekeeper, Hjordis, who opposed the idea of showing them any kindness at all. Mrs. Skoglund came to meet them and took them into a parlor where Woody introduced his father and then stepped back, quietly allowing Pop to make his case. Morris explained that he was a hard-working man who had gotten himself into financial trouble, making the case that he would be able to help children if she would just give him a break.

When Mrs. Skoglund and Hjordis left the room to pray to God about the best course of action, Pop went to a cabinet, pried open its lock with his penknife, and, to Woody's dismay, removed a silver dish. He explained that it was just in case Mrs. Skoglund did not give him the fifty dollars he needed; he would put it back if the money did appear. Woody tried to take the dish from his father, which resulted in their rolling on the floor, wrestling with each other. They broke their hold and stood up just before Mrs. Skoglund returned.

Having prayed about it, she decided to give Morris a check for the money. Woody accompanied her to her office as she wrote it and gave it to him, asking him to pray with her for his father's soul. Once they left the house, Woody asked Pop if he had returned the silver dish to its proper place, and he said that of course he had. Because of the snow, they spent the night at the Evanston YMCA, and in the morning Pop went straight to Mrs. Skoglund's bank and cashed the check.

A few days later, the dish was discovered missing. Woody denied knowing anything about it but was forced to leave the seminary. When he confronted his father about it, Pop gave him the ticket from the pawn shop when he had hocked it and invited him to redeem it.

In his apartment, Woody now remembers his father's final days. In particular, he remembers being in the hospital room when Pop tried to pull the intravenous needles out of his arms. To stop him, Woody had taken off his shoes and climbed into the bed beside him, holding his arms, denying him what he wanted for once. Prevented from removing the tubes with his hand, Pop had just shut his metabolism down, letting the heat seep out of his body until he was dead.

Characters

Halina Bujak

Halina Bujak is a Catholic woman who has worked in Morris Selbst's dry cleaning shop. When Woody is fourteen, Morris leaves his family to live with Halina, and Morris and Halina live as husband and wife for over forty years, although Halina remains married to someone else. Of all members of his extended family whom Woody sends to Disney World, Halina enjoys it most, particularly the Hall of Presidents.

Mitosh Bujak

The son of Halina, Morris Selbst's longtime companion, Mitosh is only mentioned once in the story. He plays the organ at the Stadium for basketball and hockey games.

Helen

Helen is the mistress of Woody Selbst, his "wife de facto." In his tight schedule, Woody schedules Friday nights for being with Helen.

Hjordis

Mrs. Skoglund's housekeeper, Hjordis, is a tough, suspicious old maid, unwilling to accept the good in anyone, reluctant to allow Morris Selbst into the house, even in terrible weather. When leaving the Skoglund house, Woody requests that Hjordis phone the local YMCA, where her cousin works, to get a room for Morris and himself: she does so, but reluctantly, feeling that she is being taken advantage of by people she does not like.

Aunt Rebecca Kovner

Woody's aunt, Rebecca Kovner, is the sister of his mother. She is married to the Reverend Doctor Kovner, and together they work to convert people to Christianity, including Woody, his mother, and his sisters. When he is at the seminary, Woody works under Aunt Rebecca at a soup kitchen shelter for the poor, and he pilfers food he does not need, just for spite.

Reverend Doctor Kovner

The brother-in-law of Woody's mother, Reverend Doctor Kovner is actively involved in converting people to Christianity. He despises Morris Selbst, and the feeling is mutual. Morris accuses Kovner of converting Jewish women by making them fall in love with him.

Mother

Woody's mother, who is never mentioned by name, is converted to Christianity by her sister, Aunt Rebecca Kovner, and her sister's husband. She is a self-important woman whose stern piousness drives her husband, Morris, to leave her. During the next fifty years, up to the time of this story, she lives with her two daughters. Woody accuses his mother of spoiling her daughters, making them fat and crazy, and being out of touch with the real world.

Pop

See Morris Selbst

Joanna Selbst

Woody's sister, Joanna Selbst, is depressed and mentally unstable.

Morris Selbst

Living on the streets of Liverpool, England, from the age of twelve, Morris Selbst comes to the United States at age sixteen, sneaking into the country by jumping a ship in Brooklyn; he never establishes an official identity in the country. He spends his life pursuing illegal and semi-legal means of support. In his forties, he leaves his wife and three children to live with one of his employees, Halina, with whom he remains for more than forty years until his death. Morris, or "Pop," as Woody often refers to him, is a gambler, cheat, and thief, who feels entirely justified in being the way he is. When he comes to Woody and asks for his help on the behalf of his mistress, Halina, Woody suspects that his plea is bogus, as it in fact turns out to be. When Pop takes the silver dish, he promises to put it back if Mrs. Skoglund gives him the money he asks for; when she gives him the money, he steals the dish anyway and then lectures Woody about how religious people are really taking advantage of him and deserve what they get.

Paula Selbst

Woody's sister, Paula Selbst, is cheerful but mentally unstable.

Woody Selbst

This story focuses on the life of Woody Selbst, who is now a sixty-year-old tile contractor in Chicago. Woody is the center of his extended family and the means of support for many people around him. He lives alone but has a girlfriend, Helen, whom he sees every Friday night. Every Friday he also shops for groceries for his wife, from whom he has been separated for fifteen years. He goes on Saturdays to visit his mother and his two sisters, who are in their fifties and still live at home with their mother. He has supplemented the income of his father, who has recently died, and his father's mistress, Halina.

Woody lives alone in an apartment atop his company's warehouse. He travels internationally by himself once a year. He is generally law-abiding and dependable, but he also has a criminal streak: in the previous year, for instance, he smuggles hashish in from Kampala, just for the excitement of doing so (the hashish is used to stuff the Thanksgiving turkey). He does not like to keep entirely within the limits of the law, considering it a matter of self-respect to do otherwise.

When he is in his teens during the Great Depression, Woody, by birth a Jew, converts to Catholicism and attends a seminary, which is paid for by a benefactress, Mrs. Skoglund. He takes his father to Mrs. Skoglund's house one day, and his father steals a silver dish from a curio cabinet; as a result of this theft, Woody is forced to leave school and go to work.

Mrs. Aase Skoglund

An old widow who has cooked for the wealthy Skoglund family and married their son, Aase Skoglund uses the money that she inherits to promote Christian charitable projects, such as paying Woody Selbst's tuition at a seminary. She is deeply religious, praying to God when she has a decision to make. She is charitable enough to give money to Morris Selbst, a man of whom she disapproves. She accepts no excuses when she finds out that Woody and his father have stolen from her.

Themes

Familial Love

Woody Selbst loves his father much like an indulgent father might love his irresponsible, yet self-serving son. Woody loses the opportunity to have his education paid for because of the selfish actions of his father. Because he loves his father, he gives him his savings when the old man wants to hire a taxi and leave the family. Because he loves his father, he takes him to the house of his patron, Mrs. Skoglund. Having gone that far against his better judgment, Woody distances himself from his father after the older man steals the silver dish. The brief wrestling bout on the living room floor is caused by the son trying to keep the father from misbehaving. Acting out of love rather than anger, Woody tries to restrict his father, just as later he climbs into the dying man's bed to prevent him from disconnecting his tubes.

The narrative states explicitly that Morris Selbst loved his son, too, listing him second only to Halina, his mistress, in the older man's life. Though Morris tries to take advantage of Woody, in his own mind, Morris wants to spare Woody the indignities of having to associate with people who only pretend to care for him.

Snobs and Snobbery

Pop Selbst justifies his behavior by characterizing the people who have converted Woody and his mother to Christianity—Mrs. Skoglund, the Reverend Doctor Kovland, and Aunt Rebecca Kovland—as snobs, who look down upon him because of his humble background and, perhaps, because of anti-Semitic feelings. Whether he is right, or is just using their disapproving attitude to excuse his own criminal behavior, it is nonetheless clear that Woody agrees with him. Woody characterizes his mother as waiting, like a queen, for her husband to return to her, even forty years after he left the family, but refusing their daughters to have anything to do with him: "The Empress of India speaking," Bellow writes, to show Woody's disdain for his mother's pretentious ways.

As a grown man, Woody still battles snobbery. His opponents are not religious, though: in the late twentieth century, religion is not the powerful force it once was. Woody smuggles hashish in from foreign lands and grows marijuana in the field in the back of his warehouse, not because he feels the need for such things, but in effect to snub authority. Though he is a respected and responsible member of his community, he retains the attitude that his father had, challenging, with his very respectability, the people who might look down on him.

Humility

Though the story does not show how he was able to do so, it is quite clear about the fact that Woody has been able to derive some moral advantage from what might have been a crippling humiliation. His father's actions at the house of Mrs. Skoglund resulted in his losing his scholarship and being thrown out of school. Such a traumatic event might have driven him to follow Pop into a life of crime, but, instead of becoming irresponsible, Woody grows up to be a man with a weighty conscience. He does not abandon his family, the way his father once did, but he works to support them all. An example of this is the way he shops every week for his wife, even though they have not lived together for fifteen years. Even more notable is the fact that Woody pays for vacations to Disney World for all members of his extended family (though he cannot, of course, send his mother and his father's mistress, his own wife and his mistress together). Though Woody engages in some petty crimes as a matter of self-esteem, his life is generally focused on his responsibility toward others. He does not allow himself to feel that he deserves better.

Aging

Since most of this story takes place in retrospect when Woody Selbst is a young man, it may be difficult for readers to bear in mind that he is

Topics For Further Study

- Woody is divided between the religions of his father and mother, who are, respectively, Jewish and Christian. Explain the central event of "A Silver Dish" to a rabbi or minister and record the advice that they would give to a young person who witnesses a parent committing a crime.

- Many YMCAs, including the one in Evanston, Illinois, that is mentioned in the story, have rooms to rent. Contact one near you and find out their policies: who rents their rooms, how much they charge, and what reservation policies are followed.

- Woody and his father have a bond that Morris does not have with his daughters, nor Woody with his mother. Research Sigmund Freud's theory of the "Oedipal Complex," and explain its possible relevance to the relationship between Woody and each of his parents.

- The music of the 1930s was generally about hope for a better future. Listen to the lyrics of a few songs from the Depression and describe which character would approve of it more, "Pop" Selbst or Mrs. Skoglund. Explain your reasons.

- Bellow explains that Woody is responsible for his sisters, who live with their mother. What social services could they apply for after their mother's death, so that they would be able to live independently?

---

sixty years old, well past the prime of life. Throughout the story he is overshadowed by his father. As a young man, his struggle to establish an independent identity fails, as his father ruins his chance to become a scholar and is responsible for his being thrown out of school. According to Morris Selbst, seminary did not offer Woody a true calling anyway. In adulthood, Woody has taken financial responsibilities of his family for years, but upon his father's death he awakens to a new awareness of the limits of life. Noting, at his father's hospital, the general decrepitude of his mother and his father's mistress, he muses, "everybody had lived by the body, but the body was giving out."

Solitude

Although, in his adult life, Woody is involved in the lives of people as diverse as his ex-wife, his grown sisters, his father's mistress and his own mistress, he still is alone, spending Sunday morning, the time that he has devoted to his father, alone in his apartment, listening to the mournful sounds of church bells. The root of this solitude can be plainly seen in his youth, when he was divided between his two parents when they separated. While it was easy for his sisters to sympathize with their mother, Woody only partially followed his mother's path: he converted to Christianity, but also rebelled, stealing bacon from Aunt Rebecca Kovner as a way of asserting his independence. Still, he grew up with too much conscience to follow directly in his father's larcenous footsteps. In keeping himself free of the restraints that any particular lifestyle would impose, he has also detached, to such a great extent that Helen, the woman whom he thinks of as being like a wife to him, is mentioned just once in the story and forgotten.

Style

Anti-hero

Bellow makes the character of Morris Selbst enough of a likeable rouge that readers can easily see why his son would be willing to forgive his crimes and try to help him improve. Morris may be considered a hero of the work because he is a sympathetic main character: certainly, he is something of a hero to his son, Woody. But he has many personal qualities that are less than heroic in the traditional sense. He is vain, petty, dishonest, greedy, and crude, to name just a few of his unattractive characteristics. Because he subverts the standard expectations of a hero, Morris functions as an anti-hero, making readers question their own expectations of what a hero is and does.

Foil

Traditional fiction often provides a protagonist with a foil, a character who is the opposite of the main character and whose traits contrast with the protagonist at every turn. The foil underscores the protagonist by striking a sharp contrast to him. In other words, the contrast between the two makes both more clear as it underscores the protagonist's nature.

Woody is a foil for Morris. Woody cares for his extended family, while Morris abandons his for a new life with his mistress. Woody accepts financial support to go to seminary, but he hesitates at the thought of his father borrowing money from his benefactor. When the two visit the Skoglund mansion their contrasting personalities are dramatized by their fight, which includes their wrestling with each other on the floor. This contrast played out this way makes each personality clearer to readers.

Denouement

The French word *denouement* means "unraveling." In literature, it generally refers to the part of a story that follows the climax, when the tense situations are settled and loose ends are wrapped up. The main part of "A Silver Dish" revolves around the object of the title. The story's climax may be seen as the fight that takes place between Woody and Morris, to keep him from stealing the dish; or it might be Woody's dismissal from the seminary and his steadfast decision not to blame his father; or maybe the old man's confession, later, that he took the dish, and his explanation that it was probably good for Woody that he did. Regardless of what one interprets as the story's climax, the last scene, in which Woody climbs into his father's hospital bed and holds him until he dies, is certainly the story's denouement. It is not integral to the main action of the story, but it is appropriate to the story because it dramatizes the love Woody feels for his father and the opposition he poses to his father's wishes. This final image conveys the son's love and the son's desire to prevent his father from a certain action.

Historical Context

The Great Depression

At the center of this story is Bellow's description of the night when Woody and his father, who are both poor, travel from the south side of Chicago to the affluent suburb of Evanston to the north. The contrast between the two worlds is made clear to readers, as the contrast between the rich and the poor was very clear during the Great Depression.

Like most large social phenomena, the Depression was the result of many events occurring simultaneously, such as the destruction of Europe during World War I finally taking effect and poor financial planning by the United States, which, after the war ended in 1918, failed to anticipate its rise to global financial dominance. America was a rich country throughout the 1920s, but some of that wealth was only on paper: the wealth that showed in bankbooks and stock transactions was not backed up by enough production of tangible goods. An important event that heralded the Depression was the New York Stock Market crash on October 29, 1929. Stock prices tumbled, causing other stockholders to sell their holdings at discount prices to cover their losses. People lost their savings when banks were forced out of business by large depositors pulling out. From 1929 to 1933, the U.S. gross national product fell by nearly half, from $103 billion to $55 billion. Unemployment, which usually stays under 5 percent, reached 30 percent at the height of the Depression in 1933, which is when Franklin D. Roosevelt became president and initiated new economic policies. Roosevelt's New Deal consisted of a variety of plans that gave work to many people.

Globalization in the 1980s

In this story, Bellow describes his protagonist, Woody Selbst, as a world traveler, experiencing exotic lands such as Kampala, the White Nile, and Japan, and important cities such as Istanbul, Jerusalem, and Delphi. While such international travel was of course possible then, it was by no means as common as it is in the early 2000s.

Several factors made world travel more attainable for the common person in the last two decades of the twentieth century. For one thing, the International Monetary Fund (IMF), which had been in existence since the end of World War II, became more involved in regulating commerce between countries. Previously, the IMF had been charged with tending to the interactions between a few developed countries, but in 1982 it was shaken from its slumber by an international debt crisis. With a strong regulatory body directing financial traffic between countries, international involvement increased.

Compare
&
Contrast

- **1930s:** An immigrant like Morris Selbst, who comes into the country by jumping off a ship before it docks, can live his entire lifetime without his presence documented by the government.

  Today: Government records are cross-referenced by computer. It would be virtually impossible for a man to own a business without several government agencies knowing of his existence.

- **1930s:** The World's Fair in Chicago, dubbed the "Century of Progress," draws attendance of more than 22 million people.

  Today: The ease of international travel and the knowledge of the world via the Internet make world fairs unnecessary. The last world's fair of note, Expo '98 in Lisbon, Portugal, drew 11 million people.

- **1930s:** Gambling means placing bets with a bookmaker with underground connections.

Today: Most states have casinos, lottery, and legalized horse betting. Financing bets is more often done with a credit card than with a bookie.

- **1930s:** A car is a luxury: there is one car for every three people in the United States. In cities, the main mode of transportation is the streetcar.

  Today: There is an average of one car for every person over the age of sixteen. Urban areas try to discourage car ownership and to encourage the use of public transportation to cut down on traffic congestion and pollution.

- **1930s:** Banks are going out of business, so people like Bujak in the story keep their cash hidden in their homes.

  Today: Cash is becoming obsolete: businesses encourage transactions with credit or debit cards.

Also, communications improved after the 1980s. The fax machine, which allowed a copy of a document to be transferred across phone wires, had its origins in a device that was copyrighted in 1862, but it did not become a practical tool for business offices until the late 1980s. Just as the fax machine was revolutionizing international information sharing, the Internet boom transformed business throughout the 1990s: within a matter of years, companies that had relied on verbal communications or couriers could exchange information accurately and immediately.

As businesses spread their scope throughout the world, so did individuals. The Internet and cable television brought a steady flow of information about other cultures, removing some of the fear and mystery of other lands. Tourism became a streamlined industry, so that agents in different countries could offer amenities that they knew their foreign customers wanted. Airlines became increasingly efficient at moving passengers, bringing fares down to levels that could be reached by middle-class

Americans. Since the 1980s, international travel has become much more practical and desirable for millions of vacationers who once could only dream of going abroad.

Critical Overview

By the time "A Silver Dish" was published in Saul Bellow's 1984 collection *Him with His Foot in His Mouth*, Bellow's reputation as one of the great American authors was already established. He had won most of the major awards available to writers, including the Nobel Prize for Literature in 1984. Still, even with a devout following of fans and scholars waiting for each new work, this collection was greeted with particular enthusiasm. Bellow's reputation was built by the novels that he published after the 1940s, but few readers had ever encountered his short fiction. With his reputation established, Bellow expanded the scope of his novels,

Police officer directing traffic in a snowstorm, in a scene similar to the one described in Saul Bellow's "A Silver Dish" © Wally McNamee/Corbis

inserting longer and longer passages of philosophical musings within the stories. As Sanford Pinsker explained it in his review of *Him with His Foot in His Mouth* for *Studies in Short Fiction*, "Saul Bellow's last novel, *The Dean's December*, confirmed what fans and critics alike had long suspected—namely, that the delicate balance between texture and talkiness was tilting, unhappily, toward the latter." Bellow's characters "had too much of the non-fictional essay pressing on their chests." Pinsker was pleased to report that the short story form focused Bellow's skills onto story-telling: "the sheer discipline that the short story requires has served Bellow well at this time, this place in his distinguished career."

The collection was received positively all around. D. Keith Mano started his review in the *National Review* by calling the book "a spirit-wrestler." Writing in a style that reflects Bellow's own, Mano notes, "In five stories Bellow, our best manuscript illuminator, has thrown off more stylistic improvisation and bright elegance, more body English, than ten normal-good penmen could." Janet Wiehe echoed his sentiments in the *Library Journal*, concluding as follows: "An impressive collection: Bellow's lush, intellectual fiction vigorously confronts ideas and connects individual

experience to a broad scheme of life and art and thought." By the end of the decade, the book was still influential, remembered by *Time* magazines as one of the best books of the 1980s.

By the early 2000s, critical attention that focused intensely on Bellows two decades before had dimmed. Before his death in 2005, he published short fiction so infrequently that readers look back on this collection as a particularly cherished event. "A Silver Dish." the one of his most frequently anthologized stories, is included in Bellow's 2002 *Collected Stories*. It is also included in *Best Short Stories of the Century*, edited by John Updike.

Criticism

David Kelly

Kelly is an instructor of literature and creative writing at College of Lake County and Oakton Community College in Des Plaines, Illinois. In this essay, Kelly examines Bellow's use of symbolism.

In a 1959 essay published in the *New York Times* called "The Search for Symbols, a Writer Warns, Misses All the Fun and Facts of the Story,"

Saul Bellow takes literary critics to task for reading too deeply, asserting that close scrutiny can in fact be a threat to fiction. He presents a hypothetical situation: a professor, asked why, in *The Iliad*, Achilles drags the body of Hector around the perimeter of Troy, answers that it is because doing so fits a pattern of circles, from shields to chariot wheels, that run throughout the story. To support his thesis the imaginary professor points to the fact that Plato, who was himself an ancient Greek but had no other relation to the author of *The Iliad*, favored geometric patterns, particularly the circle. Bellow submits to readers that the real answer is the simple one: Achilles circled the walls of Troy with Hector's carcass because he was angry. He says that the deep readers, who spin off symbolic importance from every little object mentioned in a work, are those who prefer meaning to feeling. Bellow's point is well taken: the search for symbolism certainly does distract a reader from nakedly experiencing a work of fiction. Still, the nature of literature is that, unlike life, the objects and events one encounters are certain to have some meaning greater than themselves, so it is more than a little disingenuous to blame the readers who want to explore possible meanings.

By the time he published the story "A Silver Dish," almost a quarter of a century later, Bellow seemed to have warmed to the idea of the responsible use of symbolism. How much of this is because he developed a more secure artist's hand over the year and how much is attributable to the fact that the short story form itself calls out for the compression that symbolism can allow is hard to say. The fact remains that "A Silver Dish" requires readers to have an appreciation of the symbolic if they are going to make meaning from it.

To start with, the title is symbolic. Titles are *always* symbolic, if we take "symbolism" to mean using one idea to represent another. A title is expected to mean much more than it says. In this particular case, three words are used to carry the same approximate meaning as thirty pages of text.

A well-formed title is transparent, at least until the other options of what it could have been are considered. "A Silver Dish" could have been called "The Bells" or "A Theft" or "A Death in the Family," but any one of these would steer the story's reader into a different direction. Something as simple as the use of "a" instead of "the," for instance, raises the tone of the story from the particular to the mythical. Describing the dish as "silver" in the story is just good, concrete, descriptive writing, but

> On the other hand, it is easy to see what Bellow was getting at when he criticized those readers who take a work to be a package full of symbols, rather than an organic entity unto itself."

mentioning it in the title tells readers that there is something special about its being silver: as it turns out, the item in question is silver plated, a counterfeit, a sham. And the fact that the title is no more specific about the item than calling it a "dish" shows that Bellow is intentionally being general, when he could have referred to it properly as a plate, platter, or tray, just as easily as he identifies the cabinet it is stolen from as an "étagère." These choices are used to signify something to the reader. Where writers disagree with critics is in determining just how much this signifying can be considered symbolism.

There are certain elements in "A Silver Dish" that are clearly symbolic, even though Bellow seemed to think that he could mute their symbolism by making the story's protagonist, Woody Selbst, aware of them. The first and most obvious of these is the buffalo calf that Woody has seen dragged underwater in Uganda. Watching the parent buffalos in their bafflement about the disappearance of their child taught Woody something about mourning. How do readers know this? For one thing, the event makes no sense being in the story if its significance is not felt; for another, Bellow introduces this episode as an "experience that was especially relevant to mourning." Similarly, the bells that chime around Woody's apartment on a Sunday morning certainly have sensual impact—thinking of church bells ringing will put readers into the state of mind that Woody is in that first Sunday without his father—but they also symbolize the larger concept of organized religion, which Bellow acknowledges when he uses the line, "he had some connection with bells and churches" to take readers into Woody's past, when he was studying for the seminary.

What Do I Read Next?

- Bellow's essay "In the Days of Mr. Roosevelt," originally written for *Esquire* magazine, is his non-fiction account of what life was like in Chicago during the Great Depression. It is reprinted in *It All Adds Up: From the Dim Past to the Uncertain Future*, a collection of his essays published by the same year as this story.

- Bellow wrote the afterward for an edition of *Con Man* (1942), an autobiography of legendary Chicago swindler J. R. "The Yellow Kid" Weil.

- Philip Roth, one of the great American novelists, wrote an appreciation of Bellow's long career in "Rereading Saul Bellow," published in Roth's collection *Shop Talk: A Writer and His Colleagues and Their Work* (2001).

- Unlike most literary biographies, Harriet Wasserman's memoir of Bellow, *Handsome Is* (1997), is steeped with personal and intimate observations about its subject and his life. Wasserman was Bellow's friend and agent, and her book brings readers close to his life.

There are, it should be said, many things in the story that point readers toward a larger significance but do not reach a level of dual meaning that would make one categorize them as symbols. Woody's one-time job pulling a rickshaw at the 1933 World's Fair is mentioned several times, and so it might seem that there is an implied connection between his life and the Chinese character that he plays for cash: this job does show him to be the hard worker that he proves to be later in life, but that is just consistent characterization, not symbolism. Riverview Park is described in more detail than most things along the streetcar route—Bellow mentions the Bobs, the Chute, and the Tilt-a-Whirl—but nothing else in the story implies that this amusement park is supposed to represent life (although if that *were* Bellow's point then his comment about "the fun machinery put together by mechanics and electricians" would make more sense). The blizzard that Woody and his father travel through might be considered symbolic of the freezing of their relationship that is to come, but the story works well enough without giving it any extra significance. Just considering the blinding snowstorm as the sort of extreme weather that writers often use for setting, to make a story all that more gripping, explains it without over explaining it. It would be easy to make too much of minute details like these and blow their significance out of proportion. This is just the sort of thing that Bellow's 1959 essay warned against.

On the other hand, there are aspects to "A Silver Dish" that are so striking that it would be off the mark to make too little of their symbolic significance. Woody and his father wrestling on the floor of Mrs. Skoglund's front room is one. Physical competition between a father and son almost always implies the Freudian concept of the Oedipal complex, in which the son tries to overcome the father, taking his sexual power from him and winning his sexual identity. Freudian interpretation is the one area that most often makes readers and writers feel that critics are going too far in the search for symbols, stretching the given facts to fit a predetermined meaning, and it was at its height when Bellow's essay was published. Still, when Bellow has a father and son grappling for what is stuffed down the front of the older man's underwear, it is difficult to avoid seeing how well the Freudian interpretation fits.

One other act in "A Silver Dish," which echoes the wrestling bout in the way that it brings the two main characters together physically again, comes when Woody takes off his shoes and crawls into the bed of his dying father to hold the old man's arms. This action is clearly meant to indicate more than just the effort to keep the father from pulling out his intravenous tubes. It shows a comfort and intimacy that the father and son never shared when the old man was vibrant; it shows Woody climbing closer to death, wrestling it to save his father's life;

it shows Woody, now sixty years old, coming to recognize his own approaching mortality. There are many interpretations that work, but the one thing that cannot be said about such a striking, prominent gesture is that it is meant to stand only for itself.

From one perspective, everything in a work of fiction must mean something beyond itself: it would be quite naïve to ask readers to please not question why the author chose to include one element or another in story. On the other hand, it is easy to see what Bellow was getting at when he criticized those readers who take a work to be a package full of symbols, rather than an organic entity unto itself. A reader who insists on torturing the slimmest connections out of each object and gesture and calling it a symbol will miss out on the fun of reading. But symbols exist, and they always will, even when the author is not aware that they occur; it is a fact that writers just have to live with.

Source: David Kelly, Critical Essay on "A Silver Dish," in *Short Stories for Students*, Thomson Gale, 2006.

Carlin Romano

In the following essay review, Romano reflects on Bellow's conservative reputation and how the pieces in It All Adds Up *do not warrant that assessment, but lack imagination nonetheless.*

Show me the Saul Bellow of the Sentences and I start to lose track of Papuans and Zulus, Proust and Tolstoy, Hutus and Tutsis. Even here in his casual nonfiction, this Canadian-Jewish-Chicago-American from pre-hyphenated days, the outsider whose '50s bolts of fusion diction knocked out the power of the WASP literary establishment, turns the mere period into a master's signature.

Edmund Wilson was "challenged by Marxism or modernism in the same way that I have seen the descendants of Orthodox Jews challenged by oysters." Khrushchev "seems to be a man of candor, just as Russia seems to be a union of socialist republics." Mayor Richard Daley's neglect of artists was preferable "to the sort of interest that Stalin took in poetry."

Watching a detective movie set in Southern California, Bellow spots "a sort of dandruff of existentialism on the shoulders of the actors." The important actors in his life get their instant of brilliant focus, whether it's his Depression-era algebra teacher, her white hair "piled in a cumulus formation," or John Berryman, "meteor-bearded like John Brown," or the "lifelong manger dogs" who accompanied him to J.F.K.'s White House Nachtmusik for artists.

> " In *It All Adds Up,* we sense that the Nobel Prize-winning arranger knows how he wants the score to sound, and it is without the bullhorns of the past, without the rebukes of the present."

Recalling his jumbled adolescent mind, "like the barrel of books at Walgreens," or announcing his one-step program for trained sensibility—"take certain masterpieces into yourself as if they were communion wafers"—Bellow hints that his attitude toward his cartwheeling metaphoric gift parallels that of mourned philosopher-friend Allan Bloom toward money: "that it was something to be thrown away, scattered from the rear platform of luxury trains."

No matter. It's the Saul Bellow of the Sentiments, not Sentences, that we've been hearing most about for a quarter century. Ever since *Mr. Sammler's Planet* (1970) supposedly blueprinted the assault of Bellow—onetime Trotskyist and Peace Now supporter, founder of a socialist club at Northwestern University—upon radicals, blacks and the "ugly, alarm-laden streets" of New York City, he's been the left's august literary golem, a clay figure written into its script of the literary right, constructed mainly to be destroyed. On this view, Artur Sammler's European-forged vision of Manhattan's urine-soaked phone booths, of darkskinned predators, simply wrapped a brown-paper cover over Saul Bellow's first travel guide, *Let's Go (Far Away From) New York.* In subsequent years, so the story goes, Albert Corde rammed it home to the "underclass" in *The Dean's December,* then the mob took over duties in *Humboldt's Gift.*

Yet Bellow's reflections outside of his fiction over this period suggest a much different story. As editors Gloria Cronin and Ben Siegel document in their forthcoming anthology, *Conversations With Saul Bellow* (University Press of Mississippi, December), Bellow's direct condemnation of alleged foes has always borne a more aesthetic cast than the broadsides of his characters. When confronted by Robert Penn Warren's Yale students about Sammler's put-down of student revolutionaries, Bellow's response addressed hypocrisy, not student policy: "The trouble with the destroyers is that they're always just as phony as what they've come to destroy. Maybe civilization is dying, but it still exists, and meanwhile we have our choice: we can either rain more blows on it, or try to redeem it." Feebly reformist, perhaps, but not Artur Sammler's idea of a crackdown.

And before the publication of *The Dean's December,* Bellow objected in a *New York Times* interview to Richard Poirier's charge that he'd been pushing "cultural conservatism" since Herzog. "People who stick labels on you are in the gumming business," remarked Bellow.

Evasion, some might say. Still, Bellow's resistance to picking up the mantle of conservative ideologue, the constancy of his harumph over the years to being cast as a politicized intellectual, deserves re-examination from the left. This spring's Bellow Gum-for-All-the combination of Brent Staple's nasty version of him in his memoir, *Parallel Time* [see Jill Nelson, "Hiding in Plain Sight," April 25], and Alfred Kazin's revival of Bellow's supposed challenge to multiculturalists in 1988 (asking to be shown the Tolstoy of the Zulus and Proust of the Papuans)—makes one wonder about the fairness of the demonizing. So do the contents of *It All Adds Up.*

Bellow's pigeonholing at this point is a cultural reflex, like praising David Letterman or bashing tabloid TV. *In Parallel Time,* Staples's memoir of growing up in Chester, Pennsylvania, then moving from his troubled neighborhood to the University of Chicago and beyond, the *New York Times* editor includes a long chapter that details his obsession with Bellow—a mix of intense admiration and resentment—during graduate school. He too once swooned before the Bellow of the Sentences.

"Bellow's people leaped more vividly from the page than any I'd encountered," Staples recalls. Still, Staples hated the horror movies of blacks in Bellow's novels, like the pickpocket in *Mr. Sammler's Planet* who exposes himself to the old man. Staples also bristled at Rinaldo, the small-time Mafioso in *Humboldt's Gift* who dismisses blacks as "crazy buffaloes" and "pork chops."

So while Staples envied and tried to emulate Bellow's ability to "kidnap people onto the page," he also began to "stalk" the writer (as the *Times*

described it in promoting the excerpt). "What would I do when I caught him?" Staples wrote. "Perhaps I'd lift him bodily and pin him against a wall. Perhaps I'd corner him on the stairs and take up questions about 'pork chops' and 'crazy buffaloes' and barbarous black pickpockets. I wanted to trophy his fear."

Bellow responded—without mentioning Staples—in a *Times* Op-Ed piece in March. He objected to how critics try to convict him "of contempt for multiculturalism and defamation of the third world," to paint him as "an elitist, a chauvinist, a reactionary and a racist—in a word, a monster." He thought it pathetic that "no writer can take it for granted that the views of his characters will not be attributed to him personally." Then, presumably addressing Kazin's revival of the 1988 remark, he denied the widespread interpretation of it as a put-down, attributing the view to a "misunderstanding" by the interviewer of a point about preliterate and literate societies.

Staples retorted that Bellow's oblique criticism of him was "so small." *The New Republic* quickly pounced on Staples, accusing him of perpetrating stereotypes of "black pimps and black prostitutes" that made Bellow's characters look "quaint." Conventional political lines neatly laid down, Bellow's sticker remained firmly affixed.

All that makes Bellow's choices for his nonfiction collection a peculiar sampler from a fifty-year career. He tells us in his preface that he rejected the option of reprinting "all the trifles" he wrote to support himself, so the collection "is not a reliquary but a gathering of some of the more readable essays." But does readable mean nonideological, nonbiting? Absent are some of Bellow's contentious interviews from the 1970s and '80s (several will be included in the Mississippi book) and the highly readable "Culture Now: Some Animadversions, Some Laughs," from the first issue of *Modern Occasions* in 1971. In it, Bellow skewered his old hangout, the *Partisan Review,* for its steep decline, comparing a piece by former colleague William Phillips on Susan Sontag to "scuba diving at Coney Island in urinous brine and scraps of old paper, orange rinds and soaked hot dog buns."

Omitted here, one presumes, with cause. For the Saul Bellow of *It All Adds Up,* the 79-year-old Bellow of the recent *Times* Op-Ed, is plainly petitioning us to recognize the paramount fact of his career since the '40s: He is an artist—not an intellectual (except by default), not a professional polemicist, not a philosopher. The crisp, exquisitely detailed ancient travel pieces here on Illinois, Spain, Vermont and Tuscany, the lovely dated commentaries on F.D.R. and Khrushchev, the overlapping reflections on the essences of American literary culture (as opposed to its current street fights)—all telegraph a desire to wave his writer's card until someone pays attention.

So does the intimation of his pragmatism. "The bitterness of my dissatisfaction in rereading some of these pieces," Bellow writes, "is due to basic revisions, radical changes in my point of view. I can see now where I went wrong. . . . I failed to understand the things I wrote, the books I read, the lessons I was taught, but I find that I am a most persistent self-educator, that I long for correction." His goal, he says, honoring William James rather than Henry for a change, is "to enter an era of improved errors."

Mysteriously, he doesn't specify. Over 300-plus pages, we find ourselves frequently guessing at what he now rejects or accepts. Yet the tone of selfreproach surfaces often. As does the subliminal postcard: How can a mindchanger be an ideologue?

As far back as 1956, in remembering his friend Isaac Rosenfeld, he admits to having been, as a young man, "peculiarly touchy, vulnerable, hard to deal with at times, as I can see now, insufferable." In his 1977 *Jefferson Lectures,* he describes himself as "aware of shameful shortcoming," and "eager for accurate diagnosis and grateful for correction and cure. The easiest way to get my attention is to approach me from the side of reform." In his 1991 *Bostonia* interviews, he concedes his much-noted early lack of humility: "I made a point of speaking down to people (the nobs) who believed that I should look up to them."

Closer to the present, in a 1993 meditation for *The National Interest,* Bellow tells us, "Politics as a vocation I take seriously. But it's not my vocation. And on the whole, writers are not much good at it." Do we take him at his word? His real aim, if we're to believe the weightier pieces here (the Jefferson and Nobel lectures), is "aesthetic bliss," sought through morally responsible art. It's much the same line as that of Charlie Citrine in *Humboldt's Gift,* who turns to Steinerian anthroposophy as aestheticism with a moral backbone, no worse than Santayana's enjoyment of Christianity's comforting beauty.

Indeed, it's much the same line he has taken in interviews for decades. One of his oldest friends, Samuel Freifeld, told an interviewer in 1963 that Bellow's commitment as a writer had always been the realist's task—"to bear witness to life"—but always, Bellow would add, through imagination, not stenography. Asked back in 1975 what the place of abstract argument should be in fiction, Bellow pointed his interviewer to T.S. Eliot's essay on Shakespeare, in which Eliot considers whether Shakespeare is a Senecan stoic or a follower of Montaigne. "He puts it there very clearly," Bellow said, "that you do not examine a playwright, a poet or a novelist as a thinker. The point is not that he creates a body of intellectual work, but that he creates something else, employing whatever he needs for the purpose."

Why, then, is the left's skepticism toward Saul Bellow, artiste, so sharp and automatic? Isn't he the senior successor of the young wannabe who, according to Kazin in *New York Jew,* "carried around with him a sense of destiny as a novelist that excited everyone around him"? Wasn't he the figure praised wildly by Leslie Fiedler and Elizabeth Hardwick, the Jewish-American novelist with the moxie to punch his way into the mainstream American literary tradition, permitting others—perhaps everyone from Toni Morrison to Sandra Cisneros to Amy Tan—to follow?

When *The New York Times Book Review* asked six American critics in the early '60s to name the writer most likely to replace Hemingway and Faulkner as a great of American literature, Bellow was the name most mentioned. More than thirty years later, this spring, the *London Sunday Times* asked thirty of Britain's leading authors and critics to name the greatest living novelist writing in English, from any country. Again Bellow was the writer most frequently named. Is it so remarkable that the man himself—who disdains such polls—insists on himself as an artist rather than an in-the-wings Crossfire substitute?

The only way to understand the odd choices of *It All Adds Up,* the scant ideological patina, is to see them as Bellow's willful—poignant?—stab at reminding a hyperpoliticized culture of his day job. To do so, he returns us to memoir, to Chicago, to his passages. "In my eyes, my parents were Russians," he recalls in a 1993 piece, and the European bent of his work—particularly the challenge of writing Sammler as a European like his parents—becomes more understandable.

Reading *It All Adds Up,* the cliche of "sound bite" becomes an ambiguous phrase, for one realizes that in a world of unsound thoughts, the sound bite, as supplied by Saul Bellow, supplants the extinct aphorism (too stilted for modern use). Bellow knocks out a remarkable number: "One must respect respect itself"; "One is more foreign in France than in other countries"; "We take foreigners to be incomplete Americans."

To reaccept Bellow as artist, to remove the "Enemy of the People" sign from round his neck, is not to excuse the stark lacuna in his nonpareil attention span. Like his novels, his pieces here—from the farewells to five male friends, to the overviews of places he has known—confirm how little women seem to have mattered to his artistic vision. An edgy reference here to Mary McCarthy as our "tiger lady," a mention there of Virginia Woolf—but almost all the rest, quotation or influence, are the same old male greats: Dostoyevsky, Proust, James, Dreiser, Forster, Conrad, Lawrence, Joyce. What a waste.

Similarly, a lack of the imagination he vaunts so regularly—what others call racism or elitism—limits his outreach to America's rainbow, its future. When he writes, in the *Jefferson Lectures,* that the country people who came to Chicago from Kentucky or Alabama, replacing earlier immigrants, "brought with them no such urban skills and customs as the immigrants had," you cringe at the presumption. When he observes, apropos of "underclass" Chicago in the same work, that the young men and women dragged before a judge are "unreachable, incomprehensible," one is bemused. Can America's most brilliantly equipped detector of personality really be stymied? Then he notes, "Among schoolchildren, you look in vain for resemblances to the past. The schools are now almost entirely black and Puerto Rican."

It can't be that his imagination is so stunted, that all resemblance is lost. Perhaps ego is the answer. For Bellow, who recycles favorite memories and quotes (the awful smell of the Seine, recamier sofas, the wisdom of Samuel Butler) like the hackiest of barroom bards, may well be so fastened to his time, to his people, that he finds it impossible to accept that others will live different lives, will crisscross his experience in different narratives. "I suspect," he remarks at one point, "that if you went to the Lake Country now to find tranquility, you might have to dig for it like an archaeologist." No, but it might help to be 18, and there for the first time.

No sensible critic would study the motorboating of George Bush, the cardoor slams of Jack Nicholson, to understand their main accomplishments better. For some, the nonfiction of a novelist falls into just such an oddball category: unrelated phenomena. Not so. Apart from the serendipitous moments that any retrieval of old material

provides—in this case, references to Arafat threatening to chop off Sadat's hands for dealing with Israel, or a portrait of Boutros-Ghali in his days as Egyptian foreign minister—the occasionals of a master provide telling clues. In *It All Adds Up,* we sense that the Nobel Prize–winning arranger knows how he wants the score to sound, and it is without the bullhorns of the past, without the rebukes of the present.

Source: Carlin Romano, "His Mouth, His Foot," in *Nation,* Vol. 259, No. 5, August 8–15, 1994, pp. 168–70.

Sanford Pinsker

In the following review, Pinsker gives the assessment that Bellow's latest work "focuses our attention . . . on Bellow's humanity, his humor, his style."

Saul Bellow's last novel, *The Dean's December* (1982), confirmed what fans and critics alike had long suspected—namely, that the delicate balance between texture and talkiness was tilting, unhappily, toward the latter. In short, Bellow's characters had too much of the non-fictional essay pressing on their fictional chests. The result tended to choke off what is most representative, and what is best, about Bellow's work.

This latest collection of five shorter pieces—ranging from a sketch/fragment ("Zetland: By a Character Witness") to "What Kind of Day Did You Have?", a novella, forces our attention, once again, on Bellow's humanity, his humor, his *style:*

> I'm a common man [Pop declares, as he puts the touch on a would-be benefactress], but I'm a hard worker and a fellow you can trust. Woody was startled when Pop used the word "trust." It was as if from all four corners a Sousa band blew a blast to warn the entire world: "Crook! This is a crook!"

Him With His Foot In His Mouth is heavy with memory, with portraits of the intellectual as a young man (Zetland, for example, is Isaac Rosenfeld in thin disguise; Harold Rosenberg figures prominently as the driving force behind the Victor Wulpy of "What Kind of Day Did You Have?") or the tugs toward family and "potato love" that Bellow's protagonists can never quite resist:

> I remembered Riva as a full-figured, dark-haired, plump, straight-legged woman. Now all the geometry of her figure had changed. She had come down in the knees like the jack of a car, to a diamond posture. She still made an effort to move with speed, as if she were dancing after the Riva she had once been.

And of course, the collection is anchored in the bang-and-blab of the Chicago pavements. The result is that gritty, quotidian texture, that deliberate roughening of syntax we immediately recognized as vintage Bellow: "I am a more disinterested Ginsberg admirer than Eddie is [the protagonist of "Him With His Foot In His Mouth" declares, as he rationalizes away an ex-colleague's accusations]. Eddie, so to speak, comes to the table with a croupier's rake. He works for the house. He skims from poetry."

Bellow's most congenial turf is the novel, with its large canvas and wide range. But the sheer discipline that the short story requires has served Bellow well at this time, this place in his distinguished career. The collection's title story ends with Professor Shawmut "ready to listen to words of ultimate seriousness." Had this wish been uttered in a Bellow novel, I'm afraid it would likely have been followed by more preachiness, more tub-thumping, more "talk" than would be good either for fiction or for us.

Source: Sanford Pinsker, Review of *Him with His Foot in His Mouth*, in *Studies in Short Fiction*, Vol. 21, No. 4, Fall 1984, p. 404.

Keith M. Opdahl

In the following essay, Opdahl discusses Bellow's writing career.

A sober evaluation of his work leaves no doubt that Saul Bellow is one of the important writers in American literature. As one of two living American Nobel Prize-winners in literature, he inherits the mantle of Hemingway and Faulkner, even though he himself has not become a culture hero. Nor has he, like Borges or Márquez, become a cult figure; when in 1979 the *New York Times Book Review* asked twenty leading intellectuals which books since 1945 would count among the hundred important books in Western civilization, Bellow was not mentioned. He *is* mentioned elsewhere, however, and with the highest praise possible. Who are "the great inventors of narrative detail and masters of narrative voice and perspective" according to Philip Roth? "James, Conrad, Dostoevski and Bellow."

Bellow has in fact always enjoyed the kind of reputation that is won by solid and accomplished work. He is a private person, and in his public appearances he is sometimes distant or moody, without those manufactured public outlines (sportsman, Southern gentleman) that give easy popular identification. But he is also our preeminent public spokesman, the writer who catches and articulates the sometimes hidden feelings of our era. Bellow puts flesh on those abstract and cliché-ridden bones, showing what alienation actually is on a

> **But the fact remains that his art is one of clearing and solidifying an abundance of materials, and when he has finished with the process the reader too has a way to go."**

winter afternoon, say, or precisely how our culture crushes a mediocre man. Does America mean opportunity? Bellow's fiction takes a larky young man about the country, exploring exactly what opportunities await him. Is life a mixture of the sublime and the vulgar? Bellow in his last novel before winning the Nobel Prize shows just what that mix can look like.

Bellow was born in Lachine, Quebec, just two years after his parents, Abraham and Liza Gordon Bellows, had emigrated from St. Petersburg, Russia. His father was a daring and not always successful businessman who in Russia had imported Egyptian onions (Bellow describes him as a "sharpie circa 1905"), and in the New World attempted several often unconventional businesses. A family portrait in 1922 shows the father to be a stocky, erect man with the touchy look one would expect from Bellow's fictionalized accounts of him. Bellow's mother in the same picture is handsome, with large gentle eyes and a broad forehead. Bellow himself—the seven-year-old Solomon Bellows—is alert and knowing, the baby among two sisters and a brother, staring down the camera with something of his father's insouciance.

The Bellows lived in a slum on St. Dominique Street "between a market and a hospital," Bellow has said. "I was generally preoccupied with what went on in it and watched from the stairs and windows." His father, who blamed himself for the family's poverty, worried that Solly would see too much; and the boy did see violence and sexuality, saying later that the raw reality of Dominique Street made all else in his life seem strange and foreign. "Little since then has worked upon me with such force," Bellow has written, as he has returned to the scene in *Dangling Man* and *Herzog*. He lived amid the color and spirituality of an earlier era, for Lachine was "a medieval ghetto. . . ; my childhood was in ancient times which was true of all orthodox Jews." By the age of four he knew the book of Genesis in Hebrew. "You never got to distinguish between that and the outer world."

Lachine was also a verbal environment, teaching young Bellow Hebrew, Yiddish, French, and English. He spent a year in the Royal Hospital (in the TB ward, he says, though he didn't have TB) with nothing to do but read. But by the time his family had moved to Humboldt Park in Chicago, when he was nine, he was healthy enough for sports as well as his many intellectual projects. Humboldt Park was a neighborhood of immigrants, filled with the cultural and intellectual activity of sidewalk orators, branch libraries, and mission houses that would provide a debating club a meeting room. By the time he attended Tuley High School, Bellow had such pals as Isaac Rosenfeld, Sydney J. Harris, who would become the newspaper columnist, Oscar Tarkov, and David Peltz, his good friend to this day, who remembers that "Solly Bellows was the most precocious of the lot—a good runner on the track team, a fair swimmer, middling tennis player, but a remarkable writer even then." The boys were leftist in politics, and at one time crazy about surrealism.

But at home all was not well, for the father—by all accounts an impetuous, pretentious man—continued to have financial problems, and a fatal accident involving his uninsured coal truck made the family labor for years to pay off the debt. Bellow's mother died when he was fifteen, and when he was seventeen he and Sydney Harris ran away to New York for a few weeks to peddle (unsuccessfully) their first novels.

If Chicago had been a shock to the young Canadian, he had persevered. He attended the University of Chicago, where he felt the dense cultural atmosphere to be suffocating, and transferred to Northwestern, where he founded a socialists' club and graduated in 1937 with honors in sociology and anthropology. He reportedly wished to study literature, but was advised that anti-Semitism would thwart his career, and so he accepted a scholarship to study anthropology at the University of Wisconsin, where his professor told him he wrote anthropology like a good novelist. In Chicago on New Year's Eve, 1937, Bellow married Anita Goshkin, a social worker, and abandoned his graduate work. "In my innocence," he has said, "I had decided to become a writer."

It was a bold decision at that time, and such boldness has characterized Bellow's work ever since. His greatest strength as a novelist is his style, which is fluid and rich, picking up the rhythms and energy of Yiddish and the plain speech (and sharply observed detail) of the Middle West. His style is precise and lucid and gives off an air of absolute integrity—an integrity that has at times gotten Bellow into trouble, for as a writer he is as stiffnecked as his father looks. Again and again over his career, Bellow has followed his imagination wherever it may lead. In an era of experimentalism he has been a realist, claiming that "the development of realism in the nineteenth century is still the major event of modern literature." During the 1940s, in a time of deep social concern, Bellow dramatized a sense of the transcendent. When alienation was popular, Bellow celebrated accommodation. He reacted to the popularity of the Jewish novel by turning to a WASP protagonist (in *Henderson the Rain King*), and he met America's new youth culture head-on with the creation of a seventy-year-old protagonist (in *Mr. Sammler's Planet*). And yet in most of these ventures he was successful, largely because of his fertile imagination and clarity of mind.

Bellow's largest difficulty as a writer lies in plot. He has confessed this difficulty, and many critics believe his novels to be formless. If Bellow's characters are colorful and his situations telling, he characteristically gives too much, too many ideas for us to know the central one and too many characters, too many memorable details, for us to discern a simple story. No doubt Bellow is not as formless as he seems, since his point is often the subtle insight of the realist, so easily lost among his comic characters and rich descriptions, and he himself is the most diligent of craftsmen, working through draft after draft. But the fact remains that his art is one of clearing and solidifying an abundance of materials, and when he has finished with the process the reader too has a way to go.

And indeed, one of Bellow's central themes is precisely this density of life. So too is the malice or nastiness of his protagonist and those around him. Another theme is the experience of transcendence and the fact that the issues that confront us are ultimately metaphysical or religious, an element that provides one of the keys to Bellow's style, as the sense of a special meaning or significance just out of reach adds another dimension to his precisely detailed physical world. A society that can invent the inner life but give it no nourishment, a universe that requires the self to twist himself to survive within its force, a protagonist seeking most of all to cure himself of some unknown malady—all of these are typical Bellow themes.

And so too is the theme of his Jewishness, but in a special and rather independent way. Although Bellow's mother wished him to become a Talmudic scholar like many others in her family, Bellow himself has insisted that he is not that exotic creature, the Jew who writes in English, but an American writer—a Western writer who happens to be Jewish. "I did not go to the public library to read the Talmud," Bellow says of his Chicago days, "but the novels and poems of Sherwood Anderson, Theodore Dreiser, Edgar Lee Masters, and Vachel Lindsay." Bellow nevertheless is singled out by Alan Guttmann in *The Jewish Writer in America* (1971) as portraying the full range of American Jewish experience, and Bellow's comedy, intellectualism, moral preoccupation and alienation, his concern with the family and with rough Eastern European immigrants, his obsession with the past and with the dangers of an alien world, his emphasis on purity, his sense, as Alfred Kazin says, "of the unreality of this world as opposed to God's"—all of these elements bespeak his deep Jewish concern.

And indeed, the fact that he is Jewish added a special tension to his decision to be a writer, for he would enter a world dominated not only by WASPS but by WASPS from New England. He worked for the Work Projects Administration doing biographical sketches of Midwestern writers and then taught at the Pestalozzi-Froebel Teacher's College. He went to Mexico in 1940, writing the never-published novel "Acatla," and lived, he says, a bohemian life. But these years were not all gaiety: "I sat at a bridge table in a back bedroom of the apartment while all rational, serious, dutiful people were at their jobs or trying to find jobs, writing something." After lunch with his mother-in-law, in whose apartment he lived, he would walk the city streets. "If I had been a dog I would have howled," he has written. He managed in 1941 to place a short story about a young man waiting for the draft in the *Partisan Review*; the next year another, about the Trotsky assassinations, appeared. And in 1943 *Partisan Review* published part of his new novel in progress.

Perhaps the most memorable quality of this first novel, published in 1944 as *Dangling Man*, is the tone of voice: modeled after that of Rilke's *Journal of My Other Self*, the voice is frank and honest, compensating for its self-pity by the depth and precision of its observation. Taking on Ernest Hemingway, the most famous writer just then, the protagonist Joseph jibs at the hard-boiled: "If you

have difficulties, grapple with them silently, goes one of their commandments. To hell with that! I intend to talk about mine, and if I had as many mouths as Siva has arms and kept them going all the time, I still could not do myself justice."

Like Bellow himself, Joseph has been kept dangling by his draft board, bound in the red tape surrounding his Canadian birth. His ostensibly formless journal is actually shaped by his increasing lack of self-control, as he records the failure of his attempts to write or prepare himself spiritually for the army, and then his disappointment with his friends and his wife, his in-laws and his mistress. Wanting to forge a self that would be "a member of the Army, but not a *part* of it," he must watch himself become overwhelmed by a hundred trivial details, as his self-control leaves him and the nasty bad temper he has remarked in others comes to dominate. When he strikes his landlord and realizes that his sense of the strangeness and impermanence of the world has grown, he, like Dostoevski's Underground Man, throws in the towel, crying "Long live regimentation."

One critic thought Joseph was a "stinker," but other reviewers gave the book a remarkably affirmative judgment. Even the names of the reviewers tell us a great deal, for Edmund Wilson, Peter DeVries, Diana Trilling, and Delmore Schwartz all felt this first novel worthy of their attention. Edmund Wilson called it "one of the most honest pieces of testimony on the psychology of a whole generation," and George Mayberry proclaimed the creation of a complex character like Joseph "an event that is rare and wonderful in modern American writing." Subsequent critics have found the book narrow and Bellow's attitude toward Joseph uncertain. To some, Joseph at the end rejoins society and thus is not ironic; to others, he is totally defeated, surrendering his individuality, a reading the echo from Dostoevski's "Notes from Underground" would support. Bellow's novel is a lively and even memorable work, with many striking figures, even if the author himself has confessed that he cannot bear to reread it.

Bellow's own dangling was ended by the army for medical reasons, and in 1943 he began to work for Mortimer Adler's "Great Books" project for the *Encyclopaedia Britannica*, reading he says some 60 of the 443 works indexed. He joined the merchant marine, which stationed him in New York, and then worked for the Maritime Commission onshore. After the war, Bellow decided to stay in New York, tasting, he has said, the intellectual life of the Village and enjoying the pleasures of father-hood with the birth of his son Gregory. He reviewed books, edited, wrote reports for the founder of Penguin books, and in a clash that served him well, spent two days as movie reviewer for *Time*, until Whitaker Chambers reportedly picked a quarrel and fired him on the spot—an event he would include in his next novel, *The Victim* (1947).

Joseph in *Dangling Man* had complained that upon awaking he went "in the body from nakedness to clothing and in the mind from relative purity to pollution" when he read the newspaper and admitted the world. To Joseph the world is a war that can kill him, but it is also the physical universe itself. In *The Victim* this impurity pursues the protagonist Asa Leventhal as Kirby Allbee comes one hot summer night to accuse the solitary and anxious Leventhal of causing his ruin. Leventhal had quarreled with Allbee's boss, prompting Allbee's loss of his job, he claims, and thus his drinking and the loss of his wife. Following Dostoevski's *The Eternal Husband*, Bellow explores the intense and ambivalent relation between the two men, as Allbee presses deeper and deeper into Leventhal's life, taking money, a bed in his apartment, liberties with his mail, and finally a whore in Leventhal's own bed—an impurity that is still not the final one, since Allbee slips into the apartment late at night to attempt suicide in Leventhal's kitchen.

Was Asa Leventhal responsible? A parallel plot suggests he was not, for he mistakenly assumes the blame in a death for which he had no responsibility at all. Both Leventhal and Allbee are victims of an oppressively dense world—one of the finest creations in the novel, as Bellow catches the summer heat of New York—and of their inability to discern a clear order in it. Each argues for a version of reality that the other cannot accept. Allbee cannot bear the notion of an impersonal universe in which he might be harmed for no reason at all. He must find an agent—a Jew. To Leventhal, on the other hand, such a "human" universe is ominous, frightening, a world in which he could be ruined overnight. Allbee appears inexplicably, emerging from a crowd in a park as an embodiment of the city streets which Leventhal, like his immigrant forebears, considers full of impurity and danger: "He really did not know what went on about him," Leventhal thinks, "what strange things, savage things."

The Victim is a remarkable advance over *Dangling Man*, for though it is dense and claustrophobic it is also rich and full of an absolutely honest life. It raised some eyebrows, coming as it did only two years after the death camps had been opened, for to critics such as Theodore Ross in the *Chicago Jewish Forum* Allbee and Leventhal are too much alike. Was this the time to show that the psychology of Jew and bigot can be similar? Bellow had insisted on paying the Jew the same tribute he would pay all human beings, neither more nor less, and in Allbee he captured the unconscious subtleties of Jewish self-hatred, making him a messenger from not just a destructive world but Leventhal's own psyche. Leventhal's alienation is that of modern man, moreover, for by showing Jew and Gentile to be alike Bellow shows that at this time we are all Jews.

Although *The Victim* was not praised as much as it deserves (critics now judge it to be one of Bellow's best works), it was sufficiently recognized to win Bellow a Guggenheim Fellowship for 1948, freeing him from teaching at the University of Minnesota, where he had been in 1946 and 1947. In France on his fellowship he began a third novel in the same serious vein as his first two, but found he needed a relief. He took to writing a "memoir" of Chicago—which in France had become exotic to him, he says—and by 1949 had turned to it almost exclusively. "Augie was my favorite fantasy," he has said of the Chicago book. "Every time I was depressed while writing the grim one I'd treat myself to a fantasy holiday." He wrote *The Adventures of Augie March* (1953) while on the move, in trains and in cafés in Paris and Rome, in Minneapolis where he returned to teach in 1949, in a cold-water flat in New York where he lectured at New York University, at Princeton where he was a Creative Writing Fellow, and even in the editorial offices at Viking Press. At some point he felt such revulsion with the "grim" work he had begun that he slid some 100,000 words down an incinerator.

Thus *The Adventures of Augie March* begins as the opposite of Bellow's serious concerns, best defined perhaps in terms of Asa Leventhal's fear of the streets. Bellow had known a lad like Augie: "He came of just such a family as I described. I hadn't seen him in 25 years, so the novel was a speculative biography." And what was particularly speculative was Bellow's definition of the young man as an enthusiast who is swept up by the people he loves, sometimes in a sexual swoon and at others as an admiring disciple. Can a young man in a harsh world of force survive without weapons other than affection and tolerance and a lack of calculation? The answer lies in the adults who surround Augie and are as large and threatening as they would appear to a child. They exist with a Balzacian vigor and importance that testifies to human worth as they act upon their environment, but they also overwhelm the passive young Augie, who becomes another Bellow hero oppressed by the world.

At first he manages to survive, and Bellow's point is clear. Augie's childhood is dominated by the wonderful Grandma Lausch, whose world is every bit as dramatic and cynical as the czar's court, and whom Bellow describes as the equal of the great politicians of the world. And so too is the crippled Einhorn, even if his kingdom is a West Side neighborhood and his courtier (and male nurse) the young Augie. Augie serves the North Shore matron Mrs. Renling (until he is taken as her gigolo and she wishes to adopt him) and acts as an aide-de-camp to his ambitious brother Simon, who marries into a wealthy family. In each case, Augie observes not only that "it wasn't so necessary to lie," as he says in the first chapter, rejecting Machiavellian cynicism, but also that these egotists finally do themselves in. Grandma Lausch's children treat her with the same impersonality she had tried to teach Augie. Simon is tormented by his position, and Einhorn outsmarts himself. Only Augie, larky, impetuous, sensual, accepting—the very opposite really of Bellow's usual protagonist and thus a true fantasy for Bellow—only Augie it seems is escaping a harsh and destructive world.

And yet Augie doesn't escape either. Bellow's insistence that these Chicago-neighborhood characters are of the same caliber as mythic and historic greats can work both ways. His references and allusions enrich and elevate the story, but they also darken it, reminding us of the terror at the heart of our myths and legends. Or to put it another way, Augie's style is Whitmanian in the way it picks up everything, relishing its energetic catalogues; but at the same time and in much the same way as Whitman, it contains a belying strain, a shrillness. Augie March is the Jew accepting all of America, Norman Podhoretz has said, and accepted in return, except for his "quality of willed and empty affirmation."

For the truth is that Augie is hit again and again, and we can measure the novel's progress by noting Augie's responses. In the first chapter Augie is beaten up by neighborhood punks (including Augie's good friend) for being a Jew: "But I never had any special grief from it," Augie says, "or brooded, being by and large too larky and boisterous to take it to heart." By the middle of the novel, when Augie is beaten up in a labor strike, he flees full of rage and terror. He goes to Mexico with his

lover Thea, another Machiavellian who plans to hunt iguanas with a trained eagle, and suffers a concussion that makes him spend depressing weeks on the mend. When he cheats on Thea, she tells him he is not a man of love at all, but isolate or indifferent, a fact that Einhorn had earlier described as Augie's "opposition." "Me, love's servant?," Augie wails. "I wasn't at all!"

Bellow's fantasy has simply turned into his old nightmare, and the book becomes the memoir of a rather scarred and saddened middle-aged man who defines himself as one singing in the middle of a desolate and frozen farm field. Like the novel after which it was modeled, *Adventures of Huckleberry Finn*, *The Adventures of Augie March* is unable to sustain its original serenity.

Reviewers in 1953 took Bellow's intention for the deed, however, praising the novel for its energy and acceptance and stylistic fireworks. Even though it won a National Book Award in 1954, Bellow himself today has reservations, commenting that "I got stuck in a Sherwood Anderson ingenue vein: here are all these people and isn't life wonderful! By the last third of the book I wasn't feeling that way any more." The novel had emancipated Bellow from grim labor, at any rate, but what seems notable today is not so much the sweep and energy of the work, particularly in the large numbers of characters, as the warm tone of its voice and the precision of its details. Augie promises to tell the truth, to close in on his experience, which makes the book not so much a picaresque novel skating on the surface of life as a deeper, closer investigation of what a life over a period of years actually is. Bellow had grown up on the naturalistic work of Dreiser, Dos Passos, and Farrell, and he retains their sense of a cruel world of force, but he transforms it here into something less mechanical, less deterministic or external, focusing more on the perception and history and feeling of the inner protagonist—who finds a triumph finally in consciousness if not in love.

Bellow taught at Bard College in 1953–1954 and at the University of Minnesota the next year. He won a second Guggenheim Fellowship which permitted him to spend 1955 in Nevada and California, and then, having terminated his troubled marriage, he was free to marry Alexandra Tschacbasov and settle down—after almost two decades of moving about—in Dutchess County, New York, near Tivoli. It was during these same five years that he wrote the short works that would make up his next book, *Seize the Day* (1956): "Looking for Mr. Green" (1951),

"A Father to Be" (1955), "The Gonzaga Manuscripts" (1956), the title novella, and a one-act play, *The Wrecker* (1954). The novella "Seize the Day" reflects the important fact that Bellow's novels are usually written over a period of years and thus do not belong to the year or even the decade in which they see publication. A friend of Bellow's reports seeing *The Victim* in two different versions by 1945, which means its composition may well have overlapped that of *Dangling Man*. When an interviewer grouped "Seize the Day" with Bellow's work in the 1940s, Bellow didn't argue with him, saying only that he had written it over a period of years. The fact remains, however, that the novella reflects a pattern of variety in Bellow's work, as each novel seems to contrast in tone with its predecessor. *The Adventures of Augie March* sprawls and attacks the world with energy; it made Bellow well known in the world of letters. "Seize the Day" is tight and sets an elegiac tone; it may well be the work that insures Bellow's position in the world of important writers.

The story recounts a day in the life of a failing middle-aged American, Tommy Wilhelm, who has made a series of poor decisions that land him jobless in his early forties at the Hotel Ansonia, where his father lives in retirement. Tommy wants his father's help—and is denied. He wants his substitute father's help too, and this father, the sometime psychologist Tamkin, is the character Bellow now finds most interesting in the tale, for "like most phony phonies, he is always somewhere near the truth. . . . But Tamkin's truths aren't really true." As he treats patients over the phone and spouts existential clichés, Tamkin promises to cure all of Tommy's troubles. He will make him strong, teaching him to "seize the day"—the very vagueness of which is Bellow's point—and he will make him financially comfortable, too, using his money to speculate on the grain market. Bellow begins the novella with Tommy emerging from his room, assuming a bold front. He gives over the first three sections to Tommy's past and his breakfast with his father, and the second three to his relations with Tamkin. In the last, climactic section, Tommy's disgusted father disowns him and Dr. Tamkin, having lost Tommy's last remaining savings, disappears.

Tommy's defeat makes many readers uncomfortable, and several reviewers termed "Seize the Day" an interim work, filling the time after *The Adventures of Augie March*. Since 1956 the novella's reputation has grown steadily, however, until, as Alfred Kazin puts it, "none of his works is so widely and genuinely admired as this short novel."

The reason lies in the calm and solidity of Bellow's art. The tone is almost Olympian in its treatment of Tommy's sloppy sentimentality, and Tommy himself is a significant creation. He is at once the ultimate antihero (Herbert Gold called "Seize the Day" "one of the central stories of our day") and yet a worthwhile man, and likable, with "a large, shaky, patient dignity." He is cheerful and without malice. He cares for his loved ones. More important, he is intelligently aware, undergoing his experience with depth and sensitivity.

But the finest accomplishment of the story, and certainly one of the remarkable conclusions in American literature, is the novella's climactic scene. Tommy at one moment is on the New York streets, desperately looking for Tamkin and feeling the pressure of the crowd, "the inexhaustible current of millions of every race and kind pouring out, pressing round, of every age, of every genius, possessors of every secret," and at the next inside a funeral parlor, where it is suddenly "dark and cool," and where "men in formal clothes and black homburgs strode softly back and forth on the cork floor, up and down the center aisle."

In a few moments he stands before the corpse, a man he had never known, and begins to cry. He sobs at first for the man, "another human creature," he thinks, but soon he cries for himself and for all his troubles. "Soon he was past words, past reason, coherence," Bellow writes. "The source of all tears had suddenly sprung open within him, black, deep." The other guests envy the dead man, to have such mourning, but Tommy does not stop. His grief becomes a definitive and strangely triumphant moment, as the flowers and lights and music fuse within him, pouring "into him where he had hidden himself in the center of a crowd by the great and happy oblivion of tears. He heard it and sank deeper than sorrow, through torn sobs and cries toward the consummation of his heart's ultimate need."

In the first version of this concluding paragraph, as originally published in the *Partisan Review*, Bellow included "and by the way that can be found only through the midst of sorrow," implying what the prose rhythms suggest, which is that the humiliating moment is some kind of victory. Critics disagree about Bellow's final meaning, puzzled, as Brendan Gill puts it, by the sense that Tommy is "sobbing his heart out over his plight and yet feeling rather better than usual," but almost all readers sense the authority of the scene. As Alfred Kazin says of the whole novella, "It has a quite remarkable intensity of effect without ever seeming to force one."

More specifically, the circumstance of Tommy finding his way to a stranger's funeral crystallizes Tommy's situation and needs. For he needs a father and has been denied, seeking help from people "dead" to him. He has sought all day to hide his failure, to put up a front, and here he is publicly reduced to truthfulness. Bellow himself has said that he wanted to dramatize the way New Yorkers fulfill intimate emotional needs through strangers, and so Tommy turns from his psychologist (the professional stranger) to an alien corpse—where he finally finds fulfillment. The scene gathers together other themes as well, for Tommy all day has been sinking in his tears and here drowns; he had rejected his Jewish heritage, anglicizing his name, and here grieves before the Star of David; Tommy has been a masochist too, seeking pain in a classic case of Reichian pathology, as Eusebio Rodríquez has shown, and here he finally lets go, dissolving his destructive rigidity to permit a healthy venting of emotion. Since Tommy has had mystical promptings that his suffering somehow has a transcendent purpose, Bellow's point is also that Tommy sinks to a truer, more spiritual level of being accessible only when he is stripped of worldly pretensions.

Henderson the Rain King (1959) did not receive effusive praise when it was published, but it did not diminish Bellow's reputation either. Bellow wrote it in 1957 in Tivoli, New York, the period during which his second son, Adam, was born, and in 1958 at the University of Minnesota (an anchor for Bellow in these years and the place where he was friends with John Berryman), and then the next year in Europe, having won a two-year Ford Foundation grant.

This book about a WASP millionaire's trip to a dreamlike Africa illustrates the fertility and variety in Bellow's imagination and his desire, as he said later, to develop "a fiction that can accommodate the full tumult, the zaniness and crazed quality of modern experience." Henderson is a gigantic man in body and emotion, six foot four inches tall with "an enormous head, rugged, with hair like Persian lambs' fur. Suspicious eyes, usually narrowed. Blustering way. A great nose." He is an heir to a fortune, a hard drinker, a bully, a fighter, a man fleeing death. When the comedy of Henderson's brawling is done, his character remains formed in malice. He is nasty to his wives, torments the neighbors, breaks glass on tourist beaches. His rages finally scare the family cook to death, making him seek a salvation in Africa where, he says, "the world which I thought so mighty an oppressor has

removed its wrath from me." Henderson (whose initials and taste in guns are the same as Hemingway's) is the militant, insecure American who attempts to prove his manhood by killing. He is also the intelligent and sensitive man who suffers from his knowledge of human limitation. Confessing that he is most like the character Henderson, "the absurd seeker of high qualities," Bellow comments that "what Henderson is really seeking is a remedy to the anxiety over death. What he can't endure is this continuing anxiety . . . which he is foolhardy enough to resist."

In Africa Henderson encounters a harsh desert environment with a fierce white light—in essence, the inhuman physical universe. Although the novel has many realistic touches, it is essentially a fantasy, a trip deep within the Africa of Henderson's mind. For in this wasteland, reminiscent of the sheer raw power of the naturalistic world, Henderson discovers first a tribe which reacts to its environment with a soft, worshiping attitude, loving its cows and its dimpled and smiling old queen, and then (after he has harmed the gentle Arnewi irremediably by blowing up their water supply) a fierce and willful and manipulative tribe that beats its gods and threatens to kill its king. Part of Bellow's point is Henderson's desire to serve a community even though it involves often bizarre and dangerous conditions, as in the case of the marvelously relaxed Wariri King Dahfu, who studies Emerson, William James, and Wilhelm Reich and who will be unceremoniously strangled if he fails to satisfy any one of his forty wives. To make the anxious Henderson equally serene, Dahfu takes him into a lion's den, where he teaches him to emulate the lion. Dahfu's tribe believes that he is not completely king until he captures the soul of his dead father . . . in a live lion. Although educated in the Western empirical tradition, which would scoff at such a view, Dahfu accepts these conditions, and is killed in the attempt.

When Henderson then feels himself cured or freed from the world's wrath, he stumbles in explaining the cause, for he claims it was not the lion's cruel indifference that freed him but the love of the Arnewi—a statement that grows more out of Bellow's desire than the novel's events. The truth seems to be that Bellow's imagination drives (as in *The Victim* and "Seize the Day") to a final scene of violence or death which once experienced leaves the protagonist relieved and joyful. Bellow's burden as the maker of plots is to justify not just the death but the joy. And when he fails to do so, as in *Henderson the Rain King*, critics complain about a murky ending.

Henderson the Rain King is an amusing novel and a good introduction to Bellow's work. Henderson is a truly comic character, and Dahfu's theories are good intellectual fun. Bellow is bolder than he had been in his previous work (it is from *Henderson the Rain King* that he dates his maturity as a writer), for he here openly makes a connection between the force of the universe, particularized in the sun, say, or in an octopus's eye, and a human or spiritual principle. But Bellow once again sought variety, turning in the hectic next five years to a realistic work. He spent much of 1959 in Europe and the next year at his country home in Dutchess County. With Keith Botsford and Aaron Asher he edited the periodical the *Noble Savage*, which published writers such as Ralph Ellison, Thomas Pynchon, Josephine Herbst, and John Hawkes. He taught at the University of Puerto Rico and then settled down to his third marriage, with Susan Glassman, whom he wed in December 1961. Much sought after as a leading novelist, he taught a course in 1962 on "The Modern Novel and its Heroes" at the University of Chicago. The next year, with a new child on the way (Daniel, born in 1963) and a desire to return to his roots, Bellow left New York for Chicago, where he accepted a permanent position at the University of Chicago on the Committee on Social Thought.

In Chicago Bellow sought a greater freedom to work, a desire which bore fruit the next year with the publication of *Herzog* and the production of *The Last Analysis*. The play was a lighthearted episodic farce Bellow hoped would survive because of its entertaining qualities. The novel was more serious, embodying the theory he had announced in 1961 that a novelist must be permitted to deal with ideas. The play flopped, and the novel was a best-seller for six months. "I received two or three thousand letters from people pouring out their souls to me, saying 'This is my life, this is what it's been like for me,'" Bellow said after the publication of *Herzog*. "And then I understood that for some reason these themes were visited upon me, that I didn't always pick them, they picked me." Since the novel covered events similar to those of Bellow's life, portraying an intellectual professor devastated by the betrayal of wife and friends, some of the interest in the novel was that of a roman à clef. But most of the people who bought it were not in on the gossip; the novel articulated their own anger, their own frustration—precisely that frame of mind that characterized the late 1960s as tempers flared (and letters flew) over the issues of free speech, racial injustice, and war. Writing as early as 1960, Bellow anticipated the mood of the coming decade.

The story consists of Moses Herzog's memories as he putters alone about his country home—technically the place at which the action takes place, since everything that follows is a memory in Herzog's mind. Herzog remembers himself in New York, where he had stayed a few days after teaching a course, and then in Chicago, where he had lurked outside his estranged wife's apartment before suffering a minor auto accident, and a brief incarceration, from which the police freed him to go back to his country home in western Massachusetts.

If the geography is simple, however, the story is not. Since Herzog writes letters to all kinds of people and remembers all kinds of earlier events, the novel seems disorganized. Critics divide largely into those who forgive this disorganization (since it reflects Herzog's mind) and those who do not. And once again the protagonist at the end feels somewhat better, but the reader is not certain why. And yet the truth is that the book, which Bellow rewrote at least thirteen times, is indeed well formed. Moses Herzog had decided early in the story to shift from an emotional, "personal" life, such as the one in which his wife Madeleine abused him, to a more rational, civil, moderate one—he will shift, as he says in a letter to Eisenhower, from Tolstoy to Hegel. And much of the novel flows from this decision: he leaves Martha's Vineyard in part two because to him it represents the emotional or personal life since he had come there seeking comfort from a friend. He reviews his intimate family and friends in part three because they too sought salvation in the personal. He carps about Ramona (who gives him gourmet dinners and what she thinks is gourmet sex) because she would cure him by means of the "personal life." Resolved to do something, he awaits his lawyer in a courtroom that portrays the horrors of the personal or sexual life and shows how the impersonal machinery of the court may give true justice.

In part six he flies to Chicago, contemplating murder of his ex-wife and her lover in order to protect his daughter Junie, reportedly locked crying in an auto outside Madeleine's apartment, but he decides once more (as the novel catches the realistic zigzags of a man trying on a new mode) that he is being extreme and indulging in personal "drama."

Thus each of the novel's sections (there are nine in all) dramatizes Bellow's theme. After he is caught the next day with the gun in his pocket, Herzog finds himself standing before a police sergeant, next to Madeleine, who in pure hatred seeks to have him imprisoned. "Her voice went up sharply, and as she spoke, Herzog saw the sergeant take a new look at her, as if he were beginning to make out her haughty peculiarities at last. . . . 'One of those was for me, wasn't it!' she says of the bullets. 'You think so? I wonder where you get such ideas? And who was the other one for?' He was quite cool as he said this, his tone was level. He was doing all he could to bring out the hidden Madeleine, the Madeleine he knew."

When the sergeant lets him go, Herzog receives a symbolic justice. The friends and relatives and even doctors who had witnessed his divorce had all failed him, but the civil authority had not. And having gotten justice he feels better. One of the problems with the novel, however, is that he feels an ecstatic joy that goes far beyond fair treatment. The truth seems to be that this novel too must be viewed as not so much a thematic statement as an experience. Herzog in Chicago undergoes a purgation, first in the pondered murder and then in being jailed. Madeleine's lover Gersbach, whom Herzog had stalked with a gun in his pocket, becomes the parallel to Allbee, Dahfu, Tommy's dead stranger—and so too, in the cell that means ruin and death, does Herzog himself.

Herzog is notable for the controversy it caused. Bellow's second National Book Award-winner, it was praised and highly criticized. Alfred Kazin called it Bellow's "most brilliant" novel while Brendan Gill termed it "faultless." Other critics worried that Herzog pondered only himself, making the novel solipsistic. The key question is whether or not Herzog succeeds in making a character of himself as he looks back. Does Herzog get out of his own mind? His ability to see himself from the outside and with precise detail suggests that he might. Bellow's theme at any rate is something very much like solipsism, as Herzog is imprisoned in the "private" life.

But however one evaluates the structure of the book, *Herzog* is perhaps most notable for the style, which represents Bellow at his very best. Herzog's double remove permits Bellow to dote on detail, to slow the action when necessary to make the scenes live. And since Herzog does a great deal of observing, the novel finds its center in its descriptions. The prose is charged, rich, full of the specifics and precisely defined impressions that create the feel of mid-1960s American life. Herzog's pain seems to intensify his perception, but in many ways the novel is almost a culmination of the realistic

movement, defining just that moment before the ripeness turned. Because Herzog is deflected from his course not by any insight or charged drama but by the sight of kindly Gersbach giving little Junie a bath, *Herzog* is a defense of the realistic mode, holding that the significant levels of life are often the common, whether in the home or outside in society—a view Herzog himself embraces (rejecting the fashionable existentialism) and then in his life dramatizes.

But once again Bellow was not content to work in a single key. *Herzog* joins *The Victim* and the novella "Seize the Day" to define Bellow's realistic work (a mode which more than one critic feels to be Bellow's best), but Bellow in 1964 also wrote a wilder, more fantastic piece in the play *The Last Analysis*, which he saw performed in fall 1964 and which climaxed a long interest in the theater. One of his early essays had been about the season's Broadway plays, and in 1952 he had seen *The Victim* as adapted for the stage by Leonard Lesley. He had collaborated on a dramatization of "Seize the Day" and had included a one-act play, *The Wrecker*, among the pieces in the collection *Seize the Day*. Bellow also seems to have been motivated financially, for his novels had not made him a great deal of money, and his coming book—about a professor who writes letters to famous intellectuals—did not promise to be a best-seller. Zero Mostel would play the lead in "Humanitis," as *The Last Analysis* was originally entitled, and the play, Bellow thought, would be easy to write. He saw the theater as a form of freedom, since the footlights required a more direct, less subtle approach. He would supply the skeleton, as it were, and string some vaudeville-like bits together on it—a play with energy and emotion and sprawl not too unlike some of the work in the Yiddish theater.

By 1964, though, Bellow complained that he was writing himself into his grave. Mostel backed out, to be replaced by Sam Levene, and Bellow found playwriting more demanding than he had imagined. He persevered, however, presenting a comedian who has slipped in his career because of his seriousness and who now, in his New York warehouse studio, seeks to combine laughter and home-style psychoanalysis. The protagonist, Bummidge, seeks a cure for "humanitis," and his technique, he says, is to act out "the main events of my life, dragging repressed material into the open by sheer force of drama." In the first act he struggles to get enough money to go on closed-circuit television before a gathering of psychoanalysts and talks about his performance with his associates and relatives—his agent Winkleman, his mistress Pamela, his sexy but platonic secretary Imogen, his sister, his wife, his son—many of whom resent the money he is squandering. He rehearses his method, and then in the second and final act gives his lecture-demonstration, taking himself through the birth trauma, conflicts with his father, sexual adolescence, marriage, and then death, the experience of the last triggering an ecstatic state in which he disposes of all those who had obstructed him and determines to proceed with an institute to advance his new therapy.

So goes the published version of the play, which Bellow tells us is a substantial rewrite of the original, much tightened and simplified—abandoning the vaudevillian looseness for form and stressing the mental comedy of Bummy's method. The Broadway version flopped after twenty-eight performances, receiving poor reviews even though journalists such as John Simon tried gallantly to save it, arguing that it was the most substantial piece of comic drama produced that season. And such, at least in Bellow's rewrite, it seems to be. Bellow plays with ideas, providing a protagonist who seeks to discover what is wrong with himself by exploring the past. Bellow finds a way to visualize the internal. He combines a comedy of ideas—having fun not only with Freud but also with the intellectual's search for health—and a physical stage comedy, reminiscent of vaudeville.

Bellow's second effort in the theater did no better. For the production *Under the Weather*, Bellow combined three one-act plays, two of which have been published: *A Wen*, a delightful comedy about a scientist who has found the experience of winning the Nobel Prize less intense than the glimpse of a birthmark on a woman's thigh (a glimpse he seeks to duplicate, in middle age, with the same surprised lady) and a somewhat darker comedy, *Orange Soufflé*, about a Polish whore who wants to move in with her elderly and wealthy WASP customer. *Under the Weather* was produced in London, Spoleto, and New York, but failed to catch on.

In the novel *Herzog* Bellow attempted something like the comedy of serious thought, while in the play *The Last Analysis* he presented a clown reaching for serious ideas. Both works define a mode that would dominate Bellow's fiction for the next eighteen years, and that is the reliving of the past. *The Adventures of Augie March*, of course, was a memoir, and Henderson attempts to reach the dead parents for whom he yearns. In *The Last Analysis* and *Herzog*, however, Bellow discovered

a new center, as the protagonist relives his memories. The result was not only the creation of a special richness and color, always contrasting past and present, but a special style, one with the leisure to look and replay and sort and arrange and explore the past. "I think of myself as horribly deprived of people whom I loved and who are dead," Bellow confessed recently. "These memories serve to resurrect feelings which, at the time, I didn't want to have. . . . Now I realize how much emotion was invested in them, and I bring them back."

This mode is expressed in the best story in Bellow's next published work, *Mosby's Memoirs and Other Stories* (1968), a more or less "made" book designed to keep Bellow's name before the public and perhaps to capitalize on the great success of *Herzog*. Bellow continued to teach in Chicago in the years following *Herzog*, although he took time out in 1967 to cover the Six-Day War for *Newsday* and in 1968 to receive the Croix de Chevalier des Arts et Lettres from France. He had begun the novel that was to become *Humboldt's Gift*, but upon hearing an anecdote about an old man witnessing a pickpocket at work, shifted to the manuscript that would become *Mr. Sammler's Planet*. He had also found time to write two short stories, "Mosby's Memoirs" (1968) and "The Old System" (1967), to which he added "Leaving the Yellow House" (1957) and several tales already published in *Seize the Day*.

The best story of the group is "The Old System," in which the well-known scientist Samuel Braun, transparently Bellow himself, indulges in what became a characteristic Bellow posture in the late 1960s and 1970s: the middle-aged man remembering his Jewish relatives, losing himself in a colorful and exotic past. The characters are mysterious to Braun, who loves them. He ponders their reality, their evolution, the strangeness of their being. They are in one sense crude and grasping immigrants from Eastern Europe who would embarrass a third-generation Jew. But they are also vital and proud and fierce. They seem to Braun to be more intensely alive, or at least more passionate, than his modern colleagues. And indeed they are, for the remarkable story begins when Braun's fierce and fat cousin Tina, having reneged on a business deal with her brother Isaac, misses out on the fortune Isaac proceeds to make. The disappointment makes her claim Isaac cheated her, and she refuses to see him even though Isaac, as an old-fashioned believer in family, is scandalized. He spends years trying to see her, but it is only on her deathbed that she sends Isaac a message: he may visit if he pays her $20,000. To Braun remembering all this, the issue is why he is so moved now, why the event seems so precious to him. As he looks at the stars which make the episode and all else seem insignificant, he still glories in the magnificence of Tina's will and of her capriciousness—as she refuses the money when it is offered—and of her sassing the fate that gave her a fat body and the death that will soon come. He glories too in the integrity of Isaac and the old system to which he clung.

And thus it seems ironic that Bellow's next novel be marred by a lack of caring. *Mr. Sammler's Planet* (1970) was well but somewhat absentmindedly received, as though the reviewers praised Bellow by rote; a few years later it was attacked by radical young critics for political reasons, in part because Bellow had declared his independence from the liberal establishment in 1965 by attending the White House dinner that Robert Lowell, protesting Vietnam, had boycotted.

A stubborn and difficult writer, Bellow had written about an elderly man in a decade obsessed with American youth. In this novel, as in *Herzog*, Bellow seemed to test both his readers and his own powers. Artur Sammler is an old Polish Jew who, having lived in London in the 1930s, where he knew many of the Bloomsbury group, and having survived Nazi atrocities, has the civilized tastes of the intellectual English and the wisdom of the survivor. Around him he finds a host of modern young nieces, nephews, and acquaintances who reject all limits on their desire. They know no sexual bounds, no moral imperatives, no common civility. Sammler alone in New York quietly pursues something like duty. When his crazed daughter Shula steals a manuscript to help her father with his study of H. G. Wells, he doggedly seeks to return the manuscript. When his friend and benefactor Elya Gruner lies mortally ill in a hospital, Sammler alone among even the man's children pays homage to the dying.

The plot, which Bellow seems to have formed with a Wellsian casualness, consists largely of the young interfering with these two tasks and is typified in the running story of Sammler's relations with the black pickpocket, whose crimes he has witnessed on a bus and who follows Sammler to his apartment foyer to threaten the old man by exposing himself. Sammler mentions the incident to his opportunistic friend Feffer, only to discover later (in too much of a coincidence) the black struggling with Feffer because he had taken pictures of the crime. And when Sammler asks his ex-son-in-law to intervene, the younger man hits to kill. In contrast to such madness, Sammler at the end praises his friend Elya Gruner, who (though sometimes an abortionist for the mob) had known how to be kind. And to do his duty. Moderation, limits, rationality—all we have, Sammler suggests, is simple human decency. Gruner had met "the terms of his contract," Sammler concludes, "The terms which, in his inmost heart, each man knows. As I know mine. As all know. For that is the truth of it—that we all know, God, that we know, that we know, we know, we know."

Mr. Sammler's Planet is vintage Bellow, full of the precise detail and lively ideas and honest feeling that provide Bellow his strengths. If it is true, as several critics have charged, that Mr. Sammler is too right and the city too wrong, it may well be that this is the best novel the reader could hope for, written as it was so close in time to the controversial period it takes as its subject. And certainly the character of Sammler, who has survived the Holocaust, waking from a pile of corpses to kill fascists in his escape, is an excellent point of view from which to examine and judge American culture. Bellow captures better than anyone the feel of American society in the late 1960s, with its blend of social rebellion, sexuality, racial unrest, and personal aggrandizement.

Those who criticize the book have a point, too, however, although it is not a political one. Sammler's rational conservatism is totally responsible, whether we agree with it or not, for it is the result of a calm choice. "Without limits you have monstrosity, always," he says. "Within limits? Well, within limits monsters also appear. But not inevitably." What does mar the novel, finally, is Sammler's basic feeling of revulsion toward the world, both in its social form, which is cheap and distracting—Gruner's daughter worries about her sex life as her father dies—and in terms of all matter. Like Yeats sailing to Byzantium, Mr. Sammler has no use for the natural physical world, or what he calls "creatureliness. . . . Its low tricks, its doggish hind-sniffing charm." Sammler yearns to be "a soul released from Nature, from impressions, and from everyday life."

Herzog had balanced precariously between a sense of the world's beauty and its ugliness. In *Mr. Sammler's Planet* the balance is tipped, and the result is not only a book that turns sour but also one that tolerates a certain contrivance of plot, as though corny or mechanical events were a true parallel to a corny or mechanical world. Sammler on the move, fending off the crazed youth, is unconvincing.

Sammler alone with his thoughts and memories, in what is now Bellow's most typical mode, is mellow and believable.

Mr. Sammler's Planet won a National Book Award in 1971. While continuing to teach at the University of Chicago (where he had become chairman of the Committee on Social Thought) and coping with the public and bitter dissolution of his third marriage, Bellow worked on two novels, segments of which were published in 1974. One of these was *Humboldt's Gift*, which in 1975 became his seventh novel and which nominally won him the 1976 Nobel Prize.

Many reviewers praised the book, and *Newsweek* did a cover story on America's leading writer, but other critics were disappointed. "The book is not very real," Alfred Kazin confessed, although large pieces of it were. Part of the trouble seemed to be the combination of the realistic and the manic: Bellow attempted to work grotesque gangsters into a finely detailed world, and it did not work. And then the plot creaked, even though Bellow had been true to his vision once again, for if the world of affairs is contrived and vulgar, what kind of plot must a realist provide? Bellow had defined his basic intention in this novel in 1963, discussing "Literature" for *Encyclopaedia Britannica*: few modern novelists, he noted, dramatize a spiritual experience. If they feel they are important, writers "ought to show us the actualities of a religious life." *Humboldt's Gift* is a fascinating book because it does precisely that.

The story is told from the point of view of Charles Citrine, a well-known dramatist who reminisces about his friendship with Humboldt, a poet who combines qualities of John Berryman, with whom Bellow had been close friends at Minnesota, and Delmore Schwartz, whom Bellow had known in New York. It was in fact shortly after Schwartz died in 1966 that Bellow began the novel, much of which consists of Citrine trying to hang on to his memories of Humboldt and do a little anthroposophical meditation while being harassed by gangsters, lawyers, bimbos, and creeps—some funny and some not. All of them are typified by Cantabile, to whom Citrine owes money and who has Citrine's car smashed in by baseball bats and later forces the playwright to watch him defecate. An ex-wife is suing Citrine, and a mistress—the sensual Renata, an uninhibited woman who makes one think of a witty and tough Ramona—is attempting to lead him to the altar. But during all these events, Citrine moves inward in memory and meditation, seeking the images that Rudolf Steiner had promised would give spiritual salvation.

What is interesting thematically in *Humboldt's Gift* is the equation within Citrine's inner life of his meditation of spirit and his memories of his friend. Both of these exist in saving opposition to the world, although Humboldt's actual gift combines the sublime and the vulgar, for it consists first of a movie scenario on which they had collaborated and which proceeds to earn Citrine a small fortune, and then of a scribbled sentence at the end of a farewell letter: "We are not natural beings but supernatural beings."

The chief critical issue in the novel, aside from Bellow's struggle to mesh his transcendental philosophy with commercial America, is how Bellow in the same book can write both brilliantly and ineptly. Bellow moves from passages such as

> She threw a very good pass—a hard, accurate spiral. Her voice trailed as she ran barelegged and made the catch on her breast. The ball in flight wagged like a duck's tail. It flew under the maples over the clothesline.

to passages such as this:

> I met Kathleen at a cafe and showed her the clippings. There was more in the same vein. I said, 'Thraxter has a terrible weakness for making major statements. I think I might just ask for the three guns to be applied to the back of my head and the triggers pulled rather than sit through those seminars.'
>
> "Don't be too hard on him. The man is saving his life," she said.
>
> "Also it's a fascinating thing, really. Where does he make the ransom pitch?"
>
> "Here."

Bellow at his worst sounds like an amateur playwright providing background information as he moves his characters on- and offstage. Thus the later parts of the novel fall off, becoming talky and cranky, as though (as reportedly is the case) Bellow took to talking his novel to a stenographer, like the later Henry James, or as though his troubled personal life had taken its toll. The truly fine early parts of the book were written not too long after *Herzog*, while the later parts, developing some of the disenchantment with the real world Bellow expressed in *Mr. Sammler's Planet*, came since 1969.

Critics have not really done justice to the fact that good writing seems to exist in a delicate balance or tension that the reader can sometimes see come and go. One thinks of Mark Twain, and then, perhaps, the Bellow of *Humboldt's Gift*, for this novel contains writing as good as any that Bellow has done and also the very worst that he has done.

Perhaps Bellow said what he had to say in *Herzog* and now marks time. Certainly *Mr. Sammler's Planet* is very much like a brilliant piece of journalism, providing a highly intelligent man pondering our civil disruption.

And yet Bellow has always surprised his readers, and the wise Bellovians would expect to be surprised again. Bellow's 1976 book is the journalistic *To Jerusalem and Back; A Personal Account*, published after Bellow had accompanied his new wife, Alexandra, professor of mathematics at Northwestern University, to Israel. There he had adopted a fascinating premise: what could a practitioner of the humanities add to the politics and propaganda and terror of the Israeli-Arab conflict? Could he penetrate the confusion to find some kind of order? Bellow had contemplated a book on Chicago and had served as a journalist during the Six-Day War. Could he now make some kind of contribution to solving Israel's troubles? The book describes Bellow's travels, his interviews with Israeli and American leaders, and his dinner conversations with the powerful and the humble, and then—and not least important—his reading and research into the problem.

Bellow's writing is lucid and detailed, and not without humor, as an Hasidim, for example, is offended by Bellow's eating habits and offers to send him money each month if he will return to orthodoxy. But at the end the rational and well-meaning Bellow is forced to conclude that the situation is even more dangerous than he had supposed, for he finds that nations (and their leaders) do not act consistently with even their own self-interest. If only they recognized their goals and sought them ruthlessly, Bellow suggests, the struggle would have some order. But both Arab and Jew act irrationally, creating a dangerous and unpredictable mix. That bystanders such as Jean-Paul Sartre or the United States will make use of the conflict for their own purposes—again inconsistently and irrationally defined—only makes the issue worse.

Bellow's most recent novel examines another situation out of control and represents again the humanist's look at an important human issue. In *The Dean's December* (1982), Bellow contrasts communism and capitalism or, more accurately, the human failure of both systems. In this novel, Albert Corde, a dean of students at a Chicago college, has accompanied his sensible astronomer wife, Minna, to Bucharest, where her mother lies ill in a hospital. There petty communist officials make it difficult for Minna to visit the dying woman, a communist official now fallen from favor, and finally permit her only one visit—she must choose the time. Corde's wife must suffer the ordeal of her mother dying alone, without her daughter at the bedside.

As Minna hurries about the city seeking help, Corde passes the time in a chilly apartment remembering the problems he left back in Chicago. He had published a set of articles on the black underclass of the city and had insisted upon the prosecution of two blacks in the murder of a white student. His articles had upset liberals, who mistook his bleak honesty for racism, and so too had his insistence that the murderers be prosecuted. Corde could lose his job as dean, since it was injudicious of him to confront a problem as intractable as the Chicago ghetto, and certainly the acquittal of the black defendants in the murder case would mean that his insistence upon prosecution had been an error. While Minna struggles with a communist bureaucracy, Corde struggles with an American one. But because Corde is isolated in the Rumanian apartment, the chief drama in this novel is in meditation: Corde *thinks* about his problems, as the story passes back and forth between the present and the past, between action and analysis, between suspense and a reflection that Henry James might have found delightful.

But of course, the issues are not a delight. Bellow places his protagonist six thousand miles from Chicago to obtain distance from America's mammoth and emotional social problems. Corde's articles (recently published in *Harper's*, he says) are in fact leftovers from Bellow's abandoned book about Chicago and include a fine description of dialysis at the Cook County Hospital as well as several interviews, one with the public defender in a troubling case. A middle-class housewife had been abducted and raped and had sought refuge in private homes only to be turned back into the arms of her captor, who then murdered her. The public defender blandly tells Corde that the white woman had acquiesced; she had been sitting alone in the abductor's car. She had been dazed, Bellow suggests, and her black murderer had been dazed too: people suffer and commit atrocities like sleepwalkers. But the point of Corde's meditation is justice: the blacks must be held responsible for their crimes, Corde believes, and so too must the whites who are callous about human suffering. Corde is especially scornful toward the "media intellectuals," or those journalists and academics who have studied the lower class and have come up with nothing but jargon.

Corde's position as a journalist and an academic is thus very much to the point. Modern problems are so large that citizens must rely upon information supplied to them. But those charged with the responsibility of supplying such information have failed: "The language of discourse had shut out experience all together." Corde wrote his articles, we understand, "to recover the world that is buried under the debris of false description or non-experience."

And does Bellow himself "recover the world?" Because the specialists have failed in terms of language and perspective, Bellow provides a rationale for the participation of the humanist in public issues. But in doing so he makes an ambitious claim for his own novel. Does he succeed? Several reviewers found *The Dean's December* to be a considerable achievement. Bellow compares not just capitalism and communism, or a world in which "people have to be human without freedom" and one in which "they succeed in not being human with it," but the intersection in each society of the State and the person. Bellow in Rumania permits us to look at the State through the eyes of personal need, as in Minna's story, and then in Chicago to glimpse the individual—the suffering black—through the eyes of the State or the public officials who administer it. In both Rumania and America, the society parcels out pain to the individual. Ironically, in this intersecting set of contrasts and similarities, the communist state works in terms of the individual, singling out Minna's mother, while the capitalistic society works in terms of the larger group, creating a community (a commune) of deprivation and despair.

And yet the novel is flawed too, by what increasingly seems to be Bellow's carelessness. Bellow's style can flash to life at any moment, but it can also go dead. The plot concerning Minna's mother seems true and right; the murder trial in Chicago is contrived and wooden, full of desperate characters who are not so much shown as discussed. Bellow's description of Bucharest is so fine that John Updike proclaimed Bellow "one of the rare writers who when we read them feel to be taking mimesis a layer or two deeper than it has gone before." But Bellow's dialogue is formal, "talky," full of information that should be shown. Bellow forgets to ground his dialogue in a human relationship that will anchor it and make it part of the story and instead attempts to reveal events by having people talk about them.

Thus the reviewers had mixed feelings about *The Dean's December*, treating Bellow with respect but acknowledging the book's deep flaws.

Those who praised the novel did so on the grounds of Bellow's style and the immediacy of his descriptions. Those who criticized it (for reasons other than political ones) tended to refer to what has come to typify Bellow's later work, the juxtaposition in the same book of two different tones, two kinds of experience, or two levels of imagination. Bellow presents in his last three novels both a quiet, realistic level of experience, usually surrounding his protagonist's personal life, and then a manic one, full of energy and color and involving the external world or an eccentric who represents that world. What seems to have happened is that history has thrown Bellow a curve: as the public realm has become progressively more complex and uncontrollable, Bellow has had greater trouble uniting his two modes. The manic tone that Bellow once used as comic relief is now a form of verisimilitude, true to the public life, and the result in the novel is a series of jolts as we move from one tone to the other, from what Bellow controls to what he simply describes. And yet Bellow himself feels this disunity, for he carefully positions his protagonist to cope with it, giving him the leisure to think and a vantage point far enough away from the chaos—in terms of his years, say, or his sojourn in far-off Rumania—to gain perspective on it.

But whatever his difficulties, Bellow continues to write fascinating fiction, struggling to close the gap between private and public experience. He himself has continued to live in Chicago, writing and teaching, and seems to have achieved his own orderly life, with the end of a public lawsuit by his third wife. Will his work last? Even as fads come and go, even as Ph.D.'s study Bellow's difficulty with plot and others study Bellow's great success in style, even as the world whirls about him, Bellow's novels give evidence of lasting. Perhaps the most accurate testimony to Bellow's strength is given by his friend Richard Stern, when he asks, "How many American writers have published first-rate imaginative books over a thirty year period? Perhaps three, Henry James, Faulkner and now Bellow."

Source: Keith M. Opdahl, "Saul Bellow," in *Dictionary of Literary Biography*, Vol. 28, *Twentieth-Century American-Jewish Fiction Writers*, edited by Daniel Walden, Gale Research, 1984, pp. 8–25.

Sources

Bellow, Saul, "The Search for Symbols, a Writer Warns, Misses All the Fun and Fact of the Story," in the *New York Times*, February 15, 1959.

Mano, D. Keith, "In Suspense," in *National Review*, Vol. 36, Issue 15, August 10, 1984, p. 48.

Pinsker, Sanford, Review of *Him with His Foot in His Mouth*, in *Studies on Short Fiction*, Vol. 21, Issue 4, Fall 1984, pp. 404–05.

Wiehe, Janet, Review of *Him with His Foot in His Mouth*, in *Library Review*, Vol. 106, Issue 11, June 15, 1984, p. 1251.

Further Reading

Atlas, James, *Bellow: A Biography*, Random House, 2000.
  This is a major literary biography, ten years in the making, by an important analyst of the literary scene.

Glaysher, Frederick, "A Poet Looks at Saul Bellow's Soul," in *Saul Bellow and the Struggle at the Center*, edited by Eugene Houlahan, AMS Press, 1996, pp. 43–55.
  Since the split between spiritual traditions of Christianity and Judaism is so much a part of the life of this story's protagonist, readers may enjoy Glaysher's examination of matters usually deemed too spiritual for literary criticism.

Kiernan, Robert F., *Saul Bellow*, Continuum Publishing, 1989.
  Kiernan is one of the few critics to devote several pages to this specific short story.

Porter, Gilbert, *Whence the Power? The Artistry and Humanity of Saul Bellow*, University of Missouri Press, 1974.
  When this book was published, Bellow had already been an important figure in American literature for two decades. Porter analyzes the early novels and ends with a summary chapter about "Bellow's Vision."

Titanic Survivors Found in Bermuda Triangle

Robert Olen Butler

1996

"*Titanic* Survivors Found in Bermuda Triangle" was published in Robert Olen Butler's 1996 short story collection *Tabloid Dreams*. As the title of the book indicates, the basic premise of the stories in this collection is the lurid exaggerations found in the headlines of newspapers such as the *National Enquirer* and the *Weekly World News*. Rather than simply sticking with the humor implied by the outlandish titles of the stories, however, Butler develops the humanity implied within each piece, exploring what the situations mean to the characters who find themselves in such bizarre circumstances.

This story consists of a monologue by a survivor of the *Titanic* disaster. She has no memory of the time that has passed from the sinking of the ship in 1912 to the time that a rescue helicopter arrived to save the lifeboat she floated in, sometime in the mid-1990s. In her time (the first decade of the twentieth century), she was active in the feminist movement, wary of men and acutely conscious of the inequalities that marked the American society she knew firsthand. Excited about the signs of social progress in the modern world that she sees on the television in her hotel room, she is also worried about what this means for her future: with the cause settled to which she once devoted her life, she cannot imagine that there is any joy left for her, a stranger in a strange land.

Though the title "*Titanic* Survivors Found in Bermuda Triangle" implies a farcical comedy, Butler is dead serious about this woman's plight,

examining her situation with the same measured care that readers expect of thoughtful works of literature.

Author Biography

Robert Olen Butler was born in Granite City, Illinois, on January 20, 1945. His father was a college professor and his mother was an executive secretary. He graduated from Northwestern University in Evanston, Illinois, in 1967, with a degree in oral interpretation. The following year he married Carol Supplee, a marriage that was to last only four years. He attended the University of Iowa for postgraduate work, receiving a master of arts in playwriting in 1969. From 1969 to 1972, he served in Vietnam as an Army Intelligence officer and later as a translator for the U.S. advisor to the mayor of Saigon. His fiction, especially in his early novels, reflects his experience during the height of the Vietnam war.

After returning to the United States in 1972, Butler served as a reporter and editor for the *New York Times* and then returned to teach at the high school in his home town for a short while. He married again in 1972, to the poet Marilyn Geller; they divorced in 1987. From 1975 to 1985 he was an editor-in-chief for the *Energy User's News* in New York City. Butler took a position as associate professor at McNeese State University in Lake Charles, Louisiana, moving into a full professorship in fiction writing in 1993. As of 2005, Butler was teaching at Florida State University; in the same year, he won the National Magazine Award for Fiction.

Butler's first novel, *The Alleys of Eden*, was published in 1981, after having been rejected by twenty-one publishers. When it was finally brought out, it was praised by critics and became a Pulitzer Prize contender. The next year, his second novel, *Sun Dogs*, was published. In all, he published six novels between 1981 and 1992. Butler's 1987 marriage to Maureen Dolan ended in 1995, when he married Elizabeth Dewberry. His short story collection in 1992, *A Good Scent from a Strange Mountain*, won the Pulitzer Prize for 1993 and was a nominee for the PEN/Faulkner Award. He published two more novels after that and, in 1996, another collection of stories, *Tabloid Dreams*, which includes "*Titanic* Survivors Found in Bermuda Triangle. " He also published another collection of stories based on a central concept: the stories in *Had a Good Time* are all based on antique postcards that Butler collected. In 2005, Butler wrote a how-to

Robert Olen Butler   © Christopher Felver/Corbis

book: *From Where You Dream: The Process of Writing Fiction.*

Plot Summary

Robert Olen Butler does not establish a setting at the start of "*Titanic* Survivors Found in Bermuda Triangle"; nor does he establish who is talking. Instead, he starts the story with the narrator, whose name will much later be given as Margaret, telling her story, leaving the situation for the reader to piece together. From the title of the story, readers can accurately suppose that she is one of the survivors of the wreck of the *Titanic*, on the night of April 14, 1912. This assumption is supported by her reference, in the first sentence, to the coldness of the North Atlantic, the location where the *Titanic* sank, and references soon after to a lifeboat and the ship's smokestacks. She is recalling that night, and her life leading up to it.

While describing the chaotic scene of the ship going down, Margaret describes having been in London just days earlier, with a group of women who were marching in protest for women's right to vote and whose demonstration was being ignored by men. She feels similarly ignored as the ship is

Media Adaptations

- Butler reads from his novel *They Whisper* and is interviewed on a 1994 audiocassette produced by the University of Missouri, recorded for the radio series "*New Letters* On the Air."

- Butler's interview for the American Audio Prose Library is available on "Robert Olen Butler: Interview with Kate Bonetti," released by AAPL. It is featured at www.audible.com for downloading.

- Butler's interview for "Soundings," the cultural affairs radio program produced by the National Humanities Center, is part of the center's audiocassette collection *New Southern Writers*, released in 1995.

- Readers accessing the official Florida State University Robert Olen Butler page at www.fsu.edu/~butler/ can see Butler develop a story, day by day.

sinking, as her immediate understanding of the situation is ignored by all but one of the men she encounters. She traveled to London to attend a convention on suffrage and is proud of herself for having traveled alone, which was highly irregular for women in 1912.

In the present, Margaret finds her modern hotel room strange, but she has come to understand and accept it. She is conscious of the cold air from the air conditioner and has learned to use the television, examining the world and pleased to see women playing more significant roles now than they did in her time. The running water in the bathtub intrigues her: she has never taken off all of her clothes to bathe and finds uncomfortable the idea of doing so.

Remembering the ship's last hours, she recalls one particular man, an Englishman, whom she met on the promenade deck soon after the ship struck the iceberg. Though she generally looked upon men with disdain, she felt a little more comfortable with this man, which she attributes to his gentle, soft eyes.

When he told her that the ship would be all right, repeating the much-advertised point that it was supposed to be unsinkable, she dismissed his words of consolation and told him that she knew that it was sinking. Rather than the patronizing attitude that men ordinarily took with women, he accepted her intelligence, earning her respect. Later, she explains that she climbed into the life boat that was filled with women because he asked her to, while he stayed on the ship and faced his death with those left behind.

She remembers being on the lifeboat a few days after the *Titanic* sank and then hearing a large, loud machine approach from overhead: a helicopter. To the amazement of all of the women on the boat, the captain who speaks to them when they are loaded onto the helicopter is a woman, which is something that would have been unheard of in their time. The advances that women have made give Margaret hope, but they also give her a sense of being unneeded, since so much of her identity was connected to the struggle for gender equality.

The memory of the Englishman haunts her. She knew all onboard the *Titanic* would all die; she smells death nearby as she did in childhood when she and her father visited a town where the coalmine had collapsed on workers. The man, whom she calls "my man" to distinguish him from another man who was treating this disaster as a joke, stopped her when she wanted to go back to her cabin to read. He asked her to get into the lifeboat, and, despite her aversion to domineering men, she listened to him and agreed. For a moment, she considered touching him—reaching out and straightening his necktie, in a gesture of familiarity, as if they were a married couple.

Looking back on the experience from the present in the hotel room, Margaret realizes that she missed a once-in-a-lifetime opportunity for human contact. Having mentioned before how she has never been comfortable with her naked body, even while bathing, she strips out of her clothes and fills the bathtub. She climbs into the tub as it is filling, and, in the end, slides under the water, imagining that drowning now will reunite her with the nameless man she left behind.

Characters

The Drunk Man

Just as the Englishman and Margaret are coming to realize that they view the world in the same way, a drunk man approaches them. He has a drink cooled with ice that was chipped off of the iceberg that has sealed their fate. In describing the drunken man, Margaret is forced to refer to the Englishman as "my man," a familiarity that she notes. Both she and "her" man disapprove of the drunken man's foolishness.

The Englishman

Margaret, the narrator of the story, is generally disdainful of men, finding them to be offensively patronizing and belittling toward women. However, on the night the *Titanic* sinks, she meets one man, an Englishman, whom she comes to trust, respect, and possibly even love.

He is described as being stiff in bearing like an Englishman but having nice, soft eyes, "a woman's eyes." He is tall, wears tweed clothes, and has a moustache. When they first meet, he tries to comfort Margaret with the idea that the ship is unsinkable, but she tells him of her certainty that it is in fact going to sink, and she is impressed that he actually listens to her opinion, instead of thinking that she, as a woman, would not know about mechanical matters. As they are talking, a drunk man approaches, and both Margaret and the Englishman share a feeling of disgust. When he tells Margaret that she should get into the lifeboat that is being filled with women, she walks away, but he finds her, and the care that he has shown in seeking her out reveals to her that he really does understand her. He is the first man for whom she feels anything like love, and she shows her feelings for him by obeying his request to leave in the lifeboat; minutes later, the ship sinks, and he drowns. After her rescue, more than eighty years later, Margaret cannot get this nameless man out of her mind, and, thinking of him, she submerges herself into the cold water of her bathtub, dying just as he has in cold water.

Margaret

The first-person narrator of this story was on the *Titanic* when it sunk on the night of April 14–15, 1912. She was evacuated to a lifeboat, and, after drifting at sea for what seemed like just a few hours, suddenly found herself in modern times, rescued by a helicopter and taken to a room in Washington, D.C., where she is left to think about her past.

Margaret is a thirty-year-old woman. Her father, with whom she was particularly close, was a newspaper editor, and his intellectual curiosity carried on to his daughter. She is well-read, being familiar with authors such as the astronomer Percival Lowell and the economist Karl Marx, whose writings would have been considered inappropriate for young ladies in her day. When she recalls her father covering a coalmine strike in West Virginia, she thinks of him as standing up against the coal company and its "excesses."

She identifies with a strong feminist sensibility she has held to throughout her life. She is a great admirer of such luminaries of the suffrage movement as Susan B. Anthony, Elizabeth Cady Stanton, and Lucy Stone. Her trip on the *Titanic* is a return passage from Europe. First, she attended a convention of the National Union of Women's Suffrage Societies in London, where she was disappointed to find, when the women took their protest to the street, that the police opposed the protestors. Then she went to Venice, but soon became discontent with travel. Her status as a woman traveling alone was remarkable for a woman of the time.

As soon as the ship crashes, Margaret knows, intuitively, that the *Titanic* is sinking. She is willing to go back to her cabin and finish reading Edith Wharton's *Ethan Fromme* before dying, but a man whom she meets on deck, an Englishman with a gentle disposition, implores her to abandon ship in one of the lifeboats reserved for women. Though Margaret hates exactly this kind of pandering toward women, treating them as if they are children, she agrees. For a moment, as he is escorting her to the lifeboat and saying good-bye, she almost reaches out and embraces him, but she is too self-conscious to do so. Out on the sea in the boat, her mind focuses on the man who had shown her so much concern.

Finding herself suddenly in the 1990s, Margaret adapts fairly well. She accepts modern conveniences such as the television and the computer, understanding them in her own terms. She is glad to see the gains that women have made socially (and assumes incorrectly that they are farther reaching than in fact they are), but these gains also leave her with a sense of loss, since the thing that she fought for her whole life no longer appears to be an issue. At the end of the story, she takes off her clothes and climbs in the bathtub, which is something that she specifically states she would never have done before, and she slides under the water, apparently drowning herself to be reunited with the man with whom she almost shared a tender moment.

Margaret's Father

It is clear that Margaret's father was an important influence on her life. He was her intellectual inspiration. He took her with him to cover the coalmine strikes while he was a newspaper editor in West Virginia, and he gave her, as a teenager, a book about the possibility of life on Mars that he found so intriguing that he reported the author's thesis on the front page of the New York newspaper he was editing at the time. Thinking about the new world of the future to which she has found herself transported, Margaret frames its wonders in terms of headlines that her father might have written for his newspaper.

Her father is the only man to whom Margaret has ever been close. She remembers his death, just a year before the *Titanic* sank, when she was nearly thirty. At his bedside, she took his hand, an act of physical intimacy that, in the story, she finds herself unable to commit with the Englishman to whom she is attracted. His final words to her were, "I'm proud of you, Margaret," which shows the source of her self-assurance, her energy, and willingness to stand up against social convention. The tears that she wept over him, she says, were "from gratitude, as much as anything else."

Captain O'Brien

When the lifeboat full of women who have escaped the sinking ship is rescued, the women are all brought on board a helicopter. Since no time has passed for them and they think it is still 1912, they are amazed to find that the captain of the rescue ship, Captain O'Brien, is a woman: this instantly shatters all of their notions of gender roles.

Themes

Edwardian Age

The term "Edwardian Age" refers to years during which Edward VII reigned. Though Edward was king from 1900 to 1910, the era named after him is often extended to the start of World War I in 1914. The Edwardian period marked the very different mood that prevailed in England and in America in the first decade of the twentieth century. In 1901, Edward ascended the throne upon the death of his mother, Victoria, who had been queen since 1837. In the early 2000s, many people probably assume that the Victorian period was one of prudishness and repressed sexuality. To whatever extent that description is accurate, Victoria's son, Edward was quite a contrast. He was self-indulgent and licentious. His own behavior matched a developing English taste for permissiveness, intellectual inquiry, and social progressiveness.

Margaret fights Victorian assumptions. She tries to liberalize nineteenth-century standards for women, remnants of the old oppressive social order. Having grown up in a household that encouraged her to challenge conventional beliefs, she is prepared for the fight, but she leaves England disappointed in Englishmen who are resistant to female suffrage. In the end, though, the man who does listen to her and respect her individuality is an Englishman.

Women's Rights

Margaret's obsession is female suffrage, a goal shared by many women and men at the start of the twentieth century. She is so involved in the National American Women Suffrage Association that she attends an international convention supporting the cause held in England.

Her concern for social justice shapes her world view: she is suspicious of men, expecting the worst of them. When she meets the Englishman on the deck of the *Titanic*, she thinks that he "seemed stupid at first, in a typical way": she expects him to dismiss her intuition about their present situation and is instead surprised to find that he takes her seriously. His acceptance, coming after years of struggling with men's patronizing attitudes, is such a surprise that it frightens and angers her, forcing her to walk away. At the end of their brief encounter, she finds that, even though she feels the right to, she cannot bring herself to reach out and touch him. At the last minute, faced with almost certain death, she is still bound by the traditional gender roles that she has spent her adult life struggling against.

Flesh versus Spirit

Though Margaret, the protagonist of this story, is strong spirited, she is unable to translate that strength into a sense of truly feeling at one with her own flesh. When she talks about going to Venice to be alone after facing crowds of hostile men at the rally in London, she describes her self-conscious inability to bathe or even to look at her own body naked. As she puts it, "For all my ideas I was not comfortable in this woman's body."

Margaret describes being told of her father's death and realizing that he "had left his body." She wonders, when faced with death at the sinking of the *Titanic*, whether her father found his body as useless as she found hers.

In the end, though, she comes to an understanding that unites her body and her spirit. In the future, far removed from the events of April 1912,

Topics For Further Study

- Interview a large number of people about what they think the Bermuda Triangle is and what causes its mysterious power. Then research the scientific theories of people who have studied the area. What psychological need do you think accounts for the difference?

- The website for the parody newspaper *The Onion* lists made-up newspaper front pages from history. Find one from around the time of the *Titanic* sinking and write a short story based on it.

- Watch the 1997 blockbuster movie *Titanic*, and the 1958 film *A Night to Remember*, which is also about the night that the ship went down. Write a comparison of the two films, explaining which story you found most compelling.

- Find the specifications of a contemporary luxury liner, and explain to your class why—in theory, at least—it will not sink.

- Research Elizabeth Cady Stanton and Susan B. Anthony, and write a report about what their personalities were like. Explain in detail what Margaret's interest in them says about her.

she thinks about the Englishman with whom she shared a spiritual bond on that night. At the time, she was too self-conscious to touch him, as she wanted: looking back now at what has been important in her life, she is able to free herself of her clothes, as she was not able to before. Sliding naked into the cold water in the bathtub makes her acutely aware of her body, and she imagines that she and this man, with whom she connected in life can be together again, spiritually, this time in death.

Love

This is a story about a woman who has worked so diligently to avoid being victimized by traditional gender roles that she suppresses the impulse to love when it occurs. The affection that Margaret shows for her father is deep, as is seen clearly in the scene where she sits by his bedside the night of his death and weeps while she holds his hand. Her love for the Englishman whom she meets on shipboard, however, is much less certain.

Throughout their brief encounter, Margaret holds this man at length. She never even learns his name. She expects a condescending attitude from him, and she is surprised to see his genuine interest in her, that he takes her seriously. Her suspicion is so strong that it keeps her from putting a hand up to his face as they are about to separate: the love impulse within her tells her to reach out

to him, but Margaret has been conditioned to check herself. It is only after she survives the ordeal and is magically transported decades into the future that she takes the time to consider the potential in that relationship. Then she realizes that it was in fact love, and she wants to rejoin him in spirit.

Style

Symbolism

Throughout "*Titanic* Survivors Found in Bermuda Triangle," water is used to symbolize Margaret's fear of being touched. This is made most obvious in the segment of the story describing her trip to Venice. The trip itself is a quick diversion: she leaves London, goes to Venice, and is quickly back in London. It is not important to the plot, but it offers great symbolic significance. In Venice, as Margaret describes it, she found herself unable to bathe naked in a tub of water, overcome with shame at her own body. This aversion to water becomes even more poignant when she recoils in terror at finding that, due to high tide and/or a storm at sea, the Piazza San Marco is covered with overflow from the canals. She flees to America immediately thereafter, only to find herself faced with the prospect of drowning in the North Atlantic.

In the end, Butler uses the fear of water to show that Margaret has discovered a willingness to be free and open with her body. Having earlier mentioned a fear of the bathtub in her hotel room, she finally fills the tub and slips into the water. This willingness to submerge herself corresponds with her willingness to accept the idea that she actually does want to open herself up to the man she met on the ship that night.

First Person Point of View

Readers may find this story difficult to follow because the first-person point of view restricts the narrative and takes them from one time frame to another without explaining what is going on. The story takes place within Margaret's head and is placed so deeply within her consciousness that it does not identify places where one thought leads to another. Because the background is not established for specific scenes, readers have to interpret the clues around them in order to figure out what is going on. The basic premise of the piece, that it is the story of a person who was on the *Titanic* and has been transported to modern times through the magic of the Bermuda Triangle, is suggested in the title, but the order within the story is only dictated by Margaret private review of events.

Historical Context

The Sinking of the Titanic

The *Titanic* was advertised heavily throughout 1911 and 1912 as illustrating the future of ocean travel, a ship too huge and too well-designed to ever sink. It sank on its first voyage.

The theory behind the ship's presumed stability was its double-lined hull, which was divided into sixteen watertight compartments. Four of these compartments could flood, and the ship would stay afloat. Worldwide attention was drawn to its maiden voyage between England and New York. On the night of April 14, 1912, two days out of Southampton, the ship collided with an iceberg in the North Atlantic, and five of the watertight compartments were ruptured, which was enough to make the *Titanic* lose its buoyancy. The initial impact was just before midnight, and by 2:30 a.m., the ship that had been called the greatest luxury liner ever was underwater. Of the 2,200 passengers, including many from the wealthiest families in the world, 1,513 drowned. Many of these could have been saved. But in their haste, people in lifeboats hurried away from the ship without being full, and the ship nearest, the *California*, did not hear the *Titanic*'s distress call: the signal operator had turned off his radio and gone to sleep.

The Bermuda Triangle

The Bermuda Triangle is an area in the southern Atlantic ocean where weird phenomena have been said to have occurred for hundreds of years. It is the area bordered by Miami, Bermuda, and Puerto Rico. More than a hundred ships and airplanes are rumored to have disappeared in this relatively small area, fueling rumors of alien abduction, government conspiracies, and paranormal activity. Hurricanes and waterspouts have been known to spontaneously flair up in this area, and strange lights have been reported in the skies.

The most popular explanation for the anomalies that occur in the Bermuda Triangle is that the area, for some reason, has a strange electromagnetic field that confuses navigational instruments. The uniqueness of the magnetism in this area is clear from the fact that it is one of only two places on Earth where true north and electromagnetic north actually align. Many theorists take the strange magnetic fields to be proof of the work of outside forces. The second most common scientific explanation for the apparent difficulty in navigating this area is the unevenness of the ocean floor: it varies widely within the Bermuda Triangle, from 5000 feet in the Florida Straits to 12,000 feet a few miles away to 30,000 feet near Puerto Rico. The floor of the ocean affects currents in ways that sailors who are used to more gradual changes cannot anticipate. In addition, the tropical weather is violent and unpredictable. There are plenty of logical explanations for the large number of ships lost in the Bermuda Triangle, just as there are plenty of supernatural explanations.

The Suffrage Movement

The struggle for women's rights in America was present at the country's founding, as is seen in a letter from Abigail Adams to her husband, John Adams, while he was attending the Continental Congress in 1976, asking him to "remember the ladies." He responded jokingly by using a line that was to be cited frequently over the next hundred and fifty years: the Declaration of Independence says that all *men* are created equal.

The first Women's Rights convention, held in Seneca, New York, in 1848, galvanized the struggle for equality, identifying the inability to vote as a primary stumbling block to it. After the Civil War, those in the suffrage movement worked

Compare & Contrast

- **1912:** Women will not have the constitutional right to vote for another eight years.

  Today: Political operatives study and preen candidates' images in order to find the best way to gain the "woman vote."

- **1912:** The fastest way to get from Europe to the United States is by steamship. Under the best conditions, the trip takes approximately six days.

  Today: British Airways' Concord airplane could make the trip between New York and London in less than three and a half hours, but it was retired in 2003 due to lack of interest.

- **1912:** The distress call from the *Titanic* is not answered by the nearest ship because the communications operator has turned off his radio.

  Today: In a crisis such as the *Titanic* faced, most of the passengers would be able to call anywhere in the world on their cell phones.

- **1912:** Sailors speculate about the mysterious Bermuda Triangle, where ships have been known to mysteriously disappear.

  Today: The phrase "Bermuda Triangle" is so well known that one can generally use it to refer to any mysterious disappearance.

- **1912:** Many cities have daily tabloid newspapers that practice "yellow journalism": printing sensationalistic articles as "news," even when they have been made up by the writers specifically to capture public attention.

  Today: Daily newspapers are usually held to standards of ethics and verifiability. Lurid, imaginary stories are the province of the low-end supermarket tabloids and bloggers.

---

equally for the rights of women and blacks to vote; when the Fifteenth Amendment granted the vote to black citizens, Elizabeth Cady Stanton and Susan B. Anthony formed the group that, in 1890, became the National American Woman Suffrage Association, mentioned in the story. Stanton resigned from the group in 1892, falling out of favor with many members, who found her ideas too radical. In 1911, the year before *Titanic* sank, the National Association Opposed to Women's Suffrage was formed as a conglomeration of shadowy financial interests, backed by society women. Nonetheless, the right to vote—suffrage—was granted to women with the Nineteenth Amendment, in 1920. Much of the organizing apparatus of the National American Woman Suffrage Association was used to form the League of Women Voters, which continued to be active into the early 2000s.

Tabloids

Almost every grocery store and convenience store in the United States has a rack near the checkout counter stocked with newspapers whose headlines pronounce lurid claims, usually combining the names of currently popular celebrities with pulse-quickening adjectives such as "bizarre," "twisted," "horrifying," "shocking," and so forth. These papers are referred to as "supermarket tabloids." The word "tabloid" refers to the papers' layouts: they are printed on half sheets that are folded in half, not in quarters, so that they can be thumbed through like books without the trouble of having to separate sections and unfold them. Traditionally, papers laid out this way have catered to the lower classes: people who might read their newspapers on a subway train or carry it in a back pocket to read during a break, as opposed to those who might have the luxury of spreading their newspaper over a breakfast table or desk. Editors of tabloids generally catered to uneducated readers with bold, gripping headlines about sensationalistic stories.

Tabloids were increasingly available throughout the nineteenth century in the United States, but

Titanic survivors in a lifeboat, seen floating near the rescue ship Carpathia *on the morning of April 15*   Photograph by Ralph White. © Ralph White/Corbis

they became even more common with the 1890s competition between William Randolph Hearst (1863–1951) and Joseph Pulitzer (1847–1911). By the 1970s, tabloids were part of the newspaper mainstream. By that decade, the *National Enquirer* had been distributed at grocery stores for twenty years. Other newspapers, such as the *Sun* and the *Weekly World News* followed in its wake, offering stories that were attributed to ambiguous sources (such as "a close friend" of the celebrity being maligned) or simply running articles so preposterous that no one could take them seriously. As of the early 2000s, all U.S. supermarket tabloids are owned by the same publishing conglomerate, American Media.

Critical Overview

Critics have generally been favorable to Robert Olen Butler's works throughout his career. When *Tabloid Dreams* was published, many critical responses focused on the book's general premise, which was to present twelve stories based on lurid-sounding titles that might have been actual headlines in some of the

more sensationalistic supermarket tabloids. Bonnie Smothers, writing a review in *Booklist*, found that Butler "fairly giggles throughout this collection over the fun he's having." Smothers found the stories to be "fabulously grotesque" and praised Butler for "inventiveness bordering on excess." In *America*, Barbara C. Ewell noted her appreciation of Butler's narrative device and also found the stories to be meaningful on their own: "But what makes these tales more than hilarious devices is how much truth Butler makes the incredible captions reveal about being human, and how well they expose the strangeness of our own daily life." She ends her review by telling readers that "if his fiction makes us probe a little more deeply into the absurd dreams we all inhabit, then he's only doing his job—very well."

There are, however, critics who understand what Butler was trying to accomplish with the form he chose for these stories and yet still find that his skills fall short. An example of this criticism came from Theo Tait, who reviewed the book for the *Times Literary Supplement*. After acknowledging the book's success in mirroring the collective consciousness of these superficial times, Tait explained, "Unfortunately, these episodes frequently degenerate into a familiar brand of occult whimsy, failing to grapple with their intriguing subject-matter." He found the subject matter of the stories to be too focused on the theme of isolation, with one story after another striking the same note. While many critics have been delighted with what Butler achieved, there are a good number, like Tait, who wished he had accomplished more.

Criticism

David Kelly

Kelly is an instructor of literature and creative writing at College of Lake County and Oakton Community College in Des Plaines, Illinois. In this essay, Kelly looks at whether Butler tries too hard to avoid the sort of sensationalism that his story's title suggests.

Robert Olen Butler's 1996 short story collection *Tabloid Dreams* has a gimmick: each of the stories that it contains is based on a title that resembles the types of titles one finds in tabloid newspapers, the kind that shoppers thumb through while waiting in line at the supermarket. "Help Me Find My Spaceman Lover," "Boy Born with Tattoo of Elvis," and "Woman Struck by Car Turns into Nymphomaniac" are some of Butler's titles that could easily have been taken from the same weeklies that promise information about Bat Boy, aliens, and unlikely medical phenomena, all peppered with superlatives such as "amazing," "shocking," "mysterious," and "miracle."

Butler's use of these titles could be considered gimmicky because they reach out to a wider audience than literary fiction usually reaches. Cynical readers and critics could assume that Butler has actively courted a wide readership of people who would find his book easy to talk about with each other, given a handy description: an ordinary collection of short stories can be referred to by its title and author, but friends can take a shorthand approach to a book with a gimmick, telling each other, "Oh, it's the one where . . . " For this reason, popular response to a book with an obvious gimmick is inclined to be favorable. Critics, though, knowing that the gimmick might gain a book more popular attention than it otherwise deserves, tend to stare at such works with more skepticism than usual. They even distrust themselves, fearing that they might be kinder to a book that promises fun than they would be to just another work of literature.

> " It is one thing to refuse to dwell on the sensational, but '*Titanic* Survivors Found in Bermuda Triangle' refuses to even acknowledge the proverbial elephant on the living room sofa."

Butler seemed to be aware of the probability of critical distrust, maybe too aware. Though the titles of the stories in *Tabloid Dreams* imply a playful sense and some tongue-in-cheek jibes at popular culture, the stories themselves are usually dry and serious. It is as if Butler has gone out of his way to curtail the charge that the fantasy, hallucinations, and paranoia implied by the titles of his stories are there for cheap thrills, and squeezed all of the thrills out of his fiction entirely. Nowhere is this more evident than in the collection's final tale, "*Titanic* Survivors Found in Bermuda Triangle." It is the story of a woman on the way home from a suffrage convention in Britain when the *Titanic* crashes into an iceberg: on the deck, a man she meets convinces her to seek safety in a lifeboat, and soon after she watches the ship sink she finds herself in the modern world. The title touches upon two elements that might capture the attention of fans of actual tabloids: the sinking of the *Titanic* off the coast of Newfoundland in 1912 and the mysterious Bermuda Triangle, where ships and aircraft are said to disappear without explanation. What the story delivers, though, is a woman in a hotel room, looking back on her life with regret.

The main thing to consider when asking whether Butler has let his gimmick affect his story too much is whether the story works on its own, regardless of its title. The story itself perches in several different, but familiar, conceits. First, there is the doomed shipboard romance. Forgetting for a moment that the narrator, Margaret, says that the ship she was on was the *Titanic*, this is just the story of two people, a man and a woman, who meet in that terrible time between a tragic event and its eventual, inevitable result. About the man, readers

What Do I Read Next?

- The narrator of this story refers to Edith Wharton's 1911 novel *Ethan Frome*, which she says she was a few pages from completing the night that the *Titanic* sank. In the book, Frome, a poor New England farmer, finds himself attracted to the enchanting, captivating Mattie Silver, who is the cousin of his homely, ill wife, Zeena.

- Butler's first short story collection, *A Good Scent from a Strange Mountain*, won the 1993 Pulitzer Prize for fiction. Its fifteen stories, centered on the lives of Americans and immigrant Americans affected by the Vietnam War, force Vietnam folk myths up against the difficult realities of modern industrial life.

- Readers can get advice from Butler about how to write in his *From Where You Dream: The Process of Writing Fiction* (2005), published by Atlantic Monthly Press.

- Unlike the titles in Butler's short stories, the works discussed in Bill Sloan's *I Watched a Wild Hog Eat My Baby: A Colorful History of the Tabloids and Their Cultural Impact* were all actually published in newspapers. Sloan, a former editor for the *National Enquirer*, gives an insider perspective on how decisions are made in the tabloid publishing business.

- *The Story of the "Titanic" as Told by Its Survivors*, edited by Jack Winocour, contains dozens of first-person accounts from the night the ship went down in 1912. Some of the voices echo the voice of Margaret in the story.

---

are told practically nothing: his story is told in detail in another story in *Tabloid Dreams*, but, considering this story on its own strength, he is just a tall, decent man with a moustache dressed in initially in tweed.

About the woman, much is known. As the narrator of the story, she darts in and out of important moments of her life, giving glimpses of herself at different ages, telling readers about her history, her family, her ambitions, her phobias. We learn that at the time of the boat crash she was thirty, a crusader for women's rights who had recently lost the father whom she adored. She distrusts men, but is uncertain about her own instincts. In some ways a Victorian, she is uncomfortable looking at her own body so she cannot comfortably take off all her clothes to bathe. She traveled to Venice, which was daring for a woman in 1912, but while there she experienced an unidentified dread when water filled the streets, and she raced for home.

Although the most of the story is concerned with Margaret's life in the year 1912 and before, the story actually takes place in modern times. She is in a hotel room in Washington D.C., where she has been for less than an hour. She has seen rescue helicopters and female army officers. She has seen television, on which she has seen "women intimately involved with machines," from which one can assume she means computers, automobiles, and the like.

Herein lies the most unsettling question about Butler's telling of the story: is Margaret's reaction to the situation she finds herself in credible? With so much new, so much unfamiliar life being introduced, is it possible that a person would spend her time dwelling on her past? The slippery thing about this question is that it concerns a possible person, not a likely one. You, yourself, might not spend your first hour in the computer age pondering your theories, or your father's theories, or the great suffragist Elizabeth Cady Stanton's, but if there *could* be one person who would do so, then Butler is certainly entitled to tell that person's story. He only has to convince readers that Margaret is that person.

It is not inconceivable nor even unlikely. Margaret is thoughtful and painfully self-conscious, and her encounter with the mustachioed man on the ship is the closest thing she has ever had to a romance. She might, after a glance at the modern world, take note of what is unfamiliar to her and then turn back to the matters that already preoccupied her on the lifeboat. Margaret is an unusual case: but then, all stories ought to have protagonists who are unique.

Making Margaret so introspective gives Butler a chance to delve into such rich, diverse fields as history, philosophy, sociology, Freudian psychology, gender issues, and love. In order to stuff all of these issues into a short story, he needs to have Margaret just barely conscious of the circumstances that surround her, such as the fact that she has been transported across decades in the wink of an eye. It is one thing to refuse to dwell on the sensational, but *"Titanic* Survivors Found in Bermuda Triangle" refuses to even acknowledge the proverbial elephant on the living room sofa.

For instance, the story makes no mention of the supernatural. The title mentions that Margaret has been moved from the familiar world to the unfamiliar by the mysterious workings of the Bermuda Triangle, but the story does not use the words "Bermuda Triangle" at all. For all that the story's narrator knows, she was in one place one minute and then somewhere else: the best she can do to understand this transformation, with her 1912 mindset, is to compare the modern world to a 1895 description of life on Mars. Butler avoids the question of just how the Bermuda Triangle works, just as he refuses to offer any realistic explanation for any of the weird events in the other stories in the book. To do so is his right as a fiction writer. What he fills the story with while avoiding an explanation of what has happened are the protagonist's random thoughts and background fears.

The other attention-grabbing element in the story's title is the *Titanic.* To people familiar with the story of the ship's sinking, who would be drawn to a headline like this if it actually appeared in a tabloid newspaper, the fascination with the *Titanic* is not that two lonely people might have met before the disaster. There are particular aspects of the sinking that have been told and retold since 1912: for example, the band played "Nearer My God to Thee" as the boat went down, people cooled their drinks with chunks of the iceberg that had sealed their doom. Butler's dour narrator refers to both, but only disparagingly. The elements that became commonly known and which ordinary people found interesting about the ship's sinking are not relevant to her. This seems to reflect the attitude of the story in general: after catching readers' eyes with an extraordinary title, Butler seems to be warning them that fiction is not supposed to be fun.

Since the story focuses on Margaret's mental state and avoids having her interact with the strange new world in which she finds herself, the options for how it can end are limited. One might imagine an ending with her embracing her new home, perhaps picking up the telephone and summoning the people who put her in the hotel room to tell them—what? To buy her different clothes, take her out to work the press circuit? No, this story would never go there. Such an ending is cut from the same sensationalistic territory that this story goes to such lengths to avoid.

The end that Butler chooses is so constricted that it is can only work by turning symbolic. Margaret, longing for the romance that she did not have time or impulse to enjoy, decides to conquer the fear of water and nakedness that overcame her in Venice and to overcome the disdain for men that has defined her adult life. She explains that sliding into a tub of cold water will reunite her with the Englishman she did too little to get to know. If such a reunion is to happen, it could only be symbolic. (Unknown to her but known to readers of *"Titanic* Victim Speaks Through Waterbed," which is also in *Tabloid Dreams,* his fate has been a transformation into water). It is a spectacularly quiet ending to an amazingly uneventful story.

"Titanic Survivors Found in Bermuda Triangle" is more static than it needs to be, pushed deep inside the main character's psyche by the need to avoid seeming a slave to its exotic origins. All of the stories in *Tabloid Dreams* stem from populist roots, but they struggle against the very idea of whimsy that gave them their original purpose for being. Butler is a terrific writer, and the idea of working with tabloid sensibilities is a compelling one, but it seems as if, in working through his ideas, his basic gimmick may have scared him.

Source: David Kelly, Critical Essay on *"Titanic* Survivors Found in Bermuda Triangle," in *Short Stories for Students,* Thomson Gale, 2006.

Michael Becker

Becker has an M.M. in musicology from the University of Texas at Austin. As of 2005, he is completing his Ph.D. in musicology from the same school. In the following essay, Becker discusses the use of form, especially the conclusion, in the short story "Titanic *Survivors Found in Bermuda Triangle."*

In a time-based creative endeavor (meaning anything with a beginning, a middle, and an end which unfold over a certain time period), devising

> "
> To put it another way, by repeatedly broaching the topic of death in such a short space, Butler paves the way for Margaret to commit suicide without completely blindsiding the reader."

a satisfying ending can perhaps present the most difficult questions for the creator. How a composer resolves the sonic tension created during a piece, what decisions a director makes about how a film's momentum slows, or how an author wraps up the situations he has presented through out his story all have a major impact on how the audience receives the work as a whole. An exemplary finish can make up for an otherwise perfunctory work; in fact, some writers and authors make entire careers out of unique endings (for example, writer/director M. Night Shyamalan of *The Sixth Sense* and *Unbreakable* fame). At the same time, a poorly executed ending can spoil an entire work for the audience, even if the rest of it is top-notch.

For example, a common tactic in poor conclusions is the use of fairy-tale endings in which the hero implausibly wins the heart of the love interest, defeats the evil-doers, and, to boot, learns some important life lesson along the way. In short, everything ends neatly tied up and totally positive. While this may work in children's stories and Walt Disney movies, it generally does not for adult literature. After spending time witnessing the drama's unfurling, such an ending short-changes the audience. It leaves them feeling cheated or snubbed, as though they wasted their time.

To circumvent blatant fairy-tale endings, authors have endings which are just as "cheap" as that described above but are not as obviously childish. One of these is the ending in which the central character is placed in a difficult situation (or usually a series of them) only to find out in the end that it all has been a dream. In the 1980s the writers of the hit television show *Dallas* tried to use this

tactic at the end of the 1985–1986 season; in the season finale, the main character wakes up one morning to find her husband alive (he was killed off at the end of the previous season) and that the events in this entire year's episodes were all figments of her imagination. Fans of the show were disappointed because they watched the show every week for months only to find out that none of it mattered—they wasted their time. A variant of the dream ending involves the character either dying suddenly or realizing he has been dead all along (for example the films *Sixth Sense* or 1990s *Jacob's Ladder* with Tim Robbins). This method is just as frustrating for an audience because killing off a character makes it easy for the author not to have to resolve the complicated situations he or she has created for that character. It all magically disappears. In other words, this type of ending feels like a cop out.

Given this discussion of types of endings, the conclusion of Robert Olen Butler's short story, "'Titanic' Survivors Found in Bermuda Triangle," from his *Tabloid Dreams* merits a close examination. On the surface it would appear to be one of these difficult-to-digest endings. The character, Margaret, agonizes over her unfulfilled life and lost chance at love only to suddenly choose to drown herself in the bathtub on the very last page. However, Butler does not allow this to play out like an awkward, sophomoric gimmick. His choice to have her commit suicide is more than just a convenient, if a tad morbid, way to bring the story to a finish. Instead, his choice of ending works for this story and this character, even though death endings are often weak. This begs the question, "How does the author manage to kill off the only character in the story, yet manage to make it seem genuine rather than an unskilled stunt?"

To begin with, Butler's choice of ending is sensible in that death appears as a topic throughout the story. While Margaret's decision to die is sudden, at least the end is not the first time the reader has encountered death in the story. Perhaps the clearest example of this foreshadowing comes when Margaret first meets "her man," as she calls him, telling him she can sense death in the air; the feeling reminds her of the time when as a little girl she saw the mine disaster in West Virginia. Thus, Butler immediately establishes the theme of dying in the initial connection between them. In fact, this discussion serves as the turning point for her, the moment in which he wins her heart by both listening intently and apologizing for doubting her. This discussion of death in essence becomes the cornerstone of her attraction to him and an inseparable part of her memory of him. Given the early references to death, readers may not be surprised that death reappears as a topic when Margaret yearns for him decades later.

Soon after this flashback about West Virginia, Butler again brings up death when Margaret claims she was not afraid of dying while on board the sinking ship. Though she is not explicit about why, the reader can infer from the next paragraph that it is because a year before she had experienced the death of her father. After remembering his death, Margaret thinks again about the *Titanic*. Butler comes back to the subject of mortality by having her decide to return to her cabin to finish the book she was reading. In this book, Edith Wharton's novel *Ethan Frome* (1911), two lovers decide to kill themselves rather than face the shame of an illicit affair. Thus, in a matter of a mere four pages, Butler makes the reader aware of death through a variety of references. These indirect omens for her suicide at the end serve to make her final act more understandable. To put it another way, by repeatedly broaching the topic of death in such a short space, Butler paves the way for Margaret to commit suicide without completely blindsiding the reader.

In addition to the way death recurs in the story, Butler's potentially self-indulgent ending is successful because it is a realistic one for his main character. To begin with, Margaret openly admits near the beginning of the story that she is alone. Further, she describes her life in the decades since the sinking as that of a deep dreamless sleep. In fact, the only time she seems to have not felt alone and catatonic was during the brief time she spent on the deck of the sinking ship with "[her] man"; this short-lived encounter was her only brush with any sort of romance. Because of this lack of exuberance in her lifetime, she paces around the hotel room, "frantic with regret," over her inability to savor the little time she had with the Englishman. At this point in her life, she desperately wants to reconnect with this fleeting moment, the only time she has felt a close personal connection and intimacy with a potential sexual partner. Now, still thirty but suddenly in the late twentieth century, Margaret realizes she has outlived her peers; thus a reunion with the Englishman in death is attractive.

Margaret chooses a highly symbolic manner of dying. How she does it is important since she believes that "the mind's energy surely crackled on beyond the body." How she dies would have an impact on the way her energy will "crackle" after her

Two suffragettes trying to attract support for the cause of women's right to vote, c. 1905
© Hulton-Deutsch Collection/Corbis

departure. Perhaps it would affect her reunion with the Englishman in the afterlife, especially considering she hopes that "his spirit has found its way to me and is gazing on this vessel of my body." If he is watching, she needs to him to approve of her actions. Since the Englishman died in icy water, her death by the same method appeals to her. In short, Butler's choice is a nearly perfect solution to Margaret's situation. She will get to reconnect with the Englishman (albeit in the afterlife) which will ease her suffering from both solitude and regret over her lost chance at love; plus the method she chooses will resonate with how he died.

But does the ending relate to the rest of the story? Any part of the narrative, be it a twist ending or a perfunctory beginning, should be more than just plausible in terms of the plot. It should play into the mood, feel, or theme of the rest of the story; a reader should be able to interpret it as easily as any other part. Gimmick endings (or any section of a story for that matter) stand out in that they have little or nothing to do thematically with the others.

In this case, Margaret's suicide underscores the message of the whole story: the importance of living fully. Margaret's actions are not heroic but they express her single regret: "if I were the woman my mind has always aspired to and even believed I was, I should have taken the initiative there, should have touched him."

Source: Michael Becker, Critical Essay on "*Titanic* Survivors Found in Bermuda Triangle," in *Short Stories for Students*, Thomson Gale, 2006.

Laura Carter

Carter is a freelance writer. In this essay, Carter considers the merits of Butler's story from a surrealistic perspective.

Robert Olen Butler's "*Titanic* Survivors Found in Bermuda Triangle," is, on the surface, a personal account of a narrator whose life has been defined by two equally profound, near-death experiences and the impact these experiences have had in shaping the course of her life and ultimate suicide. From this perspective, it is a rather dismal account. Beneath the surface, however, is a tale of supernatural proportions, punctuated with inconsistencies that suggest Butler's narrative is more than a mere survivor's tale, but a beautiful, surrealistic love story powerful enough to transcend the physicality of space and time.

At the beginning of the story, the narrator recounts the *Titanic* disaster, including here own feelings and associations. The narrator talks of her heart as "a place ripped open by ice and letting all this cold air rush in." Her experience and escape from tragedy has left a gash in her heart. The narrator speaks of being "so cold in the boat." She recalls how a "vast jagged wall of ice sought out at once" the ship on which she was a passenger. Similar images dominate the opening pages, as her focus shifts back and forth between the sinking ship and the air-conditioned hotel room; she focuses on the view of the sea and the sky, lights blazing and smoke smoldering.

Butler sets the stage for the story of a woman who, deeply traumatized, walks the world in a dreamlike state. Central to the action is the narrator, who acknowledges the emotional toll that has been taken on her spiritually. Rhetorically, the narrator asks, perhaps even pleading for a belief in the present, "Why am I still slow in believing in the reality of this hotel room in a year decades removed from the night when I fled a ship and then fell into a deep sleep?" The setting is also driven early on by other pertinent or important historical clues. Butler's protagonist expresses her displeasure for the captain of a ship, whom she calls an "arrogant man," positioning herself as "a scorned woman." Along with everyone else on the ship, she is jeopardized by his incredible shortsightedness. But for Margaret he also represents as the gender collective, "men who would not let us speak, much less gain the vote."

Buried almost casually within Margaret's recollections is yet another near miss with death. The reader discovers that she has escaped not one, but two terrible accidents at sea. She describes her mortal predicament this way: "I understand that I am alone in some surpassing way, plucked out of a place in the sea apparently notorious for mysteries, a place far from the fatal ice field." Thus readers learn that she has both survived the *Titanic* disaster and the Bermuda Triangle; she has outlived her contemporaries, yet she remains "just turned thirty." The narration moves between the past and the present in a dreamlike fashion as Margaret remembers what matters most to her. Events seem to be separated more by their emotive power than by distinct moments in time.

The story moves between the *Titanic*'s fateful voyage and the mystery of the Bermuda Triangle, from which, as the title suggests, the narrator has emerged. This claim tests credibility. Margaret is fortunate enough to survive the *Titanic* and then is safely plucked from a location in the ocean where many disappear. But the *Titanic* and the Bermuda Triangle incidents represent more than two mysterious tragedies. One is a romantic memory from the narrator's past; the other, a circumstance from which the narrator has reemerged, as if from a long sleep. Essentially the story moves between two periods in history, from the turn of the twentieth century to the late twentieth century. On an emotional level, these time periods are diametrically opposed; therefore, the movement is troubling for the narrator. She sees herself as a step out of time, out of agreement with modern society. She approaches the twentieth century as one without hope or promise, but with arguments against industrialization.

Her misery is compounded by two things: first, separation from the object of her fantasy, the Englishman, a love story lost opportunity. The narrator states, "I find myself now walking around and around this room at the end of the twentieth century and I am frantic with regret, for on that night I could find no other language with which to speak." She regrets touching him only to straighten his tie: "I wanted to take him in my arms, but I did not, I could not, I was being a lady. God forgive me," she exclaims. She is haunted by this lost opportunity and what she perceives to be a separation from the other. This is in fact the context with which she frames her reaction to escaping the *Titanic*. She is, by her own admission, not afraid to die; she welcomes the idea. Her reaction to survival is not one of elation; rather, she regrets not going down with the ship if doing so could have offered her a chance to experience equality and intimacy with a tender man who took her seriously.

The second rift is a matter of living versus existing. She is disturbed by being detached from contemporary society. From the outset, the narrator claims that she is "in a place and time as foreign to me as Planet Mars." In describing the hotel room she chooses to recall her romantic encounter as it unfolded in the moments before impending tragedy. It seems that she has kept her cloths from the *Titanic*, favoring them over those that are laid out in her room, which are to her immodestly revealing. She claims that she no longer knows what to do with her body, now that her mind has been rendered obsolete with modern advances. She remarks, "When I was a child—dear God, more than a century ago now." For her only a brief time has lapsed since the ship when down, but she now realizes decades have gone by and she is thrust into a new world.

Suddenly thrust into the late twentieth century, the narrator who has committed herself to female suffrage realizes, "I am no longer needed, for one thing. I have no proof of it, but I am certain in a world like this that women have the right to vote." Given the changes between 1912 and the 1990s, she would naturally feel uncomfortable, perhaps even frightened, by technologies that have emerged during the lapsed decades. In light of her circumstances, then, an extreme discomfort with her surroundings is no surprise.

Moreover, Margaret does not want to endure life without the connection she felt briefly to the Englishman. The narrator's world is a watery one, her story's emotive power shifting, murky, turbulent as the deep ocean waters from which she has emerged twice. Despite her good fortune or perhaps because of it, she is haunted by the souls of those not so fortunate that night on the *Titanic*, but by the modern world in which she has found herself desperately out of place, purposeless, and alone. Her suicide is an effort to transcend these circumstances in order to be again with the Englishman. In light of these circumstances, Robert Olen Butler's "*Titanic* Survivors Found in Bermuda Triangle" is a hauntingly beautiful love story about a woman's hope to transcend the physical boundaries of space and time.

Source: Laura Carter, Critical Essay on "*Titanic* Survivors Found in Bermuda Triangle," in *Short Stories for Students*, Thomson Gale, 2006.

Barbara C. Ewell

In the following review, Ewell praises Butler's stories for making "us probe a little more deeply into the absurd dreams we all inhabit."

We depend on writers to show us the unreality of our lives. If they do their job right, they remind us how we always seem to be missing what is important in our efforts to be human. But when we live in a world as bizarre as contemporary America, with its hysterical machines and ironic facades, then the writer's work becomes a bit tricky. How do you expose unreality in a world devoted to counterfeit and substitution? How can you tell which is which? Robert Olen Butler is one writer who seems to thrive on the challenge.

In his first collection of short stories, *A Good Scent From a Strange Mountain,* which won a Pulitzer Prize in 1993, Butler sharpened the sense of strangeness by focussing on exiles. Part of what makes the stories in that volume so compelling (apart from the recognition that Butler is just a white boy from Illinois), is that the exiles are mostly Vietnamese, often women, and that they live in south Louisiana, a part of the country whose peculiarity is pretty much certified by the Cajun twists it applies to what passes for normal in the southern United States. In *Tabloid Dreams,* his second collection of short stories, Butler achieves a similar angle of difference simply by going to the grocery stores and buying the perspectives of the tabloids much as we all eventually do, standing in line to exercise our habits of ridiculous comsumption.

The premise—or at least the writerly trick—of these stories is an exploration of tabloid headlines as though they were true. This is a wonderful gimmick, really—and the fact that Butler is working with HBO to produce a television series based on these stories indicates just how clever the ploy is. But what makes these tales more than hilarious devices is how much truth Butler makes the incredible captions reveal about being human, and how well they expose the strangeness of our own daily life.

One of the best stories, "Help Me Find My Spaceman Lover," illustrates the kind of depth that Butler can elicit from such an apparently silly supposition. Edna Bradshaw, a 40-year-old insomniac and divorcée, finds great comfort when the "regular old Wal-Mart" of Bovary, Ala., becomes a 24-hour Super Center. It gives her a place to go in the wee hours when her loneliness gets the best of her.

One night in the parking lot she encounters a little spaceman, whom she calls Desi—because it's the right name for someone we like even though they talk "with a funny accent." He has been waiting for her, he says, because Edna always tells the truth: "You seem always to say what is inside your head without any attempt to alter it." Edna is won by Desi's gentle courtship, something in short supply in Bovary (and not entirely approved by Desi's fellow planetary researchers), and she adjusts admirably to all the little shocks of his difference—his "eight-sucker hands" and big eyes, his telepathic ability and smaller-than-expected spaceship—"not as big as all of Wal-Mart certainly, maybe just the pharmacy and housewares departments put together."

If Desi helps Edna to "see things in the larger perspective," Edna's willingness to love a spaceman reminds us how our usual notions of what is "pretty and sweet" may need "some serious adjusments" if we hope to overcome our loneliness. The the primary antidote for such loneliness is 24-hour shopping—or loving cats ("subspecie companions") and spacemen instead of our tyrannical daddies or fellow Bovarians—is exactly the "kind of odd thing that makes you shake your head about the way life is lived on planet Earth."

Much of Butler's humor derives from the blunt naïveté of his narrators. Like Edna, they seem not to censor themselves in commenting on their lives; and, like the tabloids themselves, they willingly tell all, revealing absurdity and shallowness but also a great deal of suffering. In Butler's tabloid dreams, unloved or betrayed women become deadly—bashing thick-headed men with meteorites or setting themselves on fire at baking contests they have lost like their lives. Wives and husbands learn the bitter truth about their philandering partners by becoming glass eyes or suicidal parrots; young boys revenge their absent fathers by becoming efficient hit men or their mother's lovers.

One of Butler's gifts is his obvious sympathy for these absurd people, blundering toward love and stumbling onto truths they don't quite recognize. Like the stiffly proper narrator of "*Titanic* Victim Speaks Through Waterbed," whose icy death transforms him into water and who ends up inside a waterbed on which lovers thrash about (after experience as clouds and rain and rivers and lakes and tea and—you know), these are "solitary travellers[s]." They only become "fully conscious" after they are dead. But they do at least see something. And so do we. By showing us how really strange things could be, Butler's stories give us new ways to look at our experience. And if his

fiction makes us probe as little more deeply into the absurd dreams we all inhabit, then he's only doing his job—very well.

Source: Barbara C. Ewell, Review of *Tabloid Dreams*, in *America*, May 17, 1997, pp. 28–29.

Adam Mazmanian

In the following review, Mazmanian recommends Butler's collection highly, calling the stories "inventive, compelling fantasies."

Hearing a voice from beyond the grave is usually a chilling, blood-curdling experience. However, being such a voice, issuing unheard from an improbable source (a parrot, a waterbed), offers the lost soul plenty of time to reflect on the missed opportunities of a life not fully lived. And though a lurid sensibility permeates the titles and tableaux of the "tabloid" tales in Pulitzer Prize-winning author Butler's latest collection, this vision of post-mortem regret is at the heart of Butler's sad, mirthful stories. In "Jealous Husband Returns in Form of Parrot," a woman buys the avian reincarnation of her ex-husband in a Houston pet store and takes him home, where he ruminates on his past and present failure to express his unconditional love for his wife: "I was not enough. 'Bad bird,' I say. I'm sorry." Widowed housewife Gertie in "Woman Loses Cookie Bake-Off, Sets Self on Fire" chooses self-immolation when she is forced to realize that her whole life has been sucked away, down the ungrateful gullets of men. As rumored, John Kennedy is not dead, but has merely lost his capacity for self-censorship and is kept in seclusion by the CIA to restrain him from compulsively revealing state secrets. In "JFK Secretly Attends Jackie Auction," the 79-year-old former president travels incognito to Sotheby's to retrieve a relic of his former grandeur but is woefully short of cash. Butler's wicked humor is tempered by genuine compassion for the characters' indelible misfortunes. Readers everywhere will enjoy these inventive, compelling fantasies. Highly recommended.

Source: Adam Mazmanian, Review of *Tabloid Dreams*, in *Library Journal*, September 1, 1996, p. 212.

Joe Nordgren

In the following essay, Nordgren discusses Butler's writing career.

As of 1996 Butler's publications include eight novels, a prize-winning collection of short stories, and numerous contributions to respected journals and reviews. His defining themes are the suffering that results from thwarted desire and the intimacy that characterizes fundamental human relationships. His crafting of these topics in his collected stories about Vietnamese expatriates living in southwest Louisiana placed him at the forefront of American letters. *A Good Scent from a Strange Mountain* (1992) earned the Pulitzer Prize, the Richard and Hinda Rosenthal Foundation Award from the American Academy of Arts and Letters, the *Southern Review*/LSU Prize for Short Fiction, a PEN/ Faulkner Award nomination, and a Guggenheim Fellowship.

Robert Olen Butler was born on 20 January 1945. An only child, he grew up, as did his parents, in the small steel-mill town of Granite City, Illinois, in the river bottoms across the Mississippi from Saint Louis and a few miles northwest of Cahokia State Park. His father, Robert Olen Sr., is a retired actor and former chairman of the theater department at Saint Louis University. Speaking of their relationship, Butler said in a 1993 interview: "It was second nature for us to talk late into the night about books, movies, and theater." His mother, Lucille Hall Butler, is a retired executive secretary, and her stories about Granite City during the Depression inspired the content for *Wabash* (1987), Butler's fifth novel.

Butler moved only twice during his years with his parents. He entered grade school in Springfield, Missouri, and completed fourth grade in Overland Park, Kansas, but when he was ten, his family returned to Illinois. After junior high he went to Granite City High School, becoming president of the student body, and graduated as class covaledictorian in 1963. In the 1950s and 1960s the local steel mills attracted economic exiles from depressed areas of the Midwest and the South, and this led to a collision of cultures that Butler said shaped his personality. During high school and into college, he worked summers at Granite City Steel. He learned to talk Saint Louis Cardinals baseball with coworkers at the blast furnace operation and to discuss aesthetic theory with his father's colleagues.

Planning to major in theater, Butler enrolled at Northwestern University. As a freshman he was cast in four of the school's six major productions for 1963–1964, but in his sophomore year he turned to oral interpretation and playwriting. In addition to required creative-writing courses, he studied for five months with British author Stephen Spender and graduated summa cum laude in June 1967. That fall Butler attended graduate school at the University of Iowa, and on 10 August 1968 he married Carol Supplee. He earned an M.F.A. in play-writing.

> Butler structures events from a moment of psychological curiosity."

Butler suspected that after graduate school he would be drafted for military duty in Vietnam, so he visited the army recruiter in Granite City and enlisted. He committed to a three-year enlistment to be guaranteed a position in counterintelligence, thinking he would be placed in an American field office doing background checks on U.S. Army personnel applying for security clearances. In February 1969 he started basic training in Fort Lewis, Washington, and was then transferred to Fort Holabird, Maryland. From Fort Holabird Butler went to language school in Washington, D.C., and spent a year learning Vietnamese from a native speaker. Fully trained as a linguist, he was assigned in January 1971 to a counterintelligence unit near Bien Hoa and within six months was chosen to be the administrative assistant and interpreter for the American Foreign Service officer advising the mayor of Saigon. Butler left Vietnam in December 1971, and the following month he was mustered out of the army. He told Joseph Olshan (*People*) about his year of active service: "Vietnam ravished me sensually. I made amazing friends, from my favorite leper beggar to the highest officials. After I came back, there were a hundred flashes of memories, prompted by a smell of overripe fruit, a certain perfume, a glimpse of a woman's ankle. And I was filled with the same sense of nostalgia, loss and even aspiration that the Vietnamese in my stories feel."

After his wife and he divorced, Butler moved to New York City and became a reporter for *Electronic News*, owned by Fairchild Publications. On 1 July 1972 he married Marylin Geller. Although he advanced to editor of the journal, he and his second wife decided in mid 1973 to move to Granite City, and he worked as a high-school substitute teacher and freelance writer for a year. Following the birth of a son, Joshua, he rejoined *Electronic News* in Chicago for eighteen months, at which time Fairchild asked him to return to New York to start a newspaper of his own creating. From 1975 until 1985 he was editor in chief of *Energy User*

News, a weekly investigative business newspaper targeted for industrial and commercial consumers and managers of energy.

Butler struggled in the 1970s to think of himself as a writer. He explained to Peter Applebome of *The New York Times* that his early novels were completed "in longhand on legal pads supported by a Masonite lapboard as he commuted on the Long Island Rail Road from his home in Sea Cliff, L.I., to his job in Manhattan." Beginning in 1979 he attended four consecutive semesters of advanced creative-writing courses at the New School for Social Research taught by Anatole Broyard, who encouraged him.

Butler has been tagged a Vietnam novelist even though he finds the label disparaging. He told Jon Anderson (*Chicago Tribune*): "It's like saying Monet was a lily-pad painter; artists get at deeper truths." Three of his first four books, however, loosely form a Vietnam trilogy, each novel focusing on a different member of a common group of characters. Clifford Wilkes in *The Alleys of Eden* (1981), Wilson Hand in *Sun Dogs* (1982), and David Fleming in *On Distant Ground* (1985) served in an army intelligence unit located outside Saigon. For months they established a routing for bringing donations to a nearby Catholic orphanage, and on one of these visits, Vietcong soldiers attacked the compound and took Hand prisoner. After the raid Fleming approached Wilkes to act as his interpreter when questioning a suspected VC military insurgent picked up by the National Police. While they interrogated and tortured the man, he died of a heart attack. Within a few days Fleming discovered where Hand was being detained and set out to rescue him. Wilkes's tour would have elapsed in seven months, but his collusion in the prisoner's death upset him to the point of deserting. One morning he stole a jeep and passed Fleming and Hand returning to base camp as he was on his way toward Saigon and an uncertain future.

The Alleys of Eden begins in an alley apartment of Saigon, which is destined to fall soon to the insurgent North Vietnamese. Cliff Wilkes is in bed with the twenty-eight-year-old bar girl with whom he has been living for the past four years, and while Lanh sleeps, he remembers the people who have either by fate or choice previously forsaken him. His father died when Wilkes was fourteen. When he was at college, his mother remarried and began a new but distant life. A political activist whom he befriended at Northwestern University fled to Canada after they had hitchhiked to an antiwar rally on the

West Coast. Francine, his former wife, divorced him during his first leave from the army. She wrote to him about marriage: "It is death. It stops me from really connecting to other people. And I have to connect as myself. Not part of a tandem." Wilkes determines not to abandon Lanh. As a precursor for many of Butler's future characters, he must contend with the unforeseen, including changing identities: He deserts from the army; he and Lanh are separated as they flee in the chaos during the fall of Saigon; they are reunited in Speedway, Illinois.

A pivotal scene unfolds when Lanh and he are invited to dinner by their Speedway neighbors, Quentin and June Forbes. The Forbeses honestly wish for Lanh to feel comfortable in their home, yet everything about them—their politics, their horseradish, their expensive china, their beliefs about death and an afterlife—is alien to her. Excluded from what they know, Lanh watches Cliff sneak out of the hiding his desertion from the army has required and bond with people who have a claim on his past. At their apartment that night, she tells him: "I would have felt more comfortable stripped naked and marched through the streets of Saigon before a VC bayonet." Happiness abandons her until she is embraced by a Vietnamese refugee family in town.

Following a disastrous visit to his former wife, in which he is nearly trapped by the police seeking to arrest him, Wilkes returns to Lanh and is intimate with her for a final time. Butler shows them connecting passionately, sensually as woman and man; afterward Wilkes gets dressed and walks into Speedway's deserted main street. Going to Canada, he remembers a female reporter telling him: "A man's home is where he is innocent." He and Lanh have tried to prevail over their cultural barriers, but are unable to revive the Edenic joy they had shared in Saigon.

Vietnam was not a popular subject when Butler started shopping around his manuscript. *The Alleys of Eden* was turned away by a dozen publishers who "admitted every virtue in the book except its marketability," he said. London-based publisher Methuen finally selected the novel for the company's American trade list; however, two months before the novel was published, Methuen notified Butler that it was forgoing the trade-book business. Butler forwarded the manuscript to nine additional publishers before Ben Raeburn, editor of Horizon Press, accepted it in 1980. The book came out the next year and sold eighty-five-thousand copies in paperback.

Within a year Horizon published Butler's second novel, *Sun Dogs*. Sun dogs are "mock suns" formed by ice crystals in the upper atmosphere, and the narrator points out that in the Arctic these reflections of ice "run with the sun, speak to it of things unseen, things that claim a special knowledge." Butler's title assumes far-reaching implications as he examines the depletion of natural and human resources during the energy debate of the early 1980s.

The plot involves Wilson Hand approximately ten years after he had been a prisoner in Vietnam. A self-employed private investigator who is anxious to get away from New York City, Hand accepts Royal Petroleum's offer to find who has been stealing confidential maps and reports from its headquarters at Moonbase on Alaska's North Slope. After he visits his former wife on the afternoon before he is to leave, she jumps to her death from her fourteenth-floor apartment balcony. A newspaper photograph of her bare legs projecting from a smashed windshield and flashbacks to his week in the VC prison camp are the mock suns that pursue Hand in Alaska when winter temperatures plummet to seventy-five degrees below zero.

Butler attacks corporate ethics in his account of Royal Petroleum's propaganda war. An advocate for the U.S. president's energy independence campaign, Royal wants foreign and domestic consumers to think America has abundant natural reserves. The stolen maps and reports, however, confirm that Alaska is nearly depleted of resources. The company hopes to bury this information and thus give itself time to develop a strategy for capitalizing on the panic that will result when the news is spread. Without suspecting it, Hand has been retained to assist Royal Petroleum in its scheme.

At Moonbase Hand falls in love with a sensuous but untrustworthy woman named Marta Gregory. Marta and he agree to avoid the "emotional clutter of words" when making love, but on one occasion they break their rule of silence, and she discloses that her father's death has overshadowed her life. A cold and imposing Wall Street broker, he became ill when she was twelve and made her sit at his hospital bedside and listen to his regrets for having been so distant. When he started saying all the right things that he previously lacked the time to say, Marta began to hate him. His example has made her distrustful of everyone's sincerity, thus putting feelings connected to loyalty, as she knows, beyond her emotional grasp.

Bush pilot Clyde Mazer, in contrast, possesses a bold vitality for life. Butler creates in him a maverick who drinks, tells stories, squanders money, and flirts with both women and danger. Appalled by deception, he is the one person upon whom Hand can rely. Hand asks Clyde to fly him from Anchorage to Moonbase so he can verify that the trans-Alaskan pipeline is going dry. After crashing onto a mountain ledge in a seldom-used pass of the Brooks Range, they are without food, heat, and light as they huddle inside their makeshift ice cave. Clyde falls asleep, and while listening to his friend's agonized breathing, Hand begins stripping away his clothing as images of VC guards and of Beth stepping onto her balcony crystallize in his mind. Unafraid of dying, he whispers to Clyde in the darkness: "Eat it is finished." Thus Butler unites self-sacrifice and life-fulfilling peace, which he foreshadows in the book's epigraph from Leviticus 22:7: "And when the sun is down, he shall be clean."

Vietnam and *Energy User News* provided Butler with material for his first two books. In *Countrymen of Bones* (1983) he steps beyond personal experiences to probe dimensions of violence against the backdrop of World War II. In the Jornada del Muerto, a section of New Mexico desert known as "the journey of the dead," an archaeologist and a physicist become rivals during the weeks leading to the first experimental atomic detonation on the morning of 16 July 1945. The book's theme compresses into J. Robert Oppenheimer's pronouncement: "I am become Death, the shatterer of worlds."

The most technically innovative of Butler's early novels, *Countrymen of Bones* alternates between characters and locales, simultaneously developing two stories. Darrell Reeves has been trying for a decade, according to his former wife, to excavate his way to God. Employed by the University of Santa Fe, he is sifting through what he thinks to be a burial mound that happens to be located one thousand yards from the spot Oppenheimer has designated as ground zero. Reeves's antagonist, an army scientist named Lloyd Coulter, divides his time between Los Alamos and Trinity Base Camp, ten miles southwest of the archaeological dig. In the opening scene Reeves clutches a weaponlike trowel while looking down the desert wastes. His funds are virtually exhausted, and he worries that his professional intuition might be betraying him since his digging thus far has yielded nothing. As Reeves drifts into listlessness, Butler cuts to Los Alamos two hundred miles to the north. Having been with Oppenheimer for two years, Coulter knows they are at the brink of failure. The plutonium-gun idea is dead; the Holocaust continues in Europe. Time is running out for the Manhattan Project as scientists debate Seth Neddermeyer's implosion theory. By creating parallel narratives, Butler generates intensity for the important moment when Coulter and Reeves will collide.

Reeves has been ordered to complete his work in fifteen weeks and then evacuate. In this time, he unearths the bones of an ancient Indian death cult, meets a disabled former colleague, falls in love with army private Anna Brown, hears of President Franklin D. Roosevelt's death, and in self-defense kills an indignant rancher. Whereas Butler allows Reeves to have a measure of control over his emotions, anger destroys Lloyd Coulter. The son of an abusive father, Coulter lashes out at his coworkers, Oppenheimer, Reeves, and himself. In his worst moment he rapes Anna, driven by some hidden impulse whose mystery is "locked far tighter than the heart of an atom."

Anatole Broyard (*The New York Times*) praised Butler's depiction of Anna Brown for recognizing "love as a powerful violence too, a sublime one that can distract from other kinds." Her encouraging wide-set Indian eyes entice Reeves and Coulter to talk about themselves. Confused about why men are attracted to her, she tells Coulter when rejecting his marriage proposal: "I'm not the kind of girl I sometimes seem. I guess I just don't understand how I come across sometimes." After being raped, she escapes to be with Reeves on the morning of the atomic test.

Butler places the burden of his message on a found artifact. After the bomb detonation, in which Coulter dies, the narrative jumps ahead in time to a hotel room near Times Square. Anna and Reeves are celebrating their honeymoon and the end of the war. From among the ancient burial remains, Reeves has brought with him an ornamental stone collar shaped like a human face with wide-set eyes from which two jagged lines descend. He interprets the jagged lines to be a symbolic mournful expression of impending death, although Anna is quick to disagree. For her they encompass all of human history, conveying grief "at what men can do."

After *Countrymen of Bones* Butler changed publishing houses and editors when Horizon Press was bought out and Ben Raeburn left the firm. Butler took his manuscripts-in-progress, including half of *On Distant Ground*, the third book in his Vietnam trilogy, to New York agent Candida Donadio. Within two weeks he was a Knopf author and Lee Goerner was his editor.

Whereas *The Alleys of Eden* opens in Vietnam and closes in the United States, *On Distant Ground* begins in the United States and concludes in Vietnam. Dates, settings, and events in the two novels overlap as Capt. David Fleming's ties to Southeast Asia impel him toward surprising decisions. At Fort Holabird in April 1975, Fleming is to go on trial for assisting the enemy during his tour of duty. While awaiting formal court-martial proceedings, he privately arraigns himself for failing as a husband; for losing contact with Nguyen Thi Toyet Suong, a woman with whom he briefly fell in love in Saigon; and for helping a Vietcong prisoner to escape from his captors. Fleming's devotion to truth, in the end, secures his redemption.

Butler structures events from a moment of psychological curiosity. Fleming recalls an episode from his past in which he and his CIA team had seized key Vietcong leaders and were instructed to turn them over to the South Vietnamese. During a visit to these prisoners, he entered a vacant cell and was struck by the phrase *ve-sinh la koe* ("hygiene is healthful") scratched into one of its walls. He knew instantly that he shared a particular "detachment of the mind" that made him fear for the cell's prior occupant as he would for himself. Determined to find the person, he learned he was tracking a man named Pham Van Tuyen (twin), whom he later helped to escape from a South Vietnamese camp. Fleming's recollections thematically elevate human decency to a level above patriotism, and in the present action Butler turns to family issues to underscore Fleming's personal integrity.

Before Fleming's trial concludes, his wife gives birth to their first child. He is allowed to stay at home with Jennifer and David Junior until a verdict is reached, and during a news broadcast one evening, he watches intently as orphans, many of whom have distinctly American features, are being evacuated from Saigon. Their faces stir memories of his affair with Suong, and he is certain he has a four-year-old son whom he must rescue. "He realizes this is madness," says reviewer Joe Klein (*The New York Times*), "but is too self-absorbed to stop himself." Klein adds, "It is a tribute to Mr. Butler's skill as a writer that his story's pyramiding absurdities seem not merely plausible but inevitable." Desire becomes action when Fleming is dishonorably discharged but assigned no prison time.

When Fleming arrives in Vietnam, he is enveloped by the panic of a country on the run. Playing on hunches, he locates Suong's mother, introduces himself to his son Khai, visits the prison where Suong had died, and on two occasions comes face-to-face with Tuyen, currently the director of security in Saigon for the Provisional Revolutionary Government. Their second meeting occurs after Fleming is captured while trying to smuggle Khai out of the city. When the opportunity arises, Tuyen admits that he lacked the bravery ever to have written the words Fleming ascribes to him, but repaying a debt, he arranges for Fleming and Khai to be transported safely to Bangkok. The book's closing asserts that mutual respect is a requisite for reconciliation and peace.

With the success of his fourth novel, Butler's publishing credentials presented him with an opportunity to change careers. In the summer of 1985 he left *Energy User News* and accepted a creative-writing post at McNeese State University, in Lake Charles, Louisiana, where he still teaches. When Joseph Olshan asked about his first visit to Lake Charles, Butler said, "My God, it was [like] the Mekong Delta! The same rice paddies, the same calligraphy of marshland waterways and that subtropical kind of haze. It seemed the most natural place in the world for me to be." Although the setting was natural, he had succumbed to what he called "functional fixedness." Butler had so adapted to writing while riding commuter trains that he told David Streitfeld (*Washington Post*): "I thought I would have to buy a little electric motor and fix it to my chair, hire someone to come in and flap a newspaper. I was having a lot of trouble writing in a quiet room that wasn't moving." Once settled, he began mapping out his fifth novel, *Wabash*, by drawing on his mother's stories about Granite City during the Great Depression.

In 1932 Wabash, Illinois, is mired in corporate intimidation and escalating poverty. Wabash Steel exercises baronial power over the town, and Butler shows it financing community life, regulating local politics, and enforcing strong-arm laws. Deborah and Jeremy Cole are a couple in their early thirties who have yet to recover from the death three years earlier of their only child, Elizabeth. Jeremy carries his misery "like a lump of slag" into the blast furnaces where he works. Since Lizzy's death, physical intimacy has demanded too great an effort from him, so he retreats into his suffering. Deborah is helpless on two fronts. First, she is unable to rescue Jeremy from his pain, and second, she cannot stop the endless bickering between her mother and aunts. Deborah visits her relatives while Jeremy is at the mill, and in bed at night they grieve. When Deborah prevents Jeremy from assassinating John J. Hagemeyer, the company's owner, their passion flares "like a Wabash night, burning them until they are clean."

As in *Countrymen of Bones*, Butler juxtaposes two narratives so that Deborah's battles at home correlate to Jeremy's conflicts at work. Deborah's mother, Miriam, and her aunts, Adah, Berenice, and Della, seem trapped by their sooty lives. Bored, childless, and unmarried, Adah and Della often sit on Miriam's porch swing and fret half-heartedly about their sister Berenice going mad. There is a fifth sister, Effie, about whom the others speak as if she were dead. Deborah now and then visits her eccentric grandmother whose home borders the town dump. Continuing a family tradition, Grandma Birney writes polite but firm warning letters to the river rats clawing around in her house. Deborah hears from her that Effie is alive and residing in Saint Louis, but that she has been ostracized for becoming a Catholic and accepting the Virgin Mary as her true mother. When Grandma Birney dies, Deborah persuades Effie to attend her mother's funeral, but the sisters will not be reconciled. Berenice's suicide prompts Deborah to write her own "Dear Rats" letter in which she threatens to poison whoever is taking Jeremy from her.

Jeremy decides to kill Hagemeyer for several reasons. Cronin, an underpaid Hungarian worker, is fired and then hangs himself rather than watch his wife and children go hungry. For taking part in solidarity meetings, Nick Brenner is beaten to a pulp and evicted from his home, one of Hagemeyer's tar-paper shanty houses. A Fourth of July protest march turns into a riot between mounted police and rock-throwing dissidents, with whom Jeremy sides. Following the march, a hired thug tries to kill him. Finally, when his supervisor threatens to harm Deborah, Jeremy borrows a gun from Brenner and plans to shoot Hagemeyer during a political gathering at Lawton where President Herbert Hoover will be endorsing the company owner in his bid for Congress.

Butler invents Nick Brenner and Effie Birney to advance a lesson about losing oneself in either a political or spiritual conversion. Brenner is taken in by Marxist rhetoric and jeopardizes his family's welfare. Discovering that his wife has taken their children and left town, he tells Jeremy: "A family's a corrupt idea anyway. Capitalism in four walls." Effie, similarly, rejects her mother and sisters to join the family of the Roman Catholic Church. Christ and the Virgin Mary sustain her in her masochism as, with a childlike dependency, she clutches to rituals to make her feel clean. Presented as weak, insecure people, Effie and Nick are usurped by organizations that purport to revere their individuality.

Critic Philip Beidler suggests in *Re-Writing America: Vietnam Authors in Their Generation* (1991) that Butler's experimentation leads to "a fiction of brilliant doublings" in which "the renderings of the local and the immediate search out their larger mythic textualizations." In *Wabash* Deborah and Jeremy break from their struggles and picnic on Sun Mound, which is mentioned in *The Alleys of Eden* and which figures more prominently in *Countrymen of Bones*. Describing this and other examples as "mythic-cultural revision," Beidler sees in Butler's work "the archeology of culture at large, writing on the shared ground, the bone palimpsest of American myth itself."

Since 1985 Butler has made Lake Charles his home. In addition to teaching at McNeese, he has obtained funding from the Calcasieu Parish Arts and Humanities Council to initiate creative-writing classes for elementary, junior-high, and high-school students. On a continuing basis he contributes articles and reviews to *The New York Times Book Review*, the *Washington Post*, and the *Chicago Tribune*, and he has participated as a faculty member in well-known programs such as the Iowa Summer Writing Festival, the Port Townsend Writers' Conference, and the Antioch Writers' Workshop. In 1987 he was a charter recipient of the Tu Do Chinh Kien Award given by the Vietnam Veterans of America for "outstanding contributions to American culture by a Vietnam veteran." Butler's second marriage ended in July 1987, and he gained full legal custody of his son. On 21 July 1987 he married Maureen Donlan, his present wife. While working on *The Deuce* (1989) Butler took advantage of his theater training and discovered that he could use a first-person voice to his satisfaction. The experiment "opened realms of my artistic unconscious," he said, "that were previously unaccessible to me."

The Deuce, Butler's sixth novel, is an extended monologue in which he adopts the persona of a seventeen-year-old Amerasian who recounts a lifetime of memories to unravel his identity. Referring to the challenge of writing within a culture other than one's own, Butler told David Streitfeld: "I know the Vietnamese people probably better than I knew most of the people I grew up with. But beyond that, it is an article of faith for the artist—that we can leap in our imaginations into the minds and hearts and souls of people quite different from ourselves."

Butler's narrator states in his opening line: "I wish it was simple just to say who I am, just to say my name is so-and-so and that makes you think of a certain kind of person and that would be me." Names are meaningful to him, and to this point in his life he has been Vo Dinh Thanh, Anthony "Tony" James Hatcher, and "the Deuce," each name representing a different identity. Born in 1968, Vo Dinh Thanh is the six-year-old son of a Saigon bar girl, Vo Xuan Nghi, and an American GI. When his mother brings her clients home to their soiled apartment, Thanh runs outside and blends in with the other "children of dust," for whom war has made life surreal. Nghi is about to collapse from years of selling herself for heroin; thus, when a familiar-looking dark-haired American man named Kenneth appears one afternoon in the spring of 1974, Thanh can feel his life is going to change.

Thanh is also Tony, son of Kenneth Hatcher, a Vietnam veteran and aspiring lawyer who comes to Saigon to reclaim his child. When Kenneth arrives and sees that Nghi is desperate, he buys Thanh from her and brings him to live in Point Pleasant, New Jersey. James Patrick Sloan (*Chicago Tribune*) mentions that instead of soldiers in dirty underwear teaching him English slang, Tony is introduced to "all the appurtenances of suburban life that have about as much meaning as a roomful of rocks from Mars." After Tony's first stepmother seeks a divorce, he and Kenneth try to normalize their relationship by arranging outings to Coney Island, Yankee Stadium, and the Bronx Zoo. One night when his father carelessly refers to Nghi as a "whore and a druggie," Tony steals a few hundred dollars and runs out.

Thanh-Tony is also a sixteen-year-old runaway hiding in New York City. Tony is beaten and robbed within hours of arriving at the Port Authority Bus Terminal. He drifts, as a result, into weeks of panhandling with an alcoholic Vietnam veteran who calls him "the Deuce," the name locals use for Forty-second Street where the wrong people, Joey Cipriani warns him, will "eat you alive." Even though Tony claims to be 100 percent Vietnamese, Joey says, "You can't [b—sh—t] me. You're two things. You're Vietnamese and you're an American. A deuce."

Being half-Asian and half-American, the Deuce emerges as Butler's symbol for the collision of cultures that he finds so interesting about the Vietnam War and its aftermath. To make his point, he includes numerous details linking America to Vietnam when Tony runs away from his Jersey Shore home. Tony is sixteen when he sets out to be on his own; his mother was sixteen when she left Vinh Binh province and moved to Saigon. In New York City the Deuce loses his innocence to a sixteen-year-old runaway, Norma, who changes her name to Nicole and begins working the streets. Joey still carries a photograph of the Vietnamese prostitute with whom he fell in love sixteen years ago. On the afternoon the Deuce tracks Mr. Treen, a knife-wielding pederast, to a gay bar, he recoils when he sees a young mother sell her six-year-old boy for sexual favors in exchange for drugs. Forty-second Street, Joey notes, cuts through the city like the Mekong River, drowning the weak and disenfranchised.

Joey Cipriani is perhaps Butler's most tragic character. Claiming to be burdened by the legacies of civilian massacres and Agent Orange, Joey was, in truth, a personnel clerk who left South Vietnam before the Tet offensive of 1968. The war did not divest his life of meaning; Vietnam filled it with purpose. Kenneth tries to make this clear for his son after bringing him home from New York. He explains to Tony that some veterans like Joey have been disoriented after the war because

> What Vietnam really was for them was the only time in their lives when you'd get up in the morning and see the sky really clearly or really appreciate a shower or a dry pair of socks. And not just the little things. It was the only time in their lives when every day you knew for sure that there's something very important at stake on the planet Earth, that issues of life and death and love and even eternity, heaven and hell, are all real, these things exist. You knew that, and you never forgot it for a second, and then you came home and all of that faded away.

Back in Point Pleasant the narrator compares himself to a cicada "burrowed by the root of a tree, waiting his long wait [seventeen years] to emerge one night and play out his life." Butler uses the extended metaphor of the cicada as his vehicle for issues about personal growth and change as Tony "drags himself free" of the identities others have created for him. He leaves again for New York to avenge Joey's murder and to find out what kind of person he is inside. After leading Mr. Treen to his death, he can say with confidence: "I'm a lot of things but I'm one thing, and I have no doubt about that. I'm the Deuce." Loyalty to his past and loyalty to his friend are at the heart of his moral vision as he comes of age in the decade following the Vietnam War.

When Butler was near the end of *The Deuce*, National Public Radio contacted him about contributing to its series, the *Sound of Writing*. He returned to the more than thirty stories he had previously written and found to his interest a Vietnamese folkway about Saigon boys staging fights between insects. He sat down one afternoon, took on the voice of a middle-aged Vietnamese man in Lake Charles trying to come to terms with his Americanized son, and six hours later he had produced "Crickets." Within a few days he had jotted down notes for twenty additional stories, and after contacting Allen Peacock, then his editor at Knopf, about the possibility of doing a collection, he spent the next fourteen months on *A Good Scent from a Strange Mountain*.

Butler's displaced Vietnamese live in places in Louisiana like Gretna, Lake Charles, Versailles, and New Orleans. Some are from North Vietnam and others are from South Vietnam; some are Buddhists, and others are Catholics; some have found America to be a land of plenty, and others eke out a living the best they can. Madison Smartt Bell (*Chicago Tribune*) regards the collection as a "novelistic unit" that maps "a Vietnamese legend onto an American situation," and he believes that "any reader of this book will feel a strange and perhaps salutary sense of exposure and be made to wonder just who are the real Americans." Richard Eber (*Los Angeles Times Book Review*) says about Butler's subject matter and style that he "writes essentially, and in a bewitching translation of voice and sympathy, about what it means to lose a country, to remember it, and to have the memory begin to grow old. He writes as if it were his loss, too."

Having been a midlevel author, Butler told Peter Applebome about winning the Pulitzer Prize for his stories: "It came as a total surprise, something remarkable and wonderful that hit with the abruptness of a bolt of bayou lightning." The award lifted him considerably, leading to subsequent fellowships from the John Guggenheim Foundation and the National Endowment for the Arts. He was made an honorary doctor of humane letters by McNeese State University in 1993, and in that year he also came under contract to Ixtlan, Oliver Stone's production company, to write a screenplay for *A Good Scent from a Strange Mountain*. As demands for his time increased, Butler replaced his former Masonite lapboard with a notebook computer. Once again he was writing on the go, while flying between reading tours, book signings, and literary festivals.

His reputation secured, in *They Whisper* (1994) Butler set out to write a serious literary work about human sexuality. He had written sexual scenes into his previous novels, but *They Whisper* is devoted entirely to intimacy between women and men. Although confronted by difficulties in language and in what he had to face about himself, he said, "There was no other book I could have possibly written at that moment in my life. It was a book that was absolutely compelling." Like most writers, Butler pulls his subject matter from life experiences, but readers should guard against being lured into the biographical fallacy. He told Sybil Steinberg (*Publishers Weekly*): "[Carlos] Fuentes defines the novel as a pack of lies hounding the truth. This is a book full of the truest lies I can tell."

They Whisper is born of an image of a ten-year-old boy asking a young girl to wiggle her toes under the X-ray machine in his uncle's shoe store in Wabash, Illinois. This private moment of seeing Karen Granger's bones as no other person would ever see them is the first incident that Ira Holloway recalls in his being a lover of women. From this image Butler renders all he has learned about physically and spiritually connecting with life's unspoken sensual mysteries.

The novel is a stream-of-consciousness sojourn that takes place in 1980. Ira Holloway, now thirty-five, stands on a beach watching a parasailor glide over Puerto Vallarta. For the next 333 pages sensory impressions initiate sexual memories that span twenty-five years. In his mental flights to Wabash, New York, Zurich, Bangkok, and Saigon, he projects for each woman along the way a unique inner voice that whispers only to him of her secret desires and joys. Regardless of how intently he listens for their whispers, Ira says, "The answer of each woman does not prevent me from yearning. And it is the yearning I have to understand." From among Ira's many relationships, Butler makes his marriage to Fiona Price the crux of the narrative, demonstrating how love succumbs to obsession.

Soon after returning from Vietnam, Ira meets Fiona Price in New York's East Village. As their relationship evolves, she persuades him to speak about being attracted to other women, unwittingly establishing the groundwork for her ensuing jealousy. Within six months they are married, and while honeymooning in Paris, Ira learns that Fiona was sexually abused by her father, beginning on the night her parents' home caught on fire. Feeling her pain, he laments, "I would give up all my adult touching of Fiona to have held her sexlessly in my arms as a father just that once and cast the man from her life before he could scatter her mind and heart like sparks rising from the burning house." The morning after this secret revelation, Fiona insists that she must return to God if she is to survive.

Following the birth of their son, John, she begins attending Our Lady of Sorrows Catholic Church in Seaview, New York. Fiona wants Ira and John to share in her return to innocence, but the more insistent she becomes, the more they whisper behind her back. When his lawyer informs him that he would never gain legal custody of John should he seek a divorce, Ira decides he can either leave John with Fiona and allow her to create for their son a "terrible self," or he can stay and live two lives, "one to keep Fiona sane and one to whisper to my son all the things that I felt deeply were true." Presented as a sacrifice of his fullest sexual being, Ira forgoes his own happiness to safeguard his son, an attitude which Jane Smiley (*The New York Times*), Diane Johnson (*Vogue*), and Albert Read (*Spectator*), critics of Butler's sexual politics, perceive to be self-aggrandizing.

Fiona also suffers for her choices. Because she can intuit Ira's thoughts about other women, she needs constant reassurances that he yearns sexually only for her. As her doubts intensify, she becomes violent. Though she turns to psychiatry before the Catholic confessional, her religious zeal and escalating mistrust destroy Ira's longing for her, so when they are in bed, he fantasizes about being with other women. If he is too slow in getting an erection, Fiona is lost in envy; if they make love, she is overcome by shame and aches to confess. She wants more than anything for Ira and John to accept the church's sacraments as absolute truths. Should they not side with her, she thinks, then either they are right and she is a fool, or they are wrong and the husband and son she loves are going to hell. Christopher Lehmann-Haupt (*The New York Times*) observes, "The whiteness of burning desire, the compulsion to purify by confessing, the desired purification of death: these themes weave and tangle and knot so intricately in *They Whisper* that against all common-sensical judgments you trace them to the novel's harrowing end."

Butler told Sybil Steinberg that he knew he wanted to become a writer when he was in Saigon. He said of wandering the streets and crouching in doorways at 2 A.M.: "This ravishingly sensual experience illuminated my future as an artist. I understood that what I knew about the world was demanding expression in a fully sensual, moment-to-moment way. I saw that fiction was the medium that would permit me to do this." With seven acclaimed novels in print, he has good reason for saying, "My rich and varied life has been deeply composted in my imagination." Butler intends to write a new book every eighteen months.

Source: Joe Nordgren, "Robert Olen Butler," in *Dictionary of Literary Biography*, Vol. 173, *American Novelists Since World War II, Fifth Series*, edited by James R. Giles and Wanda H. Giles, Gale Research, 1996, pp. 3–13.

Sources

Ewell, Barbara C., Review of *Tabloid Dreams: Stories*, in *America*, May 17, 1997, pp. 28–29.

Smothers, Bonnie, "Uncommon Storytellers," in *Booklist*, October 1, 1886, p. 321.

Tait, Theo., Review of *Tabloid Dreams: Stories*, in the *Times Literary Supplement*, January 16, 1998, p. 1302.

Further Reading

Bird, S. Elizabeth, *For Enquiring Minds: A Cultural Study of Supermarket Tabloids*, University of Tennessee Press, 1992.

Bird's analysis is particularly interesting for its emphasis on the historical antecedents of the tabloid reporting that is popular in the early 2000s.

Glynn, Kevin, *Tabloid Culture: Trash Taste, Popular Power, and the Transformation of American Television*, Duke University Press, 2000.

A scholar from New Zealand, Glynn has an outsider perspective that helps Americans see the growing influence of tabloid newspapers and television shows as reflections of their contemporary life.

Sartisky, Michael, "Robert Olen Butler: A Pulitzer Profile," in *The Future of Southern Writers*, edited by Jefferson Humphries and John Lowe, Oxford University Press, 1996, pp. 155–69.

This 1994 interview, recorded when Butler was still pigeonholed as a "Vietnam" writer, chronicles the author's jump from obscurity to fame with his Pulitzer Prize win the year before.

Schumock, Jim, "Robert Olen Butler," in *Story Story Story: Conversations with American Authors*, Black Heron Press, 1999, pp. 201–13.

This interview covers Butler's life up to the end of the century and includes a long discussion of the ideas behind *Tabloid Dreams*.

Trucks, Rob, "A Conversation with Robert Olen Butler," in *The Pleasure of Influence: Conversations with American Male Fiction Writers*, NotaBell Books, Purdue University Press, 2002, pp. 65–88.

As the title of Trucks' book implies, gender is a focal point in this interview. He does focus on the genesis of and the critical responses to *Tabloid Dreams*.

Glossary of Literary Terms

A

Allegory: A narrative technique in which characters representing things or abstract ideas are used to convey a message or teach a lesson. Allegory is typically used to teach moral, ethical, or religious lessons but is sometimes used for satiric or political purposes. Many fairy tales are allegories.

Allusion: A reference to a familiar literary or historical person or event, used to make an idea more easily understood. Joyce Carol Oates's story "Where Are You Going, Where Have You Been?" exhibits several allusions to popular music.

Analogy: A comparison of two things made to explain something unfamiliar through its similarities to something familiar, or to prove one point based on the acceptance of another. Similes and metaphors are types of analogies.

Antagonist: The major character in a narrative or drama who works against the hero or protagonist. The Misfit in Flannery O'Connor's story "A Good Man Is Hard to Find" serves as the antagonist for the Grandmother.

Anthology: A collection of similar works of literature, art, or music. Zora Neale Hurston's "The Eatonville Anthology" is a collection of stories that take place in the same town.

Anthropomorphism: The presentation of animals or objects in human shape or with human characteristics. The term is derived from the Greek word for "human form." The fur necklet in Katherine Mansfield's story "Miss Brill" has anthropomorphic characteristics.

Anti-hero: A central character in a work of literature who lacks traditional heroic qualities such as courage, physical prowess, and fortitude. Anti-heroes typically distrust conventional values and are unable to commit themselves to any ideals. They generally feel helpless in a world over which they have no control. Anti-heroes usually accept, and often celebrate, their positions as social outcasts. A well-known anti-hero is Walter Mitty in James Thurber's story "The Secret Life of Walter Mitty."

Archetype: The word archetype is commonly used to describe an original pattern or model from which all other things of the same kind are made. Archetypes are the literary images that grow out of the "collective unconscious," a theory proposed by psychologist Carl Jung. They appear in literature as incidents and plots that repeat basic patterns of life. They may also appear as stereotyped characters. The "schlemiel" of Yiddish literature is an archetype.

Autobiography: A narrative in which an individual tells his or her life story. Examples include Benjamin Franklin's *Autobiography* and Amy Hempel's story "In the Cemetery Where Al Jolson Is Buried," which has autobiographical characteristics even though it is a work of fiction.

Avant-garde A literary term that describes new writing that rejects traditional approaches to literature in favor of innovations in style or content. Twentieth-century examples of the literary avant-garde include the modernists and the minimalists.

B

Belles-lettres: A French term meaning "fine letters" or" beautiful writing." It is often used as a synonym for literature, typically referring to imaginative and artistic rather than scientific or expository writing. Current usage sometimes restricts the meaning to light or humorous writing and appreciative essays about literature. Lewis Carroll's *Alice in Wonderland* epitomizes the realm of belles-lettres.

Bildungsroman: A German word meaning "novel of development." The *bildungsroman* is a study of the maturation of a youthful character, typically brought about through a series of social or sexual encounters that lead to self-awareness. J. D. Salinger's *Catcher in the Rye* is a *bildungsroman*, and Doris Lessing's story "Through the Tunnel" exhibits characteristics of a *bildungsroman* as well.

Black Aesthetic Movement: A period of artistic and literary development among African Americans in the 1960s and early 1970s. This was the first major African-American artistic movement since the Harlem Renaissance and was closely paralleled by the civil rights and black power movements. The black aesthetic writers attempted to produce works of art that would be meaningful to the black masses. Key figures in black aesthetics included one of its founders, poet and playwright Amiri Baraka, formerly known as Le Roi Jones; poet and essayist Haki R. Madhubuti, formerly Don L. Lee; poet and playwright Sonia Sanchez; and dramatist Ed Bullins. Works representative of the Black Aesthetic Movement include Amiri Baraka's play *Dutchman,* a 1964 Obie award-winner.

Black Humor: Writing that places grotesque elements side by side with humorous ones in an attempt to shock the reader, forcing him or her to laugh at the horrifying reality of a disordered world. "Lamb to the Slaughter," by Roald Dahl, in which a placid housewife murders her husband and serves the murder weapon to the investigating policemen, is an example of black humor.

C

Catharsis: The release or purging of unwanted emotions—specifically fear and pity—brought about by exposure to art. The term was first used by the Greek philosopher Aristotle in his *Poetics* to refer to the desired effect of tragedy on spectators.

Character: Broadly speaking, a person in a literary work. The actions of characters are what constitute the plot of a story, novel, or poem. There are numerous types of characters, ranging from simple, stereotypical figures to intricate, multifaceted ones. "Characterization" is the process by which an author creates vivid, believable characters in a work of art. This may be done in a variety of ways, including (1) direct description of the character by the narrator; (2) the direct presentation of the speech, thoughts, or actions of the character; and (3) the responses of other characters to the character. The term "character" also refers to a form originated by the ancient Greek writer Theophrastus that later became popular in the seventeenth and eighteenth centuries. It is a short essay or sketch of a person who prominently displays a specific attribute or quality, such as miserliness or ambition. "Miss Brill," a story by Katherine Mansfield, is an example of a character sketch.

Classical: In its strictest definition in literary criticism, classicism refers to works of ancient Greek or Roman literature. The term may also be used to describe a literary work of recognized importance (a "classic") from any time period or literature that exhibits the traits of classicism. Examples of later works and authors now described as classical include French literature of the seventeenth century, Western novels of the nineteenth century, and American fiction of the mid-nineteenth century such as that written by James Fenimore Cooper and Mark Twain.

Climax: The turning point in a narrative, the moment when the conflict is at its most intense. Typically, the structure of stories, novels, and plays is one of rising action, in which tension builds to the climax, followed by falling action, in which tension lessens as the story moves to its conclusion.

Comedy: One of two major types of drama, the other being tragedy. Its aim is to amuse, and it typically ends happily. Comedy assumes many forms, such as farce and burlesque, and uses a variety of techniques, from parody to satire. In a restricted sense the term comedy refers only to dramatic presentations, but in general usage it is commonly applied to nondramatic works as well.

Comic Relief: The use of humor to lighten the mood of a serious or tragic story, especially in plays. The technique is very common in Elizabethan works, and can be an integral part of the plot or simply a brief event designed to break the tension of the scene.

Conflict: The conflict in a work of fiction is the issue to be resolved in the story. It usually occurs between two characters, the protagonist and the antagonist, or between the protagonist and society or the protagonist and himself or herself. The conflict in Washington Irving's story "The Devil and Tom Walker" is that the Devil wants Tom Walker's soul but Tom does not want to go to hell.

Criticism: The systematic study and evaluation of literary works, usually based on a specific method or set of principles. An important part of literary studies since ancient times, the practice of criticism has given rise to numerous theories, methods, and "schools," sometimes producing conflicting, even contradictory, interpretations of literature in general as well as of individual works. Even such basic issues as what constitutes a poem or a novel have been the subject of much criticism over the centuries. Seminal texts of literary criticism include Plato's *Republic,* Aristotle's *Poetics*, Sir Philip Sidney's *The Defence of Poesie,* and John Dryden's *Of Dramatic Poesie.* Contemporary schools of criticism include deconstruction, feminist, psychoanalytic, poststructuralist, new historicist, postcolonialist, and reader-response.

D

Deconstruction: A method of literary criticism characterized by multiple conflicting interpretations of a given work. Deconstructionists consider the impact of the language of a work and suggest that the true meaning of the work is not necessarily the meaning that the author intended.

Deduction: The process of reaching a conclusion through reasoning from general premises to a specific premise. Arthur Conan Doyle's character Sherlock Holmes often used deductive reasoning to solve mysteries.

Denotation: The definition of a word, apart from the impressions or feelings it creates in the reader. The word "apartheid" denotes a political and economic policy of segregation by race, but its connotations— oppression, slavery, inequality—are numerous.

Denouement: A French word meaning "the unknotting." In literature, it denotes the resolution of conflict in fiction or drama. The *denouement* follows the climax and provides an outcome to the primary plot situation as well as an explanation of secondary plot complications. A well-known example of *denouement* is the last scene of the play *As You Like It* by William Shakespeare, in which couples are married, an evildoer repents, the identities of two disguised characters are revealed, and a ruler is restored to power. Also known as "falling action."

Detective Story: A narrative about the solution of a mystery or the identification of a criminal. The conventions of the detective story include the detective's scrupulous use of logic in solving the mystery; incompetent or ineffectual police; a suspect who appears guilty at first but is later proved innocent; and the detective's friend or confidant —often the narrator—whose slowness in interpreting clues emphasizes by contrast the detective's brilliance. Edgar Allan Poe's "Murders in the Rue Morgue" is commonly regarded as the earliest example of this type of story. Other practitioners are Arthur Conan Doyle, Dashiell Hammett, and Agatha Christie.

Dialogue: Dialogue is conversation between people in a literary work. In its most restricted sense, it refers specifically to the speech of characters in a drama. As a specific literary genre, a "dialogue" is a composition in which characters debate an issue or idea.

Didactic: A term used to describe works of literature that aim to teach a moral, religious, political, or practical lesson. Although didactic elements are often found inartistically pleasing works, the term "didactic" usually refers to literature in which the message is more important than the form. The term may also be used to criticize a work that the critic finds "overly didactic," that is, heavy-handed in its delivery of a lesson. An example of didactic literature is John Bunyan's *Pilgrim's Progress.*

Dramatic Irony: Occurs when the reader of a work of literature knows something that a character in the work itself does not know. The irony is in the contrast between the intended meaning of the statements or actions of a character and the additional information understood by the audience.

Dystopia: An imaginary place in a work of fiction where the characters lead dehumanized, fearful lives. George Orwell's *Nineteen Eighty-four,* and Margaret Atwood's *Handmaid's Tale* portray versions of dystopia.

E

Edwardian: Describes cultural conventions identified with the period of the reign of Edward VII of England (1901–1910). Writers of the Edwardian Age typically displayed a strong reaction against the propriety and conservatism of the Victorian Age. Their work often exhibits distrust of authority in religion, politics, and art and expresses strong doubts about the soundness of conventional values. Writers of this era include E. M. Forster, H. G. Wells, and Joseph Conrad.

Empathy: A sense of shared experience, including emotional and physical feelings, with someone or something other than oneself. Empathy is often used to describe the response of a reader to a literary character.

Epilogue: A concluding statement or section of a literary work. In dramas, particularly those of the seventeenth and eighteenth centuries, the epilogue is a closing speech, often in verse, delivered by an actor at the end of a play and spoken directly to the audience.

Epiphany: A sudden revelation of truth inspired by a seemingly trivial incident. The term was widely used by James Joyce in his critical writings, and the stories in Joyce's *Dubliners* are commonly called "epiphanies."

Epistolary Novel: A novel in the form of letters. The form was particularly popular in the eighteenth century. The form can also be applied to short stories, as in Edwidge Danticat's "Children of the Sea."

Epithet: A word or phrase, often disparaging or abusive, that expresses a character trait of someone or something. "The Napoleon of crime" is an epithet applied to Professor Moriarty, archrival of Sherlock Holmes in Arthur Conan Doyle's series of detective stories.

Existentialism: A predominantly twentieth-century philosophy concerned with the nature and perception of human existence. There are two major strains of existentialist thought: atheistic and Christian. Followers of atheistic existentialism believe that the individual is alone in a godless universe and that the basic human condition is one of suffering and loneliness. Nevertheless, because there are no fixed values, individuals can create their own characters—indeed, they can shape themselves—through the exercise of free will. The atheistic strain culminates in and is popularly associated with the works of Jean-Paul Sartre. The Christian existentialists, on the other hand, believe that only in God may people find freedom from life's anguish. The two strains hold certain beliefs in common: that existence cannot be fully understood or described through empirical effort; that anguish is a universal element of life; that individuals must bear responsibility for their actions; and that there is no common standard of behavior or perception for religious and ethical matters. Existentialist thought figures prominently in the works of such authors as Franz Kafka, Fyodor Dostoyevsky, and Albert Camus.

Expatriatism: The practice of leaving one's country to live for an extended period in another country. Literary expatriates include Irish author James Joyce who moved to Italy and France, American writers James Baldwin, Ernest Hemingway, Gertrude Stein, and F. Scott Fitzgerald who lived and wrote in Paris, and Polish novelist Joseph Conrad in England.

Exposition: Writing intended to explain the nature of an idea, thing, or theme. Expository writing is often combined with description, narration, or argument.

Expressionism: An indistinct literary term, originally used to describe an early twentieth-century school of German painting. The term applies to almost any mode of unconventional, highly subjective writing that distorts reality in some way. Advocates of Expressionism include Federico Garcia Lorca, Eugene O'Neill, Franz Kafka, and James Joyce.

F

Fable: A prose or verse narrative intended to convey a moral. Animals or inanimate objects with human characteristics often serve as characters in fables. A famous fable is Aesop's "The Tortoise and the Hare."

Fantasy: A literary form related to mythology and folklore. Fantasy literature is typically set in nonexistent realms and features supernatural beings. Notable examples of literature with elements of fantasy are Gabriel García Márquez's story "The Handsomest Drowned Man in the World" and Ursula K. Le Guin's "The Ones Who Walk Away from Omelas."

Farce: A type of comedy characterized by broad humor, outlandish incidents, and often vulgar subject matter. Much of the comedy in film and television could more accurately be described as farce.

Fiction: Any story that is the product of imagination rather than a documentation of fact. Characters and events in such narratives may be based in real life but their ultimate form and configuration is a creation of the author.

Figurative Language: A technique in which an author uses figures of speech such as hyperbole, irony, metaphor, or simile for a particular effect. Figurative language is the opposite of literal language, in which every word is truthful, accurate, and free of exaggeration or embellishment.

Flashback: A device used in literature to present action that occurred before the beginning of the story. Flashbacks are often introduced as the dreams or recollections of one or more characters.

Foil: A character in a work of literature whose physical or psychological qualities contrast strongly with, and therefore highlight, the corresponding qualities of another character. In his Sherlock Holmes stories, Arthur Conan Doyle portrayed Dr. Watson as a man of normal habits and intelligence, making him a foil for the eccentric and unusually perceptive Sherlock Holmes.

Folklore: Traditions and myths preserved in a culture or group of people. Typically, these are passed on by word of mouth in various forms—such as legends, songs, and proverbs—or preserved in customs and ceremonies. Washington Irving, in "The Devil and Tom Walker" and many of his other stories, incorporates many elements of the folklore of New England and Germany.

Folktale: A story originating in oral tradition. Folk tales fall into a variety of categories, including legends, ghost stories, fairy tales, fables, and anecdotes based on historical figures and events.

Foreshadowing: A device used in literature to create expectation or to set up an explanation of later developments. Edgar Allan Poe uses foreshadowing to create suspense in "The Fall of the House of Usher" when the narrator comments on the crumbling state of disrepair in which he finds the house.

G

Genre: A category of literary work. Genre may refer to both the content of a given work—tragedy, comedy, horror, science fiction—and to its form, such as poetry, novel, or drama.

Gilded Age: A period in American history during the 1870s and after characterized by political corruption and materialism. A number of important novels of social and political criticism were written during this time. Henry James and Kate Chopin are two writers who were prominent during the Gilded Age.

Gothicism: In literature, works characterized by a taste for medieval or morbid characters and situations. A gothic novel prominently features elements of horror, the supernatural, gloom, and violence: clanking chains, terror, ghosts, medieval castles, and unexplained phenomena. The term "gothic novel" is also applied to novels that lack elements of the traditional Gothic setting but that create a similar atmosphere of terror or dread. The term can also be applied to stories, plays, and poems. Mary Shelley's *Frankenstein* and Joyce Carol Oates's *Belle fleur* are both gothic novels.

Grotesque: In literature, a work that is characterized by exaggeration, deformity, freakishness, and disorder. The grotesque often includes an element of comic absurdity. Examples of the grotesque can be found in the works of Edgar Allan Poe, Flannery O'Connor, Joseph Heller, and Shirley Jackson.

H

Harlem Renaissance: The Harlem Renaissance of the 1920s is generally considered the first significant movement of black writers and artists in the United States. During this period, new and established black writers, many of whom lived in the region of New York City known as Harlem, published more fiction and poetry than ever before, the first influential black literary journals were established, and black authors and artists received their first widespread recognition and serious critical appraisal. Among the major writers associated with this period are Countee Cullen, Langston Hughes, Arna Bontemps, and Zora Neale Hurston.

Hero/Heroine: The principal sympathetic character in a literary work. Heroes and heroines typically exhibit admirable traits: idealism, courage, and integrity, for example. Famous heroes and heroines of literature include Charles Dickens's Oliver Twist, Margaret Mitchell's Scarlett O'Hara, and the anonymous narrator in Ralph Ellison's *Invisible Man*.

Hyperbole: Deliberate exaggeration used to achieve an effect. In William Shakespeare's *Macbeth,* Lady Macbeth hyperbolizes when she says, "All the perfumes of Arabia could not sweeten this little hand."

I

Image: A concrete representation of an object or sensory experience. Typically, such a representation helps evoke the feelings associated with the object or experience itself. Images are either "literal" or "figurative." Literal images are especially concrete and involve little or no extension of the obvious meaning of the words used to express them. Figurative images do not follow the literal meaning of the words exactly. Images in literature are usually visual, but the term "image" can also refer to the representation of any sensory experience.

Imagery: The array of images in a literary work. Also used to convey the author's overall use of figurative language in a work.

In medias res: A Latin term meaning "in the middle of things." It refers to the technique of beginning a story at its midpoint and then using various flashback devices to reveal previous action. This technique originated in such epics as Virgil's *Aeneid*.

Interior Monologue: A narrative technique in which characters' thoughts are revealed in a way that appears to be uncontrolled by the author. The interior monologue typically aims to reveal the inner self of a character. It portrays emotional experiences as they occur at both a conscious and unconscious level. One of the best-known interior monologues in English is the Molly Bloom section at the close of James Joyce's *Ulysses*. Katherine Anne Porter's "The Jilting of Granny Weatherall" is also told in the form of an interior monologue.

Irony: In literary criticism, the effect of language in which the intended meaning is the opposite of what is stated. The title of Jonathan Swift's "A Modest Proposal" is ironic because what Swift proposes in this essay is cannibalism—hardly "modest."

J

Jargon: Language that is used or understood only by a select group of people. Jargon may refer to terminology used in a certain profession, such as computer jargon, or it may refer to any nonsensical language that is not understood by most people. Anthony Burgess's *A Clockwork Orange* and James Thurber's "The Secret Life of Walter Mitty" both use jargon.

K

Knickerbocker Group: An indistinct group of New York writers of the first half of the nineteenth century. Members of the group were linked only by location and a common theme: New York life. Two famous members of the Knickerbocker Group were Washington Irving and William Cullen Bryant. The group's name derives from Irving's *Knickerbocker's History of New York*.

L

Literal Language: An author uses literal language when he or she writes without exaggerating or embellishing the subject matter and without any tools of figurative language. To say "He ran very quickly down the street" is to use literal language, whereas to say "He ran like a hare down the street" would be using figurative language.

Literature: Literature is broadly defined as any written or spoken material, but the term most often refers to creative works. Literature includes poetry, drama, fiction, and many kinds of nonfiction writing, as well as oral, dramatic, and broadcast compositions not necessarily preserved in a written format, such as films and television programs.

Lost Generation: A term first used by Gertrude Stein to describe the post-World War I generation of American writers: men and women haunted by a sense of betrayal and emptiness brought about by the destructiveness of the war. The term is commonly applied to Hart Crane, Ernest Hemingway, F. Scott Fitzgerald, and others.

M

Magic Realism: A form of literature that incorporates fantasy elements or supernatural occurrences into the narrative and accepts them as truth. Gabriel Gárcia Márquez and Laura Esquivel are two writers known for their works of magic realism.

Metaphor: A figure of speech that expresses an idea through the image of another object. Metaphors suggest the essence of the first object by identifying it with certain qualities of the second object. An example is "But soft, what light through yonder window breaks? / It is the east, and Juliet is the sun" in William Shakespeare's *Romeo and Juliet*. Here, Juliet, the first object, is identified with qualities of the second object, the sun.

Minimalism: A literary style characterized by spare, simple prose with few elaborations. In minimalism, the main theme of the work is often never discussed directly. Amy Hempel and Ernest Hemingway are two writers known for their works of minimalism.

Modernism: Modern literary practices. Also, the principles of a literary school that lasted from roughly the beginning of the twentieth century until the end of World War II. Modernism is defined by its rejection of the literary conventions of the nineteenth century and by its opposition to conventional morality, taste, traditions, and economic values. Many writers are associated with the concepts of modernism, including Albert Camus, D. H. Lawrence, Ernest Hemingway, William Faulkner, Eugene O'Neill, and James Joyce.

Monologue: A composition, written or oral, by a single individual. More specifically, a speech given by a single individual in a drama or other public entertainment. It has no set length, although it is usually several or more lines long. "I Stand Here Ironing" by Tillie Olsen is an example of a story written in the form of a monologue.

Mood: The prevailing emotions of a work or of the author in his or her creation of the work. The mood of a work is not always what might be expected based on its subject matter.

Motif: A theme, character type, image, metaphor, or other verbal element that recurs throughout a single work of literature or occurs in a number of different works over a period of time. For example, the color white in Herman Melville's *Moby Dick* is a "specific" motif, while the trials of star-crossed lovers is a "conventional" motif from the literature of all periods.

N

Narration: The telling of a series of events, real or invented. A narration may be either a simple narrative, in which the events are recounted chronologically, or a narrative with a plot, in which the account is given in a style reflecting the author's artistic concept of the story. Narration is sometimes used as a synonym for "storyline."

Narrative: A verse or prose accounting of an event or sequence of events, real or invented. The term is also used as an adjective in the sense "method of narration." For example, in literary criticism, the expression "narrative technique" usually refers to the way the author structures and presents his or her story. Different narrative forms include diaries, travelogues, novels, ballads, epics, short stories, and other fictional forms.

Narrator: The teller of a story. The narrator may be the author or a character in the story through whom the author speaks. Huckleberry Finn is the narrator of Mark Twain's *The Adventures of Huckleberry Finn.*

Novella: An Italian term meaning "story." This term has been especially used to describe fourteenth-century Italian tales, but it also refers to modern short novels. Modern novellas include Leo Tolstoy's *The Death of Ivan Ilich,* Fyodor Dostoyevsky's *Notes from the Underground,* and Joseph Conrad's *Heart of Darkness.*

O

Oedipus Complex: A son's romantic obsession with his mother. The phrase is derived from the story of the ancient Theban hero Oedipus, who unknowingly killed his father and married his mother, and was popularized by Sigmund Freud's theory of psychoanalysis. Literary occurrences of the Oedipus complex include Sophocles' *Oedipus Rex* and D. H. Lawrence's "The Rocking-Horse Winner."

Onomatopoeia: The use of words whose sounds express or suggest their meaning. In its simplest sense, onomatopoeia may be represented by words that mimic the sounds they denote such as "hiss" or "meow." At a more subtle level, the pattern and rhythm of sounds and rhymes of a line or poem may be onomatopoeic.

Oral Tradition: A process by which songs, ballads, folklore, and other material are transmitted by word of mouth. The tradition of oral transmission predates the written record systems of literate society. Oral transmission preserves material sometimes over generations, although often with variations. Memory plays a large part in the recitation and preservation of orally transmitted material. Native American myths and legends, and African folktales told by plantation slaves are examples of orally transmitted literature.

P

Parable: A story intended to teach a moral lesson or answer an ethical question. Examples of parables are the stories told by Jesus Christ in the New Testament, notably "The Prodigal Son," but parables also are used in Sufism, rabbinic literature, Hasidism, and Zen Buddhism. Isaac Bashevis Singer's story "Gimpel the Fool" exhibits characteristics of a parable.

Paradox: A statement that appears illogical or contradictory at first, but may actually point to an underlying truth. A literary example of a paradox is George Orwell's statement "All animals are equal, but some animals are more equal than others" in *Animal Farm.*

Parody: In literature, this term refers to an imitation of a serious literary work or the signature style of a particular author in a ridiculous manner. A typical parody adopts the style of the original and applies it to an inappropriate subject for humorous effect. Parody is a form of satire and could be considered the literary equivalent of a caricature or cartoon. Henry Fielding's *Shamela* is a parody of Samuel Richardson's *Pamela.*

Persona: A Latin term meaning "mask." Personae are the characters in a fictional work of literature. The persona generally functions as a mask through which the author tells a story in a voice other than his or her own. A persona is usually either a character in a story who acts as a narrator or an "implied author," a voice created by the author to act as the narrator for himself or herself. The persona in Charlotte Perkins Gilman's story "The Yellow Wallpaper" is the unnamed young mother experiencing a mental breakdown.

Personification: A figure of speech that gives human qualities to abstract ideas, animals, and inanimate objects. To say that "the sun is smiling" is to personify the sun.

Plot: The pattern of events in a narrative or drama. In its simplest sense, the plot guides the author in composing the work and helps the reader follow the work. Typically, plots exhibit causality and unity and have a beginning, a middle, and an end. Sometimes, however, a plot may consist of a series of disconnected events, in which case it is known as an "episodic plot."

Poetic Justice: An outcome in a literary work, not necessarily a poem, in which the good are rewarded and the evil are punished, especially in ways that particularly fit their virtues or crimes. For example, a murderer may himself be murdered, or a thief will find himself penniless.

Poetic License: Distortions of fact and literary convention made by a writer—not always a poet—for the sake of the effect gained. Poetic license is closely related to the concept of "artistic freedom." An author exercises poetic license by saying that a pile of money "reaches as high as a mountain" when the pile is actually only a foot or two high.

Point of View: The narrative perspective from which a literary work is presented to the reader. There are four traditional points of view. The "third person omniscient" gives the reader a "godlike" perspective, unrestricted by time or place, from which to see actions and look into the minds of characters. This allows the author to comment openly on characters and events in the work. The "third person" point of view presents the events of the story from outside of any single character's perception, much like the omniscient point of view, but the reader must understand the action as it takes place and without any special insight into characters' minds or motivations. The "first person" or "personal" point of view relates events as they are perceived by a single character. The main character "tells" the story and may offer opinions about the action and characters which differ from those of the author. Much less common than omniscient, third person, and first person is the "second person" point of view, wherein the author tells the story as if it is happening to the reader. James Thurber employs the omniscient point of view in his short story "The Secret Life of Walter Mitty." Ernest Hemingway's "A Clean, Well-Lighted Place" is a short story told from the third person point of view. Mark Twain's novel *Huckleberry Finn* is presented from the first person viewpoint. Jay McInerney's *Bright Lights, Big City* is an example of a novel which uses the second person point of view.

Pornography: Writing intended to provoke feelings of lust in the reader. Such works are often condemned by critics and teachers, but those which can be shown to have literary value are viewed less harshly. Literary works that have been described as pornographic include D. H. Lawrence's *Lady Chatterley's Lover* and James Joyce's *Ulysses.*

Post-Aesthetic Movement: An artistic response made by African Americans to the black aesthetic movement of the 1960s and early 1970s. Writers since that time have adopted a somewhat different tone in their work, with less emphasis placed on the disparity between black and white in the United States. In the words of post-aesthetic authors such as Toni Morrison, John Edgar Wideman, and Kristin Hunter, African Americans are portrayed as looking inward for answers to their own questions, rather than always looking to the outside world. Two well-known examples of works produced as part of the post-aesthetic movement are the Pulitzer Prize–winning novels *The Color Purple* by Alice Walker and *Beloved* by Toni Morrison.

Postmodernism: Writing from the 1960s forward characterized by experimentation and application of modernist elements, which include existentialism and alienation. Postmodernists have gone a step further in the rejection of tradition begun with the modernists by also rejecting traditional forms, preferring the anti-novel over the novel and the anti-hero over the hero. Postmodern writers include Thomas Pynchon, Margaret Drabble, and Gabriel Gárcia Márquez.

Prologue: An introductory section of a literary work. It often contains information establishing the situation of the characters or presents information about the setting, time period, or action. In drama, the prologue is spoken by a chorus or by one of the principal characters.

Prose: A literary medium that attempts to mirror the language of everyday speech. It is distinguished from poetry by its use of unmetered, unrhymed language consisting of logically related sentences. Prose is usually grouped into paragraphs that form a cohesive whole such as an essay or a novel. The term is sometimes used to mean an author's general writing.

Protagonist: The central character of a story who serves as a focus for its themes and incidents and as the principal rationale for its development. The protagonist is sometimes referred to in discussions of modern literature as the hero or anti-hero. Well-known protagonists are Hamlet in William Shakespeare's *Hamlet* and Jay Gatsby in F. Scott Fitzgerald's *The Great Gatsby.*

R

Realism: A nineteenth-century European literary movement that sought to portray familiar characters, situations, and settings in a realistic manner. This was done primarily by using an objective narrative point of view and through the buildup of accurate detail. The standard for success of any realistic work depends on how faithfully it transfers common experience into fictional forms. The realistic method may be altered or extended, as in stream of consciousness writing, to record highly subjective experience. Contemporary authors who often write in a realistic way include Nadine Gordimer and Grace Paley.

Resolution: The portion of a story following the climax, in which the conflict is resolved. The resolution of Jane Austen's *Northanger Abbey* is neatly summed up in the following sentence: "Henry and Catherine were married, the bells rang and every body smiled."

Rising Action: The part of a drama where the plot becomes increasingly complicated. Rising action leads up to the climax, or turning point, of a drama. The final "chase scene" of an action film is generally the rising action which culminates in the film's climax.

***Roman a clef*:** A French phrase meaning "novel with a key." It refers to a narrative in which real persons are portrayed under fictitious names. Jack Kerouac, for example, portrayed various friends under fictitious names in the novel *On the Road*. D. H. Lawrence based "The Rocking-Horse Winner" on a family he knew.

Romanticism: This term has two widely accepted meanings. In historical criticism, it refers to a European intellectual and artistic movement of the late eighteenth and early nineteenth centuries that sought greater freedom of personal expression than that allowed by the strict rules of literary form and logic of the eighteenth-century neoclassicists. The Romantics preferred emotional and imaginative expression to rational analysis. They considered the individual to be at the center of all experience and so placed him or her at the center of their art. The Romantics believed that the creative imagination reveals nobler truths—unique feelings and attitudes—than those that could be discovered by logic or by scientific examination. "Romanticism" is also used as a general term to refer to a type of sensibility found in all periods of literary history and usually considered to be in opposition to the principles of classicism. In this sense, Romanticism signifies any work or philosophy in which the exotic or dreamlike figure strongly, or that is devoted to individualistic expression, self-analysis, or a pursuit of a higher realm of knowledge than can be discovered by human reason. Prominent Romantics include Jean-Jacques Rousseau, William Wordsworth, John Keats, Lord Byron, and Johann Wolfgang von Goethe.

S

Satire: A work that uses ridicule, humor, and wit to criticize and provoke change in human nature and institutions. Voltaire's novella *Candide* and Jonathan Swift's essay "A Modest Proposal" are both satires. Flannery O'Connor's portrayal of the family in "A Good Man Is Hard to Find" is a satire of a modern, Southern, American family.

Science Fiction: A type of narrative based upon real or imagined scientific theories and technology. Science fiction is often peopled with alien creatures and set on other planets or in different dimensions. Popular writers of science fiction are Isaac Asimov, Karel Capek, Ray Bradbury, and Ursula K. Le Guin.

Setting: The time, place, and culture in which the action of a narrative takes place. The elements of setting may include geographic location, characters's physical and mental environments, prevailing cultural attitudes, or the historical time in which the action takes place.

Short Story: A fictional prose narrative shorter and more focused than a novella. The short story usually deals with a single episode and often a single character. The "tone," the author's attitude toward his or her subject and audience, is uniform throughout. The short story frequently also lacks *denouement*, ending instead at its climax.

Signifying Monkey: A popular trickster figure in black folklore, with hundreds of tales about this character documented since the 19th century. Henry Louis Gates Jr. examines the history of the signifying monkey in *The Signifying Monkey: Towards a Theory of Afro-American Literary Criticism*, published in 1988.

Simile: A comparison, usually using "like" or "as," of two essentially dissimilar things, as in "coffee as cold as ice" or "He sounded like a broken record." The title of Ernest Hemingway's "Hills Like White Elephants" contains a simile.

Socialist Realism: The Socialist Realism school of literary theory was proposed by Maxim Gorky and established as a dogma by the first Soviet Congress of Writers. It demanded adherence to a communist worldview in works of literature. Its doctrines required an objective viewpoint comprehensible to the working classes and themes of social struggle featuring strong proletarian heroes. Gabriel Gárcia Márquez's stories exhibit some characteristics of Socialist Realism.

Stereotype: A stereotype was originally the name for a duplication made during the printing process; this led to its modern definition as a person or thing that is (or is assumed to be) the same as all others of its type. Common stereotypical characters include the absent-minded professor, the nagging wife, the troublemaking teenager, and the kind-hearted grandmother.

Stream of Consciousness: A narrative technique for rendering the inward experience of a character. This technique is designed to give the impression of an ever-changing series of thoughts, emotions, images, and memories in the spontaneous and seemingly illogical order that they occur in life. The textbook example of stream of consciousness is the last section of James Joyce's *Ulysses.*

Structure: The form taken by a piece of literature. The structure may be made obvious for ease of understanding, as in nonfiction works, or may be obscured for artistic purposes, as in some poetry or seemingly "unstructured" prose.

Style: A writer's distinctive manner of arranging words to suit his or her ideas and purpose in writing. The unique imprint of the author's personality upon his or her writing, style is the product of an author's way of arranging ideas and his or her use of diction, different sentence structures, rhythm, figures of speech, rhetorical principles, and other elements of composition.

Suspense: A literary device in which the author maintains the audience's attention through the buildup of events, the outcome of which will soon be revealed. Suspense in William Shakespeare's *Hamlet* is sustained throughout by the question of whether or not the Prince will achieve what he has been instructed to do and of what he intends to do.

Symbol: Something that suggests or stands for something else without losing its original identity. In literature, symbols combine their literal meaning with the suggestion of an abstract concept. Literary symbols are of two types: those that carry complex associations of meaning no matter what their contexts, and those that derive their suggestive meaning from their functions in specific literary works. Examples of symbols are sunshine suggesting happiness, rain suggesting sorrow, and storm clouds suggesting despair.

T

Tale: A story told by a narrator with a simple plot and little character development. Tales are usually relatively short and often carry a simple message.

Examples of tales can be found in the works of Saki, Anton Chekhov, Guy de Maupassant, and O. Henry.

Tall Tale: A humorous tale told in a straightforward, credible tone but relating absolutely impossible events or feats of the characters. Such tales were commonly told of frontier adventures during the settlement of the west in the United States. Literary use of tall tales can be found in Washington Irving's *History of New York,* Mark Twain's *Life on the Mississippi,* and in the German R. F. Raspe's *Baron Munchausen's Narratives of His Marvellous Travels and Campaigns in Russia.*

Theme: The main point of a work of literature. The term is used interchangeably with thesis. Many works have multiple themes. One of the themes of Nathaniel Hawthorne's "Young Goodman Brown" is loss of faith.

Tone: The author's attitude toward his or her audience may be deduced from the tone of the work. A formal tone may create distance or convey politeness, while an informal tone may encourage a friendly, intimate, or intrusive feeling in the reader. The author's attitude toward his or her subject matter may also be deduced from the tone of the words he or she uses in discussing it. The tone of John F. Kennedy's speech which included the appeal to "ask not what your country can do for you" was intended to instill feelings of camaraderie and national pride in listeners.

Tragedy: A drama in prose or poetry about a noble, courageous hero of excellent character who, because of some tragic character flaw, brings ruin upon him- or herself. Tragedy treats its subjects in a dignified and serious manner, using poetic language to help evoke pity and fear and bring about catharsis, a purging of these emotions. The tragic form was practiced extensively by the ancient Greeks. The classical form of tragedy was revived in the sixteenth century; it flourished especially on the Elizabethan stage. In modern times, dramatists have attempted to adapt the form to the needs of modern society by drawing their heroes from the ranks of ordinary men and women and defining the nobility of these heroes in terms of spirit rather than exalted social standing. Some contemporary works that are thought of as tragedies include *The Great Gatsby* by F. Scott Fitzgerald, and *The Sound and the Fury* by William Faulkner.

Tragic Flaw: In a tragedy, the quality within the hero or heroine which leads to his or her downfall. Examples of the tragic flaw include Othello's jealousy and Hamlet's indecisiveness, although most great tragedies defy such simple interpretation.

U

Utopia: A fictional perfect place, such as "paradise" or "heaven." An early literary utopia was described in Plato's *Republic,* and in modern literature, Ursula K. Le Guin depicts a utopia in "The Ones Who Walk Away from Omelas."

V

Victorian: Refers broadly to the reign of Queen Victoria of England (1837–1901) and to anything with qualities typical of that era. For example, the qualities of smug narrow-mindedness, bourgeois materialism, faith in social progress, and priggish morality are often considered Victorian. In literature, the Victorian Period was the great age of the English novel, and the latter part of the era saw the rise of movements such as decadence and symbolism.

Cumulative Author/Title Index

Cumulative
Nationality/Ethnicity Index

Mistry, Rohinton
  Swimming Lessons: V6
Mukherjee, Bharati
  The Management of Grief: V7
Munro, Alice
  Boys and Girls: V5
  Meneseteung: V19
  Walker Brothers Cowboy: V13

Chilean

Allende, Isabel
  And of Clay Are We Created:
    V11
  The Gold of Tomás Vargas:
    V16

Chinese

Jin, Ha
  In the Kindergarten: V17

Colombian

García Márquez, Gabriel
  Eyes of a Blue Dog: V21
  *The Handsomest Drowned Man in
    the World:* V1
  *A Very Old Man with Enormous
    Wings:* V6
  *The Woman Who Came at Six
    O'Clock:* V16

Cuban

Calvino, Italo
  The Feathered Ogre: V12
Rivera, Beatriz
  African Passions: V15

Czech

Kafka, Franz
  A Hunger Artist: V7
  In the Penal Colony: V3
  The Metamorphosis: V12
Kundera, Milan
  The Hitchhiking Game: V10

Danish

Dinesen, Isak
  Babette's Feast: V20
  The Ring: V6
  The Sailor-Boy's Tale: V13
  Sorrow-Acre: V3
Høeg, Peter
  Journey into a Dark Heart: V18

Dominican

Díaz, Junot
  The Sun, the Moon, the Stars:
    V20

Egyptian

El-Bisatie, Mohamed
  *A Conversation from the Third
    Floor:* V17
Mahfouz, Naguib
  Half a Day: V9

English

Bates, H. E.
  The Daffodil Sky: V7
Bowen, Elizabeth
  The Demon Lover: V5
Burton, Richard
  The Arabian Nights: V21
Carter, Angela
  The Bloody Chamber: V4
  The Erlking: V12
Clarke, Arthur C.
  "If I Forget Thee, O Earth . . .":
    V18
  The Star: V4
Conrad, Joseph
  Heart of Darkness: V12
  The Secret Sharer: V1
Davies, Peter Ho
  Think of England: V21
du Maurier, Daphne
  The Birds: V16
  Don't Look Now: V14
Eliot, George
  The Lifted Veil: V8
Far, Sui Sin
  Mrs. Spring Fragrance: V4
Galsworthy, John
  The Japanese Quince: V3
Greene, Graham
  The Destructors: V14
Jacobs, W. W.
  The Monkey's Paw: V2
Kipling, Rudyard
  Mowgli's Brothers: V22
  Mrs. Bathurst: V8
  Rikki-Tikki-Tavi: V21
Lahiri, Jhumpa
  A Temporary Matter: V19
Lawrence, D. H.
  Odour of Chrysanthemums: V6
  The Rocking-Horse Winner: V2
Lessing, Doris
  Debbie and Julie: V12
  Through the Tunnel: V1
  To Room Nineteen: V20
Maugham, W. Somerset
  The Fall of Edward Barnard: V17

Okri, Ben
  In the Shadow of War: V20
Orwell, George
  Shooting an Elephant: V4
Saki
  The Interlopers: V15
  The Open Window: V1
Sayers, Dorothy L.
  Suspicion: V12
Wells, H. G.
  The Door in the Wall: V3
Wodehouse, Pelham Grenville
  Jeeves Takes Charge: V10
Woolf, Virginia
  Kew Gardens: V12
  The New Dress: V4

Eurasian

Far, Sui Sin
  Mrs. Spring Fragrance: V4

French

Balzac, Honore de
  La Grande Bretèche: V10
Beckett, Samuel
  Dante and the Lobster: V15
Camus, Albert
  The Guest: V4
Cortázar, Julio
  Axolotl: V3
  The Pursuer: V20
Flaubert, Gustave
  A Simple Heart: V6
Maupassant, Guy de
  Boule de Suif: V21
  The Necklace: V4
Merimee, Prosper
  Mateo Falcone: V8
Robbe-Grillet, Alain
  The Replacement: V15
Sartre, Jean-Paul
  The Wall: V9

German

Böll, Heinrich
  Christmas Not Just Once a Year:
    V20
Mann, Thomas
  Death in Venice: V9
  Disorder and Early Sorrow: V4
Wolf, Christa
  Exchanging Glances: V14

Haitian

Danticat, Edwidge
  Children of the Sea: V1

Cumulative Nationality/Ethnicity Index

Philippine

Santos, Bienvenido
Immigration Blues: V19

Polish

Borowski, Tadeusz
This Way for the Gas, Ladies and Gentlemen: V13
Conrad, Joseph
Heart of Darkness: V12
The Secret Sharer: V1
Singer, Isaac Bashevis
Gimpel the Fool: V2
Henne Fire: V16
The Spinoza of Market Street: V12

Russian

Asimov, Isaac
Nightfall: V17
Babel, Isaac
My First Goose: V10
Chekhov, Anton
The Darling: V13
Gooseberries: V14
The Lady with the Pet Dog: V5
Dostoevsky, Fyodor
The Grand Inquisitor: V8
Gogol, Nikolai
The Overcoat: V7

Nabokov, Vladimir
A Guide to Berlin: V6
That in Aleppo Once . . .: V15
Pushkin, Alexander
The Stationmaster: V9
Solzhenitsyn, Alexandr
One Day in the Life of Ivan Denisovich: V9
Tolstaya, Tatyana
Night: V14
Tolstoy, Leo
The Death of Ivan Ilych: V5
Yezierska, Anzia
America and I: V15

Scottish

Doyle, Arthur Conan
The Red-Headed League: V2
Scott, Sir Walter
Wandering Willie's Tale: V10

South African

Gordimer, Nadine
Town and Country Lovers: V14
The Train from Rhodesia: V2
The Ultimate Safari: V19
Head, Bessie
Life: V13
Snapshots of a Wedding: V5
Kohler, Sheila
Africans: V18

Mphahlele, Es'kia (Ezekiel)
Mrs. Plum: V11

Spanish

Unamuno, Miguel de
Saint Emmanuel the Good, Martyr: V20
Vargas Llosa, Mario
The Challenge: V14

Swedish

Gustafsson, Lars
Greatness Strikes Where It Pleases: V22
Lagerlöf, Selma
The Legend of the Christmas Rose: V18

Welsh

Dahl, Roald
Lamb to the Slaughter: V4

West Indian

Kincaid, Jamaica
Girl: V7
What I Have Been Doing Lately: V5

Subject/Theme Index